Introductory Statistics for the Behavioral Sciences

Sixth Edition

Introductory Statistics for the Behavioral Sciences

Sixth Edition

Joan Welkowitz
New York University

Barry H. Cohen
New York University

Robert B. Ewen
Gulliver Preparatory School

WILEY

John Wiley & Sons, Inc.

Library of Congress Cataloging-in-Publication Data

Welkowitz, Joan.
  Introductory statistics for the behavioral sciences / Joan Welkowitz, Barry H. Cohen, Robert B.
Ewen. — 6th ed.
    p. cm.
  Various multi-media instructional resources are available to supplement the text.
  Includes bibliographical references and index.
  ISBN-13: 978-0-471-73547-2 (cloth)
  ISBN-10: 0-471-73547-7 (cloth)
  1. Social sciences—Statistical methods. 2. Psychometrics. 3. Sociology—Statistical methods.
4. Education—Statistical methods.
  I. Cohen, Barry H., 1949– . II. Ewen, Robert B., 1940– . III. Title.
HA29.W445 2006
519.5024′3—dc22

                                                                                        2006013970

Printed in the United States of America

10 9 8 7 6 5 4 3 2 1

This book is dedicated to
our students—past, present, and future—
to Walter, Julie, Larry, David, Sara, and Ray,
to Lori, Michael, and Melissa,
to Judy and Meredith,

and especially to the memory of Joan Welkowitz,
our mentor and brilliant, much-loved friend.
She will be greatly missed by many family members,
friends, colleagues, and former students.

Contents

Preface   xv
Acknowledgments   xix
Glossary of Symbols   xxi

Part I   Descriptive Statistics   1

Chapter 1   **Introduction   3**

Chapter 2   **Frequency Distributions and Graphs   23**

Preface

This sixth edition represents a major revision of a text that was first published in 1971, and has been in print continuously ever since. However, our purpose in this edition is the same as it was in the very first edition: to introduce and explain statistical concepts and principles clearly and in a highly readable fashion, assuming minimal mathematical sophistication, but avoiding a "cookbook" approach to methodology.

In this edition we have moved to a new publisher, John Wiley & Sons, and replaced our dear, departed colleague, Jack Cohen, with another co-author of the same last name. Although not directly related to Jack in a genetic sense, Barry Cohen began teaching statistics at New York University while Jack Cohen was still doing the same, and has been influenced accordingly. Before then, he served as a teaching assistant to Joan Welkowitz at NYU more than twenty years ago. One advantage of joining John Wiley & Sons is that this text can now share supplementary materials with Barry Cohen's graduate-level statistics text, *Explaining Psychological Statistics,* also published by Wiley. (See Barry Cohen's statistics web page: www.psych.nyu.edu/cohen/statstext.html.)

There are five major changes in this edition.

1. The Inclusion of Exercises in the Text

Most of the numerical exercises from the Study Guide prepared by Bob Ewen for the fifth edition of this text have been moved to the end of the appropriate chapters in this edition. Most of the conceptual workbook problems have been moved to a separate section following the exercises in each chapter, labeled Thought Questions. Answers to selected exercises appear in an appendix to the text; answers to all of the exercises (including the thought questions) are in the instructor's manual, available from the Wiley web page for this text (instructors will need to set up a password to access this manual). For instructors who have used the Study Guide from the previous edition, the instructor's manual includes a table that will tell them where to find each of those problems in this edition. A student study guide is also available from the Wiley web page. (Links to the Wiley web page can always be found on the Cohen statistics web page.)

2. The Addition of Computer Exercises and a "Bridge to SPSS" Section at the End of Every Chapter

Although we believe that the performance of some simple hand calculations is vital for a complete understanding of the statistical procedures in this text, we also recognize that most instructors these days require their students to learn how to calculate basic statistics with Microsoft Excel, or one of the comprehensive statistical software packages (e.g., SPSS, SAS, Minitab). Therefore, we have included one large data set in the appendix, which can also be downloaded in several useful formats from the web, and end-of-chapter computer exercises, all of which refer to this data set. The use of a single data set for all of the computer exercises facilitates comparisons among seemingly disparate, yet nonetheless closely related statistical procedures.

Because SPSS for Windows (SPSS, Chicago, Illinois) seems to be the most often used statistical package among our intended audience, we have included instructions that will help students to solve the computer exercises with SPSS, and to understand the output that SPSS creates. This built-in SPSS guide cannot take the place of a more general introductory guide to the SPSS package, and students will still need instructions concerning access to SPSS at their particular college or university. However, our Bridge to SPSS sections will ensure that students can connect the statistical terms that SPSS uses, which are not always universally recognized, with the language being used in this text.

It should be possible to solve most, if not all, of our computer exercises using any major statistical software package, but instructors using packages other than SPSS will need to provide their students with some guidance in translating their output into terms that are compatible with this text. Our Bridge to SPSS sections are based on version 14.0 of SPSS for Windows, the current version at the time of publication of this edition, but users of SPSS versions as early as 8.0 should find these sections just as applicable. If newer versions of SPSS for Windows, released before the next edition of this text, require any modifications of our Bridge to SPSS sections, these will be posted on the Cohen statistics web page.

3. The Addition of an Entire Chapter on Multiple Comparisons

The material on Fisher's protected t tests and LSD has been moved from the one-way ANOVA chapter in the fifth edition to a chapter of its own in this edition, and has been joined by Tukey's HSD, the modified LSD test, and the Bonferroni adjustment. The relative advantages and disadvantages of these alternatives are explained.

4. The Addition of a Chapter on Repeated-Measures ANOVA

This new chapter extends the scope of this text into an area that is now covered commonly in introductory statistics texts. This chapter appears *after* the two-way ANOVA, and can therefore take advantage of both the formulas and concepts of the two-way ANOVA to explain the workings of the repeated-measures and randomized-blocks ANOVA procedures. The new chapter concludes with a brief description of the computation and use of the two-way mixed-design ANOVA.

5. The Reorganization of Material from the Previous Edition

An important theme of this new edition has been the drawing of connections between statistical procedures from different chapters. Towards that end, we have reanalyzed, whenever feasible, the data sets of earlier chapters by the methods of subsequent chapters. Moreover, our text examples frequently refer to, as a unifying theme, the same hypothetical experiment that we used for our computer exercises.

Another important, and somewhat related, theme has been continuity. For example, the material on discrete probability (in chapter 8 of the fifth edition) was interrupting the flow between the description of standardized (z) scores, and their use with respect to the areas of the normal distribution. Consequently, we moved this material to a new chapter, just before "Chi-Square Tests," to create an introduction to nonparametric statistics. Also, in accord with the suggestion of an anonymous reviewer, we reversed the order of chapters 6 and 7 from the fifth edition, so that the chapter on standardized scores directly precedes the description of the normal curve, and the chapter on exploratory data summaries follows directly after the chapters on central tendency and variability.

What has not changed in this edition is our continuing commitment to teaching our readers to understand the rationales that underlie the various statistical procedures explained herein, and to interpret and apply the results of those procedures without falling prey to common conceptual errors. Our emphasis therefore remains on the fundamental logic and proper use of descriptive and inferential statistics. This text was ahead of its time in highlighting the advantages of using confidence intervals and effect size measures, and making simple power calculations accessible to students at an introductory level. It is our hope that this revision brings our text not just up-to-date, but moves it once again to the forefront of statistical education for students of the behavioral sciences.

Acknowledgments

Thanks are due to our many encouraging friends and relatives, to colleagues and reviewers who made many useful comments on previous editions, and to two reviewers who gave us helpful suggestions for this latest edition: Dr. Marie S. Hammond, Tennessee State University; and Dr. Jasia Pietrzak, Columbia University. Most of all, we wish to thank our many students who, throughout the years, have provided invaluable feedback on our teaching of statistics, as well as on earlier editions of this text, and its accompanying workbook.

For the very existence of this latest edition, we owe our thanks to Patricia Rossi (senior editor) and Isabel Pratt (associate editor); without the vision and understanding of the editors and publishers at John Wiley & Sons, this revision would not have been published. We are also grateful to those responsible for the look and design of this text—especially, Linda Witzling (senior production editor, Wiley) and Susan Dodson (Graphic Composition, Inc., Athens, GA). Finally, we owe a debt of gratitude to Leona Gizzi for tirelessly typing the new chapters and sections from handwritten copy, and to Ihno Lee for her careful preparation of the answer key both in the appendix of this edition and in the accompanying instructor's manual.

Joan Welkowitz
Barry H. Cohen
Robert B. Ewen

Postscript

It is with much sadness that we note the passing of our senior author, Joan Welkowitz, early in 2006. She was very excited about the whole framework of this new edition, and remained involved in every stage of this revision, until the final copyediting. This edition is a tribute to her lifelong dedication to the teaching of statistics, and more generally, the mentoring of students of psychology. We will miss her greatly.

Barry H. Cohen
Robert B. Ewen

Glossary of Symbols

Numbers in parentheses indicate the chapter in which the symbol first appears.

a_{YX}	Y-intercept of linear regression line for predicting Y from X (12)
α	criterion (or level) of significance; probability of Type I error (9)
α_{EW}	the experiment-wise alpha (16)
α_{pc}	the alpha per comparison (16)
b_{YX}	slope of linear regression line for predicting Y from X (12)
β	probability of Type II error (9)
$1 - \beta$	power (14)
cf	cumulative frequency (2)
χ^2	statistic following the chi square distribution (20)
D	difference between two scores or ranks (11)
$\overline{D}$	mean of the Ds (11)
$\mathbf{d}$	effect size involving two populations (14)
df	degrees of freedom (9)
df_B	degrees of freedom between groups (15)
df_W	degrees of freedom within groups (15)
df_1	degrees of freedom for factor 1 (17)
df_2	degrees of freedom for factor 2 (17)
$df_{1 \times 2}$	degrees of freedom for interaction (17)
δ	delta (14)
η^2	eta squared (15)
$\mathbf{f}$	effect size involving multiple populations (15)
f	frequency (2)
f_e	expected frequency (20)
f_o	observed frequency (20)
F	statistic following the F distribution (15)
g	effect size involving two samples (14)
h	interval size (3)

H	statistic following the Kruskal—Wallis test (21)
$H\%$	percent of subjects in all intervals higher than the critical one (3)
H_0	null hypothesis (10)
H_1	alternative hypothesis (10)
HSD	Tukey's Honestly Significant Difference (16)
i	case number (1)
$I\%$	percent of subjects in the critical interval (3)
k	a constant (1)
k	number of groups (or the last group) (15)
$L\%$	percent of subjects in all intervals below the critical one (3)
LRL	lower real limit (3)
LSD	Fisher's Least Significant Difference (16)
Mdn	median (4)
MS	mean square (15)
MS_B	mean square between groups (15)
MS_W	mean square within groups (15)
MS_1	mean square for factor 1 (17)
MS_2	mean square for factor 2 (17)
$MS_{1\times2}$	mean square for interaction (17)
μ	population mean (4)
N_T	total number of subjects or observations (1)
N_i	number of observations or subjects in group i (15)
π	hypothetical population proportion (10)
p	observed sample proportion (10)
$P(A)$	probability of event A (19)
PR	percentile rank (3)
ϕ	phi coefficient (20)
ϕ_C	Cramér's ϕ (20)
q	studentized range statistic (16)
r_C	matched pairs rank biserial correlation coefficient (21)
r_G	Glass rank biserial correlation coefficient (21)
r_{pb}	point-biserial correlation coefficient (13)
r_s	Spearman rank-order correlation coefficient (21)
r_{XY}	sample Pearson correlation coefficient between X and Y (12)
$\bar{R}$	mean of a set of ranks (21)
ρ_{XY}	population correlation coefficient between X and Y (12)

s	sample standard deviation (5)
s^2	population variance estimate (5)
s_D^2	variance of the Ds (11)
s_{pooled}^2	pooled variance (11)
$s_{\overline{X}}$	standard error of the mean (10)
$s_{\overline{X}_1 - \overline{X}_2}$	standard error of the difference (11)
$s_{Y'}$	estimate of $\sigma_{Y'}$ obtained from a sample (12)
$Score_p$	score corresponding to the pth percentile (3)
SFB	sum of frequencies below the critical interval (3)
SS	sum of squares (15)
SS_T	total sum of squares (15)
SS_B	sum of squares between groups (15)
SS_W	sum of squares within groups (15)
SS_1	sum of squares for factor 1 (17)
SS_2	sum of squares for factor 2 (17)
$SS_{1 \times 2}$	sum of squares for interaction (17)
Σ	summation sign (1)
σ	population standard deviation (5)
σ^2	population variance (5)
σ_p	standard error of a sample proportion (10)
σ_T	standard error of the ranks of independent samples (21)
σ_{T_M}	standard error of the ranks of matched samples (21)
$\sigma_{\overline{X}}$	standard error of the mean when σ is known (10)
$\sigma_{Y'}$	standard error of estimate for predicting Y (12)
t	statistic following the t distribution (10)
T	T score (7)
T_E	expected sum of the ranks (21)
T_i	sum of ranks in group i (21)
x	deviation score (4)
X'	predicted X score (12)
$\overline{X}$	sample mean (4)
$\overline{X}_i$	mean of group i (15)
$\overline{X}_G$	grand mean (15)
Y'	predicted Y score (12)
z	standard score (7)

Part I
Descriptive Statistics

Chapter 1
Introduction

PREVIEW

Why study statistics?

What are three important reasons why a knowledge of statistics is essential for anyone majoring in psychology, sociology, or education?

Descriptive and Inferential Statistics

What is the difference between descriptive and inferential statistics? Why must behavioral science researchers use inferential statistics?

Populations, Samples, Parameters, and Statistics

What is the difference between a population and a sample?

Why is it important to specify clearly the population from which a sample is drawn?

What is the difference between a parameter and a statistic?

Measurement Scales

What types of scales are used to measure variables in the behavioral sciences?

What is the difference between qualitative and quantitative data?

Independent and Dependent Variables

What is the difference between observational and experimental studies?

Sara's Study

An example that provides a common thread tying together all of the subsequent chapters.

Summation Notation

Why is summation notation used by statisticians?

What are the eight rules involving summation notation?

Summary

Exercises

Thought Questions

Computer Exercises

Bridge to SPSS

Why Study Statistics?

This book is written primarily for undergraduates majoring in psychology, sociology, and education. There are three reasons why a knowledge of statistics is essential for those who wish to pursue the study of these behavioral sciences:

To understand the professional literature.   Most professional literature in the behavioral sciences includes results that are based on statistical analyses. Therefore, you will be unable to understand important articles in scientific journals and books unless you understand statistics. It is possible to seek out secondhand reports that are designed for the statistically ignorant, but those who prefer this alternative to obtaining firsthand information should not be majoring in the fields of behavioral science.

To understand the rationale underlying research in the behavioral sciences. Statistics is not just a catalog of procedures and formulas. It offers the rationale upon which much of behavioral science research is based—namely, drawing inferences about a population based on data obtained from a sample. Those familiar with statistics understand that research consists of a series of educated guesses and fallible decisions, not right or wrong answers. Those without a knowledge of statistics, on the other hand, cannot understand the strengths and weaknesses of the techniques used by behavioral scientists to collect information and draw conclusions.

To carry out behavioral science research.   In order to do competent research in the behavioral sciences, it is necessary to design the statistical analysis *before* the data are collected. Otherwise, the research procedures may be so poorly planned that not even an expert statistician can make any sense out of the results. To be sure, it is possible (and often advisable) to consult someone more experienced in statistics for assistance. Without some statistical knowledge of your own, however, you will find it difficult or impossible to convey your needs to someone else and to understand the replies.

Save for these introductory remarks, we do not regard it as our task to persuade you that statistics is important in psychology, sociology, and education. If you are seriously interested in any of these fields, you will find this out for yourself. Accordingly, this book contains no documented examples selected from the professional literature to prove to you that statistics really is used in these fields. Instead, we have devised one detailed, realistic example with numerical values that reveal the issues involved as clearly as possible.

The example we will use throughout this text is based on a hypothetical experiment performed by Sara, a first-year doctoral student. The participants are students who are enrolled in her statistics classes. We will describe this experiment in greater detail later in this chapter and return to it in all of the subsequent chapters.

We have tried to avoid a "cookbook" approach that places excessive emphasis on computational recipes. The various statistical procedures and the essential underlying concepts have been explained at length, and insofar as possible in standard English, so that you will know not only what to do but why you are doing it. Do not, however, expect to learn the material in this book from a single reading. The concepts involved in statistics, especially inferential statistics, are so challenging that it is often said that the only way to completely understand statistics is to teach it (or write a book about it). On the other hand, there is no reason to approach statistics with fear and trembling. You do not have to be a mathematical expert to obtain a good working knowledge of statistics. What *is* needed is mathematical comprehension sufficient to cope with high school–level algebra and a willingness to work at new concepts until they are understood.

Descriptive and Inferential Statistics

One purpose of statistics is to summarize or describe the characteristics of a set of data in a clear and convenient fashion. This is accomplished by what are called *descriptive statistics.* For example, your grade point average serves as a convenient summary of all of the grades that you have received in college. Part I of this book is devoted to descriptive statistics.

A second function of statistics is to make possible the solution of an extremely important problem. Behavioral scientists can never measure *all* of the cases in which they are interested. For example, a clinical psychologist studying the effects of various kinds of therapies cannot obtain data on all of the mental patients in the world; a social psychologist studying gender differences in attitudes cannot measure all of the millions of men and women in the United States; an experimental psychologist cannot observe the maze behavior of all rats. Behavioral scientists want to know what is happening in a given *population*—a large group (theoretically an infinitely large group) of people, animals, objects, or responses that are alike in at least one respect (for example, all men in the United States). They cannot measure the entire population, however, because it is so large that it would be much too time consuming and expensive to do so. What to do?

One reasonable procedure is to measure a relatively small number of cases drawn from the population (that is, a *sample*). A sample of 100 people can readily be interviewed or given a written questionnaire. However, conclusions that apply only to the 100 people who happened to be included in the sample are unlikely to be of much interest. The behavioral scientist hopes to advance scientific knowledge by drawing general conclusions—for example, about the populations of men and women from which the samples of 50 men and 50 women were drawn. *Inferential statistics* makes it possible to draw inferences about what is happening in the population based on what is observed in a sample from that population. (This point will be discussed at greater length in

Chapter 9.) The remaining parts of this book are devoted to inferential statistics, which makes frequent use of some of the descriptive statistics discussed in Part I.

Populations, Samples, Parameters, and Statistics

As the above discussion indicates, the term *population* as used in statistics does not necessarily refer to people. For example, the population of interest may be that of all white rats of a given genetic strain, or all responses of a single subject's eyelid in a conditioning experiment.

Whereas the population consists of all of the cases of interest, a *sample* consists of any subgroup drawn from the specified population. It is important that the population be clearly specified. For example, a group of 100 New York University freshmen might be a well-drawn sample from the population of all NYU freshmen or a poorly drawn sample from the population of all undergraduates in the United States. It is strictly proper to apply (that is, *generalize*) the research results only to the specified population. (A researcher *may* justifiably argue that her results are more widely generalizable, but she is on her own if she does so because the rules of statistical inference do not justify this.)

A *statistic* is a numerical quantity (such as an average) that summarizes some characteristic of a sample. A *parameter* is the corresponding value of that characteristic in the population. For example, if the average studying time of a sample of 100 NYU freshmen is 7.4 hours per week, then 7.4 is a statistic. If the average studying time of the population of all NYU freshmen is 9.6 hours per week, then 9.6 is the corresponding population parameter. Usually the values of population parameters are unknown because the population is too large to measure in its entirety, and appropriate techniques of inferential statistics are used to estimate the values of population parameters from sample statistics. If the sample is properly selected, the sample statistics will often give good estimates of the parameters of the population from which the sample was drawn; if the sample is poorly chosen, erroneous conclusions are likely to occur. Whether you are doing your own research or reading about that of someone else, you should always check to be sure that the population to which the results are generalized is proper in light of the sample from which the results were obtained.

Measurement Scales

You may have noticed that we have used the term *data* several times without talking about where the data come from. It should come as no surprise, however, that in the behavioral sciences the data generally come from measuring some aspect of the behavior of a human or animal. Unlike physics, in which there are quite a few important *constants* (values that are always the same, such as the speed of light or the mass of an electron), the behavioral sciences deal mainly with the measurement of *variables,* which can take on a range of different values. An additional complication faced by the behavioral scientist is that some of the variables of most interest are difficult to measure (e.g., anxiety).

Interval Scales

How precisely you can measure a behavioral or psychological variable depends in part on the type of scale you use. The most precise scales are the kinds that are used for physical measurement. For instance, the temperature of the skin at your fingertips can be related to the amount of stress that you experience (high stress can cause the constriction of peripheral blood vessels, resulting in a decrease in skin temperature). Using either the Fahrenheit or Celsius temperature scale allows a precise measurement of skin temperature. Because degrees on either scale are fixed units that are always the same size, you can be sure that the difference between, say, 32 and 33 degrees Celsius is exactly the same as the difference between 18 and 19 degrees Celsius. These two temperature scales are therefore called *interval* scales.

Ratio Scales

Another desirable property that scales may have is the ratio property, which requires that a measurement of zero on the scale indicates that there is really nothing left of what is being measured. If the scale has a true zero point in addition to the interval property, a measurement of 6 units, for instance, will actually indicate twice as much of what is being measured as 3 units. Therefore, such scales are called *ratio* scales. A measurement of zero degrees on the Kelvin temperature scale means that there is no temperature at all (this is absolute zero), which is not the case for the Fahrenheit or Celsius scales. Therefore, Kelvin is a ratio scale, whereas the latter two are just interval scales.

It is only the interval property that is needed for precise measurement, so it is common to make no distinction between interval and ratio scales, referring instead to interval/ratio data. We will use the less formal term *quantitative data,* as opposed to qualitative data, which we discuss next.

Nominal Scales

The crudest form of measurement is to classify items by assigning names to them (categorization), which does not involve any numerical precision at all. Such a scale is called a *nominal* scale. For example, a person's occupation can only be "measured" on a nominal scale (e.g., accountant, lawyer, carpenter, sales clerk). We can count the number of people that fall into each category, but (unlike in interval or ratio scales) there is no obvious order to the categories, and certainly no regular intervals between them. We will refer to such categorical data as being *qualitative,* as distinguished from quantitative.

Ordinal Scales

Sometimes it is possible to order your categories, even though the intervals are not precise. The most common example of this is called a Likert scale (after its creator, Rensis Likert), on which respondents rate their agreement with some statement by choosing, for instance, among "strongly agree," "agree," "uncertain," "disagree," and "strongly disagree." Because the order of the categories is clear but there is no way to be sure that they are equally spaced, this type of scale lacks the interval property and is therefore called an *ordinal scale.* Although it is a somewhat controversial practice, many behavioral researchers simply assign numbers to the categories (e.g., strongly agree is 1, agree is 2) and then treat the data as though they came from an interval/ratio scale.

Another less common way that an ordinal scale can be created is by rank ordering. It may not be possible to measure, in a precise way, the creativity of paintings produced by students in an art class, but a panel of judges could rank them from most to least creative, with perhaps a few paintings tied at the same rank.

Sometimes researchers have quantitative measurements that vary in such an odd way that it becomes more useful just to rank them and use the ranks in place of the original measurements, even though ranks are less precise. We will explain this somewhat unusual practice when we focus on statistical tests with ordinal data in Chapter 21. Until that chapter, we will deal only with purely qualitative (nominal) and purely quantitative (interval/ratio) data.

Independent and Dependent Variables

Most behavioral research can be classified into one of the following two categories: *observational* or *experimental.*

In the simplest experiment, a researcher creates two conditions. The participants assigned to one of the conditions get some form of treatment, such as a pill intended to cure depression. Those assigned to the other condition get something that superficially resembles the treatment, such as a fake pill (placebo); they are part of a control group. These two conditions are the two different levels of an *independent* variable, or one that is created by the experimenter. Commonly, an independent variable is one whose levels are qualitative (e.g., a real pill versus a placebo). The *dependent* variable, or the variable that is measured by the experimenter and is expected to change from one level of the independent variable to another, is usually quantitative (such as a self-rating of depression). We will begin to describe such experiments in Chapter 10.

Behavioral researchers often study the relationships among variables when it is not convenient, or even possible, to manipulate any of the variables of interest. If one simply measures the relationship between two dependent variables (e.g., self-esteem in teenagers and their family's annual income to see if those from more affluent families tend to have higher—or lower!—self-esteem), this is an observational study. We will begin to describe this kind of research, where both the independent and dependent variables may be quantitative, in Chapter 12. Research in which both the independent and dependent variables (or two dependent variables) are qualitative involves what are called *nonparametric statistical procedures* and will be discussed in Part V of this text. Part V will also cover the special case in which one or two of a researcher's variables have been measured on an ordinal scale.

Sara's Study

This text covers a number of statistical procedures, some of which look very different from the others. In order to emphasize the links between these seemingly disparate statistical formulas and methods, we will refer throughout the chapters ahead to the same basic set of data collected by a hypothetical first-year doctoral student named Sara (she appears later in her career as the hypothetical researcher Dr. Tonin in *Explaining Psychological Statistics* [Cohen, 2000]). Her study, whose data are available on the Web at http://www.psych.nyu.edu/cohen/statstext.html, consists of both observational and experimental aspects.

The participants in Sara's study were students who attended one of two recitation classes that she conducted each week as the teaching assistant (TA) for an undergraduate class in statistics. (Of course, all of her students voluntarily signed proper informed consent forms, and her study was approved by the appropriate review board at her hypothetical school.) Her data were collected on two different days. On the first day of classes, the 85 students who came to either Sara's morning or afternoon recitation class filled in a brief background questionnaire on which they provided contact information, some qualitative data (gender and undergrad major), some quantitative data (number of math courses already completed, latest math SAT score, and the score they received on a diagnostic math background quiz they were all required to take before registering for statistics), and some ordinal data (a rating of their math phobia on a scale from 0 to 10).

The rest of Sara's data were collected as part of an experiment that she conducted on one day in the middle of the semester. The combined results of the two class sessions on that day add up to a total of 100 students who participated in the experiment. (Due to late registration and other factors, not all of Sara's students had shown up on the first day of classes.) First, Sara explained how each student could take his or her own pulse. She then provided a one-minute interval during which they counted the number of beats and wrote down that number as their (baseline) heart rate in beats per minute (bpm). Then each student filled out an anxiety questionnaire consisting of ten items, each rated (0 to 4) on a 5-point Likert scale. The questionnaire items inquired about anxiety and how the student was feeling at the present time (e.g., "Would you say that you are now feeling tense and restless? Circle one: Not at all; Somewhat; Moderately; Quite a bit; Extremely"). Total scores could range from 0 to 40, and provided a measure of baseline anxiety.

Next, Sara announced a pop quiz. She handed out a page containing eleven multiple-choice statistics questions on material covered during the preceding 2 weeks, and asked the students to keep this page face down while taking and recording their (prequiz) pulse and filling out an anxiety questionnaire for a second time. Then Sara told the students they had 15 minutes to take the fairly difficult quiz. She also told them that the first 10 questions were worth 1 point each but that the 11th question was worth 3 points extra credit. Sara's experimental manipulation consisted of varying the difficulty of the 11th question. Twenty-five quizzes were distributed at each level of difficulty of the final question: easy, moderate, difficult, and impossible to solve. After the quizzes were collected at the end of the 15 minutes, Sara asked the students to provide heart rate and anxiety data (postquiz) one more time. Finally, Sara explained the experiment, adding that the 11th quiz question would not be scored and that, although the students would get back their quizzes with their score for the first 10 items, that score would not influence their grade for the statistics course.

We will use Sara's data set in most chapters to illustrate the main statistical procedure being taught, and in all chapters to create exercises that can be solved by a computer running statistical software. We hope that all statistics students will eventually become proficient at performing statistical procedures by computer. However, we still believe that there is important educational value in asking students to apply basic statistical formulas directly to small sets of numbers to see how the formulas work and to thus gain a greater understanding of the statistical results being generated by computer programs. The first step toward understanding the statistical formulas that will be presented in this text is to become familiar with the "workhorse" of statistics, the procedure known as *summation*.

Summation Notation

Mathematical formulas and symbols often appear forbidding. In fact, when you get to know them, you will see that they are just very convenient ways to clearly and concisely convey information that would be much more awkward to express in words. In statistics, a particularly important symbol is the one used to represent the *sum* of a set of numbers—that is, the value obtained by adding up all of the numbers.

To illustrate the use of summation notation, let us suppose that eight students take a 10-point quiz. Letting X stand for the variable in question (quiz scores), let us further suppose that the results are as follows:

$$X_1 = 7 \qquad X_2 = 9 \qquad X_3 = 6 \qquad X_4 = 10$$
$$X_5 = 6 \qquad X_6 = 5 \qquad X_7 = 3 \qquad X_8 = X_N = 4$$

Notice that X_1 represents the first score on X; X_2 stands for the second score on X; and so on. Also, the *number of scores* is denoted by N; in this example, $N = 8$. The last score may be represented by either X_8 or X_N. The *sum of all the X scores* is represented by

$$\sum_{i=1}^{N} X_i,$$

where Σ, the Greek capital letter sigma, stands for "the sum of" and is called the *summation sign*. The subscript below the summation sign indicates that the sum begins with the first score (X_i where $i = 1$), and the superscript above the summation sign indicates that the sum continues up to and including the last score (X_i where $i = N$ or 8). Thus,

$$\sum_{i=1}^{N} X_i = X_1 + X_2 + X_3 + X_4 + X_5 + X_6 + X_7 + X_8$$
$$= 7 + 9 + 6 + 10 + 6 + 5 + 3 + 4$$
$$= 50$$

In some instances, the sum of only a subgroup of the numbers may be needed. For example, the symbol

$$\sum_{i=3}^{6} X_i$$

represents the sum beginning with the third score (X_i where $i = 3$) and ending with the sixth score (X_i where $i = 6$). Thus,

$$\sum_{i=3}^{6} X_i = X_3 + X_4 + X_5 + X_6$$
$$= 6 + 10 + 6 + 5$$
$$= 27$$

Most of the time, however, the sum of *all* the scores is needed in the statistical analysis. In such situations it is customary to omit the indices i and N from the notation, as follows:

$$\sum X = \text{sum of all the } X \text{ scores}$$

The fact that there is no written indication as to where to begin and end the summation is taken to mean that all the X scores are to be summed.

Summation Rules

Certain rules involving summation notation will prove useful in subsequent chapters. Let us suppose that the eight students previously mentioned take a second quiz, denoted by Y. The results of both quizzes can be summarized conveniently as follows:

Subject (S)	Quiz 1 (X)	Quiz 2 (Y)
1	7	8
2	9	6
3	6	4
4	10	10
5	6	5
6	5	10
7	3	9
8	4	8

We have already seen that $\sum X = 50$. The sum of the scores on the second quiz is equal to

$$\sum Y = Y_1 + Y_2 + Y_3 + Y_4 + Y_5 + Y_6 + Y_7 + Y_8$$
$$= 8 + 6 + 4 + 10 + 5 + 10 + 9 + 8$$
$$= 60$$

The following rules are illustrated using the small set of data shown, and you should verify each one carefully.

Rule 1. $\sum(X + Y) = \sum X + \sum Y$

Illustration	S	X	Y	$X + Y$
	1	7	8	15
	2	9	6	15
	3	6	4	10
	4	10	10	20
	5	6	5	11
	6	5	10	15
	7	3	9	12
	8	4	8	12
		$\sum X = 50$	$\sum Y = 60$	$\sum (X + Y) = 110$
		$\sum X + \sum Y = 110$		

This rule should be intuitively obvious; the same total should be reached regardless of the order in which the scores are added.

Rule 2. $\sum(X - Y) = \sum X - \sum Y$

Illustration	S	X	Y	X – Y
	1	7	8	–1
	2	9	6	3
	3	6	4	2
	4	10	10	0
	5	6	5	1
	6	5	10	–5
	7	3	9	–6
	8	4	8	–4
		$\sum X = 50$	$\sum Y = 60$	$\sum(X - Y) = -10$
		$\sum X - \sum Y = -10$		

As with the first rule, it makes no difference whether you subtract first and then sum $[\sum(X - Y)]$ or obtain the sums of X and Y first and then subtract $(\sum X - \sum Y)$.

Unfortunately, matters are not so simple when multiplication and squaring are involved.

Rule 3. $\sum XY \neq \sum X \sum Y$

That is, first multiplying each X score by the corresponding Y score and then summing $(\sum XY)$ is *not* equal to summing the X scores $(\sum X)$ and summing the Y scores $(\sum Y)$ first and then multiplying once $(\sum X \sum Y)$.

Illustration	S	X	Y	XY
	1	7	8	56
	2	9	6	54
	3	6	4	24
	4	10	10	100
	5	6	5	30
	6	5	10	50
	7	3	9	27
	8	4	8	32
		$\sum X = 50$	$\sum Y = 60$	$\sum XY = 373$
		$\sum X \sum Y = (50)(60) = 3{,}000$		

Observe that $\sum XY = 373$, while $\sum X \sum Y = 3{,}000$.

Rule 4. $\sum X^2 \neq \left(\sum X\right)^2$

That is, first squaring all of the X values and then summing ($\sum X^2$) is *not* equal to summing first and then squaring a single quantity [$(\sum X)^2$].

Illustration	S	X	X^2
	1	7	49
	2	9	81
	3	6	36
	4	10	100
	5	6	36
	6	5	25
	7	3	9
	8	4	16
		$\sum X = 50$	$\sum X^2 = 352$

$$(\sum X)^2 = (50)^2 = 2,500$$

Here, $\sum X^2 = 352$, while $(\sum X)^2 = 2,500$.

Rule 5.   **If k is a *constant* (a fixed numerical value), then**

$$\sum k = Nk$$

Illustration	Suppose that $k = 3$. Then,
S	k
1	3
2	3
3	3
4	3
5	3
6	3
7	3
8	3
	$\sum k = 24$

$$Nk = (8)(3) = 24$$

Rule 6.   **If k is a constant,**

$$\sum (X + k) = \sum X + \sum k = \sum X + Nk$$

S	Illustration X	Suppose that $k = 5$. Then, k	$X + k$
1	7	5	12
2	9	5	14
3	6	5	11
4	10	5	15
5	6	5	11
6	5	5	10
7	3	5	8
8	4	5	9
	$\sum X = 50$	$\sum k = Nk = 40$	$\sum (X + k) = 90$

$$\sum X + Nk = 50 + (8)(5) = 90$$

This rule follows directly from Rules 1 and 5.

Rule 7.   **If k is a constant,**

$$\sum (X - k) = \sum X - Nk$$

The illustration of this rule is similar to that of Rule 6 and is left to the reader as an exercise.

Rule 8.   **If k is a constant,**

$$\sum kX = k \sum X$$

S	Illustration X	Suppose that $k = 2$. Then, k	kX
1	7	2	14
2	9	2	18
3	6	2	12
4	10	2	20
5	6	2	12
6	5	2	10
7	3	2	6
8	4	2	8
	$\sum X = 50$		$\sum kX = 100$

$$k \sum X = (2)(50) = 100$$

Summary

Descriptive statistics are used to summarize and make understandable large quantities of data. *Inferential statistics* are used to draw inferences about numerical quantities (called *parameters*) concerning *populations* based on numerical quantities (called *statistics*) obtained from *samples*. Some behavioral variables cannot be measured precisely (e.g., religion) but can only be measured qualitatively using categories (e.g., Protestant, Catholic, Jewish), which comprise a *nominal* scale. If the categories can be placed in order (e.g., the belts awarded for different levels of skill in the martial arts—black belt, brown belt, etc.), an *ordinal* scale has been created. If the scale involves precise measurement resulting in units of equal size, the data are considered to be *quantitative*, whether the scale has a true zero point (*ratio* scale) or not (*interval* scale). Experiments involve measuring dependent variables that are expected to vary somewhat as a function of the different levels of one or more independent variables created by the researcher. *Observational* research involves comparing dependent variables to each other since we are not manipulating variables.

The summation sign, Σ, is used to indicate "the sum of" and occurs frequently in statistical work. Remember that ΣX is a shorthand version of

$$\sum_{i=1}^{N} X_i$$

(where N = number of subjects or cases).

Summation Rules:

1. $\Sigma(X + Y) = \Sigma X + \Sigma Y$
2. $\Sigma(X - Y) = \Sigma X - \Sigma Y$
3. ΣXY (multiply first, then add) $\neq \Sigma X \Sigma Y$ (add first, then multiply)
4. ΣX^2 (square first, then add) $\neq (\Sigma X)^2$ (add first, then square)

If k is a constant,

5. $\Sigma k = Nk$
6. $\Sigma(X + k) = \Sigma X + Nk$
7. $\Sigma(X - k) = \Sigma X - Nk$
8. $\Sigma kX = k \Sigma X$

Exercises

The exercises in this section refer to the following set of data.[1]

Hypothetical Scores on a 20-Point Psychology Test for Students Drawn at Random from Four Universities

University A (N = 50)	17	12	6	13	9	15	11	16	4	15
	12	13	10	13	2	11	13	10	20	14
	12	17	10	15	12	17	9	14	11	15
	11	16	9	13	18	10	13	0	11	16
	9	18	12	13	12	17	8	16	12	15
University B (N = 50)	17	8	12	12	3	12	7	14	1	11
	12	11	9	14	10	13	7	13	8	12
	9	12	17	11	6	10	10	3	9	8
	6	13	5	16	10	9	19	5	12	10
	16	11	14	11	13	12	2	17	10	14
University C (N = 10)	9	11	6	5	4	9	0	4	5	7
University D (N = 5)	14	8	17	6	10					

1. Express the following words in symbols.
   (a) Add up all the scores on test X, then add up all the scores on test Y, and then add the two sums together.
   (b) Add up all the scores on test G. To this, add the following: the sum obtained by squaring all the scores on test P and then adding them up.
   (c) Square all the scores on test X. Add them up. From this, subtract 6 times the sum you get when you multiply each score on X by the corresponding score on Y and add them up. To this, add 4 times the quantity obtained by adding up all the scores on test X and squaring the result. To this, add twice the sum obtained by squaring each Y score and then adding them up. (Compare the amount of space needed to express this equation in words with the amount of space needed to express it in symbols. Do you see why summation notation is necessary?)

2. Five students are enrolled in an advanced course in psychology. Two quizzes are given early in the semester, each worth a total of 10 points. The results are as follows:

Student	Quiz 1 (X)	Quiz 2 (Y)
1	0	2
2	2	6
3	1	7
4	3	6
5	4	9

---

1. These data, the problems in this section, and most of the problems in subsequent Exercises sections come from Ewen (2000).

(a) Compute each of the following:

$\Sigma X = $ _____ $(\Sigma X)^2 = $ _____ $\Sigma(X - Y) = $ _____

$\Sigma Y = $ _____ $(\Sigma Y)^2 = $ _____ $\Sigma X - \Sigma Y = $ _____

$\Sigma X^2 = $ _____ $\Sigma (X - Y) = $ _____ $\Sigma XY = $ _____

$\Sigma Y^2 = $ _____ $\Sigma X + \Sigma Y = $ _____ $\Sigma X \Sigma Y = $ _____

$\Sigma_{i=1}^{3} X_i = $ _____ $\Sigma_{i=2}^{5} Y_i = $ _____ $\Sigma_{i=2}^{4} X_i Y_i = $ _____

(b) Using the results of part (a), show that each of the following rules listed in this chapter is true:

Rule 1: _____ = _____

Rule 2: _____ = _____

Rule 3: _____ ≠ _____

Rule 4: _____ ≠ _____ (X data)

_____ ≠ _____ (Y data)

(c) After some consideration, the instructor decides that Quiz 1 was excessively difficult and decides to add 4 points to each student's score. This can be represented in symbols by using k to stand for the constant amount in question, 4 points.

Using Rule 6, compute $\Sigma(X + k) = $ _____ + _____ = _____.

Compute $\Sigma X + k = $ _____ + _____ = _____. (Note that this result is different from the preceding one.)

Now add 4 points to each student's score on Quiz 1 and obtain the sum of these new scores.

(d) Had the instructor been particularly uncharitable, he might have decided that Quiz 2 was too easy and subtracted 3 points from each student's score on that quiz. Although this is a new problem, the letter k can again be used to represent the constant; here, $k = 3$.

Using Rule 7, compute $\Sigma(Y - k) = $ _____ - _____ = _____.

Compute $\Sigma Y - k = $ _____ - _____ = _____. (Note that this result is different from the preceding one.)

Now subtract 3 points from each student's score on Quiz 2 and obtain the sum of these new scores.

(e) Suppose that the instructor decides to double all of the original scores on Quiz 1.

Using Rule 8, compute $\Sigma kX = $ _____ · _____ = _____.

Now double each student's score on Quiz 1 and obtain the sum of these new scores.

3. Compute the following:

(a) For University C:

$\Sigma X = $ _____ $\Sigma X^2 = $ _____ $(\Sigma X)^2 = $ _____

(b) For University D:

$$\Sigma X = \underline{\quad} \qquad \Sigma X^2 = \underline{\quad} \qquad (\Sigma X)^2 = \underline{\quad}$$

If you would like some additional practice, you may verify that

For University A, $\Sigma X = 617$; $\Sigma X^2 = 8385$; $(\Sigma X)^2 = 380{,}689$

For University B, $\Sigma X = 526$; $\Sigma X^2 = 6316$; $(\Sigma X)^2 = 276{,}676$

4. For each of the following (separate) sets of data, compute the values needed in order to fill in the answer spaces. Then answer the additional questions that follow.

Data set 1:

S	X	Y		
			$N = \underline{\quad}$	
1	1	2	$\Sigma X = \underline{\quad}$	$\Sigma Y = \underline{\quad}$
2	3	5	$\Sigma X^2 = \underline{\quad}$	$\Sigma Y^2 = \underline{\quad}$
3	1	0	$(\Sigma X)^2 = \underline{\quad}$	$(\Sigma Y)^2 = \underline{\quad}$
4	0	1	$\Sigma XY = \underline{\quad}$	$\Sigma X \Sigma Y = \underline{\quad}$
5	2	3	$\Sigma(X + Y) = \underline{\quad}$	$\Sigma(X - Y) = \underline{\quad}$

Data set 2:

S	X	Y		
			$N = \underline{\quad}$	
1	7.14	0	$\Sigma X = \underline{\quad}$	$\Sigma Y = \underline{\quad}$
2	8.00	2.60	$\Sigma X^2 = \underline{\quad}$	$\Sigma Y^2 = \underline{\quad}$
3	0	4.32	$(\Sigma X)^2 = \underline{\quad}$	$(\Sigma Y)^2 = \underline{\quad}$
4	4.00	2.00	$\Sigma XY = \underline{\quad}$	$\Sigma X \Sigma Y = \underline{\quad}$
5	4.00	6.00	$\Sigma(X + Y) = \underline{\quad}$	$\Sigma(X - Y) = \underline{\quad}$
6	1.00	1.15		
7	2.25	1.00		
8	10.00	3.00		

	set 1	set 2
If every X score is multiplied by 3.2, what is the new ΣX in each set?	_____	_____
If 7 is subtracted from every Y score, what is the new ΣY in each set?	_____	_____
If 1.8 is added to every X score, what is the new ΣX in each set?	_____	_____
If every Y score is divided by 4, what is the new ΣY in each set?	_____	_____

(Hint: Use the appropriate summation rule in each case so as to make the calculations easier.)

5. Compute the values needed to fill in the blanks.

   Data set 3:

S	X	Y
1	97	89
2	68	57
3	85	87
4	74	76
5	92	97
6	92	79
7	100	91
8	63	50
9	85	85
10	87	84
11	81	91
12	93	91
13	77	75
14	82	77

$N =$ _____

$\Sigma X =$ _____ $\Sigma Y =$ _____

$\Sigma X^2 =$ _____ $\Sigma Y^2 =$ _____

$(\Sigma X)^2 =$ _____ $(\Sigma Y)^2 =$ _____

$\Sigma XY =$ _____ $\Sigma X \Sigma Y =$ _____

$\Sigma(X + Y) =$ _____ $\Sigma(X - Y) =$ _____

Thought Questions

1. What is the difference between (a) a population and a sample? (b) a parameter and a statistic? (c) descriptive statistics and inferential statistics?

2. What is the difference between a constant and a variable?

3. What is the difference between a ratio scale and an interval scale?

4. What important property do interval scales have that ordinal and nominal scales do *not* have?

5. If we want to know how many people have each of five different psychological disorders—Major Depressive Disorder, Bipolar Disorder, Generalized Anxiety Disorder, Obsessive-Compulsive Disorder, and Phobic Disorder—what kind of measurement scale are we using?

6. A poll of sportswriters ranks the 25 best college football teams in the country, where #1 is the best team, #2 is the second best team, and so on. What kind of measurement scale is this?

7. What kind of measurement scales are used for each of the following variables in Sara's study? (a) The gender of each student. (b) The undergraduate major of each student. (c) The number of math courses each student has

already completed. (d) The latest SAT score of each student. (e) The ratings of the math phobia of each student.

8. What is the difference between an independent variable and a dependent variable?

Computer Exercises

1. Read Sara's data into your statistical software package. For those not using the Statistical Package for the Social Sciences (SPSS), we have provided the data in two convenient formats: a tab-delimited text file, and an Excel spreadsheet (Microsoft Office 95). For the convenience of SPSS users, we have also included the data as an SPSS.sav file, though your instructor may want you to know how to read text or Excel files into SPSS.

2. Label the values of the categorical (i.e., qualitative) variables according to the following codes: For gender, 1 = Female and 2 = Male; for undergrad major, 1 = Psychology, 2 = Pre-med, 3 = Biology, 4 = Sociology, and 5 = Economics. Your instructor may ask you to fill in missing-value codes for any data that are missing (e.g., blank cell in the Excel spreadsheet).

3. A good many statistical functions can be performed in Excel. As a first step, use the Sum function to add up the scores for each of the quantitative variables in the Excel file of Sara's data.

4. Create a new variable that adds 10 points to everyone's math background quiz score. How does the sum of this variable compare to the sum of the original variable? What general rule is being illustrated by this comparison?

5. Create a new variable that is 10 times the statistics quiz score. How does the sum of this variable compare to the sum of the original variable? What general rule is being illustrated by this comparison?

Bridge to SPSS

SPSS is certainly not the only "statpack" available, and your instructor may prefer to teach you how to use SAS, Minitab, or another of SPSS's many competitors. However, because SPSS for Windows is the most popular statpack in the social and behavioral sciences, and is particularly easy to learn for introductory statistics students, we provide this section after the computer exercises in each chapter. (This should help students translate the terminology used by SPSS into the language that we are using to describe the same topics in this text.) We also show you briefly how to obtain from SPSS the statistics discussed in the chapter, along with a few tricks and shortcuts. However, we understand

Introduction 21

that even though you may be using SPSS in your statistics course, you may not be using the latest version, which will probably be 14.0 by the time this text is printed. Therefore, we only describe aspects of SPSS that have not changed between version 10, released in the year 2000, and version 14.

The rightmost column in SPSS's Variable View spreadsheet is labeled **Measure,** and it allows you to classify each of your variables as being measured by one of the following three types of scales: nominal, ordinal, or scale. The first two terms are used the same way by SPSS that we have defined them in this chapter. *Scale* is SPSS's term for interval/ratio data. In general, numerical data are set to **scale** by default, whereas string data—which contain letters instead of, or in addition to, numbers—are set to **nominal.** In practice, these scale designations are not very important, because SPSS uses them only to determine the way some charts are displayed.

For simplicity, Sara's data set is presented entirely in terms of numbers, even for the categorical variables of gender and undergrad major. To assign meaningful labels to the arbitrary numbers we have used to represent the different levels of the categorical variables, go down the Values column of Variable View until you reach the row for a categorical variable. Then click in the right side of that cell to open the Value Labels box. For gender, you would type **1** for Value, and then tab to Value Label, where you can type **female.** Click the **Add** button, and provide a label (male) for value **2,** then **Add** again, and **OK.** The process is similar for undergrad major. Note that if you use the Missing column to define a particular value of a variable, say 99, as meaning that the value is missing, rather than just leaving the cell blank (e.g., you could use 99 to mean "missing" for the math background quiz, because none of the real values can be that high), you can then attach a value label to that value, such as "never took the math quiz."

To create new variables that are based on ones already in your spreadsheet, click on the **Transform** menu, then **Compute.** In the Compute Variable box that opens up, Target Variable is a name that you make up (and type into that box) for the new variable (but no more than eight characters and no embedded spaces); when you have filled in a Numeric Expression and then click **OK,** the new variable will suddenly appear in the rightmost column of your Data View spreadsheet. We will leave it to your instructor, or an SPSS guide book, to teach you various ways to create Numeric Expressions that transform your existing variables into new ones.

Chapter 2
Frequency Distributions and Graphs

PREVIEW

The Purpose of Descriptive Statistics

What is the primary purpose of descriptive statistics?

What are the the most useful types of descriptive statistics?

Regular Frequency Distributions

What is a regular frequency distribution, how is it constructed, and why is it useful?

Cumulative Frequency Distributions

How does a cumulative frequency distribution differ from a regular frequency distribution, and how is it constructed?

Grouped Frequency Distributions

How does a grouped frequency distribution differ from a regular frequency distribution, and how is it constructed?

What is gained by using a grouped frequency distribution?

What is lost by using a grouped frequency distribution, and why are such distributions usually *not* used when computing means and other statistics?

Graphic Representations

What are bar charts, histograms, frequency polygons, and stem-and-leaf displays?

When is a bar chart preferable to a histogram?

When is a frequency polygon preferable to a histogram?

Shapes of Frequency Distributions

What is meant when we say that a distribution is symmetric? skewed? unimodal? bimodal? normal? rectangular? a J-curve?

Summary

Exercises

Thought Questions

Computer Exercises

Bridge to SPSS

The Purpose of Descriptive Statistics

The primary goal of descriptive statistics is to bring order out of chaos. For example, consider the plight of a professor who has given an examination to a class of 85 students and has computed the total score on each student's exam. In order to decide what represents relatively good and bad performance on the examination (e.g., in order to grade on a curve), the professor must find a way to comprehend and interpret 85 numbers (test scores). Similarly, a researcher who runs 60 rats through a maze and records the time taken to run the maze on each trial is faced with the problem of interpreting 60 numbers.

In addition to causing problems for the professor or researcher, the large quantity of numbers also creates difficulties for the audience in question. The students in the first example are likely to request the distribution of test scores so as to be able to interpret their own performance, and they also will have trouble trying to interpret 85 unorganized numbers. Likewise, the people who read the scientific paper ultimately published by the researcher interested in rats and mazes will have a difficult time trying to interpret a table with 60 numbers in it.

Descriptive statistics help to resolve problems such as these by making it possible to *summarize and describe large quantities of data.* Among the various techniques that you will find particularly useful are the following:

Frequency distributions and graphs—procedures for describing all (or nearly all) of the data in a convenient way.

Measures of "central tendency"—single numbers that describe the location of a distribution of scores: where the "center of gravity" of the scores generally falls within the infinite range of possible values.

Measures of variability—single numbers that describe how "spread out" a set of scores is: whether the numbers are similar to each other and vary very little, as opposed to whether they tend to be very different from one another and vary a great deal.

Transformed scores—new scores that replace each original number, and show at a glance how good or bad any score is in comparison to the other scores in the group.

Areas under the normal curve—proportions that tell you the probability of randomly selecting a score smaller or larger than yours from a particular normal distribution.

Each of these procedures serves a different (and important) function. Our discussion of descriptive statistics begins with frequency distributions and graphs; the other topics are treated in subsequent chapters.

Regular Frequency Distributions

One way of making a set of data more comprehensible is to write down every possible score value in order and record next to each score value the number of times that the score occurs. For example, let us look at the quiz scores for the 100 students in Sara's statistics class who participated in her experiment. Recall that the quiz consisted of 10 questions worth 1 point each (the 11th question was not graded), so that any student's score could therefore fall between 0 (none correct) and 10 (all correct), inclusive. The scores of the 100 students are shown in Table 2.1.

As you can see, the table of 100 numbers is difficult to interpret. A *regular frequency distribution,* on the other hand, will present a clearer picture. The first step in constructing such a distribution is to list every *score value* in the first column of a table (frequently denoted by the symbol X), with the highest score at the top. The *frequency* (denoted by the symbol f) of each score, or the number of times a given score was obtained, is listed to the right of the score in the second column of the table. To arrive at the figures in the "Frequency" column, you could go through the data and count all the 10s, go through the data again and count all the 9s, and so forth, until all frequencies were tabulated. A more efficient plan is to go through the data just once and make a tally mark next to the appropriate score in the score column for each score, and add up the tally marks at the end.

The complete regular frequency distribution is shown in Table 2.2 (ignore the "Cumulative Frequency" column for the moment; it will be discussed in the next section). The table reveals at a glance how often each score was obtained. For example, nine people received a score of 9 and five people received a score of 3. This makes it easier to interpret the performance of the students in Sara's class, since you can conveniently ascertain (among other things) that 6 was the most frequently obtained score, scores distant from 6 tended to occur less frequently than scores close to 6, and the majority of people got more than half the problems correct.

TABLE 2.1

Number of quiz questions answered correctly by the 100 college undergraduates in Sara's statistics class

5	8	3	6	5	8	3	7	4	7
6	8	7	4	6	5	8	7	10	6
5	3	6	1	8	6	8	5	7	10
8	9	6	9	6	5	9	9	6	3
8	5	8	4	8	6	7	4	10	5
8	7	6	8	5	7	6	9	6	10
4	8	6	8	6	5	4	7	9	6
7	4	5	5	9	6	6	7	4	5
10	3	5	7	9	10	6	7	6	6
6	9	8	7	8	5	7	4	6	8

TABLE 2.2		
Regular and cumulative frequency distributions for data in Table 2.1		
Score (X)	Frequency (f)	Cumulative frequency (cf)
10	6	100
9	9	94
8	17	85
7	15	68
6	23	53
5	15	30
4	9	15
3	5	6
2	0	1
1	1	1
0	0	0

Cumulative Frequency Distributions

The primary value of *cumulative frequency distributions* will not become apparent until subsequent chapters, when they will prove to be of assistance in the computation of certain statistics (such as the median and percentiles). To construct a cumulative frequency distribution, first form a regular frequency distribution. Then start with the *lowest* score in the distribution and form a new column of *cumulative frequencies* by adding up the frequencies as you go along. For example, the following diagram shows how the cumulative frequencies (denoted by the symbol *cf*) in the right hand column of Table 2.2 were obtained:

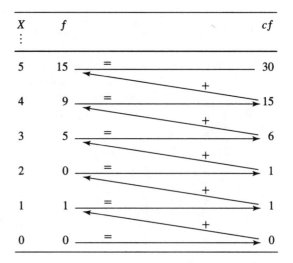

The cumulative frequency for the score of 4 is equal to 15. This value was obtained by adding the frequency (f) of that score, namely 9, to the cumulative frequency (cf) of the next lower score, which is 6. The other cumulative frequencies were obtained in a similar fashion.

The cumulative frequency distribution is interpreted as follows: the cumulative frequency of 15 for the score of 4 means that 15 people obtained a score of 4 *or less*. This can be readily verified by looking at the frequencies (f): nine people scored 4, five people scored 3, and one person scored 1, for a total of 15 people with scores at or below 4:

X	f	cf	
$\vdots$			
5	15	30	
4	9	15	scores of 4 or less
3	5	6	
2	0	1	
1	1	1	
0	0	0	

The *cf* for the score of 7 in Table 2.2 is 68, which means that 68 people obtained a score of *7 or less*. Since everyone obtained a score of *10 or less,* the *cf* for a score of 10 equals 100, the total number of subjects. (The *cf* for the *highest* score should always equal *N*.) Now, can you tell how many people obtained a score of *6 or more?* The cumulative frequency distribution reveals that 30 people obtained scores of 5 or less, so there must be 70 people who scored 6 or more. This can be checked by using the frequencies; there were *23* scores of 6 + *15* scores of 7 + *17* scores of 8 + *9* scores of 9 + *6* scores of 10. Although no unique information is presented by the cumulative frequency distribution, it allows you to arrive at certain needed information more quickly and conveniently than is possible using the regular frequency distribution.

Grouped Frequency Distributions

When the number of *different scores* to be listed in the score (X) column is not too large, regular frequency distributions are an excellent way to summarize a set of data. If, however, there are more than 15 or 20 values of X to be written, constructing a regular frequency distribution is likely to prove tedious. One way of avoiding an excessive case of writer's cramp, and a summary that does not summarize enough, is to use a *grouped frequency distribution.* Instead of

TABLE 2.3

Scores of 85 students on a 50-point math background quiz

39	42	30	11	35	25	18	26	37	15
29	22	33	32	21	43	11	11	32	29
44	26	30	49	13	38	26	30	45	21
31	28	14	35	10	41	15	39	33	34
46	21	38	26	26	37	37	14	26	24
32	15	22	28	33	47	9	22	31	20
37	40	20	39	30	18	29	35	41	21
26	25	29	33	23	30	43	28	32	32
34	28	38	32	31					

listing single scores in the score column (for example, 0, 1, 2, 3, 4, 5, 6, 7, . . .), several score values are grouped together into a *class interval* (for example, 0–4, 5–9, 10–14, 15–19, . . .), and frequencies are tallied for each interval.

As we mentioned in the first chapter, the students who attended one of Sara's first recitation classes filled out a background questionnaire, which asked them (among other things) to write in the score they had recently received on a diagnostic quiz of their basic math skills. The data in Table 2.3 represent the scores of the 85 students who filled out that questionnaire. Scores on the quiz could have ranged from zero to a maximum score of 50, but inspection of the data shows that the actual scores range from a low of 9 to a high of 49. Even so, if a regular frequency distribution were to be used, some 41 separate scores and corresponding frequencies would have to be listed.[1] To avoid such a tiresome task (and such a cumbersome table to look at), a grouped frequency distribution has been formed in Table 2.4. An *interval size* of 3 has been chosen, meaning that there are three score values in each class interval. (The symbol h will be used to denote interval size.) Then, successive intervals of size 3 are formed until the entire range of scores has been covered. Next, frequencies are tabulated, with all scores falling in the same interval being treated equally. For example, a score of 39, 40, or 41 would be entered by registering a tally mark next to the class interval 39–41. When the tabulation is completed, the frequency opposite a given class interval indicates the number of cases with scores in that interval.

Note that grouped frequency distributions lose information, since they do not provide the exact value of each score. They are very convenient for purposes of summarizing a set of data, but should not generally be used when computing means and other statistics.

In the illustrative problem, the interval size of 3 was specified. In your own work, there will be no such instructions, and it will be up to you to construct the proper intervals. The conventional procedure is to select the intervals in such a way as to satisfy the following guidelines:

---

1. There are 49 – 9 + 1 or 41 numbers between 9 and 49, inclusive.

TABLE 2.4
Grouped and cumulative frequency distributions for data
in Table 2.3

Class interval	Frequency (f)	Cumulative frequency (cf)
48–50	1	85
45–47	3	84
42–44	4	81
39–41	6	77
36–38	7	71
33–35	9	64
30–32	14	55
27–29	8	41
24–26	10	33
21–23	8	23
18–20	4	15
15–17	3	11
12–14	3	8
9–11	5	5

1. Have a total of approximately 8 to 15 class intervals.
2. Use an interval size of 2, 3, 5, or a multiple of 5, selecting the smallest size that will satisfy the first rule. (All intervals should be the same size.)
3. Make the lowest score in each interval a multiple of the interval size.

For example, suppose that scores range from a low of 49 to a high of 68. There is a total of 20 score values (68 – 49 + 1), and an interval size of 2 will yield 20/2 or 10 class intervals. This falls within the recommended limits of 8 and 15, and size 2 should therefore be selected. It would waste too much time and effort to list all the nonoccurring scores between zero and 48. Make the first interval 48–49, the next interval 50–51, and so on, so that the first score in each interval will be evenly divisible by the interval size, 2.

If instead scores range from a low of zero to a high of 52, there are 53 score values in all. An interval size of 2 or 3 will yield too many intervals (53/2 = 26 + ; 53/3 = 17 +), and size 4 is customarily avoided (being so close to 5, which produces intervals more like the familiar decimal system). Therefore, interval size 5, which will produce 11 intervals, should be chosen. Begin with the class interval 0–4 and continue with 5–9, 10–14, 15–19, and so on.

What if scores range from 14 to 25? In this case, there are only 12 possible score values and you *should not group* the data, because the loss of information would not be justified by the advantages of having such a small, easy-to-read table. Use a regular frequency distribution.

Just as was the case with regular frequency distributions, a cumulative frequency distribution can be formed from grouped data, and you will find one in Table 2.4. The cumulative frequencies are formed by starting with the lowest interval and adding up the frequencies as you go along, and are interpreted in the usual way. For example, the value of 64 corresponding to the class interval

33–35 means that 64 people obtained scores at or below this interval—that is, scores of 35 or less.

Graphic Representations

It is often effective to express frequency distributions pictorially as well as in tables. Four procedures for accomplishing this are discussed next.

Bar Charts

Suppose that just for the 25 pre-med students in her class, Sara tabulated the number of math courses that each had taken prior to enrolling in statistics, and the results are as follows:

Number of math courses (X)	f
7 or more	0
6	1
5	0
4	3
3	4
2	8
1	5
0	4

A *bar chart* (or *bar graph*) of these data is shown in Figure 2.1. To construct a bar chart, the Y-axis (vertical axis) is marked off in terms of *frequencies,* and the X-axis (horizontal axis) is marked off in terms of *score values.* The frequency of any value is expressed by the height of the bar above that value. For example, to show that a score of 3 (courses) occurred 4 times, a bar 4 units in height is drawn above this score.

Bar charts can be used for any kind of data, but they are particularly appropriate for *discrete* data, where results between the score values shown *cannot* occur. In the present example it is impossible for a student to have taken 2.4 courses, and this fact is well expressed in the bar chart by the separate and distinct bars above each score value. Categorical data (e.g., each student's undergraduate major) are always discrete, and are therefore good candidates for being displayed as bar charts.

Histograms

A *histogram* is very similar to a bar chart except that adjacent bars are allowed to touch, because the variable being graphed is considered *continuous.* When

FIGURE 2.1

Bar chart expressing number of prior math courses taken by 25 pre-med students

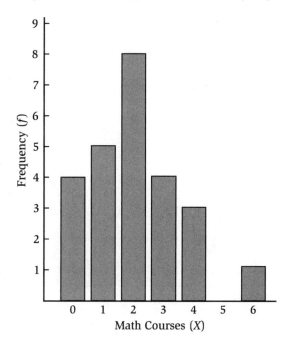

dealing with continuous data, results between whole score values can occur, or could if it were possible to measure with sufficient refinement. Interval or ratio data, whether or not fractions can occur, are almost always treated as continuous. For simplicity, the math background quiz was graded in terms of whole numbers, but it could have been graded even more precisely (at least in theory), resulting in scores like 32.7 or 38.4. Ordinal data (e.g., somewhat agree, strongly agree, etc.) are sometimes graphed as a histogram but are usually more appropriately displayed in a bar chart.

Treating the math quiz scores as continuous data, the frequencies in Table 2.4 are presented as a histogram in Figure 2.2. As in the bar chart, the Y-axis is marked off in terms of frequencies, and the frequency corresponding to a score (or class interval, as found in Table 2.4) is expressed by the height of the bar above the X-axis. However, because the scale being marked off on the X-axis is treated as continuous, it is marked off in terms of the *real limits* of each class interval, rather than its *apparent limits*. For instance, the apparent limits of the two lowest class intervals in Table 2.4, 9–11 and 12–14, do not appear to touch, but if the scale is considered continuous the real limits of those intervals are 8.5–11.5 and 11.5–14.5. As you can see, the real limits of adjacent intervals do touch for continuous data and do not allow any fractional scores to fall between intervals. Real limits are discussed in greater detail in the next chapter.

Histogram representing the grouped data in Table 2.4

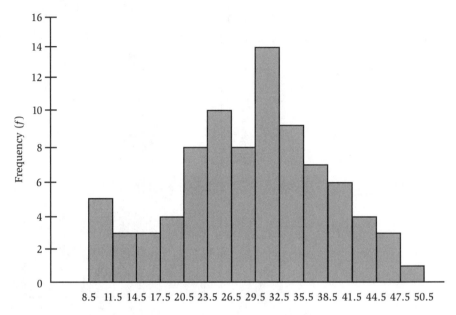

Scores on the math background quiz (X)

Frequency Polygons

In some cases, line graphs are easier to look at than a series of bars. Line graphs can be used to represent various kinds of frequency distributions, as described next.

Regular Frequency Polygons

An alternative to the histogram that is also appropriate only for continuous data is the *frequency polygon*. The frequency data in Table 2.4, which were graphed in Figure 2.2, are presented again as a *regular frequency polygon* in Figure 2.3. The strategy is the same as in the case of the histogram: the frequency of a score (or score interval) is expressed by the height of the graph above the X-axis (as measured along the Y-axis), and the scores are measured horizontally along the X-axis. The difference is that points, rather than bars, are used for each entry. Thus, the frequency of 5 for the class interval of 9–11 is shown by a dot 5 units up on the Y-axis above the score of 10 (the midpoint of the 9–11 interval; with a regular frequency distribution, as in Table 2.2, each score would be entered on the X-axis). All dots are connected with straight lines, and the leftmost and rightmost dots are connected to the X-axis at the midpoints of the next intervals to the left and right, respectively (see Figure 2.3). Regular frequency polygons are particularly appropriate when many different scores (or

FIGURE 2.3

Regular frequency polygon for data in Table 2.4

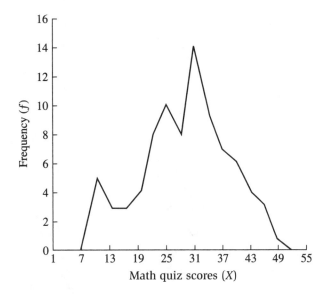

intervals) are being represented on the *X*-axis, because a histogram with many very narrow bars is particularly tedious to look at. Also, it is relatively easy to draw two frequency polygons on the same graph if, for example, you wanted to compare the math quiz distribution for this semester with the corresponding distribution from the previous semester. Imagine how hard it would be to look at and compare two histograms drawn on the same set of axes.

Cumulative Frequency Polygons

Cumulative frequency distributions are also commonly graphed in the form of frequency polygons, and the resulting figure is called (not very surprisingly) a *cumulative frequency polygon* (and sometimes called an *ogive*). An example, based on the data in Table 2.2, is provided in Figure 2.4. Note that, reading from left to right, the cumulative frequency distribution always remains level or increases and can never drop down toward the *X*-axis. This is because the cumulative frequencies are formed by successive additions. Thus, the *cf* for an interval can be at most equal to, but never less than, the *cf* for the preceding interval.

Stem-and-Leaf Displays

A simple and useful technique for summarizing a set of data, the *stem-and-leaf display* is a hybrid that combines features of the frequency distribution and the histogram (see Tukey, 1977). The "stems" consist of class intervals, while the "leaves" are strings of specific values within each interval.

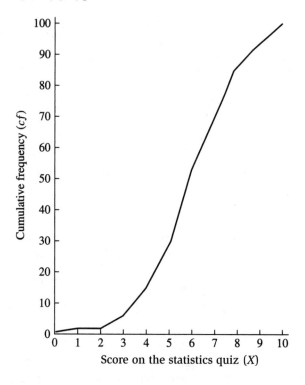

FIGURE 2.4

Cumulative frequency polygon for data in Table 2.2

TABLE 2.5

Stem-and-leaf display for data in Table 2.3

Stems (intervals)	Leaves (observations)	Frequency (f)	Cumulative frequency (cf)
5–9	9	1	1
10–14	0 1 1 1 3 4 4	7	8
15–19	5 5 5 8 8	5	13
20–24	0 0 1 1 1 1 2 2 2 3 4	11	24
25–29	5 5 6 6 6 6 6 6 6 8 8 8 8 9 9 9 9	17	41
30–34	0 0 0 0 0 1 1 1 2 2 2 2 2 2 3 3 3 3 4 4	20	61
35–39	5 5 5 7 7 7 7 8 8 8 9 9 9	13	74
40–44	0 1 1 2 3 3 4	7	81
45–49	5 6 7 9	4	85

To illustrate, consider once again the scores of the 85 students shown in Table 2.3 (and presented as a grouped frequency distribution in Table 2.4). In the interest of variety, let us choose an interval size of 5 for the stem-and-leaf display, and order the stems (intervals) from small to large going down the page. (See Table 2.5.) Each leaf is made up of the scores within a given interval, with each score represented solely by its units digit, and the scores in each leaf are ordered from low to high. Because each observation takes up one space, the stem-and-leaf display provides the same graphic representation as the histogram (rotated 90° counterclockwise), while at the same time explicitly giving each score value. Thus you can see both the overall shape of the distribution and such particulars as the largest and smallest observations. The stem-and-leaf display may be supplemented by the frequency distribution and/or the cumulative frequency distribution, as needed.

Since the stem-and-leaf display is used primarily to help understand a set of data, you may use or invent whatever variations best accomplish this purpose. For data that cover a wide range of values, you can use the last two digits to represent each score in the leaf (e.g., 460–479 | 63, 68, 74, 74, 78). Or, if there are a great many observations, you might choose to let each leaf entry represent not one but two or more cases.

Shapes of Frequency Distributions

It is often useful to talk about the general shape of a frequency distribution. Some important definitions commonly used in this regard are as follows. (Note that the distributions shown in the following definitions are *theoretical* frequency polygons, based on infinite populations, which is why they look so smooth.)

Symmetry versus Skewness

A distribution is *symmetric* if and only if it can be divided into two halves, each the "mirror image" of the other. For example, Distributions A, B, C, and G in Figure 2.5 are symmetric. Distributions D, E, F, and H are *not* symmetric, however, since they cannot be divided into two similar parts.

A markedly asymmetric distribution with a pronounced "tail" is described as *skewed* in the direction of the tail. Distribution E is *skewed to the left* (or negatively skewed), since the long tail is to the left of the distribution. Such a distribution indicates that most people obtained high scores but some (indicated by the tail) received quite low scores, as might happen if an instructor gave an exam that proved easy for all but the poorest students. If you create a frequency polygon for the data in Table 2.2, you will see that the statistics quiz scores have a mildly negative skew. Distribution F, on the other hand, is *skewed to the right* (or positively skewed), as is indicated by the position of the tail. This distribution indicates many low scores and some quite high scores, as could occur if an instructor gave a difficult examination on which only relatively few students excelled. If you were to inspect the distribution of baseline anxiety scores for all of Sara's students, you would see a positive skew. Most of the students have fairly low anxiety scores when not facing a threat (like a statistics quiz), but a few of the students are chronically anxious.

FIGURE 2.5

Shapes of frequency distributions. (A) Normal curve (symmetric, unimodal). (B) Symmetric, unimodal. (C) Symmetric, bimodal. (D) Asymmetric, bimodal. (E) Unimodal, skewed to the left. (F) Unimodal, skewed to the right. (G) Rectangular. (H) J-curve.

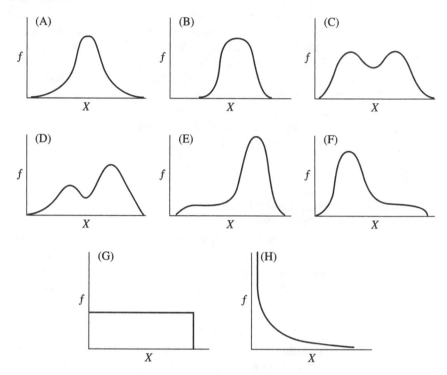

Modality

Modality refers to the number of clearly distinguishable high points or "peaks" in a distribution. In Figure 2.4, Distributions A, B, E, and F are described as *unimodal* because there is one peak; Distributions C and D are *bimodal* because there are two clearly pronounced peaks; and Distribution G has no modes at all. Be careful, however, not to be influenced by minor fluctuations when deciding whether to consider a distribution unimodal or bimodal. For example, the curve shown in Figure 2.3 is properly considered unimodal: with just one less case in the 24–26 interval and one more case in the 27–29 interval, the second "peak" would disappear entirely.

Special Distributions

Certain frequency distributions have names of their own. A particular bell-shaped, symmetric, and unimodal distribution shown in Example A of Figure

2.5 is called the *normal distribution,* about which much more will be said in subsequent chapters. In this distribution, frequencies are greatest at the center, and more extreme scores (both lower and higher) are less frequent. Many variables of interest to the behavioral scientist, such as intelligence, are approximately normally distributed. The distribution of math quiz scores, as shown in Figure 2.3, may look more like Example B than Example A in Figure 2.5, but it is similar enough to the normal distribution for most statistical purposes. This will be made clear in later chapters.

Example G illustrates a *rectangular* distribution, in which each score occurs with the same frequency. A distribution approximately like this would occur if one fair die were rolled a large number of times and the number of 1s, 2s, and so on were recorded. (This would, however, be a discrete distribution.)

Example H is an illustration of a *J-curve,* wherein the lowest score is most frequent and the frequencies decrease as the scores become larger. An example of such a distribution would be the number of industrial accidents per worker over a 2-month period: the majority of workers would have no accidents at all, some would have one accident, a few would have two accidents, and very few unfortunate souls would have a larger number of accidents. The mirror image of this distribution, which is shaped almost exactly like a "J," is also called a J-curve.

Summary

In *regular frequency distributions,* all score values are listed in the first column and the frequency corresponding to each score is listed to the right of the score in the second column. *Grouped frequency distributions* sacrifice some information for convenience by combining several score values in a single *class interval* so that fewer intervals and corresponding frequencies need be listed. *Cumulative frequency distributions* are obtained by starting with the frequency corresponding to the lowest score and adding up the frequencies as you go along. *Bar charts* and *histograms* are two similar methods for graphing frequency distributions, but bar charts are particularly appropriate for discrete data and histograms are preferred for continuous data. *Frequency polygons* are a useful alternative to histograms when you want to compare the shapes of two distributions. The *stem-and-leaf display* combines features of the frequency distribution and histogram and facilitates the comprehension of a data set by allowing the reader to see it all at once and with as much detail as is needed.

1. Regular Frequency Distributions

List every score value in the first column, with the highest score at the top. List the *frequency* (symbolized by f) of each score to the right of the score in the second column.

2. Grouped Frequency Distributions

List the *class intervals* in the first column and the frequencies in the second column. It is usually desirable to do the following:

1. Have a total of from 8 to 15 class intervals.
2. Use an interval size of 2, 3, 5, or a multiple of 5, selecting the smallest size that will satisfy the first rule. (All intervals should be the same size.)
3. Make the lowest score in each interval a multiple of the interval size.

Do not use grouped frequency distributions if all scores can be quickly and conveniently reported, because grouped frequency distributions lose information.

3. Cumulative Frequency Distributions

To the right of the frequency column, form a column of cumulative frequencies (symbolized by *cf*) by starting with the frequency for the lowest score and adding up the frequencies as you go along.

4. Graphic Representations

Bar charts, in which the frequency of any score is expressed by the height of the bar above that score, and the bars do not touch, are particularly appropriate for discrete data (where results between the score values shown cannot occur). *Histograms* are similar to bar charts except that adjacent bars are allowed to touch, so these types of graphs are particularly appropriate for continuous data (in which results between the score values shown can occur, or could if it were possible to measure with sufficient refinement). *Frequency polygons* are a good alternative to histograms, especially when the frequencies of many scores (or class intervals) are being represented on the X-axis and you want to see the shape of the distribution at a glance, or you want to compare two distributions on the same graph. *Stem-and-leaf displays* are formed by listing class intervals ("stems") in a column at the left, with specific values within each interval ("leaves") on a horizontal line next to that interval (often represented solely by the units digit).

Exercises

1. Create regular and cumulative frequency distributions for the data from Universities A, B, and C (see Chapter 1).
2. Create grouped and cumulative grouped frequency distributions for Universities A and B.
3. Plot a histogram corresponding to the grouped frequency distribution that you created for University A in exercise 2.

4. Using the grouped frequency distributions you created for Universities A and B in exercise 2, plot the two corresponding frequency polygons on the same set of axes (i.e., in one graph).

5. Redo exercise 4 for the cumulative grouped frequency distributions of Universities A and B.

6. Create a stem-and-leaf plot for the data from University A using an interval size of 3.

7. For each of the frequency distributions shown in the following table, state whether it is

(a) (approximately) normal

(b) unimodal, skewed to the right

(c) unimodal, skewed to the left

(d) bimodal, approximately symmetric

(e) bimodal, skewed to the right

(f) bimodal, skewed to the left

(g) (approximately) rectangular

(h) J-curve

(1)		(2)		(3)		(4)		(5)		(6)	
X	f	X	f	X	f	X	f	X	f	X	f
10	0	45–49	2	27–29	2	55–59	0	10	3	80–89	5
9	0	40–44	3	24–26	8	50–54	1	9	4	70–79	4
8	1	35–39	1	21–23	17	45–49	3	8	10	60–69	4
7	0	30–34	4	18–20	24	40–44	3	7	6	50–59	3
6	1	25–29	2	15–17	16	35–39	8	6	2	40–49	5
5	3	20–24	5	12–14	6	30–34	13	5	5	30–39	6
4	0	15–19	12	9–11	8	25–29	19	4	11	20–29	5
3	2	10–14	9	6–8	2	20–24	12	3	6	10–19	4
2	6	5–9	3	3–5	3	15–19	10	2	2	0–9	4
1	14	0–4	0	0–2	1	10–14	4	1	1		
0	21					5–9	2	0	0		
						0–4	0				

Thought Questions

1. Why would it be a bad idea to make up a *grouped* frequency distribution for the University C data or the University D data in Chapter 1?

2. For which of the following should you use a bar chart, and for which should you use a histogram? Why? (a) Scores on a midterm examination in psychology taken by 50 students. (b) The number of children in each of the families of the 50 students taking the psychology course.

3. What is the difference between a regular frequency polygon and a cumulative frequency polygon?

4. What is a symmetric distribution?

5. In a *positively* skewed distribution, are the unusual scores extremely large or extremely small? At what end of the graph is the "tail"?

6. In a *negatively* skewed distribution, are the unusual scores extremely large or extremely small? At what end of the graph is the "tail"?

7. What is a bimodal distribution? If a distribution of grades in a college course is bimodal, what does this imply about the students who took the course?

Computer Exercises

1. Request a frequency distribution and a bar chart for the variable Undergraduate Major across all 100 of Sara's students.

2. Repeat exercise 1 for the variables Math Courses and Math Phobia. Would it make sense to request a histogram instead of a bar chart for Math Phobia? Discuss.

3. Request a frequency distribution and a histogram for the variable Quiz Score across all students. Describe the shape of this distribution.

4. Request a frequency distribution and a histogram for the variables Baseline Anxiety and Baseline Heart Rate for all students. Comment on your statistical software's choice of class intervals for each histogram.

5. Repeat exercise 4 separately for male and female students. Describe the shapes of all four of the resulting distributions.

6. Request a stem-and-leaf plot for the variables Baseline Anxiety and Baseline Heart Rate for all students. Did your statistical package use the stem-and-leaf arrangement that you would have used for maximum clarity? Explain.

Bridge to SPSS

Frequency distributions can be obtained from SPSS by clicking on **Analyze Descriptive Statistics,** and **Frequencies. . . .** For whichever dependent variable (DV) you move into the Variable(s) box, you get a table with five columns, the first of which contains every different score on that DV. That is, SPSS gives you a regular frequency distribution and does not create a grouped frequency distribution no matter how many different scores you have. The second column is Frequency (the number of times each different score occurs). Note that at the bottom of this table there is a row for Total, followed by a row for Missing Values, and then another Total (which includes the number of missing values). These three bottom rows are critical for understanding the remaining columns.

The third column from the left is called Percent; each of its entries is the Frequency divided by the Total number of cases (i.e., rows) in your spreadsheet—the bottom-row total that includes any missing values—multiplied by 100. The fourth column is Valid Percent, which differs from the third column in that each frequency is divided by the total number of actual scores in your data (i.e., the total that does not include the missing values—we will call this the Valid Total). This is the percentage you are more likely to be interested in. Finally, the last column contains the cumulative values of the Valid Percents. If you want the cumulative frequency distribution, you will just have to multiply each of these entries by the Valid Total, divide by 100, and round off to the nearest whole number.

Along the bottom of the Frequencies dialog box are three buttons. We will discuss the results that can be obtained by clicking on the **Statistics . . .** button in the next chapter. For now, let's consider your choices if you click on the **Charts . . .** button. The two choices that are relevant to this chapter are Bar Charts and Histograms. If you select Bar Charts, SPSS will create a graph based on a regular frequency distribution of your variable; class intervals will not be created, no matter how many different score values your data contain. Moreover, a bar chart will treat your variable not only as discrete (inserting slim spaces between adjacent bars) but as though it were measured on a nominal or ordinal scale. For instance, no place is held for a value within your variable's range that has zero frequency (e.g., if three students each took one, two, and four prior math courses but no student took three math courses, you would see three equally high and equally spaced bars, with no extra gap to represent the zero frequency for three prior math courses taken). Selecting Bar Charts gives you two choices with respect to the scaling of the vertical axis: frequencies (the default choice), and percentages. The relative heights of the bars will look the same, but if you choose percentages the Y-axis will be marked off to correspond with the fact that the frequencies are being divided by the valid N and multiplied by 100.

If your variable has been measured on a scale that can be considered quantitative (interval or ratio), you will most likely want to choose Histograms, instead of Bar Charts, in the **Frequencies** dialog box. If you choose Histograms for your selected variables, each variable will be treated as though measured on an interval/ratio scale: adjacent bars will touch, and if there are many different values, they will be grouped into convenient class intervals (a full bar width will be left for each empty class interval within your range of scores). However, the bars are labeled in terms of the midpoints of the intervals; the real limits of the intervals are not shown (we put them in our Figure 2.2 for educational rather than descriptive purposes).

Finally, if you want stem-and-leaf plots for any of your DVs, you cannot request them from the Frequencies dialog box. Instead, after clicking **Analyze** and **Descriptive Statistics,** click on **Explore. . . .** If you click on **Plots . . .** in the **Explore** dialog box, you will have the choice of selecting Stem-and-Leaf as well as Histogram.

Chapter 3
Transformed Scores I: Percentiles

PREVIEW

Interpreting a Raw Score

What is a raw score?

Why is it often necessary to compare a raw score to the specific group of scores in which it appears?

What is a transformed score?

Definition of Percentile and Percentile Rank

What is a percentile rank?

What is a percentile?

What is the primary purpose of percentile ranks and percentiles?

Why must we take careful note of the reference group to interpret a percentile rank correctly?

Computational Procedures

How is a raw score transformed into a percentile rank?

Given a percentile, how do we determine the corresponding raw score?

How can percentile ranks be determined more easily when a stem-and-leaf display has been prepared?

Deciles, Quartiles, and the Median

What is a decile?

What is a quartile?

What is the median?

Summary

Exercises

Thought Questions

Computer Exercises

Bridge to SPSS

Interpreting a Raw Score

If you obtain a score of 41 on a 50-point examination, you will need additional information in order to determine how well you did. You can draw some useful conclusions from the fact that your score represents 82% of the total (for example, it is unlikely that you have failed the examination). But you also need to know how your score compares to the specific group of scores in which it appears, namely the scores of the other students in the class. If the examination has proved easy for most students and there are many high scores, your score of 41 may represent only average (or even below-average) performance. If the examination was a difficult one for most students, your score may be among the highest (or may even be the highest).

One way of providing this additional information is to transform the original score (called the *raw score*) into a new score that will show at a glance how well you did in comparison to other students in the class. There are several different kinds of transformed scores. We will discuss one of them in this chapter—percentiles—and defer a discussion of others (which depend on material in the following chapters) until Chapter 7.

Definition of Percentile and Percentile Rank

A *percentile rank* of a score is a single number that gives the *percent of cases in the specific reference group scoring at or below* that score. If your raw score of 41 corresponds to a percentile rank of 85, this means that 85% of your class obtained scores equal to or lower than yours, while 15% of the class received higher scores. If instead your raw score of 41 corresponds to a percentile rank of 55, this would signify that your score was slightly above average; 55% of the class received equal or lower scores, while 45% obtained higher scores.

A *percentile* is the score at or below which a given percent of the cases lie. A score that would place you at the 5th percentile would be a cause for concern, since 95% of the class did better and only 5% did as poorly or worse.

As these examples illustrate, percentile ranks and percentiles show directly how an individual score compares to the scores of a specific group. In order to interpret a percentile rank correctly, however, you must take careful note of the reference group in question. A college senior who obtains a test score with a percentile rank of 90 would seem to have done well, since his score places him just within the top 10% of some reference group. But if this group consists of high school seniors, the student should not feel proud of his performance! A score at the 12th percentile is usually poor, since only 12% of the reference group did as badly or worse. But if the score was obtained by a high school freshman and the reference group consists of college graduates, the score may actually represent good performance relative to other high school freshmen.

It is unlikely that anyone would err in extreme situations such as the foregoing, but there are many practical situations where misleading conclusions can easily be drawn. Scoring at the 85th percentile on the Graduate Record Examination, where the reference group consists of college graduates, is superior to scoring at the 85th percentile on a test of general ability, where the reference group consists of the whole population (including those people not intellectually capable of obtaining a college degree). Conversely, if you score at the 60th percentile on a midterm examination in statistics and a friend in a different class scores at the 90th percentile on her statistics midterm, she is not necessarily superior. The students in her class might be poorer, which would make it easier for her to obtain a high standing in comparison to her reference group. Remembering that a percentile *compares* a score to a *specific group of scores* will help you to avoid pitfalls such as these.

Computational Procedures

Case 1: Given a raw score, compute the corresponding percentile rank.

In order to illustrate the computation of percentile ranks, let us consider the case of a student who received a score of 41 on the math background quiz whose scores were initially displayed in Table 2.3. The grouped and cumulative frequency distributions for these data (Table 2.4) are reproduced in Table 3.1.

To find the percentile rank corresponding to any particular raw score, do the following:

TABLE 3.1

Hypothetical math quiz scores for 85 students: Transforming a raw score of 41 to a percentile rank

Class interval	Frequency (f)		Cumulative frequency (cf)
48–50	1	⎫	85
45–47	3	⎬ 8	84
42–44	4	⎭	81
39–41	6		77
36–38	7	⎫	71
33–35	9		64
30–32	14		55
27–29	8		41
24–26	10	⎬ 71	33
21–23	8		23
18–20	4		15
15–17	3		11
12–14	3		8
9–11	5	⎭	5

1. Locate the class interval in which the raw score falls. (This interval has been boxed in Table 3.1.) Let us call this the "critical interval."

2. Combine the frequencies (f) into three categories: those corresponding to all scores *higher* than the critical interval, those corresponding to all scores in the critical interval, and those corresponding to all scores *lower* than the critical interval, as follows:

    As is shown in Table 3.1, a total of 8 people obtained scores higher than the critical interval; 6 people obtained scores in the critical interval; and 71 people obtained scores lower than the critical interval. The last figure is readily obtained by referring to the *cumulative* frequency for the interval just below the critical interval, which shows that 71 people obtained scores of 36–38 or less. Each frequency is then converted to a percent by dividing by N, the total number of people (in this example, 85). We will denote the percent of people scoring in intervals higher than the critical interval by $H\%$ (for *higher*), the percent of people scoring in the critical interval by $I\%$ (for *in*), and the percent of people scoring lower than the critical interval by $L\%$ (for *lower*).

	f	Percent ($= f/N$)
All *higher* intervals	8	$8/85 =$ 9.4% ($H\%$)
Critical interval (39–41)	6	$6/85 =$ 7.1% ($I\%$)
All *lower* intervals	71	$71/85 =$ 83.5% ($L\%$)
		Check: $= 100.0\%$

3. It is now apparent that a score of 41 is better than at least 83.5% of the scores, namely those below the critical interval. If 41 were *your* score, your rank in the class expressed as a percentile (or, more simply, your *percentile rank*) would have to be at least 83.5%. It is also apparent that 9.4% of the scores, the ones above the critical interval, are better than yours. But what of the 7.1% of the scores within the critical interval? It would be too optimistic to assume that your score is higher than the scores of all the other people in the critical interval, since some of these people may also have obtained scores of 41. On the other hand, it would be too pessimistic to assume that you did not do better than anyone in your class interval. The solution is to look at your score in comparison to the size of the interval: The higher your score in relation to the critical interval, the more people in that interval you may assume that you outscored.

In order to determine accurately your standing in the critical interval, you must first ascertain the *lower real limit* of the interval. It may seem as though the lower limit of the 39–41 interval is 39, but appearances are often deceiving. If a score of 38.7 were obtained, in which interval would it be placed? Since this score is closer to 39 than 38, it would be tallied in the 39–41 interval. If a score of 38.4 were obtained, it would be tallied in the 36–38 interval because

38.4 is closer to 38 than to 39. The *real* dividing line between the critical interval of 39–41 and the next lower interval of 36–38 is not 39, but 38.5. (This is the same principle we used to graph the histogram of these data in Figure 2.2.) Any score between 38.5 and 39.0 belongs in the 39–41 interval, and any score between 38.0 and 38.5 belongs in the 36–38 interval. (For a score of exactly 38.5, it would be necessary to flip a coin or use some other random procedure.) A convenient rule is that the lower real limit of an interval is halfway between the lowest score in that interval (39) and the highest score in the next lower interval (38).

Your score of 41 is 2.5 points (41 – 38.5) up from the lower real limit of the interval. Since the size of the interval is 3, this distance expressed as a fraction is equal to 2.5 points/3 points, or .83 of the interval. Consequently, in addition to the 83.5% of the scores that are clearly below yours, you should credit yourself with .83 of the 7.1% of people in your interval, so that your percentile rank is equal to

$$83.5\% + (.83)(7.1\%) = 83.5\% + 5.9\%$$

$$= 89.4\%$$

This procedure is conveniently summarized by the following formula:

$$percentile\ rank = L\% + \left(\frac{Score - LRL}{h} \cdot I\%\right),$$

where

$$L\%\ and\ I\%\ are\ obtained\ from\ step\ 2$$

$$Score = raw\ score\ in\ question$$

$$LRL = lower\ real\ limit\ of\ critical\ interval$$

$$h = interval\ size$$

In our example, this is equal to

$$83.5\% + \left(\frac{41 - 38.5}{3} \cdot 7.1\%\right) = 83.5\% + 5.9\%$$

$$= 89.4\%$$

So your percentile rank is equal to 89.4%, which indicates that approximately 89% of the class received equal or lower scores and only about 11% received higher scores. This result is depicted in Figure 3.1.

This procedure is also suitable for use with regular frequency distributions, where the interval size (*h*) equals 1. You will find that the fraction

FIGURE 3.1

FIGURE 3.1

Illustration of percentile rank corresponding to a raw score of 41 for data in Table 3.1

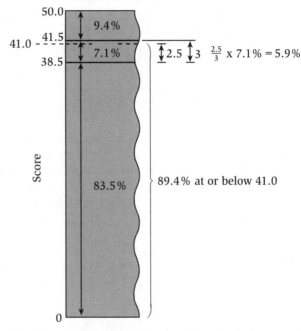

Note: This percentile rank is computed for a particular *point* on the scale—that is, a score of exactly 41.00. The fact that a score of 41 actually occupies the interval 40.5 to 41.5 is deliberately disregarded in this instance so that we can talk of a percentage above and a percentage at or below the given point, which together sum to 100%. Thus, the point is a "razor-thin" dividing line that divides the group into two parts, and not an interval in which scores may fall.

$$\left(\frac{Score - LRL}{h} \right)$$

always equals one-half for regular frequency distributions.

When you are able to use a regular frequency distribution, you will get somewhat more accurate results, since grouped frequency distributions lose information. For purposes of descriptive statistics, however, the loss of accuracy incurred by grouping will usually not be important, and you can follow the guidelines for forming frequency distributions given in the preceding chapter.

Case 2: Given a percentile, compute the corresponding raw score.

In the previous problem, we focused on a raw score (41) and wished to find the corresponding percentile rank. It is also useful to know how to apply the percentile procedures in reverse—to find the raw score that corresponds to a specified percentile value. For example, suppose that Sara wishes to recommend a brief refresher course to the students who scored in the bottom 25% of the class on the math background quiz. What raw score should be used as the cutting line? In this example, the percentile (25%) is specified and the raw score is needed, and the steps are as follows:

1. Convert the percentile to a case number by multiplying the percentile by N. In the present example, this is equal to $(.25) \times (85)$ or 21.25. Thus, the score that corresponds to the individual whose rank is 21.25 from the bottom of the class (the person scoring at the 25th percentile) is the cutting line that you need.

2. Find the interval in which the case number computed in step 1 falls. This is easily accomplished by starting at the *bottom* of the *cumulative* frequency distribution and proceeding upward until you find the *first* value equal to or greater than the critical case (21.25); the corresponding interval is the "critical interval." This step is illustrated in Table 3.2.

3. The 21.25th case must have a score of at least 20.5, the lower real limit of the interval in which it appears. However, the critical interval covers 3 score points (from 20.5 to 23.5); what point value corresponds to the 25th percentile? The solution lies in considering how far up from the lower end of the interval the 21.25th case falls, and assigning an appropriate number of additional score points. If the 21.25th case falls near the bottom of the interval, very little will be added to 20.5; if the 21.25th case falls near the top of the interval, a larger quantity will be added to 20.5. In our present ex-

TABLE 3.2

Hypothetical math quiz scores for 85 students: Finding the raw score corresponding to the 25th percentile

Class interval	Frequency (f)	Cumulative frequency (cf)	
48–50	1	85	
45–47	3	84	
42–44	4	81	
39–41	6	77	
36–38	7	71	
33–35	9	64	
30–32	14	55	
27–29	8	41	
24–26	10	33	
21–23	8 = f	23	first $cf \geq 21.25$
18–20	4	15	
15–17	3	11	
12–14	3 15 = SFB	8	
9–11	5	5	

$$pN = .25 \times 85 = 21.25$$

ample, there are 15 cases *below* the critical interval, so the 21.25th case falls (21.25 – 15) or 6.25 cases up in the interval. The total number of cases in the interval is 8, so this distance expressed as a fraction is 6.25 cases/8 cases or .78. Therefore, in addition to the lower real limit of 20.5, .78 of the 3 points included in the critical interval must be added in order to determine the point corresponding to the 21.25th case. The desired cutting score is therefore equal to

$$20.5 + (.78 \times 3) = 20.5 + 2.3$$
$$= 22.8$$

This procedure is conveniently summarized by the following formula:

$$Score_p = LRL + \left(\frac{pN - SFB}{f} \cdot h \right),$$

where

$$Score_p = \text{score corresponding to the } p\text{th percentile}$$
$$LRL = \text{lower real limit of critical interval}$$
$$p = \text{specified percentile}$$
$$N = \text{total number of cases}$$
$$SFB = \text{sum of frequencies below critical interval}$$
$$f = \text{frequency within critical interval}$$
$$h = \text{interval size}$$

In our example,

$$Score_{.25} = 20.5 + \left(\frac{(.25)(85) - 15}{8} \cdot 3 \right)$$
$$= 20.5 + \left(\frac{6.25}{8} \cdot 3 \right)$$
$$= 22.8$$

Students with scores of 22 or less are candidates for a refresher course on basic math skills, whereas those with scores of 23 or more are not. The calculations are depicted in Figure 3.2.

Remember that percentiles refer to the percent at or *below*, not above, a particular score. Therefore, questions about the top X% of a distribution are more easily answered in terms of the *bottom* (100 – X)%. For example, suppose that

FIGURE 3.2

Illustration of raw score corresponding to percentile rank of 25% for data in Table 3.2

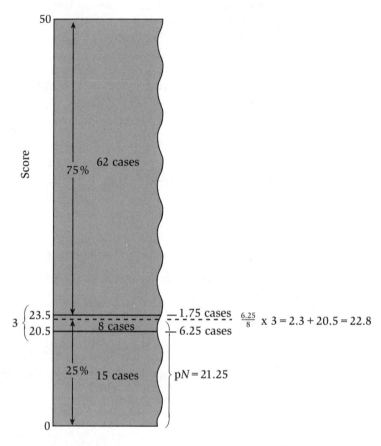

the top 10% of the students who took the math quiz are to be invited to take a more advanced statistics class. What cutting line should be used? Before doing any calculations you must note that the top 10% corresponds to the *90th percentile;* therefore, p = .90. The solution:

$$pN = 76.5$$

$$\text{Critical interval} = 39 - 41$$

$$Score_{.90} = 38.5 + \frac{76.5 - 71}{6} \cdot 3$$

$$= 38.5 + 2.75$$

$$= 41.2$$

This result should not prove surprising, since we found in the previous section that a score of 41.00 corresponded to the 89.4th percentile. You will obtain a surprising (and erroneous) result, however, if you unthinkingly set p equal to .10 rather than 1 − .1.

Alternative Method Using Stem-and-Leaf Displays

An easier procedure for determining percentile ranks (Case 1) is available when a stem-and-leaf display has been prepared, since it offers a ranking of all the observations. Given Table 2.5, which provides a stem-and-leaf display of the same data shown in Tables 2.4 and 3.1, all that is necessary to ascertain a percentile rank is some counting.

For example, the raw score of 41 appears in the second stem from the bottom (40–44). It is exceeded by four scores in that stem and four more scores in the last stem (45–49), a total of eight scores. Since there are 85 scores in all, there are 85 − 8 = 77 scores at or below a score of 41. Therefore, the raw score of 41 has a corresponding percentile rank of 77/85 = 90.6%. Why does this not agree with the value of 89.4% obtained from the formula in the preceding section? Because the latter interpolates within the interval, treating its scores as though they were uniformly distributed in that interval. Conversely, with the stem-and-leaf display, you determine the percentile rank exactly. This discrepancy is usually not important, however, so you might well decide not to expend the effort to make up a stem-and-leaf display solely for the purpose of computing a percentile rank. The primary advantage of this method occurs when such a display already exists (or is needed for other purposes), and when the number of observations is small enough to make such a display feasible (say, less than 100).

If a stem-and-leaf display has been prepared, the determination of the raw score corresponding to a given percentile (Case 2) is also simplified. Thus, for p = .25, first compute pN = .25(85) = 21.25 (as before). Now refer to the cumulative frequency distribution included with the stem-and-leaf display in Table 2.5, and observe that the 21.25th score occurs in the 20–24 stem (interval). Since 13 scores fall below this stem, you need to cumulate an additional 8.25 scores (21.25 − 13). Therefore, simply count along the leaf to the 8.25th score. The 8th score is the second 2 (standing for 22) and the ninth score also happens to be 2, so the 8.25th score—and, therefore, the score corresponding to the 25th percentile—must also be 22.

Deciles, Quartiles, and the Median

Certain percentile values have specific names, as follows:

Percentile		Decile		Quartile		
90th	=	9th				
80th	=	8th				
75th	=			3rd		
70th	=	7th				
60th	=	6th				
50th	=	5th	=	2nd	=	MEDIAN
40th	=	4th				
30th	=	3rd				
25th	=			1st		
20th	=	2nd				
10th	=	1st				

Whereas the percentile divides the total number of cases into 100 equal parts, the *decile* divides the number of cases into 10 equal parts and the *quartile* divides the number of cases into four equal parts. The score corresponding to the 50th percentile has the unique property that exactly half the scores in the group are higher and exactly half the scores in the group are equal or lower. It is called the *median,* and it is one of the measures of central tendency that will be discussed in the next chapter.

Summary

The *percentile rank* corresponding to a given score refers to the percent of cases in a given reference group *at or below* that score. A specified raw score may be converted to the corresponding percentile rank to express its standing relative to the reference group, or the raw score corresponding to a specified percentile may be determined, as follows:

1. Case 1: Given a score, find the corresponding percentile rank (PR).

1. Find the class interval in which the score falls.
2. Set up the following diagram and fill in the missing values:

	f	Percent $(= f/N)$
All *higher* intervals	_____	$H\%$ = _____
Interval in which score falls	_____	$I\%$ = _____
All *lower* intervals	_____	$L\%$ = _____
		Check = 100%

3. Let

LRL = *lower real limit* of the interval in which the score falls (The lower real limit of an interval is the number halfway between the lowest number in that interval and the highest number in the next lower interval.)

h = interval size

Then,

$$PR = L\% + \left(\frac{Score - LRL}{h} \cdot I\% \right)$$

2. **Case 2: Given a percentile (p), find the corresponding raw score ($Score_p$).**

1. Compute $p \times N = N$th case.
2. Find the interval in which this case falls.
3. Let

LRL = lower real limit of this interval

SFB = *s*um of *f*requencies *b*elow this interval

f = frequency within this interval

h = interval size

Then,

$$Score_p = LRL + \frac{pN - SFB}{f} \cdot h$$

Exercises

1. Use the regular (ungrouped) frequency distribution that you created for University B in the first exercise of the previous chapter to solve this exercise. (a) What is the percentile rank corresponding to a score of 5? (b) What is the percentile rank corresponding to a score of 10?

2. Use the same distribution for this exercise that you used for exercise 1. (a) What score corresponds to the 25th percentile? (b) What score corresponds to the 75th percentile?

3. Use the grouped frequency distribution that you created for University B in the second exercise of the previous chapter to solve this exercise. (a) What is the percentile rank corresponding to a score of 16? (b) What is the percentile rank corresponding to a score of 7?

4. Use the same (grouped) distribution for this exercise that you used for exercise 3. (a) What score corresponds to the 3rd decile? (b) What score corresponds to the 60th percentile?

Thought Questions

1. Why might you want to convert a raw score into a percentile rank?
2. What is the difference between a percentile rank and a percentile?
3. For each of the following, state which one represents better performance or if they are the same: (a) The 3rd quartile and the 70th percentile. (b) The 1st quartile and the 3rd decile. (c) The median and the 50th percentile. (d) The median and the 2nd quartile. (e) The 6th decile and the 80th percentile.
4. Mary's percentile rank on a psychology test is 93. John's percentile rank on a physics test is 80. Why is it potentially incorrect to conclude that Mary did better than John?

Computer Exercises

1. Request the deciles for the variable Quiz Score across all students.
2. Request the quartiles for the variables Baseline Anxiety and Prequiz Anxiety for all students. Describe the shift in anxiety scores between these two measurement points.
3. Repeat exercise 2 separately for male and female students.
4. Request the following percentiles for the variables Baseline Heart Rate and Prequiz Heart Rate for all students: 15, 30, 42.5, 81, and 96.

Bridge to SPSS

Percentiles can be obtained from SPSS by clicking on **Analyze, Descriptive Statistics, and Frequencies. . . .** Move the DVs for which you want to find percentiles into the Variable(s) box. Then, click on the **Statistics . . .** button along the bottom of the dialog box. The upper-left quadrant of the Frequencies: Statistics box that opens presents three choices for obtaining percentiles. The topmost choice, Quartiles, will give you, of course, the 25th, 50th, and 75th percentiles. The second choice, Cut points for . . . , will give you the deciles, if you use the default number of 10. If you change that number to 5, for instance, you will obtain the 20th, 40th, 60th, and 80th percentiles.

The third choice, Percentile(s), allows you to specify any number of particular percentiles that you would like to see—just click **Add** after typing in each one. Click **Continue** to return to the main **Frequencies** dialog box, and then click **OK.** You will get a table of all of the percentiles you requested in numerical order (e.g., if you requested quartiles, as well as the particular percentiles 35 and 60, the table will list the scores corresponding to the 25th, 35th, 50th, 60th, and 75th percentiles, in that order). Following the table of requested percentiles, SPSS will print the regular frequency distribution that we described in the Bridge to SPSS in the previous chapter unless you uncheck the little box labeled "Display frequency tables" under the list of all your variables on the left side of the Frequencies dialog box.

Chapter 4
Measures of Central Tendency

PREVIEW

Introduction

What is a measure of central tendency?

What do we gain by using a measure of central tendency instead of a regular frequency distribution?

What important information is *not* conveyed by a measure of central tendency?

The Mean

How do we compute the mean of a set of scores?

Is the population mean computed any differently from the sample mean?

How is the mean computed from a regular frequency distribution?

How is a weighted mean calculated?

What must the sum of the deviations of all scores from the mean be equal to?

> What does this imply about the way in which very large or very small scores affect the mean?

When should the mean be used as the measure of central tendency?

The Median

What is the median and how is it computed?

How do very large or very small scores affect the median?

In what kind of distribution is the median larger than the mean?

In what kind of distribution is the mean larger than the median?

When should the median be used as the measure of central tendency?

The Mode

What is the mode?

Why is the mode usually *not* used as the measure of central tendency?

When is the mode your only choice as a measure of central tendency?

Summary

Exercises

Thought Questions

Computer Exercises

Bridge to SPSS

Introduction

The techniques presented in Chapter 2 are useful when you wish to provide a detailed summary of all of the data in a convenient format. Often, however, your primary objective will be to highlight certain important characteristics of a group of data. For example, suppose that an inquisitive friend wants to know how well you are doing in college. You might hastily collect all of your semester grade reports and compile a regular frequency distribution such as the one in Table 4.1.

TABLE 4.1

Grade distribution for 20 courses taken by one hypothetical student

Grade	f
A	4
B	9
C	6
D	1
F	0

This would show that you received four grades of A, nine grades of B, and so forth. But all this detail is not essential in order to answer the question, and it would undoubtedly prove tiresome both for you and for your audience. In addition, presenting the data in this form would make it awkward for your friend to compare your performance to his own college grades. A better plan would be to select one or two important attributes of this set of data and summarize them so that they could be reported quickly and conveniently.

One item of information that you would want to convey is the general *location* of the distribution of grades. You could simply state that your college work was slightly below the B level. If you wished to be precise, you would report your numerical grade point average—a single number that describes the general location of this set of scores. In either case, you would sum up your performance by referring to a central point of the distribution. It would be misleading to describe your overall performance as being at the A or D level, even though you did receive some such grades.

This is one of many situations that benefit from the use of a *measure of "central tendency"—a single number that describes the general location of a set of scores.* Other examples include the average income of families in the United States, the number of cents gained or lost by an average share of stock on the New York Stock Exchange in a single day, and the number of seconds taken by the average rat to run a T maze after 24 hours of food deprivation.

It should be stressed, however, that *the overall magnitude of a set of data is not its only important attribute.* Suppose that the average score on a statistics quiz that you have just taken is 5.0. This average provides information as to the general location of these scores along the possible range of quiz scores, but it does not tell you how many high and low scores were obtained. Consequently, you cannot determine what score will be needed to ensure an A (or to just pass with a D!). In a distribution such as the following one, a score of 7 would rank very highly:

7 7 6 5 4 4 4 3

On the other hand, a score of 7 would not seem so illustrious in a distribution like this:

10 10 9 7 5 4 3 2 0 0

In both examples, however, the average, measured as the mean, is equal to 5.0. This indicates that there are important aspects of a set of data that are *not* conveyed by a measure of central tendency; a second vital characteristic will be considered in the next chapter.

The Mean

When people use the word *average* in everyday language, they are usually referring to what statisticians call the *arithmetic mean.* There are other types of means in statistics (e.g., the harmonic mean, which will be introduced in Chapter 14), but in this text the term *mean* by itself will always refer to the arithmetic mean.

Computation

The *mean* of a set of scores is computed by adding up all the scores and dividing the result by the number of scores. In symbols,

$$\overline{X} = \frac{\sum X}{N},$$

where

$$\overline{X} = \text{sample mean (it is often read aloud as ``X bar'')}$$
$$\sum X = \text{sum of the } X \text{ scores (see Chapter 1)}$$
$$N = \text{total number of scores}$$

In the case of the first set of quiz scores given above, the mean is equal to 5.0:

$$\frac{7+7+6+5+4+4+4+3}{8} = \frac{40}{8} = 5.0$$

Note that simply computing $\sum X$ is not sufficient to identify the location of these scores. What is further required is to divide by N (the number of scores). This step ensures that the means of two different samples will be comparable, even if they are based on different numbers of scores. The mean of the second set of quiz scores presented in the previous section is equal to 50/10 or 5.0; $\sum X$ is different, but the mean correctly shows that the overall location is the same.

In the case of populations, the Greek letter mu, μ, is used to represent the *population mean*. Nevertheless, the procedure is the same—sum all scores and divide by N. Because we will be applying the computational formulas in this part of the text only to samples, rather than entire populations, we will be using the symbol $\overline{X}$ instead of μ to represent the mean.

Computation from a Regular Frequency Distribution

If scores are available in the form of a regular frequency distribution, the mean is most easily computed from the following formula:

$$\overline{X} = \frac{\sum fX}{N}$$

where

$\overline{X}$ = sample mean

fX = X score multiplied by the frequency of that score

$\sum fX$ = sum of fX values

N = total number of scores

Perhaps because of the extra symbol f in the numerator, this equation is often a source of confusion. It gives exactly the same result as would the preceding formula applied to the same data in an untabulated format. It may be helpful to think of the first formula for the sample mean as a special case of the second in which $f = 1$.

The two procedures for computing the mean are compared in Figure 4.1. Note that the value $N = 20$ is easily recovered from the regular frequency distribution by computing $\sum f$: the total of the *frequencies* shows *how many scores* there are.

As an example, we will apply the foregoing formula to the data in Table 2.2:

$\Sigma fX = 6 \times 10 + 9 \times 9 + 17 \times 8 + 15 \times 7 + 23 \times 6 + 15 \times 5 + 9 \times 4 + 5 \times 3 + 0 \times 2 + 1 \times 1 + 0 \times 0 = 60 + 81 + 136 + 105 + 138 + 75 + 36 + 15 + 0 + 1 + 0 = 647$. $\overline{X} = \Sigma fX/N = 647/100 = 6.47$. Note that the value of N is easily found by computing Σf; the total of the frequencies shows you just how many scores there are. Of course, we could obtain the same value for $\overline{X}$ by adding up all of the scores in Table 2.1 and dividing by N (which equals 100), but if you are not using a computer, dealing with Table 2.2 is easier. Also, the procedure just illustrated is useful for finding a weighted average, as we will show in the next section.

As is mentioned in Chapter 2, means (and other statistics) should in general not be computed from *grouped* frequency distributions, which do not give the exact value of every score. They may be approximated by treating all the scores in any interval as if they fell at the midpoint of the interval. For instance, there is no reason to calculate an approximate mean from Table 2.4 if you have the raw data, as in Table 2.3. Summing all of the numbers in Table 2.3 and dividing by 85, we see that the mean of the math quiz scores is 29.07.

The Weighted Mean

The mean of a regular frequency distribution can be viewed as a *weighted mean* (also called "weighted average") of the different possible scores in the distribution, each weighted by its frequency. For example, a student's *grade point average* (GPA) is usually found by first assigning a numerical value or score to each possible letter grade (commonly A = 4, B = 3, C = 2, etc., and sometimes with intermediate grades such as B+ = 3.3), and then weighting each possible grade by the number of courses that received that grade. (We are assuming that all courses carry the same number of credits. Otherwise you would have to use the numbers of credits for your weights.)

Figure 4.1 illustrates the calculation of the weighted mean for the letter grades in Table 4.1. Notice that the GPA is 2.8, which is usually considered to be just a little higher than a B– average. Figure 4.1 also demonstrates that you get the same mean by simply adding up all of the individual scores and dividing by N, rather than using the shortcut of multiplying each possible score by its frequency before finding the sum of the scores and dividing by N. We make use of the weighted mean when we are comparing two samples in Chapter 11.

Properties

One important property of the mean is that if you add a *constant* (i.e., a fixed number of points) to every score in a distribution, the mean of the new distribution will be the original $\overline{X}$ plus that constant, which we will call k (as we did

FIGURE 4.1

GPA computed as a weighted mean of the grades shown in Table 4.1 and from the untabulated data

Grade (X)	f	fX	X
A = 4	4	16	A = 4 A = 4 A = 4 A = 4
B = 3	9	27	B = 3 B = 3 B = 3 B = 3 B = 3 B = 3 B = 3 B = 3 B = 3
C = 2	6	12	C = 2 C = 2 C = 2 C = 2 C = 2 C = 2
D = 1	1	1	D = 1
F = 0	0	0	
	$N = \Sigma f = 20$	$\Sigma fX = 56$	$\Sigma X = 56$

$$\overline{X} = \frac{\Sigma fX}{N} = \frac{56}{20} = \boxed{2.8} = \frac{56}{20} = \frac{\Sigma X}{N} = \overline{X}$$

in Chapter 1). It is easy to prove that this is true by expressing each new score as $(X + k)$, and then following these steps:

$$\overline{X}_{new} = \frac{\sum (X + k)}{N}$$

$$= \frac{\sum X + Nk}{N} \quad \text{(Rule 6, Chapter 1)}$$

$$= \frac{\sum X}{N} + \frac{Nk}{N}$$

$$= \overline{X}_{old} + k$$

Similarly, we could use Summation Rule 7 from Chapter 1 to show that if we subtract k from every score, $\overline{X}_{new} = \overline{X}_{old} - k$. A related property of the mean follows from Summation Rule 8. If every score is multiplied by k, then the mean of the new scores (i.e., the mean of kX) can be shown to be k times the old mean by the following steps:

$$\overline{X}_{new} = \frac{\sum kX}{N}$$

$$= k \frac{\sum X}{N} \quad \text{(Rule 8, Chapter 1)}$$

$$= k\overline{X}_{old}$$

Because dividing by k is the same as multiplying by $1/k$, it is just as easy to show that when all of the scores are divided by k, $\overline{X}_{new} = \overline{X}_{old}/k$. We make use of these properties in Chapter 7.

Another important property of the mean is that the sum of distances (or *deviations*) of all scores from the mean is zero. That is,

$$\sum(X - \overline{X}) = 0$$

It can readily be proved that this must always be true.[1] As an illustration, consider once again the small set of quiz scores discussed previously.

Score	Deviation from mean $(X - \overline{X})$	
7	+2	
7	+2	
6	+1	
5	0	$(\overline{X} = 5)$
4	−1	
4	−1	
4	−1	
3	−2	
$\sum(X - \overline{X}) = +5 - 5 = 0$		

The mean balances or equates the sums of the positive and negative deviations. It is in this sense that it gives the location of the distribution. This implies that the mean will be sensitive to extreme values on one side that are not balanced by extreme values on the other side, as the following example shows:

Score	$(X - \overline{X})$	
39	+30	
7	−2	
6	−3	
5	−4	$(\overline{X} = 9)$
4	−5	
4	−5	
4	−5	
3	−6	
$\sum(X - \overline{X}) = +30 - 30 = 0$		

---

1. $\sum(X - \overline{X}) = \sum X - N\overline{X}$ (Rule 7, Chapter 1) but $\sum X = N\overline{X}$ because $\overline{X} = (\sum X)/N$. Therefore, $\sum(X - \overline{X}) = N\overline{X} - N\overline{X} = 0$.

As a result of the change in one score from 7 to 39, the mean shows a substantial 4-point increase. In addition, all of the other seven scores now fall below the mean in order to balance the effects of the large positive deviation introduced by the score of 39. One might well question the use of the mean to describe the location of a set of data in a situation where it is so influenced by one extreme score!

As another example of the sensitivity of the mean to unbalanced extreme values, consider the case of an unethical manufacturing company in which the president earns one million dollars per year and the 99 assembly-line workers earn only $16,500 per year. The president might attempt to refute criticism of the company's miserly tactics by arguing that the mean annual income of all 100 people in the company is $26,335. The workers would undoubtedly object to the appropriateness of this figure, which is more than 2 1/2 times their actual salaries! Here again, the use of the mean as the index of location is questionable. It almost always is with income data, since almost all income distributions are positively skewed.

Usage

The mean has many other advantageous properties. It takes all of the scores into account, so it makes the most of the information provided by the data. Also, the mean is the most stable of the measures of central tendency for most distributions encountered in practice: It is the most consistent across different samples drawn from the same population. For this and other reasons, many of the procedures of inferential statistics make use of the mean. Thus, a third advantage of the mean is that it is usable as a datum in further statistical analyses, while other measures of central tendency usually are not. For these reasons, the mean is the most frequently suitable measure of central tendency.

At times, however, the first advantage becomes a liability instead of an asset. As we have seen, extreme scores at one end of a distribution exert a strong influence on the mean and cause it to give a misleading picture of the location of the distribution. Therefore, when a distribution is highly skewed and when you do not intend to use the measure of central tendency in subsequent statistical analyses, you should seek an alternative to the mean that will not be affected by unbalanced extreme scores.

In some cases, the actual size of the extreme scores may be unknown. For example, suppose that a few subjects in a learning experiment do not learn the task even after a great many trials. You might have to terminate the experiment for anyone failing to learn after (say) 75 trials. Such subjects would therefore have learning scores of "at least 75 trials." They would be the slowest learners (and should not be discarded from the experiment, as the results would then be biased); but their exact scores would be unknown, so you could not compute a sample mean.

In situations such as these, a measure of central tendency is needed that does *not* take the exact value of extreme scores into account. Such a measure is available, and it is called the median.

The Median

The median (Mdn) is defined as the score corresponding to the 50th percentile. It is computed using the procedures given in the previous chapter (simply compute $Score_{.50}$).

Computation

As an illustration, the computation of the median for the "grade" data given at the beginning of this chapter is shown in Figure 4.2. There are 20 observations in all, so the median is the score such that 10 cases (*half* of the total) fall above it and 10 cases fall below it. If you were to take the score of 2.50 (the dividing line between B and C) as your median, there would be only 7 cases below it (6 Cs and 1 D) and 13 cases above it (4 As and 9 Bs). So you must also take 3 of the 9 cases from the B interval and add them to the group below the cutting line, and this is accomplished by moving up 3/9 of a point from the starting place of 2.50. Thus the median is equal to 2.50 + 3/9, or 2.83.

The median is the *middle* score in the distribution when scores are put in order of size. If there is an even number of scores (so that there is no single middle score), the median is computed by averaging the two middle scores. There are an odd number of scores in Table 2.3, so when they are placed in numerical order there is a single middle score (the 43rd score from the lowest) with 42 scores below it and 42 scores above it. For these data, the median is 30. You can see from Table 2.6 that there are five scores tied at 30, but unless there is an overwhelming proportion of tied scores (which is not the case for

FIGURE 4.2

The median computed from a regular frequency distribution

X	f	cf	
A = 4	4	20	
B = 3	9	16	first $cf \geq 10$
C = 2	6	7	
D = 1	1	1	
F = 0	0	0	

$p = .50, N = 20$
$pN = (.50)(20) = 10$
"Critical interval" (c.i.)
is the "B" interval.

$LRL = 3.0 - 0.5 = 2.5$
$SFB = 7$ (cases below c.i.)
$f = 9$ (cases in c.i.)
$h = 1$ (interval size)

$Mdn = Score_{.50}$

$$= LRL + \frac{pN - SFB}{f} \cdot h$$

$$= 2.5 + \frac{(.50)(20) - 7}{9} \cdot 1$$

$$= 2.5 + \frac{3}{9}$$

$$= 2.83$$

these data), you can use 30 as the value for the median without being concerned about interpolating between 29.5 and 30.5.

Properties

When the distribution of scores is symmetric, the mean and the median will be equal (as is almost exactly true for the "grade" data). In a *positively skewed* distribution, where there are extreme values at the higher end, the mean will be pulled upward by the extreme high scores and will therefore be larger than the median:

$$3 \ 4 \ 4 \ 4 \ 5 \ 6 \ 7 \ 39$$

We have seen that the *mean* of these data is 9.0. The *median* is only 4.5, however; it is *not* affected by the size of any extremely large (or extremely small) values. In fact, the median will remain 4.5 even if the value of 39 is changed to a huge number such as 39,000. (The median will also remain 4.5 if the value of 3 is changed to an extremely small number, such as minus one million. But the median *will* change somewhat if the value of 39 is changed to a small number like 3, for there will no longer be 4 cases above it and 4 cases below it.) Similarly, in a learning experiment where some subjects fail to learn the task even after the full 75 trials, you would call the highest class interval "75 trials or more" and compute the median, which is not affected by the numerical value of extremely high (or low) scores.

In a *negatively skewed* distribution where the extreme values are at the lower end, the mean will be pulled downward by the extreme low scores and will therefore be smaller than the median:

$$3 \ 6 \ 25 \ 26 \ 27 \ 27 \ 27 \ 29$$

Here the mean is equal to 21.25, while the median is equal to 26.5. Recall that the mean we calculated for the math quiz scores (Table 2.3) was 29.07, and the median we just determined for the same data set was only slightly higher at 30. This indicates, at most, a very slight negative skew for the math quiz distribution.

Usage

Use the median when either (1) the data are highly skewed or (2) there are inexact data at the extremes of the distribution. This will enable you to profit from the fact that the median is not affected by the size of extreme values. In almost all other cases, use the mean so as to benefit from its numerous advantages. Except for a few infrequent situations that require the median (Chapter 18), the mean is the measure of location that is usually used in inferential statistics, with the median reserved for situations where the objectives are purely descriptive.

The Mode

The mode is the score that occurs most often. For example, the mode of the data in Figure 4.1 is 3 (or B) since this score was obtained more often than any of the others (9 times). In a bar chart or histogram (e.g., Figure 2.1 or 2.2), the mode is the score on the X-axis that has the highest bar over it. In a frequency polygon (e.g., Figure 2.3), the mode is the score (or class interval) that corresponds to the highest point on the graph. A distribution can have two or more modes, because two or more scores can have exactly the same frequency (e.g., Figure 2.5C). The mode can also be viewed in a less exact, relative sense, as when a distribution is referred to as bimodal even though its two peaks are not equally high (e.g., Figure 2.5D).

The mode is a crude descriptive measure of location that ignores a substantial part of the data. Therefore, it is not often used in research in the behavioral sciences. However, when the variable you are dealing with has only categorical levels, the mode is the only measure of central tendency available. For instance, a marketing researcher may allow the children in a study to take home only one toy each but may offer that toy in a choice of five bright colors. If a manufacturer wants to produce the toy in only one color, it would make sense to use the "modal" (i.e., most frequently chosen) color from the research study, especially if there were many children participating in the study.

Summary

One important attribute of a set of scores is its *location:* where in the possible range between minus infinity and plus infinity the scores tend to fall. This can be described in a single number by using either the *mean,* the best measure in most instances, or the *median* (the score corresponding to the 50th percentile), which is preferable when data are highly skewed or there are extreme data whose exact values are unknown, and when the objectives are purely descriptive.

1. The Sample Mean

$$\bar{X} = \frac{\sum X}{N}$$

1. Use the formula $\bar{X} = (\sum fX)/N$ with regular frequency distributions.
2. The sample mean $(\bar{X})$ is an estimate of the population mean (μ).

2. The Median

For either grouped or ungrouped data, compute the score corresponding to the 50th percentile. Recall from Chapter 3 that:

$$Score_{.50} = \text{Mdn} = LRL + \frac{.50N - SFB}{f} \cdot h$$

3. The Mode

This is the most frequently obtained score. The mode is at best a rough measure and is usually inappropriate when dealing with quantitative data. However, it is the only measure of central tendency that can be used with qualitative levels of a variable (e.g., different colors, different diagnoses for mental illness).

Exercises

1. Calculate the means of Universities A, B, C, and D.

2. Recalculate the mean of University C as a weighted mean of the seven different scores in that distribution. (Hint: Use the regular frequency distribution you created for University C when solving the first exercise of Chapter 2.)

3. Compute the median of University A from the regular frequency distribution you created for that university when solving the first exercise of Chapter 2.

4. Compute the median of University A from the *grouped* frequency distribution you created for that university when solving the *second* exercise of Chapter 2.

5. Find the mode of University B by inspecting the regular frequency distribution you created for that university when solving the first exercise of Chapter 2.

6. Using the raw data of University C, demonstrate that the sum of the deviations from the mean equals zero.

Thought Questions

1. For each of the following problems, which measure of central tendency should be computed? (a) An experimental psychologist wants a measure of central tendency for the number of trials taken to learn a task by 45 eight-year-old children. The maximum number of trials allowed is 30. Most of the children took between 14 trials and 30 trials to learn the task, but five children did not learn the task at all even after 30 trials. (b) A student who has taken 25 college courses, each of which is worth 3 credits, wants to compute her grade point average. (c) A student who has taken 25 college courses, some of which are worth 3 credits and some 4 credits, wants to

compute his grade point average. (d) A researcher wants a measure of central tendency for the income of a sample of 100 people that includes Bill Gates and Michael Jordan. (e) The editor of a college student yearbook wants to decide the color of the cover and asks the 30 students working on the yearbook to vote for burgundy, blue, green, or black.

2. (a) In a *positively* skewed distribution, which is larger, the mean or the median? (b) In a *negatively* skewed distribution, which is larger, the mean or the median? (c) In a *symmetric* distribution (such as the normal distribution), which is larger, the mean or the median?

3. Consider the following set of data, which represents 15 scores on a 10-point quiz: 0, 1, 3, 3, 4, 4, 4, 5, 5, 5, 7, 8, 9, 9, 10. (a) If the score of 10 is changed to 225,000,000, but the other numbers remain the same, what is the general effect on the mean and the median? (b) If the score of 10 is changed to 0, what is the general effect on the mean and the median? Why does the median change in this example, but not in the preceding example?

4. The mean grade for an exam is 57.3. (a) The instructor decides to add 5 points to each score because the exam was too difficult. What is the new mean? What would the new mean be if the instructor (b) subtracts 4 points from each score? (c) multiplies each score by 2? (d) divides each score by 3?

Computer Exercises

1. Use your statistical package to find the mode, median, and mean for each of the quantitative variables in Sara's data set.

2. Use your statistical package to find the mode for each of the categorical (i.e., qualitative variables) in Sara's data set.

Bridge to SPSS

The three measures of central tendency discussed in this chapter can be obtained from SPSS by opening the Frequencies: Statistics box described in the previous chapter (click on **Analyze, Descriptive Statistics,** and **Frequencies . . .** , and then click on the **Statistics** button). The upper-right quadrant of this box is labeled "Central Tendency" and allows you to select any number of the following choices: Mean, Median, Mode, and Sum (we don't know why SPSS includes the sum of the scores under the heading of Central Tendency). The mean of a distribution can actually be obtained from quite a few of the choices under **Analyze;** we point out a number of these options in later chapters.

Chapter 5
Measures of Variability

PREVIEW

The Concept of Variability

What is meant by the variability of a set of scores?

Why is it usually essential to know about the variability of a set of scores, rather than just the central tendency? For example, how might your grade on a midterm exam be strongly affected by the variability of the examination scores?

The Range

What is the range, and how is it computed?

Why is the range usually *not* used as the measure of variability?

The Semi-Interquartile Range

What are the interquartile and semi-interquartile ranges?

How are these measures computed, and when should they be used?

The Standard Deviation and Variance

Why can't we use the average of the deviation scores as a measure of variability? How does squaring all of the deviations solve this problem?

What is the sum of squares of a set of scores?

What is the variance of a set of scores?

What is the standard deviation of a set of scores? What advantage does the standard deviation have over the variance as a measure of variability?

When computing the variance or standard deviation, when should the sum of the squared deviations be divided by N? When should you divide instead by $N - 1$?

Why is it usually easier to calculate the value of the variance or standard deviation by using the computing formulas?

What are some of the useful mathematical properties of the standard deviation?

Summary

Exercises

Thought Questions

Computer Exercises

Bridge to SPSS

In addition to general location, there is a second important attribute of a distribution of scores—its *variability*. Measures of variability are used extensively in the behavioral sciences, so it is essential to understand the meaning of this concept as well as the calculational procedures.

The Concept of Variability

Variability refers to how *spread out or scattered* the scores in a distribution are (or how like or unlike each other they are). As an illustration, a few distributions involving a small number of scores are shown in the following table.

		Distribution			
1	2	3	4	5	6
7.0	7.2	40.2	7.0	10.0	97.8
7.0	7.1	40.1	7.0	10.0	88.5
7.0	7.1	40.1	6.0	9.0	83.4
7.0	7.1	40.1	5.0	7.0	76.2
7.0	7.1	40.1	4.0	5.0	69.9
7.0	7.0	40.0	4.0	4.0	67.3
			4.0	3.0	58.4
			3.0	2.0	44.7
				0.0	
				0.0	

The minimum possible variability is zero. This will occur only if all of the scores are exactly the same, as in Distribution 1, and there is no variation at all.

In Distribution 2, there is a very small amount of variability. The scores are somewhat spread out, but only to a very slight extent.

Distribution 3 is equal in variability to Distribution 2. The locations of these two distributions differ, but variability is not dependent on location. The distance between each score and any other, and hence the amount of spread, is identical.

Each of the remaining three distributions is more variable than the ones that precede it. At the opposite extreme to Distribution 1 would be a distribution with scores spread out over the entire range from –1,000,000 to +1,000,000 (or more). Such extreme variabilities, however, are rarely encountered in practice.

Variability is important in many areas, although it is frequently not reported (or described vaguely in words) because it is less familiar to nontechnical audiences than is central tendency. We list a few examples:

Testing

Suppose that you score 75 on a statistics midterm examination and that the mean of the class is 65; the maximum possible score is 100. Although your score cannot be poor because it is above average, its worth in comparison to

FIGURE 5.1

Frequency polygons of two distributions with the same mean but different variability

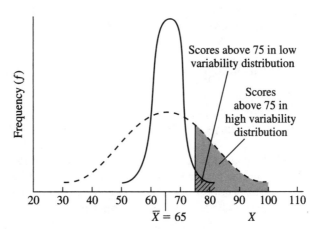

the rest of the class will be strongly influenced by the variability of the distribution of examination scores. If most scores are clustered tightly around the mean of 65, your score of ten points above average will stand out as one of the highest (and may well merit a grade of A). But if the scores are widely scattered, and values in the 80s and 90s (and 40s and 50s) are frequently obtained, being ten points above average will not be exceptional because many will have done better. In this case, your score may be worth no more than a B– or C+. A mean of 65 together with low variability would indicate that you did very well, whereas a mean of 65 together with high variability would imply that your performance was less than outstanding compared to the group that took the test. These two possibilities are illustrated graphically in Figure 5.1. (Note that the spread of a frequency polygon indicates the variability of the distribution.)

Consider Distributions 4 and 5, which happen to be the two sets of scores discussed at the end of the introduction to Chapter 4. The mean of both distributions is 5.0. Yet a score of 7 ranks higher in Distribution 4, where the scores are less variable, than in Distribution 5, where the scores are more variable. Looking at the lower end of these distributions, a score of 3 is poorer in comparison to the group in Distribution 4. Being two points above or below average stands out more in a distribution in which there is less spread.

Sports

Suppose that two professional basketball players average 20.3 points per game. Although their mean performance is the same, they may be different in other respects. One player may be consistent (low variability) and always score close to 20 points in each game, rarely scoring as high as 25 but also rarely falling to

15 or less. The second player may be very erratic (high variability); he scores more than 30 points in some games, but drops to below 10 in others. The second player is likely to be a much greater source of frustration to his coach and to the fans. Here again, a measure of variability would provide useful additional information to that given by the mean.

Psychology

Modern psychology is based on the idea that people differ. On any trait of interest—musical ability, throwing a baseball, introversion, height, mathematical ability—people are distributed over the entire range from low to high. If all people were the same, the behavior of the entire population could be predicted from a knowledge of one individual, and psychological research would be unnecessary; anything true about you would be true about everyone else. Since this is not the case, the psychologist has the essential task of measuring and explaining variation—why some people are more neurotic and others less so, why some people do better in school or on the job than others, why one person performs differently on different occasions, and so on. Thus, variability is the *raison d'être* of the psychologist.

Statistical Inference

Another reason for the importance of variability will become evident when statistical inference is discussed beginning in Chapter 9. Other things being equal, the more variable a phenomenon is, the less precise is the estimate you can get of the population's location (for example, mean) from sample information.

Rather than describe variability in ambiguous terms such as "small" or "large," it is preferable to summarize the variability of a distribution of scores in a single number. Techniques for accomplishing this are discussed next.

The Range

One possible way of summarizing the variability of a distribution is to look at the distance between the smallest and largest scores. The *range* of a distribution is defined as the largest score minus the smallest score. For example, the range of Distribution 4 is (7.0 – 3.0) or 4.0.

While this procedure makes intuitive sense, it is likely to give misleading results on many occasions because the extreme values are frequently atypical of the rest of the distribution. Consider the following two distributions:

DISTRIBUTION A:	10	10	10	9	7	6	5	4	4	3	2	0	0
DISTRIBUTION B:	10	6	6	5	5	5	5	5	5	5	4	4	0

In both of these examples, the range is equal to 10. Yet Distribution A, with scores spread out over the entire 10-point range, is more variable than Distribution B, where all but two scores are concentrated near the middle of the distribution. The range is a poor measure of the variability of Distribution B because the extreme values are not typical of the total variation in the distribution; if the two extreme scores are excluded, the range drops to 2. Since this type of distortion occurs fairly often, the range (like the mode) is best regarded as a crude measure that should not generally be used in behavioral science research. It is always a good idea to take note of the minimum and maximum values obtained for each of your variables, especially to check for errors and anomalous findings. Looking back at Table 2.3, we can see that the smallest score is 9 and the largest is 49, so the range of the math background quiz scores is $49 - 9 = 40$.

The Semi-Interquartile Range

You may recall that a major advantage of the median as a measure of central tendency is that it is not affected by making an extreme score even more extreme. In fact, the median is still valid if there are some scores on either end of the distribution that are undetermined. For example, on a survey question about how many different jobs the respondent has held, several participants may have checked "10 or more." Obviously, the ordinary range is very much affected by extreme scores and cannot be used with open-ended responses.

There is a type of range measure, called the *interquartile range,* that has advantages similar to those of the median. It is found by subtracting the score at the 25th percentile (the 1st quartile) from the score at the 75th percentile (the 3rd quartile). The median, of course, is the score at the 2nd quartile. This range measure tells you the total spread for the middle 50% of the scores, and it is clearly not affected by extreme or indeterminate scores (unless the latter comprise as much as 25% of the scores on either end of the distribution). For example, in Chapter 3 we calculated the 25th percentile for the math quiz and found it to be a score of 22.8. Using the same method, the 75th percentile turns out to be 35.4. Thus, the interquartile range for those quiz scores is 35.4 – 22.8, which equals 12.6.

Dividing the value for the interquartile range by 2 results in a useful variability measure called the *semi-interquartile range* (SIQR). The main advantage of the SIQR is that it gives you an immediate idea of the distance of the typical score from the median. (About half the scores in the distribution are further from the median than the SIQR, and about half are closer than the SIQR.) For the math quiz scores, the SIQR is 12.6/2 = 6.3. This means that if you need to come up with a single number that characterizes how much the scores tend to vary from the median of that distribution, 6.3 points would serve the purpose. Although the SIQR is a good descriptive measure of variability, it does not play a role in more advanced statistical methods, so it will not be discussed further in this text. A more sophisticated way of determining how much the "typical" score differs from the center of the distribution will be described in detail next.

The Standard Deviation and Variance

We have seen that the mean, an average that takes all of the scores into account, is usually the best measure of central tendency. Similarly, an "average" variability that is based on all the scores will usually provide the most accurate information. Before an *average* variability can be computed, however, this concept must be defined in terms of an individual score.

Variability actually refers to the difference between each score and every other score, but it would be quite tedious to compute this in practice (especially if N is large). If there are 100 scores, you would have to compute the difference between the first score and each of the 99 other scores, compute the difference between the second score and each of the 98 remaining scores, and so on—4,950 differences in all.

A more feasible plan, which will serve the purpose equally well, is to define the "differentness" or *deviation* of a single score in terms of how far it is from the center of the distribution. In a distribution of scores that is closely packed together, most scores are close to each other and hence close to their center. Conversely, in a highly variable distribution, some scores are quite a distance from each other and hence far from their center. Since the mean is the most frequently used measure of central tendency, a reasonable procedure is to define the deviation of a single score as its *distance from the mean:*[1]

$$\text{Deviation score} = X - \overline{X}$$

Extremely deviant scores (ones far away from the mean) will have numerically large deviation scores, while scores close to the mean will have numerically small deviation scores.

The next step is to derive a measure of variability that will take into account the deviations of all of the scores. There are several possible ways to do this. If we were to average the deviation scores by the usual procedure of summing and dividing by N, we would get

$$\frac{\sum(X - \overline{X})}{N}$$

---

1. A reference point other than the mean could be used, but the choice of the mean has certain statistical advantages as well as making good intuitive sense. For example, it can be proved that the mean is the value of c about which $\sum(X - c)^2$, the sum of squared deviations, is a minimum (the importance of which will become apparent in the following discussion).

It will prove extremely frustrating to try and use this as the measure of variability because, as was proved in Chapter 4, $\Sigma(X - \overline{X})$ is *always* equal to zero. As a result, this "measure" cannot provide any information as to the variability of any distribution.

This problem could be overcome if we were to focus on the *size* of the deviations and ignore whether they are positive or negative. We might therefore first take the *absolute value* of each deviation, its numerical value ignoring the sign, and then compute the average variability. That is, we might compute

$$\frac{\Sigma \left| X - \overline{X} \right|}{N},$$

where $\left| X - \overline{X} \right|$ is the absolute value of the deviation from the mean. This is not an unreasonable procedure, and in fact yields a good descriptive measure called the *mean* or *average deviation* (often symbolized as MD). But, unfortunately, measures based on absolute values are unsuitable for use in further statistical analyses (one awkward property of the mean deviation is that it is smaller when deviations are calculated from the *median,* rather than from the mean). The measure that is most frequently used circumvents this difficulty by *squaring* each of the deviations prior to taking the average. The sum of the squared deviations from the mean, $\Sigma(X - \overline{X})^2$, is symbolized by *SS* and is called the *sum of squares.* The measure of variability produced by taking the average of the sum of squares is called the *variance* and is symbolized by σ^2:

$$\sigma^2 = \frac{\Sigma(X - \overline{X})^2}{N} = \frac{SS}{N}$$

This is a basic measure of the variability of any set of data. However, when the data of a sample are used to estimate the variance of the population from which the sample was drawn, the *population variance estimate* (symbolized by s^2) is computed instead:

$$s^2 = \frac{\Sigma(X - \overline{X})^2}{N - 1} = \frac{SS}{N - 1}$$

In each of these formulas, the order of operations is as follows: (1) Subtract the mean from each score; (2) square each result; (3) sum; (4) divide. The sample estimate of the population variance, s^2, is computed somewhat differently from σ^2; the sum of squared deviations is divided by $N - 1$ instead of N. This is to enable s^2 to be an *unbiased* estimate of the population variance—that is, an estimate that on the average will be too large no more often than it is too small. Hence, it is common to refer to s^2 simply as the "unbiased variance" and to σ^2 as the "biased variance."

There is one remaining difficulty. Having squared the deviations to eliminate the negative numbers that otherwise would have led to a total of zero with annoying regularity, the variance is in terms of the original units *squared*. For example, if you are measuring height, the variance indexes variability in terms of square inches. Especially for descriptive purposes, it is preferable to have a measure of variability that is in the same units as the original measure, and this can be accomplished by taking the positive square root of the variance. This yields a commonly used measure of variability called the *standard deviation,* symbolized by σ or s depending on whether the variance or the population variance estimate is used:

$$\sigma = +\sqrt{\sigma^2} = \sqrt{\frac{\sum (X - \bar{X})^2}{N}} = \sqrt{\frac{SS}{N}}$$

$$s = +\sqrt{s^2} = \sqrt{\frac{\sum (X - \bar{X})^2}{N-1}} = \sqrt{\frac{SS}{N-1}}$$

Following the naming convention applied to σ^2 and s^2, σ is often called the "biased standard deviation," and s is called the "unbiased standard deviation."

Whereas the mean represents the "average *score*," the standard deviation represents a kind of "*average variability*"—similar to the average of the deviations of each score from the mean $(X - \bar{X})$—with two minor complications: squaring and subsequently taking the positive square root, to eliminate the minus signs before averaging and to return to the original unit of measurement afterwards; and dividing by $N - 1$ instead of N when estimates of the population are involved. Although the standard deviation is not literally the average deviation, it can be thought of, less precisely, as a typical deviation. The formulas we have given are called the *definition* formulas for σ and s because their primary function is to define the meaning of these terms; they are not necessarily the formulas by which σ and s are most easily computed.

Illustrative examples of the computation of σ^2 and σ, and s^2 and s using the definition formulas are shown on the left-hand side of Table 5.1. If the eight scores in Table 5.1 represent the entire population, σ is computed; however, if these eight scores are a sample from a larger population, s is computed. Note that a partial check on the calculations is possible in that $\sum (X - \bar{X})$ should always equal zero. As expected from the previous discussion concerning these distributions, Distribution 5 has a larger standard deviation (is more variable) than Distribution 4. The typical deviation from the mean is 3.66 points in Distribution 5, but only 1.5 points in Distribution 4.

Computing Formulas

Using the definition formulas to calculate σ and s can be awkward for several reasons. If the mean is not a whole number, subtracting it from each score will yield a deviation score with decimal places, which when squared will produce

TABLE 5.1

Computation of σ^2 and σ, and s^2 and s, for two small samples using the definition and computing formulas

Example 1. Distribution 4 (where $\overline{X} = 5.0$)

X	$X - \overline{X}$	$(X - \overline{X})^2$		X	X^2
7	$7 - 5 = 2$	4		7	49
7	$7 - 5 = 2$	4		7	49
6	$6 - 5 = 1$	1		6	36
5	$5 - 5 = 0$	0		5	25
4	$4 - 5 = -1$	1		4	16
4	$4 - 5 = -1$	1		4	16
4	$4 - 5 = -1$	1		4	16
3	$3 - 5 = -2$	4		3	9
		$\Sigma(X - \overline{X})^2 = 16$		$\Sigma X = 40$	$\Sigma X^2 = 216$

A. Definition formulas

$$\sigma^2 = \frac{\Sigma(X - \overline{X})^2}{N} = \frac{16}{8} = 2.00$$

$$\sigma = \sqrt{2.00} = 1.41$$

$$MD = \frac{\Sigma |X - \overline{X}|}{N}$$

$$= \frac{2 + 2 + 1 + 0 + 1 + 1 + 1 + 2}{8}$$

$$= \frac{10}{8}$$

$$= 1.25$$

B. Computing formulas

$$\sigma^2 = \frac{1}{N}\left[\Sigma X^2 - \frac{(\Sigma X)^2}{N}\right]$$

$$= \frac{1}{8}\left[216 - \frac{(40)^2}{8}\right]$$

$$= \frac{1}{8}(216 - 200)$$

$$= \frac{1}{8}(16) = 2.00$$

$$\sigma = \sqrt{2.00} = 1.41$$

$$s^2 = \frac{\Sigma(X - \overline{X})^2}{N - 1}$$

$$= \frac{16}{7}$$

$$= 2.29$$

$$s = \sqrt{2.29} = 1.51$$

$$s^2 = \frac{1}{N - 1}\left[\Sigma X^2 - \frac{(\Sigma X)^2}{N}\right]$$

$$= \frac{1}{7}\left[216 - \frac{(40)^2}{8}\right]$$

$$= \frac{1}{7}(216 - 200) = \frac{1}{7}(16) = 2.29$$

$$s = \sqrt{2.29} = 1.51$$

table continues

still more decimal places. This can make the computations quite tedious. Second, the mean must be calculated before the formula can be used, which necessitates two steps in the computation of the standard deviation (although normally the mean will be desired anyway). Therefore, before the advent of handheld statistical calculators and personal computers made these calculations so easy to perform, *computing formulas* for σ and s were derived by ma-

TABLE 5.1

(continued)

Example 2. Distribution 5 (where $\bar{X}$ = 5.0)

X	$X - \bar{X}$	$(X - \bar{X})^2$		X	X^2
10	10 – 5 = 5	25		10	100
10	10 – 5 = 5	25		10	100
9	9 – 5 = 4	16		9	81
7	7 – 5 = 2	4		7	49
5	5 – 5 = 0	0		5	25
4	4 – 5 = –1	1		4	16
3	3 – 5 = –2	4		3	9
2	2 – 5 = –3	9		2	4
0	0 – 5 = –5	25		0	0
0	0 – 5 = –5	25		0	0
		$\Sigma(X - \bar{X})^2 = 134$		$\Sigma X = 50$	$\Sigma X^2 = 384$

A. Definition formulas

$$\sigma^2 = \frac{\Sigma(X - \bar{X})^2}{N} = \frac{134}{10} = 13.40$$

$$\sigma = \sqrt{13.40} = 3.66$$

$$MD = \frac{\Sigma |X - \bar{X}|}{N}$$

$$= \frac{5 + 5 + 4 + 2 + 0 + 1 + 2 + 3 + 5 + 5}{10}$$

$$= \frac{32}{10} = 3.2$$

B. Computing formulas

$$\sigma^2 = \frac{1}{N}\left[\Sigma X^2 - \frac{(\Sigma X)^2}{N}\right]$$

$$= \frac{1}{10}\left[384 - \frac{(50)^2}{10}\right]$$

$$= \frac{1}{10}(384 - 250)$$

$$= \frac{1}{10}(134) = 13.40$$

$$\sigma = \sqrt{13.40} = 3.66$$

$$s^2 = \frac{\Sigma(X - \bar{X})^2}{N - 1}$$

$$= \frac{134}{9}$$

$$= 14.89$$

$$s = \sqrt{14.89} = 3.86$$

$$s^2 = \frac{1}{N - 1}\left[\Sigma X^2 - \frac{(\Sigma X)^2}{N}\right]$$

$$= \frac{1}{9}\left[384 - \frac{(50)^2}{10}\right]$$

$$= \frac{1}{9}(384 - 250) = 14.89$$

$$s = \sqrt{14.89} = 3.86$$

nipulating the definition formulas algebraically. Because the computing and definition formulas are algebraically equivalent to each other, they always yield identical results. Although there is no longer much need for them, for historical purposes, as well as to facilitate comparison with the many texts that still present them, the computing formulas for the standard deviation and variance are shown next.

$$\sigma^2 = \frac{1}{N}\left[\sum X^2 - \frac{(\sum X)^2}{N}\right], \quad \sigma = \sqrt{\frac{1}{N}\left[\sum X^2 - \frac{(\sum X)^2}{N}\right]}$$

$$s^2 = \frac{1}{N-1}\left[\sum X^2 - \frac{(\sum X)^2}{N}\right], \quad s = \sqrt{\frac{1}{N-1}\left[\sum X^2 - \frac{(\sum X)^2}{N}\right]}$$

Examples of the use of the computing formulas for σ^2 and σ, and s^2 and s, are shown on the right-hand side of Table 5.1. For comparison purposes, we have included the calculation of the mean deviation, which is often similar to, but can never be larger than, the standard deviation.

The Variability of the Math Background Quiz Scores

The variance of the math quiz scores (see Table 2.3) is equal to 88.82. As usual, the population variance estimate is a bit larger: $s^2 = 89.88$. These measures are not useful for descriptive purposes because they are in squared units. We therefore take the square root of the variance and find that σ equals 9.42, while the unbiased standard deviation of these quiz scores is of course slightly larger: $s = 9.48$. Recall that the mean of this distribution is about 29. The standard deviation tells us that it is not unusual for scores to vary about 9.4 points from the mean, so scores as high as 38.4 or as low as 19.6 could be considered fairly typical.

Note that σ is considerably larger than the SIQR for this distribution (6.3). This will make more sense when you see in Chapter 8 that for common distributions, *more* than half of the scores tend to vary within a distance of σ from the mean.

Properties of the Standard Deviation

The properties we will discuss here for σ also hold for its unbiased cousin, s. Although σ shares several important properties with the mean, one property it does *not* share is its response to adding a constant to all of the scores in the distribution. (The properties that are associated with addition also hold for subtraction, which can be viewed as the adding of a negative constant.) We demonstrated in the previous chapter that if the same constant (k) is added to all of the scores, $\overline{X}_{new} = \overline{X}_{old} + k$. However, it is easy to show that adding (or subtracting) a constant to all of the scores has no effect on σ. Consider any one deviation score: $X - \overline{X}$. If you add k to all of the scores, each new deviation score will look like this: $(X + k) - (\overline{X} + k)$. (Remember that the mean is also increased by k.) So the new deviation score equals $X + k - \overline{X} - k = X - \overline{X}$, which is exactly the same as the old deviation score.

Because all of the deviation scores remain the same, σ, which is based on these deviation scores, also remains unchanged. It is as though everyone in a large crowd were to move exactly 12 inches in exactly the same direction. After the move, the people are standing in exactly the same way in relation to each other; only the overall location of the crowd (like the mean of the distribution) has changed. On the other hand, multiplying by a constant *does* have the same effect on σ as it does on the mean: $\sigma_{new} = k\sigma_{old}$. (The same properties hold for division.) Again, we will look at what happens to any one deviation score when all of the scores are multiplied by k. The new deviation equals $kX - k\overline{X}$ $= k(X - \overline{X}) = k$ times the old deviation. Because the size of each deviation score is multiplied by k, σ is multiplied by k as well.

Like the mean, the standard deviation has the statistically desirable property of being based on *all* of the scores in the distribution. This implies, however, that σ also has the often *un*desirable property that it can be strongly influenced by one very extreme score. It can therefore produce a value for variability that gives a misleading picture of the entire distribution. Unlike the case of the mean, equally extreme scores on both sides of the distribution will not cancel each other out (because their deviations are squared before being added), so σ can be misleading even with symmetrical distributions. Extreme scores have less of an impact on the mean deviation (MD) than they do on σ, because large deviations are not squared in the process of calculating the MD as they are in finding σ. Therefore, the MD could be a useful measure of variability for purely descriptive purposes. However, because it is not suitable for further statistical analyses, it is rarely used at all. In cases where you want to use the median instead of the mean to describe the central tendency of your distribution, it would make sense to use the SIQR as your measure of variability rather than the standard deviation.

As we mentioned earlier, σ has an undesirable property (i.e., bias) that can be corrected by calculating s instead when we wish to estimate the variability in the population from which a sample was drawn. It is the latter measure, the unbiased standard deviation (and its square, the unbiased variance), that is used most frequently as the basis for the more advanced statistical procedures that we will begin to describe in Chapter 9.

Summary

A second important attribute of a set of scores is its *variability*, or how much the scores *differ from one another*. In the behavioral sciences, this is customarily summarized in a single number by computing the *variance* or its positive square root, the *standard deviation*. The larger the variance or standard deviation, the more different the numbers are from one another. The concept of variability has many practical applications and is particularly important in statistical work.

1. The Range

The simplest (and crudest) measure of variability encountered in the behavioral sciences is the range, which is equal to the highest score minus the lowest score. Although it is sometimes useful to know the maximum separation of your scores, as a measure of variability the range is rather unreliable and is therefore generally less useful than the other available variability measures.

2. The Interquartile and Semi-Interquartile (SIQ) Ranges

The interquartile range is the distance from the 1st to the 3rd quartile of the distribution. The formula is 75th percentile – 25th percentile. The SIQR is half of that distance. These measures are useful for descriptive purposes, especially when your distribution contains extreme or indeterminate scores, but are not used for inferential statistics.

3. The Mean Deviation

This is the average of the absolute values of all the deviations from the mean. It is less susceptible to extreme scores (called *outliers*) than the standard deviation, and it makes intuitive sense, but it is not used for drawing inferences about populations. The formula for the MD is

$$MD = \frac{\sum |X - \bar{X}|}{N} \quad \text{where } |X - \bar{X}| = \text{the absolute value of the}$$
$$\text{deviation from the mean}$$

4. The Biased Variance and Standard Deviation

Variance (definition formula):

$$\sigma^2 = \frac{\sum (X - \bar{X})^2}{N}$$

Variance (computing formula):

$$\sigma^2 = \frac{1}{N}\left[\sum X^2 - \frac{(\sum X)^2}{N} \right]$$

Standard deviation formula (in terms of variance):

$$\sigma = +\sqrt{\sigma^2}$$

When calculated for samples, σ^2 and σ tend to underestimate their corresponding values in the population. Therefore, these measures are acceptable only for descriptive purposes; they are not used to make estimates of, or draw inferences about, population parameters.

5. The (Unbiased) Population Variance Estimate and the Unbiased Standard Deviation

When the data of a sample are to be used to estimate the variance of the population from which the sample was drawn, compute the *population variance estimate*.

Unbiased variance (definition formula):

$$s^2 = \frac{\sum(X - \bar{X})^2}{N - 1}$$

Unbiased variance (computing formula):

$$s^2 = \frac{1}{N - 1}\left[\sum X^2 - \frac{(\sum X)^2}{N}\right]$$

Unbiased standard deviation formula:

$$s = +\sqrt{s^2}$$

Exercises

1. Insert the sums you found for exercise 3 of Chapter 1 into the *computing* formulas given in this chapter to find σ^2, σ, s^2, and s for Universities A, B, C, and D. (We highly recommend that you also learn to obtain these results directly with an inexpensive handheld calculator.)

2. Recalculate σ^2, σ, s^2, and s for University C using the *definition* formulas, and compare them to the corresponding results from the previous exercise. Which type of formula (computing or definition) usually leads to greater error due to rounding off before the final result?

3. Compute the range for each of the four universities.

4. Using the results you found for exercise 2 in Chapter 3, compute the interquartile range and SIQR for University B. Using the same methods, calculate these measures for University A as well.

5. Using the definition formula, calculate the "variance" of University D in terms of deviations from the median, rather than the mean, of that distribution (just put the five scores in numerical order, and use the middle one as the median). How does this "variance" compare to the ordinary variance that you calculated in exercise 1? What property of the ordinary variance is illustrated by this exercise?

6. Calculate the mean deviation for University D, and compare it to σ (as calculated in exercise 1). What do you think would happen to the difference of these two measures if you were to add an extreme score to the data of University D?

Thought Questions

1. Why is the range much less informative (and much less useful) as a measure of variability than the standard deviation?

2. What is the difference between the variance of a set of scores and the standard deviation of a set of scores? Which one is preferable when our sole purpose is to describe a set of data? Why?

3. When determining the variability of a set of scores, why is it necessary to square the deviations from the mean (or take the absolute value), rather than simply using the sum of the deviations from the mean?

4. The mean of a statistics examination is 77.0. (a) If your score is 85, would you prefer the standard deviation to be large or small for purposes of getting a better grade? Why? (b) If your score is 69, would you prefer the standard deviation to be large or small? Why?

5. Two college students have each taken twenty 3-credit courses and have precisely the same C+ average. However, Beth's set of grades has a large standard deviation, while Joe's set of grades has a small standard deviation. Which student might be considered to have a greater potential for success? Why? Which student might pose more difficulties for his or her college adviser? Why?

6. (a) When computing the standard deviation of a set of scores, when do we divide by N, and when do we divide by $N - 1$? (b) What is the difference between σ and s?

7. If the standard deviation of a set of scores is zero, what does this imply about the scores?

8. Can a standard deviation be negative? Why or why not?

9. The mean of an exam is 57.3 and the standard deviation is 9.6. What will happen to the standard deviation of these scores if the instructor (a) adds 5 points to each score? (b) subtracts 4 points from each score? (c) multiplies each score by 2? divides each score by 3?

10. (a) When is it desirable to use the SIQR as the measure of variability? (b) When is it desirable to use the mean deviation (MD) as the measure of variability?

Computer Exercises

1. Use your statistical package to find the range, semi-interquartile range, unbiased variance, and unbiased standard deviation for each of the quantitative variables in Sara's data set (see if your statistical package offers you the option of obtaining the biased versions of the variance and standard deviation).

2. (a) Use your statistical package to create a new variable that is equal to 2 times the diagnostic quiz score, so that the new variable is measured on a 0 to 100 scale. How do the measures of variability found in the previous exercise compare between the new variable and the original math quiz score? What general principle is being illustrated with respect to the standard deviation?

(b) Use your statistical package to create a new variable that adds 50 points to the math quiz score. How have the measures of variability changed for this new variable as compared to the same measures calculated for the original math quiz score? What general principle is being illustrated with respect to the standard deviation?

Bridge to SPSS

There are three choices on the **Analyze/Descriptive Statistics** menu that will give you measures of variability (along with measures of central tendency). The one that is labeled **Descriptives . . .** is obviously intended for use with continuous, quantitative data only. For measures of variability (SPSS refers to variability as "dispersion"), its **Options . . .** box offers only the standard deviation, variance, and range. Note that with respect to the first two measures just mentioned only the "unbiased" versions are given. In response to how infrequently the biased versions are used in the social sciences, it appears that SPSS does not offer the biased variance or biased standard deviation from any of its menus.

The **Frequencies . . .** dialog box is intended to accommodate a broader range of data types, including ordinal data and open-ended distributions. By clicking on the **Statistics** button, you can select **Quartiles,** and then calculate the interquartile and SIQ ranges from those results. The third relevant choice on the Analyze/Descriptive Statistics menu is **Explore . . . ,** and this selection is clearly intended for the thorough exploration of distributions that may be problematic. If you click on the **Statistics** button in the **Explore** dialog box, and then click on **Descriptives** in the **Explore: Statistics** box, you will get, in addition to the standard deviation, variance, and range (and a few measures that are too advanced to be mentioned in this text), the interquartile range. If you want the SIQ range, just divide this result by 2.

Chapter 6
Additional Techniques for Describing Batches of Data

Thus far, we have discussed various graphic and numerical techniques for describing sets of data. In some situations, pictorial representations will be worth the proverbial thousand words (e.g., histograms; frequency polygons). In others, a tabular format may prove best (e.g., frequency distributions; stem-and-leaf displays). And in still others, a few numbers may be most convenient and effective (e.g., means; medians; standard deviations; percentiles). The purpose of descriptive statistics is to summarize a set of data, and the best summary is one that discards the greatest number of minor details while retaining and highlighting important information.

Since the definition of what is important varies from one situation to another, there is no one universally accepted way to describe a set of data. The more techniques you have at your disposal, the better you will be able to choose one that emphasizes those aspects of the data that you deem to be most crucial. Therefore, let's expand our investigation of descriptive statistics by examining some additional, relatively modern summarization procedures. The first two procedures described in the following sections were devised by the same pioneering statistician, J. W. Tukey, who created the stem-and-leaf display described in Chapter 2. These techniques are part of a larger statistical approach known as *exploratory data analysis* (Tukey, 1977).

Numerical Summaries

As we observed in Chapters 4 and 5, the two most important characteristics of a set of numerical observations are its location and variability. Many distributions are well described by just two numbers: the mean and standard deviation. For example, a class of high school students' IQ scores might be found to have a mean of 105.2 and a standard deviation of 13.6, conventionally represented as 105.2 ± 13.6.

The kind of distribution that is particularly well described by its mean and standard deviation is one that is symmetric, and has a single mode in the middle of the range of values. This is the "bell-shaped" curve, illustrated in Figure 2.4A and discussed in detail in Chapter 8. Bell-shaped distributions occur frequently in the behavioral sciences, hence the great popularity of the mean and standard deviation as descriptive tools. But some distributions depart substantially from this shape, in which case the mean and standard deviation may be inadequate or even misleading as numerical summaries. (Recall the salary example in Chapter 4.) In such instances, therefore, you will need to seek out more accurate alternatives.

Percentiles and the Five-Number Summary

In Chapter 3, we observed that a percentile rank describes a specific score in terms of the proportion of cases falling at or below that score. If a college student's score of 146 on an entrance examination places him at the 80th percentile of the freshman class, then he exceeds (or is at least equal to) 80% of this group.

In addition to individual scores, entire distributions may be summarized by reporting the score values for various specific percentile ranks (e.g., quartiles or deciles). A particularly effective method using such "order" statistics is the five-number display devised by Tukey. The five numbers referred to are the median, the first and third quartiles (i.e., the 25th and 75th percentiles), and the lowest and highest scores. These five numbers are conventionally represented in a box, as follows:

Median		30
First, third quartile	22	35
Lowest, highest score	9	49

The values of the five numbers are readily obtained from a stem-and-leaf display (see Chapter 3), and they convey a considerable amount of information about the distribution. The ones shown above are from the stem-and-leaf display in Table 2.5, generated from the math quiz scores in Table 2.3. You can see at a glance that a score of 30 divides the class into top and bottom halves, that the lower half is further divided in half by a score of about 22 (the 25th percentile, or 1st quartile), and that the upper half is further divided in half by a score of about 35 (the 75th percentile, or 3rd quartile). The poorest (9) and best (49) scores show you exactly the limits within which the observations fall, and are frequently of interest in their own right.

By providing the limits of the four quarters of the ordered observations, the five numbers convey considerable information about the location, spread, and shape of the distribution. Recall that the quartiles give the limits of the *middle* 50% of the distribution. That is, the middle 50% of the scores occupy the span from 22 to 35. This also indicates that the middle 50% is not symmetric about the median, since the quarter below the median covers a greater range (30 – 22 = 8 score points) than does the quarter above the median (35 – 30 = 5 score points). Similar asymmetry is shown by the extreme scores: the bottom half occupies a slightly greater range (30 – 9 = 21 points) than does the top half (49 – 30 = 19 points).

Now let us compare this distribution with one obtained in the previous year by a different instructor, whose five-number summary was

Median		29
First, third quartile	24	33
Lowest, highest score	8	48

Notice that this distribution does not differ much from the preceding one in location (median of 29 vs. 30), and not at all in overall range (48 – 8 = 49 – 9

= 40). However, the middle half of this distribution is more symmetric about its median, which is 5 points from the 1st quartile and 4 points from the 3rd quartile. The most striking difference is that the middle half of the cases occupy much less of the full range (interquartile range = 33 – 24 = 9 points, compared with 35 – 22 = 13 points for the former distribution). Thus, the second distribution is much less variable, even though its overall spread is the same. (This should not be overly surprising, since we noted in the previous chapter that the range is a relatively poor measure of variability.) This in turn implies that the lowest and highest quarters of the students' scores are each considerably more heterogeneous than the comparable groups in the first instructor's course.

The five-number summary provides a fairly good indication of the shape of the distribution, as well as giving information about its location and spread, so you can use it with all kinds of data. In fact, the second distribution is approximately bell shaped, while the first is clearly skewed.

Graphic Summaries

The field of exploratory data analysis is responsible for several innovative methods for displaying data in such a way that important features can be noticed in just one glance. The most popular of these graphic techniques is described next.

Box-and-Whisker Plots

The information contained in a five-number summary may be expressed graphically in a figure called the "box-and-whisker plot" (Tukey, 1977). Although this device may be used to represent a single distribution, it is particularly valuable when two or more distributions are to be compared. Box-and-whisker plots (sometimes called "boxplots," for short) for the two math quiz distributions discussed above are presented in Figure 6.1, together with their corresponding five-number summaries.

In a box-and-whisker plot, the middle half of the observations in a given distribution is presented as a vertical rectangle whose top and bottom fall at the 3rd and 1st quartiles, respectively. Note that the vertical height of the box is equal to the interquartile range, as defined in the previous chapter. The box is divided by a line that represents the median. Then, lines ("whiskers") may be extended up to the largest and down to the smallest observation. (There are other schemes for determining the lengths of the whiskers, but these are best left to a statistical package.) This enables the span and endpoints of each quarter of the observations to be clearly represented, which in turn provides a clear sense of the distribution as a whole.

With the two box-and-whisker plots side by side on the same scale, it is possible to see even more clearly their similarities and differences. This is because

FIGURE 6.1

Box-and-whisker plots of the math background quizzes for the two classes and their 5-number summaries

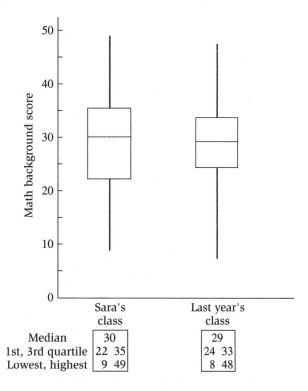

	Sara's class	Last year's class
Median	30	29
1st, 3rd quartile	22 35	24 33
Lowest, highest	9 49	8 48

it is easier to see and compare lengths of lines than it is to mentally compute differences (and differences between differences). Note in Figure 6.1 how easy it is to perceive the narrower spread of the middle half of the cases in the second class, and the concomitant greater spread of the lowest and highest quarters. Also, with the distributions summarized in this way, you can better appreciate how similar the two classes are otherwise.

Mean-on-Spoke Representations

Whereas box-and-whisker plots are particularly useful for irregular or skewed data, a more concise summary can be achieved when a distribution is approximately bell shaped. This graphic representation makes use of the mean and standard deviation, as would be expected in such instances, and is known as the "mean-on-spoke."

As an illustration, consider the three heart rate measurements in Sara's experiment. Fortunately for this example, all three distributions of scores are approximately bell shaped, and the means and standard deviations for the three

FIGURE 6.2

Means-on-spokes for the three sets of heart rate measurements and their respective values for mean ± standard deviation

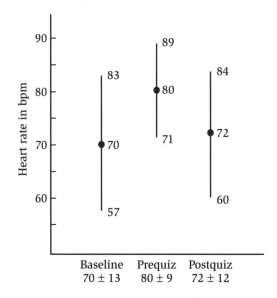

sets of measurements are the following: baseline, 70 ± 13; prequiz, 80 ± 9; and postquiz, 72 ± 12. You can see from these statistics that while students waited for the quiz, their heart rates rose on the average and exhibited less variability. But you can see this better still if these variables are represented on a graph, with each mean plotted as a point and a spoke running through it that is one standard deviation long on each side. (See Figure 6.2.)

Various implications of bell-shaped distributions can be used to understand the mean-on-spoke representation. For example, in a bell-shaped curve, approximately two thirds of the observations fall within the limits defined by the mean ± one standard deviation. Thus, at the pre-quiz interval described by 80 ± 9, you can expect about two thirds of the students to have heart rates between 71 and 89 beats per minute. (How we arrive at two thirds will become clear when we discuss the characteristics of the normal distribution in Chapter 8.) The graph also shows at a glance that the students at the lower end of the spoke at prequiz have heart rates at about the same level as those at the mean during the baseline and after the quiz.

The methods described in this chapter are descriptive only. You could not use them to draw inferences about whether heart rate will rise reliably before a statistics quiz for students in general, rather than just for those who happened to be included in this particular sample. (We will deal with methods for drawing inferences about three or more repeated measures in Chapter 18.) In order to extrapolate from Sara's students to the entire population of possible statistics students, we will need to use inferential statistics, but we have not yet presented the tools you will need to make such extrapolations. The next two chapters will help you to locate more precisely any particular score in a distribution and then translate that location into a statement about probability.

Summary

Some additional techniques for describing sets of data were discussed in this chapter. These include the following:

1. The Five-Number Summary

This numerical summary provides a good indication of the shape of a distribution by specifying five important values in box form:

	Median	
First quartile		Third quartile
Lowest score		Highest score

2. Box-and-Whisker Plots

This graphic summary is particularly valuable when two or more distributions are to be compared. Score values are shown on the vertical axis, with the name of the distribution(s) on the horizontal axis. The middle half of the observations in a given distribution is presented as a vertical rectangle whose top and bottom fall at the 3rd and 1st quartiles, respectively. The box is divided by a line that represents the median, and lines (whiskers) are extended up to the largest and down to the smallest observation.

3. Mean-on-Spoke Representations

This graphic summary is preferable to box-and-whisker plots when a distribution is approximately bell shaped. Here again, score values are shown on the vertical axis, but the mean of a given distribution is plotted as a point, with a vertical spoke running through it that is one standard deviation long on either side.

Exercises

1. Use the regular (ungrouped) frequency distributions that you created for the exercises in Chapter 2 to create five-number summaries for Universities A and B.

2. Using the results of exercise 1, create box-and-whisker plots for Universities A and B, displaying them on the same graph for comparison.

3. Create mean-on-spoke representations as another way to compare the distributions of Universities A and B.

Thought Questions

1. When is it preferable to use a five-number summary and/or a box-and-whisker plot to describe a set of data instead of the mean and standard deviation?

2. What is the relationship between the five-number summary and the box-and-whisker plot?

3. When is it preferable to use a mean-on-spoke representation to describe a set of data rather than a box-and-whisker plot?

Computer Exercises

1. Use your statistical package to create five-number summaries and boxplots for the anxiety and heart rate measures both at baseline and prequiz in Sara's data set. Request that the baseline and prequiz boxplots be displayed adjacent to each other on separate graphs for anxiety and heart rate.

2. Use your statistical package to create a new variable that is equal to the difference between the baseline and prequiz anxiety scores. Do the same for heart rate. Create boxplots for both the anxiety and heart rate difference scores. What do these boxplots tell you?

3. Using descriptive statistics that you have already calculated, create a mean-on-spoke representation for the stats quiz score. Do the same for the math background quiz.

Bridge to SPSS

The values you need in order to create a 5-number summary are easily obtained from SPSS by clicking on **Analyze, Descriptive Statistics,** and **Frequencies....** After moving the DV(s) of interest into the Variable(s) box, click on the **Statistics...** button, and then check Quartiles. Also, select Minimum and Maximum under the Dispersion section of the same Frequencies: Statistics box.

Box-and-whisker plots can be obtained directly from the Graphs rather than the Analyze menu, but you can obtain the values for the 5-number summary *and* boxplots from the Analyze/Descriptive Statistics menu if you click on Explore.... Make sure that **Both** is selected in the lower-left corner of the initial Explore dialog box. You can then click on the **Statistics...** button to make sure that the default selection, Descriptives, is checked. Click **Continue** so that you can go back to the initial Explore box, and this time click on the **Plots...** button. The Boxplot choices are in the upper-left corner of the Explore: Plots box; you can select None if you don't want to see boxplots at all. The other two choices, Factor levels together, and Dependents together, depend on the variables that you moved in the initial Explore box.

Let us say that you moved Gender into the Factor List in the Explore dialog box, and both base_HR and preqz_HR into the Dependent List area. If **Factor levels together** is selected in the Plots box, you will get side-by-side boxplots of men and women for base_HR, and then a separate set of men/women boxplots for preqz_HR. If **Dependents together** is selected instead, you will get side-by-side boxplots of base_HR and preqz_HR for both men and women (all on the same graph, if there's room, in different colors for the two DVs). If you now remove Gender from the factor list, you will get side-by-side boxplots of base_HR and preqz_HR, across all of Sara's students (select **Factor levels together,** and these two boxplots will be displayed separately).

Chapter 7
Transformed Scores II: *z* and *T* Scores

PREVIEW

Interpreting a Raw Score

What is the advantage of using a transformed score, such as a percentile rank?

When comparing two (or more) scores from different distributions, why is it necessary to refer each score to its mean and standard deviation? What errors are we likely to make if we look only at the raw scores?

Rules for Changing $\overline{X}$ and σ

What will happen to the mean and standard deviation of a set of scores if we do the following: Add a constant to every score? Subtract a constant from every score? Multiply every score by a constant? Divide every score by a constant?

How can these rules be used to obtain transformed scores with *any* desired mean and standard deviation?

Standard Scores (*z* Scores)

What is the mean and standard deviation of a set of *z* scores? Why is this desirable?

How are *z* scores computed?

When raw scores are transformed into *z* scores, what happens to the shape of the distribution?

T Scores and SAT Scores

Why might we prefer to use *T* scores or SAT scores instead of *z* scores?

How are *T* scores and SAT scores computed?

What is the mean and standard deviation of a set of *T* scores or a set of SAT scores?

IQ Scores

What is the mean and standard deviation of a set of IQ scores, and how are these scores computed?

Summary

Exercises

Thought Questions

Computer Exercises

Bridge to SPSS

Interpreting a Raw Score

In Chapter 3, we saw that it can be helpful to transform a raw score into a percentile rank. The percentile rank shows at a glance how the score stands in comparison to a specific reference group.

In Chapters 4 and 5, we identified two important characteristics of a group of scores: its location, frequently summarized by the mean $(\bar{X})$, and its variability, for which we will use the standard deviation (σ). It is possible to deduce how well a given score compares to the reference group by using the mean and standard deviation of that group. As was the case with percentiles, we can build this information into the score itself. That is, we can derive a transformed score that shows at a glance the relationship of the original raw score to the mean, using the standard deviation of the reference group as the unit of measurement.

To illustrate, let us suppose that a college student takes three midterm examinations in three different subjects and obtains the following raw scores:

	English	Mathematics	Psychology
X	80	65	75

On the surface, it might seem as though the student's best score is in English and his poorest score is in mathematics. It would be unwise to jump to such a conclusion, however, since there are several reasons why the raw scores may not be directly comparable. For example, the English examination may have been easy and resulted in many high scores, while the mathematics examination may have been extremely difficult. Or the English examination may have been based on a total of 100 points, and the mathematics examination on a total of only 80 points. The raw scores provide information about the absolute number of points earned, but they give no indication as to how good the performance is, and certainly no indication of how good the performance is compared to others.

Suppose that we specify the mean and standard deviation of each test:

	English	Mathematics	Psychology
X	80	65	75
$\bar{X}$	85	55	60
σ	10	5	15

This additional information changes the picture considerably. Looking at the means, we can see that the scores on the English examination were high, so much so that the score of 80 is below average. On the other hand, both the mathematics and psychology scores are above average. Therefore, the student's poorest result is in English.

The unwary observer might now conclude that the student's best score is in psychology, since that score is 15 points above average while the mathematics score is only 10 points above average. But as we pointed out in Chapter 5, the variability of a distribution of scores also influences the relative standing of a given score. The standard deviation indicates that the "average" variability on the psychology test was 15 points from the mean; some scores were more than 15 units from the mean and some were less. So the student's psychology score of 75, which is 15 points or one standard deviation above average, was exceeded by a number of better scores.[1] The average variability on the mathematics examination, however, was only five points from the mean. Hence the student's mathematics score of 65 is 10 points or *two* standard deviations above average. It is unusually far above the mean, and is therefore likely to be one of the best scores.[2]

The picture presented by the raw scores was quite misleading in this instance. It turns out that the student's best score is in mathematics, the next best score is in psychology, and the poorest score is in English, all relative to the other students in each course.

The raw scores of 80, 65, and 75 cannot be compared directly because they come from distributions with different means and different standard deviations. That is, the units in which the raw scores measure are not the same from test to test. This difficulty can be overcome by transforming the scores on each test to a common scale with a specified mean and standard deviation. This new scale will then serve as a "common denominator," enabling us to compare directly the transformed scores of different tests.

Two questions remain: How do we change the scores so that they will have the desired common mean and standard deviation? And what values of the mean and standard deviation are useful choices for the "common denominator"?

Rules for Changing $\overline{X}$ and σ

Suppose that the mathematics instructor in the previous example suffers a pang of conscience about the low mean, and decides to add 5 points to everyone's score. Since she has added a *constant* amount to each score (one that is exactly the same for all the scores), she does not have to recompute a new mean via the usual formula; we already showed in Chapter 4 that adding 5 points to everyone's score increases the mean by 5 points. Thus, the mean of the transformed scores (symbolized by $\overline{X}_{new}$) will be 60.

We know from the properties of the mean described in Chapter 4 that if the

---

1. The exact number depends on the shape of the distribution of scores. For example, if the scores are normally distributed, approximately 16% of the scores are more than one standard deviation above the mean (as will be shown in Chapter 8).

2. If the distribution is normal, less than $2^1/_2$% of the scores are more than two standard deviations above the mean.

English instructor subtracts 7.5 points from every score, the new mean is 77.5. If he multiplies every score by 4, the new mean is 340. And if he divides every score by 2, the new mean is 42.5. Recall that these rules for conveniently determining the new mean work only if every original score is altered by exactly the same amount.

Insofar as the variability of the distribution is concerned, we saw in Chapter 5 that adding a constant to every score or subtracting a constant from every score does *not* change the standard deviation or variance. However, we also showed the following:

If every score is *multiplied* by a positive constant k,

$$\sigma_{new} = k\sigma_{old},$$

and if every score is *divided* by a positive constant k,

$$\sigma_{new} = \sigma_{old}/k.$$

Therefore, if the English instructor adds 10 points or subtracts 6 points from every score, the standard deviation remains 10 (and the variance remains 10^2 or 100), but if he multiplies every score by 4, the new standard deviation equals 4×10 or 40 (and the new variance equals $4^2 \times 100$ or 1,600). If he divides every score by 2, the new standard deviation equals 10/2 or 5 (and the new variance equals $100/2^2$ or 25).

These rules make it possible to obtain transformed scores with any desired mean and standard deviation. For example, scores on the English test can be transformed to scores comparable to those on the mathematics test in two steps:

Procedure	New $\overline{X}$	New σ
1. Divide every score on the English examination by 2.0.	85/2 = 42.5	10/2 = 5
2. Add 12.5 to each of the scores obtained in Step 1.	42.5 + 12.5 = 55	5 (no change)

The first step is to change the standard deviation to the desired value by multiplying or dividing each score by the appropriate constant, which affects the value of both $\overline{X}$ and σ. Then, the desired mean is obtained by adding or subtracting the appropriate constant, which does not cause any further change in σ. When the student's English score of 80 is subjected to these transformations, it becomes $(80/2) + 12.5$ or 52.5, and it is evident that this score is not nearly as good as the student's mathematics score. Note that both the original and the transformed English scores are half a standard deviation below the means of their respective distributions.

Standard Scores (z Scores)

The techniques discussed in the preceding section make it possible to switch to any new mean and standard deviation. Therefore, the next logical step is to choose values of $\overline{X}_{new}$ and σ_{new} that facilitate comparisons among the scores. One very useful procedure is to convert the original scores to new scores with a mean of 0 and a standard deviation of 1, called *z* scores or *standard scores.*

Standard scores have two major advantages. Since the mean is zero, you can tell at a glance whether a given score is above or below average; an above-average score is positive and a below-average score is negative. Also, since the standard deviation is 1, the numerical size of a standard score indicates *how many standard deviations* above or below average the score is. We saw at the beginning of this chapter that this information offers a valuable clue as to how good the score is; a score one standard deviation above average (that is, a standard score of +1) would demarcate approximately the top 16% in a normal distribution, while a score two standard deviations above average (a standard score of +2) would demarcate approximately the top 2½% in a normal distribution.

To convert a set of scores to standard scores, the first step is to subtract the original mean from every score. According to the rules given in the previous section, the new mean is equal to

$$\overline{X}_{new} = \overline{X}_{old} - \overline{X}_{old}$$
$$= 0,$$

while the standard deviation is unchanged. Next, each score obtained from the first step is divided by the original standard deviation. As a result,

$$\overline{X}_{new} = \frac{0}{\sigma_{old}} = 0$$

$$\sigma_{new} = \frac{\sigma_{old}}{\sigma_{old}} = 1$$

That is, the mean remains zero, while the standard deviation becomes 1. Summarizing these steps in a single formula gives

$$z = \frac{X - \overline{X}}{\sigma},$$

where *z* is the symbol for a standard score.

Converting each of the original examination scores given at the beginning of this chapter to *z* scores yields the following:

	English	Mathematics	Psychology
X	80	65	75
$\overline{X}$	85	55	60
σ	10	5	15
z	$\dfrac{80-85}{10}=-0.50$	$\dfrac{65-55}{5}=+2.00$	$\dfrac{75-60}{15}=+1.00$

The standard scores show at a glance that the student was half a standard deviation below the mean in English, two standard deviations above the mean in mathematics, and one standard deviation above the mean in psychology.

When raw scores are transformed into z scores, *the shape of the distribution remains the same.* We just measure from a new point (the mean instead of zero), with a new unit size (the standard deviation instead of the raw units). To illustrate this point, the baseline heart rates for the 20 low-phobic men from Sara's statistics class are presented in Table 7.1 along with the corresponding z scores. The scores have been arranged in increasing order for clarity. The mean of the baseline heart rate (HR) scores is 67.80 beats per minute (bpm)

TABLE 7.1

Distribution of 20 baseline heart rate scores expressed in beats per minute (bpm), z scores, and beats per second (bps)

Low-phobic male	Heart rate (bpm)	Heart rate z score	Heart rate (bps)
1	72	+2.36	1.200
2	70	+1.24	1.167
3	70	+1.24	1.167
4	70	+1.24	1.167
5	69	+0.67	1.150
6	69	+0.67	1.150
7	68	+0.11	1.133
8	68	+0.11	1.133
9	68	+0.11	1.133
10	68	+0.11	1.133
11	67	−0.45	1.117
12	67	−0.45	1.117
13	67	−0.45	1.117
14	67	−0.45	1.117
15	67	−0.45	1.117
16	67	−0.45	1.117
17	66	−1.01	1.100
18	66	−1.01	1.100
19	66	−1.01	1.100
20	64	−2.14	1.067
$\overline{X}$	67.80	0.00	1.13
σ	1.78	1.00	0.0296

and the standard deviation is 1.78 bpm, and the z scores were obtained using the formula given above. For example, the z score corresponding to 72 bpm is equal to

$$z = \frac{72 - 67.80}{1.78} = +2.36$$

In accordance with the previous discussion, the mean of the z scores is 0.00 and the standard deviation is 1.00. The raw score and z score distributions are plotted in Figure 7.1; note that a single graph suffices because the shape of the distribution is the same for both sets of scores. Thus, the relationship of the scores to one another is *not* changed by transforming them to standard scores. All that change are the location and the scaling.

Although the HR scores are measured in beats per minute, identical z scores would be obtained (within rounding-off error) for each individual if HR were measured in beats per *second*, as is shown in the rightmost column of Table 7.1. For example,

HR in beats per minute	z score	HR in beats per second
$\dfrac{70 - 67.80}{1.78} =$	$+1.24$	$= \dfrac{1.167 - 1.13}{.0296}$

This indicates that z scores give an accurate picture of the standing of each score relative to the reference group even after the original scores have been divided by a constant (60, in this case). In fact, the properties of the mean and standard deviation are such that the original scores can be subjected to any combination of addition, subtraction, multiplication, or division by constants without affecting the corresponding z scores.

Standard scores are used extensively in the behavioral sciences. They also play an important role in statistical inference, as we will see in subsequent chapters.

T Scores and SAT Scores

Standard scores have one disadvantage: They are difficult to explain to someone who is not well versed in statistics. A college professor once decided to report the results of an examination as z scores. He was quickly besieged by anxious students who did not understand that a z score of 0 represents average performance (and not zero correct!), not to mention the agitated ones who received negative scores and wondered how they could ever repay the points they owed the professor.

FIGURE 7.1

Frequency distribution of raw HR scores and their z scores from Table 7.1

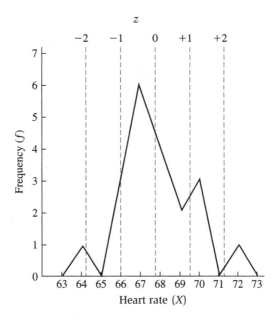

T Scores

Since one task of behavioral scientists is to report test scores to people who are not statistically sophisticated, several alternatives to z scores have been developed. The mean and standard deviation of each such "common denominator" have been chosen so that all of the scores will be positive, and so that the mean and standard deviation will be easy to remember. One such alternative, called *T scores,* is defined as a set of scores with a mean of 50 and a standard deviation of 10. The T scores are obtained from the following formula:

$$T = 10z + 50$$

Each raw score is converted to a z score, each z score is multiplied by 10, and 50 is added to each resulting score. For example, a heart rate of 69 in Table 7.1 is converted to a z score of $+0.67$ by the usual formula. Then, T is equal to $(10)(+0.67) + 50$ or 56.70. It is easy to prove that the above formula does produce the desired mean and standard deviation:

Procedure	New $\bar{X}$	New σ
1. Convert raw scores to z scores.	0	1
2. Multiply each z score by 10.	$10 \times 0 = 0$	$10 \times 1 = 10$
3. Add 50 to each score obtained in Step 2.	$0 + 50 = 50$	10 (no change)

Common physical measurements (including heart rates) are rarely transformed to T scores, because they are already expressed in units that are familiar. A T score would still provide additional information in locating a particular individual within a distribution. (You may know that a man who is 6 feet tall is taller than average, but a T score of 60 for height would tell you immediately that he is one standard deviation above the mean.) But T scores are even more helpful when dealing with psychological tests that are measured in arbitrary units. For example, scores on the anxiety scale that Sara used can range from 10 to 50. Whereas it may be clear that 10 represents very little or no anxiety and 50 a great deal of anxiety, it is certainly not obvious just how to interpret a score of, say, 20 or 30. However, once you become familiar with T scores, you can tell at a glance that a student whose baseline anxiety T score is 45 is below average in anxiety and, more specifically, that he or she is exactly one half of a standard deviation below average. (A z score of $-.5$ yields the same information but requires dealing with a minus sign and a decimal point.) Although a negative T score is mathematically possible, it is very unlikely. It would require that a person be more than five standard deviations below average, and scores more than three SDs above or below the mean rarely occur with real data.

SAT Scores

Scores on some nationally administered examinations, such as the Scholastic Aptitude Test (SAT), the College Entrance Examination Boards, and the Graduate Record Examination, are transformed to a scale with a mean of 500 and a standard deviation of 100. These scores, which we will refer to as SAT scores (based on their best-known application), are obtained as follows:

$$\text{SAT} = 100z + 500$$

As in the case of T scores, the raw scores are first converted to z scores; each z score is then multiplied by 100, and 500 is added to each resulting score. A comparison with the T score formula should make it obvious that an SAT score is just 10 times a T score. This explains the apparent mystery of how you can obtain a score of 642 on a test with only 30 or 40 items. And you may well be pleased if you obtain a score of 642, since it is 142 points or 1.42 standard deviations above the mean (and therefore corresponds to a z score of $+1.42$ and a T score of 64.2).

IQ Scores

Another common score that is based on transforming z scores to a more convenient form is the *IQ score*. The well-known Stanford-Binet test creates its intelligence quotient (i.e., IQ) scores by transforming its z scores according to the following formula:

$$IQ = 16z + 100$$

It is because of this formula, rather than some convenient coincidence, that the average IQ of the population happens to be about 100. You can also see why IQ scores above 148 or below 52 are very unusual: They differ from the mean by 3 SDs. The newer Wechsler Adult Intelligence Scale (WAIS) uses a slightly different formula to create IQ scores. The WAIS is also based on a mean of 100, but unlike the Stanford-Binet test, it uses a standard deviation of 15 instead of 16 (i.e., WAIS-IQ = $15z + 100$).

Summary

In order to compare scores based on different means and standard deviations, it is desirable to convert the raw scores to *transformed scores* with a common mean and standard deviation. Some frequently used transformed scores are *z scores* (*standard scores*), with a mean of 0 and a standard deviation of 1; *T scores,* with a mean of 50 and a standard deviation of 10; "*SAT scores,*" with a mean of 500 and a standard deviation of 100; and IQ scores, with a mean of 100 and a standard deviation of 15 or 16 (depending on the test). A transformed score shows at a glance whether a score is above or below average, and how far in terms of standard deviation units, with respect to a specified reference group.

1. General Transformations

Operation	Effect on $\overline{X}$	Effect on σ	Effect on σ^2
1. *Add* a constant, k, to every score	New mean = old mean + k	No change	No change
2. *Subtract* a constant, k, from every score	New mean = old mean – k	No change	No change
3. *Multiply* every score by a constant, k	New mean = old mean $\times k$	New σ = old $\sigma \times k$	New σ^2 = old $\sigma^2 \times k^2$
4. *Divide* every score by a constant, k	New mean = old mean/k	New σ = old σ/k	New σ^2 = old σ^2/k^2

2. z Scores (Standard Scores)

$$z = \frac{X - \overline{X}}{\sigma}$$

3. T Scores

$$T = 10z + 50$$

4. SAT Scores

$$\text{SAT} = 100z + 500 = 10T$$

5. IQ Scores

$$\text{IQ} = 15z + 100$$

or

$$16z + 100$$

Exercises

1. The mean of a set of scores is 8 and the standard deviation is 4. What will the new mean, standard deviation, and variance be if you:

   (a) add 6.8 to every number?

   (b) subtract 4 from every number?

   (c) multiply every number by 3.2?

   (d) divide every number by 4?

   (e) add 6 to every number, and then divide each new number by 2?

2. For each of the following, compute the z score; then compute the T score.

   (a) A University A student with a score of 17.

   (b) A University A student with a score of 11.

   (c) A University B student with a score of 11.

   (d) A University C student with a score of 9.

   (e) A University C student with a score of 6.

   (f) A University D student with a score of 6.

3. Consider the following data:

	Psychology test	English test
Student's score	73	67
$\overline{X}$	81.0	77.0
σ	5.0	10.0

A student believes that he has done better on the psychology test for two reasons: His score is higher, and he is only 8 points below average (as opposed to 10 points below average on the English test). Convert each of his test scores to a z score. Is he right?

4. Which of each pair is better, or are they the same? (You should be able to answer by inspection.)

   (a) A T score of 47 and a z score of +0.33

   (b) A T score of 64 and a z score of +0.88

   (c) A T score of 42 and a z score of –1.09

   (d) A T score of 60 and a z score of +1.00

   (e) A T score of 50 and a raw score of 26 (mean of raw scores = 26, $\sigma = 9$)

   (f) A z score of +0.04 and a raw score of 1092 (mean of raw scores = 1113, $\sigma = 137$)

   (g) A z score of zero and a T score of 50

5. For data set 3 in Chapter 1 (see exercise 5), transform each subject's score on X to a z score. Then transform each subject's score on Y to a z score.

S	X	Y	z_X	z_Y
1	97	89	_____	_____
2	68	57	_____	_____
3	85	87	_____	_____
4	74	76	_____	_____
5	92	97	_____	_____
6	92	79	_____	_____
7	100	91	_____	_____
8	63	50	_____	_____
9	85	85	_____	_____
10	87	84	_____	_____
11	81	91	_____	_____
12	93	91	_____	_____
13	77	75	_____	_____
14	82	77	_____	_____

6. Transform each raw score in the data set that follows into a z score, a T score, and an SAT score.

   68.36, 15.31, 77.42, 84.00, 76.59, 68.43, 72.41, 83.05, 91.07, 80.62, 77.83

Thought Questions

1. What are the advantages of having a set of scores that has a mean of zero and a standard deviation of 1 (z scores)?

2. A college student takes two introductory courses for first-year students. On her psychology exam, she scores 73; the mean is 81.0, and the standard deviation is 5.0. On her English exam, she scores 67; the mean is 77, and the standard deviation is 10.0. Both distributions are approximately normal. She concludes that she did better on the psychology exam because her score on that exam is 6 points higher. Is she correct? Why or why not?

3. For the same exams as in the previous question, another student scores 91 on the psychology exam and 93 on the English exam. He concludes that he did better on the English exam because his English score is 16 points above average, while his psychology score is only 10 points above average. Is he correct? Why or why not?

Computer Exercises

1. Use your statistical package to create new variables consisting of the z scores for the anxiety and heart rate measures both at baseline and prequiz in Sara's data set. Request means and SDs of the z-score variables to demonstrate that the means and SDs are 0 and 1, respectively, in each case.

2. Use your statistical package to create a z-score variable corresponding to the math background quiz score, and then transform the z-score variable to a T score, an SAT score, and an IQ score.

3. Repeat exercise 2 for the statistics quiz score that was part of Sara's experiment.

Bridge to SPSS

After SPSS has calculated the mean and SD for one of the variables in your spreadsheet, you could find the corresponding z scores by creating a new variable in the Compute Variable box available from the Transform menu (just click on the first choice: **Compute...**). However, an easier way to obtain z scores is available from the Analyze/Descriptive Statistics menu; just choose **Descriptives....** Under the list of variables that appears in the Descriptives dialog box, you will see the phrase "Save standardized values as variables" preceded by a small checkbox. Check the box, and move over the variables for which you would like to see the z scores. After you click **OK,** two things will happen. You will get the usual Descriptives output for the variables you moved over, and for each of these variables SPSS will have added a new variable at the end of your spreadsheet, containing the z scores that correspond to the scores of that variable.

We have two warnings for those who create z scores automatically in SPSS. Note that the first of these does not apply to users of SPSS for Windows, version 14.0 or later. SPSS names the new *z*-score variables by putting the letter z at the beginning of the original name. If the original name consists of the maximum eight characters allowed, the last character will be dropped; for example, if the variable is named anxiety1, the *z*-score variable will be named zanxiety. However, if you are creating *z*-score variables for both anxiety1 and anxiety2, the second of these cannot also be called zanxiety, so SPSS will name it zsc001, instead. Choose a shorter original name if you want to ensure that all of your new *z*-score variable names will have some mnemonic value.

Second, because SPSS does not deal at all with the biased variance or standard deviation, it creates *z* scores by dividing deviations from the mean by the *unbiased* standard deviation. We described *z* scores in this chapter as based on σ rather than s, because that is the more common method. When you are calculating *z* scores for individuals, it is usually the case that you are viewing the entire set of individuals as a population instead of just a sample. Because SPSS creates *z* scores based on s, calculating σ for the set of *z* scores created will not yield a value of 1.0; it is s that will equal 1.0, in this case. Of course, the mean of the set of *z* scores will always be zero, even if they were produced by SPSS. To get *z* scores based on σ instead of s, you would have to multiply all of the *z* scores created by SPSS by the square root of the ratio of your total N to $N-1$.

Chapter 8
The Normal Distribution

PREVIEW

Introduction

What is meant by saying that the normal distribution is a *theoretical* distribution?

How can the normal curve model be useful when dealing with real data?

What is the shape of the normal curve? Is it unimodal? Is it symmetric?

Score Distributions

How is the total population depicted in a graph? As a probability?

In a graph, how do we depict the proportion of the population with scores between two specified values?

Parameters of the Normal Distribution

What are the two parameters of the normal distribution?

Table of the Standard Normal Distribution

How is the normal curve table used?

How do we find the percent of the area under the normal curve that falls between the mean and any particular z score?

Characteristics of the Normal Curve

Where in the normal curve are values more likely to occur?

What percent of the area under the normal curve falls between the mean and one standard deviation unit? Between the mean and two standard deviation units?

Illustrative Examples

How do we calculate the proportion of the population that can be expected to have scores between two specified values, or above or below one specified value?

How do we calculate the score that is required to be within a specified proportion of the population (for example, the top 10%)?

Summary

Exercises

Thought Questions

Computer Exercises

Bridge to SPSS

Introduction

In the previous chapter, we showed that a standard score can be more inform-ative than a raw score—for example, when trying to interpret an individual's performance on a very difficult exam for which the average could be as low as 40 points out of 100. A z score of $+1.0$ has to be relatively good no matter what the mean is. However, just how good that z score is depends on the *shape* of the distribution you are dealing with.

Suppose that the scores on an exam have an extremely positive skew: The bulk of the scores are a bit below 40, but some scores are over 80, and there are even a few in the 90s. In this case, a z score of $+1.0$ is not nearly as im-pressive as it would be in a very negatively skewed distribution because there are many high scores. Conversely, suppose that the scores are clustered slightly above 40 with a "tail" that narrows down as you get near a score of zero, but there are no really high scores. Here, a z score of $+1.0$ is likely to be one of the highest scores in the class, and therefore much more impressive than in the preceding case. Two z scores, each from a different distribution, can be more easily compared if we know that the two distributions have similar shapes.

In this chapter, you will see that z scores become especially informative when you are dealing with a very well-known distribution called the *normal distribution* (less formally referred to as the "normal curve"). Any distribution of real data will never match the normal distribution (ND) exactly. The ND is a *theoretical* distribution—a mathematical abstraction like a perfect circle, or a line that has length but no width. The normal curve is unimodal and symmet-ric (as was illustrated in Chapter 2) and is most often described as a bell-shaped curve because it is high in the middle and low at both ends or *tails*. However, the ND is not just any bell-shaped curve; its shape is defined by a particular mathematical equation.[1] As a theoretical distribution, the ND con-tains an infinite number of scores. Its tails on either side keep falling closer to the X axis, but do not actually touch it until you go an infinite distance in either direction.

On the other hand, the ND is a distribution that tends to arise, at least ap-proximately, rather frequently in nature. For example, if you look at the heights of all people of one gender in a large population, their distribution will look rather similar to the ND. However, you can tell immediately that your empiri-cal height distribution cannot match the ND exactly. Your distribution will end abruptly on either side, when you get to the shortest and tallest people in the population. Nonetheless, for many purposes, the ND will be an acceptable ap-proximation for the variable you are dealing with, and it is much easier to work with mathematically than any finite distribution of real data. College Board

---

1. The formula for the normal curve is fairly complicated:

$$f(X) = \frac{1}{\sigma\sqrt{2\pi}}\, e^{-(X-\mu)^2/2\sigma^2},$$

where $\pi = 3.1416$ and $e = 2.7183$, both approximately.

scores, for which a very large number of data points are available, will be used later in this chapter as our example of a population that has a distribution similar to the ND.

The statistical procedures described in this chapter may seem relevant only when measuring dependent variables that have approximately normal distributions in a population. However, we will show in the next chapter that the ND has a much broader use as a statistical model when used with groups of scores rather than individuals, even when the variable being measured has a very skewed distribution in the population (e.g., annual income).

Score Distributions

As with any frequency distribution, the horizontal axis of the normal distribution in Figure 8.1 represents score values and the vertical axis is related to frequency. Also, all values in Figure 8.1 are located *under* the curve. So the *total population* is expressed in the graph as the *total area under the normal curve,* and we can arbitrarily define this area as 100% without bothering about the exact number of cases in the population. Alternatively, we may move the decimal point two places to the left and define the total area under the normal curve as 1.00. This definition is useful when we wish to answer questions that deal with probability, since the sum of all the specific probability values in any distribution is 1.00.

Now suppose that you are asked to find the proportion of the population with values between points X_1 and X_2 in Figure 8.1. Graphically, the answer is given by the percent *area between* these two points. This is equivalent to the

FIGURE 8.1

The normal curve: A theoretical distribution

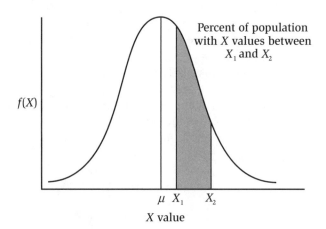

percent frequency of these values, and/or to the probability of occurrence of these values.

If you have taken an elementary calculus course, you know that the numerical value of the area between these two X values may be found by integrating the normal curve equation. However, you also know how tedious it would be to carry out an integration every time you wished to use the normal curve model. Fortunately, all necessary integrations have been performed and summarized in a convenient table, which shows the percent frequency of values within any distance (in terms of standard deviations) from the population mean. We will explain the use of the normal curve table next.

Parameters of the Normal Distribution

Normal distributions can differ from each other in just two ways: their locations (represented by their central point, μ), and their variability or spreads (as measured by σ). Just as any rectangle can be specified by giving both its length and width, any ND can be completely determined by giving its μ and σ. These two quantities are referred to as the *parameters* of the normal distribution. (This usage is consistent with the meaning of a parameter as a population value as defined in Chapter 1.) Note that these two parameters appear in the equation for the normal distribution (see footnote on page 109) and must be specified before that equation can be solved for any value of X. Because Parts II and III of this text deal with statistical procedures whose purpose is to estimate or make inferences about the parameters of some ND of interest, procedures in those chapters are referred to collectively as *parametric statistics.*

Table of the Standard Normal Distribution

Although integral calculus could be used *in theory* to create a table of areas for every possible ND, *in practice* this would require an infinite number of tables—one table for each possible combination of μ and σ. Instead, a very convenient table has been created for just one special ND, the one whose parameters are $\mu = 0$ and $\sigma = 1$. This ND is called the *standard normal distribution,* and it arises whenever you transform all the scores in any normal distribution into z scores. It is important to recall that transforming raw scores into z scores does *not* change the shape of a distribution at all. Only if a population of raw scores follows a normal distribution will its z scores also form a normal distribution—specifically, the standard normal distribution.

In order to use the table for the standard ND (presented as Table A in the Appendix) to solve problems about *any* ND, it is necessary to convert the scores you are interested in to z scores. Fortunately, as you have seen in the previous chapter, this is easy to do. To illustrate the way areas can be looked up in terms of z scores in Table A, a portion of that table is reproduced next.

	Percents calculated from area under the normal curve					
z	.00	.01	.02	.03	. . .	.09
0.0						
⋮						
1.0	34.13	34.38	34.61	34.85		
1.1	36.43	36.65	36.86	37.08		
1.2	38.49	38.69	38.88	39.07		
1.3	40.32	40.49	40.66	40.82		
⋮						
∞						

The vertical column on the left represents z values expressed to one decimal place, while the top horizontal row gives the second decimal place. The values within the table represent the *percent area between the mean and the z value,* expressed to two decimal places. For example, to find the percent of cases between the mean and 1.03 standard deviations from the mean, select the 1.0 row and go across to the .03 column; the answer is read as 34.85%.

The table gives percents on one side of the mean only, so that the maximum percent given in the table is 50.00 (representing half of the area). However, the normal curve is *symmetric,* which implies that the height of the curve at any positive z value (such as $+1$) is exactly the same as the height at the corresponding negative value (-1). Therefore, the percent between the mean and a z of $+1$ is exactly the same as the percent between the mean and a z of -1, and presentation of a second half of the table to deal with negative scores is unnecessary. It is up to you to remember whether you are working in the half of the curve above the mean (positive z) or the half of the curve below the mean (negative z). Also, do not expect the value obtained from the table to be the answer to your statistical problem in every instance. Since the table only provides values between the mean and a given z score, some additional calculations will be necessary whenever you are interested in the area between two z scores (neither of which falls at the mean) or the area between one end of the curve and a z score. These calculations will be illustrated in the following sections.

Characteristics of the Normal Curve

In Figure 8.2, the normal curve is presented with the X axis marked off to illustrate specified z distances from the mean. The percent areas between the mean and those z values have been determined from Table A. Notice that the percent of the total area between μ (the population mean where $z = 0$) and a z of $+1.00$ is 34.13%, and the area between μ and $z = -1.00$ is also 34.13%.

FIGURE 8.2

Normal curve: Percent areas from the mean to specified z distances

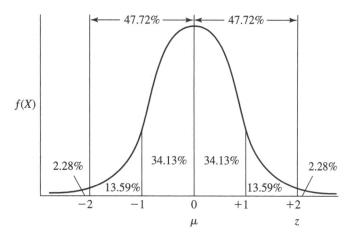

Thus, 68.26% of the total area under the normal curve lies between $z = -1.00$ and $z = +1.00$.

Looking at the shape of the normal distribution, you should expect z values between 0 and 1 to occur more frequently than z values between 1 and 2. Even though the score distances between the mean and $z = +1$ and between $z = +1$ and $z = +2$ are the same, the *area* between the mean and $z = +1$ is much greater than the area between $z = +1$ and $z = +2$. As you can see from Figure 8.2, the area between a z of $+1$ and a z of $+2$ is only about 13.6%.

Adding up the areas in Figure 8.2, you can see that just over 95% of the normal curve lies within approximately two standard deviation units of μ (more exactly, between $z = -1.96$ and $z = +1.96$). For example, if the heights of American adult males were assumed to be normally distributed with the mean at 5 ft. 8 in. and the standard deviation equal to 3 in., you would expect close to 95% of these males to have heights within 5 ft. 8 in. ± 6 in., or between 5 ft. 2 in. and 6 ft. 2 in. Table A can be used to answer more complex questions about areas of the normal curve, as we will see next.

Illustrative Examples

The College Boards are administered each year to many thousands of high school seniors, and the scores are transformed in such a way as to yield a mean of 500 and a standard deviation of 100, as discussed for SAT scores in the previous chapter. These scores are close to being normally distributed, so we can use the normal curve model in our calculations. Because Sara included the math SAT scores of her students as part of the background data she collected,

FIGURE 8.3

Percent of population with math SAT scores between 500 and 675

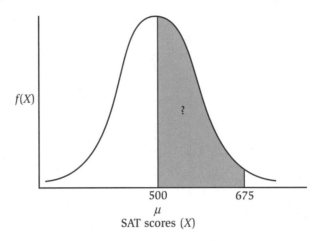

we express our examples in terms of that particular test. Since we know both μ and σ for the math SAT, we can convert any score on that test to a z score and refer it to Table A in the Appendix, using

$$z = \frac{X - \mu}{\sigma}$$

$$= \frac{X - 500}{100}$$

In situations where μ and σ are not known, they can be estimated from the sample $\overline{X}$ and s provided that the sample size is large; we will demonstrate this in the next chapter.

There are many problems that can be solved by the use of this model:

1. What percent of high school seniors in the population can be expected to have math SAT scores between 500 and 675?

The first step in any normal curve problem is to draw a rough diagram and indicate the answer called for by the problem; this will prevent careless errors. The desired percent is expressed as the shaded area in Figure 8.3.

To obtain the percent area between the mean (500) and a raw score of 675, convert the raw score to a z score:

$$z = \frac{675 - 500}{100} = +1.75$$

Table A reveals that the percent area between the mean and a z score of $+1.75$ is equal to 45.99%. Therefore, approximately 46% of the population is

FIGURE 8.4

Percent of population with math SAT scores between 450 and 500

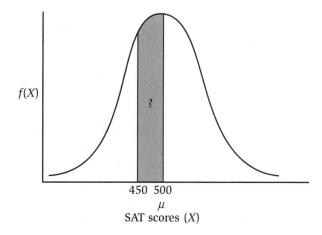

expected to have scores between 500 and 675. By using the normal curve model as an approximation, you can reach this conclusion even though you cannot measure the entire population.

2. What percent of the population can be expected to have scores between 450 and 500?

The diagram for this problem is shown in Figure 8.4. Converting the raw score of 450 to a z score yields

$$z = \frac{450 - 500}{100} = -0.50$$

Table A does not include any negative z values, but entering the table at the z score of $+.50$ will produce the right answer because of the symmetry of the normal curve. The solution is that 19.15%, or about 19% of the population, is expected to have scores between 450 and 500.

3. What percent of the population can be expected to have scores between 367 and 540?

This problem is likely to produce some confusion unless you use the diagram in Figure 8.5 as a guide. Table A gives values only between the mean and a given z score, so two steps are required. First obtain the percent between 367 and the mean (500); then obtain the percent between the mean and 540. Then *add* the two percents together to get the desired area. The z values are as follows:

$$z = \frac{367 - 500}{100} = -1.33; \quad z = \frac{540 - 500}{100} + 0.40$$

FIGURE 8.5
Percent of population with math SAT scores between 367 and 540

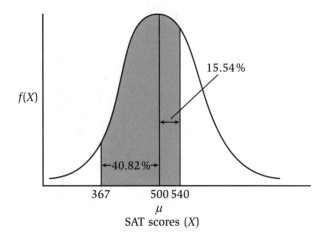

Table A indicates that 40.82% of the total area falls between the mean and a z of -1.33, and 15.54% falls between the mean and a z of $+0.40$. So the percent of the population expected to have scores between 367 and 540 is equal to 40.82% + 15.54% or 56.36%.

4. What percent of the population can be expected to have scores between 633 and 700?

Once again, you are likely to encounter some difficulty unless you draw a diagram such as the one shown in Figure 8.6. The z score corresponding to a

FIGURE 8.6
Percent of population with math SAT scores between 633 and 700

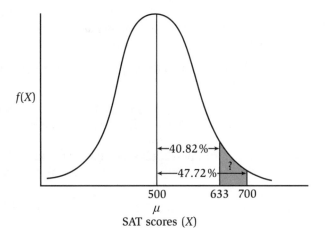

FIGURE 8.7

Percent of population with math SAT scores above 725

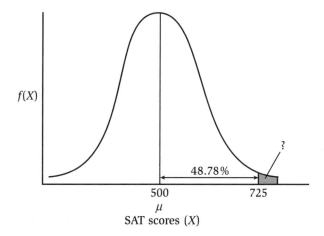

raw score of 633 is equal to $(633 - 500)/100$ or $+1.33$, and the z score corresponding to a raw score of 700 is equal to $(700 - 500)/100$ or $+2.00$. According to Table A, 40.82% of the curve falls between the mean and $z = +1.33$, and 47.72% of the curve falls between the mean and $z = +2.00$. So the answer is equal to 47.72% *minus* 40.82%, or 6.90%. In this example, subtraction (rather than addition) is the route to the correct answer, and drawing the illustrative diagram will help you decide on the proper procedure in each case.

5. What percent of the population can be expected to have scores above 725?

The percent to be calculated is shown in Figure 8.7. The z score corresponding to a raw score of 725 is equal to $(725 - 500)/100$ or $+2.25$, and the area between the mean and this z score as obtained from Table A is equal to 48.78%. At this point, avoid the incorrect conclusion that the value from the table is the answer to the problem. As the diagram shows, you need to find the percent *above* 725. Since the half of the curve to the right of the mean is equal to 50.00%, the answer is equal to $50.00\% - 48.78\%$, or 1.22%. A score of 725 is at about the 99th percentile, since about 1% of the population exceeds it.

6. What is the probability that a person drawn at random from the population will have a score of 725 or more?

This problem is identical to the preceding one, but is expressed in different terminology. As before, convert 725 to a z score, obtain the percent between the mean and 725, and subtract from 50% to obtain the answer of 1.22%. To express this as a probability, move the decimal point two places to the left. The probability that any one individual drawn at random from the population will have a score of 725 or more is $.0122$, or about $.01$.

FIGURE 8.8
Math SAT score that demarcates the top 10% of the population

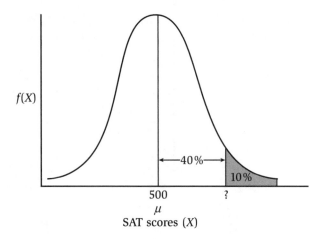

7. A math professor wishes to invite only the top 10% of the student population to join a competitive math team that he is forming. What cutoff math
   SAT score should he use to accept and reject candidates?

   This problem is the reverse of the ones we have looked at up to this point.
Previously, you were given a score and asked to find a percent; this time, the
percent is specified and a score value is needed. The problem is illustrated in
Figure 8.8.
   The needed value is the raw score value corresponding to the cutoff line in
Figure 8.8. The steps are exactly the reverse of the previous procedure:

   1. If 10% are above the cutoff line, then 40% (50% – 10%) are between the
      mean and the cutoff line.
   2. Enter Table A in the *body* of the table (where the percents are given) with
      the value 40.00 (= 40%). Read out the z score corresponding to the per-
      cent nearest in value to 40.00 ($z = 1.28$ for 39.97).
   3. Determine the *sign* of the z score. Since the diagram shows that the de-
      sired cutoff score is *above* the mean, the z score is positive and equals
      +1.28.
   4. Convert the z score to a raw score. Since $z = (X - \mu)/\sigma$, some simple al-
      gebraic manipulations yield $X = z\sigma + \mu$. Thus, $X = (+1.28)(100) + 500$,
      or 628. Any student with a score of 628 or more may try out for the new
      math team; individuals with scores of 627 or less are not invited.

8. What cutoff score separates the top 60% of the population from the bottom
   40%?

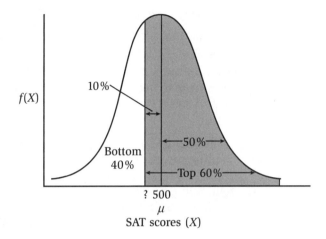

FIGURE 8.9

Math SAT score demarcating the top 60% of the population

Since you are given a percent and asked to find a score, this is another "reverse" problem; you need to find the raw score illustrated in Figure 8.9.

The percent with which to enter the table is not immediately obvious, and a hasty reliance on any percent that seems to be handy (such as 60% or 40%) will produce an incorrect answer. The area between the mean and the cutoff line is 10%, and it is this value that must be used to enter Table A. As in the previous problem, enter the table in the center; find the value nearest to 10.00 (here, 09.87), and read out the corresponding z score (0.25). Next, determine the sign. Since the diagram shows that the desired cutoff score is *below* the mean, the sign is negative and $z = -0.25$. Finally, convert this value to a raw score: $X = (-0.25)(100) + (500)$, or 475. Thus the cutoff score between the top 60% and the bottom 40% of the population is 475.

As you can see, the normal curve is useful for solving various types of problems involving scores and percentage distributions. Of even greater importance is its use with certain sampling distributions, such as means, to which we now turn.

Summary

One frequently used theoretical distribution is the *normal curve.* One use of this model is as follows: If it is assumed that raw scores in the population are normally distributed, and that we know or can estimate the population mean and standard deviation, we can obtain (1) the percent of the population with raw scores above or below or between specified values and/or (2) the raw score that demarcates specified percents in the population.

1. Type 1 Problem: Given a raw score, find the corresponding frequency or percent frequency.

1. Convert the raw score to a z score: $z = (X - \mu)/\sigma$.
2. Enter the normal curve table in the z column, and read out the percent area from the mean to this z value.
3. Compute the answer to the problem. Note that Table A gives only the area from the mean to the z value; be sure your final answer is the one called for by the problem.

2. Type 2 Problem: Given a frequency or percent frequency, find the corresponding raw score.

1. Compute the percent frequency (if it is not given) and enter the normal curve table in the area portion. Read out the corresponding z score. If the desired raw score is *below* the mean, assign a negative sign to this z score.
2. Convert the z score to a raw score: $X = z\sigma + \mu$.

Exercises

The following exercises are based on SAT scores, with the assumption that they follow the normal distribution with $\mu = 500$ and $\sigma = 100$.

1. What percent of the population obtains scores of 410 or less?
2. What percent of the population obtains scores between 430 and 530?
3. What percent of the population obtains scores between 275 and 375?
4. How do you explain the fact that the answer to exercise 3 is smaller than the answer to exercise 2, even though each problem deals with a 100-point range of scores?
5. What is the minimum score needed to rank in the top 5% of the population?
6. A psychologist wishes to test a new learning strategy on the bottom 15% of those who took the math SAT. What cutoff score should she use to select participants for her study?
7. A single student is drawn at random from the population. What is the probability that this student has a score (a) of 410 or less? (b) between 430 and 530? (c) between 275 and 375? (d) in the top 5% of the population? (Hint: base your answers to this exercise on the percentages you found for the previous exercises.)

Thought Questions

1. Why is Table A given in terms of z scores rather than raw scores?

2. Why is it *not* necessary to know the exact number of cases in the population being studied in order to use the procedures described in this chapter?

3. The distributions of scores on two exams are approximately normal. The mean of the first exam is 80, and the mean of the second exam is 95. The standard deviation of each exam is 15. Use the properties of the normal distribution to show that there *must* be some scores on the first exam that are greater than the mean of the second exam.

4. Suppose that in the previous question, the standard deviation of each exam is changed to 3. How would this affect the likelihood that there are scores on the first exam that are greater than the mean of the second exam?

5. If you know that a distribution of scores is bimodal, or asymmetric, or a J-curve, or any other shape that departs significantly from the normal distribution, would it be correct to use Table A to solve problems, as was done in this chapter? Why or why not?

Computer Exercises

Use your statistical package to find the following areas under the normal curve (your answer should include six digits past the decimal point):

1. The area below a z score of +3.1.

2. The area above a z score of +3.3.

3. The area below a z score of −3.7.

4. The area between the mean and a z score of +.542.

5. The area between the mean and a z score of −1.125.

Bridge to SPSS

You can use SPSS to obtain areas under the normal distribution with more accuracy (i.e., digits past the decimal point) than available in Table A, and for z scores not found in Table A or most other tables available from books. Start by opening a new (i.e., empty) data sheet, and entering the z score of interest in the first cell. For convenience, you can assign the simple variable name "z" to this first column. Then open the Compute Variable box by selecting Compute... (the first choice) from the Transform menu. In the Target Variable space, type an appropriate variable name like "area." In the Numeric Expression space, type **CDFNORM** and then, in parentheses, the name of the first variable—for example, CDFNORM (z). (Note: We are using uppercase letters here, but SPSS does not distinguish between upper- and lowercase letters in variable or function names.) CDFNORM is a function name that stands for the *Cumu*lative *D*ensity *F*unction for the *NORM*al distribution; therefore it returns a value equal to all of the area to the left of (i.e., below) the z score you entered. If you multiply this value by 100, you get the percentile rank associated with the z score in question (this works for both positive and negative z scores, as long as you include the minus sign for any negative z score).

If you want the area between the mean and your z value, just subtract .50 from the area obtained by the CDFNORM function (this will work for negative z scores, if you enter them without the minus sign). If you want the area above, rather than below, a particular z score, just change the sign in front of the z score (add a minus sign to a positive z score or remove the minus sign from a negative z score); because the normal curve is symmetric around z = 0, the area below –z is the same as the area above +z. Note that the larger the z score you enter in the first cell of your SPSS datasheet, the more "decimals" you will need to display the answer accurately. The fourth column in Variable View lets you set the number of digits that will be displayed to the right of the decimal point—as long as this number is less than the number in the third column (Width) for that variable. For instance, if you are looking for the area below a z score of 3 or 4, you will want to set the "decimals" number to at least 6.

Part II
Basic Inferential Statistics

Chapter 9
Introduction to Statistical Inference

PREVIEW

Introduction

The typical population of interest to the behavioral science researcher is extremely large; what serious problem does this create? How does the use of samples help to solve this problem?

What new difficulty is created by the use of samples? What type of statistics helps to solve this problem?

The Goals of Inferential Statistics

What are the three major varieties of inferential statistics?

Sampling Distributions

What is an experimental sampling distribution? Why is this type of statistical model *not* used in inferential statistics?

What is a theoretical sampling distribution? When is it reasonable to use the normal curve as the theoretical distribution (i.e., statistical model)?

The Standard Error of the Mean

We wish to draw inferences about the mean of one population, based on a statistic whose sampling distribution is normal—namely, the sample mean. Why should the standard deviation of the raw scores *not* be used as the measure of variability? How does the variability of a distribution of *sample means* differ from that of *raw scores?*

What is the standard error of the mean? Why can't it be measured directly? How is it estimated?

What does the standard error of the mean tell us about the trustworthiness of a single sample mean as an estimate of the population mean?

The *z* Score for Sample Means

How is the *z* score calculated when dealing with sample means instead of individuals?

What is a *p* value?

Null Hypothesis Testing

What two hypotheses are made prior to conducting the statistical analysis?

Which of these hypotheses is assumed to be true?

(continued next page)

PREVIEW (continued)

What is a Type I error?

What is the criterion of significance, and how is it related to a Type I error?

What is the probability of a Type I error?

How does the one-tailed p value differ from the two-tailed p value?

What are critical values? How are critical values used in null hypothesis testing?

What are the critical values for z in a two-tailed significance test using the .05 criterion?

What are the critical values using the .01 criterion of significance?

What advantage does the .05 criterion of significance have over the .01 criterion of significance? What is the advantage of the .01 criterion? Which is used more often in behavioral science research?

What is a Type II error?

Why is the probability of a Type II error harder to determine than the probability of a Type I error?

What is the relationship between the probabilities of Type I and Type II errors?

What is a one-tailed test of significance? What are the advantages and disadvantages of this procedure? Why is the two-tailed test more commonly used?

Assumptions Required by the Statistical Test for the Mean of a Single Population

What assumptions underlie the use of the z score for sample means in conjunction with the normal distribution?

What can be done when σ is not known?

Summary

Exercises

Thought Questions

Computer Exercises

Bridge to SPSS

Introduction

One distressing fact greatly complicates the lives of behavioral scientists: The populations from which they seek to collect data are usually far too large for them to measure every element in the population, or even a sizable portion of the population.

Suppose that a psychologist wishes to test the hypothesis that a new computer software package will improve the performance of students in college-level statistics courses. In this study, the population consists of all college students in the United States who are studying statistics. This is enough to frighten off even the most dedicated researcher! No behavioral scientist can afford the time, effort, and money needed to obtain and analyze data from so many thousands of people.

Therefore, the psychologist might decide to limit the study to 100 statistics students selected in some way from the population. This procedure will provide him with a group that can be measured in its entirety, but it creates a serious problem. Since the data are obtained from only a very small part of the population, there is no assurance that these data will accurately reflect what is happening in that population. If this sample of 100 students is atypical of the population as a whole, the psychologist will suffer some unhappy consequences: The results that he publishes, and his decision concerning the merits of the software package, will subsequently be contradicted by other researchers who try to verify his findings with different samples of students drawn from this population. When it is discovered that the psychologist's research findings were incorrect, he will suffer professional loss of face. More importantly, the effort to advance our scientific knowledge in this area will undergo a setback while researchers try to untangle the various conflicting results. Unfortunately, the only sure way to prevent this calamity would be to measure the entire population—which, as we noted above, is impossible.

In sum: Behavioral scientists need to draw conclusions about populations, but they usually can measure only a small part of those populations. This problem affects all areas of the behavioral sciences. For example, an industrial psychologist studying the effects of pay on job satisfaction cannot measure the entire population of all paid employees in the United States. Even if he were to restrict his attention to one type of job, the population would still be far too large to measure in its entirety. An experimental psychologist studying the performance of rats in a maze under varying conditions cannot run all laboratory rats in the world in her experiment, nor can she obtain all possible runs from any one rat. An anthropologist interested in the effects of different cultures on motivation in children cannot study all of the children from each of the cultures in which she is interested. In fact, this predicament is so common that most behavioral science research would not be possible without some effective resolution. As you may have guessed from the title of this chapter, the answer lies in the use of *inferential statistics*—techniques for drawing inferences about an entire population, based on data obtained from a sample drawn from that population.

The Goals of Inferential Statistics

There are three kinds of inferences that the behavioral scientist wishes to make about a population. One useful procedure is to estimate the values of population parameters. Given a sample whose mean and variance have been computed, we may wish to estimate the mean and variance of the parent population. Any statistic computed from a single sample (such as $\overline{X}$ or s) that provides an estimate of the corresponding population parameter (such as μ or σ) is called a *point estimate*.

For some purposes, a point estimate is not sufficiently informative, since it leaves us with no idea of how far off from the parameter it may be. Such information is supplied by an *interval estimate,* a range of values that has a known probability of including the true value of the parameter. For example, suppose that a sample of white mice runs through a maze in an average of 60 seconds. A point estimate would state that the most reasonable value of μ is 60. If an estimate in terms of a single number is *not* essential, the researcher may decide to use appropriate techniques of inferential statistics to determine an *interval* that is likely to include the population mean. Suppose she finds this interval to be 54–66, or 60 ± 6. This interval estimate divides all numerically possible values of μ into two sets: "likely" (54–66) and "unlikely" (less than 54 and more than 66), with "unlikely" having a precise meaning to be discussed in subsequent sections.

A third important use of inferential statistics is to assess the probability of obtaining certain kinds of sample results under certain population conditions. The aforementioned psychologist might wish to determine the probability that a sample of 100 statistics students, who have been switched to computer learning techniques and have gained an average of 5 points in their examination scores, come from a population where the mean gain in examination scores is zero. In other words, if the computer learning techniques do *not* work on the average for the *population,* how likely are we to get a *sample* of 100 statistics students that improved by 5 points? In order to determine probabilities when dealing with samples instead of individuals, you will need to learn about *sampling distributions.* It is to this topic that we turn next.

Sampling Distributions

In the preceding two chapters you learned how to transform a raw score into a new score that shows at a glance how that score stands in comparison to a separate reference group, and how to find the proportion of scores above or below that score in a normal distribution. These procedures will be useful in the chapters ahead, but not for the descriptive purposes discussed previously. Behavioral researchers are rarely concerned with the score of any one individual in a distribution. Such studies usually involve a group of individuals, all of whom share some common characteristic (e.g., the same psychopathology diagnosis), or all of whom have been subjected to the same experimental treatment. Therefore, the remainder of this text will focus on the performance of a group as a whole—for instance, on some word-recall task. This is where descriptive statistics becomes immediately useful. To describe the performance of an entire group, rather than an individual, we need a measure of central tendency. As we have seen, the arithmetic mean is usually the most suitable of such measures for advanced statistics. Therefore, throughout this part of the text, groups will be dealt with in terms of their means. Also, our interest will not be in the particular groups we are dealing with but in how these groups serve as samples of (and therefore representations of) the entire populations from which they were drawn. Consequently, we will refer to all of the groups that we deal with from now on as *samples,* and we will focus primarily on the means $(\overline{X})$ of these samples.

Before we can introduce statistical inference, we must first apply the descriptive tools you have already learned to entire collections of groups (i.e., samples), rather than to collections of individuals. We will begin with a simple example in which the variable of interest is height and the population is American men. We know from large-scale studies that the heights of American men follow an approximately normal distribution with a mean of (about) 68 inches, and a standard deviation of 3.2 inches. For the purposes of this chapter, we want to know what the distribution would look like if we were to take millions of random samples of American men (all samples being the same size), calculate the mean for each sample, and then plot the distribution of the millions of sample means. If we were to do this for an *infinite* number (not merely millions) of sample means, the resulting distribution would be called the *sampling distribution of the mean.* (If, instead, we found the median of each sample and then plotted all of the sample medians, we would be creating the sampling distribution of the *median.*)

To obtain an approximate sampling distribution of the mean, one possible (but still not practical) way would be to draw a large number of samples of the same size from the defined population, and determine on an empirical basis how often the various alternatives occur. It is important that the samples are *random*—that is, drawn in such a way as to minimize bias and make the sample typical of the population insofar as possible. A *random sample* is defined as a sample drawn in such a way as to (1) give each element in the population an equal chance of being drawn *and* (2) make all possible samples of that size equally likely to occur. If the mean of each sample is computed and a frequency distribution of the many means is plotted, we will have an idea how often to expect a sample with a particular mean. Such a frequency distribution is called an *experimental sampling distribution* because it is obtained from observed or experimental data.[1] Note that this is not how distributions of sample values are ordinarily determined, but merely how one *could* determine them.

To get concrete about it, suppose that we decide on a sample size of 100 American men. We could begin by measuring the height of each man in our first random sample and computing the mean height of the sample. We would then replace the sample into the population, draw another random sample of

---

1. It is also sometimes called a *Monte Carlo distribution,* particularly when it is generated by a computer.

TABLE 9.1

Hypothetical frequency distribution of mean height for 1,000 samples (sample $N = 100$)

(A) Mean height (in.)	(B) Number of samples (f)	(C) Proportion of samples ($p = f/N$)
68.55 or more	0	.000
68.50–68.54	1	.001
68.45–68.49	1	.001
68.40–68.44	4	.004
68.35–68.39	11	.011
68.30–68.34	19	.019
68.25–68.29	31	.031
68.20–68.24	56	.056
68.15–68.19	81	.081
68.10–68.14	112	.112
68.05–68.09	116	.116
68.00–68.04	141	.141
67.95–67.99	131	.131
67.90–67.94	103	.103
67.85–67.89	76	.076
67.80–67.84	57	.057
67.75–67.79	28	.028
67.70–67.74	21	.021
67.65–67.69	7	.007
67.60–67.64	2	.002
67.55–67.59	2	.002
67.54 or less	0	.000
Total	1,000	1.000

100 American men, and compute the mean height of *that* sample. If we were to obtain a total of 1,000 samples (each of $N = 100$), the frequency distribution of mean heights of the 1,000 samples might resemble the one in Table 9.1. Figure 9.1 represents the data in Table 9.1 as a frequency polygon.

Fortunately, it is rarely necessary to perform this procedure for determining an experimental sampling distribution; it was presented just to make the concept of a sampling distribution more concrete. In practice, you will refer to *theoretical sampling distributions.* Observe that in the experimental sampling distribution of height, most of the sample means cluster about the grand mean of 68.00, and there are fewer and fewer observations as one goes further away from the grand mean. This distribution closely approximates the theoretical *normal curve,* a statistical model that can describe the sampling distributions of several statistics of interest, including means. Use of the theoretical normal curve model in the proper situations will enable you to avoid the toil and trouble of determining an experimental sampling distribution in order to ascertain the probabilities in which you are interested.

An important law of statistics tells us that when a population is normally

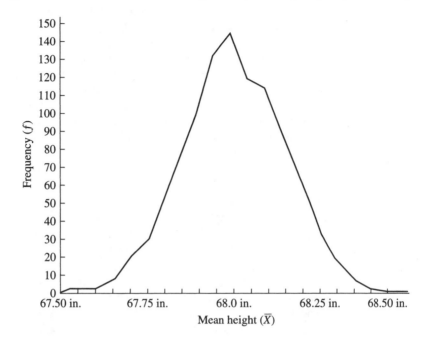

FIGURE 9.1

Hypothetical distribution of mean height for 1,000 samples (sample $N = 100$)

distributed for a particular variable, the corresponding sampling distribution of the mean will also follow the normal distribution (ND). Although actual populations in behavioral research never follow the ND exactly, variables that have a distribution close to the ND (e.g., height for one gender) will lead to sampling distributions of the mean that are approximated very well by the ND. A statistical law known as the *Central Limit Theorem* states that as the *size* of the samples increases (remember that a sampling distribution requires an infinite number of samples *all of which are the same size*), the sampling distribution of the means becomes closer to the ND, regardless of the shape of the original distribution for individual measurements in the population. However, the more the original population distribution departs from the ND, the larger the samples have to be before the sampling distribution of the mean begins to resemble a normal distribution.

Let us use N to represent the size of each sample in a sampling distribution. Even for a small N, there will be very little error involved in using the theoretical normal curve to represent the sampling distribution of the mean *if* the original distribution in the population even roughly resembles the ND. For highly skewed distributions (e.g., reaction times; annual income), an N of 30 or 40 is often needed before the sampling distribution begins to follow the ND fairly closely. An even larger N is needed in those rare cases when the population distribution is nearly the opposite of the ND.

It should come as no surprise that the mean height of our 1,000 samples of men (summarized in Table 9.1), 68 inches, is the same as the mean of the entire population of men. As the number of samples becomes infinite, the *mean* of this infinite number of sample means will always equal the mean of the population (μ), regardless of the size of each sample (N). However, if we want to use z scores to compare the mean of any *one* sample to the whole distribution of sample means, we will also need to know the standard deviation of these sample means (i.e., the SD of the sampling distribution of the mean). It is important to note that the standard deviation of the individual scores, σ (or its estimate s), is *not* the correct measure to use. To see why, consider once again the normal distribution of math SAT scores in the population ($\mu = 500$). Selecting one person at random with a score of 725 is fairly unlikely. But drawing *a whole sample of people* with scores so extreme that the sample averages out to a mean of 725 is much less likely, since a greater number of low probability events must occur simultaneously. This implies that the variability of the distribution of sample means is *smaller* than the variability of the distribution of raw scores. In fact, it decreases as the sample N increases.

If a large number of sample means were actually available (as in Table 9.1), you could measure the variability of the means directly. You would simply calculate the standard deviation *of the sample means,* using the usual formula for computing the standard deviation (Chapter 5) and treating the sample means just like ordinary numbers. However, behavioral scientists rarely have *many* samples of a given size. They usually have only a few.

The Standard Error of the Mean

Fortunately, there is a simple statistical law that relates the standard deviation of the sampling distribution of means to the sample size N and the standard deviation of the population.

$$\sigma_{\bar{x}} = \frac{\sigma}{\sqrt{N}},$$

where

σ = the population standard deviation

N = number of observations in each sample

This quantity estimates the variability of means for samples of the given N, so it is a *standard deviation* of *means.* But since it does that, it also tells you how trustworthy is any single mean that you have, hence it is called the *standard error of the mean.* A *small* value of $\sigma_{\bar{x}}$ indicates that if you were to draw many different random samples of the same size from this population, the vari-

FIGURE 9.2

Distribution of observations of heights (in inches) for a population of 5,000,000 adult males

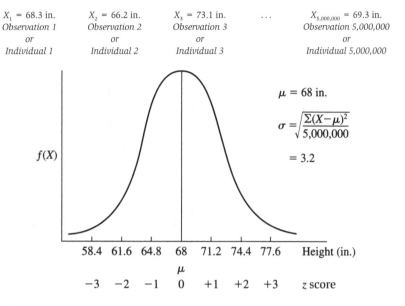

X_1 = 68.3 in.
Observation 1
or
Individual 1

X_2 = 66.2 in.
Observation 2
or
Individual 2

X_3 = 73.1 in.
Observation 3
or
Individual 3

. . .

$X_{5,000,000}$ = 69.3 in.
Observation 5,000,000
or
Individual 5,000,000

μ = 68 in.

$$\sigma = \sqrt{\frac{\Sigma(X-\mu)^2}{5,000,000}}$$

$$= 3.2$$

$f(X)$

58.4	61.6	64.8	68	71.2	74.4	77.6	Height (in.)
			μ				
−3	−2	−1	0	+1	+2	+3	z score

ous values of $\overline{X}$ would be relatively close to one another (since they would have a small standard deviation). Therefore, any single value of $\overline{X}$ that you may have is likely to be a rather accurate estimate of μ. But if $\sigma_{\overline{X}}$ is *large,* and you were to draw many different random samples of the same size from this population, the various values of $\overline{X}$ would differ markedly from one another (since they would have a large standard deviation). Therefore, any one value of $\overline{X}$ would be a less trustworthy indication of the true value of μ.

As you can see from the formula, the standard error of the mean must be smaller than the standard deviation of the raw scores. It becomes smaller as the sample size grows larger. The term *standard error* signifies that the difference between a population mean and the mean of a sample drawn from that population is an "error," caused by the cases that happened by chance to be included in the sample. If *no* error existed (as would happen if the "sample" consisted of the entire population and $N = \infty$), all of the sample means would exactly equal each other, and the value of the standard error of the mean would be zero. This situation would be ideal for purposes of statistical inference, since the mean of any one sample would exactly equal the population mean. Sad to say, it never happens; actual data are always subject to sampling error.

To clarify the preceding discussion, let us return to our example concerning the heights of samples of American men, and compare the distribution of raw scores to the distribution of sample means. A hypothetical distribution of five million height observations for American men is shown in Figure 9.2; each X

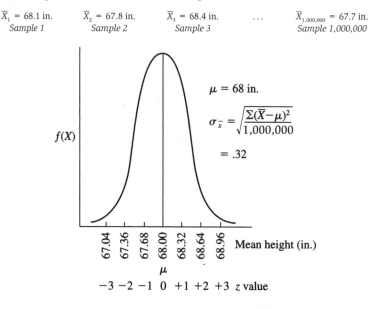

FIGURE 9.3

Distribution of mean heights (in inches) for 1,000,000 randomly selected samples of $N = 100$ height observations in each sample

$\overline{X}_1 = 68.1$ in. $\overline{X}_2 = 67.8$ in. $\overline{X}_3 = 68.4$ in.   . . . $\overline{X}_{1,000,000} = 67.7$ in.
Sample 1   Sample 2   Sample 3   Sample 1,000,000

$f(X)$

$\mu = 68$ in.

$\sigma_{\overline{x}} = \sqrt{\dfrac{\Sigma(\overline{X}-\mu)^2}{1,000,000}}$

$= .32$

67.04 67.36 67.68 68.00 68.32 68.64 68.96   Mean height (in.)

μ

−3 −2 −1 0 +1 +2 +3 z value

represents one *raw score.* Now suppose that one million random samples of N = 100 observations each are randomly selected from the population, and the mean of each sample is calculated. The resulting distribution of *sample means* would closely resemble the particular normal curve that is illustrated in Figure 9.3.

Notice that the shape of *both* distributions (original distribution of raw scores or single observations, and distribution of sample means) is normal and centered around μ (68 in.).[2] However, the distribution of sample means is *less variable* than is the distribution of raw scores. The standard deviation of the raw scores shown in Figure 9.2 would be calculated directly by applying the usual formula for the standard deviation to the 5,000,000 raw scores; let us suppose that σ is found to be equal to 3.2 in. The standard deviation of the sample means in Figure 9.3 could be calculated directly by applying the usual formula for the standard deviation to the 1,000,000 sample means. More conveniently, we can use the formula to find that the means of the samples, each based on $N = 100$ observations, will have a σ equal to one tenth ($= 1/\sqrt{N}$) the σ of the individual observations. As you can see in Figure 9.3, the value of $\sigma_{\overline{x}}$ is $3.2/\sqrt{100}$ or .32.

---

2. Theoretically, you need an infinite number of samples before your sampling distribution fits the normal curve perfectly, but a million samples is at least imaginable, and would lead to a very smooth curve.

The *z* Score for Sample Means

The sampling distribution of the means for height will closely resemble the normal distribution. Because we know both the mean and standard deviation of this distribution, we can use *z* scores in conjunction with Table A to answer questions about the proportion of samples that will be shorter or taller than a particular sample. (Why anyone would want to do this will be explained in the second half of this chapter.)

Suppose you measure, at random, 100 men who are currently enrolled in statistics, and their average height turns out to be 67.4 inches. What proportion of all such samples ($N = 100$) will be less than (or equal to) 67.4 inches? First, we need to calculate a *z* score for samples rather than individuals, which means that the formula must be based on the *standard error of the mean* as the measure of variability.

That is,

$$z = \frac{\overline{X} - \mu}{\sigma_{\overline{X}}},$$

where

$\overline{X}$ = the observed value of the sample mean

μ = the hypothesized value of the population mean

$\sigma_{\overline{X}}$ = the standard error of the mean ($= \sigma/\sqrt{N}$)

Given that $\mu = 68$ and $\sigma = 3.2$ for height in the male population,

$$\sigma_{\overline{X}} = \frac{3.2}{\sqrt{100}} = .32, \text{ and}$$

$$z = \frac{67.4 - 68}{.32}$$

$$= \frac{-.60}{.32}$$

$$= -1.875$$

To find the proportion of the ND that is below $z = -1.875$, draw a diagram similar to Figure 8.4, but label it with *z* scores: 0 at the mean (where Figure 8.4 has 500), and −1.875 where that figure has 450. Ignoring the negative sign of the *z* score, look between $z = 1.87$ and $z = 1.88$ in Table A, and you can see that the shaded area of your figure contains about 46.96% of the distribution. However, we are not interested this time in the shaded area. We want to know the percentage below −1.875, so we need to subtract the area we just found from 50%. The area below $z = -1.875$ equals $50 - 46.96 = 3.04\%$. As a proportion, this comes to .0304. Stated as a probability, the chance of randomly selecting 100 men whose height averages out to 67.4 inches or less is only .0304, or just a little over 3 out of 100. We can conclude that these 100 men are unusually short *as a group,* even though the group average is only a little more than half an inch less than the population mean. As random samples get larger, their means tend to vary less from the population mean. Therefore, a fairly large random sample does not need to have a mean very different from that of the population to be considered unusual. Probabilities such as the value of .0304 calculated here, are a valuable tool for a procedure called *null hypothesis testing,* which will be discussed next. We will introduce this procedure by applying the z score for sample means to a hypothetical experiment.

College Boards and similar tests are usually taken in a group setting with many other students nearby, and this can be distracting for some students. Let us suppose that you want to test the possibility that taking the math section of the SAT in a comfortable private setting will lead to higher exam scores. To do this, you select 30 names at random from a list of students about to take this test, and arrange for these students to take the test individually. After the scores are sent back, you calculate the mean math SAT for your group, and you are delighted to find that this average is 534.25. It seems unlikely that a random sample of 30 students would have such a high mean, and we can use the z score for samples to find this probability rather precisely. Recall that for SAT scores, the population mean (μ) is set at 500, and the standard deviation (σ) is 100. Therefore,

$$z = \frac{\overline{X} - \mu}{\dfrac{\sigma}{\sqrt{N}}} = \frac{534.25 - 500}{\dfrac{100}{\sqrt{30}}} = \frac{34.25}{18.26} = 1.875$$

Generally, we will be interested in the probability of obtaining a sample as extreme as or even more extreme than the one we have observed. So in this case we want to look up the area above (i.e., to the right of) a z score of $+1.875$. Because of the symmetry of the normal distribution, this area will be the same as the area below $z = -1.875$, which we found for the height example to be .0304. Thus, the probability of selecting 30 students at random from the ordinary population (i.e., the population of students taking the exam in the usual setting), which has a mean of 500, and obtaining a sample whose mean is 534.25 or larger is only .0304. Knowing this probability, which we will call a *p value,* will help us to make a decision about whether or not our experiment worked—that is, whether we will conclude that individual testing would produce any difference in math SAT scores if given to the entire population.

Null Hypothesis Testing

The decision process just alluded to is known as *null hypothesis testing* (NHT). In terms of the present example, we can say that we will *test the hypothesis* that the mean of the population of individually tested students is equal to 500 on the math SAT. When the testing of a statistical hypothesis is designed to help make a decision about a population parameter (here, μ), the overall method is called *inferential parametric statistics*.

The Null and Alternative Hypotheses

The first step in NHT is to state the *null hypothesis* (symbolized by H_0), which specifies the hypothesized population parameter. In the present example,

$$H_0: \mu = 500$$

This null hypothesis implies that the sample, with mean equal to 534.25, is a random sample from the population with μ equal to 500 (and that the difference between 534.25 and 500 is due to sampling error). The probability of obtaining a sample mean of the observed value (534.25) is calculated under the assumption that H_0 is true (that is, that $\mu = 500$), as we did above ($p = .0304$).

Next, an *alternative hypothesis* (symbolized by H_1) is formed. It specifies another value or set of values for the population parameter. In the present study,

$$H_1: \mu \neq 500$$

This alternative hypothesis states that the population from which the sample comes does *not* have a μ equal to 500. That is, the difference of 34.25 between the sample mean and the null-hypothesized population mean is due to the fact that the null hypothesis is false (e.g., that individual testing changes the mean of the population, so that the sample of 30 individually tested students is not actually coming from a population whose mean is 500).

The null hypothesis gets its name from the idea that nothing is going on. That is, the null hypothesis states that there is *no* effect or *no* difference of the kind that the experiment is seeking to establish. Usually, the theory that the scientist hopes to support is identified with the *alternative* hypothesis. Rejecting H_0 will cause the scientist to conclude that his theory has been supported, and failing to reject H_0 will cause him to conclude that his theory has not been supported. This is a sensible procedure, since scientific caution dictates that the researcher should not jump to conclusions. He should claim success only when there is a strong indication to that effect—that is, when the results are sufficiently striking to cause rejection of H_0.

The Criterion of Significance

Having set up the null and alternative hypotheses, we need to define *how unusual* a sample mean must be to cause you to reject H_0 and accept H_1. Intuitively, an observed sample mean of 501 would hardly represent persuasive evidence against the null hypothesis that $\mu = 500$, even though it is not exactly equal to the hypothesized population value. Conversely, an observed sample mean of 600 would do more to suggest that the hypothesized population value was incorrect. Where should the line be drawn? This is where the p value can be helpful.

To simplify our terms let us refer to an experiment for which the null hypothesis is actually true (e.g., individual testing did *not* affect math SAT scores) as a *null experiment.* The object of NHT can then be described as trying to keep under control the number of null experiments that get reported as working when, in fact, the results look good only because of sampling error (e.g., by chance, our sample included a disproportionate number of students who were very good at math). Rejecting the null hypothesis for an experiment in which the null hypothesis is actually true is called a *Type I error.* Although we can never know whether H_0 is true for any particular experiment, and we don't even know how often null experiments are performed by various researchers, we can try to control the rate at which Type I errors are made. We do this by deciding on what proportion of all null experiments we will allow to be declared *statistically significant.* This is not something that an individual researcher decides; this is something that a research community decides as a whole.

The proportion of null experiments that will be considered "significant" is called the *criterion of significance* and is symbolized by the first letter of the Greek alphabet, alpha (α). Due in large part to the pioneering work of Sir Ronald Fisher, the largest alpha level commonly used in behavioral research is .05. Note that setting alpha to .05 fixes only the Type I error *rate* and does not determine the *total number* of Type I errors. Although no attempt is made to control how many null experiments are performed, universal adoption of the .05 level ensures that only (about) 5% of null experiments (i.e., experiments for which the null hypothesis is actually true) that *are* performed will lead to a rejection of H_0 and therefore to results that are (mistakenly) regarded as statistically significant. Let us see how the p value for a particular experiment can be used to make a decision about the null hypothesis.

Critical Values

The p value for the math SAT experiment was .0304. This means that if individual testing has no effect at all (H_0 is true), about 3% of experiments like ours would nonetheless result in sample means even higher than ours. It may seem that because .0304 is less than .05, we should reject the null hypothesis using the .05 decision rule. However, this is a *one-tailed p* value, in that it applies only to the upper end of the distribution. Our null and alternative hypotheses were set up for a *two-tailed* test, which implies that we would also have tested our sample mean for statistical significance if it were *below* the population mean. The two-tailed test is the more cautious option and the one usually required by the better scientific journals. To perform a two-tailed instead of a one-tailed test, all you have to do is double your one-tailed p value (which you obtained from Table A) and compare it to your alpha level. For this example, the two-

FIGURE 9.4

Areas for rejecting H_0 in both tails of the normal sampling distribution using the .05 criterion of significance when H_0 actually is true

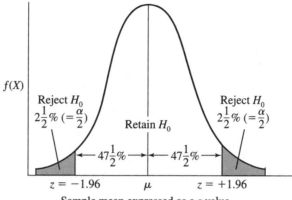

Sample mean expressed as a z value

tailed p equals $2 \times .0304 = .0608$. This is *not* less than .05, so H_0 cannot be rejected at the .05 level for a two-tailed test. We will elaborate on the distinction between one- and two-tailed tests shortly.

There is a simpler way to make decisions about the null hypothesis that does not require finding the p value for your experiment. If you are planning to conduct a two-tailed test with, say, $\alpha = .05$, you can find the minimum z score needed for significance ahead of time, and then just check the z score for your sample to see if it is larger than the borderline z score. The z scores that fall right at the borderline between the significant and nonsignificant portions of the null hypothesis distribution are called *critical values* (or, less formally, *cutoff scores*). For a two-tailed test there is a critical value on each side of the distribution, as illustrated in Figure 9.4.

When the normal curve model is appropriate, the critical values beyond which H_0 should be rejected are easily ascertained using the normal curve table (Table A). Since 2.5% of the area of the curve is in each tail, 50.0 – 2.5% or 47.5% falls between the mean and the cutoff score. Entering Table A in the center with a value of 47.5%, the cutoff scores expressed as z values are found to be equal to –1.96 and +1.96. Once the sample mean has been expressed as a z value, the .05 criterion of significance states that H_0 should be rejected if z is less than or equal to –1.96 or z is greater than or equal to +1.96. Conversely, H_0 should be retained if z is between –1.96 and +1.96. Note that the area in each rejection region is equal to $\alpha/2$, or .05/2 or .025, and that the total *area of rejection* (or *critical region*) is equal to the significance criterion α or .05.

Another traditional, but more stringent, criterion is the 1% or *.01 criterion of significance*. Using this criterion, two-tailed hypotheses about the population mean are rejected if, when H_0 is true, a sample mean is so unlikely to occur that

FIGURE 9.5

Areas for rejecting H_0 in both tails of the normal sampling distribution using the .01 criterion of significance when H_0 is true

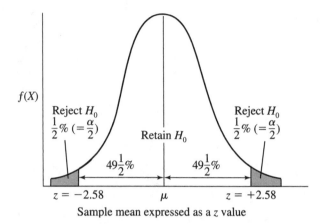

$f(X)$

Reject H_0
$\frac{1}{2}\% \left(= \frac{\alpha}{2}\right)$

Retain H_0

Reject H_0
$\frac{1}{2}\% \left(= \frac{\alpha}{2}\right)$

$49\frac{1}{2}\%$ $49\frac{1}{2}\%$

$z = -2.58$ μ $z = +2.58$

Sample mean expressed as a z value

no more than 1% of sample means would be so extreme. Here again, $\alpha/2$ or .005 (or 1/2 of 1%) is in each tail. This criterion is illustrated in Figure 9.5.

When the normal curve model is appropriate, the critical values beyond which H_0 should be rejected using the .01 criterion are ascertained by entering Table A in the body of the table with the value 49.5%. These cutoff scores, expressed as z values, are –2.58 and +2.58. Once the sample mean has been expressed as a z value, the .01 criterion of significance states that H_0 should be rejected if z is less than or equal to –2.58 or z is greater than or equal to +2.58. Conversely, H_0 should be retained if z is between –2.58 and +2.58. Once again, the area of rejection is equal to α (0.5% + 0.5% = 1% or .01), the criterion of significance.

Consequences of Possible Decisions

Admittedly, an event that occurs 1 in 20 times (i.e., that has a probability of occurrence of .05) is not a very rare event. Yet when we set alpha to .05, we are saying that whenever our experiment produces a result that is likely to be exceeded by a similar experiment, for which H_0 is actually true (a "null" experiment) no more than 1 in 20 times we will consider the null hypothesis "sufficiently unlikely" as an explanation for our findings and can therefore reject it.[3] Given that Type I errors are undesirable, why doesn't the behavioral research community

---

3. Since this is a matter of convention and is not based on any mathematical principle, common sense is essential in borderline cases. If, for example, $p = .06$, the technically correct procedure is to call the event "not sufficiently unlikely," but .06 is so close to .05 that the best plan is to repeat the experiment and gain additional evidence. The reason that a guide such as the ".05 rule" is needed is that NHT would quickly become useless if each researcher were free to set alpha to any value he or she found convenient for each result being reported.

agree to set .01 as the minimum alpha for ordinary circumstances, rather than .05? The short answer is that as you make alpha smaller, the critical value that an experimental result has to exceed to be statistically significant becomes larger. Therefore, more and more experiments for which the null hypothesis is *not* true will fail to yield significant results. When the null hypothesis is *not* true but you fail to reject H_0 because your experimental results are not extreme enough, you are making an error that can be thought of as the opposite of a Type I error. It is appropriately called a *Type II error* and is symbolized by the second letter of the Greek alphabet, beta (β). Whereas alpha is fixed by the researcher, the value for beta associated with any particular experiment depends on a number of factors. Usually it can only be estimated roughly, as we will demonstrate in Chapter 14.

For the math SAT experiment, there are two possibilities with respect to the mean of the theoretical population in which all students are individually tested: either $\mu = 500$ (H_0 is true), or μ is not equal to 500 (H_0 is false) and individual testing has at least some effect. There are also just two possible decisions you could make based on the results of this experiment: reject H_0, or retain H_0. The four possible combinations of the actual mean of the experimental population and the decision that is made about the experiment can be summarized as follows (see Table 9.2):

1. The population mean for individually tested students is actually 500 (that is, individual testing would not change the mean of the population) and you *incorrectly reject H_0*. You have committed a Type I error.

2. The population mean for individually tested students is actually *not* 500 and you *incorrectly retain H_0*. Failing to reject a *false* null hypothesis is a Type II error.

3. The population mean for individually tested students is actually *not* 500 and you *correctly reject H_0*. The probability of reaching this correct decision is called the *power* of the statistical test, and is equal to $1 - \beta$.

4. The population mean for individually tested students is actually 500 and you *correctly retain H_0*. The probability of making this correct decision is equal to $1 - \alpha$.

TABLE 9.2

Model for error risks in hypothesis testing

Outcome of experiment dictates:	State of the population	
	H_0 is actually true	H_0 is actually false
Retain H_0	*Correct decision:* probability of retaining true H_0 is $1 - \alpha$	*Type II error:* probability (risk) of retaining false H_0 is β
Reject H_0	*Type I error:* probability (risk) of rejecting true H_0 is α	*Correct decision:* probability of rejecting false H_0 (power) is $1 - \beta$

One- versus Two-Tailed Tests of Significance

The statistical tests described thus far in this chapter (see, for example, Figures 9.4 and 9.5) are called *two-tailed* tests of significance. This means that the null hypothesis regarding the population mean, μ, is rejected if a z value is obtained that is either extremely high (far up in the upper tail of the curve) *or* extremely low (far down in the lower tail of the curve). Consequently, there is a rejection area equal to $\alpha/2$ in each tail of the distribution. As we have seen, the corresponding null and alternative hypotheses are

H_0: μ = a specific value

H_1: $\mu \neq$ this value (that is, μ is greater than the value specified by H_0 *or* is less than this value)

Let us suppose, on the other hand, that a researcher argues as follows: "My theory predicts that the mean of population X is *less than* 100." (For example, she may predict that children from homes in which there are few books and little emphasis on verbal skills score below average on a standardized test of intelligence.) "It's all the same to me whether μ_X is equal to 100 or much greater than 100; my theory is disconfirmed in either case. If I use a two-tailed test, I am forced to devote $2\frac{1}{2}\%$ of my rejection region (using $\alpha = .05$) to an outcome that is meaningless insofar as my theory is concerned. Instead, I will place the entire 5% rejection region in the lower tail of the curve." (See Figure 9.6.) "In other words, I will test the following null and alternative hypotheses:

$$H_0: \mu_X \geq 100$$

$$H_1: \mu_X < 100$$

$$\alpha = .05$$

"Note that I am being properly conservative by assuming at the outset that my results are due to chance (the null hypothesis). Only if I obtain a result very unlikely to be true if H_0 is true will I conclude that my theory is supported (switch to the alternative hypothesis). Looking at Table A, I see that a z score of -1.65 encloses about 45% of the normal curve between it and the mean, leaving 5% of the distribution in the lower tail (as shown in Figure 9.6). Therefore, I will use -1.65 as my only critical value. (Actually -1.64 is just as close an approximation to cutting off 5% of the curve, but -1.65 is the more cautious choice with respect to controlling Type I errors.) This means that I will retain H_0 if z is anywhere between -1.65 and $+\infty$ and reject H_0 if z is -1.65 or less. Since a two-tailed test of significance would lead to rejection of H_0 only if z were -1.96 or less (or $+1.96$ or more), the one-tailed value of -1.65 quite properly makes it easier for me to reject H_0 (and conclude that my theory is supported) when the results are in the direction that I have predicted."

Similar reasoning could be applied if the researcher claimed to be interested

FIGURE 9.6

One-tailed test of the null hypothesis that $\mu_x \geq 100$ against the alternative that $\mu_x < 100$.

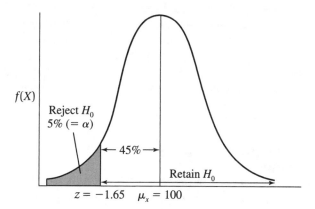

only in the outcome that the population mean was *greater* than 100. The entire rejection region would be placed at the upper end of the curve, and H_0 would be retained if z were between $-\infty$ and $+1.65$ and rejected if z were $+1.65$ or more.

Although behavioral researchers often have a theory that predicts the direction of their results, to be conservative (i.e., particularly cautious about Type I errors) they usually report their results in terms of two-tailed tests. Consider once again our math SAT example. The z score calculated in that example, 1.875, is larger than the critical value for a one-tailed test at the .05 level, 1.65. Therefore, the null hypothesis would be rejected using a one-tailed test. We had good reason to expect the individually tested sample to have a *higher*, rather than lower, average on the math SAT, because such test conditions are usually more conducive to concentration. So it would seem fair to use the one-tailed test in this case and declare statistical significance. However, a one-tailed test implies a promise that we would not have presented our results if our sample mean had been very much *lower* than the mean of the population— even if it were so low as to easily exceed the critical value for a two-tailed test in the other (i.e., lower) direction. If such a promise were routinely made and obeyed, researchers could not ethically report extreme results in the unexpected direction. This could cause serious problems. For example, the individually tested students might feel that they were under very close scrutiny and become much more anxious, making them *less* likely to perform well on the test. This could be a finding of interest that deserves to be reported, although it could be argued that the experiment should first be replicated.

If you were to lower your critical value by putting your entire alpha in one tail, and then put even just half of your alpha in the other tail *after* seeing the results, you would be violating the .05 decision rule. That is, you would really be using an alpha of .05 + .025 = .075, which would make the probability of a Type I error greater than .05. Whenever we recognize the significance of a one-tailed test, we are implicitly accepting the promise that the researchers would not have tested and presented their results no matter how extreme their results might have been in the opposite direction. Because the research community does not want to discourage the reporting of paradoxical findings, but also does not want alpha to creep above the .05 level, the two-tailed test is the norm. However, one-tailed tests may be justified if the results would make no sense in the opposite direction, and would therefore never be tested in that direction.

Assumptions Required by the Statistical Test for the Mean of a Single Population

Our use of the z score for sample means, in conjunction with the normal curve table to obtain a p value for our hypothetical math SAT experiment, was based on several assumptions. The most important of these are that the individuals in our sample were selected randomly (and independently) from the population, and that the variable being measured (e.g., math SAT) is normally distributed in the population. The Central Limit Theorem tells us that for fairly large samples we will get reasonably accurate p values even if the original distribution is not very "normal." However, to use the z-score formula at all, we had to know σ, the standard deviation of the individual scores in the population. Unfortunately, we will know σ only for a few variables that have been studied extensively in the population. More often we will not know σ, and we will have to estimate it from the data we do have. Estimating σ is an additional step that slightly complicates our test of a single population mean. This complication involves a new theoretical distribution that is similar to the normal distribution, which will be described in the next chapter.

Summary

Although behavioral researchers are usually interested in the average response of an entire population to some treatment or experimental condition, practical constraints generally lead them to select and study a relatively small, random sample from the population of interest. After the members of the sample have been measured, the following steps can be applied in order to draw some conclusion about the population.

1. The Standard Error of the Mean

To test null hypotheses about the *mean of one population,* first compute the *standard error of the mean.* This is a measure of how accurate the sample mean is likely to be as an estimate of the population mean. Then, use the standard error of the mean to determine whether the difference between the observed sample mean and the hypothesized value of the population mean is or is not "sufficiently unlikely" to occur if H_0 is true (that is, if the hypothesized value of the population mean is correct).

The formula for the standard error of the mean is

$$\sigma_{\bar{x}} = \frac{\sigma}{\sqrt{N}},$$

where

$$N = \text{the number of scores in each sample}$$

$$\sigma = \text{standard deviation of the population}$$

2. The z Score for Sample Means

To draw inferences about the population mean, first calculate

$$z = \frac{\bar{X} - \mu}{\sigma_{\bar{x}}}$$

Then, look in Table A to find the percentage of the normal curve that extends beyond your calculated z. Converted to a proportion, this is the one-tailed p value corresponding to your sample mean.

3. Null Hypothesis Testing: General Considerations

1. State the *null hypothesis* (denoted by the symbol H_0) and the *alternative hypothesis* (denoted by H_1). It is important to understand that you cannot *prove* whether H_0 or H_1 is true because you cannot measure the entire population.

2. Begin with the assumption that H_0 is true. Then obtain the data and test out this assumption. If this assumption is unlikely to be true, you will abandon it and switch your bets to H_1; otherwise, you will retain it.

   Before you collect any data, it is necessary to define in numerical terms what is meant by "unlikely to be true." In statistical terminology, this is called selecting a *criterion* (or *level*) *of significance*, represented by the symbol α.

   (a) Using the .05 criterion of significance, "unlikely" is defined as having a probability of .05 or less. In symbols, $\alpha = .05$.

   (b) Using the .01 criterion of significance, "unlikely" is defined as having a probability of .01 or less. In symbols, $\alpha = .01$.

   Other criteria of significance can be used, but these are the most common.

3. Having selected a criterion of significance, obtain your data and compute the appropriate statistical test. If the test shows that H_0 is unlikely to be true, reject H_0 in favor of H_1. Otherwise, retain H_0.

4. Though you are backing the hypothesis indicated by the statistical test (H_0 or H_1), you could be wrong. You could make either of the following two kinds of error, depending on your decision:

(a) Type I error: rejecting H_0 when H_0 is in fact true. This error is less likely when the .01 criterion of significance is used. In fact, the probability of this kind of error (that is, the risk you run that your decision to reject H_0 is incorrect) is equal to the chosen criterion of significance, α.

(b) Type II error: retaining H_0 when H_0 is in fact false. This error is less likely when the .05 criterion of significance is chosen. The probability of this kind of error, denoted by the symbol β, is not so conveniently determined. (See Chapter 14.)

Thus, the relative importance of each kind of error helps to determine what criterion of significance to use.

4. One- versus Two-Tailed Tests of Significance

The use of one-tailed tests of significance is sometimes justified in behavioral science research. If the results are in the direction predicted by the researcher, it is more likely that statistical significance will be obtained. But if the results are in the opposite direction, the entire experiment should be repeated using a two-tailed design before any conclusions are drawn. Therefore, the two-tailed test is more commonly reported.

Exercises

1. Assume that the mean height for women at a large university (to be viewed as a population) is 65 inches with a standard deviation of 3 inches.

(a) If the women are placed randomly into physical education classes of 36 each, what will be the standard deviation of the class means for height (i.e., the standard error of the mean)?

(b) Using your answer to part (a), what is the z score for a phys ed class whose average height is 64.2 inches? What are the one- and two-tailed p values for this class?

(c) If you were testing the null hypothesis (i.e., $\mu = 65$), would you reject H_0 for this class at the .05 level for a one-tailed test? For a two-tailed test?

(d) Repeat part (b) for a class whose mean height is 67.4 inches. Would you reject the null hypothesis for this class with a two-tailed test at the .05 level? At the .01 level?

2. Assume that the mean IQ for all 10th graders at a large high school (i.e., population) is 100 with $\sigma = 15$ and that the students are assigned at random to classes with an N of 25.

   (a) What is the z score for a class whose IQ averages 104? What is the one-tailed p value for this z score? What is the two-tailed p?

   (b) Repeat part (a) for a class whose mean IQ is 92.

   (c) Perform two-tailed null hypothesis tests for the classes in part (a) and part (b) at both the .05 and .01 levels. In each case explain whether you could be making a Type I or Type II error.

3. Given that for SAT scores, $\mu = 500$ and $\sigma = 100$:

   (a) Test the claim of students at Bigbrain University that they have SAT scores that are statistically significantly higher than the ordinary population, because a random sample of 25 of their students averaged 530 on this test. Make your statistical decision by comparing the z score for the Bigbrain sample with the appropriate critical value for a two-tailed test. Would a one-tailed test be significant in this case?

   (b) Repeat part (a) for a random sample of 64 students, who also have a mean of 530 on the SAT.

4. This exercise is designed to give you a more direct understanding of the standard error of the mean. Create a population as follows: Get 20 identical small slips of paper or file cards. On eight of these slips, write the number 50; on five of the slips, write the number 51; on another five, write the number 49. For the last two slips of paper, write the number 48 on one and 52 on the other. Place all the slips in a bowl and mix thoroughly.

   (a) Draw one slip at random from the bowl and write down its number. Then replace the slip in the bowl, mix thoroughly, and draw at random again (this is called *sampling with replacement*). Keep repeating this process until you have written down the numbers for five random selections. Calculate the average for these five numbers. This is your first sample mean.

   (b) Repeat the process described in part (a) until you have calculated a total of six sample means.

   (c) Calculate the mean and (unbiased) standard deviation of the six sample means you found in part (b). The latter statistic is the standard error of the mean calculated directly from the sample means rather than estimated from a sample standard deviation divided by $\sqrt{N}$. Is the mean of the sample means about what you expected?

   (d) Estimate the standard error of the mean separately from the standard deviation of each of the six samples you drew. How do these six estimates compare to each other, and to the standard error you calculated directly in part (c)?

5. Repeat exercise 4 for a different population using the following set of numbers: 5, 10, 15, 20, 25, 30, 35, 40, 45, 50, 50, 55, 60, 65, 70, 75, 80, 85, 90, 95.

Thought Questions

1. What is the difference between descriptive statistics and inferential statistics (statistical inference)?

2. (a) Do researchers in the behavioral sciences want to draw conclusions about populations or about samples? Why? (b) Why, then, must researchers use samples? (c) What problems are caused by having to use samples? Include and explain the term *sampling error* in your answer.

3. (a) What is a random sample? (b) Why are random samples desirable in behavioral science research? (c) Why is it often difficult or impossible to obtain a sample that is truly random?

4. Which of the following are random samples from the specified populations and which are not? Why? (a) An experimenter selects every 10th name in the telephone book for her city, starting with one name that is chosen blindly. Population: all those with listed telephone numbers in her city. (b) Teenage American students taking introductory psychology at University X are selected to participate in an experiment. Population: all American teenagers. (c) The names of all students at a college in the United States are written on slips of paper and placed in an extremely large hat. The slips are well shuffled, and 50 names are drawn blindly to serve as participants in an experiment. Population: all students at this college. (d) The procedure is the same as in part (c) but the population is all college students in the United States.

5. (a) What is the difference between the standard deviation of a set of scores and the standard error of the mean? (b) Do behavioral science researchers want the standard error of the mean to be small or large? Why? (c) What happens to the standard error of the mean as the sample size (N) becomes smaller? Why? What does this imply about the dangers of using samples in behavioral science research that are very small? (d) What happens to the standard error of the mean as the standard deviation of the original scores in the population becomes larger? Why?

6. A behavioral science researcher conducts an experiment and hopes to publish the results. (a) What are the practical consequences of making a Type I error? (b) What are the practical consequences of making a Type II error?

7. You are using the .05 criterion of significance. (a) If the two-tailed p value (that is, the probability of obtaining the results you got if H_0 is true and the hypothesized value of the population mean is correct) is .03, what decision should you make about H_0? Why? (b) If the two-tailed p value is .33, what

decision should you make about H_0? Why? (c) Should you treat a result that has a two-tailed p value of .06 the same as a result that has a two-tailed p value of .45? Why or why not?

8. The probability of making a Type I error when using the .01 criterion of significance is lower than when using the .05 criterion of significance. Why, then, don't researchers use the .01 criterion instead of the .05 criterion?

9. (a) What is the difference between a one-tailed test of significance and a two-tailed test of significance? (b) What are the disadvantages of using one-tailed tests of significance?

Computer Exercises

1. Assuming that a normative study has shown that the mean anxiety level for college students (μ) is 18 ($\sigma = 11$) on the scale that Sara used, what is the z score for the baseline anxiety scores in Sara's class? What are the one- and two-tailed p values that correspond to this z score?

2. Assuming that the mean resting heart rate for all college-aged men (μ) is 70 bpm, with $\sigma = 6$, what is the z score for the baseline HR of the men in Sara's data set? What are the one- and two-tailed p values that correspond to this z score?

3. Repeat exercise 3 for the women in Sara's statistics class.

Bridge to SPSS

You can use SPSS to obtain accurate p values from the normal distribution using the CDFNORM function described in the previous chapter. For a p value, you will always want the area "beyond" your z score—that is, below a negative z score and above a positive z score. When you enter a negative z score, the area returned by CDFNORM is the one-tailed p value. Just multiply it by 2 if you want a two-tailed p value. If you want the p value associated with a positive z score, just enter it with a minus sign in front of it to make it negative.

Chapter 10

The One-Sample *t* Test and Interval Estimation

In the previous chapter, we described how you could use a z score for sample means to test a null hypothesis concerning the mean of one population. We explained how to find a p value and use it to decide whether it is reasonable to suppose that your sample is just a random selection from the ordinary population (i.e., H_0 is true) or whether your sample mean is so extreme (and therefore p is so small) that the null hypothesis can be rejected on the basis of being "sufficiently unlikely" to account for your results. The latter decision would support the alternative hypothesis that your sample actually represents a population whose mean differs from the null hypothesized value, either because the treatment applied to the participants in the sample had some effect on your dependent variable (as in an experimental study) or because the characteristic for which the participants were selected (e.g., people who exercise regularly) is related to the variable you are measuring (e.g., subjective level of stress). The second case might be called an observational study or quasi-experiment. Unfortunately, the z test requires that you know the standard deviation of your dependent variable in the population (i.e., σ), and this is rarely known for the variables studied by behavioral science researchers. The good news is that you can estimate σ from the data you do have and then use a formula very similar to the z score for sample means, as we will demonstrate next.

When you do not know σ, the best that you can do is to estimate it by calculating the value of s for your sample. When divided by the square root of N, the resulting quantity, expressed symbolically as $s_{\bar{X}}$ can be used as an estimate of $\sigma_{\bar{X}}$ in the z-score formula. The new formula looks like this:

$$\frac{\bar{X} - \mu}{\dfrac{s}{\sqrt{N}}} = \frac{\bar{X} - \mu}{s_{\bar{X}}}$$

The Statistical Test for the Mean of a Single Population When σ Is Not Known: The t Distributions

Although this formula may look similar to the one in the preceding chapter, there is an important difference. Values obtained from the formula given here are *not* normally distributed (although the normal curve will yield a good approximation if the sample size is greater than 25 or 30). This is because $s_{\bar{X}}$ is only an estimate of $\sigma_{\bar{X}}$. So using the normal curve procedure will give wrong answers, primarily when the sample size is small, because the statistical model is incorrect. You must instead refer to the exact distribution of $(\bar{X} - \mu)/s_{\bar{X}}$, which is appropriate for all sample sizes but particularly necessary for small samples. This new statistical model is known as the t *distributions.*

In contrast to the normal curve, there is a *different* t distribution for every sample size. The sampling distribution of means based on a sample size of 10 has one t distribution, while the sampling distribution of means based on a sample size of 15 has a different t distribution. Fortunately, you do not have to know the shape of each of the various t distributions. Critical values for the curves corresponding to each sample size have been determined by mathematicians. All you need do is note the size of your sample and then refer to the proper t distribution. Such a t table is presented as Table B in the Appendix. (The assumptions of t distributions are discussed in Chapter 11.)

Statisticians could have created a table just like Table A (for the normal curve) for each of the t distributions, but that would require a very large number of tables. Theoretically, an infinite number of tables would be needed (one for each possible sample size), but the t distribution resembles the normal distribution more closely as the sample size increases. When N is about 100 or more, the difference between the t table and the normal curve table becomes small enough to ignore for most purposes. Unfortunately, that would still require too many tables. Providing a t table that contains only critical values saves a great deal of space. Unlike Table A, therefore, Table B does not make it possible for you to find the p value that corresponds to a particular value for t, but you can look up critical values for several commonly used alphas, for both one- and two-tailed tests.

Degrees of Freedom

The t table is given in terms of *degrees of freedom* (df) rather than sample size. When you have a sample mean and a hypothesized population mean (and σ is not known),

$$df = N - 1$$

That is, degrees of freedom in the present situation are equal to 1 *less* than the sample size. Recall that this is equal to the divisor of s^2 (Chapter 5).

"Degrees of freedom" is a concept that arises at several points in statistical inference; you will encounter it again in connection with other statistical tests in later chapters. The number of degrees of freedom is the number of freely varying quantities in the kind of repeated random sampling that produces sampling distributions. In connection with the test of the mean of a single population, it refers to the fact that each time a sample is drawn and the population variance is estimated, it is based on only $N - 1$ df. That is, there are $N - 1$ freely varying quantities. When you find for each of the N observations its deviation from the sample mean, $X - \overline{X}$, not all of these N quantities are free to vary in any sample. Since they must sum to zero (as was shown in Chapter 4), the Nth value is automatically determined once any $N - 1$ of them are fixed at given observed values. For example, if the sum of $N - 1$ deviations from the mean is -3, the Nth must equal $+3$ so that the sum of all deviations from the mean will equal zero. So in this situation, there are only $N - 1$ df, and therefore the t distribution is here based on $N - 1$ df. The df and not the N is the fundamental consideration, because df need not be $N - 1$ in other applications of t.

Using the *t* Distributions to Test Null Hypotheses

The following is a section of the *t* table:

df	...	$t_{.05}$	$t_{.01}$	...
⋮				
4		2.78	4.60	
⋮				
10		2.23	3.17	
11		2.20	3.11	
12		2.18	3.06	
13		2.16	3.01	
14		2.15	2.98	
15		2.13	2.95	
⋮				
40		2.02	2.70	
⋮				
120		1.98	2.62	
⋮				
∞		1.96	2.58	

Each horizontal row represents a separate distribution that corresponds to the *df*. The row labeled with the symbol for infinity (∞) represents the normal distribution.

To illustrate the use of the *t* table, suppose that you wish to test the null hypothesis H_0: $\mu = 17$ against the alternative H_1: $\mu \neq 17$ using the .05 criterion of significance. You obtain a sample of $N = 15$ and find that $\overline{X} = 18.80$ and $s = 3.50$. Then compute

$$t = \frac{\overline{X} - \mu}{s_{\overline{X}}},$$

where

$\overline{X}$ = the observed value of the sample mean

μ = the hypothesized value of the population mean

$s_{\overline{X}}$ = the estimated standard error of the mean ($= s/\sqrt{N}$)

In the present example,

$$t = \frac{18.80 - 17}{(3.50/\sqrt{15})} = \frac{1.80}{.90} = 2.00$$

You now compare the *t* value that you have computed to the critical value obtained from the *t* table. For 14 degrees of freedom (one less than your *N* of

15) and using the two-tailed .05 criterion of significance, the critical value is 2.15. A t value larger than this *in absolute value* (that is, ignoring the sign) is "sufficiently unlikely" to occur if H_0 is true for you to reject H_0. That is, the probability of obtaining t values absolutely larger than 2.15 when $df = 14$ is .05. Therefore, if the absolute value of the t that you compute is *less than* 2.15, *retain H_0*. If, however, your result is *greater* in absolute value than 2.15, *reject H_0* in favor of H_1. (In the unlikely event that your computed t value exactly equals the t value obtained from the table, reject H_0.) In our example, the obtained t value of 2.00 is not larger in absolute value than 2.15. So you should retain H_0, and conclude that the data do *not* warrant concluding that the population mean is not 17.

If instead your sample size were 12, you would have 11 degrees of freedom. The corresponding critical value from the table, again using the .05 criterion of significance, would be 2.20. You would retain H_0 if the absolute size of the t value you computed were less than 2.20, and you would reject H_0 in favor of H_1 if this value were equal to or greater in absolute value than 2.20. Similarly, for the same sample size, the critical value of t using the .01 criterion of significance is 3.11. Here, retain H_0 if your computed t value is no greater than 3.11 in absolute value and reject H_0 otherwise.

The t and z Distributions Compared

The t distribution for nine degrees of freedom and the normal curve are compared in Figure 10.1. Note the fatter tails in the case of the t distribution, so that you have to go further out on the tails to find points that set off the .05 or .01 areas of rejecting H_0. While 95% of the normal curve lies between the z values -1.96 and $+1.96$, 95% of the t distribution for nine degrees of freedom lies between -2.26 and $+2.26$. So using the two-tailed .05 criterion, 2.26 (and *not* 1.96) must be used as the critical value when σ is not known and $df = 9$.

Notice also in the t table that the *smaller* the sample size, the *larger* t must be in order to reject H_0 at the same criterion of significance. Also, when the sample size is large, z and t are virtually equivalent. Thus, for 40 degrees of freedom, $t = 2.02$ (using the .05 criterion). For 120 degrees of freedom, $t = 1.98$. These values are so close to the z value of 1.96 that it makes little difference which one you use.

Suppose Sara suspects that the math aptitude of statistics students at her school is on the rise and that her class in particular is from a population with a higher math aptitude than the population that existed over the previous decade. She finds the means for previous statistics classes on the math background quiz and calculates an average over the previous 10 years. This 10-year average can be viewed as the population mean against which she wishes to test her current class. If this average were to equal 27.31, then the null hypothesis that Sara would be testing is $H_0: \mu = 27.31$. Because Sara has only the means from previous classes and not the raw scores, she does not know σ; she will have to estimate the standard error of the mean from the data for her class. We

FIGURE 10.1

A comparison between the normal curve and the *t* distribution for *df* = 9

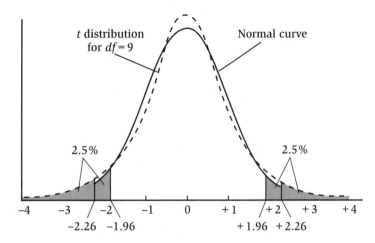

showed in previous chapters that for the 85 students who took the math quiz in Sara's class, $\overline{X} = 29.07$ and $s = 9.48$. Therefore:

$$s_{\overline{X}} = \frac{s}{\sqrt{N}} = \frac{9.48}{\sqrt{85}} = \frac{9.48}{9.22} = 1.028$$

and

$$t = \frac{\overline{X} - \mu}{s_{\overline{X}}} = \frac{29.07 - 27.31}{1.028} = 1.71$$

Sara would decide to retain H_0 whether she compared 1.71 to the critical *t* value of 1.99 for *df* = 84 (i.e., 85 − 1), or to the *z* value of 1.96. In behavioral science research, it is customary to report the obtained value as a *t* value even for large samples. The reason is that although *z* is a good approximation in large samples, it is still an approximation. So you should use the critical *t* value obtained from the *t* table, rather than the *z* value of 1.96 for the .05 criterion or 2.58 for the .01 criterion, unless you happen to know the exact value of σ. *Retain* H_0 if your computed *t* value (ignoring the sign) is smaller than the critical value, and *reject* H_0 otherwise.

Interval Estimation

Hypothesis testing is still very popular in the behavioral sciences despite the fact that this method has several serious (and much-debated) drawbacks. One difficulty is that when the results are statistically significant, the researcher is entitled to reject *only* the exact value specified by the null hypothesis.

Suppose that a researcher wishes to test the hypothesis that students at a particular high school differ from the average IQ (namely, a score of 100). In this study, the null hypothesis states that these students come from a population where $\mu = 100$. The alternative hypothesis states that $\mu \neq 100$. The researcher obtains a sample of 50 students, finds that the mean IQ for this sample is 115.72, performs the appropriate *t* test, and finds that the results are statistically significant using the .05 criterion of significance. The researcher therefore rejects the null hypothesis, switches to the alternative hypothesis, and concludes that the mean IQ of all students in this high school is greater than 100.

Although the researcher was able to reject the null hypothesis that $\mu = 100$, the researcher *cannot* reject the hypothesis that $\mu = 102$, that $\mu = 101$, or even that $\mu = 100.1$. The research study tested one and only one null hypothesis, namely $\mu = 100$, so only this hypothesis can be rejected when the results are statistically significant. To be sure, it is likely that values very close to the null-hypothesized value of 100 should also be rejected. But it is not certain, nor is it clear what "very close" means numerically.

If the population mean does happen to be 101 or 102, the students in this high school are actually about average in intelligence. A person with an IQ of 101 or 102 does not behave very differently from a person with an IQ of 100; a difference of one or two IQ points is virtually meaningless. Despite the statistically significant results, important issues remain unresolved. The students in this sample are very unlikely to have come from a population where $\mu = 100$. But it may be likely that they have come from a population where μ is so close to 100 that, for all practical purposes, it is the same. Without additional information, there is no way to tell.

One good way to resolve this difficulty is by estimating a *confidence interval* within which the population mean is likely to fall. Rather than specifying a single numerical value (as does H_0), a confidence interval specifies a *range of values* within which a parameter (here, the population mean) is likely to fall. How likely? If you are using the .05 criterion of significance, you can be 95% confident that the population mean falls within the range specified by the confidence interval. The end points of the confidence interval are called *confidence limits*.

Computation

To illustrate the use of confidence intervals, consider the example involving the math aptitude of Sara's class. We wish to determine an interval that will include all "not sufficiently unlikely" values of μ (all values for which H_0 should be retained). Using the .05 criterion of significance and $df = 84$, the furthest that any sample mean can lie from μ and still be retained as "not sufficiently unlikely" is $\pm 1.99 s_{\bar{x}}$ (where 1.99 is the critical value of *t* for the specified df, 84). So the lower limit of the confidence interval may be found by solving the following equation for μ:

$$+1.99 = \frac{\bar{X} - \mu}{s_{\bar{X}}}$$

The upper limit of the confidence interval may be found by solving the following equation for μ:

$$-1.99 = \frac{\bar{X} - \mu}{s_{\bar{X}}}$$

This is readily done as follows:

$$\pm 1.99 s_{\bar{X}} = \bar{X} - \mu$$

$$\mu = \bar{X} \pm 1.99 s_{\bar{X}}$$

or

$$\bar{X} - 1.99 s_{\bar{X}} \le \mu \le \bar{X} + 1.99 s_{\bar{X}}$$

Thus,

$$29.07 - 1.99(1.028) \le \mu \le 29.07 + 1.99(1.028)$$

$$29.07 - 2.05 \le \mu \le 29.07 + 2.05$$

$$27.02 \le \mu \le 31.12$$

You should retain any hypothesized value of μ between 27.02 and 31.12, inclusive, using the confidence interval corresponding to the .05 criterion of significance (called the *95% confidence interval*). Conversely, reject any hypothesized value of μ outside this interval.

The general formula for computing confidence intervals when σ is not known is

$$\bar{X} - t s_{\bar{X}} \le \mu \le \bar{X} + t s_{\bar{X}},$$

where

$$t = \text{critical value from the } t \text{ table for } df = N - 1$$

$$\bar{X} = \text{observed value of the sample mean}$$

The confidence interval corresponding to the .01 criterion of significance is called the *99% confidence interval.* In the math quiz example, the critical value of t for $df = 84$ and the .01 criterion is 2.62. Thus, the 99% confidence interval is equal to

$$29.07 - 2.62(1.028) \leq \mu \leq 29.07 + 2.62(1.028)$$

$$29.07 - 2.69 \leq \mu \leq 29.07 + 2.69$$

$$26.38 \leq \mu \leq 31.76$$

Note that the 99% confidence interval is *wider* than the 95% confidence interval. You can be more sure that the population mean falls in the 99% confidence interval, but you must pay a price for this added confidence: the interval is larger, so μ is less precisely estimated. (You could be absolutely certain that the population mean falls within the "confidence interval" $-\infty \leq \mu \leq +\infty$, but such a statement is useless—it tells nothing that you did not know beforehand.) For $\alpha = .05$, you can be 95% confident that the true population mean falls within the stated interval (narrower, hence more informative). For $\alpha = .01$, you can be 99% confident (more sure) that the true population mean falls within the stated interval (wider, hence less informative).

If σ *is known,* use the critical z values (1.96 for the 95% confidence interval, 2.58 for the 99% confidence interval) instead of t.

Confidence Intervals and Null Hypothesis Tests

The scientific journals in the behavioral sciences still place a good deal of emphasis on testing null hypotheses, but there is a rapidly growing recognition that interval estimation has important advantages.

Confidence intervals allow you to do everything that null hypothesis testing does. If a value of μ specified by a null hypothesis falls within the confidence interval, that null hypothesis is retained. If a value of μ specified by a null hypothesis falls outside the confidence interval, that null hypothesis is rejected. And confidence intervals do more, because they provide a range of population means that should be retained. For example, the 95% confidence interval (CI) that Sara found for the mean of the population from which her statistics class was (theoretically) randomly selected is 27.02 to 31.12. Any value for μ that falls within this range should be considered a reasonable possibility for the true value of μ. Because the average math background score for the previous 10 years (27.31) falls inside the 95% CI, it cannot be rejected as a null hypothesis at the .05 level. This is consistent with the conclusion drawn from Sara's t test. Because her t (1.71) was less than the .05 two-tailed, critical value for a t distribution with 84 degrees of freedom (1.99), the null hypothesis ($\mu = 27.31$) could not be rejected.

Confidence intervals provide an alternative way of interpreting your data that can be more informative than a simple null hypothesis test. To illustrate, let us consider four very different but possible CIs that Sara's class data could have led to:

(1) $28.8 \leq \mu \leq 32.9$

(2) $27.2 \leq \mu \leq 31.3$

(3) $24.4 \leq \mu \leq 28.5$

(4) $22.0 \leq \mu \leq 26.1$

The first set of results supports Sara's suspicion. She can conclude with 95% confidence that the population mean corresponding to her class is well above 27.31. That is, it can be expected to fall between 28.8 and 32.9.

The second set of results is less encouraging. To be sure, the population mean is likely to be greater than 27.31. But Sara cannot reject the hypothesis that μ is very close to 27.31 or even slightly lower, since the confidence interval extends as low as 27.2. Because there is little difference in aptitude between math quiz scores of 28 or even 29 and an aptitude of 27.31, this confidence interval includes quite a few values that do not provide much support for Sara's theory. Yet because most of the confidence interval is above 27.31, she may be on the right track.

The third set of results is discouraging. It is unlikely that the population mean is much above 27.31. Therefore, these results provide little support for Sara's idea that her class comes from a "better" population.

The fourth set of results is completely inconsistent with Sara's notion about her class. Because 27.31 is well *above* the *upper* confidence limit, these results would lead to the conclusion that Sara's class is actually from a population whose mean is *lower* in math aptitude than the population of previous students.

Confidence intervals provide considerably more information than the results of testing a specific null hypothesis. Therefore, confidence intervals should be used more widely in behavioral science research.

The Standard Error of a Proportion

Suppose that a few weeks before an election, a worried politician takes a poll by drawing a random sample of 400 registered voters. He finds that 53% intend to vote for him, while 47% prefer his opponent.[1] He is pleased to observe that he has the support of more than half of the sample, but he knows that the sample may not be an accurate indicator of the population because an unrepresentative number of his supporters may have been included by chance. What should he conclude about his prospects in the election?

This problem is similar to the preceding ones in this chapter. There is one population in which the politician is interested (registered voters), and he wishes to draw an inference about the mean of this population based on data obtained from a sample. In particular, he would like to know if the percent sup-

---

1. For simplicity, we assume that there are no undecided or "won't say" voters in this sample. There will be some such in reality, and omitting them we make the possibly incorrect assumption that they will break the same way as those who make a choice.

porting him is greater than 50% (in which case he will win the election). There is one important difference in the present situation, however: his data are in terms of percents or *proportions.*

While the general strategy is the same as in the case of the standard error of the mean, special techniques must be used to deal with proportions. The needed formula is

$$z = \frac{p - \pi}{\sqrt{\pi(1 - \pi)/N}},$$

where

p = proportion observed in the sample

π = hypothesized value of the *population* proportion

N = number of people in the sample

The denominator of this formula, $\sqrt{\pi(1 - \pi)/N}$, is the *standard error of a proportion,* symbolized by σ_p. It serves a similar purpose to the standard error of the mean, but it is a measure of the variability of *proportions* in samples drawn at random from a population where the proportion in question is π. (Notice that in this formula, π is used to represent the hypothesized value of the population proportion. It does *not* represent the usual mathematical value of approximately 3.14159.)

Since the population π is specified, and the σ of the population in question is known—it can be proved equal to $\sqrt{\pi(1 - \pi)}$—the results are referred to the z table. In the case of the anxious politician, the critical population value in which he is interested is .50: He wants to know whether the observed sample proportion of .53 is sufficiently different from .50 to enable him to conclude that a majority of the population of voters will vote for him. Thus,

π = hypothesized population proportion = .50

p = proportion observed in sample = .53

The statistical analysis is as follows:

$H_0: \pi = .50$

$H_1: \pi \neq .50$

$\alpha = .05$

$$z = \frac{.53 - .50}{\sqrt{.50(1 - .50)/400}} = \frac{.03}{.025} = 1.20$$

The value of 1.20 is smaller than the critical z value of 1.96 needed to reject

FIGURE 10.2

Sampling distribution of *p* when $\pi = .50$ and $N = 400$

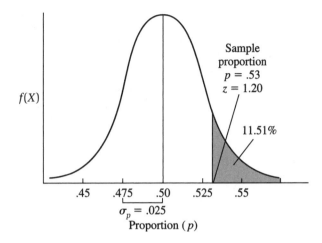

H_0. Therefore, the politician *cannot* conclude that he will win the election. It is "not sufficiently unlikely" for 53% of a sample of 400 voters to support him, even if only 50% of the population will vote for him. The politician will therefore have a nervous few weeks until the votes are in, and he may well conclude from the results that he should increase his campaigning efforts. The results are illustrated in Figure 10.2.

There is one important caution regarding the use of the standard error of the proportion. When the hypothesized value of the population proportion (π) is quite large or small (i.e., close to 1.0 or 0) and the sample size is small, computing a *z* value and referring it to the normal curve table will yield incorrect results. As a rough guide, you should *not* use this procedure when either $N\pi$ or $N(1 - \pi)$ is less than 5. For example, if you wish to test the null hypothesis that $\pi = .85$ with a sample size of 20,

$$N\pi = (20)(.85) = 17 \quad \text{and} \quad N(1 - \pi) = (20)(.15) = 3$$

Since $N(1 - \pi)$ is less than 5, the procedures discussed in this section should *not* be used. The tested value of π is too extreme, and the sample size is too small, to give an accurate answer. You should either use the appropriate statistical techniques to deal with this situation (the binomial distribution, as discussed in Chapter 19) or increase the size of your sample.

Confidence Intervals for π

Suppose you wish to determine all reasonably likely values of the population proportion (π) using the .05 criterion of significance. The confidence interval is

$$(p - 1.96\sigma_p) \leq \mu \leq (p + 1.96\sigma_p)$$

There is one difficulty: σ_p depends on the value of π, which is not known. In the previous section, a value of π was specified by H_0 and used in the calculation of σ_p. However, there is no single hypothesized value of π in interval estimation.

One possibility, which yields a fairly good approximation *if the sample size is large,* is to use p as an estimate of π. With a large sample, p is unlikely to be so far from π as to greatly affect σ_p and hence the size of the confidence interval. In the case of the nervous politician in the previous section, $p = .53$; and $\sqrt{.53(1 - .53)/N}$ is equal to .025. Then, the 95% confidence interval is equal to

$$.53 - 1.96(.025) \leq \mu \leq .53 + 1.96(.025)$$

$$.53 - .049 \leq \mu \leq .53 + .049$$

$$.48 \leq \mu \leq .58$$

Since the sample size is large ($N = 400$), the politician can state with 95% confidence that between approximately 48% and 58% of the population will vote for him. Note that the value of .50 *is* within the confidence interval, as would be expected from the fact that the null hypothesis that $\pi = .50$ was retained. To determine the 99% confidence interval, the procedure would be the same except that the z value of 2.58 would be used instead of 1.96.

Summary

The use of the normal distribution to test hypotheses requires that the standard deviation of the population be known. If you have a very large sample, its standard deviation can be used in place of σ with negligible error. However, if your sample is fairly small you will need to use one of the t distributions.

1. Testing the Mean of a Single Population with the t Distributions

The formula for estimating the standard error of the mean from a single sample is

$$s_{\bar{X}} = \frac{s}{\sqrt{N}},$$

where

$s_{\bar{X}} =$ the estimated standard error of the mean

$s =$ standard deviation of the sample of observations

Then, to draw inferences about the population mean, use

$$t = \frac{\overline{X} - \mu}{s_{\overline{X}}} \quad \text{with} \quad df = N - 1$$

Use *z* instead of *t* if σ is known. For large samples, *t* and *z* are approximately equal.

2. Confidence Intervals

Confidence intervals establish all reasonably likely values of a population parameter, such as a mean or proportion. Confidence intervals provide considerably more information than the results of testing a specific null hypothesis, because they show the decision that should be made for every conceivable null-hypothetical value rather than only one.

Use $s_{\overline{X}}$ when determining confidence intervals for the mean of one population. Obtain the critical value of *t* from the *t* table ($df = N - 1$; $\alpha = 1.0 -$ confidence) and compute

$$(\overline{X} - ts_{\overline{X}}) \leq \mu \leq (\overline{X} + ts_{\overline{X}}),$$

where

$$t = \text{critical value from } t \text{ table}$$

Use *z* instead of *t* if σ is known. For large samples, *z* and *t* are approximately equal.

3. The Standard Error of a Proportion

If the data are in the form of proportions,

1. Compute

$$\sigma_p = \sqrt{\frac{\pi(1 - \pi)}{N}}$$

2. Compute

$$z = \frac{p - \pi}{\sigma_p}$$

where

$$\sigma_p = \text{the standard error of a proportion}$$

$$p = \text{proportion observed in the sample}$$

$$\pi = \text{hypothesized value of the population proportion}$$

Do *not* use this procedure if $N\pi$ or $N(1 - \pi)$ is less than 5.

Exercises

1. Answer these problems by calculating a *t* value and comparing it to the critical value for a two-tailed test at the .05 level. (Note: You can save time by using the means and SDs you calculated for Universities A and B for the exercises in Chapters 4 and 5.)

   (a) Would you retain or reject the null hypothesis that the population mean for University A is 14?

   (b) Would you retain or reject the null hypothesis that the population mean for University B is 10?

2. For University B, compute each of the following:

   (a) The 99% confidence interval.

   (b) The 95% confidence interval.

   (c) The 90% confidence interval.

   (d) Explain why the size of the CIs becomes larger as the level of confidence increases.

3. This exercise is based on the following data set: 1, 3, 6, 0, 1, 1, 2, 1, 4.

   (a) Perform a *t* test in order to decide whether you can reject the null hypothesis of $\mu = 2.5$ at the .05 level (two-tailed) for these data.

   (b) Redo your *t* test in part (a) for a null hypothesis of $\mu = 6.0$.

   (c) Compute the 95% CI for the population mean from which these data were drawn. Explain how this CI could be used to draw conclusions about the null hypotheses in parts (a) and (b).

4. This exercise is based on the following data set: 68.36, 15.31, 77.42, 84.00, 76.59, 68.43, 72.41, 83.05, 91.07, 80.62, 77.83.

   (a) Perform a *t* test in order to decide whether you can reject the null hypothesis of $\mu = 52.3$ at the .01 level (two-tailed) for these data.

   (b) Redo your *t* test in part (a) for a null hypothesis of $\mu = 85.0$.

   (c) Compute the 99% CI for the population mean from which these data were drawn. Explain how this CI could be used to draw conclusions about the null hypotheses in parts (a) and (b).

5. A politician has staked his political career on whether or not a new state constitution will pass. To find out which way the wind is blowing, he obtains a random sample of 100 voters a few weeks prior to the election and finds that 60% of the sample says that they will vote for the new constitution. Assuming that the constitution will fail if it receives 50% or less of the vote, should he conclude that the electorate as a whole will support the new constitution? Perform the appropriate statistical test to answer this question.

6. A certain business concern needs to obtain at least 20% of the market in order to make a profit. A random sample of 200 prospective buyers is asked

whether they will purchase the product. What should the company conclude if

(a) 26 of those asked said they would buy the product?

(b) 46 of those asked said they would buy the product?

(c) 58 of those asked said they would buy the product?

Thought Questions

1. You are drawing inferences about the mean of one population. (a) When should you use the t distributions as the theoretical model rather than the normal curve model? (b) Why is there a different critical t value for different degrees of freedom?

2. What advantages do confidence intervals have over testing a specific null hypothesis?

3. (a) What happens to the size of a confidence interval as the standard error of the mean becomes larger? Why? (b) What happens to the size of a confidence interval as the sample size becomes larger? Why? (c) What are the advantages of having a smaller confidence interval?

4. (a) Why does the size of the confidence interval become larger when we change from a 95% confidence interval to a 99% confidence interval? (b) We can be more certain that the unknown population mean falls within the 99% confidence interval than within the 95% confidence interval. Why, then, don't we always use 99% confidence intervals?

5. On a test of scholastic ability administered to college students in the United States, the mean is 500 and the standard deviation is 100. Each of the following 95% confidence intervals for the mean of one population was computed from a random sample of students from the university in question: University Y, 601.63–642.75; University Z, 502.42–534.68. Both universities claim that their students are superior to the national average of 500. (a) Is this claim correct? (b) How do these results illustrate the advantages that confidence intervals have over testing a specific null hypothesis, such as whether the population mean is equal to 500?

6. A behavioral science researcher wishes to draw inferences about the proportion of one population. (a) Would she prefer that the standard error of a proportion be small or large? Why? (b) Should she use the normal curve model or the t distributions as her theoretical model? Why? (c) When should she *not* use the procedures for drawing inferences about the proportion of one population discussed in this chapter? (d) Why might she prefer to use confidence intervals for the proportion of one population rather than testing a specific null hypothesis?

Computer Exercises

1. Use your statistical package to perform a one-sample t test to determine whether the baseline anxiety of Sara's students differs significantly from the mean ($\mu = 18$) found by a very large study of college students across the country. Find the 95% CI for the population mean represented by Sara's students.

2. Use your statistical package to perform a one-sample t test to determine whether the average baseline heart rate of Sara's male students differs significantly from the mean HR ($\mu = 70$) for college-aged men. Find the 99% CI for the population mean represented by Sara's male students.

3. Use your statistical package to perform a one-sample t test to determine whether the average *postquiz* heart rate of Sara's *female* students differs significantly from the mean resting HR ($\mu = 72$) for college-aged women. Find the 95% CI for the population mean represented by Sara's female students.

Bridge to SPSS

To perform a one-sample t test in SPSS, select **Compare Means** from the ANALYZE menu, and then choose **One-Sample T Test....** In the dialog box that opens, move the variable you want to test to the Test Variable(s) area, and enter the hypothesized population mean that you want to test against in the space labeled **Test Value.** The **Options...** button allows you to select the percentage that will be used to create a confidence interval for the population mean. The other choice you can make in the Options box applies only when you move more than one variable to the Test Variables area, in order to perform several t tests in the same run (all against the same population value, however). The default choice for handling missing values deals with missing values separately for each test variable. However, if you select **Exclude cases listwise,** any case (i.e., row in the data sheet) that is missing a value for *any* of the variables that appeared together in the Test Variables area, will be deleted for *all* of the t tests in that run (you may want the t tests of all your variables to involve exactly the same participants). You will see the **Exclude cases listwise** option presented for a number of other statistical procedures in SPSS, which we will describe in subsequent chapters.

Chapter 11

Testing Hypotheses about the Difference between the Means of Two Populations

PREVIEW

The Standard Error of the Difference

We wish to draw inferences about the *difference* between the means of *two* populations. What is the correct standard error term to use in this situation? Why can't it be measured directly?

What is an experimental group? A control group?

Why is it desirable to use random samples?

How does sampling error affect the difference between the means of the experimental group and the control group?

What does the standard error of the mean tell us about the trustworthiness of a single difference between two sample means as an estimate of the difference between the population means?

Estimating the Standard Error of the Difference

What are the procedures for estimating the value of the standard error of the difference?

How is the standard error of the difference related to the variance of the population? To the size of the sample?

The *t* Test for Two Sample Means

What is the correct statistical model to use in this situation?

How do we test hypotheses about the difference between the means of two populations (independent samples)?

Confidence Intervals for $\mu_1 - \mu_2$

How do we estimate an interval in which the difference between the two population means is likely to fall?

What is gained by using confidence intervals?

Using the *t* Test for Two Sample Means: Some General Considerations

What assumptions underlie the use of this *t* test?

What is the separate-variances *t* test and under what circumstances would its use be considered?

(continued on next page)

In the preceding two chapters we looked at techniques for drawing inferences about the mean of one population. More often, scientists wish to draw inferences about differences between two or more populations. For example, a social psychologist may want to know if the mean of the population of urban Americans on a pencil-and-paper test of spatial abilities is equal to the mean of the population of suburban Americans. Or an experimental psychologist may wish to find out whether rats perform better on a discrimination learning task to gain a reward or to avoid punishment—that is, whether the mean number of correct responses is greater for the "reward" population or for the "punishment" population. In both cases, the question of interest begins with a comparison between the means of *two* samples.

In this chapter, we will discuss techniques for drawing inferences about the *difference between the means of two populations* ($\mu_1 - \mu_2$) based on the data from two samples. Procedures for drawing inferences about the means of more than two populations, or about other aspects of two or more populations, will be considered in later chapters.

The Standard Error of the Difference

Suppose that you wish to conduct a research study to determine whether the use of caffeine improves performance on a college mathematics examination. To test this hypothesis, you could obtain two *random* samples of college students taking mathematics, an *experimental group* and a *control group.* But while random sampling is theoretically the ideal method to avoid obtaining two groups that differ greatly in ability, motivation, or any other variable that might obscure the effects of caffeine, a more common approach is to select one (twice-as-large) convenient sample and then randomly assign the participants to either the experimental or control group. This procedure is called *random assignment.* Unlike random sampling, random assignment is very easy to do because it simply involves dividing a sample of participants that you already have into two (or more) groups. For example, you might flip a coin and assign a participant to group 1 if a "head" comes up and group 2 if a "tail" comes up.

Once you have formed two groups, you then give all members assigned to the experimental group a small dose of caffeine one hour prior to the test. At the same time, the control group is given a placebo (a pill that, unknown to them, has no biochemical effect whatsoever). This is to control for the possibility that administering *any* pill will affect the students' performance. (For example, they may become more psychologically alert and obtain higher scores.) Thus, the control group serves as a baseline against which the performance of the experimental group can be evaluated. Finally, the mean test scores of the two groups are compared. Suppose that the mean of the experimental group equals 81, and the mean of the control group equals 78. Should you conclude that caffeine is effective in improving the test scores?

As was shown in Chapter 10, any sample mean is almost never exactly equal to the population mean because of sampling error; the cases that happened, by chance, to be included in the sample may be unusually high or low on the variable being measured. Therefore, the two populations in question (a hypothetically infinite number of test takers given caffeine and a hypothetically infinite number of test takers given a placebo) may have equal means even though the sample means are different. Consequently, you cannot tell what conclusion to reach just by looking at the sample means. You need additional information: namely, whether the 3-point difference between 81 and 78 is likely to be a trustworthy indication that the population means are different (and that caffeine *has* an effect), or whether this difference may be due solely to which cases

FIGURE 11.1

Illustration of procedure for obtaining the empirical sampling distribution of differences between two means ($N = 30$)

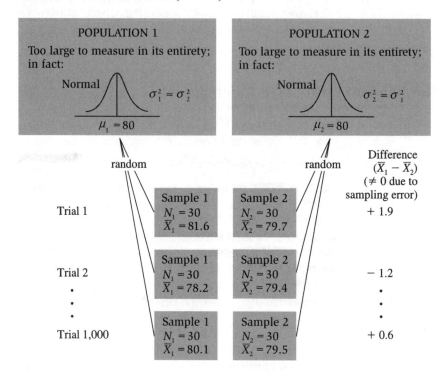

happened to fall in each sample (in which case you should *not* conclude that caffeine has an effect).

How can this additional information be obtained? In Chapter 10 we saw that the estimated variability of the sampling distribution of means drawn from one population, $s_{\bar{X}}$, provides information as to how trustworthy is any one $\bar{X}$ as an estimate of μ. The present problem concerns how trustworthy is any one *difference*, $\bar{X}_1 - \bar{X}_2$, as an estimate of the difference between the population means, $\mu_1 - \mu_2$. This problem is also solved by making use of an appropriate sampling distribution: the sampling distribution of the *difference* between *two* sample means.

Suppose that a variable is normally distributed in each of two defined populations, and that the populations have equal means and equal variances (that is, $\mu_1 = \mu_2$ and $\sigma_1^2 = \sigma_2^2$). If many pairs of random samples of equal size were drawn from the two populations, a distribution of differences between the paired means could be established empirically. For each pair, you would subtract the mean of the second sample ($\bar{X}_2$) from the mean of the first sample ($\bar{X}_1$). Since the means of the two populations are equal, any difference between the sample means must be due solely to sampling error.

Figure 11.1 illustrates the procedure needed to obtain an empirical sampling

TABLE 11.1

Empirical sampling distribution of 1,000
differences between pairs of sample means
($N = 30$) drawn from two populations
where $\mu_1 = \mu_1 = 80$ (hypothetical data)

Difference between sample means $\overline{X}_1 - \overline{X}_2$	Number of samples (f)
Greater than $+11.49$	0
$+10.50$ to $+11.49$	1
$+9.50$ to $+10.49$	0
$+8.50$ to $+9.49$	1
$+7.50$ to $+8.49$	4
$+6.50$ to $+7.49$	7
$+5.50$ to $+6.49$	21
$+4.50$ to $+5.49$	32
$+3.50$ to $+4.49$	54
$+2.50$ to $+3.49$	77
$+1.50$ to $+2.49$	107
$+.50$ to $+1.49$	122
$-.50$ to $+.49$	153
-1.50 to $-.51$	114
-2.50 to -1.51	95
-3.50 to -2.51	82
-4.50 to -3.51	60
-5.50 to -4.51	31
-6.50 to -5.51	22
-7.50 to -6.51	10
-8.50 to -7.51	4
-9.50 to -8.51	1
-10.50 to -9.51	2
Smaller than -10.50	0
Total	1,000

distribution of 1,000 differences in the case where $\mu_1 = \mu_2 = 80$ and the size of each random sample is 30. The resulting frequency distribution is shown in Table 11.1, and the frequency polygon plotted from this distribution is shown in Figure 11.2. The sample means are not in general exactly equal to 80, and the differences between pairs of means are not in general exactly equal to zero, due to sampling fluctuations. Notice that the distribution is approximately symmetric, which indicates that chance differences are equally likely to occur in either direction—that is, $(\overline{X}_1 - \overline{X}_2) > (\mu_1 - \mu_2)$ or $(\overline{X}_1 - \overline{X}_2) < (\mu_1 - \mu_2)$. Thus the mean of the distribution of differences tends to be equal to $\mu_1 - \mu_2$, which in this case is zero.

Given the data in Table 11.1, you could calculate the standard deviation of the distribution of differences for the given sample size by using the usual formula for the standard deviation (Chapter 5). This standard deviation would tell you how much, on the average, a given $\overline{X}_1 - \overline{X}_2$ is likely to differ from the "true"

FIGURE 11.2

Frequency polygon of data in Table 11.1

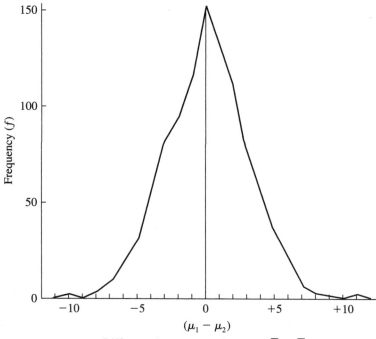

$(\mu_1 - \mu_2)$

Difference between sample means $(\overline{X}_1 - \overline{X}_2)$

difference of zero (the central point of the distribution of differences). Consequently, it would indicate how trustworthy is the single difference that you have on hand as an estimate of $\mu_1 - \mu_2$. This standard deviation is therefore called the *standard error of the difference.*

A relatively *large* standard error of the difference indicates that any single difference between a pair of sample means must be viewed with grave suspicion. Since large discrepancies between $\overline{X}_1$ and $\overline{X}_2$ are likely *even if they come from populations with equal means,* you need a sizable difference before you can safely conclude that μ_1 is not equal to μ_2. If, on the other hand, the standard error of the difference is relatively *small,* you can place more confidence in any one sample difference as an estimate of the population difference. Large discrepancies between $\overline{X}_1$ and $\overline{X}_2$ are *not* likely to occur (and mislead you) if in fact $\mu_1 = \mu_2$, so a large difference between the sample means *is* a trustworthy sign that the population means differ.

In practice, behavioral scientists never have many paired random samples of a given size. Therefore, it is impossible to compute the standard error of the difference empirically. Instead, as in Chapter 10, you must make use of estimation procedures developed by statisticians. In the present situation, you need a formula that enables you to *estimate* the standard error of the difference based on the *one* pair of samples that you have measured.

Estimating the Standard Error of the Difference

As was the case with $s_{\bar{x}}$, developing the estimation formula for the standard error of the difference by means of a formal proof is beyond the scope of this book. Instead, we will attempt to explain the formula in nonmathematical terms.

If it is assumed that the two population variances are equal, the variances of each of the two samples may be combined into a single estimate of the common value of σ^2. If the sizes of the two samples are exactly equal, you can obtain this combined or *pooled* estimate by computing the ordinary average of the two sample variances. Often, however, the sample sizes are not equal, in which case greater weight must be given to the larger-sized sample. That is, a *weighted* average must be computed. The general formula for the *pooled variance* (symbolized by s^2_{pooled}), which may be used for equal or unequal sample sizes, is

$$s^2_{pooled} = \frac{(N_1 - 1)s_1^2 + (N_2 - 1)s_2^2}{N_1 + N_2 - 2},$$

where

$$s_1^2 = \text{population variance estimate of sample 1}$$
$$s_2^2 = \text{population variance estimate of sample 2}$$
$$N_1 = \text{number of cases in sample 1}$$
$$N_2 = \text{number of cases in sample 2}$$

Then, the estimation formula for the standard error of the difference is

$$s_{\bar{X}_1 - \bar{X}_2} = \sqrt{\frac{s^2_{pooled}}{N_1} + \frac{s^2_{pooled}}{N_2}}$$

$$= \sqrt{s^2_{pooled}\left(\frac{1}{N_1} + \frac{1}{N_2}\right)},$$

where

$$s_{\bar{X}_1 - \bar{X}_2} = \text{estimated standard error of the difference}$$

This formula should not look totally unfamiliar. We saw in Chapter 10 that the estimation for the standard error of the mean ($s_{\bar{X}}$) is equal to $s/\sqrt{N}$. Consequently, $s_{\bar{X}}^2$ is equal to s^2/N. Here, since a difference is subject to sampling error from *two* means, the sampling error variance reflects both sources of error. In addition, it uses a more stable estimate of the population variance by pooling the variance information from the two samples.

It should be obvious that the larger the variance of the population (as estimated by s_{pooled}^2), the larger the estimated standard error of the difference. Only slightly less obvious is the fact that the *larger* the sample sizes, the *smaller* the standard error. Differences based on large samples will have smaller sampling error (and are thus likely to be more accurate estimates of the population difference) than are differences based on small samples, just as is the case for a single mean.

The two steps given previously can be combined into a single formula, as follows:

$$s_{\bar{X}_1 - \bar{X}_2} = \sqrt{\frac{(N_1 - 1)s_1^2 + (N_2 - 1)s_2^2}{N_1 + N_2 - 2} \left(\frac{1}{N_1} + \frac{1}{N_2} \right)}$$

The *t* Test for Two Sample Means

When you test hypotheses about the difference between two population means, the correct statistical model to use is the *t* distributions. Once the estimated standard error of the difference has been computed, a *t* value (and therefore a probability value) may be found for any given obtained difference, as follows:

$$t = \frac{(\bar{X}_1 - \bar{X}_2) - (\mu_1 - \mu_2)}{s_{\bar{X}_1 - \bar{X}_2}}$$

Notice that the two sample means yield a single difference score, $\bar{X}_1 - \bar{X}_2$, which is compared to the null-hypothesized mean of the difference scores, $\mu_1 - \mu_2$.

It is possible to test any hypothesized difference between the means of two populations. For example, you could test the hypothesis that the mean of the first population is 20 points greater than the mean of the second population by setting $\mu_1 - \mu_2$ equal to 20 in this equation. Much more often than not, however, you will want to test the hypothesis that the means of the two populations are equal (that is, $\mu_1 = \mu_2$ or $\mu_1 - \mu_2 = 0$). In this situation, the *t* formula can be simplified to

$$t = \frac{\bar{X}_1 - \bar{X}_2}{s_{\bar{X}_1 - \bar{X}_2}}$$

or

$$t = \frac{\overline{X}_1 - \overline{X}_2}{\sqrt{\dfrac{(N_1 - 1)s_1^2 + (N_2 - 1)s_2^2}{N_1 + N_2 - 2}\left(\dfrac{1}{N_1} + \dfrac{1}{N_2}\right)}}$$

$$df = N_1 + N_2 - 2$$

The degrees of freedom on which this t value is based, which is needed to obtain the critical value of t from the t table, is determined from the fact that the population σ^2 is estimated using $N_1 - 1$ degrees of freedom from sample 1 and $N_2 - 1$ degrees of freedom from sample 2 (see Chapter 10). Therefore, the estimate is based on the combined degrees of freedom:

$$(N_1 - 1) + (N_2 - 1) \qquad \text{or} \qquad N_1 + N_2 - 2$$

Recall the problem of caffeine and mathematics test scores posed at the beginning of this chapter; the first step in the statistical analysis would consist of stating the hypotheses and establishing a significance criterion, α:

$$H_0: \mu_{caf} = \mu_{con}$$
$$H_1: \mu_{caf} \neq \mu_{con}$$
$$\alpha = .05$$

H_0 states that the caffeine and control samples come from populations with equal means, while H_1 states that these two samples come from populations with different means. The customary .05 criterion of significance is specified. Because Sara had good reason to be concerned with the obvious possible effects of caffeine on the heart rates of her students, we will reframe the problem in terms of HR rather than test scores.

Wisely, Sara had asked her students, immediately after they had written down their baseline heart rates, to report their usage of caffeine from the time they woke up that morning until the time they entered the classroom. (She told them as they entered not to drink any caffeinated beverage during the class.) From the variety of responses she received, Sara selected 22 students who clearly had ingested a good deal of caffeine shortly before class to have their heart rates analyzed as part of her caffeine group,[1] and another 20 students who were quite certain they had had no caffeine that day or the day before to be in her control group. Suppose that the heart rate results for her two groups are as follows:

---

1. This is not a truly experimental group, as these students decided for themselves to ingest caffeine before class, perhaps because they found statistics to be particularly boring (if you can believe that).

Caffeine group	Control group
$N_1 = 22$	$N_2 = 20$
$\overline{X}_1 = 81.0$	$\overline{X}_2 = 68.0$
$s_1 = 12.0$	$s_2 = 16.8$

The estimated standard error of the difference is equal to

$$s_{\overline{X}_1 - \overline{X}_2} = \sqrt{\frac{(21)(12^2) + 19(16.8^2)}{22 + 20 - 2}\left(\frac{1}{22} + \frac{1}{20}\right)}$$

$$= \sqrt{(209.664)\left(\frac{1}{22} + \frac{1}{20}\right)}$$

$$= 4.474$$

The t value is equal to

$$t = \frac{81.0 - 68.0}{4.474} = 2.91, \qquad df = 22 + 20 - 2 = 40$$

Referring to the t table for 40 degrees of freedom, we find that a t value greater in absolute value than 2.02 is needed to justify rejection of H_0 using the .05 criterion of significance. Since the obtained value of t is greater in absolute value than the critical value found in Table B, the difference between the sample means observed by Sara is not likely to arise from sampling error. So she should reject H_0 and conclude that the caffeine and control groups are random samples from populations with *different* means. More specifically, caffeine *has* a positive effect on resting heart rates. (The rejection areas for this experiment are illustrated in Figure 11.3.)

Although we can conclude that caffeine has *some* effect on heart rate, the null hypothesis test alone does not allow us to estimate the amount of that effect.[2] The fact that an effect is statistically significant does *not* by itself tell us whether the effect is large enough to be of any *practical* interest. For some well-known variables, however, the difference between two sample means does provide a good idea of the size of the effect that we are dealing with. For this example $\overline{X}_1 - \overline{X}_2$ equals 13 bpm, which represents a substantial increase in heart rate associated with caffeine.

In any case, $\overline{X}_1 - \overline{X}_2$ is the best point estimate for the difference between the two population means ($\mu_1 - \mu_2$). However, as we pointed out in the previous chapter, a point estimate alone does not tell you how accurate the estimate is. Interval estimation is much more informative, so we will now apply this procedure to the two-sample case.

---

2. Strictly speaking, we shouldn't even say that caffeine *affects* heart rate, because we did not assign students to the caffeine group and therefore cannot make causal conclusions. The issue of proving causation will be discussed further in the next chapter.

FIGURE 11.3

Acceptance and rejection regions for the caffeine/control comparison in the *t* distribution for *df* = 40

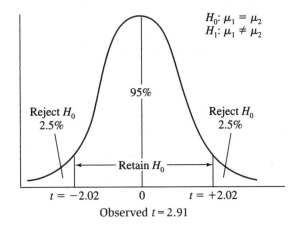

$$H_0: \mu_1 = \mu_2$$
$$H_1: \mu_1 \neq \mu_2$$

95%

Reject H_0
2.5%

Reject H_0
2.5%

Retain H_0

$t = -2.02$ 0 $t = +2.02$

Observed $t = 2.91$

Confidence Intervals for $\mu_1 - \mu_2$

The use of confidence intervals to determine all reasonably likely values of the mean of a *single* population was discussed in Chapter 10. In a similar fashion, all reasonably likely values of the *difference between two population means* can be found by using the following confidence interval:

$$[(\overline{X}_1 - \overline{X}_2) - ts_{\overline{X}_1 - \overline{X}_2}] \leq \mu_1 - \mu_2 \leq [(\overline{X}_1 - \overline{X}_2) + ts_{\overline{X}_1 - \overline{X}_2}],$$

where

t = critical value obtained from the *t* table for the specified criterion of significance for the appropriate *df*

Since this confidence interval pertains to the *difference* between two population means, the appropriate error term is the standard error of the difference $(s_{\overline{X}_1 - \overline{X}_2})$.

For example, in Sara's caffeine study, the observed sample means were 81.0 for the caffeine group and 68.0 for the control group; the standard error of the difference was 4.474, and the critical value of t for $df = 40$ and $\alpha = .05$ was 2.02. The 95% confidence interval for the difference between the population means is

$$[(81.0 - 68.0) - (2.02)(4.474)] \leq \mu_1 - \mu_2$$

$$\leq [(81.0) - 68.0) + (2.02)(4.474)]$$

$$(13.0 - 9.04) \leq \mu_1 - \mu_2 \leq (13.0 + 9.04)$$

$$3.96 \leq \mu_1 - \mu_2 \leq 22.04$$

You can state with 95% confidence that the mean of the caffeine population is included in the interval that runs from 3.96 points to 22.04 points greater than the mean of the control population. Note that zero is *not* in this interval, indicating that it is *not* likely that $\mu_1 = \mu_2$.

To determine the 99% confidence interval, the procedure would be the same except that the critical value of t for 40 *df* for $\alpha = .01$, which is 2.70, would be used instead of 2.02. The 99% confidence interval would therefore be

$$(13.0 - 12.08) \leq \mu_1 - \mu_2 \leq (13.0 + 12.08)$$

$$.92 \leq \mu_1 - \mu_2 \leq 25.08$$

As always, the 99% confidence interval is wider than the 95% confidence interval. You can be more certain that the true difference between the two population means falls in the 99% confidence interval, but you must pay a price for this added confidence: the interval is larger, so $\mu_1 - \mu_2$ is estimated less precisely.

Here again, confidence intervals allow you to do everything that null-hypothesis testing does. If a value of $\mu_1 - \mu_2$ specified by the null hypothesis (such as the frequently used value of zero) falls within the confidence interval, that null hypothesis is retained. If a value of $\mu_1 - \mu_2$ specified by the null hypothesis falls outside the confidence interval, that null hypothesis is rejected. And by specifying a range of population differences that should be retained, confidence intervals provide us with more information.

For example, in the caffeine study, a 95% confidence interval of 7.62 – 13.74 would indicate that the effect of caffeine on resting heart rate is a probable mean increase of at least 7 beats per minute and not more than 14 bpm. However, a 95% confidence interval of 0.62 – 20.74 would tell a different story. Here, caffeine may cause an increase of as much as 20 beats per minute or as little as one. Since an increase of 1 bpm is virtually negligible, the possibility would remain that caffeine has no important practical effect on heart rate. (Such a wide confidence interval suggests the likelihood of substantial sampling error. The best way to improve accuracy is to repeat the experiment with a larger sample.) Yet in both cases, a null hypothesis test will yield identical results: It will tell us only that the null-hypothesized value of zero between the two population means should be rejected.

Confidence intervals (CIs) are highly recommended by the American Psychological Association (2001) to supplement null hypothesis testing (NHT) when submitting a study for publication. Many behavioral researchers feel that CIs should be used more widely than they are at present; some even suggest that the reporting of CIs should replace NHT entirely. However, CIs are less meaningful when your dependent variable is measured on a scale that is not very commonly used, as when you measure the ability to memorize verbal material in terms of how many words are recalled from a list that you created for your experiment. A more universally interpretable measure of the size of an experiment's effect is discussed shortly.

Using the *t* Test for Two Sample Means: Some General Considerations

It is easy to perform and report two-sample *t* tests, but some care must be taken in deciding when such a test is appropriate, and what practical conclusions can be drawn. The following points should help you to use and interpret *t* tests appropriately.

Violations of the Underlying Assumptions

In theory, the use of the independent-samples *t* test is justified only if two assumptions are met:

1. The observations within each group are independent of each other, and all of the observations in one group are independent of all of the observations in the other group.
2. The dependent variable is normally distributed within each population.

In practice, however, you should not be deterred from using the *t* test even if the assumption concerning normality is not exactly met. This test is *robust* with regard to this assumption—it gives fairly accurate results even if the assumption is not satisfied. The pooled-variance version of the two-sample *t* test requires an additional assumption:

3. The variances of the two populations are equal ($\sigma_1^2 = \sigma_2^2$).

The assumption concerning the equality of the two population variances can also be ignored in practice *if* the two sample sizes are equal. But if the sample sizes are fairly unequal (say, the larger is more than 1.5 times greater than the smaller) *and* the population variances are markedly unequal, the *t* test presented in this chapter may well yield erroneous results. So if there is reason to believe that the population variances differ substantially, it is a good idea to obtain approximately equal sample sizes. Then, any differences between the population variances will have little ability to bias the results obtained from the *t* test.

If you are stuck with a combination of rather unequal sample sizes and the variance for one of your samples is more than twice as large as the variance of the other sample, you should consider the possibility of using a different type of *t* test. The test described previously is often called the *pooled-variances t test* for reasons that should be obvious from its formula. The other type of *t* test does *not* assume that the two population variances are equal, so it does *not* pool the two sample variances. A glance at the following formula should make it clear why this procedure is often referred to as the *separate-variances t test:*

$$t = \frac{\overline{X}_1 - \overline{X}_2}{\sqrt{\dfrac{s_1^2}{N_1} + \dfrac{s_2^2}{N_2}}}$$

The tricky part of using the separate-variances t test is finding the right t distribution to use for your critical values. The number of degrees of freedom associated with this test is usually less than the df used for the pooled-variances test (i.e., $N_1 + N_2 - 2$) and often involves fractional values, so this form of the t test is best performed by statistical software. The separate-variances t test is rarely reported in journal articles (other procedures, such as data transformations and nonparametric statistics, are more often employed to deal with large discrepancies in sample variances), so we will not discuss this procedure further in this text.

Implications of Retaining H_0

Suppose that a different caffeine study yielded an obtained t value of 1.14 for $df = 40$. Since 1.14 is smaller than the critical value of t obtained from Table B, you would decide to retain H_0. This does *not* imply that you have shown that the population means are equal. You do not know the probability that your decision to retain H_0 is wrong (that is, how likely you are to have made a Type II error), so you should limit yourself to a cautious statement such as "there is not sufficient reason to reject the hypothesis that caffeine has no effect."

"Retaining" H_0 merely means that we have not refuted it. It does *not* mean that we have shown H_0 to be true!

Implications of Rejecting H_0

When the results of the statistical analysis indicate that you should *reject H_0* (that is, the results are *statistically significant*), you may then conclude that your independent variable (e.g., presence versus absence of caffeine) has some effect. But there is still some chance that you have committed a Type I error and that the population means actually are equal. Therefore, it is usually *not* a good idea to regard any one such statistical finding as conclusive. You should wait to see if repetitions (*replications*) of your study also indicate similar effects before reaching firm conclusions.

It is also important *not* to confuse statistical significance with practical significance. Depending on your sample sizes, effects too small to be of any consequence can end up statistically significant, and effects that look fairly large can fail to reach statistical significance. We will return to the topic of effect size in the next section of this chapter.

Reporting the Results of a t Test

A common way to express the results of a two-sample experiment in a journal article is in the context of a sentence like this one: "The group that reported having ingested caffeine before the session exhibited a higher resting heart rate ($M = 81$ bpm) than the group that had not ingested caffeine that day ($M = 68$

bpm); this difference was statistically significant, $t(40) = 2.91, p < .01$.[3] (The number in parentheses after t is, of course, the df.) It is becoming increasingly common to include the standard error (the denominator of the t formula) to make it easier for the reader to calculate a CI if it is not actually reported by the article's author.

Measuring the Size of an Effect

If the 95% CI for a new 6-month weight-loss program goes from 10 to 30 pounds lost, you can easily decide for yourself whether you are interested. But if a new memory improvement program announces, with 95% confidence, that you will recall between 10 and 20 more names from a list after 3 weeks of training, should you be impressed? When the scale used to measure the dependent variable is not a familiar one, it can be more informative to standardize the obtained difference in sample means rather than to report that difference in its original units. This standardized measure of effect size in your data is often called g, and its formula looks like a z score:

$$g = \frac{\overline{X}_1 - \overline{X}_2}{s_p}$$

Note that s_p is the square root of the pooled variance (s^2_{pooled}) that is calculated as part of a t test. For the caffeine study, s_p equals $\sqrt{209.664} = 14.48$, so $g = (81 - 68)/14.48 = 13/14.48 = .9$. This tells us that the two sample means are nearly an entire standard deviation apart, which is considered a rather large effect.

The interpretation of effect sizes, and the possibility of creating CIs for effect sizes, will be discussed in Chapter 14. An alternative measure of effect size, based on the principle of correlation, will be described in Chapter 13. Note that if you have already calculated g, and your two samples are the same size, you can calculate your t value from g and the sample sizes by using the following formula. (When the two samples are the same size, it is convenient to use n to represent the size of just one of those samples—i.e., $n = N_1 = N_2$.)

$$t = g\sqrt{\frac{n}{2}}$$

3. These days it is common either to report the exact two-tailed p value provided by the computer program that performed the statistical test (e.g., $p = .017$) or to state that p is lower than some potential alpha level that ends in a 1 or a 5, such as $p < .005$ or $p < .001$ (whichever is lower). The traditionalist sets one alpha level (usually .05) at the outset of a study and then reports p only as less than or greater than that alpha—for example, $p < .05$ or $p > .05$.

If $N_1 \neq N_2$, you must compute the *harmonic mean* of the two sample sizes in order to use the preceding formula. The harmonic mean of any two numbers can be calculated as follows:

$$\overline{X}_{\text{harmonic}} = \frac{2N_1 N_2}{N_1 + N_2}$$

Combining the formula for the harmonic mean with the formula for t in terms of g and n yields the following formula for unequal Ns:

$$t = g \sqrt{\frac{N_1 N_2}{N_1 + N_2}}$$

Applying the above formula to the caffeine study yields the same t value, of course, that we calculated with the more direct formula:

$$t = .9 \sqrt{\frac{440}{42}} = .9 \times 3.237 = 2.91.$$

The t Test for Matched Samples

Suppose that you want to test the hypothesis that in families with two children, the first-born is more introverted than the second-born. Once again, the question of interest concerns a comparison between the means of two populations, and the null and alternative hypotheses are as follows:

$$H_0: \mu_{\text{first-born}} = \mu_{\text{second-born}}$$

$$H_1: \mu_{\text{first-born}} \neq \mu_{\text{second-born}}$$

To obtain your samples, you randomly select *matched pairs* of children, with each pair consisting of the first-born child and the second-born child from a given family. You then administer an appropriate measure of introversion. The general format of the resulting data would be as follows:

Pair	First-born (X_1)		Second-born (X_2)
1	65	matched	61
2	48	matched	42
3	63	matched	66
⋮	⋮		⋮
N	66	matched	69

The first-born child from family 1 has an introversion score of 65, and the second-born child from family 1 has an introversion score of 61. Similarly, each pair of children is matched by virtue of coming from the same family.

To illustrate a second (and perhaps more common) use of matched samples, let us suppose that you wish to test the effect of a persuasive message on people's attitudes toward gun control. Each subject's attitude is measured *before* receiving the message (X_1) and again *after* receiving the message (X_2). For pair 1, the score of 65 could represent the attitude of the first subject before hearing the persuasive message, and the score of 61 could represent the *same* subject's attitude after hearing the message. Each subject therefore serves as his or her own control, and each pair of scores is matched by virtue of coming from the same subject. (It would be desirable to have additional control groups in this study, but this is beyond the present point.)

The statistical analysis described previously in this chapter involved *independent* random samples. That is, there was no connection between any specific individual in sample 1 and any specific individual in sample 2. This approach is *not* suitable for matched samples. To analyze matched pair data (of either of the two types described above), procedures are used that are similar to those already developed in Chapter 10. Since each score in sample 1 has a paired counterpart in sample 2, you can subtract each X_1 from each X_2 and obtain a difference score (denoted by D). Then, you can use the techniques of the previous chapter for drawing inferences about the mean of one population— the mean of the population of difference scores.

To illustrate this procedure, let us look at the heart rates for 10 students from Sara's class; the data for the baseline and prequiz heart rates are shown in Table 11.2. The difference scores are shown in the last column of the table; note that the *sign* of each difference score must be retained. The null and alternative hypotheses are now as follows:

$$H_0: \mu_D = 0$$

$$H_1: \mu_D \neq 0$$

H_0 states that the mean of the population of difference scores is zero, and H_1 states that the mean of the population of difference scores is not zero. The next step is to compute the mean difference score obtained from the sample, $\overline{D}$:

$$\overline{D} = \frac{\sum D}{N} = \frac{60}{10} = 6.0$$

Note that N is not necessarily the number of different participants, but the number of *paired measurements*, which may be the number of *pairs* of subjects. As is shown in Table 11.2, $\overline{D}$ is equal to $\overline{X}_2 - \overline{X}_1$.[4] Thus, testing the hy-

---

4. We are subtracting X_1 from X_2 in this example to reduce the number of difference scores that are negative. This changes the sign, but not the magnitude, of the t value that we will calculate. Therefore, the order of subtraction does not affect our chances of attaining statistical significance.

TABLE 11.2

Heart rate in bpm before and after the announcement of a pop statistics quiz

Student	Baseline HR (X_1)	Prequiz HR (X_2)	$D = (\bar{X}_2 - \bar{X}_1)$
1	70	77	+7
2	66	75	+9
3	73	68	−5
4	62	62	0
5	74	89	+15
6	63	74	+11
7	64	62	−2
8	65	73	+8
9	71	76	+5
10	72	84	+12
Σ	680	740	+60
Mean	68.0	74.0	6.0
SD	4.472	8.59	6.48

pothesis that $\mu_D = 0$ is equivalent to testing the hypothesis that $\mu_1 - \mu_2 = 0$, or that $\mu_1 = \mu_2$.

To test the hypothesis about the mean of one population, you compare the sample mean to the hypothesized value of the population mean and divide by the standard error of the mean, as follows:

$$t = \frac{\bar{D} - \mu_D}{\sqrt{\dfrac{s_D^2}{N}}}$$

Here, s_D^2 is equal to the estimated population variance of the difference scores, computed by the usual formula:

$$s_D^2 = \frac{\sum (D - \bar{D})^2}{N - 1} \quad \text{or} \quad s_D^2 = \frac{\sum D^2 - \dfrac{(\sum D)^2}{N}}{N - 1}$$

Since the hypothesized value of μ_D is generally zero, the t formula may be simplified to

$$t = \frac{\bar{D}}{\sqrt{s_D^2/N}}$$

These two steps may be summarized by the following (algebraically identical) computing formula:

$$t = \frac{\sum D}{\sqrt{\dfrac{N \sum D^2 - (\sum D)^2}{N - 1}}}$$

As is normally the case in tests concerning one population mean, the number of degrees of freedom on which t is based is equal to one less than the number of scores, or

$$df = (\text{number of } pairs) - 1$$

If the computed t is smaller in absolute value than the value of t obtained from the table for the appropriate degrees of freedom, retain H_0; otherwise reject H_0 in favor of H_1.

Returning to Sara's heart rate study, the analysis of the data is as follows:

$$\alpha = .05$$

$$\sum D = 60, \qquad \bar{D} = 6.0, \qquad \sum D^2 = 738$$

$$s_D^2 = \frac{738 - \dfrac{(60)^2}{10}}{9} = \frac{378}{9} = 42$$

$$t = \frac{6.0}{\sqrt{42/10}} = \frac{6}{2.05} = 2.93$$

The critical value of t obtained from Table B for $(10 - 1)$ or 9 degrees of freedom is 2.26. Since the obtained t value of 2.93 is larger in absolute value than the critical value, you can reject H_0: There is sufficient reason to believe that the announcement of a surprise quiz increases the mean heart rate of the population being sampled.

Confidence intervals may be established in the usual way. The critical value of t is 2.26, and the standard error of the mean is equal to $\sqrt{42/10}$ or 2.05. The 95% confidence interval is

$$6 - (2.26)(2.05) \leq \mu_D \leq 6 + (2.26)(2.05)$$

$$1.37 \leq \mu_D \leq 10.63$$

As would be expected from the rejection of the null hypothesis, the value of zero does *not* fall within this interval.

Comparing the t Test for Matched Pairs with the t Test for Independent Samples

To demonstrate more clearly the usual advantage of the matched-pairs design, let us perform an independent-samples t test on the heart rate data. For this demonstration, we will ignore the connection between the two columns of HR data in Table 11.2. Instead, we will treat the 10 baseline HR measurements as though they come from one group of students, while the 10 prequiz HR measurements come from another, completely separate, group of students. Because our two "independent" sets of HR data are the same size, we can use the following simplified formula for the independent-samples t test:

$$t = \frac{\overline{X}_1 - \overline{X}_2}{\sqrt{\dfrac{s_1^2 + s_2^2}{n}}},$$

where n is the size of *each* sample. The numerator of the t test remains the same whether you apply the matched-pairs t test or the independent-samples t test to a given set of data (in this example the numerator is 6 bpm); it is the denominator that is likely to change. We will now use the standard deviations we included at the bottom of each column of HR data in Table 11.2. They are squared to yield variances and inserted in the foregoing formula to obtain the following result:

$$t = \frac{74 - 68}{\sqrt{\dfrac{73.8 + 20}{10}}} = \frac{6}{3.063} = 1.96$$

We do gain additional degrees of freedom by treating the two sets of measurements as independent. For the matched-pairs design, the df was one less than the number of *pairs,* or 9. For the independent-samples design, the df would be $10 + 10 - 2 = 18$. This lowers the critical value of the independent test relative to the matched-pairs test from 2.262 to 2.101. However, the t value calculated for the independent-samples t test (1.96) is smaller than even this reduced critical value (2.101), so the independent-samples t test would *not* be statistically significant. In contrast, matching the HR scores in pairs (based on the two measures coming from the same student) resulted in a decrease in the denominator of the t test from 3.063 for the independent t test to 2.05 for the matched-pairs test, and this increased the calculated t value from 1.96 to 2.93. This increase made the results statistically significant, enabling Sara to conclude that her heart rate study "worked."

The extent to which matching the scores in pairs increases the t value relative to the independent-samples test, and thus makes statistical significance more likely, depends on how highly the two sets of scores are correlated. We will discuss correlation in detail in the next chapter. For now, we will simply state that when two sets of scores are positively correlated, one score *tends* to increase when the score paired with it increases. (For example, higher baseline HRs *tend* to be associated with higher prequiz HRs.) In general, measuring the same experimental participant twice, called the *repeated-measures* (RM) design, leads to higher correlations than matching separate participants into pairs. However, the latter design can be very helpful when the RM design is not feasible.

The Different Types of Matched-Pairs Designs

The matched-pairs (difference-score) t formula we just described can be applied to the results of several different experimental designs, which are described next.

The Repeated-Measures (RM) Design

The RM design works well if your experiment consists of many similar trials of one type that can be randomly mixed with the same number of trials of some other type. Suppose that participants are told to indicate, as soon as they know it, the missing letter of a word presented on a screen (e.g., POLI_E). Before each word is presented, a priming word is flashed subliminally on the same screen. There are two types of trials: Either the priming stimulus is a word that is relevant to one of the solutions (e.g., "crime" for POLICE, or "manners" for POLI*T*E), or it is an irrelevant word (e.g., "basket"). Because the two types of trials are mixed together in a random order, the experimental participant cannot know which type of trial will be presented next. The reaction times can then be averaged separately for the two types of trials for each participant, so each participant ultimately contributes a pair of scores that can be used to create a difference score for the matched-pairs t test.

The RM design is potentially more problematic when you cannot mix the two conditions together but must present one condition before the other. The simplest type of *successive* RM design is the before-after design. Our heart rate example falls into this category because HR was measured both *before* and *after* the announcement of the quiz. In order to draw conclusions from a before-after design, a separate control group is usually required. We will not discuss this issue further until Chapter 18.

The other type of successive RM design involves two different experimental conditions. Suppose you want to see if more clerical tasks are correctly performed in a given time interval while participants listen to happy, as compared to sad, music. It would not be a fair comparison of the two conditions to present the same type of music first for all of the participants; it is possible, for instance, that the participants will perform better in the second condition because of the practice they received during the first condition. The common solution to this problem is *counterbalancing:* Half of the subjects perform the tasks first with happy music and then with sad music, while the other half of the subjects are assigned to the reverse order (i.e., sad music first). Counterbalancing averages out *simple order effects,* such as those due to practice or fatigue, but it does not help if you have *differential carry-over effects.* For example, if you want to compare the effects of two different types of strategies on problem solving, participants may not be able to stop themselves from employing the first strategy they are given when it is time for them to solve similar problems with a second strategy. To avoid carry-over effects while still gaining at least some of the benefit of correlated sets of scores, you can match your participants into pairs based on some relevant similarity. Although the same statistical procedure (i.e., the matched-pairs *t* test) is used for both designs, from now on we will use the term *RM design* when the same participant is measured twice, and reserve the term *matched-pairs* (MP) *design* for the case in which two different participants have been matched together based on some relevant similarity.

The Matched-Pairs (MP) Design

For some types of experiments, the RM design is not a reasonable option. Suppose you want to compare two methods for teaching children to read. It would make little sense to teach a child to read by one method for 6 months, measure his or her reading ability, and then teach the same child for another 6 months with the other method. The potential for misleading carry-over effects rules out the possibility of counterbalancing. However, the RM design can be approximated by testing the children on various prereading skills and then matching the children into pairs based on the similarity of their prereading scores, as well as their ages and genders. Some random event, like the flip of a coin, should be used to decide which child in each pair is assigned to each reading method. When the experiment is completed, and all the children have had their reading abilities measured, the reading scores of the two children in a pair are treated as though they were two scores from the same child measured twice: The difference is calculated for the two members of each pair, and then these difference scores are subjected to a matched-pairs *t* test as described for the heart rate example.

There are situations in which the RM design is not feasible but there is no relevant information that can be used to match the participants in pairs. For example, you may wish to test the effects of the level of the experimenter's apparent aggressiveness on the willingness of the participants to donate their time for future experiments. Because you will not have the advantage of correlated sets of scores, you need to make sure that your samples are large enough to have a good chance of attaining significance with the effect size you expect. We show how you can estimate the sample size that you will need when we discuss the topic of power in Chapter 14.

Summary

To test null hypotheses about *differences between the means of two populations,* perform one of the following procedures.

1. For Independent Samples

First compute

$$s^2_{pooled} = \frac{(N_1 - 1)s_1^2 + (N_2 - 1)s_2^2}{N_1 + N_2 - 2}$$

Then use

$$t = \frac{\overline{X}_1 - \overline{X}_2}{s_{\overline{X}_1 - \overline{X}_2}} = \frac{\overline{X}_1 - \overline{X}_2}{\sqrt{s^2_{pooled}\left(\dfrac{1}{N_1} + \dfrac{1}{N_2}\right)}}$$

with

$$df = N_1 + N_2 - 2,$$

where

$$s_{\overline{X}_1 - \overline{X}_2} = \text{the estimated standard error of the difference}$$

a measure of how accurate the observed difference between the sample means is likely to be as an estimate of the difference between the population means.

Reject H_0 if the computed value of t, ignoring the sign, is greater than the critical value of t obtained from the t table. Note that this t formula may well yield misleading results if σ_1^2 and σ_2^2 are markedly unequal *and* also N_1 and N_2 are markedly unequal. In such a case, the separate-variances t test may be preferable.

When you reject H_0 it is likely that you will want to estimate the true difference between the population means with a confidence interval. The formula for the CI in the two-group case is very similar to the CI for a single population:

$$[(\overline{X}_1 - \overline{X}_2) - ts_{\overline{X}_1 - \overline{X}_2}] \leq \mu_1 - \mu_2 \leq [(\overline{X}_1 - \overline{X}_2) + ts_{\overline{X}_1 - \overline{X}_2}],$$

where

$$t = \text{critical value obtained from the } t \text{ table for the specified criterion of significance for the appropriate } df$$

Another useful way to describe the size of the effect you found in your data is by calculating a standardized measure of effect size, such as g:

$$g = \frac{\overline{X}_1 - \overline{X}_2}{s_p},$$

where s_p is the square root of the pooled variance (s^2_{pooled}).

2. For Matched Samples

First compute a difference score (symbolized by D) for each pair, where

$$D = X_1 - X_2$$

Next, compute the *variance* of the D scores, using the usual formula for the variance of a sample (Chapter 5). Then use

$$t = \frac{\overline{D}}{\sqrt{\dfrac{s_D^2}{N}}}$$

with

$$df = (\text{number of pairs}) - 1,$$

where

$$\overline{D} = \text{mean of the } D \text{ scores}$$

$$s_D^2 = \text{variance of the } D \text{ scores}$$

$$N = \text{number of pairs}$$

This procedure may be summarized in the following computing formula, which yields exactly the same result:

$$t = \frac{\sum D}{\sqrt{\dfrac{N \sum D^2 - (\sum D)^2}{N - 1}}}$$

with

$$df = (\text{number of pairs}) - 1$$

Here again, reject H_0 if the computed value of t (ignoring the sign) is greater than the critical value of t obtained from the t table.

For matched samples, confidence intervals can be computed in the usual way, using the standard error of the mean of the differences. The formula looks like this:

$$\overline{D} - t_{\text{crit}} s_{\overline{D}} \leq \mu_D \leq \overline{D} + t_{\text{crit}} s_{\overline{D}},$$

where

$$s_{\bar{D}} = \sqrt{\frac{s_D^2}{N}}$$

Note once again that confidence intervals provide considerably more information than do null hypothesis tests.

The formula for the matched-pairs t test can be used whether the same individual is being measured twice (RM design) or participants are being matched in pairs (MP design). The RM design usually leads to the larger t value, but it may produce misleading results if there are strong carry-over effects. The MP design provides much of the benefit of the RM design without the possibility of carry-over effects. As long as there is a reasonably high, positive correlation between the two sets of scores, the MP design can be counted on to yield higher t values than an independent-samples t test on the same data, due to a reduction in the denominator of the t formula.

Exercises

1. Use the two-sample t test to determine whether the difference in means between University A and University B is significant at the .05 level, two-tailed. Given your decision with respect to the null hypothesis, which type of error could you be making: Type I or Type II? Report the results of your t test in a sentence that includes the means of the two universities.

2. An industrial psychologist obtains scores on a job-selection test from 41 men and 31 women, with the following results: men, $M = 48.75$ (SD $= 9.0$); women, $M = 46.07$ (SD $= 10.0$). Test this difference for significance at both the .05 and .01 levels (two-tailed).

3. Suppose that the industrial psychologist from the previous exercise is testing the difference in performance on the job-selection test of two different ethnic groups. Given the following data, can the psychologist reject the null hypothesis (alpha $= .05$) that the population means of these two groups are the same for the job-selection test she is investigating?

Group 1	Group 2
62	46
54	53
59	50
56	52
59	54

4. Repeat exercise 3 for the following two sets of summary statistics. In each case, determine if the results would be significant for a one-tailed as well as a two-tailed test.

(a)		Group 1	Group 2
	$\bar{X}$	17.34	21.58
	s	5.83	4.42
	N	32	30

(b)		Group 1	Group 2
	$\bar{X}$	76.57	69.72
	s	20.15	22.87
	N	17	15

5. An educational psychologist has developed a new textbook based on programmed instruction techniques and wishes to know if it is superior to the
conventional kind of textbook. He therefore obtains subjects who have had
no prior exposure to the material and forms two groups: an experimental
group, which learns via the programmed text, and a control group, which
learns via the old-fashioned textbook.

   The psychologist is afraid, however, that one group may differ from the
other in intelligence. If such is the case, differences in the effectiveness of
one or the other of the learning procedures may be obscured by differences
in ability to learn. Therefore, he matches his subjects on intelligence and
forms 10 pairs of subjects such that each pair is made up of two people
roughly equal in intelligence test scores.

   After both groups have learned the material, the psychologist measures
the amount of learning by means of a 10-item quiz. The results are as follows:

Pair	Experimental group (programmed text)	Control group (standard text)
1	9	7
2	6	4
3	5	6
4	7	3
5	3	5
6	7	3
7	3	2
8	4	5
9	6	7
10	10	8

Test the results for statistical significance at the .05 level. What should the
psychologist decide about his new programmed text?

6. For the following set of data, assume that the X score represents the subject's performance in the experimental condition and that the Y score represents the subject's performance in the control condition. (Thus, each sub-

ject serves as his or her own control.) Compute the *matched t* test for these data.

Data set 3, Chapter 1		
S	X	Y
1	97	89
2	68	57
3	85	87
4	74	76
5	92	97
6	92	79
7	100	91
8	63	50
9	85	85
10	87	84
11	81	91
12	93	91
13	77	75
14	82	77

7. Now carry out a matched *t* test for the same set of data as in exercise 6, but with *X* rearranged as shown.

S	X	Y
1	92	89
2	82	57
3	85	87
4	81	76
5	87	97
6	93	79
7	68	91
8	85	50
9	63	85
10	100	84
11	74	91
12	77	91
13	92	75
14	97	77

Thought Questions

1. (a) What is the difference between *random sampling* and *random assignment?* (b) What similar purpose do these two procedures have? (c) Which one is usually much easier to do? Why?

2. A behavioral science researcher wishes to test a null hypothesis about the difference between the means of two populations. (a) What statistical

model should the researcher use? (b) Would the researcher prefer that the standard error of the difference be relatively small or large? Why? (c) If the size of one or both samples becomes larger, what happens to the standard error of the difference? Why? (d) If the standard deviation of the individual scores in one or both populations becomes larger, what happens to the standard error of the difference? Why?

3. The difference between two means is statistically significant. (a) What decision should the researcher make about the null hypothesis? (b) Assuming that all of the procedures and calculations in this experiment were done correctly, why might this decision still be incorrect? (c) If this decision is incorrect, which type of error would the researcher be making, Type I or Type II? (d) What are the practical consequences of making this error?

4. A behavioral science researcher uses a standardized measure of intelligence that has a mean of 100 and a standard deviation of 15. The researcher obtains a very large sample of American men and a very large sample of American women and finds that the mean for men is 102.56, the mean for women is 104.84, and this difference is statistically significant. Use this example to show that a statistically significant difference does *not* necessarily indicate that the results have any practical importance.

5. The difference between two means is *not* statistically significant. (a) What decision should the researcher make about the null hypothesis? (b) Assuming that all of the procedures and calculations in this experiment were done correctly, why might this decision still be incorrect? (c) Does the criterion of significance give the probability that this decision is incorrect? (d) If this decision is incorrect, which type of error would the researcher be making, Type I or Type II? (e) What are the practical consequences of making this error? (f) Should the researcher conclude that the two population means are equal? Why or why not?

6. If the difference between two means is statistically significant, will zero be included in the 95% confidence interval for the difference between the two population means? Why or why not?

7. Students at University Z claim that their school is superior to vaunted Bigbrain University with regard to achievement on a national aptitude test, where the mean is 500 and the standard deviation is 100. A random sample of students is obtained from each university, the mean for the University Z sample is found to be higher than the mean for the Bigbrain University sample, and the 95% confidence interval for the difference between two means is computed. What should the University Z students conclude if this confidence interval is (a) –7.63 to 13.44? (b) 2.27 to 19.85? (c) 97.22 to 122.44? (d) Compare examples (b) and (c). How does this comparison illustrate the advantages that confidence intervals have over testing a specific null hypothesis, such as whether the difference between the means of University Z and Bigbrain University is zero?

8. (a) What is the difference between the t test for two independent sample means and the matched-pairs t test? (b) Since the same statistical procedure is used for both, what is the difference between the matched-pairs design and the repeated-measures design?

Computer Exercises

1. Use your statistical package to perform a two-sample t test to determine whether there is a statistically significant difference in baseline anxiety between the men and the women of Sara's class. Find the 95% CI for this gender difference. Report your results as they might appear in a journal article.

2. Repeat exercise 1 for heart rate.

3. Perform a two-sample t test to determine whether the students in the "impossible to solve" condition exhibited significantly higher postquiz heart rates than the students in the "easy to solve" condition at the .05 level. Is this t test significant at the .01 level? Find the 99% CI for the difference of the two population means and explain its connection to your decision regarding the null hypothesis at the .01 level.

4. Repeat exercise 3 for the postquiz anxiety scores.

5. Perform a matched-pairs t test to determine whether there is a significant increase in heart rate from baseline to the prequiz measurement. Also, test the difference between the pre- and postquiz measurements. (Advanced exercise: Repeat these paired t tests separately for men and women.)

6. Repeat exercise 5 for the anxiety measurements.

Bridge to SPSS

Before you perform an independent-samples t test in SPSS, you should have one column for your grouping variable (usually, "1"s and "2"s), and one for your dependent variable. The matched-pairs t test requires instead that you have two columns for your dependent variable; each column represents your DV measured under a different condition.

Independent-Samples t Test

To perform a two-sample t test in SPSS, select Compare Means from the Analyze menu, and then choose **Independent-Samples T Test. . . .** In the dialog box that opens, move the variable that distinguishes your two groups (e.g., gender) to the area labeled **Grouping Variable:**. Doing that activates the **Define Groups . . .** button; click this button and then enter the numeric values of your two groups. If your grouping variable has more than two values (e.g., undergrad major), you can compare any two of them by specifying their values as Group 1 and Group 2. Move the dependent variable (DV) you want to test to the Test Variable(s) area (the grouping variable is often thought of as the independent variable, but in many cases it is not truly an IV, because it is just selected for, and not created by, the experimenter). Note that you can test many DVs at the same time. The **Options . . .** button allows you to exclude cases listwise (as explained in the previous chapter), and also to select the percentage that will be used to create a confidence interval for the difference of the two population means.

The default output for this test consists of two boxes, the first of which presents descriptive statistics for the two groups. The second box contains both the pooled-variances t test (labeled "Equal variances assumed") and the separate-variances t test (labeled "Equal variances not assumed"). To the left of the t values is a test for homogeneity of variance ("Levene's Test for Equality of Variances"); if the "Sig." (the term SPSS uses for p value) for this test is less than .05, reliance on the separate-variances t test is recommended, particularly if the two samples are not the same size. To the right of the "df" (which usually involves a fraction for the separate-variances test) is the two-tailed p value for each version of the t test, labeled "Sig. (2-tailed)."

Matched-Pairs t Test

To perform a matched-pairs t test in SPSS, select Compare Means from the Analyze menu, and then choose **Paired-Samples T Test. . . .** In the dialog box that opens, under the list of variables, you will see an area labeled **Current Selections,** which contains space for "Variable 1" and "Variable 2." The first time that you click on a variable in the list, the name of that variable appears to the right of Variable 1; the second time you select a variable, it appears to the right of Variable 2, and the right-facing triangle becomes active, allowing you to move the *pair* of variables you selected over to the "Paired Variables:" area. Before you move a pair of variables over, you can change one or both of the variables in the pair, and, of course, you can always remove a pair of variables from the Paired Variables area by highlighting it, and clicking the triangle that will then be pointing to the left. The Options are the same as for the Independent-Samples test.

The default output for the paired-samples t test consists of three boxes, the first of which is the same as the first box for the Independent-Samples test. The second box presents the correlation between the two sets of scores and its p value (labeled "Sig.," as usual); we will have more to say about this statistical measure in the next chapter. The third box contains the t value for the matched-pairs test, its df, and its two-tailed p value. Notice that to the left of these values, the box contains descriptive statistics for the Paired Differences. The first three entries are labeled Mean (the mean of the difference scores, which is the numerator of the t formula), Std. Deviation (the unbiased standard deviation of the difference scores), and Std. Error Mean (the standard error of the mean for the difference scores, which is the denominator of the t formula).

Chapter 12
Linear Correlation and Prediction

PREVIEW

Introduction

What is meant by the correlation between two variables?

What is a positive correlation? A negative correlation?

What is a scatter plot?

How is the ability to make predictions related to correlation?

What is a linear relationship?

Describing the Linear Relationship between Two Variables

What does the z score difference formula for r tell us about the meaning of the correlation coefficient?

Why is it easier to determine the numerical value of r by using the computing (or raw score) formula?

Interpreting the Magnitude of a Pearson r

If two variables are significantly correlated, does this mean that one of the variables causes the other?

How can restriction of range lead to misleading conclusions about the correlation between two variables?

How can the presence of bivariate outliers in a data set lead to misleading conclusions about the correlation between two variables?

When Is It Important That Pearson's r Be Large?

What are the different types of reliability for which the Pearson r is frequently used?

What is the validity of a measure, and why is it important that it be large?

Testing the Significance of the Correlation Coefficient

What are the procedures for testing hypotheses about the population correlation coefficient (usually, that it is equal to zero)?

How much confidence can we have in our conclusion, if we must retain the null hypothesis?

How is it possible for two variables to have a Pearson r near zero and yet be closely related?

Under what condition can we obtain a statistically significant Pearson r that is too small to be of any practical importance?

(continued on next page)

Introduction

The independent-samples t test described in the previous chapter can be viewed as a test of association between two variables: a dichotomous (i.e., two-valued) grouping variable (e.g., gender) and a continuous dependent variable (e.g., height). This is just a special case of a more general principle: Knowing an individual's value on one variable can help you to predict his or her value on another, related variable (e.g., knowing someone's gender is certainly helpful if you need to guess that individual's height). In this chapter, we will show how you can quantify the degree of the relationship between two continuous variables, and how you can use that relationship to make predictions about the values of one variable given values on the other variable.

For example, you learn early in your scholastic career that the amount of time spent in studying is related to grades. True, there are exceptions. Some stu-

FIGURE 12.1
Possible relationship between income of a family and their child's IQ

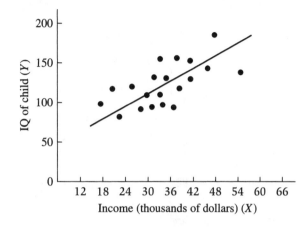

dents may study for many hours and obtain poor grades, while others may achieve high grades despite short study periods. Nevertheless, the general trend holds. In the majority of cases, you can accurately predict that little or no studying will lead to poor grades, while more studying will result in better grades. So if you are dissatisfied with grades that you feel are too low, one likely way to improve this aspect of your environment is by studying more. In statistical terminology, the two variables of "hours studying" and "grades" are said to be co-related or *correlated.*

Many pairs of variables are correlated, while many are unrelated or *uncorrelated.* For example, sociologists have found that the incomes of families are positively related to the IQs of the children in the families; the more income, the higher the children's IQs. These variables are said to be *positively correlated.* This relationship is depicted graphically in Figure 12.1, which is called a *scatter plot* (or scatter diagram) because the points scatter across the range of scores. Note that each point on the graph represents two values for one family, income (X variable) and IQ of the child (Y variable). Also, in the case of a positive correlation, the straight line summarizing the points slopes *up* from left to right.

The golf enthusiast will readily agree that the number of years of play is negatively related to his golf score: The more years of practice, the fewer strokes needed to complete a round of 18 holes. These two variables are said to be *negatively correlated.* (See Figure 12.2.) Notice that in the case of a negative correlation, the straight line summarizing the points slopes *down* from left to right.

A different picture results when two variables are uncorrelated. For example, length of big toes among male adults is uncorrelated with IQ scores, and the corresponding scatter plot is shown in Figure 12.3.

When you can demonstrate that two variables are correlated, you can use the score of an individual on one variable to *predict* or *estimate* his score on the

FIGURE 12.2

Possible relationship between years of play and average golf score

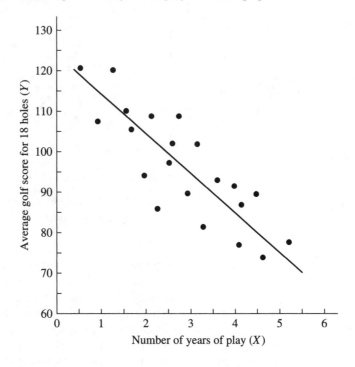

FIGURE 12.3

Possible relationship between the length of big toe and male IQ scores

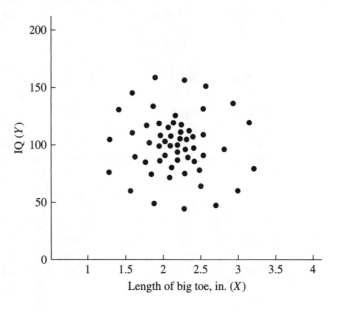

other variable. In Figure 12.2, a fairly accurate prediction of an individual's golf score can be made from the number of years she has played golf. The more closely the two variables are related, the better the prediction is likely to be; if two variables are uncorrelated (as in the case of toe length and IQ), you cannot accurately predict an individual's score on one of them from his score on the other. Thus the concepts of correlation and prediction are closely related.

This chapter deals with three main topics: (1) the *description* of the relationship between two variables for a set of observations; (2) making *inferences* about the strength of the relationship between two variables in a population, given the data of a sample; and (3) the *prediction* or estimation of values on one variable from observations on another variable with which it is paired. We will deal with one very common kind of relationship between two variables, namely a *linear* or straight-line relationship. That is, if values of one variable are plotted against values of the other variable on a graph, the trend of the plotted points is well represented by a straight line. Notice that the data plotted in Figures 12.1 and 12.2 tend to fall near or on the straight line drawn through the scatter plot; this indicates that the two variables in question are highly linearly correlated. The points in Figure 12.3, on the other hand, are scattered randomly throughout the graph and cannot be represented well by a straight line. Therefore, these two variables are linearly uncorrelated.

Many pairs of variables that are of importance to behavioral scientists tend to be linearly related. Although there are many other ways of describing relationships, the linear model is generally the one most frequently used in such fields as psychology, education, and sociology.

Describing the Linear Relationship between Two Variables

Suppose you want to measure the degree of linear relationship between a scholastic aptitude test (SAT) and college grade point average (GPA). It would be reasonable to expect these two variables to be positively correlated. This means that students with high SAT scores, on the average, obtain relatively high GPAs and students with low SAT scores, on the average, obtain low GPAs. The phrase "on the average" alerts us to the fact that there will be exceptions: Some students with low SAT scores will do well in college and obtain high GPAs, while some with high SAT scores will do poorly and receive low GPAs. That is, the relationship between SAT scores and GPA is not perfect. Thus the question arises: Just how strong *is* the relationship? How can it be summarized in a single number?

The z Score Difference Formula for r

We have seen in Chapter 7 that in order to compare scores on different variables (such as a mathematics test and a psychology test), it is useful to transform the raw scores into standard scores. These transformed scores allow you to compare paired values directly. Similarly, in order to obtain a coefficient of

TABLE 12.1

Raw scores and z scores on SAT (X) and GPA (Y) for 25 students in an eastern U.S. college

Student	X	Y	z_X	z_Y
1	650	3.8	1.29	1.67
2	625	3.6	1.08	1.31
3	480	2.8	−.16	−.09
4	440	2.6	−.50	−.44
5	600	3.7	.86	1.49
6	220	1.2	−2.37	−2.89
7	640	2.2	1.21	−1.14
8	725	3.0	1.93	.26
9	520	3.1	.18	.44
10	480	3.0	−.16	.26
11	370	2.8	−1.09	−.09
12	320	2.7	−1.52	−.26
13	425	2.6	−.62	−.44
14	475	2.6	−.20	−.44
15	490	3.1	−.07	.44
16	620	3.8	1.04	1.67
17	340	2.4	−1.35	−.79
18	420	2.9	−.67	.09
19	480	2.8	−.16	−.09
20	530	3.2	.27	.61
21	680	3.2	1.55	.61
22	420	2.4	−.67	−.79
23	490	2.8	−.07	−.09
24	500	1.9	.01	−1.67
25	520	3.0	.18	.26
$\bar{X} = 498.4$	$\bar{Y} = 2.85$		$\sigma_X = 117.33$	$\sigma_Y = .57$

relationship which describes the similarity between paired measures in a single number, it is convenient to transform the raw score into z units:

$$z_X = \frac{X - \bar{X}}{\sigma_X} \qquad z_Y = \frac{Y - \bar{Y}}{\sigma_Y}$$

In Table 12.1, a distribution of SAT scores (X) and GPAs (Y) is presented along with the corresponding descriptive statistics for 25 students at a college in the eastern United States. The SAT scores were obtained when the students were high-school seniors, and the GPAs are those received by the students after one year of college. In addition to the raw scores, the z equivalents are also shown in the table. Notice that students with high SAT scores do tend to have high GPAs and consequently large z_X and z_Y values. Conversely, students with low SAT scores tend to have low GPAs. So the paired z values are similar for most students, and the two variables are therefore highly positively correlated. The *raw scores,* however, need not be numerically similar for any pair, since they are measured in different units for each variable.

FIGURE 12.4

Perfect linear relationship between two variables: (A) Perfect positive linear relationship; (B) perfect negative linear relationship.

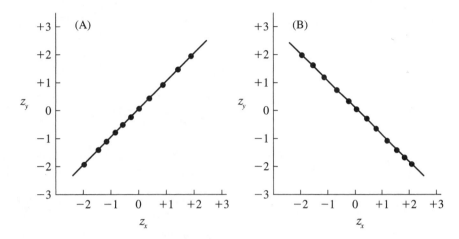

If the association between the two selected variables were perfect and in a positive direction, each person would have exactly the same z score on both variables. If the relationship were perfect but in a negative direction, each z_X value would be paired with an identical z_Y value but they would be *opposite in sign*. (See Figure 12.4.) These perfect relationships are offered for illustration and almost never occur in practice.

Since the size of the difference between paired z values is related to the amount of the relationship between the two variables, some kind of *average* of these differences should yield information about the closeness or *strength* of the association between the variables. Because the mean of the differences $z_X - x_Y$ is necessarily zero, it is helpful that the coefficient of correlation is actually obtained by *squaring* differences between paired z values. The size of the average of these squared differences,

$$\frac{\sum (z_X - z_Y)^2}{N},$$

is an index of the strength of the relationship. For example, a small value indicates a high positive correlation (little difference between the paired z values). If this average is a large number, it indicates a high negative relationship (most paired z values are "opposite" to one another). A "medium-sized" average indicates little or no relationship. This average, however, is not convenient to interpret, since (as can be proved) it ranges from zero in the case of a perfect positive correlation to 4.0 in the case of a perfect negative relationship. A much more readily interpretable coefficient is obtained by subtracting half of this average from one:

$$r_{XY} = 1 - \frac{1}{2} \frac{\sum (z_X - z_Y)^2}{N},$$

where

r_{XY} = symbol for the correlation coefficient between X and Y

N = number of *pairs*

(It should be noted that this is *not* a conventional computing formula.)
   This correlation coefficient has the following desirable characteristics:

1. A value of zero indicates no linear relationship between the two variables (that is, they are linearly uncorrelated).
2. The *size* of the numerical value of the coefficient indicates the *strength* of the relationship. Large absolute values mean that the two variables are closely related, and small absolute values mean that they are only weakly related.
3. The *sign* of the coefficient indicates the *direction* of the relationship.
4. The largest possible positive value is +1.00, and the largest possible negative value is −1.00.

   Thus, if the correlation between two variables is +.20, you can tell at a glance that the relationship between them is positive and weak (since it is far from the maximum of +1). A correlation of −.80 would indicate a strong negative relationship.
   The correlation coefficient may be symbolized more simply by r when there is no possible confusion as to which two variables are involved. This coefficient is often referred to as the Pearson r in honor of Karl Pearson, who did the early work on this measure starting with an idea of Francis Galton's.
   To clarify the meaning of the above formula, let us suppose that we have a small set of four paired X and Y scores, obtained from two quizzes in a small college seminar. (Four pairs would be far too few to permit a useful conclusion in a real experiment, but it will be easier to illustrate the concept if very few numbers are involved.) Let us first suppose that the results are as follows:

Student	X	Y	z_X	z_Y	$z_X - z_Y$
1	8	29	+1.266	+1.266	0
2	7	26	+.633	+.633	0
3	5	20	−.633	−.633	0
4	4	17	−1.266	−1.266	0

Note that the paired z values are identical in each case, indicating a perfect positive relationship. There is no difference between any of the corresponding z values, so the correlation coefficient is equal to

$$r = 1 - \frac{1}{2}\,\frac{(0)^2 + (0)^2 + (0)^2 + (0)^2}{4}$$

$$= 1 - \frac{1}{2}(0)$$

$$= +1.00$$

Thus, the smallest possible mean of $(z_X - z_Y)^2$ is 0. So the largest possible positive value of r is +1, the value that occurs when the relationship between the two variables is perfect and positive.

Now let us suppose that the results are instead as follows:

Student	X	Y	z_X	z_Y	$z_X - z_Y$
1	8	17	+1.266	−1.266	+2.532
2	7	20	+.633	−.633	+1.266
3	5	26	−.633	+.633	−1.266
4	4	29	−1.266	+1.266	−2.532

In this case, the relationship between the two variables is perfect and negative. This is indicated by the fact that the paired z values for each person are equal but opposite in sign. In other words, high scores on X are paired with low scores on Y, and low scores on X are paired with high scores on Y. The correlation coefficient is equal to

$$r = 1 - \frac{1}{2}\,\frac{(+2.532)^2 + (+1.266)^2 + (-1.266)^2 + (-2.532)^2}{4}$$

$$= 1 - \frac{1}{2}\left(\frac{16}{4}\right)$$

$$= 1 - \frac{1}{2}(4)$$

$$= 1 - 2$$

$$= -1.00$$

Thus the largest possible value of the mean of $(z_X - z_Y)^2$ is 4, as stated above. So the largest possible negative value of r is −1, the value that occurs when the relationship between the two variables is perfect and negative.

Finally, let us suppose that the results are instead as follows:

Student	X	Y	z_X	z_Y	$z_X - z_Y$
1	8	20	+1.266	−.633	+1.899
2	7	29	+.633	+1.266	−.633
3	5	17	−.633	−1.266	+.633
4	4	26	−1.266	+.633	−1.899

Here there is no linear relationship at all between X and Y, as is shown by the paired z values, and the correlation coefficient is equal to

$$r = 1 - \frac{1}{2} \frac{(+1.899)^2 + (-.633)^2 + (+.633)^2 + (-1.899)^2}{4}$$

$$= 1 - \frac{1}{2}\left(\frac{8}{4}\right)$$

$$= 1 - \frac{1}{2}(2)$$

$$= 1 - 1$$

$$= 0$$

The correlation coefficient can take on any value between −1.00 and +1.00. Equal numerical values of r describe equally strong relationships between variables. For example, coefficients of +.50 and −.50 describe relationships which are equally strong but are in opposite directions.

Computing Formulas for r

The preceding procedure for obtaining r, although helpful for understanding the meaning of r, is much too tedious computationally even with a calculator. (Proofs of the equivalence of all of the various formulas for r are given in the Appendix at the end of this chapter.) It can be shown, however, that identical results are obtained by calculating the mean of the *product* of the paired z values:

$$r_{XY} = \frac{\sum z_X z_Y}{N}$$

We can avoid the necessity for converting to z values by rewriting the preceding formula as

$$r_{XY} = \frac{\sum (X - \bar{X})(Y - \bar{Y})}{N\sigma_X \sigma_Y}$$

The preceding formula can be rearranged algebraically to produce the following convenient *raw-score formula for the Pearson correlation coefficient:*

$$r = \frac{\dfrac{\sum XY}{N} - \overline{X}\overline{Y}}{\sigma_X \sigma_Y},$$

where N is the number of *pairs* of observations (i.e., the number of cases).

The numerator of this formula (the average of the raw-score cross-products minus the cross-product of the two averages) is called the *covariance*. When relatively large scores on one variable are paired with relatively large scores on the other, and small scores with small scores, the average of the cross-products tends to be larger than the cross-product of the averages, producing a positive correlation. When relatively large scores on one variable are paired with relatively small scores on the other, this relationship is reversed, leading to a negative correlation. When scores are paired randomly, the two parts of the numerator of r tend to be about the same, leading to an r that is near zero.

The calculation of the Pearson r for the SAT and GPA data in Table 12.1, using both the raw-score and z product formulas, is shown in Table 12.2. Note that the discrepancy in the results of these two formulas (.64 for raw scores vs. .65 for z products) is due to rounding off the means and standard deviations in Table 12.1, which were then used in the calculations in Table 12.2. The raw-score formula is only as accurate as the number of digits you retain for the means and SDs of the two variables.

Another limitation of the raw-score formula used in Table 12.2 is that it is based on using the biased SDs in its denominator (the numerator is a *biased* estimate of the covariance), and it is more likely that you will have calculated the unbiased SD if you were thinking of drawing inferences from your data. If you want to use s's rather than σ's in the denominator of the raw-score formula, the bias of the covariance in the numerator must be corrected as well. The resulting formula is not as neat as the one used on the left side of Table 12.2, but it always gives the same answer for r (except for any differences in rounding off):

$$r = \frac{\dfrac{1}{N-1}[\sum XY - N\overline{X}\overline{Y}]}{s_X s_Y}$$

The obtained value of $+.65$ indicates that for this group of 25 students, there is a fairly high positive correlation between these two variables. (In fact, this value is higher than most correlations that you would get in the behavioral sciences, unless you are measuring essentially the *same* variable in two different ways.) A scatter plot of the data in Table 12.1 is shown in Figure 12.5.

The Before-After Heart Rate Example

In the previous chapter we mentioned that the larger the correlation between two sets of scores, the more the denominator of the matched-pairs t formula

TABLE 12.2

Calculation of Pearson correlation coefficient between SAT (X) and GPA (Y) by the raw score and z product methods

	Raw-score method			z product method		
Subject	X	Y	XY	z_X	z_Y	$z_X z_Y$
1	650	3.8	2470	1.29	1.67	2.1543
2	625	3.6	2250	1.08	1.31	1.4148
3	480	2.8	1344	−.16	−.09	.0144
4	440	2.6	1144	−.50	−.44	.2200
5	600	3.7	2220	.86	1.49	1.2814
6	220	1.2	264	−2.37	−2.89	6.8493
7	640	2.2	1408	1.21	−1.14	−1.3794
8	725	3.0	2175	1.93	.26	.5018
9	520	3.1	1612	.18	.44	.0792
10	480	3.0	1440	−.16	.26	−.0416
11	370	2.8	1036	−1.09	−.09	.0981
12	320	2.7	864	−1.52	−.26	.3952
13	425	2.6	1105	−.62	−.44	.2728
14	475	2.6	1235	−.20	−.44	.0880
15	490	3.1	1519	−.07	.44	−.0308
16	620	3.8	2356	1.04	1.67	1.7368
17	340	2.4	816	−1.35	−.79	1.0665
18	420	2.9	1218	−.67	.09	−.0603
19	480	2.8	1344	−.16	−.09	.0144
20	530	3.2	1696	.27	.61	.1647
21	680	3.2	2176	1.55	.61	.9455
22	420	2.4	1008	−.67	−.79	.5293
23	490	2.8	1372	−.07	−.09	.0063
24	500	1.9	950	.01	−1.67	−.0167
25	520	3.0	1560	.18	−.26	.0468

$$\sum X = 12{,}460 \quad \overline{X} = 498.4$$
$$\sum Y = 71.2 \quad \overline{Y} = 2.85$$
$$\sum XY = 36{,}582 \quad N = 25$$

$$\sum z_X z_Y = 16.35$$
$$N = 25$$

$$r = \frac{\dfrac{\sum XY}{N} - \overline{X}\overline{Y}}{\sigma_X \sigma_Y} = \frac{\dfrac{36{,}582}{25} - (498.4)(2.85)}{(117.33)(.57)}$$

$$= \frac{1{,}463.28 - 1420.44}{66.8781} = \frac{42.84}{66.8781}$$

$$= +.64$$

$$r = \frac{\sum z_X z_Y}{N}$$

$$= \frac{16.35}{25}$$

$$= +.65$$

decreases relative to the denominator of the independent-samples test. As another example of calculating r, let us see just how large the correlation is between the baseline (i.e., prequiz) and postquiz heart rates of the first 10 students in Sara's data set. Because we have already calculated the s's for these data in the previous chapter, we will use the Pearson r formula that is based on the unbiased standard deviations.

FIGURE 12.5

Scatter plot for data in Table 12.1 ($r = +.65$)

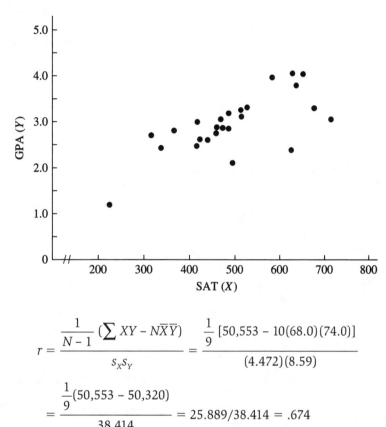

$$r = \frac{\dfrac{1}{N-1}\left(\sum XY - N\overline{X}\,\overline{Y}\right)}{s_X s_Y} = \frac{\dfrac{1}{9}\left[50{,}553 - 10(68.0)(74.0)\right]}{(4.472)(8.59)}$$

$$= \frac{\dfrac{1}{9}(50{,}553 - 50{,}320)}{38.414} = 25.889/38.414 = .674$$

Once you have calculated r for sets of paired scores, you can use an alternative formula for the matched-pairs t test that is based on r. This formula is not really easier to use than the one we introduced in the previous chapter, but it is instructive to see how it uses the Pearson r to obtain its result. This formula, applied to the heart rate data, yields the following result:

$$t = \frac{\overline{X}_1 - \overline{X}_2}{\sqrt{\dfrac{s_1^2 + s_2^2}{n} - \dfrac{2rs_1 s_2}{n}}} = \frac{74 - 68}{\sqrt{\dfrac{20 + 73.79}{10} - \dfrac{2(.674)(4.472)(8.59)}{10}}}$$

$$= \frac{6}{\sqrt{9.379 - 5.178}} = \frac{6}{2.05} = 2.93$$

Note that this alternative formula always yields the same t value as the formula for difference scores. However, an inspection of the alternative formula reveals an important principle: As Pearson's r increases (all else remaining the same), a larger portion is subtracted from the denominator, making the t value larger. When r is zero, the second term in the denominator drops out and you are left with the equal-N formula for the independent-samples t test. Also note that a Pearson r does not have to be large or statistically significant to be helpful. Moreover, a large, statistically significant r certainly does not guarantee a significant matched-pairs t test. The difference between the two means in the numerator can override either a small or large denominator to determine whether the matched-pairs t test will reach statistical significance.

Interpreting the Magnitude of a Pearson r

A correlation coefficient is a very useful way to summarize the relationship between two variables with a single number that falls between -1 and $+1$. However, any one statistic that is used to summarize a whole set of data is bound to have its limitations, and this is certainly true for Pearson's r. A small value for r, especially one that is much smaller than expected, should never be interpreted without looking at the corresponding scatter plot. We will point out several problems to look for when r is small, but first we must caution you about a potential fallacy that is particularly tempting when the magnitude of r is relatively large.

Correlation and Causation

Several cautions should be noted at this point. First, you cannot determine the *cause* of the relationship from the correlation coefficient. Two variables may be highly correlated for one or more of three reasons: (1) X causes Y, (2) Y causes X, or (3) both X and Y are caused by some third variable.

A well-known story illustrates the danger of inferring causation from a correlation coefficient. A researcher once obtained a high positive correlation between the number of storks and the number of births in European cities (that is, the more storks in a city, the more births). Instead of issuing a dramatic announcement supporting the mythical powers of storks, further investigation was carried out. It was found that storks nest in chimneys, which in turn led to the conclusion that a third variable was responsible for the relationship between storks and births—size of city. Large cities had more people, and hence more births. They also had more houses, and hence more chimneys, and hence more storks. Smaller cities had fewer people, births, houses, chimneys, and storks. Thus, attributing causality is a logical or scientific problem, not a statistical one.

Correlation and Restriction of Range

A second important caution has to do with the effect of the variability of the scores on the correlation coefficient. Suppose you calculate the correlation be-

FIGURE 12.6

Effect of restriction of range on the correlation coefficient

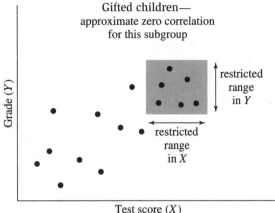

tween achievement test scores and elementary school grades for public school children in New York City. You will probably find a strong linear trend when the data are plotted. But what if you were to calculate the correlation between the same two variables for a group of children in a class for the highly gifted? Here, the range of scores on both variables is considerably narrowed, as is shown in Figure 12.6. Because of this, the correlation between the two variables is markedly reduced.

It is much harder to make fine discriminations among cases that are nearly equal on the variables in question than it is to make discriminations among cases that differ widely. More specifically, it is difficult to predict whether a gifted child will be an A or A– student. It is much easier to distinguish among a broad range of A to F students. Thus, *when the variability of scores is restricted* on either or both of two variables, the correlation between them usually decreases in absolute value. Conversely, when the variability of scores is increased on either of two variables (for example, by dropping cases in the middle of the range), the correlation can be expected to increase in absolute value.

Correlation and Bivariate Outliers

A third important caution concerns the disproportionate effect that a single case can have on r if that case represents a *bivariate outlier*. To illustrate this effect, we have reproduced Figure 12.5 as Figure 12.7 with one important difference: We changed the GPA of the student with the highest SAT score (725) from 3.0 to 1.0. A glance at Figure 12.7 makes it easy to identify this case as a bivariate outlier. A case need not be very extreme on either variable to be a bivariate outlier, as long as that case represents an unusual combination of values (e.g., a 6-foot 4-inch man who weighs 140 pounds). Changing the GPA of this one par-

FIGURE 12.7

Scatter plot for data in Table 12.1 ($r = +.324$) with one data point moved to create a bivariate outlier

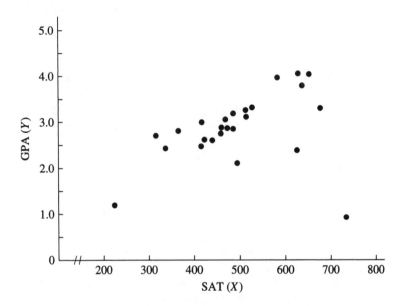

ticular student results in the Pearson r decreasing from .65 to .324. One of the main reasons for creating a scatter plot of your data is to look for such cases.

Bivariate outliers are often, but not always, due to mistakes in recording or entering the data, or to special circumstances involving the participant in question. For example, upon further investigation you might discover that the student with the 725 SAT score got a 1.0 GPA because he or she fell ill that semester and decided to "tough it out" instead of taking a medical leave of absence. It is acceptable to remove an outlier from your data when you find an objective reason to do so (e.g., you know that a participant was confused about the experiment's instructions), but it is certainly not acceptable to discard a data point merely because it *is* a bivariate outlier and discarding it would move the statistical results in the direction of your research hypothesis. Note that a single data point can also increase the magnitude of r a great deal; without the student who obtained a 2.2 GPA and scored 220 on his or her SAT, the correlation calculated in Table 12.2 would have been only .25 for the remaining 24 students.

When Is It Important That Pearson's r Be Large?

In the next section we will discuss how to determine whether the r for a sample differs significantly from zero. However, there are a number of important uses for r for which a fairly small r, even if statistically significant at a very low alpha level (e.g., .001), would be quite disappointing. These include measures of reliability and validity, as discussed in the upcoming sections.

Reliability

The simplest form of reliability involves measuring participants twice with the same scale (usually a self-report questionnaire), always with the (approximately) same time interval between the two measurements. The Pearson r between these two sets of measurements is a measure of *test-retest reliability*. When measuring some trait that is expected to be stable over time (e.g., spatial aptitude; degree of introversion), a scale should have a test-retest reliability that is at least about .7. Otherwise, it would seem that the scale is not measuring the trait in question reliably enough to be trusted. Often, researchers will then modify the scale in an attempt to improve its reliability.

Another commonly used measure of reliability involves the *internal consistency* of the scale. One way to assess this attribute of a scale is to average all of the odd-numbered items together to create an "odd" score, and, in an analogous fashion, create an "even" score. The Pearson r between the odd and even scores across all participants is a measure of the scale's *split-half reliability*—an indication of the degree to which the scale is measuring only one distinct trait. However, in the last couple of decades computers have made it easy to calculate more sophisticated measures of a scale's internal consistency (e.g., *Cronbach's alpha*).

Sometimes measurements are necessarily subjective but are not based on self-reports. For instance, the dependent variable in a study could be the creativity exhibited by a child's painting. To be sure that such a quality can be measured reliably, it is necessary that the measurements of two raters—acting without knowledge of each other—be highly correlated. A low correlation would call into question whether this quality can be measured reliably and would likely spur attempts to use better methods of training to increase the *interrater reliability* of the scale. High interrater reliability can also be important when preparing stimuli for an experiment. A common example is rating the attractiveness of yearbook photos so that the attractiveness of the photo can be controlled on any given trial by the experimenter. Without a high degree of interrater reliability, the experimenter cannot trust the attractiveness ratings of the photo stimuli. (If the raters find it too difficult to assign creativity or attractiveness scores but can place the paintings or photos in rank order, a nonparametric measure of correlation can be used, as described in the last part of this text.)

Validity

Once the reliability of a measurement scale has been established—that is, we know that the scale measures just *one* quality and does so in a stable, reproducible fashion—our attention would turn to establishing whether our scale is measuring what we think it is measuring. For example, items in a questionnaire are often chosen for their obvious *face* (or content) *validity,* but then it is important to confirm these choices by using some objective criteria. One possible goal for a new scale is to measure some human trait in a way that is quicker, less expensive, or more convenient when compared to some well-established measure. In order to replace a traditional scale, a high Pearson *r* needs to be found between the new and old scales after both are administered to the same set of participants. We do not expect such a measure of *criterion validity* to be larger than the reliability of the new scale, but it should approach that magnitude.

When trying to measure a quality for which no traditional scale exists, a very desirable form of validity involves correlating the new scale (after establishing its reliability) with some objective measure of actual behavior, if possible. For example, a new scale for measuring generosity could be validated by asking participants (who had already filled out the generosity questionnaire in some different, unrelated context) to contribute their time to some future experiment, or to give back part of the money they were given for their participation so that "additional participants could be recruited after the grant runs out." We would not expect our new scale's correlation with an objective criterion to be larger than .7, as we would expect for a reliability measure. But we would not be satisfied merely to draw conclusions based on a significance test of whether Pearson *r* is zero or not. On the other hand, when investigating the relationship between two variables that are not obviously connected, except on the basis of the researcher's theory, statistical significance can be very encouraging. We turn to this topic next.

Testing the Significance of the Correlation Coefficient

The correlation coefficient of +.65 for the group of 25 students whose scores are shown in Table 12.1 conveniently describes the linear relationship between SAT scores and GPA *for this group.* It would be very useful to know, however, whether these two variables are correlated in the population of all students. To answer this question, we must draw an inference about likely values of the population correlation coefficient (symbolized by rho, ρ). Is it likely that there is actually no correlation in the population, and that the correlation in the sample of 25 students was due to sampling error (the cases that happened to wind up in the sample)? Or, is the value of .65 large enough for us to conclude that there is some nonzero positive correlation between SAT scores and GPA in the population?

The strategy for testing hypotheses about likely values of ρ is similar to that used in previous chapters. The null hypothesis most often tested is that ρ is equal to zero:[1]

---

1. Other null hypotheses are possible, but a different statistical procedure is required in order to test them. See, for example, Cohen (2000), pp. 267–268.

$$H_0: \rho = 0$$

$$H_1: \rho \neq 0$$

A criterion of significance, such as the .05 or .01 criterion, is selected. The correct statistical model to use in this situation is the t distributions, so the appropriate t ratio may now be computed[2] with degrees of freedom equal to $N - 2$. Then, H_0 is retained if the computed t is less than the critical value of t from the t table. Otherwise H_0 is rejected in favor of H_1, and r is said to be *significantly different from zero* (or, simply, *statistically significant*).

However, you do not necessarily need to compute the t ratio. This has (in a sense) already been done for you by statisticians who have constructed tables of significant values of r. Therefore, the procedure for testing a correlation coefficient for statistical significance can be quite simple: you compare your computed value of r to the value of r shown in Table C in the Appendix for $N - 2$ degrees of freedom, where N is equal to the number of pairs. If the absolute value of your computed r is smaller than the tabled value, retain H_0; otherwise, reject H_0.

As an illustration, suppose that you wish to test the significance of the correlation between SAT scores and GPAs, using $\alpha = .05$. Referring to Table C, you find that for $25 - 2$ or 23 degrees of freedom, the smallest absolute value of r that is statistically significant is .396. Since the obtained r of .65 exceeds this value, you reject H_0 and conclude that there *is* a positive correlation in the population from which the sample of 25 students was randomly selected. Note that a correlation of $-.65$ would indicate a statistically significant negative relationship; the sign of r is ignored when comparing the computed r to the tabled value of r. Thus the test described is two-tailed—it guards against chance departures of r from zero in either the positive or negative direction.

As we observed in Chapters 10 and 11, confidence intervals provide valuable additional information about the probable values of a population parameter. However, the procedures for calculating confidence intervals for correlation coefficients are beyond the scope of this book (see Cohen, 2000, pp. 266–267).

Implications of Retaining H_0

If you fail to reject H_0, you have *not* established that the two variables are linearly uncorrelated in the population. Unless you know the probability of a Type II error (see Chapter 14), you cannot tell to what extent your decision to retain H_0 is likely to be wrong. Therefore, you should limit yourself to a conservative

---

2. The formula for the t ratio to test the significance of a Pearson r is

$$t = \frac{r\sqrt{N-2}}{\sqrt{1-r^2}},$$

where N = number of *pairs* of scores.

Example of perfect relationship between two variables where $r = 0$

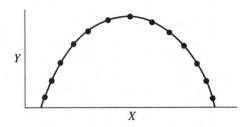

statement such as "there is not sufficient reason to believe that ρ is different from zero."

Also, the Pearson r detects only linear relationships. Thus the possibility remains that the two variables are related, but not in a linear fashion. It is possible for two variables to be even perfectly related yet to have r equal to zero. In Figure 12.8, for example, you can predict Y without error given X, but *not* linearly.

The *curvilinear relationship* depicted in Figure 12.8 represents an exception to the usual situation in which restricting the range of either or both of the variables reduces the magnitude of their linear correlation. In this example restricting the range of X to values that are to the left of the center would result in a fairly high positive correlation, whereas restricting X to values to the right of the center would yield an equally strong negative correlation. When X is not restricted, the correlations for each half of the range of X average out to an r near zero. Looking for evidence of a curvilinear relationship is another good reason for inspecting the scatter plot that corresponds to a correlation in which you are interested, especially if the Pearson r is considerably lower than you expected it to be.

Implications of Rejecting H_0

If a Pearson r is statistically significant, the significance denotes *some* degree of linear relationship between the two variables in the population. It does *not* denote a "significantly high" or "significantly strong" relationship; it just means that the relationship in the population is unlikely to be zero.

Notice that the larger the sample size, the smaller the absolute value of the correlation coefficient that is needed for statistical significance. For example, for $N = 12$ ($df = 10$), a correlation of .576 or larger is needed for significance using the .05 criterion. For $N = 102$ ($df = 100$), a correlation of only .195 or larger is needed. This implies that the importance of obtaining statistical significance can easily be exaggerated. Suppose that for a very large sample (say, $N = 1,000$), a statistically significant Pearson r of .08 is obtained. This statistical test indicates that ρ is greater than zero. But the obtained r of .08 is so close

to zero that the relationship in the population, although not zero and not necessarily equal to .08, is likely to be *very* weak—too weak, in fact, to allow you
to make any accurate statements about one variable based on knowledge of the
other. Consequently, such a finding would add little or nothing to our immediate knowledge, even though it is statistically significant. (It might conceivably
be useful in appraising a theory.) Therefore, you need to have *both* statistical
significance *and* a reasonably high absolute value of r before you can conclude
that ρ is large enough to be useful in applied work.

Correlation coefficients *cannot* be interpreted as percents. For example, you
cannot conclude that a correlation of .60 is 60% of a perfect relationship or that
it is twice as much as a correlation of .30. As we will see later in this chapter,
however, the *squared* correlation coefficient (r^2) does permit an interpretation,
in percentage terms, of the strength of the relationship between the two variables.

As usual, given that H_0 is true, the probability of erroneously rejecting it (a
Type I error) is equal to the criterion of significance that is selected. Using $\alpha =$
.05, when H_0 is true, you will reject it 5% of the time.

Assumptions Underlying the Use of r

The most important assumption underlying the use of the Pearson r is that X
and Y are linearly related. If X and Y have a curvilinear relationship (as in Figure 12.8), the Pearson r will not detect it. Even this is not, strictly speaking, an
assumption. If r is considered a measure of the degree of *linear* relationship, it
remains such a measure whether or not the best-fitting function is linear. Ordinarily, however, one would not be interested in the best linear fit when it is
known that the relationship is not linear.

Otherwise, no assumptions are made at all in using r to *describe* the degree
of linear relationship between two variables for a given set of data. When testing a correlation coefficient for statistical significance, it is, strictly speaking,
assumed that the underlying distribution is the so-called bivariate normal—
that is, scores on Y are normally distributed for each value of X, and scores on
X are normally distributed for each value of Y. However, when the degrees of
freedom are greater than 25 or 30, failure to meet this assumption has little
consequence for the validity of the test, unless your data contain some extreme
bivariate outliers—in which case an even larger sample may be required for an
accurate significance test.

Prediction and Linear Regression

Behavioral scientists are indebted to Sir Francis Galton for making explicit
some elementary concepts of relationships and prediction. Galton wrote his

now-classic paper "Regression toward Mediocrity in Hereditary Stature" in 1885. In it he presented the theory that the physical characteristics of offspring tend to be related to, but are on the average less extreme than, those of their parents. That is, tall parents on the average produce children *less tall* than themselves, and short parents on the average produce children *less short* than themselves. In other words, physical characteristics of offspring tend to "regress" toward the average of the population. If you were to predict the height of a child from a knowledge of the height of the parents, you should predict a less extreme height—one closer to the average of all children.

Plotting data on the stature of many pairs of parents and offspring, Galton calculated the median height of offspring for each height category of parents. For example, he plotted the median height for all offspring whose fathers were 5 ft. 7 in., the median height for all offspring whose fathers were 5 ft. 8 in., and so forth. By connecting the points representing the medians, Galton found not only that there was a positive relationship between parental height and height of the offspring, but also that this relationship was fairly linear. The line connecting each of the medians (and after Pearson, the means) came to be known as the *regression line.* This term has been adopted by statisticians to indicate the straight line used in predicting or estimating values of one variable from a knowledge of values of another variable with which it is paired. The statistical procedure for making such predictions is called *linear regression.*

Rationale and Computational Procedures

Let us assume that we wish to predict scores on Y from scores on X. Y, the variable being predicted or estimated, is called the *dependent* variable or *criterion.* X, which provides the information on which the predictions are based, is referred to as the *independent* variable (even if it is not manipulated by the experimenter) or *predictor.* In this book, we will discuss the simplest method of prediction—an equation that produces a *straight line.* One way of writing such an equation is

$$Y' = b_{YX}X + a_{YX},$$

where

$Y' = predicted$ score on Y

$b_{YX} = slope$ of the line, also called the *regression coefficient* for predicting Y

$a_{YX} = Y\text{-}intercept,$ or the value of Y' when $X = 0$

The value of b_{YX} summarizes the average rate of change in Y score per unit increase in X score, while the value of a_{YX} indicates the Y value at which the

FIGURE 12.9

Use of regression line to obtain predicted scores on Y

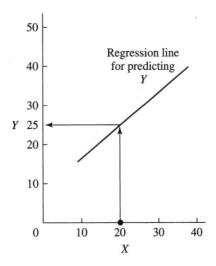

line crosses the Y-axis. For any given set of data, b_{YX} and a_{YX} are constant values in the equation. A straight line has only one slope, and there is only one value of Y' for which X equals zero. We wish to keep our errors in prediction (especially the *squared* errors) to a minimum, and the actual values of b_{YX} and a_{YX} are chosen with this objective in mind.

The way in which a regression line is used to obtain a predicted score is illustrated in Figure 12.9. Suppose a person has a score of 20 on X, and you want to predict what her score on Y will be. Given the regression line for predicting Y shown in Figure 12.9, you enter the X axis at 20 and proceed up to the regression line. You then read out the predicted Y score; Y' for this subject is equal to 25. In practice, predicted scores are computed according to the regression equation, since graphic estimates are likely to be rather inaccurate.

The regression (or prediction) line is the straight line that best represents the trend of the dots in a scatter plot. In any real situation, the dots will *not* all fall exactly in a straight line. Therefore, you will make *errors* when you use a regression line to make predictions. The error in predicting a particular Y value is defined as the difference (keeping the sign) between the *actual* Y value and the *predicted* Y value, Y'. That is,

$$\text{error in predicting } Y = Y - Y'$$

A graphic representation of errors in prediction for one set of data is shown in Figure 12.10. For example, the predicted Y value for the individual with an X score of 68 is equal to approximately 159.8. His actual Y value, however, is equal to 148. The difference of approximately –11.8 between the actual and

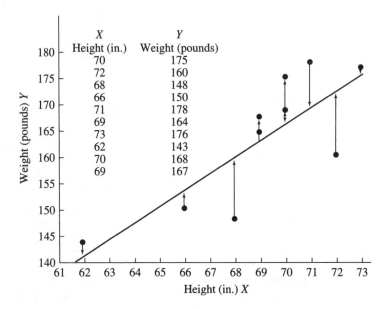

FIGURE 12.10

Regression line of Y on X showing extent of error (difference between actual weight score and predicted weight score)

X Height (in.)	Y Weight (pounds)
70	175
72	160
68	148
66	150
71	178
69	164
73	176
62	143
70	168
69	167

predicted values represents an error in prediction for this individual, and the negative sign indicates that the actual value is smaller than the prediction. These errors are also called *residual scores,* and they always sum to zero (just like deviations from the mean).

In Figure 12.10, vertical lines have been drawn between each observed Y score (actual weight) and the predicted weight score (Y'). This has been done for each value of X (actual height). These vertical distances are the errors in prediction (or residuals). All *predicted* scores lie on the straight line. Since there are two height scores of 70 inches with two different weight scores, and two height scores of 69 inches with two different weight scores, the smaller error has been superimposed upon the larger in each of these cases.

The linear regression prediction line minimizes the sum of *squared* errors in prediction, symbolized as

$$\sum(Y - Y')^2$$

That is, values are chosen for b_{YX} and a_{YX} that define a particular regression line for predicting Y: the line that makes $\Sigma(Y - Y')^2$ smaller than you would get using any other prediction line for that set of data. This line is therefore called the *least-squares* regression line of Y on X.

To see why the sum of *squared* errors is minimized, rather than the sum of unsquared errors, let us suppose that you wish to predict students' college

GPAs from scores on the SATs. After making your predictions, you wait until the students finish college and see what their actual GPAs turn out to be. The results for two students are as follows:

Student	Actual GPA (Y)	Predicted GPA (Y')	Error ($Y - Y'$)
1	3.8	3.4	+0.4
2	2.1	2.5	−0.4

The actual GPA of the first student is about half a grade point above the prediction, whereas the GPA of the second student is a similar amount below the prediction for that student. Thus, some error in prediction has been made. (This is unavoidable unless $r = \pm 1$, which never happens with real data.) Yet if you were to compute the average of the error column, it would equal zero! The same misleading result would be obtained had the predicted Y' values been 2.4 for student 1 and 3.5 for student 2, yielding substantial errors of +1.4 and −1.4.

As this example shows, it is not sufficient to have a prediction line whose errors balance out (have a mean of zero); *all* lines that go through the point $\bar{X}$, $\bar{Y}$ have this property. In order to obtain a meaningful measure of the total amount of prediction error, we must find the line about which the variation of the Y values, and hence the *squared* errors, is as small as possible. (As we will see later in this chapter, a good measure of the magnitude of prediction error can be computed by averaging these squared errors and taking the square root.)

In the general formula for a straight line, therefore, the values of b_{YX} and a_{YX} are chosen so as to minimize the value of $\Sigma(Y - Y')^2$. Equations that produce these values are found (by means of the differential calculus) to be

$$b_{YX} = r_{XY}\frac{\sigma_Y}{\sigma_X} = r_{XY}\frac{s_Y}{s_X}$$

$$a_{YX} = \bar{Y} - b_{YX}\bar{X}$$

The first formula for b_{YX} is used when values of σ_X and σ_Y are available, and the second version of the formula is used when working with the unbiased standard deviations.

To illustrate, let us return once again to our example of SAT and GPA. We have already seen that $\bar{X} = 498.4$, $\bar{Y} = 2.85$, $\sigma_X = 117.33$, $\sigma_Y = .57$, and $r_{XY} = +.65$, so

$$b_{YX} = (+.65)\frac{.57}{117.33}$$

$$= .0032$$

Since b_{YX} is the slope of the line, this result indicates that each unit of increase in X is associated with .0032 units of increase in Y. While it is not obvious from the equation, the value of b_{YX} does not change even if σ_X changes, while r_{XY} does. Thus, the rate of change in Y units per X remains the same whether the range of X is wide or narrow.

$$a_{YX} = 2.85 - (0.0032)(498.4)$$
$$= 1.26$$

This is the value of Y' when X is equal to zero. Such a value need not be a *logical* possibility for a given set of data. This is the case here, since SAT scores of zero are outside the observed range.

Combining the above two results gives the linear regression equation for predicting Y (GPA):

$$Y' = b_{YX} X + a_{YX}$$
$$= .0032X + 1.26$$

This equation can now be used to obtain predicted GPAs (Y'), given an SAT score (X). For example, the predicted GPA for a student with an SAT score of 400 is

$$Y' = (.0032)(400) + 1.26 = 2.5$$

This is the *best* linear prediction you can make, the one that on the average would yield the smallest squared error.

Note that a sample with scores on *both* the X and Y variables is needed in order to compute a linear regression prediction equation. Thus, to predict GPA from SAT, you must first obtain a sample of college students who have scores on both the SAT and GPA and compute such essential values as r_{XY}. Once you have determined the regression line, you can then use it to *make predictions for new cases for whom you have data on only the predictor*—that is, to make predictions for graduating high school seniors based on their SAT scores. However, you *must* be careful to ensure that the original sample of college students upon whom the regression equation is calculated is representative of the future groups for whom the predictions will be made.

Properties of Linear Regression

The linear regression procedure has numerous important properties. We have already seen that there is precisely one predictor and one criterion, a straight line is used to make predictions, and the line is such that the sum of squared errors in prediction is minimized. Some additional principles of importance include the following.

1. If there is no good information on which to base a prediction, the same estimate—the mean of the criterion—is made for everyone.

Suppose that a group of graduating high school seniors asks you to predict what each one's college GPA will be, but the only information that they give you is the length of each student's right big toe. Since big toe length is useless for purposes of forecasting someone's GPA (that is, $r_{XY} = 0$), you should refuse to make any predictions in this situation.

When there is no relevant information on which to base a prediction, linear regression also refuses to forecast any differences on the criterion. Instead, it "predicts" that each person will be average. That is, when the correlation between the predictor and the criterion is zero, the linear regression formula becomes

$$b_{YX} = .00 \frac{\sigma_Y}{\sigma_X} = 0$$

$$a_{YX} = \bar{Y} - (.00)\bar{X} = \bar{Y}$$

$$Y' = b_{YX} X + a_{YX}$$

$$= (0)X + \bar{Y}$$

$$= \bar{Y}$$

Thus, scores on X are ignored, since they are irrelevant for purposes of predicting Y, and the mean of the criterion is predicted for everyone. Of course, no behavioral scientist uses linear regression unless the predictor and criterion are nontrivially correlated, but it is desirable to understand this "worst of all possible worlds" in order to follow the logic of linear regression.

2. When all scores are expressed as z scores, the predicted z score on Y is equal to r multiplied by the z score on X.

It can be shown algebraically that[3]

$$z'_Y = r_{XY} z_X,$$

where

$$z'_Y = \text{predicted } z \text{ value on } Y$$

$$z_X = \text{actual } z \text{ value on } X$$

This equation may prove helpful in understanding linear regression. It

---

3. When the scores are expressed in deviation units, the standard deviation of both z_X and z_Y is equal to 1. Therefore, $b_{YX} = r(1/1) = r$. Since the mean of both z_X and z_Y is equal to zero, $a_{YX} = 0$. Thus, we have $Y' = rX + 0$, or $z'_Y = r_{XY} z_X$.

shows that the predicted score (z'_Y) will be less extreme (that is, closer to its mean) than the score from which the prediction is made (z_X), because z_X is multiplied by a fraction (r_{XY}). This illustrates the statement, made previously, about regression toward the mean of Y. The equation also shows once again that if r_{XY} is equal to zero, all predicted z'_Y values will equal the mean of Y (they will equal zero, which is the mean of z scores). This incidentally shows that the mean is a least squares measure—that is, the sum of squared deviations of the values in the sample from it is a minimum. Finally, the equation indicates that the regression line passes through the point ($\overline{X}, \overline{Y}$). If $z_X = 0$ (the mean of the X scores expressed as z scores), then $z'_Y = 0$ (the mean of the Y scores expressed as z scores).

Although this equation looks simple, it is not in general convenient for calculating predicted scores. To use it for this purpose, you would first have to transform X to a z value, then compute the value of z'_Y, and then transform z'_Y to a raw score equivalent Y'. Most of the time, it will be easier to use the raw score regression equation.

3. The closer the correlation between X and Y is to zero, the greater is the amount of prediction error.

It should be emphasized that while linear regression *minimizes* the sum of squared errors in prediction, this sum may still be prohibitively large. If the correlation between the predictor and the criterion is numerically small, such as $+.07$, even linear regression will make a substantial amount of prediction error because the relationship between the two variables is so weak. This implies that a correlation near zero is likely to be useless for practical prediction purposes, even if it is statistically significant (as could happen with a very large sample). The *sign* of the correlation coefficient, however, is *not* related to prediction error. A correlation of (say) $+.55$ and one of $-.55$ are equally good for prediction purposes, because the *strength* of the relationship between the predictor and the criterion is the same.

4. Transforming either X or Y or both by a linear transformation will not affect the linear correlation between them.

Suppose that the correlation between the high temperature for the day in a small town, as measured in degrees Fahrenheit, and the total weight of ice cream eaten that day by the people in that town, as measured in pounds, is equal to .4. If we wished to publish this result in a European journal, and its editors insisted that we convert our temperature measurements to degrees Celsius and our weights to kilograms, the Pearson r would not be affected by these transformations ($°C = .556 \times °F - 17.778$; wt. in kg $= .4 \times$ wt. in lbs.), because they are *linear transformations* (only multiplication, division, addition, and/or subtraction by constants are involved). Linearly transforming an entire set of raw scores will not change the z score for any individual, and the Pearson r depends only on the pairing of the z scores for the two variables and not the raw scores. Of course, a z score is itself just a linear transformation of a raw score, so the correlation between the raw scores on some variable and their corresponding z scores will always be perfect (i.e., $r = +1.0$).

A Technical Note: Formulas for Predicting X from Y

Since the assignment of "X" and "Y" to the two variables in a linear regression problem is usually up to the researcher, you can usually assign the Y designation to the criterion and X to the predictor and use the formulas given previously. If you should then wish to make predictions in the other direction (because you want to entertain the opposite causal theory), you can simply *change the designations* (relabel X as Y and Y as X) and use the same formulas. Note that it *is* necessary to recompute a new linear regression equation if you wish to predict in the other direction (unless $r = \pm 1$).

For purposes of reference, we will note briefly the linear regression procedure for predicting scores on X from scores on Y. The equation is

$$X' = b_{XY}\, Y + a_{XY},$$

where

$$X' = \text{predicted score on } X$$

$$b_{XY} = r_{XY}\, \frac{\sigma_X}{\sigma_Y} = r_{XY}\, \frac{s_X}{s_Y}$$

$$a_{XY} = \overline{X} - b_{XY}\, \overline{Y}$$

This procedure minimizes $\Sigma(X - X')^2$, the sum of squared errors when predicting X. While $r_{XY} = r_{YX}$, b_{XY} (the b value or slope for predicting X from Y) does *not* equal b_{YX} (the b value or slope for predicting Y from X), nor does $a_{XY} = a_{YX}$. Also, the regression line for predicting X is *not* the same as the regression line for predicting Y unless the correlation between X and Y is perfect (numerically equal to 1), $\sigma_X = \sigma_Y$, and $\overline{X} = \overline{Y}$.

Measuring Prediction Error: The Standard Error of Estimate

We have seen that when predicting scores on Y, the amount of squared error made for a given individual is equal to $(Y - Y')^2$. The *average* squared error for the entire sample can be obtained by summing the squared errors and dividing by N. Such a measure of error, the variance of errors, is in terms of squared units. As was the case with the standard deviation (Chapter 5), a measure in terms of actual score units can be obtained by taking the positive square root. This gives a useful measure of prediction error that is called the *standard error of estimate,* symbolized by $\sigma_{Y'}$:

Relationship between the standard error of estimate ($\sigma_{Y'}$), the standard deviation of Y (σ_Y), and the accuracy of prediction

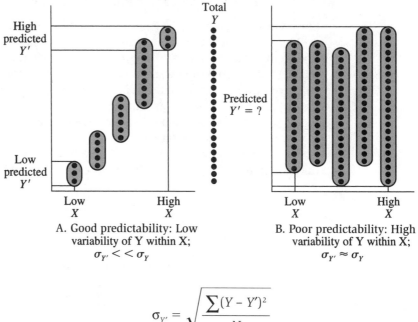

A. Good predictability: Low variability of Y within X; $\sigma_{Y'} << \sigma_Y$

B. Poor predictability: High variability of Y within X; $\sigma_{Y'} \approx \sigma_Y$

$$\sigma_{Y'} = \sqrt{\frac{\sum (Y - Y')^2}{N}}$$

In practice, the standard error of estimate (which is also the standard deviation of the residuals) can more easily be obtained by the following formula, which can be proved to be equivalent to the one above by algebraic manipulation:

$$\sigma_{Y'} = \sigma_Y \sqrt{1 - r_{XY}^2}$$

Note that if $r = \pm 1$, there is no error ($\sigma_{Y'} = 0$); while if $r = 0$, the standard error of estimate reaches its maximum possible value, which is the standard deviation of Y, or σ_Y.

The standard error of estimate of Y may be thought of as the variability of Y about the regression line for a particular X value, averaged over all values of X. This is illustrated in Figure 12.11. In panel A of Figure 12.11, the variability of the Y scores within each X value is relatively low, since the scores within each X value cluster closely together. The total variability of Y (for all X combined), which is given by σ_Y, is relatively large. Thus, $\sigma_{Y'}$ is *small compared to* σ_Y; the standard error of estimate is considerably smaller than the standard deviation of Y, whenever the correlation is fairly high. This is good for purposes of prediction, since an individual with a low score on X is likely to have a low score on Y while an individual with a high score on X is likely to have a high score on Y. Thus, in this instance, Y takes on a narrow range of values for any given X.

Figure 12.11B, on the other hand, illustrates a situation in which prediction will be very poor. The average variability within each X value is about equal to the total variability of Y; that is, the standard error of estimate $(\sigma_{Y'})$ is *about equal to* the standard deviation of Y (σ_Y) whenever the correlation is very small. In this instance, therefore, knowing an individual's X score will *not* permit you to make a good prediction as to what his Y score will be. Thus, Figure 12.11 shows that prediction will be good to the extent that for any given X, Y shows little variability.

Note that in Figure 12.11A the correlation between X and Y is fairly close to 1.0; in Figure 12.11B, the correlation is approximately zero. The standard error of estimate is also helpful in interpreting the meaning of a given numerical value of r, for it can be shown by algebraic manipulation that

$$r_{XY}^2 = 1 - \frac{\sigma_{Y'}^2}{\sigma_Y^2}$$

$$= \frac{\sigma_Y^2 - \sigma_{Y'}^2}{\sigma_Y^2}$$

That is, the *squared* correlation coefficient shows *by what proportion the reduction in the variability* (specifically the variance) *in predicting Y has been achieved by knowing X.* If this reduction has been great (as in Figure 12.11A), $\sigma_{Y'}^2$ is small compared to σ_Y^2, and r^2 is large. If, on the other hand, little reduction has been achieved (as in Figure 12.11B), $\sigma_{Y'}^2$ is about equal to σ_Y^2, and r^2 is about equal to zero. In the example involving GPA and SAT scores, r^2 is equal to $(.65)^2$ or .42. So in this example, 42 % *of the variance of the GPAs is explained by the SAT scores,* and a fairly good job has been done of identifying a (linear) relationship between two important variables.

The standard error of estimate computed from the formula given earlier is a descriptive statistic. (You may have inferred this from the fact that we used the Greek letter σ.) When you wish to draw inferences about the standard error of estimate in a population, you should correct for bias by using the following formula:

$$s_{Y'} = \sqrt{\frac{\sum (Y - Y')^2}{N - 2}} = s_Y \sqrt{\frac{N - 1}{N - 2}} (1 - r_{xy}^2),$$

where s_Y is the unbiased standard deviation of your Y scores. Note that whereas s_Y is based on $N - 1$ degrees of freedom, $s_{Y'}$, like the Pearson r, is based on $N - 2$ degrees of freedom (with the variance you lose one *df* for the mean; with regression you lose one *df* for the slope and another *df* for the Y-intercept).

Summary

Correlation refers to the co-relationship between two variables. The Pearson *r* coefficient is a useful measure of *linear* correlation.

1. The Pearson Correlation Coefficient

z score difference formula:

$$r_{XY} = 1 - \frac{1}{2} \frac{\sum (z_X - z_Y)^2}{N}$$

raw score definition formulas:

$$r_{XY} = \frac{\sum (X - \bar{X})(Y - \bar{Y})}{N \sigma_X \sigma_Y} = \frac{\dfrac{\sum XY}{N} - \bar{X}\bar{Y}}{\sigma_X \sigma_Y} = \frac{\dfrac{1}{N-1} \left(\sum XY - N\bar{X}\bar{Y}\right)}{s_X s_Y}$$

z score product formula:

$$r_{XY} = \frac{\sum z_X z_Y}{N}$$

raw score computing formula (see the end of this chapter's Appendix):

$$r_{XY} = \frac{N \sum XY - \sum X \sum Y}{\sqrt{[N \sum X^2 - (\sum X)^2][N \sum Y^2 - (\sum Y)^2]}}$$

In the foregoing formulas, N = number of *pairs*.

Points to Remember

1. The numerical value of *r* indicates the *strength* of the relationship between the two variables in your sample, while the sign indicates the *direction* of the relationship.
2. $-1 \le r \le +1$.
3. The population correlation is symbolized by ρ.
4. *r cannot* be interpreted as a percent, but r^2 can.
5. *r* may be tested for statistical significance by referring the obtained value to the appropriate table with $df = N - 2$.
6. *r* may also be used as a descriptive statistic.
7. *r* detects only *linear* relationships.

8. Correlation does not imply causation.

9. A restricted range on one or both of your variables, or a single bivariate outlier, can lead to a correlation considerably lower than you were expecting.

10. Even a tiny, inconsequential correlation can become statistically significant with a large enough sample.

11. When using correlation for various practical purposes, especially when measuring the various types of reliability and validity, it is important that the Pearson r be not only statistically significant but large in magnitude as well.

2. Linear Regression

The goal is to obtain the predicted score Y', given a score on X. The formula to use is

$$Y' = b_{YX}X + a_{YX},$$

where

$$b_{YX} = r_{XY}\frac{\sigma_Y}{\sigma_X} = r_{XY}\frac{s_Y}{s_X}$$

$$a_{YX} = \overline{Y} - b_{YX}\overline{X}$$

The standard error of estimate for predicting Y from X, a measure of error in the prediction process, is equal to

$$\sigma_{Y'} = \sqrt{\frac{\sum(Y - Y')^2}{N}} = \sigma_Y\sqrt{1 - r_{XY}^2}$$

This measure is a descriptive statistic. If instead you wish to draw inferences about the standard error of estimate in a population, use the following formula:

$$s_{Y'} = \sqrt{\frac{\sum(Y - Y')^2}{N - 2}} = s_Y\sqrt{\frac{N - 1}{N - 2}(1 - r_{xy}^2)}$$

Points to Remember

1. The foregoing procedure minimizes the sum of squared errors in prediction, $\Sigma(Y - Y')^2$.

2. The closer r is to zero, the greater the errors in prediction. If $r = \pm 1$, $\sigma_{Y'} = 0$ (prediction is perfect). If $r = 0$, $\sigma_{Y'}$ equals its maximum possible value σ_Y (prediction is useless).

3. If r is not statistically significant, linear regression should *not* be used.

4. The regression line always passes through the point $\overline{X}, \overline{Y}$.

5. The foregoing procedure is used only for purposes of predicting scores on Y (Y is the criterion and X is the predictor). Different formulas are needed to predict scores on X, and the simplest procedure in such cases is to change the designations (relabel X as Y and Y as X) so that the foregoing procedure may be used.

Exercises

1. A college dean would like to know how well he can predict sophomore grade point average for first-semester freshmen so that students who are headed for trouble can be given appropriate counseling. After students have been in school for one semester, the dean obtains their numerical final examination average for the first semester (based on a total of 100 points) and the average number of "cuts" per class during the semester. He then waits for a year and a half, and when the students have finished their second year he obtains their sophomore grade point average.

A large sample would be desirable for such a study. Since the purpose of this problem is to see how correlation and regression procedures work, let us keep the computations within reason by assuming that the dean has a sample of only seven cases, remembering that in a real study there would be many more subjects (but exactly the same procedures would be used).

Student	Test score (X)	Cuts (C)	Sophomore average (Y)
1	70	2	2.50
2	90	1	4.00
3	75	2	3.50
4	85	3	3.00
5	80	5	3.00
6	70	3	2.00
7	90	5	3.00
Mean	80	3	3.00
σ	8.02	1.41	.60

(a) Convert the test scores (X) and sophomore averages (Y) to z scores. By inspection of the paired z scores, estimate whether the correlation between these two variables is strong and positive, about zero, or strong and negative. Then verify your estimate by computing r using the *z score difference formula.*

(b) Now recompute r_{YX} by the *z score product formula* and verify that the result is the same. Briefly, state in words what this r_{XY} indicates.

(c) Use the raw-score formula from Table 12.2 to compute the Pearson r between the number of cuts (C) and the sophomore average (Y). Can you reject the null hypothesis at the .05 level with a two-tailed test? (Use Table C.)

(d) Repeat part (c) for the correlation between the number of cuts (C) and the test score (X). Is this correlation significant at the .01 level with a *one*-tailed test?

2. The data from exercise 5 in the previous chapter are reproduced in the following table. Calculate the mean and the *unbiased* standard deviations for both the experimental and control groups, and then compute the Pearson r with the raw-score definitional formula that uses the s's rather than the σ's in its denominator. Is the correlation coefficient significant? Given your decision with respect to the null hypothesis, what type of error could you be making, Type I or Type II? (Advanced exercise: Recompute the matched-pairs t test with the formula that is based on Pearson's r, and compare it to the t value you calculated for these data in the previous chapter.)

Pair	Experimental group (programmed text)	Control group (standard text)
1	9	7
2	6	4
3	5	6
4	7	3
5	3	5
6	7	3
7	3	2
8	4	5
9	6	7
10	10	8

3. The data from exercises 6 and 7 in the previous chapter are reproduced in the tables that follow.

(a) Compute the Pearson r for data set 3, Chapter 1, and test for significance at the .05 level.

(b) Use the z scores you calculated for these data in the exercises of Chapter 7 to recompute the r with the z-product formula. Is it the same?

(c) Compute the Pearson r for data set 3, chapter 1, with X rearranged, and test for significance at the .01 level.

Data set 3, Chapter 1		
S	X	Y
1	97	89
2	68	57
3	85	87
4	74	76
5	92	97
6	92	79
7	100	91
8	63	50
9	85	85
10	87	84
11	81	91
12	93	91
13	77	75
14	82	77

Same data, but with X rearranged		
S	X	Y
1	92	89
2	82	57
3	85	87
4	81	76
5	87	97
6	93	79
7	68	91
8	85	50
9	63	85
10	100	84
11	74	91
12	77	91
13	92	75
14	97	77

4. Use the data and your results from exercise 1 to compute the linear regression equation for predicting the sophomore average (Y) from the test score (X). (Advanced exercise: Compute the linear regression equation for predicting the test score [X] from the sophomore average [Y].)

(a) Use the linear regression equation you just calculated to compute the predicted (Y') sophomore average for each particular student. Then compute the error (or residual, $Y - Y'$) for each student, and the squared error as well.

(b) Using the results of part (a) compute the standard error of the estimate for predicting Y from X (i.e., the test score). Verify that this value ($\sigma_{Y'}$) is indeed equal to the value you would calculate from the expression $\sigma_Y(1 - r_{xy}^2)$.

5. Use the data and your results from exercise 1 to compute the linear regression equation for predicting the sophomore average (Y) from the number of cuts (C). What sophomore average would be predicted for a student who cut class eight times during the semester in question?

6. Compute the linear regression equation for predicting Y from X for each of the data sets in exercise 3. What proportion of the variance in Y is accounted for by X in each data set? For each data set, use the appropriate formula to calculate the *unbiased* standard error of the estimate (s_Y).

Thought Questions

1. For each of the following, state whether you would expect the Pearson r correlation between X and Y to be positive, zero, or negative. Assume that each correlation is based on a sample of 50 participants who have scores on both X and Y. (a) X = grades in a high school advanced placement psychology course, Y = scores on the advanced placement psychology test. (b) X = intelligence, Y = size of big toe on right foot. (c) X = number of years spent playing golf, Y = average golf score per 18 holes. (d) X = number of hours spent watching television per week, Y = grades in high school. (e) X = self-esteem (low number indicates low self-esteem), Y = depression (low number indicates more depressed). (f) X = number of hours spent studying for a test, Y = number of mistakes made on that test.

2. A student obtains scores of 72 on Test X and 72 on Test Y. The student therefore concludes that there is a high correlation between Test X and Test Y. Why is this conclusion incorrect?

3. In a Pearson r correlational study, X is the number of hours of violent television programs that participants watch, and Y is the number of violent acts committed by the participants in real life. Suppose that there is a moderately high correlation (say, $+.48$) between X and Y for a sample of 100 American males, and this result is statistically significant. Explain why we *cannot* infer causation from a correlational study by showing that each of the following is possible: (a) X could cause Y. (b) Y could cause X. (c) The relationship between X and Y could be caused by a third variable. (Hint: Consider physiological causes of violent behavior.)

4. In a research study using a sample of 30 participants, the Pearson r correlation between X and Y is $+.09$ and is *not* statistically significant. (a) Should linear regression be used to predict scores on Y given scores on X? Why or why not? (b) Should the researcher conclude that there is little or no correlation between X and Y? Why or why not?

5. The SAT is used to predict the success of high school students in college. Suppose that the Pearson r correlation between scores on the SAT and grades at University Z during the freshman year, based on a sample of 500 participants,

is +.53. A student complains that a friend of hers did poorly on the SAT but was admitted to University Z anyway and earned high grades during the first year, while another friend did very well on the SAT but flunked out of University Z in the first year. Should the student conclude from these two results that the SAT is inaccurate and worthless? Why or why not?

6. Using a very large sample of participants, a statistically significant Pearson r correlation of +.11 is obtained between X and Y. Does this mean that there is a strong relationship between X and Y? Why or why not?

7. (a) What is the difference between the reliability of a measure and the validity of a measure? (b) What is the difference between test-retest reliability and split-half reliability? (c) What is criterion validity?

8. (a) When using linear regression, does the researcher want the standard error of estimate to be small or large? Why? (b) If the standard error of estimate is large, what does this imply about the variability of scores on Y for any given value of X? Why does this make predicting scores on Y from scores on X less accurate? (c) If the standard error of estimate is small, what does this imply about the variability of scores on Y for any given value of X? Why does this make predicting scores on Y from scores on X more accurate?

Computer Exercises

1. Use your statistical package to compute the Pearson r between baseline and prequiz heart rates for all students; also, find the Pearson r between the pre- and postquiz heart rate measurements. (Advanced exercise: Recalculate these two r's separately for men and women.)

2. Compute the Pearson r between baseline heart rate and baseline anxiety for all students; also, find the Pearson r between prequiz heart rate and prequiz anxiety measurements.

3. Create two new variables: prequiz minus baseline heart rate and prequiz minus baseline anxiety. Compute Pearson's r between these two difference scores, and interpret the meaning of this correlation.

4. Use your statistical package to create a scatter plot of the relation between the math background quiz score and the statistics quiz score for the 85 students who have both scores. Describe the pattern that you see. If possible, request that your statistical package add a linear regression line to the scatter plot.

5. Use your statistical package to perform a linear regression predicting the statistics quiz score from the math background quiz score. Write out the formula for the raw-score regression line. What statistics quiz score would be predicted for a student who obtained a score of 20 on the math background quiz? For a score of 40?

6. Perform a linear regression to predict the statistics quiz score from the student's self-reported math phobia level, and write out the raw-score regression formula. Use a scatter plot to help you interpret this result. Repeat the linear regression and scatter plot using math phobia to predict prequiz anxiety. (Advanced exercise: Redo these two regressions for just the psychology majors in Sara's class.)

Bridge to SPSS

SPSS handles correlation quite separately from regression. These two procedures require different selections from the Analyze menu, as described in the two sections that follow.

Linear Correlation

To compute the Pearson r in SPSS, select **Correlate** from the Analyze menu, and then choose **Bivariate....** In the dialog box that opens, move the variables you wish to see correlated to the area labeled "Variables:" to the right of the variable list, and click **OK.** You can select as few as two variables from the list or as many as all of the numeric variables. By default, your output will contain a single matrix with the variables you chose as the labels of the rows, as well as of the columns; the same Pearson r will appear twice for each possible pair of variables from your selected list (the matrix also contains a diagonal, in which each variable is correlated with itself, always yielding a value of 1.000). The two-tailed p value (labeled "Sig.," of course) appears under each Pearson r, with the sample size (i.e., the number of pairs, labeled "N") under that. Any Pearson r with a "Sig." less than .05 is marked with an asterisk; if "Sig." is less than .01, that r is marked with two asterisks.

The Bivariate Correlations dialog box allows you to select the Kendall's tau-b (not discussed in this text) and/or the Spearman correlation coefficient (see Chapter 21) instead of, or in addition to, the Pearson r. This dialog box also allows you to select one-tailed rather than two-tailed p values, and to suppress the "flagging" of significant correlations. In addition, the **Options...** button allows you to add some descriptive statistics to your output, and to exclude cases listwise instead of pairwise. If you choose to exclude cases *listwise,* N will not appear under each Pearson r. Because N will be the same for each correlation (N will equal the number of cases that do not have a missing value for *any* variable in the selected list), it appears just once, under the entire matrix.

Linear Regression

To compute a linear regression in SPSS, select **Regression** from the Analyze menu, and then choose **Linear....** In the dialog box that opens, move the variable that *you want to predict* to the area labeled "Dependent:" (there is room for only one variable in this space). Then move the variable that you want to use as your *predictor* to the area labeled "Independent(s):"; this space can accommodate more than one variable, in case you want to perform multiple regression (beyond the scope of this text). The various Options, Plots, and Statistics you can request deal mainly with evaluating the assumptions (such as the linearity of the relation between the two variables) that underlie the use of linear regression, and are especially useful when performing multiple regression. (For *simple* [i.e., bivariate] regression, the default selection for Method [i.e., "Enter"] is used.) The space labeled **Selection Variable:** allows you to perform your regression on a particular subgroup of cases. For example, to perform your regression on participants of one gender only, move your gender variable to "Selection Variable," which will activate the **Rule . . .** button. Clicking on the **Rule** button will allow you to specify the numeric code (i.e., value) for the gender you want to select.

The default output for linear regression consists of four boxes. In simple (one-predictor) regression, the first box contains the independent variable (IV), under "Variables Entered," and the dependent variable (DV) is indicated below the box. The second box (Model Summary) provides the Pearson r between the IV and the DV, and some related statistics (an uppercase R is used, because with more than one predictor this value is the coefficient of multiple correlation). The third box (ANOVA) provides a significance test for the Pearson r, in terms of an F ratio—a statistic that will be described in Chapter 15. Finally, it is the fourth box (Coefficients) that provides you with the slope and intercept for the least-squares regression line, though the labels do not make this clear. Under the first column, headed "Model," the term "(Constant)" refers to the Y-intercept of the regression line. The second column, headed "B" (under the larger heading of Unstandardized Coefficients), gives you the value for the Y-intercept of the raw-score equation (next to Constant), and the value for the slope (next to the name of your IV). These values are divided by the ones in the next column ("Std. Error") to create t values for testing both the intercept and the slope for significance. You will rarely be interested in the significance test for the intercept, and the t value for the slope is exactly the same as the one you would get from the t formula for testing r, as given in the second footnote for this chapter. In fact, squaring this t value will give you the F value in the ANOVA box, and the "Sig." value in the ANOVA box will always be the same as the Sig. for your IV in the Coefficients box, when you are using only one IV (i.e., predictor).

Appendix: Equivalence of the Various Formulas for r

$$1.\ 1 - \frac{1}{2}\ \frac{\sum (z_X - z_Y)^2}{N} = \frac{\sum z_X z_Y}{N}$$

PROOF: Expanding the term in parentheses gives

$$r = 1 - \frac{1}{2} \frac{\sum (z_X^2 - 2z_X z_Y + z_Y^2)}{N}$$

$$= 1 - \frac{1}{2} \frac{\sum z_X^2 - 2 \sum z_X z_Y + \sum z_Y^2}{N} \quad \text{(Rules 1, 2, and 8, Chapter 1)}$$

$$= 1 - \frac{1}{2} \left(\frac{\sum z_X^2}{N} - \frac{2 \sum z_X z_Y}{N} + \frac{\sum z_Y^2}{N} \right)$$

It can readily be shown that the sum of squared z scores divided by N is equal to 1:

$$\sigma^2 = \frac{\sum (z - \bar{z})^2}{N} \quad \text{(definition of } \sigma^2\text{)}$$

$$1 = \frac{\sum (z - 0)^2}{N} \quad \text{(mean of } z \text{ scores} = 0\text{; variance of } z \text{ scores} = 1\text{)}$$

$$1 = \frac{\sum z^2}{N}$$

Thus,

$$r = 1 - \frac{1}{2} \left(1 - \frac{2 \sum z_X z_Y}{N} + 1 \right)$$

$$= 1 - 1 + \frac{\sum z_X z_Y}{N}$$

$$= \frac{\sum z_X z_Y}{N}$$

Incidentally, we know that the correlation of z_X (or any other variable) with *itself* is $+1$, so $(\sum z_X z_X)/N = +1$. But this is the same as $(\sum z_X^2)/N = 1$, which we have already seen.

$$2. \ \frac{\sum z_X z_Y}{N} = \frac{\sum (X - \bar{X})(Y - \bar{Y})}{N \sigma_X \sigma_Y}$$

PROOF: By definition,

$$z_X = \frac{X - \bar{X}}{\sigma_X}, \qquad z_Y = \frac{Y - \bar{Y}}{\sigma_Y}$$

Therefore,

$$r = \frac{\sum\left(\dfrac{X-\overline{X}}{\sigma_X}\right)\left(\dfrac{Y-\overline{Y}}{\sigma_Y}\right)}{N}$$

$$= \frac{\sum(X-\overline{X})(Y-\overline{Y})}{N\sigma_X\sigma_Y} \quad \text{(Rule 8, Chapter 1)}$$

3. $\dfrac{\sum(X-\overline{X})(Y-\overline{Y})}{N\sigma_X\sigma_Y} = \dfrac{\dfrac{\sum XY}{N} - \overline{X}\,\overline{Y}}{\sigma_X\sigma_Y}$

PROOF: Expanding the numerator gives

$$\sum(X-\overline{X})(Y-\overline{Y}) = \sum(XY - X\overline{Y} - \overline{X}Y + \overline{X}\,\overline{Y})$$

$$= \sum XY - \overline{Y}\sum X - \overline{X}\sum Y + N\overline{X}\,\overline{Y}$$

(Rules 1, 2, 5, and 8, Chapter 1)

Substituting $(\sum X)/N$ for $\overline{X}$ and $(\sum Y)/N$ for $\overline{Y}$ gives

$$\sum XY - \frac{(\sum Y)(\sum X)}{N} - \frac{(\sum X)(\sum Y)}{N} + \frac{N(\sum X)(\sum Y)}{(N)(N)}$$

$$= \sum XY - 2\frac{(\sum X)(\sum Y)}{N} + \frac{(\sum X)(\sum Y)}{N}$$

$$= \sum XY - \frac{\sum X\sum Y}{N}$$

Dividing the numerator by N yields

$$\frac{\sum XY}{N} - \frac{\sum X\sum Y}{N\cdot N} = \frac{\sum XY}{N} - \left(\frac{\sum X}{N}\right)\left(\frac{\sum Y}{N}\right) = \frac{\sum XY}{N} - \overline{X}\,\overline{Y}$$

Now that we have divided the numerator by N, we must do the same to the denominator:

$$\frac{N\sigma_X\sigma_Y}{N} = \sigma_X\sigma_Y$$

Put the transformed numerator over the transformed denominator to obtain the raw-score formula used in Table 12.2. This formula is sometimes called a raw-score *definition* formula; the terms in the formula are meaningful, but the format may not be optimal for computation.

4. Without the final step in the previous proof—dividing both numerator and denominator by N—we had obtained the following formula:

$$\frac{\sum XY - \dfrac{\sum X \sum Y}{N}}{N\sigma_X \sigma_Y}$$

This formula can easily be transformed into an old-fashioned raw-score *computational* formula—that is, a formula expressed entirely in terms of sums of scores, sums of cross-products, and sums of squared scores, with no intermediate statistics (e.g., mean, SD), and therefore no rounding off, until the final stage. This type of formula was popular when the only calculators that were readily available were of the simple four-function (i.e., add, subtract, multiply, divide) type. We show such a formula below, and the steps required to get to it from the formula above, mostly for reasons of historical continuity.

Turning first to the denominator, we have seen in Chapter 5 that

$$\sigma_X = \sqrt{\frac{1}{N}\left[\sum X^2 - \frac{(\sum X)^2}{N}\right]}$$

$$\sigma_Y = \sqrt{\frac{1}{N}\left[\sum Y^2 - \frac{(\sum Y)^2}{N}\right]}$$

Therefore,

$$N\sigma_X \sigma_Y = N \sqrt{\frac{1}{N}\left[\sum X^2 - \frac{(\sum X)^2}{N}\right]} \sqrt{\frac{1}{N}\left[\sum Y^2 - \frac{(\sum Y)^2}{N}\right]}$$

Since $[N(\sqrt{1/N})(\sqrt{1/N})]$ equals N/N or 1, these terms cancel out, leaving

$$\sqrt{\left[\sum X^2 - \frac{(\sum X)^2}{N}\right]\left[\sum Y^2 - \frac{(\sum Y)^2}{N}\right]}$$

If we now combine the numerator and denominator, we have

$$r = \frac{\sum XY - \dfrac{\sum X \sum Y}{N}}{\sqrt{\left[\sum X^2 - \frac{(\sum X)^2}{N}\right]\left[\sum Y^2 - \frac{(\sum Y)^2}{N}\right]}}$$

Finally, if we multiply this by $N/\sqrt{N^2}$, which is equal to 1, we have

$$r = \frac{N \sum XY - \sum X \sum Y}{\sqrt{[N \sum X^2 - (\sum X)^2][N \sum Y^2 - (\sum Y)^2]}},$$

which is the raw score computing formula for r.

Chapter 13
The Connection between Correlation and the *t* Test

PREVIEW

Introduction

What is a dichotomous variable?

If one of the two variables in a correlational study has only two possible values, why can those two values be changed to *any* two numbers without changing the magnitude of the correlation coefficient?

The Point-Biserial Correlation Coefficient

What are the procedures for computing the correlation between one continuous and one dichotomous variable (the point-biserial correlation coefficient)?

How is a point-biserial correlation coefficient tested for statistical significance?

When we obtain a statistically significant value of *t* for the difference between two means, why is it desirable to convert this value to a point-biserial correlation coefficient? How is this done?

What is the relationship between r_{pb} and the effect-size measure known as *g*?

The Proportion of Variance Accounted For in Your Samples

What does squaring r_{pb} tell you about the proportion of the total variance that is accounted for by the dichotomous variable?

Estimating the Proportion of Variance Accounted For in the Population

How can the formula for r_{pb}^2 be adjusted to create an unbiased estimator of the variance accounted for in the population?

What is ω^2 and how is it related to the population effect-size measure known as **d**?

Summary

Exercises

Thought Questions

Computer Exercises

Bridge to SPSS

Introduction

Now that you have learned how to calculate the correlation between two variables, you do not really need to know the procedure for testing a difference of two independent sample means (as shown in Chapter 11). Instead, you can treat the two-sample comparison as a form of correlation. That is, you can compute the correlation between a two-valued (i.e., *dichotomous*) variable and a continuous variable. It can be useful to think of the two-sample *t* test as a special case of correlation, as we will demonstrate in this chapter. However, the two-sample *t* test is a very commonly used procedure in the behavioral sciences, and so it was well worth describing it in detail, as we did in Chapter 11.

Let us return to the problem of predicting weight from height (as depicted in Figure 12.10). This time, suppose that your data set contains five men and five women. By a strange coincidence, all of the women are the same height (i.e., 64 inches), and all of the men are the same height as each other (i.e., 69 inches) but taller than the women. There is still variability in weight for each group, as you can see in the scatterplot in Figure 13.1. The data for Figure 13.1 are shown, and the Pearson *r* is calculated for the height/weight relationship (using the *z*-product method), in Table 13.1.

It should not be surprising that the linear correlation is high ($r = .894$) for these data (note the similarity between Figure 13.1 and Figure 12.11A), even

FIGURE 13.1

A scatter plot in which one of the variables has only two values

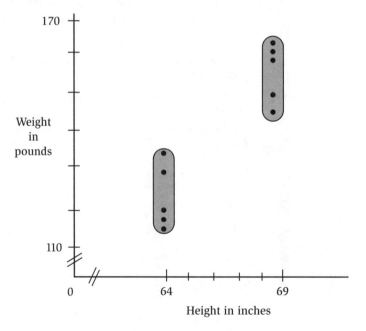

TABLE 13.1
Height and weight data for Figure 13.1

Height (in.) X	z_X	Weight (lbs.) Y	z_Y	$z_X z_Y$	
64	-1	116	-1.31	$+1.31$	
64	-1	118	-1.20	$+1.20$	$\overline{X}_1 = 123.8$
64	-1	120	-1.10	$+1.10$	$\sigma_1 = 8.635$
64	-1	125	-0.83	$+0.83$	$s_1 = 9.654$
64	-1	140	-0.03	$+0.03$	
69	$+1$	145	$+0.24$	$+0.24$	
69	$+1$	150	$+0.51$	$+0.51$	$\overline{X}_2 = 157.2$
69	$+1$	162	$+1.15$	$+1.15$	$\sigma_2 = 8.134$
69	$+1$	164	$+1.26$	$+1.26$	$s_2 = 9.094$
69	$+1$	165	$+1.31$	$+1.31$	
$\Sigma X = 665$	$\Sigma z_X = 0$	$\Sigma Y = 1405$	$\Sigma z_Y = 0$	$\Sigma z_X z_Y = +8.94$	

$$\overline{X} = 66.5 \qquad\qquad \overline{Y} = 140.5 \qquad\qquad r = \frac{\Sigma z_X z_Y}{N}$$

$$\sigma_X = 2.5 \qquad\qquad\qquad \sigma_Y = 18.69 \qquad\qquad\qquad = \frac{8.94}{10} = .894$$

though the X variable has only two values in this case. What *is* surprising is that the correlation would be exactly the same if the X values were simply 1 for all women and 2 for all men. In fact, *any* two different values for X would yield the same magnitude for Pearson's r. (However, the r would have a negative sign if women were assigned the higher of the two X values.) This phenomenon becomes much less surprising when you look carefully at the calculation of r in terms of z scores (see Table 13.1). It is easy to show that whenever you have only two different numbers the z score for the smaller one will be -1 and the z score for the larger one will be $+1$, regardless of which two numbers you are working with.

The Point-Biserial Correlation Coefficient

In our height/weight example, all of the women have one height and all of the men have another (i.e., height and *gender* are perfectly correlated). Therefore, the correlation between height and weight is also the correlation between *gender* and weight. You can correlate any variable with gender (as long as you have measured your dependent variable on at least some individuals of each gender) by arbitrarily assigning an X value to each gender (e.g., 1 and 2) and then correlating these X values with your continuous variable as the Y value for each individual. For instance, suppose you correlate gender with height. After assigning the X value of 1 to females and 2 to males, you will be measuring the tendency for height to be higher whenever the gender value (1 vs. 2) is higher.

The type of correlation just described is usually called a *point-biserial corre-lation,* symbolized as r_{pb}, because one of the variables being correlated has only two levels, which are assigned arbitrary values. The main problem with r_{pb} is that its sign will change if you reverse the assignment of the X values (e.g., r_{pb} for gender with height will become negative if males are assigned a value that is *lower* than the one assigned to the females). Therefore, we routinely ignore the sign of r_{pb} and look at the means of the two groups to determine the direction of the relationship.

When squared, r_{pb} is interpreted in the same way as any squared correlation coefficient. Note that any time you can calculate an r_{pb}, you can also compute a t value to compare the two group means instead. The information you get from the r_{pb} complements the information you get from the t value, as we will now demonstrate for the gender/weight example.

The Relationship between r_{pb} and the t Test

In the rightmost column of Table 13.1 we included the means, and the biased and unbiased SDs, for weight separately for each height (i.e., gender). Using the t formula for equal sample sizes (see the end of Chapter 11), we can calcu-late t for comparing the mean weights of the two groups:

$$t = \frac{\overline{X}_1 - \overline{X}_2}{\sqrt{\dfrac{s_1^2 + s_2^2}{n}}} = \frac{123.8 - 157.2}{\sqrt{\dfrac{93.2 + 82.7}{5}}} = \frac{-33.4}{\sqrt{35.18}} = \frac{-33.4}{5.93} = -5.63$$

This t value shows that the difference in weight between the two genders is statistically significant. Recall that the r_{pb} between height and weight (and therefore, in this example, between gender and weight) was high—in fact, it was .894. However, even such a large r should be tested for significance, which we will do by using the t formula found in the second footnote of Chapter 12. (We could look up the critical value in Table C, but we want to make a point about the t value.)

$$t = \frac{r_{pb}\sqrt{N - 2}}{\sqrt{1 - r_{pb}^2}} = \frac{.894\sqrt{8}}{\sqrt{1 - .8}} = \frac{2.5286}{.4472} = 5.65,$$

where N represents the total number of men and women, which is also the number of pairs on which r_{pb} was calculated.

The slight difference in magnitude between these two t values of .02 is due entirely to rounding off intermediate terms (e.g., the variance of each group). The sign of the t value can be ignored in each case. The point is that when you test r_{pb} for significance you are testing the relative separation of two means in a way that is equivalent to testing the difference of those means with a t test for two independent samples.

The Relationship between r_{pb} and g (Effect Size)

Recall that we have already introduced a measure of the relative separation of two sample means, called g. The ordinary (pooled-variance) two-sample t test can be viewed as a test of g, where

$$t = g\sqrt{\frac{N_1 N_2}{N_1 + N_2}}$$

In fact, both r_{pb} and g are alternative measures of effect size. It is useful to solve the preceding formula for g so that you can calculate g from a published t value (if you know the sample sizes):

$$g = t\sqrt{\frac{N_1 + N_2}{N_1 N_2}}$$

Similarly, you can modify the formula for testing the significance of r_{pb} so that you can also calculate r_{pb} from a published t value:

$$r_{pb} = \sqrt{\frac{t^2}{t^2 + df}},$$

where $df = N - 2$ (N is the *total* $N = N_1 + N_2$). If in the formula for r_{pb} you substitute the expression for t in terms of g, N_1, and N_2, you will get a formula that relates r_{pb} directly to g and the sample sizes:

$$r_{pb} = \sqrt{\frac{g^2}{g^2 + 4(df/N)}}$$

For the data in Table 13.1, g equals $t\sqrt{(10/25)} = 5.65\,(.632) = 3.57$—a very large value for an effect size. (We could also have calculated this value by dividing the difference between the male and female means by the square root of the pooled variance.) Computing r_{pb} from g yields

$$r_{pb} = \sqrt{\frac{3.57^2}{3.57^2 + 4(8/10)}} = \sqrt{\frac{12.75}{12.75 + 3.2}} = \sqrt{\frac{12.75}{12.75 + 3.2}} = \sqrt{.8} = .894$$

Given these two choices for measuring effect size, the question is this: Under what circumstances would r_{pb} be preferred, and when would g be considered more desirable? As you will see in the next chapter, g is the preferred effect-size measure for power analysis. Also, g has a very straightforward interpretation when dealing with roughly symmetric, bell-shaped curves; it gives you a clear sense of the degree to which the scores in one group overlap with the scores of the other group. This aspect of g will be described further in the next chapter as well.

The Proportion of Variance Accounted For in Your Samples

As with any correlation coefficient, squaring r_{pb} gives the proportion of variance in your dependent variable (DV) that is *accounted* for by your independent variable (IV). We will illustrate this property of r_{pb} in terms of the data in Table 13.1. First, we find the total variance in weight by squaring the (biased) standard deviation at the bottom of the Weight column in Table 13.1: $\sigma^2 = 349.25$. The variance in weight that is *not* explained by gender is the average (a weighted average if the n's are not equal) of the variances *within* the two genders. Therefore, we square and average the σ's of the two groups: $(8.635^2 + 8.134^2)/2 = 140.725/2 = 70.36$. Now we can find the explained variance (i.e., the *variance accounted for*) by subtracting the unexplained variance from the total:

$$\sigma^2_{explained} = \sigma^2_{total} - \sigma^2_{unexplained} = 349.25 - 70.36 = 278.89.$$

The proportion of the total variance in weight that is accounted for is therefore $278.89/349.25 = .799$, or approximately 80%. Note that r^2_{pb} equals $.894^2 = .799$. This shows that we did not have to go through the trouble of dividing variances; squaring the point-biserial r gives us the proportion of variance accounted for.

Even when a large t value is obtained that easily reaches statistical significance, it is possible that very little variance is being accounted for. This consideration is true of all procedures in inferential statistics. Statistical significance does *not* imply a *large* relationship or effect; it just suggests that the effect in the population is *unlikely to be zero*. A t value does *not* offer a solution to this problem, since it does not provide a ready measure of how large the relationship is (the effect size). So it is very desirable to convert values of t obtained from the procedures in Chapter 11 into point biserial correlation coefficients and to report *both* t (and statistical significance) and r_{pb}. A glance at the formula for r_{pb} in terms of t and df reveals that any particular t that is obtained with large samples (hence, many df) is less impressive (i.e., it will be associated with a smaller r_{pb}) than the same t value obtained with smaller samples.

As an illustration, consider once again the caffeine study discussed in Chapter 11. It was found that caffeine did have a positive association with heart rates; a statistically significant value of t was obtained. The question remains, however, as to *how strong* is the relationship between the presence or absence of that dosage of caffeine and test scores. Recalling that $t = 2.91$ and $df = (22 + 20 - 2) = 40$, we have

$$r_{pb} = \sqrt{\frac{(2.91)^2}{(2.91)^2 + 40}}$$

$$= \sqrt{\frac{8.47}{48.47}}$$

$$= \sqrt{.175}$$

$$= .42$$

Thus, there is a moderately strong relationship between the presence or absence of caffeine and test scores. Since r_{pb}^2 can be interpreted in the same way as r^2, $(.42)^2$ or 17% of the variance in test scores is explained by whether or not caffeine is present. You therefore know that caffeine is a fairly important factor that accounts for differences among people on this test, though far from the only one—83% of the variance in test scores is still not accounted for. If it could be assumed that caffeine has no known harmful side effects, a cautious recommendation that students take caffeine before a mathematics examination would be justified.

Suppose instead that, using a very large sample, the statistically significant t had yielded a value of r_{pb} of .10. Here, only $(.10)^2$ or 1% of the variance in test scores is explained by the presence or absence of caffeine. You are therefore warned that this experimental finding, while statistically significant, is probably not of much practical value. You certainly would *not* recommend that caffeine actually be used, for the probable effect on test scores would be too small to matter. (The possibility does exist, however, that such a finding might be of theoretical importance in understanding brain functioning.)

Estimating the Proportion of Variance Accounted For in the Population

As we have seen, squaring r_{pb} produces a useful descriptive statistic. However, r_{pb}^2 tends to *over*estimate the proportion of variance that would be accounted for in the data for the entire population from which you drew your samples. Fortunately, the formula for r_{pb}^2 can easily be adjusted to remove nearly all of its *bias*.

It would be reasonable to expect that calculating r_{pb}^2 for the entire population would produce a quantity referred to as ρ_{pb}^2. However, the proportion of variance accounted for in the *population* is usually referred to as ω^2 (the lowercase Greek letter omega, squared). To create a nearly unbiased estimate of ω^2, we need only square the formula for r_{pb} and modify it slightly, as shown:

$$\text{est. } \omega^2 = \frac{t^2 - 1}{t^2 + df + 1}$$

If we apply this formula to the heart rate data, we see that whereas 17.47% of the heart rate variance is accounted for by caffeine in *Sara's data*, her best guess about the percent of variance that would be accounted for in the *population is* a bit less: 15.1%.

$$\text{est. } \omega^2 = \frac{2.91^2 - 1}{2.91^2 + 40 + 1} = \frac{7.468}{8.468 + 41} = \frac{7.468}{49.468} = .151$$

The Relationship between ω^2 and d^2

If you were to calculate r_{pb}^2 on an entire population, you would refer to the result as ω^2. Now suppose that you have calculated g for an entire population. What would you call that quantity? Although there is no universal agreement on a symbol for the effect size in a population, we will follow the convention established by J. Cohen (1988), one of the original authors of this text. The lowercase letter d (for "difference") will be printed in boldface (like this: **d**) as a reminder that, even though it is not a Greek letter, it does represent a quantity in the population rather than in a sample. Although g is a slightly biased estimator of **d**, the bias is so small for fairly large sample sizes that you rarely see g being corrected when it is used to estimate **d**. We will have a great deal to say about **d** when we discuss power in the next chapter.

Just as there is a simple relationship between r_{pb} and g for the data in your samples, there is a correspondingly simple relationship between ω^2 and $\mathbf{d}^2$ in the population. To express this relationship as a formula, all that needs to be done is to square both sides of the equation relating r_{pb} to g, drop out the df/N term (there is no distinction between df and N when you are dealing with an entire population), and change the notation:

$$\omega^2 = \frac{\mathbf{d}^2}{\mathbf{d}^2 + 4}$$

When **d** is 2 (i.e., the means of the two populations are 2 standard deviations apart), the proportion of variance accounted for is .5, or $[4/(4 + 4)]$. That is, the average variance within the populations is only half as large as the variance measured across both populations. If the gender difference in height in an entire population were such that $\mathbf{d} = 2$, then you would know that the variance in height for all humans is twice as large as the variance measured separately for each gender. You can use the formula to verify for yourself that $\omega^2 = .2$ when $\mathbf{d} = 1$, and it is .8 when $\mathbf{d} = 4$.

Publishing Effect-Size Estimates

As we mentioned in Chapter 10, supplementing the results of a t test by reporting a corresponding confidence interval is especially helpful when you are dealing with familiar units (inches, kilograms, IQ points). When you are not, it is highly recommended to report a measure of effect size. Sometimes the quantity that we are calling g is used for this purpose, but it is more likely to be referred to as d, or Cohen's d (often without using boldface), even though it has been calculated from sample data and has not been corrected for bias. More often, researchers use a correlational measure, such as r_{pb} or r_{pb}^2, to represent effect size. Given that such sample measures tend to overestimate the true effect in the population, some of the most scientifically rigorous journals prefer that an (approximately) unbiased estimate of ω^2 be reported. We will see in subsequent chapters that one major advantage of estimates of ω^2 is that they can be easily modified to accommodate more than just two groups or populations.

Summary

An r_{pb} is calculated like any other Pearson r, except that the two X values may be assigned arbitrarily to two distinct groups. Therefore, the sign of the correlation is usually ignored.

1. Testing the Point-Biserial Correlation Coefficient for Significance

The magnitude of r_{pb} can be tested for significance with a t test, like any other Pearson r:

$$t = \frac{r_{pb}\sqrt{N-2}}{\sqrt{1-r_{pb}^2}},$$

where N is the total number of pairs = the total number of cases in the two groups = $n_1 + n_2$.

2. Converting Significant Values of t to r_{pb}

When a statistically significant value of t in a test of the difference between two means is obtained, it is very desirable to convert it to r_{pb} so as to determine the *strength* of the relationship. This is readily done as follows:

$$r_{pb} = \sqrt{\frac{t^2}{t^2 + df}},$$

where

$$df = N_1 + N_2 - 2$$

3. Comparing r_{pb} to Another Measure of Effect Size, g

Both r_{pb} and g are alternative measures of the strength of the relationship between a dichotomous grouping variable and a continuous dependent variable. You can compute r_{pb} directly from g with the following formula:

$$r_{pb} = \sqrt{\frac{g^2}{g^2 + 4(df/N)}}$$

4. Estimating the Proportion of Variance Accounted For in the Population

Squaring r_{pb} gives you the proportion of variance accounted for in your data, but this a *biased* estimate of that proportion in the population, which is called ω^2. A nearly unbiased estimate of ω^2 is given by the following formula:

$$\text{est. } \omega^2 = \frac{t^2 - 1}{t^2 + df + 1}$$

Exercises

1. Use the t value you calculated for exercise 1 in Chapter 11 to find the point-biserial r that corresponds to the difference in means between University A and University B. Then use the appropriate t formula to test the r_{pb} you just computed for significance. How does this t value compare with the original t value you calculated for exercise 1 in Chapter 11?

2. An industrial psychologist obtains scores on a job-selection test from 41 men and 31 women, with the following results (see exercise 2 in Chapter 11): men, M = 48.75 (SD = 9.0); women, M = 46.07 (SD = 10.0). First, calculate g for these data. Then use the appropriate formula to calculate r_{pb} directly from g. What proportion of variance in these data is accounted for by gender?

3. The following data come from exercise 3 in Chapter 11. Calculate r_{pb} for these data by assigning an X value of 0 to Group 1 and an X value of 1 to Group 2. What proportion of the variance in the scores is accounted for by group membership?

Group 1	Group 2
62	46
54	53
59	50
56	52
59	54

4. An industrial psychologist asks a group of 9 assembly-line workers and 11 workers not on an assembly line (but doing similar work) to indicate how much they like their jobs on a 9-point scale (9 = like, 1 = dislike). The results are as follows:

Assembly-line workers:	4	4	4	2	1	5	3	4	3		
Other workers:	6	5	7	5	3	7	6	8	7	3	3

Test the null hypothesis that there is no relationship between the assembly line variable and job satisfaction by computing r_{pb}. What should the psychologist decide? (Use Table C.)

5. Convert each of the following statistically significant values of t, obtained from the t test for the difference between two independent means, to r_{pb}.

t	N_1	N_2
2.11	12	8
2.75	12	8
6.00	12	8
2.11	19	23
2.75	19	23
6.00	19	23
2.11	51	51
2.75	51	51
6.00	51	51

Thought Questions

1. Explain why each of the following statements is true: (a) The data from any research study that uses the t test for the difference between two independent sample means can also be analyzed by computing a point-biserial correlation coefficient. (b) Any researcher using the t test for the difference between two independent sample means should also compute a point-biserial correlation coefficient (or other measure of effect size) for the same data. (c) When computing a point-biserial correlation coefficient, it does not matter what two numbers you assign to the dichotomous variable.

2. (a)How do the variables in a research study that uses the Pearson r correlation coefficient differ from the variables in a study that uses the point-biserial correlation coefficient? (b) Is the procedure for computing a point-biserial correlation coefficient different from the procedure for computing a Pearson r correlation coefficient? Why or why not? (c) Is the procedure for testing a Pearson r correlation coefficient for statistical significance different from the procedure for testing a point-biserial correlation coefficient for statistical significance? Why or why not? (d) In what way is the meaning of a squared point-biserial correlation coefficient the same as the meaning of a squared Pearson r correlation coefficient? Are there any differences between these two squared measures?

3. When using the Pearson r correlation coefficient (and virtually all other statistical procedures), it is important to pay attention to the sign of a coefficient (plus or minus). Why, then, do we ignore the sign when interpreting a point-biserial correlation coefficient?

4. Explain what information we obtain from each of the following and when each one is used: (a) *g*. (b) est. ω^2 (the lowercase Greek letter omega, squared). (c) **d**.

Computer Exercises

1. Use your statistical package to compute the Pearson *r* between gender and baseline anxiety for Sara's students; calculate the *t* value for testing *r*, using the formula given in the second footnote of Chapter 12, and compare it to the *t* value you obtained for exercise 1 of Chapter 11.

2. Repeat exercise 1 for baseline heart rate (compare to Chapter 11, exercise 2). How can you interpret the sign of the correlation for this and the previous exercise?

3. Create a new variable whose value is 1 for psychology majors and 2 for all other majors. Compute Pearson's *r* between this new variable and the math background quiz score. Interpret both the sign and the magnitude of this correlation.

Bridge to SPSS

There is nothing special about computing a point-biserial correlation with SPSS; as long as a variable is not a *string* variable, it can be selected in the Bivariate Correlations dialog box as described in the previous chapter. And, as long as the variable contains at least two different values in the data sheet, it will produce a correlation coefficient when selected along with any other variable that meets the same criterion. Whether the magnitude of that correlation will be meaningful depends on the nature of the variables involved. In particular, if one of the variables has only two values, representing two distinct groups, and the other variable is measured on a continuous scale, the resulting correlation coefficient is called the point-biserial *r*, and its magnitude should be interpretable. If a variable has values for more than two groups (e.g., undergrad major), you can compute a point-biserial correlation involving any two of the groups by using **Select Cases…** from the Data menu, and then specifying a condition to be satisfied after activating and clicking the **If…** button (e.g., ugmajor = 1 | ugmajor = 3). Note that the vertical line in the preceding expression functions as a logical operator that means "or"; it may appear as a broken vertical line on your keyboard, and it is sometimes referred to as the "pipe." In another situation, you may want to perform a *t* test comparing the mean of one of several groups with the mean of all the other cases combined (or compute the corresponding point-biserial *r*). In such a case, it is convenient to create a new variable for which participants in the group of interest are given one value (e.g., 1), whereas all other participants from all other groups are given a second value (e.g., 2). You can do this in SPSS with the Recode function.

Recoding

To create a new, two-valued variable from an existing multivalued one, select **Recode** from the Transform menu, and then choose **Into Different Variables...** (this preserves the original multivalued variable, which is what you will usually want to do). In the dialog box that opens, select and move the multivalued variable to the "Input Variable -> Output Variable:" space. Then type in a name for the two-valued variable you will be creating in the "Output Variable" space, and click the **Change** button to the right of that space. Then click on the **Old and New Values...** button to open yet another dialog box. Under "Old Value" insert the value of the group that you want to compare to all of the others, and then under "New Value" insert the value you want this group to have in the new variable (usually "1," for simplicity), and click **Add.** Unless there are missing values to deal with, you can click on **All other values** in the lower-left corner, enter **2** (usually) under New Value, click on **Add** once more, and then click **Continue.** Finally, click **OK** to create the new variable. The new, two-valued variable will then appear in the rightmost column of your data sheet, and at the bottom of your variable list when, for instance, you open the Bivariate Correlations box. (It is highly recommended to go to Variable View right away to create two Value labels for your new variable, as a useful mnemonic—for example, "psych majors" and "nonpsych majors.")

Using the Syntax Window

Before there was Windows, one had to type a series of commands to tell SPSS what to do with your data. Now that list of commands is conveniently created for you, behind the scenes, when you make various selections from the pull-down menus and dialog boxes. Depending on the preferences you set, SPSS may or may not show you the command list you created when it displays your output. However, whether you see it or not, SPSS is creating a Syntax file from your command selections, which can be displayed and even modified, in a Syntax Window. This is a third window (along with the Data window and the Output window) that can be saved as a file for future use (the automatic extension given by SPSS is ".sps"). There are two major uses for the Syntax window: saving a long list of complex commands (e.g., computing many new variables) that you may want to repeat in the future (even if you may need to modify them slightly before running them again); and accessing program features that are not included in any of the SPSS menus (obviously, these are features that the SPSS company believes are potentially useful, but not used very often). We will describe one of these not-available-by-menu features next.

For many purposes, it is easier not to type a syntax file from scratch but rather to create one by first making selections in the relevant dialog box and then by clicking on **Paste** instead of **OK.** As an example, we will show you how to modify a syntax file for performing correlations so that you do not produce the usual square matrix, with its redundant correlation coefficients. Suppose you want to compute the correlations between one particular criterion variable, and each of several potential predictors of that variable, but you are not interested in computing the correlations among the various possible predictors in this run. In the Bivariate Correlations dialog box, move over the criterion variable first, followed by all of the variables you would like to see correlated with the first one. Choose any Options that you want, and then click on the **Paste** button (it is always just beneath or next to the **OK** button). A Syntax file will open automatically, containing the command list needed to perform the analyses you specified in the dialog box.

For instance, if you select one criterion variable and three potential predictors, the syntax file will look something like this:

CORRELATIONS
    /VARIABLES= s_esteem salary friends body_img
    /PRINT=TWOTAIL NOSIG
    /MISSING=PAIRWISE.

Note that this file consists of just one command, called Correlations, with several (default) subcommands, each of which begins with a slash—the command must be closed by including a period at the end of the last subcommand. Running this command produces the usual square matrix containing 4×4 or 16 correlations. However, if you want to compute only three correlations—self-esteem with each of the potential predictors—you can add the keyword **with** after the first variable, so that the Variables subcommand looks like this:

    /VARIABLES= s_esteem with salary friends body_img

As you would guess, **with** is a "reserved" word in SPSS, and therefore cannot be used (for obvious reasons) as the name of a variable. Running the above syntax file after adding the keyword "with" produces an output box with just a single row containing the three correlation coefficients desired (with Sig. and *N*, as usual). You would get the same output by putting the criterion variable at the *end* of the Variables subcommand, preceded by "with," except that the Output box will be in the form of a single column, instead of a single row. If you wanted to compute a series of point-biserial *r*'s, you could put a two-valued variable first in the Variables subcommand followed by "with" and then a list of continuous variables. If you were to include *two* two-valued variables to the left of "with," your correlation output box would contain two rows of point-biserial *r*'s—one for each variable to the left of the keyword "with"—and so forth.

Chapter 14
Introduction to Power Analysis

PREVIEW

Introduction

What is the power of a statistical test? How is it related to a Type II error?

What are the practical consequences of making a Type II error?

Concepts of Power Analysis

How is the power of a statistical test related to the criterion of significance? To the size of the sample?

What is the population effect size, and how is it related to the power of a statistical test?

How large must the sample size be in order to use the procedures described in this chapter?

The Significance Test of the Mean of a Single Population

What are the procedures for determining the power of statistical tests about the mean of a single population?

What are the procedures for determining the sample size required to have a specified power?

The Significance Test of the Proportion of a Single Population

What are the procedures for determining the power of statistical tests about the proportion of a single population?

What are the procedures for determining the sample size required to have a specified power?

The Significance Test of a Pearson r

What are the procedures for determining the power of statistical tests about the Pearson r?

What are the procedures for determining the sample size required to have a specified power?

Testing the Difference between Independent Means

What are the procedures for determining the power of statistical tests about the difference between two means, using independent samples?

What are the procedures for determining the sample size required to have a specified power?

(continued on next page)

Introduction

Thus far, this text has been chiefly concerned with procedures for controlling the rate of Type I errors (incorrect rejections of the null hypothesis). This reflects a long-term emphasis among behavioral researchers and statisticians. However, in hypothesis testing, there is a second important type of error to consider. You also run the risk that even if H_0 is false, you may fail to reject it. Incorrectly retaining a null hypothesis is called a Type II error. Of the cases in which the null hypothesis is *not* true, the proportion for which H_0 is nonetheless retained is the (conditional) probability of a Type II error, symbolized by β. The complement of this probability, $1 - \beta$, is the probability of getting a significant result when H_0 is false, and it is called the *power* of the statistical test.

To truly understand null hypothesis testing, you must also understand the factors that affect the rate of Type II errors and, therefore, statistical power.

Since the behavioral scientist who tests a null hypothesis almost certainly wants to reject it, he wants the power of the statistical test to be high rather than low. That is, he hopes that there is a good chance that the statistical test will indicate that he can reject H_0. Despite its importance, this topic has received relatively little stress in introductory statistical textbooks used in the behavioral sciences. The unfortunate result of this ignorance about power is that research may be done in which, unknown to the investigator, power is low (and, therefore, the probability of a Type II error is high), a false null hypothesis is not rejected (that is, a Type II error is actually made), and much time and effort are wasted. Worse, a promising line of research may be prematurely and mistakenly abandoned because the investigator does not know that he should have relatively little confidence concerning his failure to reject H_0.

This chapter deals first with the concepts involved in power analysis. Then, methods are presented for accomplishing the two major kinds of power analysis, which can be applied to the null hypothesis tests discussed thus far.

Concepts of Power Analysis

The material in this section, since it holds generally for a variety of statistical tests, is abstract and requires careful reading. In ensuing sections, these ideas will be incorporated into concrete procedures for power and sample size analysis of five types of hypothesis tests.

There are four major factors involved in power analysis:

1. *The significance criterion,* α. This, of course, is the familiar criterion for rejecting the null hypothesis. It equals the probability of a Type I error given that H_0 is true (usually .05). A little thought should convince you that the more stringent (the smaller) this criterion, other things being equal, the harder it is to reject H_0 even when it is *not* true, and therefore the lower is the power.

2. *The sample size, N.* Whatever else the accuracy of a sample statistic may depend upon, it *always* depends on the size of the sample on which it has been determined. Thus, all the standard errors you have encountered in this book contain some function of N in the denominator. It follows that, other things being equal, error decreases and power increases as N increases.

3. *The population "effect" size,* **d.** Effect size is a critical concept for understanding power, and a very general one that applies to many statistical tests. When a null hypothesis about a population is false, it is false to some degree. (In other words, H_0 might be very wrong, or somewhat wrong, or only slightly wrong.) The parameter **d,** as described in the previous chapter, is a

standardized measure of the *degree* to which the null hypothesis is false, or how large the "effect" is in the population. Within the framework of hypothesis testing, **d** can be looked upon as a *specific* value that is an alternative to H_0. Specific alternative hypotheses, in contrast to such universal alternative hypotheses as H_1: $\mu_1 - \mu_2 \neq 0$ or H_2: $\rho \neq 0$, are what make power analyses possible. We will consider **d** in detail in subsequent sections.

Other things being equal, power increases as **d,** the degree to which H_0 is false, increases. That is, you are more likely to reject a false H_0 if H_0 is very wrong. Similarly, other things including power being equal, the larger the **d** the smaller the N that is required for significance to be obtained.

4. *Power, or* $1 - \beta$. The fourth parameter is power, the probability of rejecting H_0 at the given significance criterion when H_0 is not true. It is equal to the complement of the probability of a Type II error. That is, power $= 1 - \beta$.

These four factors are mathematically related in such a way that any one of them is an exact function of the other three. We will deal with the two most useful ones:

1. *Power determination.* Given that a statistical test is performed with a specified α and N and that the population state of affairs is **d,** the power of the statistical test can be determined.

2. *N determination.* Given that the population state of affairs is **d** and a statistical test using α is to have some specified power (say .80), the necessary sample size, N, can be determined.

One final concept that will prove useful in statistical power analysis is δ (lowercase delta), where

$$\delta = \mathbf{d} \times f(N)$$

That is, δ is equal to **d** times a function of N. Thus, δ combines the population effect size and the sample size into a single index. The table from which power is read (Table D in the Appendix) is entered using δ.

In the sections that follow, the general system described above for analyses of power determination and sample size determination will be implemented for five different statistical tests:

1. Tests of hypotheses about the mean of a single population (Chapter 9).

2. Tests of hypotheses about the proportion of a single population (Chapter 10).

3. Tests of the significance of a Pearson correlation coefficient (Chapter 12).

4. Tests of the difference between the means of two independent populations (Chapter 11).

5. Tests of the difference between the means of two matched populations (Chapter 11).

The procedures to be described are approximate, and applicable for large samples (N at least 25 or 30). This is because the system uses the normal curve, which (as we have seen) not only is useful in its own right but is also a good approximation to the t distribution once N is that large.

The Test of the Mean of a Single Population

In Chapter 9, we introduced null hypothesis testing in an example involving the math SAT. The value of 500 was known to be the mean of the population, and the issue was whether or not the mean of individually tested students differed from that value. Thus, the null hypothesis is H_0: $\mu = \mu_0 = 500$.

The alternative hypothesis stated in Chapter 9 was merely that H_1: $\mu \neq 500$. However, power analysis is impossible unless a *specific* H_1 is stated.

Power Determination

For the purposes of power analysis, let us assume that you suspect (or are interested in the possibility) that the population mean of individually tested participants is 25 points higher than 500, so that H_1: $\mu = 525$. Assume further that, to be cautious, a two-tailed .05 decision rule is to be used, and that the sample size is to be $N = 164$. Finally, assume you know that the population standard deviation (σ) for the math SAT is 100. The power determination question can then be formulated as follows: If we perform a test at $\alpha = .05$ of H_0: $\mu = 500$ using a random sample of $N = 164$, and in fact μ is 525, what is the probability that we will get a significant result and hence reject H_0?

The size of the effect postulated in the population, which is 25 points in *raw score* terms, must be expressed as a **d** value to accomplish the power analysis. For a test of the mean of a single population, **d** is expressed essentially as a z score:

$$\mathbf{d} = \frac{\mu_1 - \mu_0}{\sigma}$$

In the present example,

$$\mathbf{d} = \frac{525 - 500}{100} = \frac{25}{100} = .25$$

Note that this is *not* a statement about actual or prospective *sample* results. It expresses, as an alternative hypothesis, the *population* state of affairs. That is, μ_1 is postulated to be .25σ away from μ_0, the value specified by H_0. Note also that the sign of **d** is ignored; an effect size of $-.25$ (i.e., $\mu_1 - 475$) would lead to the same results for power.

Having obtained the measure of effect size, the next step is to obtain δ. In the previous section, we pointed out that $\delta = \mathbf{d} \times f(N)$. For the test of the mean of a single population, the specific function of N is $\sqrt{N}$, so that

$$\delta = \mathbf{d}\sqrt{N}$$

In the present example,

$$\delta = .25\sqrt{164} = 3.2$$

Entering Table D in the Appendix with $\delta = 3.2$ and $\alpha = .05$, the power is found to be .89. Thus, if the mean of the population of individually tested participants is 25 points away from 500, the probability of rejecting H_0 in this situation is .89 (or, the probability of a Type II error is .11). If the mean of the population of individually tested participants is more than 25 points away from 500, the power will be greater than .89. Conversely, if the population mean is less than 25 points away from 500, the power will be less than .89.

It is important to understand that power analysis proceeds completely with population values. It does *not* utilize sample results, either actual or prospective. The above analysis could well take place before the data were gathered to determine what the power would be under the specified α, $\mathbf{d}$ and N. Or it could take place after an experiment was completed to determine the power the statistical test *had*, given α, $\mathbf{d}$, and N with no reference to the obtained data. If the power for a reasonably postulated $\mathbf{d}$ were equal to .25 when the results of the experiment were not statistically significant, the nonsignificant result would be inconclusive, since the *a priori* probability of obtaining significance is so small (and the probability of a Type II error is so high). On the other hand, power of .90 associated with a nonsignificant result tends to suggest that the actual $\mathbf{d}$ is not likely to be as large as postulated.

In order to compute $\mathbf{d}$ in the above example, it was necessary to posit a specific value of μ_1 (525) and also to know σ (100). This can sometimes be difficult when the unit is not a familiar one. (For example, extensive *a priori* data may not be available for a new test.) For situations like this, it is useful to specify conventional values corresponding to "small," "medium," and "large" values of $\mathbf{d}$, which although arbitrary are reasonable (in much the same way as the .05 decision rule). For the test of the mean of a single population, the values suggested by J. Cohen (1988) are

small: $\mathbf{d} = .20$

medium: $\mathbf{d} = .50$

large: $\mathbf{d} = .80$

If you are unable to posit specific values of μ_1 or σ, you can select the value of $\mathbf{d}$ corresponding to how large you believe the effect size in the population to

FIGURE 14.1

Sampling distribution of means ($N = 164$) assuming $\mu_0 = 500$ and $\mu_1 = 525$

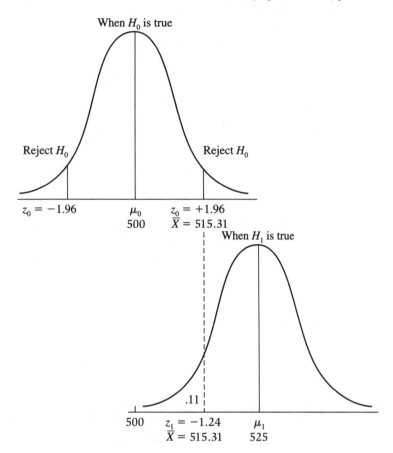

When H_0 is true

Reject H_0 Reject H_0

$z_0 = -1.96$ μ_0 $z_0 = +1.96$
                        500          $\overline{X} = 515.31$

When H_1 is true

.11

500        $z_1 = -1.24$ μ_1
           $\overline{X} = 515.31$ 525

be. Do *not* use the above conventional values if you can specify **d** values that are appropriate to the specific problem or field of research in which the statistical test occurs, for conventional values are only reasonable approximations. As you get to know a substantive research area, the need for reliance on these conventions should diminish. Later in this chapter, we discuss how previously published research results can help you to estimate **d** for your study.

To clarify the general logic of power analysis, let us reconsider the preceding problem in terms of the concepts introduced in Chapter 9. The null hypothesis states that $\mu_0 = 500$ and the standard error of the mean is equal to 7.81 ($\sigma/\sqrt{N}$ is equal to $100/12.81$), so the sampling distribution of means postulated by H_0 can be illustrated by the graph shown at the *top* in Figure 14.1. Assume that the true value of μ is equal to 525, for which the sampling distribution of means is as shown by the graph at the *bottom* in Figure 14.1. How likely is it that you will retain the incorrect μ_0 of 500?

Since we are using the normal curve as an approximation to the appropriate t distribution, the critical value (z_0) is equal to ± 1.96. If a sample mean is obtained that (when expressed as a z value) is numerically less than 1.96, the incorrect H_0 will be retained. This z_0 value can readily be converted to a critical value of the sample mean:

$$z_0 = \frac{\bar{X} - \mu_0}{s_{\bar{X}}}$$

$$1.96 = \frac{\bar{X} - 500}{7.81}$$

$$\bar{X} = (1.96)(7.81) + 500$$

$$\bar{X} = 515.31$$

So the incorrect H_0 will be rejected if the sample mean is greater than 515.31. To see how likely this is to occur when the population mean is actually equal to 525, consider only the bottom graph in Figure 14.1 and convert the mean value of 515.31 to a z value:

$$z_1 = \frac{\bar{X} - \mu_1}{\sigma_{\bar{X}}}$$

$$z_1 = \frac{515.31 - 525}{7.81} = \frac{9.69}{7.81} = -1.24$$

The percent of the area under the normal curve to the right of this z value can be found by using Table A: at $z = -1.24$, it is about 89% (= 39.25% + 50.00%). Therefore, when $\mu = 525$, about 89% of the sample means which one can obtain would be greater than 515.31 and thus significant. So the probability of rejecting H_0 when $\mu = 525$, and hence the power of this test, is .89. Since the test is two-tailed and the analysis symmetrical, the same argument would lead to the same conclusion if the true $\mu = 475$, 25 points *below* $H_0 = 500$. Thus, we can conclude that, under these conditions, if $\mu = 525$ *or* 475, the probability of rejecting H_0 ($\mu_0 = 500$) is .89.

If the null hypothesis is so wrong that there is virtually no chance of a Type II error (that is, if the effect size is extremely large), power will be virtually perfect (approaching 1.0). This does *not* indicate that the research is necessarily good, for the researcher may be testing a proposition so obviously wrong that the research would be pointless. (For example, his null hypothesis might be that the mean IQ of college graduates is 68!) If, on the other hand, the null hypothesis is only slightly wrong (the researcher is studying a small-sized effect), a large sample size will be needed in order for the research to have acceptable power.

Sample Size Determination

We now turn to the other major kind of statistical power analysis, sample size determination. Here, α, **d,** and the desired power are specified, and you wish to determine the necessary sample size. This form of analysis is particularly useful in experimental planning, since it provides the only rational method for making the crucially important decision about the size of N.

First, we must consider the concept of "desired power." Your first inclination might be to set power very high, such as .99 or .999. But, as your intuition might suggest, the quest for near certainty is likely to result in the requirement of a very large N, usually far beyond your resources. This is similar to the drawback of choosing a very small significance criterion, such as .0001: Although a Type I error is very unlikely with such a criterion, you are also very unlikely to obtain statistical significance unless the effect size and/or sample size is unrealistically large. Therefore, just as it is prudent to seek less than certainty in minimizing Type I errors by being content with a significance criterion such as .05 or .01, a prudent power value is also in order insofar as Type II errors are concerned.

Although a researcher is of course free to set any power value that makes sense to her, we suggest the value .80 (which makes the probability of a Type II error equal to .20) when a conventional standard is desired. Why is this suggested value larger than the customary .05 value for the probability of a Type I error? In most instances in science, it is seen as less desirable to mistakenly reject a true H_0 (which leads to false positive claims) than to mistakenly fail to reject H_0 (which leads only to the failure to find something and no claim at all: "the evidence is insufficient to warrant the conclusion that...."). Besides, if desired power were conventionally set at .95 (making β = .05), most studies would demand larger samples than most investigators could muster. We repeat, however, that the .80 value should be used only as a general standard, with investigators quite free to make their own decision based on the availability of participants, the cost of running the study, and other pertinent factors.

Let us return to the individual SAT test study, but now with a different purpose. Instead of assuming that N is to be 164, suppose you are now interested in the following question: "If I test at α = .05 the null hypothesis that μ = 500 when in fact μ = 525 or 475 (and σ = 100), how large must N be for me to have a .80 probability of rejecting H_0 (that is, to have power = .80)?" To answer this question, the first step is to obtain two values: **d,** determined by the same methods as in the preceding section and equal to $(\mu_1 - \mu_0)/\sigma$ or .25, and the desired power, specified as .80. Next, δ is obtained by entering Table E in the Appendix in the row for desired power = .80 and the column for α (two-tailed) = .05; δ is found to be 2.80. Finally, for this test of the mean of a single population, N is found as follows:

$$N = \left(\frac{\delta}{\mathbf{d}}\right)^2$$

In the present example,

$$N = \left(\frac{2.80}{.25}\right)^2$$

$$= (11.2)^2$$

$$= 125$$

To have power $= .80$ in the present situation, the sample must have 125 cases in it. Note that this is consistent with the previous result where we saw that, other things ($\mathbf{d}, \alpha$) being equal, $N = 164$ resulted in power $= .89$.

To illustrate the consequences of demanding very high power, consider what happens in this problem if desired power is set at .999. From Table E in the Appendix, $\delta = 5.05$. Substituting,

$$N = \left(\frac{\delta}{\mathbf{d}}\right)^2 = \left(\frac{5.05}{.25}\right)^2 = (20.2)^2 = 408$$

In this problem, to go from .80 to .999 power requires increasing N from 125 to 408. This is more than many researchers can manage. Of course, if data are easily obtained or if the cost of making a Type II error is great, no objection can be raised about such a "maximum" power demand.

The Significance Test of the Proportion of a Single Population

The structure of the power analysis procedures remains the same as before; only the details need to be adjusted. The null hypothesis in question is that the population proportion, π, is equal to some specified value. That is, $H_0: \pi = \pi_0$. H_0 is tested against some specific alternative, $H_1: \pi = \pi_1$.

Power Determination

Let us return to the worried politician in Chapter 10, who wants to forecast the results of an upcoming two-person election by obtaining a random sample of $N = 400$ voters and testing the null hypothesis that the proportion favoring him is $\pi_0 = .50$. He thinks that he is separated from his opponent by about .08. That is, he expects the vote to be .54 to .46 or .46 to .54. (His expectations are stated in both directions because a two-tailed significance test is intended.) The question can be summarized as follows: If a statistical test is performed at $\alpha = .05$ of $H_0: \pi = .50$ against the specific alternative $H_1: \pi = .54$ (or .46) with $N = 400$, what is the power of this statistical test?

For the test of a proportion from a single population, the effect size, $\mathbf{d}$, and δ are defined as follows:

$$d = \frac{\pi_1 - \pi_0}{\sqrt{\pi_0 (1 - \pi_0)}}$$

$$\delta = d\sqrt{N}$$

For the data of this problem,

$$\mathbf{d} = \frac{.54 - .50}{\sqrt{.50 (1 - .50)}}$$

$$= \frac{.04}{.50}$$

$$= .08$$

$$\delta = .08\sqrt{400}$$

$$= 1.60$$

Entering Table D with $\delta = 1.60$ and $\alpha = .05$, the power is found to be .36. So our worried politician has something else to worry about: As he has planned the study, he has only about one chance in three of coming to a positive conclusion (rejecting the null hypothesis that $\pi = .50$) if the race is as close as he thinks ($H_1: \pi = .54$ or $.46$). If the poll had already been conducted as described and the results were not statistically significant, he should consider the results inconclusive. Even if π is as far from .50 as .54 or .46, the probability of a Type II error (β) is .64.

Sample Size Determination

Let us now invert the problem to one of determining N, given the same $\mathbf{d} = .08$, $\alpha = .05$ and specifying the desired power as .80. The formula for N for the test of a proportion from a single population, like the previous formula for δ, is the same as in the case of the mean of a single population:

$$N = \left(\frac{\delta}{\mathbf{d}}\right)^2$$

The value of δ for the joint specification of power $= .80$, α (two-tailed) $= .05$ is found from Table E to be 2.80. Therefore,

$$N = \left(\frac{2.80}{.08}\right)^2$$

$$= (35)^2$$

$$= 1,225$$

This sample size is considerably larger than the $N = 400$ that yielded a power of .36 under these conditions. It is hardly a coincidence that in surveys conducted both for political polling and market and advertising research, sample sizes typically run about 1,500.

If conventional values for effect size for this test are needed, the following **d** values can be used: small, .10; medium, .30; large, .50.

The Significance Test of a Pearson *r*

Recall from Chapter 12 that for testing Pearson's *r* the null hypothesis is usually H_0: $\rho = 0$. For the purpose of power analysis, the alternative hypothesis is that the population value is some *specific* value other than zero: H_1: $\rho = \rho_1$. For example, you might be testing an *r* for significance when expecting that the population value is .30. In this case, H_1: $\rho = .30$. (Again, for two-tailed tests, the value is taken as either +.30 or –.30.)

Power Determination

When dealing with a Pearson *r*, you do not need a formula to define the effect size; the value for **d** is simply the value of ρ specified by H_1 (.30 in this example). To find δ, the appropriate function of *N* to be combined with **d** is $\sqrt{N-1}$:

$$\delta = \mathbf{d} \sqrt{N-1} = \rho_1 \sqrt{N-1}$$

Let us consider again the study in Chapter 12 in which we measured the degree of linear relationship between GPA and SAT scores in a random sample of 25 college students. Suppose we had planned a two-tailed statistical test with $\alpha = .01$, and we had expected the population ρ to be .43; thus $\rho_1 = .43$, whereas H_0: $\rho = 0$. What is the power of this test?

We can go directly to

$$\delta = .43 \sqrt{25-1}$$
$$= 2.10$$

Entering Table D for $\delta = 2.10$ and $\alpha = .01$, power is found to be .32. One chance in three of finding significance may strike the researcher as hardly worth the effort. He may then reconsider the stringency of his significance criterion and check $\alpha = .05$; the power of .56 with this more lenient criterion may still not satisfy him. He might then plan to increase his sample size (as shown in the next section). If ρ were equal to the obtained sample *r* of .65, δ would be about 3.2 and power would be as high as .73 even for $\alpha = .01$.

If the investigator has difficulty in formulating an alternative-hypothetical value for ρ_1, the following conventional values are offered (J. Cohen, 1988): small, .10; medium, .30; large, .50. The value of .50 may not seem "large," but over most of the range of behavioral science where correlation is used, correlations between different variables do not often get much larger than that.

Sample Size Determination

Returning to the SAT/GPA study, we can ask what N is necessary for a test at α (two-tailed) = .05, assuming $\mathbf{d} = \rho_1 = .30$, in order to have power of (let us say) .75. The value of N is just one more than for the other two one-sample tests previously described:

$$N = \left(\frac{\delta}{\mathbf{d}}\right)^2 + 1 = \left(\frac{\delta}{\rho_1}\right)^2 + 1$$

δ is found from Table E for power = .75, α = .05, to be 2.63, so

$$N = \left(\frac{2.63}{.30}\right)^2 + 1$$

$$= (8.77)^2 + 1$$

$$= 78$$

To have a .75 chance (that is, three-to-one odds) of finding r to be significant if $\rho_1 = +.30$ (or $-.30$), he needs a sample of 78 cases.

Testing the Difference between Independent Means

The next significance test whose power analysis we consider is the test of the difference between the means of two independently drawn random samples. This is probably the most frequently performed test in the behavioral sciences.

As stated in Chapter 11, the null hypothesis most frequently tested is H_0: $\mu_1 - \mu_2 = 0$ (often written as $\mu_1 = \mu_2$). For power analysis, a *specific* alternative hypothesis is needed. We will write this as H_1: $\mu_1 - \mu_2 = \theta$ (theta), where θ is the difference between the means expressed in *raw* units. To obtain $\mathbf{d}$, the standard measure of effect size, this difference must be standardized. This is done using the standard deviation of the population, σ (which is a single value since we assume that $\sigma_1 = \sigma_2$ for the two populations). Thus, the value of $\mathbf{d}$ in this instance is conceptually the same as for the test of a single population mean, namely

$$\mathbf{d} = \frac{\text{alternative-hypothetical } \mu_1 - \mu_2}{\sigma} = \frac{\theta}{\sigma}$$

This can be looked upon as the difference between z score means of the two populations, or, equivalently, the difference in means expressed in units of σ. Again, the direction of the difference (the sign of θ) is ignored in two-tailed tests.

This device of "standardizing" the difference between two means is generally useful, and not only for purposes of power analysis. Frequently in behavioral science, there is no sure sense of how large a unit of raw score is. How large *is* a point? Well, they come in different sizes: An IQ point comes about 15 to the standard deviation (σ_{IQ}), while an SAT point is much smaller, coming 100 to the standard deviation (σ_{SAT}). By always using σ as the unit of measurement, we achieve comparability from one measure to another, as was the case with z scores.

This device helps us with regard to other related problems. One occurs whenever we have not had much experience with a measure (a new test, for example) and we have little if any basis for estimating the population σ, which the foregoing formula for $\mathbf{d}$ requires. Paradoxically enough, we can use this σ as our unit, despite the fact that it is unknown, by thinking directly in terms of $\mathbf{d}$. Thus, a $\mathbf{d}$ of .25 indicates a difference between two population means (whose exact value we do not know) equal to $.25\sigma$ (whose exact value we also do not know). It is as if our ignorance cancels out, and in a most useful sense $\mathbf{d} = .25$ is always the same size difference whether we are talking about IQ, height, socioeconomic status, or a brand-new measure of "oedipal intensity."

How large *is* a $\mathbf{d}$ of .25, or any other? Here, as before, it is possible (and sometimes necessary) to appeal to some conventions, and they are the same as in the test of the mean of a single population: small, .20; medium, .50; large, .80. In this framework, a $\mathbf{d}$ of .25 would be characterized as a "smallish" difference. To gain a more concrete feeling with respect to the size of $\mathbf{d}$, it may help to think about $\mathbf{d}$ in terms of the overlap of the two distributions involved. When $\mathbf{d}$ is 2.0, the mean of one population is two SDs away from the mean of the other; only a little more than 2% of the population with the lower mean, for instance, will extend above the mean of the "higher" population. When $\mathbf{d}$ is merely "large" (see Figure 14.2A) about 21% of the lower population exceeds the mean of the higher population, and when $\mathbf{d}$ is "small," more than 42% of the lower population is above the mean of the higher one (see Figure 14.2B). By contrast, with a $\mathbf{d}$ of 4.0 there would be so little overlap between the two distributions that relatively few scores from the lower population would surpass *any* of the scores from the higher population (see Figure 14.2C).

Power Determination

For the comparison of two means, the value of δ is equal to

$$\delta = \mathbf{d}\sqrt{\frac{n}{2}},$$

where

> n = size of *each* of the two samples (thus $2n$ cases are needed in all)

Compare this formula to the formula in Chapter 11 for finding t in terms of g (the effect size in your samples) and n:

$$t = g\sqrt{\frac{n}{2}}$$

Over many exact replications of a particular experiment, the values of g will average out (approximately) to $\mathbf{d}$, the effect size in the population. And the t's for these replications should, in the long run, average out to (approximately) δ (delta), which can be thought of as the *expected t value* for an experiment with a particular value for $\mathbf{d}$ and a fixed size of n for each of the two samples.

FIGURE 14.2

Overlap of populations as a function of effect size

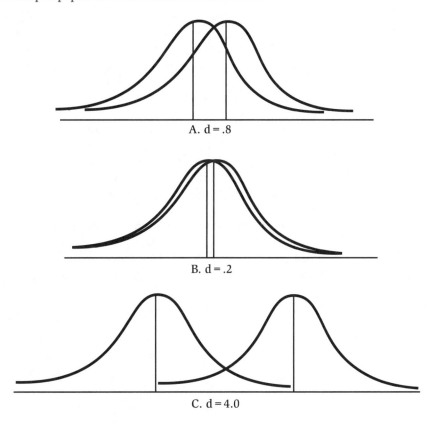

A. d = .8

B. d = .2

C. d = 4.0

As an illustration, consider the caffeine study in Chapter 11 (revised to make it a true experiment). Given two groups, each with $n = 40$ cases, one of which is given a dose of caffeine and the other a placebo, we will test at $\alpha = .05$ (two-tailed) the difference between their means on a mathematics test following the treatment. If between the populations there is a mean difference of medium size, operationally defined as $\mathbf{d} = .50$, what is the power of the test? With $\mathbf{d}$ given on the basis of convention, there is no need to compute it, and hence no need to estimate μ_1, μ_2, or σ. Thus, all we need is

$$\delta = .50 \sqrt{\frac{40}{2}}$$

$$= 2.24$$

Entering Table D in the column for $\alpha = .05$, we find for $\delta = 2.2$ that power $= .59$ and for $\delta = 2.3$ that power $= .63$. Interpolating between these two values to obtain the power corresponding to $\delta = 2.24$ yields power of $.59 + .4(.63 - .59) = .61$. Thus, for medium differences (as defined here), samples of 40 cases each have only a .61 probability of rejecting H_0 for a two-tailed test using $\alpha = .05$.

Ordinarily, in research where variables are to be manipulated, such as the caffeine experiment described here, it is possible to arrange the experiment so that the total available pool of subjects is divided equally among the groups. This division is usually optimal. But it is not always possible or desirable to have equal sample sizes. For example, it would be a mistake to reduce the larger of two available samples to make it equal to the smaller. Instead, to determine power when $N_1 \neq N_2$, we can use the same device we employed in Chapter 11; we can compute the *harmonic mean* of the two Ns and then use this obtained value for n in the formula for δ. As an example, consider a psychiatric hospital study where there are resources to place a random sample of 50 newly admitted schizophrenic patients into a special experimental treatment program. After one month, their progress is compared with a control group of 150 cases receiving regular treatment for the same period. It is planned to rate each patient on an improvement scale 30 days following admission and to test for the significance of the difference in means for rated improvement, using a two-tailed test where $\alpha = .05$. If it is anticipated that $\mathbf{d} = .40$ (between "small" and "medium"), what is the power of the test?

Since $N_1 \neq N_2$, compute

$$\overline{X}_{\text{harmonic}} = \frac{2N_1 N_2}{N_1 + N_2} = \frac{2(50)(150)}{50 + 150} = 75$$

Then enter this value as n in the formula for δ:

$$\delta = .40 \sqrt{\frac{75}{2}}$$

$$= 2.45$$

Interpolating between $\delta = 2.4$ and $\delta = 2.5$ in Table D in the $\alpha = .05$ column yields power $= .69$.

Note that a total of $N_1 + N_2 = 200$ cases will be studied. But since $N_1 \neq N_2$, the resulting power is the same as if two samples of 75 cases each, or 150 cases, were to be studied. There is a smaller effective n, and hence less power. This demonstrates the nonoptimality of unequal sample sizes. Were it possible to divide the total of 200 cases into two equal samples of 100, δ would equal $.40 \sqrt{100/2}$ or 2.83, and the resulting power at $\alpha = .05$ obtained from Table D by interpolation is .81.

Sample Size Determination

The sample size needed for *each* independent sample when means are to be compared can be found for specified values of α, **d,** and the desired power, as was shown for the other statistical tests in this chapter. The combination of α and power is expressed as δ by looking in Table E, and the values for δ and **d** are substituted in the equation appropriate for this statistical test, which is

$$n = 2\left(\frac{\delta}{\mathbf{d}}\right)^2$$

For example, it was found in the caffeine experiment that for $\alpha = .05$ and **d** $= .50$, the plan to use samples of $n = 40$ each resulted in power $= .61$. If power $= .90$ is desired, what n per sample is needed?

For a two-tailed test where $\alpha = .05$ and power $= .90$, Table E yields $\delta = 3.24$. Substituting,

$$n = 2\left(\frac{3.24}{.50}\right)^2$$

$$= 84 \text{ cases in each group, or 168 cases in all}$$

Again we see that large desired power values demand large sample sizes. Were the more modest power of .80 specified, δ would equal 2.80 (Table E) and n would equal $2(2.80/.50)^2$ or 63, a materially smaller number.

Testing the Difference between the Means of Two Matched Populations

The last significance test whose power analysis we will consider is the test of the difference between *dependent* or *correlated* means—that is, the test that is applied to the data of a matched-pairs design. The formulas and procedures for power analysis in this case differ from the preceding one (i.e., the difference between two independent means) by the inclusion of one additional term that depends on the degree to which the two sets of scores are matched in the population, as expressed by the correlation coefficient ρ.

Power Determination

Given that **d** is defined as in the case of two independent means, the value of δ for a matched (or repeated-measures) design is

$$\delta = \mathbf{d}\sqrt{\frac{1}{1-\rho}}\sqrt{\frac{n}{2}},$$

where ρ is the correlation between the two sets of scores in the population. Note that as ρ gets closer to $+1.0$, the denominator of the first term gets smaller, making the first term larger. When ρ is .75, the first term is 2.0, and δ therefore becomes twice as large as it would be for an otherwise similar experiment without matching. The power boost from this degree of matching is substantial; it is equivalent to the boost you would get by quadrupling your sample sizes.

A ρ of zero would leave δ unchanged. A negative ρ, which is unlikely when you are making an effort to match participants, would actually *reduce* your δ and therefore your power. To illustrate, let us return to the before-after heart rate comparison as shown in Table 11.2 of Chapter 11. Suppose that you expect a large effect size (**d** = .8), and a population correlation (ρ) of .5, for the 10 participants in the study. You plan to perform a two-tailed matched-pairs *t* test at the .05 level. Given these values,

$$\delta = .8\sqrt{\frac{1}{1-.5}}\sqrt{\frac{10}{2}} = .8\sqrt{2}\sqrt{5} = (.8)(1.414)(2.236) = 2.53$$

From Table D, we can see that a δ of 2.53 corresponds to a power of about .72 for a two-tailed significance test using .05 for alpha. This is a barely adequate level of power for conducting an experiment, and if a lower value of **d** or ρ were expected, the sample size would have to be increased to maintain even this minimal level of power.

Sample Size Determination

The formula for finding the sample size required for a given level of power, with values specified for **d** and ρ, is the same as the one for independent samples multiplied by a factor of $(1 - \rho)$. So if you expect a matching correlation of .9 in the population, you will only need one-tenth the number of participants $(1 - .9)$ to achieve the level of power that would result with no matching at all.

For the heart rate comparison, suppose you want power to be .8 for a .05, two-tailed test ($\delta = 2.8$, from Table D), and you expect a medium effect size ($\mathbf{d} = .5$) and a ρ of only .3. The number of pairs of scores that would be required is

$$ n = 2(1 - \rho)\left(\frac{\delta}{d}\right)^2 = 2(1 - .3)\left(\frac{2.8}{.5}\right)^2 = 1.4(31.36) = 43.9 $$

Therefore, 44 participants would each have to be measured twice in order to attain the desired level of power.

Choosing a Value for d for a Power Analysis Involving Independent Means

Students often feel uneasy when they first discover that power analysis is only as accurate as your estimate of **d.** Unless you are replicating an experiment for which you already have the results, it is not obvious how you can make a reasonable guess about the **d** that corresponds to your new experiment. So let us now consider the relatively simple case in which you *are* contemplating the replication of a published result.

Estimating d from Previous Research

Suppose you read a journal article reporting that a group of participants listening to music composed by Mozart produced significantly higher scores on a test of spatial ability than a control group who listened to popular (e.g., "soft rock") music. Further suppose that the chief result was reported as "$t(34) = 2.4, p < .05$." If you know that the two groups were the same size, then you know that n was 18 ($2n - 2 = 34$), and you can find g from t and n by reversing the formula for t from g and n given in Chapter 11:

$$ g = t\sqrt{\frac{2}{n}} = 2.4\sqrt{\frac{2}{18}} = 2.4\left(\frac{1}{3}\right) = .8 $$

If you were to replicate this study exactly, it would be reasonable to use g from the previous study as the estimated **d** for your new study when calculating power for different possible sample sizes. Even if you planned to use a different spatial ability measure whose mean and SD were quite different from those in the previous study, it would not be unreasonable to suppose that **d** (which is in standardized units) would be fairly similar for both studies.

At what point is your new study so different from a previously published study that you can no longer use g from the previous study as an estimate of **d** for your new study? This is a judgment call that requires a thorough knowledge of your research domain. It is the same kind of judgment that underlies the increasingly popular statistical procedure known as *meta-analysis*. In meta-analysis, the gs for any number of similar studies are averaged together to arrive at an improved estimate of **d**. This average g can then be tested for significance using the combined N of all the studies involved. This method creates one large "meta" study, which greatly increases power relative to any one individual study and thus makes a Type II error much less likely.

If the two samples are not equal in size in a previous study but you are given both N_1 and N_2, you can still calculate g from t by using the unequal-N formula for g (based on the harmonic mean) given in the previous chapter, and reproduced here.

$$g = t \sqrt{\frac{N_1 + N_2}{N_1 N_2}}$$

Suppose that the Ns for the Mozart study were as follows: N_1 = 30 and N_2 = 6 (*df* is still 34). In order for t to be 2.4, g would have to be

$$g = 2.4 \sqrt{\frac{36}{180}} = 2.4 \sqrt{\frac{1}{5}} = 1.07$$

Note that as the two Ns diverge, the harmonic mean decreases (the harmonic mean of 30 and 6 is only 10), which tends to lower your power and therefore increases the likelihood of committing a Type II error. This is one reason why equal sample sizes are often recommended when planning a two-group experiment.

Trying Extreme Values for d

One possible approach to sample-size determination begins with deciding on the smallest effect size for which you would like to have adequate power. For instance, suppose you feel that for your experiment there would be little point to having an adequate level of power (say, .7) for an effect size of only .1. This constraint corresponds to a size for each sample of

$$n = 2\left(\frac{\delta}{\mathbf{d}}\right)^2 = 2\left(\frac{2.48}{.1}\right)^2 = 2(24.8)^2 = 2(615) = 1230$$

Thus, you would not consider running your experiment with more than about twelve hundred participants in each group, because that would give you adequate power for an effect size too small to be of interest.

Conversely, you can begin by deciding on the largest reasonably possible value for your effect size. Suppose you think it very unlikely that **d** is greater than 1.0. Again using the value of .7 for barely adequate power, your target sample size would be

$$n = 2\left(\frac{2.48}{1}\right)^2 = 2(6.15) = 12.3$$

This calculation tells you that there would be little point to running your experiment with *fewer* than 13 participants per group, because in that case you would expect your power to be less than adequate (i.e., below .7).

Using Power Analysis to Interpret the Results of Null Hypothesis Tests

Whether or not you ever perform a power analysis before running an experiment, it is important to understand the factors that affect the power of a statistical test. This can help you to interpret the results of null hypothesis tests correctly, and avoid some serious misconceptions.

Lack of Statistical Significance Does Not Imply That the Null Hypothesis Is Likely to Be True

The smaller your samples (all else being equal) the less power you will have to detect a given effect size in the population. In many common situations, power is surprisingly low. For instance, if your two-group experiment involves 32 participants in each group, your power will be only about .5 whenever you test medium-sized effects at the .05 level. For a medium effect size, $\mathbf{d} = .5$; therefore,

$$\delta = .5 \sqrt{\frac{32}{2}} = .5(4) = 2.0$$

Looking up δ in Table D, you can see that you will reject H_0 (correctly) 52% of the time, but you will retain H_0 (and therefore commit a Type II error) nearly half of the time. So when you see a study involving small samples and H_0 is *not* rejected, you should be aware that H_0 could easily be false, nonetheless. Unfortunately, even when the true effect size is considerably more than zero, there is a good chance that the null hypothesis will not be rejected, if the samples are small.

Statistical Significance Is More Impressive When the Samples Are Smaller

For a given value of t, the *smaller n is*, the larger g has to be. And a larger g for your samples suggests a larger $\mathbf{d}$ in the population, which is more impressive than a smaller effect size. (For any particular set of experimental results, g

could accidentally be much larger or much smaller than the **d** of which it is just an estimate, but on the average, a large g implies a large **d**.) By itself a large t value only suggests that H_0 is not very likely to be true, but a large t obtained with a small n tells you that g is fairly large and that **d** therefore is not likely to be even near zero. Although it may be counterintuitive, significant results are more impressive when obtained with *small* rather than large samples, because it is so rare for the results from small samples to attain statistical significance unless the effect size in the population is fairly large.

Large Samples Tend to Produce More Accurate Results but Can Lead to Misleading Conclusions

The larger your samples, the more accurate is g as an estimate of **d.** Because it is the magnitude of **d** that you would really like to know (not just whether it is unlikely to be zero, which is all you can conclude from NHT), larger samples are always more informative. However, there is usually some economic cost that comes with increasing your sample size (e.g., paying participants, paying research assistants), and the additional information may not be worth the cost. Moreover, very large samples make it easy to obtain statistically significant t values even when g (and probably **d**) is rather small. So you should not be overly impressed with statistically significant results that are obtained from large samples; in such cases you need to pay extra attention to effect-size estimates.

Also, remember that using repeated measures or matched samples can be similar to using larger samples without matching, in terms of attaining statistical significance with experimental treatments that are quite weak in their effects. Note that *statistical* significance is less likely to imply *practical* significance, when the samples are very large, or the correlation between matched sets of scores is very high.

The Null Hypothesis Testing Controversy

There is much confusion concerning what NHT does and does not tell you about the state of affairs in a population, and there has been much debate in the literature on this topic, especially in recent years. Many improvements and alternatives to NHT have been suggested. (A good way to learn more about these issues is by reading *Beyond Significance Testing* [Kline, 2004]). Although there does seem to be some increased reporting of confidence intervals and effect-size estimates, NHT, with its reporting of p values and decisions about H_0 still dominates the results sections of articles published in many branches of behavioral science research.

There is one major advantage of NHT that would be difficult to achieve with any new system: the widespread agreement on the .05 level as the largest, routinely acceptable value for alpha. This fixed criterion of significance, coupled with the usual constraints on sample sizes (behavioral researchers rarely employ very large samples), tends to make it likely that *statistically* significant results will be associated with effect sizes that are large enough to be interesting. Conversely, whereas NHT screens out 95% of studies in which the null hypothesis is actually true (i.e., with $\alpha = .05$, 95% of the null experiments will fail to attain statistical significance), it also screens out about 93% of very small effect sizes (e.g., $\mathbf{d} \leq .1$) when using small samples (e.g., about 30 participants in each of the two groups being compared).

Technically, failing to reject H_0 when $\mathbf{d}$ is anything more than zero is a Type II error, but given all of the small effects that behavioral researchers may explore, many of these Type II errors save us the trouble of dealing with effects too small to be practical or even worthy of further exploration. For example, consider the "Mozart effect": the finding that listening to music composed by Mozart improves performance on a spatial ability test (Rauscher, Shaw, & Ky, 1993). It is not really interesting if Mozart's music produces an extremely tiny, temporary effect on spatial ability (especially when compared to popular music, as in the original study). Did anyone think that listening to Mozart's music was likely to reduce spatial ability? And would anyone be surprised if the music of other classical composers also produced such an effect?

On the other hand, (effect) size isn't everything. Sometimes even a tiny effect can be very interesting indeed, especially if it represents a phenomenon that was thought to be impossible (e.g., learning to control directly and voluntarily the function of your kidneys). It is often important to look carefully at estimates of effect size when a result is statistically significant, but it is also important to consider the theoretical significance of a study.

Summary

Power is the *probability of getting a significant result* in a statistical test for which H_0 is true. Power is equal to $1 - \beta$, where $\beta =$ the probability of a Type II error.

1. The Importance of Power

If power is not known, a researcher may waste a great deal of time by conducting an experiment that has little chance to produce significance even if H_0 is false. Worse, he may abandon a promising line of research because he does not know that he should have relatively little confidence concerning his failure to reject H_0 (that is, the probability of a Type II error is large).

2. The Four Major Parameters of Power Analysis

1. *The significance criterion, α.* A Type II error is more likely as α gets smaller because you fail to reject H_0 more often. Thus, power decreases as α decreases.

2. *The sample size, N.* Larger samples yield better estimates of population parameters and make it more likely that you will reject H_0 when it is correct to do so. Thus, power increases as N increases.

3. *The population "effect" size,* **d.** You are less likely to fail to reject a false H_0 if H_0 is "very wrong"—that is, if there is a large effect size in the population. Thus, power increases as **d** increases.

4. *Power,* $1 - \beta$.

Any one of these four parameters is an exact mathematical function of the other three.

3. The General Procedure for the Two Most Important Kinds of Power Analysis

1. Power determination

   (a) Compute or posit the value of **d.**

   (b) Compute δ (delta), which combines N and **d.**

   (c) Obtain power from the appropriate table.

2. Sample size determination

   (a) Specify desired power. (If a conventional value is needed, use .80.)

   (b) Compute or posit the value of **d.**

   (c) Obtain δ from the appropriate table.

   (d) Compute N.

If you have no basis for estimating the population values needed to compute **d**, you can use the appropriate conventional value of **d**, as devised by J. Cohen (1988), for the statistical test in question.

4. The Specific Formulas for d, δ, and N

These depend on the statistical test that is being performed.

1. The test of the mean of a single population

   (a) $\mathbf{d} = \dfrac{\mu_1 - \mu_0}{\sigma}$,

   where

   > μ_0 = value of μ specified by H_0
   >
   > μ_1 = value of μ specified by H_1
   >   (a *specific* H_1 is always necessary in power analysis)
   >
   > σ = population standard deviation

   (b) $\delta = \mathbf{d}\,\sqrt{N}$

(c) $N = \left(\dfrac{\delta}{\mathbf{d}} \right)^2$

(d) Conventional values of **d**: small, .20; medium, .50; large, .80

2. The test of the proportion of a single population

(a) $\mathbf{d} = \dfrac{\pi_1 - \pi_0}{\sqrt{\pi_0 (1 - \pi_0)}}$,

where

$$\pi_0 = \text{value of } \pi \text{ specified by } H_0$$
$$\pi_1 = \text{value of } \pi \text{ specified by } H_1$$

(b) $\delta = \mathbf{d}\,\sqrt{N}$

(c) $N = \left(\dfrac{\delta}{\mathbf{d}} \right)^2$

(d) Conventional values of **d**: small, .10; medium, .30; large, .50

3. The significance test of a Pearson r (includes r_{pb})

(a) $\mathbf{d} = \rho_1$, the value specified by H_1

(b) $\delta = \mathbf{d}\,\sqrt{N - 1}$

(c) $N = \left(\dfrac{\delta}{\mathbf{d}} \right)^2 + 1$

$ = \left(\dfrac{\delta}{\rho_1} \right)^2 + 1$

(d) Conventional values of **d**: small, .10; medium, .30; large, .50

4. The test of the difference between independent means

(a) $\mathbf{d} = \dfrac{\theta}{\sigma}$,

where

$$\theta = \text{value of } \mu_1 - \mu_2 \text{ specified by } H_1$$
$$\sigma = \text{population standard deviation (a single value}$$
$$\text{because it is assumed that } \sigma_1 = \sigma_2)$$

(b) $\delta = \mathbf{d}\,\sqrt{\dfrac{n}{2}}$,

where

> n is the size of *each* sample
> (thus, $2n$ cases are used in the experiment)

If the sample sizes are unequal, use

$$n = \frac{2N_1 N_2}{N_1 + N_2}$$

(c) $n = 2\left(\dfrac{\delta}{\mathbf{d}}\right)^2$,

where

> n is the size of *each* sample
> (so $2n$ cases will be needed in all)

(d) Conventional values of **d**: small, .20; medium, .50; large, .80

5. The test of the difference between *dependent* (i.e., correlated) means

(a) $\mathbf{d} = \dfrac{\theta}{\sigma}$ as defined for the test of the independent means

(b) $\delta = \mathbf{d}\sqrt{\dfrac{1}{1-\rho}}\sqrt{\dfrac{n}{2}} = \sqrt{\dfrac{1}{1-\rho}}\,\delta_{\text{independent}}$,

where $\delta_{\text{independent}}$ is δ as defined for independent means

ρ = linear correlation of the two sets of scores in the population

(c) $n = 2(1-\rho)\left(\dfrac{\delta}{d}\right)^2$

Note: All of the procedures given here are approximate and are applicable for large samples (n at least 25 or 30).

6. Estimating **d** from published research

You can calculate g from a published t value if you are given the two sample sizes:

$$g = t\sqrt{\frac{N_1 + N_2}{N_1 N_2}}$$

If the sample sizes are equal, this formula reduces to

$$g = t\sqrt{\frac{2}{n}},$$

where n is the size of each of the two samples.

Exercises

1. Suppose that the students at Bigbrain University are planning to test whether the mean math SAT score for their school is higher than the national average (μ) of 500 (assume that $\sigma = 100$).

   (a) If they believe that their mean is 520, and they plan to sample 25 students, what is the power of their statistical test at the .05 level, two-tailed? What would the power be for a one-tailed test? Explain why power is higher for the one-tailed test.

   (b) Recalculate the power values in part (a) assuming that the Bigbrain students expect their average to be 50 points higher than the national average. Explain why these power values are higher than the ones you calculated in part (a).

   (c) Redo part (a) assuming that a sample of 100 Bigbrain students is being planned. Explain why these power values are higher than the ones you calculated in part (a).

   (d) Given the expected effect size in part (a), what sample size would be needed to obtain power = .8 for a two-tailed .05 test? For a two-tailed .01 test?

   (e) Repeat part (d) given the expected effect size in part (b).

2. Calculate the power for the tests you conducted for Universities A and B in exercise 1 of Chapter 10. (Use the t values you calculated for that exercise as the values for δ in your power calculation.)

3. (a) A politician needs 50% or more of the vote to win an election. To find out how his campaign is going, he plans to obtain a random sample of 81 voters and see how many plan to vote for him. He is willing to posit a specific alternative hypothesis of 60% (or 40%) and wishes to use the .01 criterion of significance. Compute the power of the statistical test. How do you evaluate this research plan?

   (b) Suppose the politician decides to switch to the .05 criterion of significance (but that the other values are not changed). Will this improve the power of the statistical test to a satisfactory level?

   (c) The politician finally resigns himself to doing more work and obtaining a larger sample. He wishes power = .75. How large a sample does he need (using the .05 criterion)?

4. (a) A personality theorist feels that if two traits are correlated, the correlation should be on the order of .40. She wishes to test the null hypothesis that the correlation between the two traits is .00, using the .05 criterion of significance and a random sample of 65 subjects. Is the power of this statistical test satisfactory?

   (b) How large a sample would the theorist in part (a) need to obtain power = .9 with alpha set at .01 for a two-tailed test? For a one-tailed test?

5. If the sample r you calculated in exercise 2 of Chapter 12 were equal to ρ for the population, how large a sample would you need to obtain power = .7 for a two-tailed test at the .05 level?

6. (a) Calculate g for the comparison of the means of Universities A and B. Use that value for g as your estimate of **d,** and compute the sample sizes you would need for power = .75, for a .05 two-tailed test, comparing the two universities.

   (b) Given the sizes of the samples from Universities A and B, how large would **d** have to be to obtain power = .85, for a .01, two-tailed test?

7. (a) Calculate g from the t value you computed to solve exercise 2 in Chapter 11. Use that value for g as your estimate of **d,** and compute the sample sizes you would need for power = .7, for a .05 two-tailed test, assuming that you plan to use two equal-sized samples.

   (b) Given the sizes of the samples in exercise 2 of Chapter 11, how large would **d** have to be to obtain power = .8, for a .05, two-tailed test?

8. Calculate the missing values in the following table, assuming that you are comparing two independent, equal-sized samples with a two-tailed t test. (Note: Small = .2, Medium, = .5, Large = .8.)

Proposed n in each sample	Effect size	Power, $\alpha = .05$	Power, $\alpha = .01$	n in *each* sample needed for power of .85 if: $\alpha = .05$	$\alpha = .01$
30	Small	_____	_____		
100	Small	_____	_____	_____	_____
30	Medium	_____	_____		
100	Medium	_____	_____	_____	_____
30	Large	_____	_____		
100	Large	_____	_____	_____	_____

9. Suppose that you plan to match students between Universities A and B so that the population correlation corresponds to .4. Given the **d** you found in part (b) of exercise 6, and the sizes of the samples from Universities A and B, how much power would you have for a two-tailed matched-pairs t test at the .05 level?

10. Recalculate the required sample sizes for part (a) of exercise 7 if the two populations are matched with $\rho = .6$.

11. (a) Calculate the power your test would have in exercise 5 of Chapter 11 if the two sets of scores were not correlated at all in the population (use g for those data as **d** in your power calculation).

    (b) Calculate the power your test would have in exercise 5 of Chapter 11 if the two sets of scores had a population correlation of $\rho = .5$ (again, use g for those data as **d** in your power calculation).

Thought Questions

1. What is the power of a statistical test? Why is it important when planning a research study?

2. "Using the .05 criterion of significance, the probability of a Type I error is .05. Using the .001 criterion of significance, the probability of a Type I error is .001 (much smaller). Therefore, researchers should always use the .001 criterion of significance." Use the concept of statistical power to explain why the last sentence in the preceding quotation is incorrect.

3. A researcher argues as follows: "I performed a correlational study with a very large sample. Because my sample was so large, I obtained a correlation of $r = .07$ that was statistically significant. But this correlation is too small to be of any practical value, as there is very little (linear) relationship between the two variables that I studied. I therefore warn other researchers *not* to use large samples so as to avoid getting such misleading results." (a) Use the concept of statistical power to explain why the last sentence in the preceding quotation is incorrect. (b) Why is it always statistically desirable to obtain the largest sample that a researcher can afford?

4. In the following table, decide which of the numbered statements belongs in each box:

Sample size	You retained H_0	You rejected H_0
Very small		
Very large		

(1) You are studying an effect that is likely to be quite large.

(2) Caution is indicated because you are studying an effect that may be quite small.

(3) Power is likely to be so low, and the probability of a Type II error so large, that no conclusions of any kind should be drawn.

(4) Power is likely to be high, so it may well be that H_0 is (approximately) true.

Computer Exercises

1. Suppose that Sara is planning to compare the men with the women in her class. Use the noncentral t distribution function in your statistical package to answer the following questions. Assume that alpha is .05 and that each test is two-tailed.

    (a) Use the t value you computed for the gender difference in baseline anxiety (first computer exercise of Chapter 11) as your value for delta to determine the power of that test.

    (b) If the population effect size for another DV were only .3, how much power would Sara have for that gender comparison?

    (c) If Sara had equal-sized groups of men and women, how large would each have to be to attain power = .8, given the effect size in part (b)?

    (d) Repeat part (b) for **d** = .7.

2. Solve this problem using the same methods and assumptions that you used for exercise 1.

    (a) Use the t value you computed to compare the students in the "impossible to solve" condition with those in the "easy to solve" condition in terms of postquiz heart rates (computer exercise 3 of Chapter 11) as your value for delta to determine the power of that test.

    (b) Had the population effect size for this DV been medium in size (**d** = .5), how many students would Sara have needed to have in each condition to attain power = .7?

Bridge to SPSS

In this chapter we simplified power analysis by using the normal distribution as an approximation of the t distribution; that is why we needed only two brief tables (Tables D and E) to complete our analysis. Unfortunately, as the samples you are dealing with get smaller, the normal approximation becomes less accurate. In fact, the distribution we really need for power analysis when comparing the means of two fairly small samples is not the family of t distributions but an even more complex family known as the noncentral t distributions. A noncentral t distribution (NCTD), unlike the ordinary null hypothesis distribution for a two-sample t test, does not have zero at its center. For power analysis we use an NCTD that is centered on δ (delta). Note that there is a different NCTD for each possible combination of δ and df. There are printed tables that can deal with this complexity (see J. Cohen, 1988), but you can use SPSS to get an even more accurate value with very little effort. (You can also find various "power calculator" programs on the web.)

To find the power that corresponds to a particular combination of δ and df, first look up the critical *t* value that corresponds to your *df* and desired alpha. Then, open a new data sheet and type the value of δ into the first cell. Name the first column something like "delta." Next, click on **Compute** from the Transform menu, and in the dialog box that opens type a name like **power** in the target variable box. In the Numeric Expression box, type **1 – NCDF.T (t_{crit}, df, delta),** but in place of t_{crit} type the actual critical value you looked up, and in place of *df* type the appropriate number (note that the commas between numbers in the parentheses are necessary). For "delta," type whatever variable name you assigned to the first column of your data sheet.

For example, suppose that you have two samples available, and each has 10 participants (*df* = 18). For a .05, two-tailed test, the critical *t* is 2.101. If you expect **d** to be .8 (or just want to check what your power would be *if* **d** were large), delta equals .8 $\sqrt{5}$ = 1.79. This is the value you would type into the first cell of your data sheet. If you named your first data column "delta," then you would type the following expression in the appropriate space in the Compute dialog box: **1 – NCDF.T (2.101, 18, delta),** and then click **OK.** (If instead of typing in this expression you select it from the Function list in the Compute dialog box, you will get NCDF.T (q, df, nc), where "q" must be replaced by the critical value, "df" by *df*, and "nc" by the name of your first column. Don't forget to precede the expression by **1–** unless you want to get beta instead of power.) (Note: starting with version 14.0, type or select NPDF.T instead of NCDF.T)

A new column will appear in your data sheet bearing whatever name you typed in as the Target Variable, and it will contain the power value for your test—for this example, it is .40 (you can get an even more accurate value by requesting 3 or 4 under Decimals in Variable View). Note that if you use Table D to look up power for a delta of 1.79, you will see that power is listed as .44 for 1.8 and .40 for 1.7 (Table D is using 1.96 as the critical value instead of the more accurate value of 2.101, and it is using the normal distribution instead of the appropriate noncentral *t* distribution).

Suppose, however, that you are not starting out with fixed sample sizes but are trying to determine what sample size to use for a particular value of **d,** and a desired level of power. First, calculate your needed sample size with the formula given in this chapter. Then you can use trial and error with the SPSS expression described above to arrive at a more accurate answer. For instance, if you want power to be .8 (for a .05, two-tailed test) for an effect size of 1.0, δ (from Table E) is 2.8, and the calculated *n* is $2(2.8/1.0)^2 = 2(7.84) = 15.68$. Now you can plan to use 16 participants per group, giving you a *df* of 30, which corresponds to a critical *t* of 2.042. However, if you insert these values into the SPSS expression above, you will find that the power is .77, not .8. The normal approximation contained in Table E is overly optimistic. So you might next try *n* = 18 (*df* = 34), which gives you a critical *t* of 2.03. With **d** still at 1.0, delta equals $1.0\sqrt{9}$ = 3.0, and SPSS will return a value for power of .83. This time we made *n* a bit too large. If you try *n* = 17, you will see that this sample size yields the desired level of power (approximately) for an effect size of 1.0.

Part III
Analysis of Variance Methods

Chapter 15
One-Way Analysis of Variance

PREVIEW

Introduction

We wish to draw inferences about the differences between *more* than two population means. Why is it a poor idea to perform numerous t tests between the various pairs of means?

What is the experimentwise error rate?

In what way is one-way analysis of variance similar to the t test for the difference between two means? How does it differ?

The General Logic of ANOVA

We wish to draw inferences about population means. Why then does the statistical analysis use variances?

What is the within-group (or error) variance estimate? What is the between-group variance estimate?

What is the F ratio?

Computational Procedures

What are the procedures for drawing inferences about any number of population means by computing a one-way analysis of variance? What are sums of squares? Mean squares?

What is the correct statistical model to use in this situation?

How do we test the F ratio for statistical significance?

Comparing the One-Way ANOVA with the t Test

What is the relationship between the t value and the F ratio in the two-group case? What is the relationship between the pooled variance of the t test and MS_w in ANOVA?

How can a one-way ANOVA be calculated from means and SDs, without access to the raw scores?

A Simplified ANOVA Formula for Equal Sample Sizes

How does the equal-n formula show that the magnitude of the F ratio depends on the variance of the sample means, the variance within the samples, and the size of the samples?

Effect Size for the One-Way ANOVA

How can the formula for F be separated into a measure of effect size and a measure of sample size?

(continued next page)

Introduction

Chapter 11 provided techniques for testing the significance of the difference between two means. These techniques enable you to determine the effect of a single independent variable (for example, the presence or absence of a particular dosage of caffeine) on the mean of a dependent variable (mathematics test scores) when there are *two* samples of interest, such as an experimental group and a control group.

Suppose that you would like to determine whether *different dosages* of caffeine affect performance on a 20-item English test. As before, there is one independent variable (amount of caffeine), but this time you wish to include the following *five* samples:

Sample 1: very large dose of caffeine

Sample 2: large dose of caffeine

Sample 3: moderate dose of caffeine

Sample 4: small dose of caffeine

Sample 5: placebo (no caffeine)

As usual, you would like the probability of a Type I error in this experiment to be .05 or less. It would *not* be correct to perform 10 separate *t* tests for the difference between two means (that is, first test H_0: $\mu_1 = \mu_2$; then test H_0: $\mu_1 = \mu_3$; and so on) and then compare each obtained *t* value to the appropriate critical *t* value for $\alpha = .05$.

The more statistical tests you perform, the more likely it is that some will be statistically significant purely by chance. That is, when $\alpha = .05$, the probability that one *t* test will yield statistical significance when H_0 actually is true is .05. This is the probability of committing a Type I error. If you run 20 *t* tests when H_0 is always true, an average of 1 of them ($.05 \times 20 = 1.0$) will be statistically significant just on the basis of chance, so it is very likely that you will commit at least one Type I error somewhere along the line. Similarly, if you run 10 separate *t* tests in order to test the null hypothesis that different dosages of caffeine do not affect English test scores, the probability that you will commit at least one Type I error is clearly *greater* than the desired .05. (It can be shown that this probability is closer to .3.) The greater the number of sample means among which you perform pairwise significance tests, the more likely you are to make at least one Type I error. In statistical terminology, the rate of occurrence of *any* Type I errors over a *series* of individual but related statistical tests is called the *experimentwise* error rate.

Fortunately, there is a procedure for testing differences among three or more means for statistical significance which overcomes this difficulty. This procedure is the *analysis of variance,* abbreviated as ANOVA. ANOVA can also be used with just two samples, in which case it yields equivalent results to the procedures given in Chapter 11. The null hypothesis tested by ANOVA is that the means of the populations from which the samples were randomly drawn are all equal. For example, the null hypothesis in the caffeine experiment is

$$H_0: \mu_1 = \mu_2 = \mu_3 = \mu_4 = \mu_5$$

The alternative hypothesis merely states that H_0 taken as a whole is *not* true. There are many ways in which it may be false: it may be that $\mu_1 \neq \mu_2$, or that $\mu_3 \neq \mu_5$, or both, or that all five population means are unequal, or only two are equal, and so forth. The rejection of the ANOVA H_0 tells us only that *some* inequality exists. In the next chapter, we will describe a separate procedure for testing pairwise mean differences following an ANOVA. This procedure enables us to specify the meaning of rejecting the ANOVA H_0.

The General Logic of ANOVA

Since it may seem paradoxical to test a null hypothesis about *means* by testing *variances,* the general logic of ANOVA will be discussed before proceeding to the computational procedures. The ANOVA procedure is based on a mathematical proof that the sample data can be made to yield two independent estimates of the population variance:

1. **Within-group (or "error") variance estimate.** This estimate is based on how different each of the scores in a given sample (or *group*) is from other scores in the same group.

2. **Between-group variance estimate.** This estimate is based on how different the *means* of the various samples (or *groups*) are from one another.

If the samples all come from the same normally distributed population (or from normally distributed populations with equal means and variances), it can be proved mathematically that the between-group variance estimate and the within-group variance estimate will be about equal to each other, and equal to the population variance (σ^2). The larger the between-group variance estimate is in comparison to the within-group variance estimate, the more likely it is that the samples do *not* come from populations with equal means.

As an illustration, consider the hypothetical data in Table 15.1A. There are five groups, each of which listened to music by a different classical composer, while completing a spatial ability test. Group 1 listened to Mozart, Group 2 to Chopin, and so on. Each group contains five people, so there are 25 subjects in all, and the entries in the table represent the score of each person on the spatial ability test. There is some between-group variation and some within-group variation. The means of the five groups may differ because the composer of the music does have an effect on test scores, or merely because they are affected by the presence of sampling error (that is, the accident of which cases happened to be in each sample), or for both reasons. Whether to retain or reject the null hypothesis that the samples all come from the same population is decided by applying ANOVA procedures to the data. Inspection of Table 15.1A should suggest that the between-group variation and within-group variation are about equal, as would be expected if H_0 is true.

What if the composer of the music *does* have an effect? Suppose that one particular composer (e.g., Mozart) causes a real increase in test scores. This implies that music by Mozart produces about the same helpful effect on all subjects in the Mozart group. The variability *within* that group will not be affected, since adding a constant to all scores or subtracting a constant from all scores does *not* change the variance or standard deviation. Thus, the within-group variance estimate also will not be affected. The mean of this group, however, will be higher than the mean of the other groups. Therefore, the *between*-group variance estimate will increase. Similarly, if several different classical composers have different effects on test scores (for example, some composers increase test scores more than others), the within-group variance estimate will not increase but the between-group variance estimate will be larger. The greater the differences among the group means, the larger will be the between-group variance estimate.

As an illustration, consider the data in Table 15.1B. Imagine that the groups in this version of the experiment heard very different *types* of music (e.g., clas-

TABLE 15.1

Two versions of the music experiment (hypothetical data)

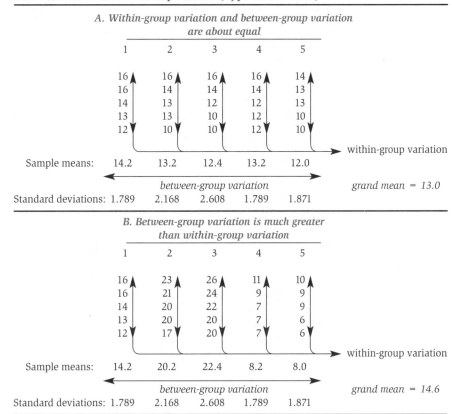

A. *Within-group variation and between-group variation*
are about equal

	1	2	3	4	5
	16	16	16	16	14
	16	14	14	14	13
	14	13	12	12	13
	13	13	10	12	10
	12	10	10	12	10
Sample means:	14.2	13.2	12.4	13.2	12.0
Standard deviations:	1.789	2.168	2.608	1.789	1.871

within-group variation

between-group variation

grand mean = 13.0

B. *Between-group variation is much greater*
than within-group variation

	1	2	3	4	5
	16	23	26	11	10
	16	21	24	9	9
	14	20	22	7	9
	13	20	20	7	6
	12	17	20	7	6
Sample means:	14.2	20.2	22.4	8.2	8.0
Standard deviations:	1.789	2.168	2.608	1.789	1.871

within-group variation

between-group variation

grand mean = 14.6

sical, jazz, New Age, bluegrass, etc.). (In reality, these data were obtained from the data in Table 15.1A as follows: Scores in Group 1 were not changed; 7 was added to each score in Group 2; 10 was added to each score in Group 3; 5 was subtracted from each score in Group 4; and 4 was subtracted from each score in Group 5.) The variance of each of the groups in Table 15.1B, and hence the within-group variance estimate, is equal to that of Table 15.1A. However, the between-group variance estimate is much greater in the case of Table 15.1B. Thus it is more likely that the five samples of scores in Table 15.1B do *not* come from the same population.

To clarify further the meaning of between-group variation and within-group variation, consider the score of the first person in Group 1 of Table 15.1A, which is equal to 16. This person's score deviates by 1.8 points from the mean of Group 1. This is "error" in the sense that it cannot be explained by the composer variable, since all people in Group 1 listened to the same music. It simply reflects the basic variance of the spatial ability scores. The difference between the mean of Group 1 and the grand mean (14.2 – 13.0) is equal to 1.2 points.

This reflects how much the music of Mozart (listened to by Group 1) caused the mean test score of this group to differ from the *grand mean* (i.e., the mean of all of the scores across all of the groups in the study), *plus* this same basic variance of the spatial ability scores. Finally, the within-group variation of 1.8 and the between-group variation of 1.2 sum to 3.0, which equals the total variation of this score from the grand mean (16 – 13.0). The three deviation scores involving this person are

1. Total deviation = 3.0
2. Within-group (from own group) deviation (*error*) = 1.8
3. Between-group (from own group to grand mean) deviation = 1.2

The total variance, the within-group variance estimate, and the between-group variance estimate express the magnitude of these deviations, respectively, for everyone in the experiment. It can readily be shown that the total sum of squared deviations from the grand mean (the total sum of squares) is equal to the sum of the between-group sum of squares and the within-group sum of squares. (The proof is given in the Appendix at the end of this chapter.)

The between-group variance estimate includes *both* the effects of the type of music (if any) *and* error variance. The group means will be affected both by the experimental treatment and by individual differences in spatial ability plus the error variance of the scores used to measure spatial ability. The within-group variance estimate, however, reflects solely the error variance (which includes individual differences, as well as measurement error). The effect of the different types of music can therefore be determined by computing the following F ratio:

$$F = \frac{\text{treatment variance} + \text{error variance}}{\text{error variance}}$$
$$= \frac{\text{between-group variance estimate}}{\text{within-group variance estimate}}$$

If H_0 is true, there is no treatment variance. The between-group and within-group variance estimates will therefore be approximately equal, so that F will be approximately equal to 1.0. The more F is greater than 1.0, the more sure you can be that music type does have an effect on test scores. You reject H_0 when F is so large as to have a probability of .05 or less of occurring if H_0 is true.

Values of F less than 1.0 would indicate that H_0 should be retained, since the between-group variance estimate is smaller than the within-group variance estimate. Since the value of F expected if H_0 is true is about 1.0, one might conceive of a *significantly small* value of F (for example, 0.2). There would be no obvious explanation for such a result other than chance, or perhaps failure of one of the assumptions underlying the F test. Thus, you would retain H_0 in such instances, and check the possibility that some systematic factor like non-random sampling has crept in.

Computational Procedures

Although we do not expect that you will be using these formulas to calculate ANOVAs on research data you collect in the future, we feel that calculating a few ANOVAs by hand will give you a deeper appreciation of both the numerator and denominator of an ANOVA F ratio than you could ever get by clicking on the menu of a statistical program and then inspecting the results.

Sums of Squares

The first step in the calculation of any ANOVA is to compute the *sum of squares between groups* (symbolized by SS_B), the sum of squares *within groups* (symbolized by SS_W), and the *total sum of squares* (symbolized by SS_T). *A sum of squares* is nothing more than a sum of squared deviations, the numerator of the variance formula defined in Chapter 5.

1. *Total sum of squares* (SS_T). The definition formula for the total sum of squares is

$$SS_T = \sum (X - \overline{X}_G)^2,$$

where

$$\overline{X}_G = \text{grand mean for all observations in the experiment}$$

$$\sum = \text{summation across all } observations$$

In Table 15.1A, for example,

$$
\begin{aligned}
SS_T &= (16 - 13)^2 + (16 - 13)^2 + (14 - 13)^2 \\
&\quad + \ldots + (13 - 13)^2 \\
&\quad + (10 - 13)^2 + (10 - 13)^2 \\
&= 3^2 + 3^2 + 1^2 + \ldots + 0^2 + (-3)^2 + (-3)^2 \\
&= 100
\end{aligned}
$$

As was the case with the variance (Chapter 5), however, it is also possible to compute SS_T by using a shortcut computing formula:

$$SS_T = \sum X^2 - N_T \overline{X}_G^2,$$

where

$$N_T = \text{total number of observations in the experiment}$$

For the data in Table 15.1A,

$$\sum X^2 = 16^2 + 16^2 + 14^2 + \ldots 13^2 + 10^2 + 10^2$$

$$= 4{,}325$$

$$N_T \overline{X}_G^2 = 25(13)^2 = 25 \times 169 = 4{,}225$$

$$SS_T = 4{,}325 - 4{,}225$$

$$= 100$$

2. Sum of squares between groups (SS_B). The definition formula for the sum of squares between groups is

$$SS_B = \sum_{i=1}^{k} N_i (\overline{X}_i - \overline{X}_G)^2$$

where

N_i = number of scores in group i

$\overline{X}_i$ = mean of group i

$\overline{X}_G$ = grand mean

k = the number of groups

$\sum_{i=1}^{k}$ = summation across all the *groups* (*not* the subjects)

As we have seen, the between-groups sum of squares deals with the difference between the mean of each group and the grand mean. The squared difference is effectively counted once for each person in the group. (Samples need not be of equal size.) In Table 15.1A,

$$SS_B = 5(14.2 - 13.0)^2 + 5(13.2 - 13.0)^2$$

$$+ 5(12.4 - 13.0)^2 + 5(13.2 - 13.0)^2 + 5(12.0 - 13.0)^2$$

$$= 5(1.2)^2 + 5(.2)^2 + 5(-.6)^2 + 5(.2)^2 + 5(-1.0)^2$$

$$= 14.4$$

When all of the samples are the same size the formula for SS_B can be simplified to

$$SS_B = n \sum_{i=1}^{k} (\overline{X}_i - \overline{X}_G)^2,$$

where

n = number of scores in *each* of the k groups

This is the same as finding the SS for the k sample means and then multiplying it by the common sample size. For example, let us apply this formula to the data in Table 15.1B.

$$SS_B = 5[(14.2 - 14.6)^2 + (20.2 - 14.6)^2 + (22.4 - 14.6)^2$$
$$+ (8.2 - 14.6)^2 + (8.0 - 14.6)^2]$$
$$= 5[(-.4)^2 + 5.6^2 + 7.8^2 + (-6.4)^2 + (-6.6)^2]$$
$$= 5(176.88)$$
$$= 884.4$$

3. Sum of squares within groups (SS_W). The definition formula for the sum of squares within groups is

$$SS_W = \sum^{n_1} (X - \overline{X}_1)^2 + \sum^{n_2} (X - \overline{X}_2)^2 + \ldots + \sum^{n_k} (X - \overline{X}_k)^2,$$

where

$\overline{X}_1$ = mean of first group, $\overline{X}_2$ = mean of second group, and so on

$\sum$ = summation across the n_i cases of the group in question (i.e., the ith group)

This is the same as calculating the SS separately for the scores in each group and then adding all of these SSs together.
   In Table 15.1A,

$$SS_W = (16 - 14.2)^2 + (16 - 14.2)^2 + (14 - 14.2)^2 + (13 - 14.2)^2$$
$$+ (12 - 14.2)^2 + (16 - 13.2)^2 + (14 - 13.2)^2 + (13 - 13.2)^2$$
$$+ \ldots + (10 - 12.0)^2 + (10 - 12.0)^2$$
$$= 85.6$$

That is, the difference between each score and the mean of the group containing the score is squared. (In this example, there is a total of 25 squared differences, but we are showing only the first 8 and the last 2.) Once this has been done for every score, the results are summed. This is the most tedious of the three sums of squares to compute, and it is possible to make use of the fact that

$$SS_T = SS_B + SS_W$$

That is, the sum of squares between groups and the sum of squares within groups must add up to the total sum of squares. (See the Appendix at the end of this chapter.) Therefore, the within-group sum of squares can readily be computed as follows:

$$SS_W = SS_T - SS_B$$
$$= 100 - 14.4$$
$$= 85.6$$

You should be careful in using this shortcut, however, because it provides no check on computational errors. If SS_W is found directly, the foregoing formula can be used as a check on the accuracy in computation.

Mean Squares

Next, SS_B and SS_W are each divided by the appropriate degrees of freedom. The values thus obtained are called *mean squares,* and are estimates of the population variance. The degrees of freedom between groups (symbolized by df_B) are equal to

$$df_B = k - 1,$$

where

$$k = \text{number of groups}$$

The degrees of freedom within groups (symbolized by df_W) are equal to

$$df_W = N_T - k,$$

where

$$N_T = \text{total number of observations}$$

This is equivalent to obtaining the degrees of freedom for each group separately ($n_i - 1$) and then adding the *df* across all groups. The *total* degrees of freedom, helpful as a check on the calculations of *df*, is equal to $N_T - 1$.

In Table 15.1A, $df_B = (5 - 1) = 4$; $df_W = (25 - 5) = 20$. The total $df = N_T - 1$ or 24, which is in fact equal to 4 + 20.

The mean squares between groups (symbolized by MS_B) and the mean squares within groups (symbolized by MS_W) are equal to

$$MS_B = \frac{SS_B}{df_B}$$

$$MS_{\text{w}} = \frac{SS_{\text{w}}}{df_{\text{w}}}$$

Thus, for Table 15.1A,

$$MS_{\text{B}} = \frac{14.4}{4}$$

$$= 3.60$$

$$MS_{\text{w}} = \frac{85.6}{20}$$

$$= 4.28$$

For Table 15.1B, MS_{w} is the same, but $MS_{\text{B}} = 884.4/4 = 221.1$.

The *F* Ratio

Having computed the mean squares, the last step is to compute the *F* ratio, where

$$F = \frac{MS_{\text{B}}}{MS_{\text{w}}}$$

For Table 15.1A,

$$F = \frac{3.60}{4.28} = .84$$

For Table 15.1B,

$$F = \frac{221.1}{4.28} = 51.66$$

Testing the *F* Ratio for Statistical Significance

As noted earlier, we encounter a new statistical model when we wish to test the ANOVA H_0 for statistical significance: the *F distributions.* Here again, the correct model (i.e., the null hypothesis distribution) enables us to determine the probability of obtaining the results observed in the samples *if H_0 is true.*

Just as there are different *t* distributions for different degrees of freedom, so are there different *F* distributions for all combinations of different df_{B} and df_{w}. While the exact shape of an *F* distribution depends on df_{B} *and* df_{w}, all *F* distributions are positively skewed. Two are illustrated in Figure 15.1.

F distributions for $df_B = 4$ and $df_W = 20$, and $df_B = 6$ and $df_W = 6$

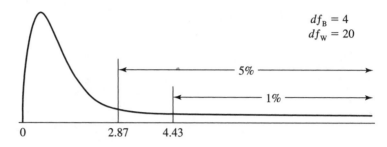

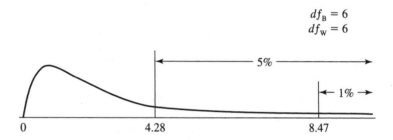

To obtain the minimum value of *F* needed to reject H_0, you can refer to Table F in the Appendix. Consult the *column* corresponding to df_B (the degrees of freedom in the *numerator* of the *F* ratio), and the *row* corresponding to df_W (the degrees of freedom in the *denominator* of the *F* ratio). The critical *F* values for 4 *df* (numerator) and 20 *df* (denominator) are as follows:

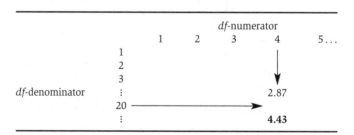

The critical values for 20 *df* (numerator) and 4 *df* (denominator) are *not* the same; be sure to enter the table in the proper place. The smaller of the two values is the .05 criterion; the larger (in boldface) is the .01 criterion. In the case of Table 15.1A, the obtained value of 0.84 is less than the critical value of 2.87. Therefore, using $\alpha = .05$, you retain H_0 and conclude there is not sufficient reason to believe that there are any differences among the five population means. (Since the computed value of *F* is less than 1.0, you could have reached this

TABLE 15.2

Summary of one-way ANOVA of music experiment

Source of Variation	SS	df	MS	F	p
Between groups	884.4	4	221.1	51.66	<.01
Within groups (error)	85.6	20	4.28		
Total	970.0	24			

conclusion without bothering to consult the table in this instance. The *expected* or mean value of any F distribution is never less than 1, so no value of 1 or less can be significant.)

For Table 15.1B, the calculated F value of 51.66 easily exceeds the critical value for the .05 level (2.87), and even the .01 level (4.43). We will present these statistically significant results in the form of a table.

The ANOVA Table

It is customary to summarize the results of an analysis of variance in a table such as the one shown in Table 15.2. Note that the between-groups source of variation is listed first, and that the value of F (and sometimes p, as well) is entered at the extreme right of the between-groups row.

Comparing the One-Way ANOVA with the *t* Test

When you compare the means of only two groups, you have a choice. You can test the difference of the means with a t test or a one-way ANOVA. Although both procedures lead to the same p value, it is instructive to see how closely connected these two seemingly diverse statistical methods are. For an example, we will retest the comparison of the caffeine and control groups from Chapter 11 using the one-way ANOVA method. Following are the summary statistics for this comparison:

	Caffeine Group	Control Group
$\overline{X}$	81	68
s	12.0	16.8
N	22	20

Before we can use the formula for SS_B, we need to calculate the grand mean for these data. If the two groups were the same size, $\overline{X}_G$ would be the simple average of the two group means (74.5 in this case). When the n's are not equal, a weighted average of the two means is more appropriate. Therefore, the grand mean is

$$\overline{X}_G = \frac{22(81) + 20(68)}{22 + 20} = \frac{3142}{42} = 74.8$$

Now we can calculate SS_B:

$$SS_B = n_1(\overline{X}_1 - \overline{X}_G)^2 + n_2(\overline{X}_2 - \overline{X}_G)^2$$
$$= 22(81 - 74.8)^2 + 20(68 - 74.8)^2 = 845.68 + 924.8 = 1770.48$$

To find SS_W when given SDs but not the raw data, you must first square each s to obtain the variance, and then multiply each s^2 by its df. (Recall that $s^2 = SS/df$, so $SS = s^2df$, where $df = N - 1$ for that group.) In our example, $SS_{caffeine} = 21(12)^2 = 3024$, and $SS_{control} = 19(16.8)^2 = 5362.56$. Therefore, $SS_W = 3024 + 5362.56 = 8386.6$.

Next, we calculate the two MSs by dividing each SS by the appropriate df term: $df_B = k - 1 = 2 - 1 = 1$; $df_W = N_T - k = 42 - 2 = 40$. Therefore, $MS_B = SS_B/1 = 1770.48$, and $MS_W = 8386.6/40 = 209.66$. Finally, we calculate the F ratio: $MS_B/MS_W = 1770.48/209.66 = 8.44$.

If you take the t value calculated for these same data in Chapter 11 (2.91) and square it, you will get (within rounding error) the F ratio just calculated for the one-way ANOVA. In fact, F always equals t^2 in the two-group case. This is also true for the critical values. The critical t that we used in Chapter 11 for this example was 2.02, and the critical F for this example, $F_{.05}(1, 40)$, equals $2.02^2 = 4.08$.

Comparing the t and F calculations for this example reveals further illuminating connections. Consider once again the calculation of the standard error of the difference in Chapter 11:

$$s_{\overline{X}_1 - \overline{X}_2} = \sqrt{209.664\left(\frac{1}{22} + \frac{1}{20}\right)}$$

Note that the value for s^2_{pooled} in this formula is 209.664, which rounds off to the value we calculated for the denominator of the F ratio, MS_W. Indeed, MS_W is just a new label for the pooled variance when more than two groups are involved; it is a weighted average of the variances of all the groups in an ANOVA. When you add the SSs from all the groups to create SS_W and then divide by the sum of the df's from all the groups (i.e., df_W), what you are actually finding is the weighted average of the variances.

A Simplified ANOVA Formula for Equal Sample Sizes

When all of the samples are the same size in a one-way ANOVA, the F ratio formula can be reduced to a simple expression that is easy to interpret. If we divide the expression for SS_B when the n's are equal (shown previously) by df_B, we get

$$MS_B = \frac{n \sum (\overline{X}_i - \overline{X}_G)^2}{df_B} = n \frac{\sum (\overline{X}_i - \overline{X}_G)^2}{df_B}$$

Notice that the part of this formula that is multiplied by n is really a formula for the variance of the sample *means*, so we can simplify the formula to $n\, s_{\overline{X}}^2$. When all the n's are equal, MS_W has a simple form as well; it is just the ordinary average of the sample variances. So

$$MS_W = \frac{\sum s_i^2}{k}$$

Putting the two halves of the F ratio together, we come up with a convenient formula for the (fairly common) case when all the samples are the same size:

$$F = \frac{n s_{\overline{X}}^2}{\dfrac{\sum s_i^2}{k}}$$

From this formula we can see at a glance that the magnitude of F depends entirely on three important factors: how far apart the sample means are from each other (the larger the spread, the larger is $s_{\overline{X}}^2$); how large the samples are (n is the size of *each* sample); and how much individuals vary from each other within each group. Because all of the n's are equal in Table 15.1, we can illustrate the use of this simplified formula by applying it to the music/spatial ability data. We begin by finding the (unbiased) variance of the five sample means in Table 15.1B. For 14.2, 20.2, 22.4, 8.2, and 8.0, $s_{\overline{X}}^2 = 44.22$.[1] MS_B equals $n\, s_{\overline{X}}^2$, so $MS_B = (5)(44.22) = 221.1$. (Note that this value agrees with the entry for MS_B in Table 15.2.)

Next, we find MS_W by squaring the (unbiased) s's for the five groups and averaging them. (The s's are the same in both the A and B sections of Table 15.1.) MS_W equals $(1.789^2 + 2.168^2 + 2.608^2 + 1.789^2 + 1.871^2)/5 = 21.4/5 = 4.28$. (Again, this value agrees with Table 15.2.) Dividing MS_B by MS_W yields the same F ratio that we calculated previously with the more tedious raw-score formula.

Effect Size for the One-Way ANOVA

Just as we were able to write a t formula in terms of the effect size in the samples (g) and the size of the sample (n), we can begin with the equal-n formula for F and separate it into an effect size term and a sample size term. If we

---

1. What makes this formula so easy to use is the ready availability of scientific or statistical calculators that give you the unbiased SD at the touch of a button after the scores are entered. This SD is then squared to obtain the (unbiased) variance.

define f^2 as $s_{\bar{X}}^2/MS_W$, then the one-way ANOVA formula can be written as $F = nf^2$. If we don't square it, f is an effect size measure comparable to g for the two-sample t test. (In fact, in the two-group case, f is just half the size of g, because it measures the standardized distance of each sample mean to the grand mean rather than the distance between the two sample means). Just as g is an estimate of **d** in the population, f can be viewed as an estimate of a corresponding population quantity that J. Cohen referred to as **f.** Although estimates of **f** are sometimes used as the basis of a power analysis (J. Cohen, 1988) for one-way ANOVA, they are not routinely reported as effect-size measures in journal articles. The commonly reported measures of effect size for ANOVA are correlational measures related to the square of the point-biserial r.

The analysis of variance procedure begins (at least conceptually) by dividing SS_{total} into two components: SS_B and SS_W. These components can be thought of, in regression terms, as the variability explained and unexplained, respectively. Therefore, dividing SS_B by SS_T gives the proportion of variance explained in your dependent variable by the ANOVA factor. Although this proportion comes from sample data, it is most commonly referred to as eta squared, as in the following formula:

$$\eta^2 = \frac{SS_B}{SS_T}$$

In the two-group case, η^2 will always be exactly equal to r_{pb}^2. And just as r_{pb}^2 can be calculated from a t value without access to the raw data, η^2 can be calculated from your F ratio by the following formula:

$$\eta^2 = \frac{df_B\, F}{df_B\, F + df_W}$$

For example, the F ratio for testing the group differences in Table 15.1B was 51.66, with $df_B = 4$ and $df_W = 20$. Such a large F ratio associated with moderate sample sizes tells us that a large proportion of variance has been accounted for. We can confirm this by using the foregoing formula:

$$\eta^2 = \frac{4(51.66)}{4(51.66) + 20} = \frac{206.64}{226.64} = .91$$

Such a large value for η^2 will not often occur in behavioral research, unless you are performing something like a manipulation check (e.g., did the participants who were moved to tears by watching a sad movie clip report more sadness than those participants who were laughing at a comedy clip?). Note that you will get the same value for η^2 if you divide SS_B by SS_T, as given in Table 15.2: $\eta^2 = 884.4/970 = .91$.

Just as in the two-group case, the proportion of variance accounted for in the population is designated by ω^2. Like r_{pb}^2, η^2 is a biased (over)estimate of ω^2.

More than one way has been recommended to correct this bias, but the simplest correction is to subtract 1 from the calculated F ratio before using the formula for η^2, as follows:

$$\text{est. } \omega^2 = \frac{df_{\text{B}}\,(F - 1)}{df_{\text{B}}\,F + df_{\text{W}}}$$

One advantage of this correction formula is that you can see at a glance that it is pointless to estimate ω^2 if your F ratio is less than 1.0 (ω^2 cannot be negative). Whenever F is less than 1, the separation between the sample means is *less* than you would expect from sampling error, so the data are suggesting that the effect in the population, and therefore ω^2, is zero.

Some Comments on the Use of ANOVA

The general considerations we included in Chapter 11 under the heading "Using the t Test for Two Sample Means" apply equally well to the ANOVA, with minor modifications, as described next.

Underlying Assumptions

The procedures discussed in this chapter assume that observations are *independent* both within and between all of the samples. The value of any observation should *not* be related in any way to that of any other observation (as would be the case if the three samples were selected to be equal on average IQ). It is also formally assumed that the variances are equal for all treatment populations (that is, homogeneous), and that the populations are normally distributed. ANOVA is fairly robust with regard to these assumptions, however, and will yield accurate results even if population variances are not homogeneous (provided that sample sizes are about equal) and even if population shapes depart (but only moderately) from normality. If you are dealing with sample sizes and variances that both vary a great deal, or small samples that are very skewed, you should consider using the *Kruskal-Wallis* test, described in the last chapter of this text.

Publishing Your Results

In behavioral research journals, the syntax for reporting an F ratio is as follows (as applied to the results presented in Table 15.2): "The different types of music produced large differences in spatial ability, and yielded a significant one-way ANOVA on the group means, $F(4,20) = 51.66$, $p < .01$, est. $\omega^2 = .89$." Note that df_{B} and df_{W} are always given, in that order, in parentheses after F. However, p may be given exactly (except when four or more zeroes are required to the right of the decimal point) or in terms of an even smaller alpha (e.g., $p < .001$), if applicable. As was pointed out in previous chapters, statistical significance (even at an unusually small alpha level) does not necessarily imply a strong relationship between the IV and DV. It is therefore desirable, and becoming increasingly common, to report a measure of effect size (e.g., g of f), or strength of relationship (e.g., estimated ω^2) in addition to the test of significance. However, effect-size measures are generally not reported if the results fail to reach significance at the .05 level. Instead of estimated ω^2, η^2 is often reported without correction. (However, in the example given here, F is so large that it would make little difference.)

Following Up on a Significant ANOVA

An investigator is rarely satisfied with knowing that a set of k (three or more) population means is not equal, yet this is all that the rejection of the ANOVA null hypothesis signifies. Instead, the researcher would usually like to conclude that certain population means are larger (or smaller) than others. Therefore, it is usually necessary to make more specific comparisons among the k means. Depending upon the structure and purpose of the experiment, these *multiple comparisons* may take many forms and are subject to many considerations.

Sometimes the investigator wishes to make all $k(k - 1)/2$ of the possible mean comparisons. At other times, only some of them may be needed (for example, when several experimental groups are each to be compared with a single control group). Another important issue is whether a given comparison was planned in advance of the research (*a priori*) or was suggested by the results (*post hoc*, also known as "data-snooping"). And we must be concerned with keeping the *experimentwise* error rate at a reasonably low level, while maintaining adequate power.

The area of multiple comparisons is a rather complex one. Therefore, in the next chapter we will provide only a brief survey of the simplest and most popular methods now available for testing multiple comparisons.

Summary

Analysis of variance (ANOVA) permits null hypotheses to be tested that involve the means of three or more samples (groups). One-way ANOVA deals with one independent variable made up of membership in one of k groups or levels. Total variance is partitioned into two sources: *between-group variance* and *within-group (error) variance*. These are compared by using the F ratio to determine whether or not the independent variable has an effect on the dependent variable. A significant F ratio in ANOVA indicates that not all k population means are equal. Follow-up procedures can be used to specify which pairs of means differ significantly.

1. Meaning of Symbols

Symbol	General Meaning
k	Number of groups (or the last group)
N_T	Total number of observations
N_i	Number of observations in group i
$\bar{X}_G$	Grand mean
$\bar{X}_i$	Mean of group i
X_i	A score in group i

2. Definition and Computing Formulas

1. Total sum of squares

$$\text{Definition: } SS_T = \sum (X - \bar{X}_G)^2$$

$$\text{Computing formula: } SS_T = \sum X^2 - N_T \bar{X}_G^2$$

2. Between-groups sum of squares

$$\text{Definition: } SS_B = \sum_{i=1}^{k} N_i (\bar{X}_i - \bar{X}_G)^2$$

$$\text{For equal-}n\text{'s only: } SS_B = n \sum_{i=1}^{k} (\bar{X}_i - \bar{X}_G)^2$$

where n is the size of *each* sample

3. Within-groups sum of squares

$$\text{Definition: } SS_W = \sum^{n_1} (X - \bar{X}_1)^2 + \sum^{n_2} (X - \bar{X}_2)^2 + \ldots + \sum^{n_k} (X - \bar{X}_k)^2$$

Shortcut computing formula: $SS_W = SS_T - SS_B$

3. Steps in One-Way Analysis of Variance

1. Compute SS_T, SS_B, and SS_W.
2. Compute

$$df_B = k - 1$$
$$df_W = N - k$$

3. Compute mean squares (MS):

$$MS_B = \frac{SS_B}{df_B}$$

$$MS_W = \frac{SS_W}{df_W}$$

If n's are equal:

$$MS_B = ns_{\bar{X}}^2$$

where $s_{\bar{X}}^2$ is the unbiased variance of the sample means, and

$$MS_W = \frac{\sum s_i^2}{k}$$

where s_i^2 is the unbiased variance within group i.

4. Compute

$$F = \frac{MS_B}{MS_W}$$

5. Obtain the critical value from the F table ($df = k - 1, N - k$) and test for significance. If the computed F is equal to or greater than the tabled F, reject H_0 (that all population means are equal) in favor of H_1 (that H_0 is not true). Otherwise, retain H_0.

6. Especially if F *is statistically significant,* a corresponding effect-size measure should be computed. The most commonly used strength-of-relationship measure is the proportion of variance accounted for as determined by the following formula:

$$\eta^2 = \frac{SS_B}{SS_T}$$

Eta squared can also be calculated from the F ratio using this formula:

$$\eta^2 = \frac{df_B F}{df_B F + df_W}$$

A less biased estimate of the variance accounted for in the population requires the following adjustment:

$$\eta^2 = \frac{df_B (F - 1)}{df_B F + df_W}$$

Exercises

1. Below are two hypothetical (separate) sets of data that are somewhat exaggerated to help clarify the procedures underlying analysis of variance. In each case, the experimenter is interested in the number of errors made by rats in a maze as a function of the kind of reward. Group 1 receives 100% water reward; group 2 receives a solution of 50% water and 50% sugar as the reward; and group 3 receives 100% sugar reward.

	Experiment 1				Experiment 2		
	Group 1	Group 2	Group 3		Group 1	Group 2	Group 3
	1	8	6		4	10	10
	3	7	5		0	0	0
	2	5	3		5	9	8
	1	4	3		0	1	1
	3	6	3		1	10	1
$\overline{X}$	2	6	4		2	6	4

(a) By inspection, in which case would you guess that the difference among groups is more likely to be statistically significant? Why?

(b) Carry out the analysis of variance for Experiment 1. Are the results significant at the .05 level? Calculate eta squared.

(c) Carry out the analysis of variance for Experiment 2. Are these results significant at the .05 level? Calculate eta squared.

(d) Briefly describe why the F ratio and eta squared statistics differ dramatically for the two experiments even though the sample means (i.e., 2, 6, and 4) are the same in both cases.

(e) Calculate an unbiased estimate of ω^2 for whichever experiment is significant.

2. Using the means and standard deviations you have already calculated for the data from the four universities, perform an analysis of variance to decide whether you can reject the null hypothesis that the four samples come from populations with identical means. Calculate eta squared for this comparison, and comment on the proportion of variance accounted for by the different universities.

3. For each of the following two experiments, calculate the means and variances for each group first, and then use those statistics to perform the ANOVA.

(a) Can you reject the null hypothesis for Experiment 1? Display your results in an ANOVA summary table, and state the significance of your F ratio in a sentence, using the proper format. Include the value for eta squared.

	Experiment 1	
Group 1	Group 2	Group 3
17	15	9
12	11	21
3	4	3
10	26	7
1	18	20
14	23	
5		

(b) Can you reject the null hypothesis for Experiment 2? Display your results in an ANOVA summary table, and state the significance of your
F ratio in a sentence, using the proper format. Include an estimate of
omega squared.

	Experiment 2	
Group 1	Group 2	Group 3
1	4	26
10	17	21
3	11	15
12	20	9
3	14	23
5	18	
7		

4. Calculate the one-way ANOVA and determine its statistical significance for
the following data:

	Group				
	1	2	3	4	5
$\overline{X}$	23	30	34	29	26
s	6.5	7.2	7.0	5.8	6.0
N	12	15	14	12	15

Thought Questions

1. A researcher wishes to test the hypothesis that the means of five populations are different. Why would it be a bad idea to test the researcher's hypothesis by computing 10 separate t tests (first test population 1 vs. population 2, then test population 1 vs. population 3, then test population 1 vs.
population 4, and so on)?

2. If there are only two groups (that is, the researcher wishes to test the hypothesis that the means of two populations are different), will a one-way ANOVA yield the same results as the t test for two independent sample means? Explain.

3. A researcher using one-way ANOVA computes the sum of squares within groups and the sum of squares between groups. (a) What causes scores within each group to differ from other scores in the same group? (b) What causes the means of different groups to differ from one another? (c) Therefore, which does the researcher want to be larger, the sum of squares within groups or the sum of squares between groups?

4. One-way ANOVA is used to test the difference between two or more *means.* Why, then, is the analysis performed using *variances?*

5. If the results of a one-way ANOVA are statistically significant, why is it desirable to compute a measure of effect size?

6. The results of a one-way ANOVA involving four groups are statistically significant. The means of the four groups are as follows: Group 1, 17.5; Group 2, 8.6; Group 3, 12.2; Group 4, 6.1. Based solely on this information, can the researcher conclude that the mean of population 1 is different from the mean of population 3, or that the mean of population 3 is different from the mean of population 2? Why or why not? What additional information is needed?

Computer Exercises

1. Perform a one-way ANOVA to test whether the different quiz conditions (last question easy, moderate, difficult, or impossible) had a significant effect on postquiz anxiety and postquiz heart rate. Request descriptive statistics and draw a graph of the sample means, with the levels of the IV on the horizontal axis. Use the sample means to explain the results of your ANOVA.

2. Using college major as the independent variable, perform a one-way ANOVA to test for significant differences in the math background quiz and the statistics quiz. Request descriptive statistics and a homogeneity of variance (HOV) test. Use the sample means to explain the results of your ANOVA. Do the standard deviations of the samples seem consistent with the results of the HOV test?

3. Create a grouping variable from the number of math courses taken (Group 1 = none; Group 2 = one or two; Group 3 = three or more), and perform a one-way ANOVA on the math background quiz and the statistics quiz. Explain your results in terms of the means of the three groups.

Bridge to SPSS

There are two ways to perform a one-way ANOVA in SPSS: by selecting **One-Way ANOVA** from the Analyze/Compare Means menu, or by selecting **Univariate** from the Analyze/General Linear Model (GLM) menu. The latter method, because it allows for a variety of complex ANOVA procedures, lacks some of the useful features found in the more specific One-Way ANOVA sub-program. So we will describe the Compare Means method here and postpone a description of the GLM method until Chapter 17.

One advantage of the One-Way ANOVA dialog box not shared by its GLM counterpart is that you can move a large number of variables into the Dependent List (but, of course, only one IV into the Factor slot), and after you click **OK,** separate one-way ANOVAs will be performed for each DV in the list. You do not have to specify the levels of your factor; every different value of your factor variable will be assumed to indicate a different group of cases. The results of each one-way ANOVA are presented in a summary table very like the one in Table 15.2, except that the exact p value is displayed under the heading "Sig." Unlike the t test procedure, descriptive statistics and homogeneity of variance tests are not reported automatically for one-way ANOVA; they must be requested by checking the appropriate choices in the Options box. In addition to **Options,** there are two other buttons along the bottom of the One-Way ANOVA dialog box: **Contrasts** and **Post Hoc.** We will describe the function of these buttons in the next chapter.

Appendix: Proof That the Total Sum of Squares Is Equal to the Sum of the Between-Group and the Within-Group Sum of Squares

It is obvious that

$$X - \overline{X}_G = (X - \overline{X}_i) + (\overline{X}_i - \overline{X}_G)$$

Squaring both sides of the equation and summing over *all* people gives

$$\sum (X - \overline{X}_G)^2 = \sum (X - \overline{X}_i)^2 + \sum (\overline{X}_G - \overline{X})^2 + 2 \sum (X - \overline{X}_i)(\overline{X}_i - \overline{X}_G)$$

For any one group, $(\overline{X}_i - \overline{X}_G)$ is a constant, and the sum of deviations about the group mean must equal zero. The last term is therefore always equal to zero, leaving

$$\sum (X - \overline{X}_G)^2 = \sum (X - \overline{X}_i)^2 + \sum (\overline{X}_i - \overline{X}_G)^2$$

For ANOVA purposes, the sums of squares are then divided by the appropriate degrees of freedom to yield estimates of the population variance, which are then compared by the F ratio.

Chapter 16
Multiple Comparisons

PREVIEW

Introduction

What is the problem with performing t tests for each possible pair of groups in your study rather than beginning with an ANOVA?

Fisher's Protected t Tests

Why is the error term used by Fisher's protected t tests an improvement over the one used by the ordinary t test for comparing two independent means? How can these tests be simplified when all of the samples are the same size?

Tukey's Honestly Significant Difference (HSD)

What do Fisher's protected t tests "protect" against, and under what conditions does that protection break down?

How does Tukey's HSD test use the studentized range statistic to provide greater protection against Type I errors than Fisher's protected t tests? What is meant by the statement that the HSD test is overly "conservative" when dealing with a three-group study?

Other Multiple Comparison Procedures

Why did the Newman-Keuls test become so popular for multiple comparisons, and why has its use decreased in recent years?

How does the Fisher-Hayter test combine elements of both the LSD and HSD tests to optimize power while remaining acceptably conservative?

Planned and Complex Comparisons

How does the Bonferroni correction provide greater power when you are planning to test a small subset of the comparisons that are possible? Why is the Bonferroni test overly conservative if you want to test all of the possible pairwise comparisons?

What is a complex comparison, and how can it lead to greater power if you predict the pattern of sample means correctly?

Summary

Exercises

Thought Questions

Computer Exercises

Bridge to SPSS

Introduction

Suppose that the dean of a small college wishes to survey student attitudes about participating in determining college curricula and requirements. She circulates a five-item questionnaire in which students respond to each item on a Likert scale that goes from 1 (no interest in student participation) to 5 (very interested). Therefore, total scores on this questionnaire can range from 5 to 25. Although the students do not give their names, they do provide such demographic items as their college major, year in school, and gender.

Looking only at the data she has collected so far for seniors, the dean notices that student attitudes seem to differ according to their principal areas of study. She decides to arrange the scores of the seniors according to whether they are majoring in a natural science, a social science, or one of the humanities. The (hypothetical) data, broken down by these three areas, are shown in Table 16.1.

The results of the ANOVA on these data are shown in summary form. (We leave it to the reader as an exercise to verify the values for SS_B and SS_W in Table 16.1.) Because the critical F at the .05 level for 2 and 24 df is 2.064, the null hypothesis for these data ($\mu_1 = \mu_2 = \mu_3$) can be rejected. Unfortunately, this does *not* allow us to conclude that all three population means are different from each other ($\mu_1 \neq \mu_2 \neq \mu_3$). There are three other possibilities that are consistent with rejecting the null hypothesis: $\mu_1 = \mu_2 \neq \mu_3$; $\mu_1 \neq \mu_2 = \mu_3$; and $\mu_1 = \mu_3 \neq \mu_2$. To decide which of the four possibilities (including $\mu_1 \neq \mu_2 \neq \mu_3$) is true requires what are called, in this context, *pairwise comparisons*. These comparisons are just the ordinary two-sample t tests you learned about in Chapter 11.

TABLE 16.1

ANOVA of attitudes of students from three areas of study at a small college to student participation in determining college curricula

Areas of study			
Natural sciences	Social sciences	Humanities	
15	17	6	$H_0: \mu_1 = \mu_2 = \mu_3$
18	22	9	$H_1: H_0$ is untrue
12	5	12	$\alpha = .05$
12	15	11	
9	12	11	
10	20	8	
12	14	13	
20	15	14	
	20	7	
	21		
$N_1 = 8$	$N_2 = 10$	$N_3 = 9$	$N_T = 27$

Source of variation	SS	df	MS	F
Between groups	170.21	$3 - 1 = 2$	$170.21/2 = 85.10$	$85.10/16.74 = 5.08$
Within groups (error)	401.79	$27 - 3 = 24$	$401.79/24 = 16.74$	

If you must follow your ANOVA with t tests anyway, why not just skip the ANOVA and proceed directly to the t tests? In the three-group case, there are only three pairwise comparisons to perform (e.g., natural vs. social sciences, and each of these vs. humanities), so the problem with performing multiple t tests is not so obvious. However, suppose that the dean has collected enough data for her to conduct a one-way ANOVA on the means from *eight* different college majors. As mentioned in the previous chapter, the number of possible pairwise comparisons is given by the formula $k(k-1)/2$, so in the eight-group case there would be $8 \times 7/2 = 28$ t tests to perform. If you were to use .05 (i.e., 1 in 20) as your alpha, the chances would be better than 50% of obtaining at least one Type I error even if all eight of the corresponding population means were exactly the same. In fact, the *experimentwise alpha* (symbolized as α_{EW}) in this case would be at least .6. The advantage of performing an ANOVA at the .05 level first is that it will screen out about 95% of those experiments in which all of the population means are equal, and follow-up t tests will be performed only on the 5% that accidentally reach significance. For this reason, Fisher, who was the first to formalize the ANOVA procedure back in the 1920s, devised the following *protected t test* procedure.

Fisher's Protected t Tests

If *and only if* an ANOVA F test has resulted in the rejection of the overall null hypothesis that all k means are equal, any (or all) of the paired means may be compared by t tests using the usual (.05) decision rule. These t tests take advantage of the more stable estimate of the population variance provided by the ANOVA's MS_W, which is based on $df = N_T - k$. In comparison, an ordinary t test between any $\overline{X}_i$ and $\overline{X}_j$ (where the subscript i represents any one of the samples, and the subscript j represents any *other* sample) would be based on only the N_i and N_j observations, and it would only have $df = N_i + N_j - 2$. By requiring that the ANOVA F be significant, we protect the resulting ts from the large experimentwise Type I error rate that would otherwise occur. At the same time, these t tests are more powerful in detecting real population mean differences.

We will illustrate the protected t procedure using the example of the ANOVA analysis of student attitudes given in Table 16.1. Since the F test for the ANOVA was significant at $\alpha = .05$, we may proceed to compare the three pairs of means by t tests. The null hypothesis for any pair of means, $\overline{X}_i$ and $\overline{X}_j$, is tested by

$$t = \frac{\overline{X}_i - \overline{X}_j}{\sqrt{MS_W\left(\dfrac{1}{N_i} + \dfrac{1}{N_j}\right)}}$$

Here, $df = N_T - k$, and MS_W is taken from the ANOVA results. Notice that this is just the ordinary formula for the two-group t test, with MS_W serving as the pooled-variance estimate.

TABLE 16.2

Protected *t* tests among the three mean attitude scores following a significant ANOVA *F*

Means	$\bar{X}_1 = 13.50$ $N_1 = 8$	$\bar{X}_2 = 16.10$ $N_2 = 10$	$\bar{X}_3 = 10.11$ $N_3 = 9$

$$MS_w = 16.74$$

$\bar{X}_1$ versus $\bar{X}_2$:
$$t = \frac{13.50 - 16.10}{\sqrt{16.74\left(\frac{1}{8} + \frac{1}{10}\right)}} = \frac{-2.60}{1.94} = -1.34$$

$\bar{X}_1$ versus $\bar{X}_3$:
$$t = \frac{13.50 - 10.11}{\sqrt{16.74\left(\frac{1}{8} + \frac{1}{9}\right)}} = \frac{-3.39}{1.99} = 1.70$$

$\bar{X}_2$ versus $\bar{X}_3$:
$$t = \frac{16.10 - 10.11}{\sqrt{16.74\left(\frac{1}{10} + \frac{1}{9}\right)}} = \frac{-5.99}{1.88} = 3.19$$

df for t's $= df_w = N_T - k = 24$

Table 16.2 uses the means, group sizes, and MS_w of Table 16.1 to illustrate the computation of these t's. For $df = 24$, the critical value for t at $\alpha = .05$ (two-tailed) is 2.064. Therefore, only the difference between the means of Groups 2 and 3 is significant. We can thus specify the rejection of the overall ANOVA null hypothesis (all three population means are not equal) by rejecting one of its composite pairwise null hypotheses and asserting that $\mu_2 \neq \mu_3$.

When all groups are of the same size, $N_i = N_j$, and therefore the denominator of the foregoing t test becomes a constant for all the pairwise comparisons. It then becomes possible to greatly simplify the protected t test procedure. There must be some difference between the two means that is just large enough so that when it is divided by the (constant) denominator it yields a t value exactly equal to the critical t needed for significance at a given alpha level. This particular difference between the means is called the *least significant difference* (LSD). When it is inserted into the t formula given previously, we get

$$t_{crit} = \frac{LSD}{\sqrt{MS_w\left(\frac{2}{n}\right)}} = \frac{LSD}{\sqrt{\frac{2MS_w}{n}}},$$

where n is the size of each sample.

Solving for LSD, we obtain the following easy-to-use formula:

$$LSD = t_{crit}\sqrt{\frac{2MS_w}{n}}$$

The value of t_{crit} is chosen for $df = N_T - k$ and the two-tailed α of the decision rule. Assume that all of the sample sizes were 10 ($= n$) in the preceding example, and the usual $\alpha = .05$ decision rule is to be used. Then MS_W ($= 16.74$) would be based on $df = N_T - k = 30 - 3 = 27$, and t for $\alpha = .05$ and $df = 27$ is found in Table B to equal 2.052. Then,

$$\text{LSD} = 2.052 \sqrt{16.74 \left(\frac{2}{10} \right)} = 2.052(1.83) = 3.75$$

Finding LSD saves you the work of performing all of the follow-up t tests. Instead, you need only look at the amount of difference for each pair of means. In this example, all pairs of means differing by at least 3.75 attitude scale points would be significantly different at $\alpha = .05$ (two-tailed).

Although the protected t procedure provides good control and balance of Type I and Type II errors when you are dealing with only three population means, the protection afforded by requiring F to be significant drops unacceptably as k increases. Some other procedure should be used (which will be described shortly) when k is more than three, especially when exact control of the experimentwise Type I error rate is desired. Also, it is possible (though highly unlikely) to find F significant and none of the pairwise t's significant, in which case the proper conclusion is that the k means are not all equal but the data do not justify any further specification (*not* that all paired means are equal, which would be a contradiction).

Confidence Intervals for the Protected t Test

In the previous section, we tested the null hypothesis for each pair of means using three protected t tests. An alternative procedure would be to calculate three confidence intervals, as discussed in Chapters 10 and 11. This has the advantage of specifying all reasonably likely values of the difference between the two population means in each comparison.

To use the confidence interval procedure for the protected t test, the ANOVA F test must have resulted in the rejection of the overall null hypothesis that all k means are equal. As we observed in Chapter 11, the confidence interval for the difference between two population means is:

$$[(\overline{X}_1 - \overline{X}_2) - ts_{\overline{X}_1 - \overline{X}_2}] \le \mu_1 - \mu_2 \le [(\overline{X}_1 - \overline{X}_2) + ts_{\overline{X}_1 - \overline{X}_2}]$$

To calculate the critical value of t, you must use the correct degrees of freedom. For the data illustrated in Table 16.2, $df = N_T - k$ or 24, the degrees of freedom associated with the within-groups mean square (MS_W). For $df = 24$ and $\alpha = .05$, and a two-tailed test, the critical value of t is 2.052.

For each comparison, the standard error of the difference is equal to $\sqrt{MS_W(1/N_i + 1/N_j)}$. Since $MS_W = 16.74$, $N_1 = 8$, $N_2 = 10$, and $N_3 = 9$, the three standard errors of the difference that we need are

1. Group 1 versus Group 2: $\sqrt{16.74(1/8 + 1/10)} = 1.94$
2. Group 1 versus Group 3: $\sqrt{16.74(1/8 + 1/9)} = 1.99$
3. Group 2 versus Group 3: $\sqrt{16.74(1/10 + 1/9)} = 1.88$

Therefore, the three confidence intervals are

1. Group 1 versus Group 2:

$$-2.60 - (2.052)(1.94) \leq \mu_1 - \mu_2 \leq -2.60 + (2.052)(1.94)$$
$$-6.58 \leq \mu_1 - \mu_2 \leq 1.38$$

2. Group 1 versus Group 3:

$$3.39 - (2.052)(1.99) \leq \mu_1 - \mu_3 \leq 3.39 + (2.052)(1.99)$$
$$-0.69 \leq \mu_1 - \mu_3 \leq 7.47$$

3. Group 2 versus Group 3:

$$5.99 - (2.052)(1.88) \leq \mu_2 - \mu_3 \leq 5.99 + (2.052)(1.88)$$
$$2.13 \leq \mu_2 - \mu_3 \leq 9.85$$

As would be expected from the results in Table 16.2, only for the comparison between groups 2 and 3 does zero fall outside the confidence interval. Here again, confidence intervals provide us with important additional information about the probable difference between the population means in each comparison.

Tukey's Honestly Significant Difference (HSD)

The problem with using Fisher's procedure when you are dealing with more than three groups is that you are "protected" only in experiments for which the *complete* null hypothesis is true (e.g., for four groups, H_0: $\mu_1 = \mu_2 = \mu_3 = \mu_4$). As the number of groups increases there is an increasing number of ways that the null hypothesis can be *partially* true.

For five groups, a worst-case scenario for Fisher's procedure would be an experiment for which $\mu_1 = \mu_2 = \mu_3 = \mu_4 \neq \mu_5$. Perhaps four antidepressant drugs are being tested against each other and against a placebo, and the drugs have identical effects, all of which exceed the placebo effect. If the ANOVA involving the five means reaches statistical significance (this would not be surprising, given the difference of the placebo from the drugs), then, according to Fisher, it is acceptable to test each of the six possible pairs of drugs for significance, in addition to testing each drug against the placebo. But in this example all of the drug-to-drug comparisons are "null." If any accidentally reach significance, you have committed a Type I error within the experiment, even though you were correct to reject the (complete) null hypothesis of the ANOVA.

We cannot know how many "partial-null" experiments are being conducted. But the more that are tested, the more α_{EW} will rise above .05. J. W. Tukey understood this problem and was able to find a distribution that could keep α_{EW} below .05, regardless of how many groups are involved in the study and how complete the null hypothesis might be. This distribution is known as the *studentized range.*

The Studentized Range Statistic

Tukey recognized that when you draw, say, five samples from the same population, and compare the smallest sample mean to the largest, the difference is likely to be considerably larger than if you had only drawn two sample means and compared them. Therefore, his *studentized range statistic* (symbolized by q) grows appropriately larger as the total number of samples becomes larger. Also, the statistic is "studentized," like the t distributions, in that it gets smaller as the size of each sample gets larger, although it changes very little after the size of the samples rises above 40 or so.

It is not unreasonable to think of q as a t statistic that has been adjusted for the total number of groups being compared. We can see the extent of this adjustment by looking at Table G, which is a table of the critical values of the studentized range statistic for alpha = .05, two-tailed. An excerpt of this table is reprinted here as Table 16.3.

Notice that the value of q increases as you move to the right in any of the rows in Table 16.3. However, by the time you are dealing with six groups,

TABLE 16.3

Selected critical values of Tukey's studentized range statistic

df_W	Number of groups						
	2	3	4	5	6	7	8
...	...	...	...	...	...	...	...
4	3.93	5.04	5.76	6.29	6.71	7.05	7.35
...	...	...	...	...	...	...	...
8	3.26	4.04	4.53	4.89	5.17	5.40	5.60
...	...	...	...	...	...	...	...
12	3.08	3.77	4.20	4.51	4.75	4.95	5.12
...	...	...	...	...	...	...	...
16	3.00	3.65	4.05	4.33	4.56	4.74	4.90
...	...	...	...	...	...	...	...
40	2.86	3.44	3.79	4.04	4.23	4.39	4.52
...	...	...	...	...	...	...	...
∞	2.77	3.31	3.63	3.86	4.03	4.17	4.29

adding another group or two does not have nearly the impact on q that it does when you are dealing with only two or three groups.

Although increasing the size of the groups (i.e., going down the columns in Table 16.3) decreases the size of q, these decreases get smaller as the samples become large (as is the case with t). It may seem odd that q is larger than t even for only two groups (e.g., at infinity, q for two groups equals 2.77, while the critical t equals 1.96). This is not an actual adjustment in the test statistic but rather an artifact of how Tukey decided to present his formula, as we will show next.

Using Tukey's HSD Formula

Tukey's original formula merely substitutes q_{crit} for t_{crit} in Fisher's formula and calls the minimal difference for significance the *honestly significant difference* (HSD):

$$\text{HSD} = q'_{crit} \sqrt{\frac{2MS_W}{n}}$$

where q'_{crit} refers to a value from Tukey's original q table. However, Tukey decided to simplify the formula. He separated it, like this,

$$q'_{crit} \sqrt{2} \sqrt{\frac{MS_W}{n}},$$

and then multiplied his original q values by the square root of 2. The resulting formula is

$$\text{HSD} = q_{crit} \sqrt{\frac{MS_W}{n}},$$

where q_{crit} is a value from Table G and equals $\sqrt{2}$ times q'_{crit}. Thus, the first column of Table G actually consists of the .05, two-tailed critical values of t, each multiplied by the square root of 2 (e.g., $2.77 = 1.96 \sqrt{2}$). Unfortunately, this change in the formula from LSD to HSD, originally intended just to simplify its calculation (at a time before there were handheld calculators and personal computers), serves these days only to confuse students of statistics. Let us see what happens when we apply Tukey's formula to the data in Table 16.2.

For three groups and $df = 24$, the critical q from Table G is 3.53. For the purpose of comparison with LSD, we will once again use 10 for the common n. Therefore,

$$\text{HSD} = 3.53 \sqrt{\frac{16.74}{10}} = 3.53(1.294) = 4.57$$

Comparing HSD to LSD

Although HSD (4.57) is considerably larger than LSD (3.75), the conclusions do not change. The difference between Group 2 and Group 3, which is 5.99, is still statistically significant. Given that HSD can never be smaller than LSD, you cannot have a difference that exceeds HSD but not LSD. However, the reverse is certainly possible (e.g., a mean difference in this example of 4.0 would be significant by the LSD but not the HSD procedure).

Both the LSD and HSD formulas assume that all of the samples have the same size (n). If your sample sizes differ only slightly, as when equal groups were planned but some data have been lost, it is acceptable to calculate the harmonic mean of your actual sample sizes and use that value as n in the formula for LSD or HSD. (See B. Cohen, 2000, for a general formula for the harmonic mean.)

Tukey's HSD procedure does a better job of controlling Type I errors than Fisher's LSD. That is, HSD keeps α_{EW} below .05 for any number of groups. Therefore, it is said to be more *conservative.* In fact, Tukey's test is *overly* conservative in the case of three groups, whereas Fisher's procedure maintains α_{EW} at the value used to look up the critical t. Therefore, Fisher's protected t tests should be used whenever you are dealing with only three groups, and the LSD formula can be used in particular whenever the samples are the same size or nearly so. On the other hand, Fisher's system is too *liberal* when dealing with more than three groups: The larger the number of groups, the more Fisher's procedure allows α_{EW} to increase.

Other Multiple Comparison Procedures

Although Tukey's HSD test is acceptable for any number of groups (as long as they are all about the same size), it is more conservative and therefore less powerful than is desirable (e.g., it is less likely to detect small effects). This realization has led many statisticians to devise alternative (and sometimes highly complex) multiple comparison procedures designed to keep α_{EW} at a predetermined rate while maximizing power. One such test, which uses the studentized range statistic in a way that makes it more powerful than HSD, is called the Newman-Keuls (N-K) test. This test was the most popular multiple comparisons method in the behavioral sciences a few decades ago, but its use has declined sharply in recent years. This decline is due to the results of computer simulation studies that have demonstrated that the N-K test was not keeping α_{EW} fixed, as was previously thought. Rather, the N-K test was gaining most of its extra power by letting α_{EW} increase as the number of groups increased. Although the N-K test is not as liberal as LSD when many groups are involved, it is no longer considered acceptably conservative.

In the last twenty years or so, a number of multiple comparison procedures have been shown to keep α_{EW} at the desired level without being overly conservative. Unfortunately, most of these methods are unreasonably tedious to calculate by hand, and only some of them have been included in major statistical software packages. However, there is one procedure that combines elements of both Fisher's and Tukey's approaches to create a test that is not only more powerful than HSD *and* acceptably conservative, but is easy to use as well. This test, proposed by Hayter (1986), is known as the *Fisher-Hayter* (F-H) test, or the *modified* LSD test.

The Fisher-Hayter (Modified LSD) Test

In keeping with Fisher's approach, the F-H test begins with a one-way ANOVA. If the null hypothesis of the ANOVA cannot be rejected, the test does not proceed. If the ANOVA is significant (usually at the .05 level), HSD is calculated. However, the critical value of q that is used is the one that corresponds to $k - 1$ (rather than k) groups.

To illustrate the use of the F-H test, let us return to the example in the previous chapter, in which different types of music differentially affected performance on a spatial ability test. The means for each music type are shown in the following table.

Bluegrass	Jazz	Classical	New Age	Heavy metal
14.2	20.2	22.4	8.2	8.0

We will ignore the standard deviations from Table 15.1, and assume that MS_W equals 62 for the one-way ANOVA. The size of MS_B depends on the variance of these sample means and the size of the samples ($n = 5$), so we will use the value calculated in the previous chapter, namely, $MS_B = 221.1$. Therefore, the F ratio for this example is $221.1/62 = 3.57$. The critical value for F at the .05 level with df's equal to 4 and 20 is 2.87, so the null hypothesis of the ANOVA can be rejected; we can say that the population means for the five music conditions are not all equal to each other. This allows us to proceed to the next step of the F-H test. The critical q for 4 (i.e., $k - 1$) groups and $df_W = 20$ is 3.96, so

$$\text{HSD} = 3.96 \sqrt{\frac{62}{5}} = 3.96(3.52) = 13.94$$

Table 16.4, which illustrates the differences between pairs of means, makes it easy to see which music conditions differ significantly.

According to the F-H test, classical music differs significantly from both New Age and heavy metal. In both cases, the difference of sample means is greater than 13.94. No other differences are statistically significant.

By comparison, Tukey's method requires that the critical q be based on k (i.e., 5) groups. For this example, Tukey's HSD is equal to $4.23(3.52) = 14.9$.

> ### TABLE 16.4
> **Difference between each pair of means in Table 15.1B**
>
> | | Jazz | Classical | New Age | Heavy metal |
> |---|---|---|---|---|
> | Bluegrass | 6.0 | 8.2 | 6.0 | 6.2 |
> | Jazz | | 2.2 | 12.0 | 12.2 |
> | Classical | | | 14.2 | 14.4 |
> | New Age | | | | 0.2 |

Thus, Tukey's method would not find any pair of conditions to differ significantly, as no differences are greater than 14.9. It should be clear from this example that the F-H test is more powerful than Tukey's HSD. The original LSD test is more powerful still, as you can see from the following calculation:

$$LSD = 2.086 \sqrt{\frac{124}{5}} = 2.086(4.98) = 10.4$$

According to Fisher's LSD test, jazz also differs significantly from New Age and heavy metal. However, this test is widely considered to be too liberal for use with more than three groups and should therefore not be used in this example.

Which Multiple Comparison Test Should I Use?

Our recommendation is clear. For multiple pairwise comparisons, use Fisher's protected t tests (LSD, if all n's are equal) when dealing with only three groups, and use the F-H test with more than three groups. However, when presenting your results to researchers who are unfamiliar with the (relatively) new F-H test, you may have to resort to the more conservative but much more widely known (and respected) Tukey HSD test.

  If you are dealing with more than three samples and their sizes differ considerably, it is not legitimate to use any of the tests mentioned above. You may have to use an even more conservative general purpose comparison test, like the Bonferroni or Scheffé tests described in the next section.

Planned and Complex Comparisons

Whenever we have used the expression *multiple comparisons,* we were referring only to *post hoc* pairwise comparisons. The Latin term *post hoc* means "after the fact." In this context, it implies that no decision was made about which particular t tests to compute before looking at the data or performing the ANOVA. If you inspect your sample means and then test the difference between the largest and the smallest, you need the same α_{EW} protection that you would if you had conducted all of the possible t tests. Selecting specific pairs of means for comparison based on your theoretical research questions *before* seeing your actual data can give you a boost in power much like the added power that you can derive from planning a one- rather than a two-tailed test. You can get "credit" for predicting the statistical significance of a few particular *planned comparisons*.

The Bonferroni Correction

If you want to keep α_{EW} at .05, say, you should not use .05 as your alpha for each comparison (symbolized as α_{pc}, for α per comparison). But if you plan on testing relatively few of the possible comparisons, you do not need to increase your critical value as much as you would for Tukey's HSD. The simplest and most common procedure for finding the appropriate alpha for each of several planned (also called "a priori") comparisons is based on a formula for the maximum accumulation of probabilities, derived by the Italian mathematician Carlo Bonferroni in the 1930s. Applied to the problem of multiple comparisons, Bonferroni's "inequality" can be stated as follows: $c \times \alpha_{pc} \leq \alpha_{EW}$, where c is the number of comparisons being performed.

For example, if you use an alpha of .01 for each of five null comparisons, the chance that one or more of the five tests will turn out to be statistically significant (i.e., α_{EW}) will not be greater than $c \times \alpha_{pc} = 5 \times .01 = .05$. This fact leads to a simple rule for adjusting alpha for each comparison, based on the number of comparisons planned and the experimentwise value for alpha that you do not want to exceed. The formula for the *Bonferroni correction* (or "adjustment") is

$$\alpha_{pc} = \frac{\alpha_{EW}}{c}$$

To illustrate the use of the Bonferroni correction, let us return to the example mentioned at the beginning of the HSD section—that is, the study of four similar drugs and a placebo. If you plan to test each drug against the placebo but you do not plan to compare one drug to another, you are planning 4 comparisons out of a total of 10 (i.e., $5 \times 4/2$). To keep α_{EW} from rising above .05, you should use the following alpha for each of the 4 drug-to-placebo comparisons: $\alpha_{pc} = .05/4 = .0125$.

Before the ready availability of statistical software, special tables were needed to find critical t values corresponding to the various possible values of α_{pc}. If you are using statistical software to conduct your planned t tests, you will get an exact p value for each of your comparisons (the two-tailed p value is usually the default option). For this example, any t test producing a p value less than .0125 would be declared significant, but H_0 would not be rejected whenever p was .0125 or larger.

For the purpose of comparison with other procedures, note that the critical t for $df_W = 20$ and $\alpha_{pc} = .0125$ equals 2.744. This is a rather drastic increase over the critical t for the .05 level, which equals 2.086. The Bonferroni correction is very conservative. That is, it tends to keep α_{EW} well below .05. But if you are planning relatively few comparisons, the Bonferroni test gives you more power than Tukey's HSD. Recall that q for five groups and $df_W = 20$ is 4.23. This is equivalent to a critical t of $4.23/\sqrt{2}$, which equals 2.99, and is even larger than the Bonferroni-corrected critical t of 2.744.

The Bonferroni correction is too conservative to be used as a post hoc test when you are performing all of the possible t tests. In the five-group case, a total of 10 pairwise comparisons is possible. So α_{pc} would equal .005, which corresponds to a Bonferroni-corrected critical t ($df_W = 20$) of 3.15. This is even larger than the equivalent t for the HSD test (2.99), which is already a bit more conservative than is necessary. A reasonable compromise would be to use the Bonferroni correction to test a few planned pairwise comparisons and then use Tukey's HSD (basing q on the total number of groups) to test the rest of the pairs.

Complex Comparisons

Selecting a few pairs of conditions for planned tests is one way to increase power. A more sophisticated (and increasingly popular) way is to create a *complex comparison,* which involves more than two conditions in one test.

For example, if your study included a drug, an herbal remedy, and a placebo, you could subtract the average of the herbal remedy and placebo means from the drug mean to create a single difference, or *contrast.* This contrast can then be tested for significance as a planned comparison. Such contrasts allow you to get "credit" for correctly predicting the pattern, or relative spacing, of the means. If it turns out that the sample mean for the herbal remedy is much closer to the placebo mean than the drug mean, our contrast (the average of herbal and placebo vs. drug) will be larger than if the herbal and drug means were close together and very different from the placebo. (Conversely, planning to average the drug and herbal means for comparison with the placebo would imply that you are predicting that the effect of the herbal remedy will be comparable to the drug and that both are better than the placebo.) If the pattern of the sample means fits well with your prediction, a planned comparison can attain significance, legitimately, even when the ANOVA would not. With very few planned comparisons, it is reasonable to test each at the .05 level. When testing more than a few such comparisons, a Bonferroni correction on alpha may be called for.

Although it is not commonly done, when trying to follow up the results of a significant one-way ANOVA, you could devise and test a complex comparison based on a pattern you have seen in your data. For such post hoc complex contrasts, the Scheffé test is widely recommended to keep α_{EW} under control. The Scheffé test is so conservative that when the ANOVA is not significant you can be sure that you will not be able to create any comparison that will be found significant by Scheffé's test (see B. Cohen, 2000).

Summary

When the F ratio for a one-way ANOVA is statistically significant, it is very likely that the researcher will want to run multiple comparisons on the data to determine which of the population means can be said to differ from one another. A general procedure for post hoc pairwise comparisons, which can be applied whether or not the sample sizes are equal or even similar, is the Fisher protected t test. It is "protected" only if the null hypothesis for the one-way ANOVA can be rejected.

1. Fisher's Protected t Tests

For any (or every) pair of groups, compute as follows:

$$t = \frac{\overline{X}_i - \overline{X}_j}{\sqrt{MS_W \left(\dfrac{1}{N_i} + \dfrac{1}{N_j} \right)}}, \qquad df = N - k,$$

where

$$\overline{X}_i = \text{mean of group } i$$
$$\overline{X}_j = \text{mean of group } j$$
$$MS_W = \text{within-groups mean square}$$
$$N_i = \text{number of observations in group } i$$
$$N_j = \text{number of observations in group } j$$

If all of the sample sizes are equal, Fisher's procedure can be simplified by calculating LSD. Any pair of means that differs by more than LSD can be said to differ significantly. The formula is

$$LSD = t_{crit} \sqrt{\frac{2MS_W}{n}}$$

where n is the size of *each* sample and t_{crit} is two-tailed and is based on df_W and the alpha used to test the one-way ANOVA. Fisher's procedure is not recommended for following up an ANOVA that involves more than three groups, because it allows α_{EW} to increase as k increases, for $k > 3$.

2. Tukey's HSD Test

This test is appropriate for any number of samples, as long as the samples are all the same size, or nearly so. (In the latter case, the harmonic mean of the sample sizes is used as n.) It is not necessary to perform a one-way ANOVA before applying this test, but Tukey's test will rarely find a pair of means to differ significantly when the ANOVA would not be significant. The difference between each pair of means is compared to

$$HSD = q_{crit} \sqrt{\frac{MS_W}{n}},$$

where n is the size of each sample and q_{crit} is a value from Table G, based on k groups and df_W. The HSD test is more conservative than is desirable, but it is simpler and better-known than most alternative multiple comparison procedures.

3. The Fisher-Hayter (or Modified LSD) Test

This test requires that the one-way ANOVA be statistically significant before proceeding. The difference between each pair of means is compared to HSD, as calculated previously, except that q_{crit} is based on $k - 1$, rather than k, groups. Although this test is acceptably conservative, and more powerful than Tukey's test, it is not yet well known.

4. The Bonferroni Correction

If a relatively small number of comparisons are planned in advance, each one can be tested using the following value for alpha:

$$\alpha_{pc} = \frac{\alpha_{EW}}{c},$$

where c is the number of planned comparisons and α_{EW} is the largest acceptable value for the experimentwise alpha. This test is too conservative to be used as a post hoc test—for example, to test all possible pairwise comparisons following an ANOVA.

Exercises

1. Calculate LSD for the two experiments in exercise 1 of the previous chapter. For which experiment is the calculation of LSD justified? Determine which pairs of means differ significantly in the experiment for which the calculation of LSD is justified.

2. Calculate protected t tests to compare all possible pairs of the four universities, using the error term for exercise 2 of the previous chapter. Which pairs differ significantly at the .05 level? Why would it not be appropriate to calculate LSD or HSD for the data from the four Universities? Which pairs

differ significantly at the .01 level? Explain why using the .01 level for these t tests is overly conservative, and why using the .05 level is not conservative enough.

3. Calculate both LSD and HSD for the two experiments in exercise 3 of the previous chapter, using the simple average of the three sample sizes as your value for n. (Note: The harmonic mean of the Ns would be slightly more accurate.) What conclusions can you draw for each experiment? Use your values for LSD and HSD to compare the relative statistical power of these two procedures.

4. For your convenience, the data from exercise 4 from the previous chapter are reprinted in the following table:

	Group				
	1	2	3	4	5
$\overline{X}$	23	30	34	29	26
s	6.5	7.2	7.0	5.8	6.0
N	12	15	14	12	15

(a) Using the simple average of all the sample sizes as your value for n, calculate HSD for these data, and determine which pairs of groups differ significantly.

(b) Recalculate HSD according to the rules of the Fisher-Hayter test. Would the use of the F-H test be justified in this case? Assuming the F-H test is justified, what conclusions can be drawn from this test? Use the values for HSD in this part and part (a) to compare the power of Tukey's test with the modified LSD test.

Thought Questions

1. An F test from an ANOVA using five samples is statistically significant. The researcher now wishes to determine which of the five population means differ significantly from each other. Why are multiple comparisons procedures necessary?

2. If a multiple comparisons procedure involves the use of t tests, why can't a researcher skip the ANOVA and just do these t tests?

3. (a) When should you use Tukey's Honestly Significant Difference (HSD) test rather than Fisher's protected t tests? (b) When should you use Fisher's protected t tests rather than Tukey's HSD test?

4. What are the advantages of using the Fisher-Hayter (Modified LSD) test? When should this test be used?

5. (a) What is the difference between post hoc comparisons and a priori comparisons? (b) What advantage results from using a priori comparisons?

6. When should the Bonferroni correction be used?

7. Suppose that a multiple comparisons procedure shows that the critical value needed to conclude that two population means are different is 5.3. A study using five samples finds that the mean of each sample is as follows: sample 1 = 6.7; sample 2 = 14.2; sample 3 = 13.8; sample 4 = 10.4; sample 5 = 15.8. Which population means should be regarded as different from each other?

Computer Exercises

1. Redo the one-way ANOVAs requested in exercise 1 of the previous chapter, selecting both LSD and Tukey from the list of post hoc tests in each case. For postquiz anxiety, which pairs of quiz conditions (last question easy, moderate, difficult, or impossible) differ significantly from each other, according to each multiple comparison procedure (MCP)? Answer this question again for postquiz heart rate. Use Table G in your text, and your own calculations, to perform the Fisher-Hayter test for each DV, and state the conclusions for this test. Compare the three MCPs with respect to power, using the results you found in this exercise to illustrate the differences.

2. Redo the one-way ANOVAs requested in exercise 2 of the previous chapter, selecting both Tukey and Bonferroni from the list of post hoc tests in each case. What is the problem with using HSD to make comparisons between groups in this exercise? Use the results for this exercise to compare the power of Tukey and Bonferroni for testing all possible pairs of means.

3. Redo the one-way ANOVAs requested in exercise 3 of the previous chapter, selecting LSD as your MCP. Also, use your statistical software to perform ordinary t tests for each pair of math groups for each DV. Explain the differences between the LSD test and ordinary t tests as applied to the data in this exercise.

Bridge to SPSS

Whether you use the Analyze/Compare Means or the Analyze/General Linear Model menu to perform your one-way ANOVA, you can obtain the same selection of multiple-comparison procedures by clicking on the **Post Hoc...** button from the initial dialog box. If you choose to assume that all of the population variances are equal (you can request a homogeneity of variance test under Options, to help you decide), there are 14 choices for multiple comparisons, only a few of which we have discussed in this chapter. The choice labeled "Tukey" corresponds to the HSD test we have described; "Tukey's-b" refers to a less-used modification that we did not discuss. "S-N-K" refers to the Student Newman-Keuls test, which we discussed briefly and did not recommend.

For each Post Hoc test selected, SPSS will give you an appropriately adjusted and interpretable p value for each possible pairwise comparison, assuming that your goal is to keep the experimentwise alpha at .05. For instance, if you choose "Tukey," your output will not present you with the size of HSD. Rather, t tests will be performed for each possible pair of levels of your factor, and the exact p level will be given for each, adjusted according to the studentized range statistic. As an example, if the difference between a pair of means is exactly equal to HSD, its p value (labeled "Sig.") will be given as .05, because it is just on the borderline of significance for Tukey's test. For LSD, no adjustment is made to the p values, so it is up to you to note whether the ANOVA is significant, and to decide whether to use LSD if dealing with more than three groups (not recommended). For a pair of means that yields a p value of .05 for "Tukey," the p value for LSD will be smaller (i.e., more "significant"), because the latter is not adjusted.

If Bonferroni is selected, the p value from the LSD test is simply multiplied by the total number of possible pairwise comparisons. For example, if there are four conditions in your one-way ANOVA (and therefore six possible pairs), and the p value for comparing a particular pair by the LSD test is .01, the Bonferroni p for that pair will be given as $6 \times .01 = .06$, and therefore that pair will not differ significantly at the .05 level, when using the Bonferroni correction. (Note that this method yields the same conclusions as dividing .05 by 6 to get a Bonferroni-adjusted alpha of .00833. Because .01 is not less than .00833, a pair associated with that p value will not differ significantly when the Bonferroni procedure is used.) The other post hoc choices are beyond the level of this text, but they are rarely used, anyway.

Both the Analyze/Compare Means/One-Way ANOVA and the Analyze/General Linear Model/Univariate dialog boxes contain a **Contrasts** button, but only the former allows you to create your own customized combination of means to test a complex comparison. However, a discussion of how to choose the "coefficients" needed to create a particular contrast is well beyond the scope of this text.

Chapter 17

Introduction to Factorial Design:
Two-Way Analysis of Variance

PREVIEW

Introduction

When should you use a factorial design instead of a one-way analysis of variance? In what way are these two procedures similar? What are some of the important differences between them?

What is meant by the interaction between two variables?

Computational Procedures

What are the procedures for computing a two-way (factorial) analysis of variance?

Why do we calculate the sums of squares for the main effects *before* the SS for the interaction?

How do we test the *F* ratios for statistical significance?

What are the multiple comparison procedures in two-way analysis of variance?

The Meaning of Interaction

What is meant by a zero interaction versus some interaction between two variables?

What are the two major types of interaction for a 2×2 factorial design?

Why are we cautious about interpreting the results of the main effects when the interaction is significant?

Following Up a Significant Interaction

What are *simple* main effects, and when is it appropriate to test them?

How can tests of simple main effects lead to more specific conclusions from a two-way ANOVA?

How do you follow up a significant simple main effect that involves three or more levels of a factor?

Summary

Exercises

Thought Questions

Computer Exercises

Bridge to SPSS

Introduction

The one-way analysis of variance presented in Chapter 15 is used to investigate the relationship of a *single* independent variable to a dependent variable, where the independent variable has two or more levels (that is, groups). For example, the music experiment in Chapter 15 dealt with the effect of five different types of music (five levels of the independent variable) on performance on a spatial ability test (the dependent variable).

The *factorial design* is used to study the relationship of *two or more* independent variables (called *factors*) to a dependent variable, where each factor has two or more levels. Suppose you are interested in the relationship between four different dosages of caffeine (four levels: large, moderate, small, zero) and sex (two levels: male and female) to scores on a 20-item English test. There are several hypotheses of interest: Different dosages of caffeine may affect test scores; males and females may differ in test performance; certain caffeine dosages may affect test scores more for one sex than for the other. These hypotheses may be evaluated in a single statistical framework by using a factorial design. This example would be called a "two-way" analysis of variance, since there are two independent variables. It could also be labeled as a 4 × 2 factorial design, because there are four levels of the first independent variable and two levels of the second independent variable.

The logic of the factorial design begins with the logic of the more simple one-way design. The total sum of squares is partitioned into within-group (error) sum of squares and between-group sum of squares. In the factorial design, however, the between-group sum of squares is itself partitioned into several parts: variation due to the first factor, variation due to the second factor, and variation due to the joint effects of the two factors (called the *interaction*). (See Figure 17.1.) An example of an interaction effect would be if a particular dosage of caffeine improved test scores for males but *not* for females, while other dosages had no effect on test scores for either sex. (The interaction, a par-

FIGURE 17.1

Partitioning of variation in a two-way factorial design

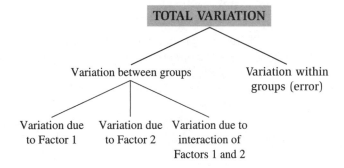

ticularly important feature of factorial design, will be discussed in detail later in this chapter.)

It can be shown algebraically that the total sum of squares is equal to the sum of these various parts: (1) the within-group (error) sum of squares, (2) the sum of squares due to factor 1, (3) the sum of squares due to factor 2, and (4) the sum of squares due to the interaction of factors 1 and 2. Thus a factorial design makes it possible to break down the total variability into *several* meaningful parts. That is, it permits several possible explanations as to why people are different on the dependent variable. As was pointed out in Chapter 5, explaining variation—why people differ from one another—is the *raison d'être* of the behavioral scientist.

Computational Procedures

The outline of the raw-score computational procedure for the two-way factorial design is as follows:

1. (a) Compute SS_T.
   (b) Compute SS_B.
   (c) Subtract SS_B from SS_T to obtain SS_W (error).
   (d) Compute SS_1 (the sum of squares for factor 1).
   (e) Compute SS_2 (the sum of squares for factor 2).
   (f) Subtract SS_1 and SS_2 from SS_B to obtain the sum of squares for the interaction of factors 1 and 2 ($SS_{1 \times 2}$).
2. Convert the sums of squares in steps (c), (d), (e), and (f) to mean squares by dividing each one by the appropriate number of degrees of freedom.
3. (a) Test the *main effect* for factor 1 (MS_1) for statistical significance by computing the appropriate F ratio (i.e., divide MS_1 by MS_W).
   (b) Test the main effect for factor 2 (MS_2) for statistical significance by computing the F ratio, as in (a).
   (c) Test the interaction of the two factors ($MS_{1 \times 2}$) for statistical significance by computing the F ratio, as in (a) and (b).

The two-way factorial design permits you to test three null hypotheses—one concerning the effect of factor 1, one concerning the effect of factor 2, and one concerning the *joint effect* of factor 1 and factor 2—in a single statistical framework. The separate effects of factors 1 and 2 are referred to as the *main effects* of those factors.

As an illustration, consider the hypothetical results for the music experiment shown in Table 17.1. There are five observations in each *cell;* for ex-

TABLE 17.1

Scores on a 20-item spatial ability test as a function of classical composer and musical background (4×2 factorial design)

	Musical composer (Factor 1)				Row means
	Mozart	Chopin	Bach	Beethoven	
No musical training	16 16 $\bar{X} = 14.2$ 14 13 $s = 1.79$ 12	16 14 $\bar{X} = 13.2$ 13 13 $s = 2.17$ 10	16 14 $\bar{X} = 12.4$ 12 10 $s = 2.61$ 10	14 13 $\bar{X} = 12.0$ 13 10 $s = 1.87$ 10	12.95
Musical background (Factor 2)					
Professional musician	16 18 $\bar{X} = 17.4$ 20 15 $s = 1.95$ 18	17 10 $\bar{X} = 13.2$ 13 12 $s = 2.95$ 14	14 14 $\bar{X} = 12.2$ 11 10 $s = 1.79$ 12	16 10 $\bar{X} = 12.8$ 13 14 $s = 2.39$ 11	13.90
Column means	15.8	13.2	12.3	12.4	Grand mean $= \bar{X}_{\text{G}}$ $= 13.425$

ample, the scores of 16, 16, 14, 13, and 12 are the test scores of five participants with no musical training who completed a spatial ability test while listening to Mozart. Just as in the one-way design, the within-group variance
estimate is based on the variability *within* each of the eight cells. Variation
due to the composer factor is reflected by the variability across the four *column* means, while variation due to the musical background factor is reflected
by the variability (that is, difference) of the two *row* means. (Note that the
data for the participants with no musical training in Table 17.1 come from
Table 15.1A, after deleting group 4.)

Sums of Squares

1. ***Total sum of squares (SS$_{\text{T}}$).*** The total sum of squares is computed in the
same way as in Chapter 15:

$$SS_{\text{T}} = \sum X^2 - N_{\text{T}} \bar{X}_{\text{G}}^2,$$

where

$$N_{\text{T}} = \text{total number of observations}$$
$$\sum = \text{summation across all observations}$$

In Table 17.1,

$$\sum X^2 = 16^2 + 16^2 + 14^2 + \ldots + 13^2 + 14^2 + 11^2$$

$$= 7{,}467$$

$$N_T \overline{X}_G^2 = 40(13.425)^2 = 7{,}209.2$$

$$SS_T = 7{,}467 - 7{,}209.2$$

$$= 257.8$$

2. Sum of squares between groups (SS_B). We can ignore for a moment the fact that this is a factorial design, treat the data in Table 17.1 as eight groups, and find SS_B as in Chapter 15. Because this is a *balanced* ANOVA design[1] (i.e., all of the groups, or cells, are the same size), we can use the equal-N version of the SS_B formula (see Chapter 15). However, to reduce the amount of hand calculation, we can use another, less tedious version of that formula. A convenient computing formula for SS_B for balanced designs is

$$SS_B = n \sum_{i=1}^{k} \overline{X}_i^2 - N_T \overline{X}_G^2,$$

where n is the size of *each* cell.

For the data in Table 17.1, $k = 8$ and $n = 5$. Therefore,

$$n \sum_{i=1}^{k} \overline{X}_i^2 = 5(14.2^2 + 13.2^2 + 12.4^2 + 12.0^2 + 17.4^2 + 13.2^2 + 12.2^2 + 12.8^2)$$

$$= 5(1{,}463.32)$$

$$= 7{,}316.6$$

We have already calculated $N_T \overline{X}_G^2$ as part of the formula for SS_T, so

$$SS_B = 7{,}316.6 - 7{,}209.2 = 107.4$$

3. Sum of squares within groups (error) (SS_W). The within-groups sum of squares may be found by subtraction:

$$SS_W = SS_T - SS_B$$

$$= 257.8 - 107.4$$

$$= 150.4$$

Later we will divide SS_W by df_W to obtain the usual denominator of our F ratios, MS_W. However, MS_W can be found directly from the unbiased SDs given

---

1. The calculation of factorial ANOVAs that are *not* balanced is a rather complex topic, which is beyond the scope of an introductory statistics text.

in Table 17.1. You may recall from Chapter 15 that in the equal-n one-way ANOVA, MS_W is the average of all the group variances. Similarly, in a balanced factorial design, MS_W is just the average of the *cell* variances. If you square all of the s's in Table 17.1, sum them, and then divide by 8, you will get 4.7061. This agrees, within rounding error, with SS_W/df_W.

Computing MS_W directly from the SDs can act as a check on the accuracy of your other calculations, but it has a more important function. If for any reason you need to calculate a factorial ANOVA from a table of means and SDs, and you do *not* have the individual scores, you will not be able to calculate SS_T directly. Therefore, you will not have the option of finding SS_W by subtraction. But that's not a problem, because you can always square and average the SDs to find MS_W directly.

Before we proceed to divide SS_B into smaller, more specific pieces, some additional notation will help to prevent confusion. Let us arbitrarily define factor 1 as the *column factor* and represent the number of columns by c. Similarly, we will define factor 2 as the *row factor* and use r to represent the number of rows. Thus, the number of cells in a two-way design can be written as rc, and the total N (N_T) therefore equals rcn. (For the design in Table 17.1, $N_T = rcn = 2 \times 4 \times 5 = 40$.)

4. Sum of squares for factor 1 (SS_1). We have defined the column factor as factor 1. In this example, the columns vary by musical composer. The sum of squares for the composer factor, *which ignores differences in musical background,* is

$$SS_1 = rn \sum_{i=1}^{c} \overline{X}_i^2 - N_T \overline{X}_G^2,$$

where $\overline{X}_i$ is the mean of any *column* and rn is the number of scores in any column (i.e., the number of rows times the size of each cell).

If composer has an effect on test scores (ignoring musical background), the means of the *columns* of Table 17.1 should show high variability. The value of $N_T \overline{X}_G^2$ has already been found to be equal to 7,209.2. Then,

$$SS_1 = 10(15.8^2 + 13.2^2 + 12.3^2 + 12.4^2) - 7,209.2$$

$$= 7,289.3 - 7,209.2$$

$$= 80.1$$

5. Sum of squares for factor 2 (SS_2). In this example, musical background is the row factor, and hence factor 2. The sum of squares for the background factor, *which ignores differences in musical composer,* is

$$SS_2 = cn \sum_{i=1}^{r} \overline{X}_i^2 - N_T \overline{X}_G^2,$$

where $\overline{X}_i$ is the mean of any *row* and *cn* is the number of scores in any row (i.e., the number of columns times the size of each cell). If musical background has an effect on test scores (ignoring composer), the means of the *rows* of Table 17.1 should be quite different.

$$SS_2 = 20(12.95^2 - 13.90^2) - 7,209.2$$

$$= 7,218.2 - 7,209.2$$

$$= 9.0$$

6. Sum of squares for interaction ($SS_{1\times2}$). The interaction sum of squares is part of the variability of the eight cells and is obtained by subtraction:

$$SS_{1\times2} = SS_B - SS_1 - SS_2$$

For the data in Table 17.1,

$$SS_{1\times2} = 107.4 - 80.1 - 9.0$$

$$= 18.3$$

Mean Squares

The next step is to convert each sum of squares to an estimate of the population variance, or mean square. This is done by dividing by the appropriate degrees of freedom, as shown in the following table and illustrated in Figure 17.2.

Source	Degrees of freedom	Computation for Table 17.1
Total	$N_T - 1$	$df_T = 40 - 1 = 39$
Within groups	$N_T - k$	$df_W = 40 - 8 = 32$
Between groups	$k - 1$	$df_B = 8 - 1 = 7$
Factor 1	c (i.e., number of levels of factor 1) $- 1$	$df_1 = 4 - 1 = 3$
Factor 2	r (i.e., number of levels of factor 2) $- 1$	$df_2 = 2 - 1 = 1$
Interaction	$df_1 \times df_2$ (i.e., $[r - 1] \cdot [c - 1]$)	$df_{1\times2} = 3 \times 1 = 3$

Note: N_T = total number of observations
k = number of cells = rc

The first three values in the preceding table are the same as in the case of the one-way design (Chapter 15). The total degrees of freedom equals $N_T - 1$, or one less than the total number of observations. The within-group degrees of freedom is equal to $N_T - k$, where k equals the number of cells (or groups). This is equivalent to obtaining the degrees of freedom for each cell (one less than the number of observations in the cell, or 4), and summing over all cells (4 × 8 = 32). The between-group degrees of freedom equals one less than the number of cells (i.e., $rc - 1$).

FIGURE 17.2

Partitioning of degrees of freedom in the music experiment

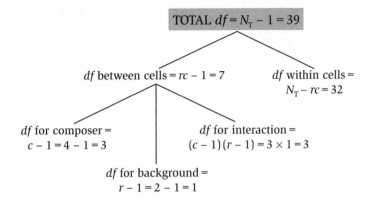

It is also necessary, however, to partition the between-group degrees of freedom in the same way as the between-group variance is partitioned. The degrees of freedom for factor 1 is one less than the number of levels of factor 1. In Table 17.1, there are four different composers, so the degrees of freedom are $4 - 1 = 3$. Similarly, the degrees of freedom for factor 2, musical background, are $2 - 1 = 1$. The degrees of freedom for the interaction of composer and background is found by *multiplying* the degrees of freedom for each factor ($3 \times 1 = 3$).

The mean squares are then found by dividing each sum of squares by the corresponding degrees of freedom:

Mean square within groups:

$$(MS_W) = \frac{SS_W}{df_W} = \frac{150.4}{32} = 4.70$$

Mean square for composer:

$$(MS_1) = \frac{SS_1}{df_1} = \frac{80.1}{3} = 26.7$$

Mean square for background:

$$(MS_2) = \frac{SS_2}{df_2} = \frac{9.0}{1} = 9.0$$

Mean square for interaction:

$$(MS_{1\times2}) = \frac{SS_{1\times2}}{df_{1\times2}} = \frac{18.3}{3} = 6.1$$

F Ratios and Tests of Significance

As with the one-way analysis of variance, the appropriate statistical model to use with factorial designs is the F distributions. The first null hypothesis to be tested is that regardless of which of the four classical composers they listen to the populations will have equal means. The mean square for the composer factor is divided by the mean square within groups, yielding the following F ratio:

$$F = \frac{MS_1}{MS_w} = \frac{26.7}{4.70} = 5.68$$

The critical value from the F table for three degrees of freedom in the numerator and 32 degrees of freedom in the denominator and $\alpha = .05$ is 2.90. Since the computed F of 5.68 is greater than this value, you reject H_0 and conclude that the four groups do *not* come from populations with equal means—that is, different musical composers *do* have an effect on spatial ability test scores.

The second null hypothesis to be tested is that the musicians and novices come from populations with equal means for spatial ability (we will refer to the participants who lack musical training as "novices," for convenience). The mean square for the background factor is divided by the mean square within groups, yielding the following F ratio:

$$F = \frac{MS_2}{MS_w} = \frac{9.0}{4.70} = 1.915$$

The critical value from the F table for one degree of freedom in the numerator and 32 degrees of freedom in the denominator and $\alpha = .05$ is 4.15. (Note that the critical values for the various F tests differ if the *df*s differ, since they are different F distributions.) Since the computed value of 1.915 is less than the critical value, you retain H_0 and conclude that there is not sufficient reason to believe that musical training is associated with differences in spatial ability.

The third null hypothesis to be tested is that the interaction effect is zero:

$$F = \frac{MS_{1\times2}}{MS_w} = \frac{6.1}{4.70} = 1.30$$

This computed value of F is less than the critical value obtained from the F table of 2.90 for 3 and 32 *df* and $\alpha = .05$. So you retain H_0 and conclude that there is not sufficient reason to reject the null hypothesis of no interaction effect.

ANOVA Summary Table

The results of the foregoing analysis of variance are summarized in Table 17.2. Note that the factors are identified by name for the convenience of the reader. Also, as was the case with the one-way analysis of variance, within-group vari-

TABLE 17.2

Summary of two-way ANOVA of music experiment

Source	SS	df	MS	F
Composer	80.1	3	26.7	5.68
Music background	9.0	1	9.0	1.92
Composer × background	18.3	3	6.1	1.30
Error (i.e., within cells)	150.4	32	4.7	

ation (error) is listed last. No F value is listed for error because error is used as the denominator of the various F ratios and is not itself the subject of a statistical test.

Multiple Comparisons in Factorial Design

We saw in the previous chapter how we could specify the meaning of a significant F ratio by means of a multiple comparison procedure. In a two-way factorial design, there are potentially three F tests that may require further specification as to which means differ from which others, and the same types of procedures may be followed.

When the F for interaction is *not* significant, it is meaningful to follow up each of the independent variables (factors) as if it were from a one-way ANOVA. If the F for a factor is *not* significant, there is nothing to follow up. Doing so is not only unnecessary but improper, since the resulting tests would not be protected. Or if a significant factor has only two levels, there is nothing to follow up. There is only one difference, so it must be significant. But a significant F for a factor of three or more levels requires specification just as in the one-way design.

In the foregoing example, the interaction F is not significant, but the F for composer is. So you may proceed to perform follow-up tests among the column means corresponding to the four different classical composers. Table 17.1 gives these as 15.8, 13.2, 12.3, and 12.4. Since all of the levels have the same $N_i = rn = 10$, and more than three levels are being compared, Tukey's HSD test is recommended, as modified thus:

$$\text{HSD} = q\sqrt{\frac{MS_{\text{w}}}{rn}},$$

where q (from Table G) is based on four groups (i.e., columns), df_{w} is from the ANOVA, and rn is the number of scores in each group (i.e., column).

Filling in the appropriate values in the formula, we find that

$$\text{HSD} = 3.84\sqrt{\frac{4.70}{10}} = 3.84(.686) = 2.63$$

Thus, two column means must differ by at least 2.63 points on the spatial ability test to be declared statistically significant at the .05 level. By this criterion, the mean for the Mozart condition (15.8) is significantly larger than the means for both the Bach (12.3) and Beethoven (12.4) conditions [and very nearly significantly larger than the Chopin mean (13.2)], thus further refining the "Mozart Effect" we first mentioned in Chapter 15. There are no significant differences among the other three composers. (The Fisher-Hayter, or modified LSD, test can be used instead of Tukey's test, as described in the previous chapter.)

Alternatively, a confidence interval may be established for each pairwise comparison. The formula for finding a CI in terms of HSD, as in the case of LSD, is very simple. In general,

$$\mu_i - \mu_j = \overline{X}_1 - \overline{X}_2 \pm HSD$$

Thus, the 95% confidence interval for the difference between column 1 (Mozart) and column 3 (Bach) is

$$[(15.8 - 12.3) - 2.63)] \leq \mu_1 - \mu_3 \leq [(15.8 - 12.3) + 2.63)]$$
$$+ .87 \leq \mu_1 - \mu_3 \leq +6.13$$

The value of zero falls outside (below) this interval, indicating that this comparison is statistically significant. In addition, the confidence interval specifies all reasonably likely values of the difference between the two population means. Other confidence intervals for the composer factor may be obtained in a similar fashion.

When the *F* for interaction *is* significant, it indicates that the factors operate *jointly.* Under these circumstances, our interest may be drawn to differences between *cells*—that is, specific combinations of the two factors. In the previous example, the *F* for interaction was not significant, so the focus was on the two main effects. But an alternative set of results for this experiment, illustrating a large interaction, is posited in Table 17.4B in the next section. The way follow-up tests are conducted for a two-way ANOVA is quite different when the interaction of the factors is found to be statistically significant. We will describe procedures for further specifying a significant interaction after we have discussed several ways to interpret the meaning of an interaction.

The Meaning of Interaction

Interaction refers to the *joint* effect of two or more factors on the dependent variable. As an illustration, consider once again the music experiment. The interaction effect of composer and music background refers to the unique ef-

TABLE 17.3

Cell means illustrating some interaction and zero interaction

Music background	Classical composer				Row means
	Mozart	Chopin	Bach	Beethoven	
	A. Cell means from Table 17.1 (some interaction)				
Novices	14.2	13.2	12.4	12.0	12.95
Musicians	17.4	13.2	12.2	12.8	13.90
$\overline{X}_{musician} - \overline{X}_{novice}$	3.2	0.0	−.2	.8	.95
	B. Cell means illustrating zero interaction				
Novices	14.2	13.2	12.4	12.0	12.95
Musician	12.6	11.6	10.8	10.4	11.35
$\overline{X}_{musician} - \overline{X}_{novice}$	1.6	1.6	1.6	1.6	1.60

fect of particular combinations of levels of the two factors, such as the musicians listening to Mozart or the novices listening to Bach, and *not* to the sum of the separate effects of the two factors. It is the joint effect *over and above* the sum of the separate effects.

Comparing Zero to Some Interaction

The interaction in the music experiment is highlighted in Table 17.3A, which displays the cell means from Table 17.1, along with the differences between the two background groups for each composer. The fact that these differences (3.2, 0, −.2, .8) are not all the same tells you that the amount of interaction is not zero. If, on the other hand, the professional musicians always scored exactly the same number of points higher (or lower) in spatial ability than the musical novices (say 1.6 points higher, as in Table 17.3B), regardless of the classical composer being listened to, the interaction would indeed be equal to zero. Also, note that a zero amount of interaction implies that the difference between mean test scores for any two composers would be the same for both musicians and novices. (See Table 17.3B.) If the mean differences for each composer were considerably different from one another, there could be a significant interaction effect; the composer factor would affect test scores differently for participants with different musical backgrounds. (One possible illustration is shown in Table 17.4.) Since the interaction effect for the data in Table 17.3A was found to be *not* significant, the differences among the observed mean differences of 3.2, 0, −.2, and .8 are likely enough to have occurred by chance (random sampling error) that there is *not* sufficient reason to believe that there is an interaction effect in the population from which the samples in this experiment were drawn.

A graphic illustration of the examples in Table 17.3 is shown in Figure 17.3. When the interaction effect is zero (Figure 17.3B), the line connecting the points corresponding to the cell means for musicians follows the same pattern

Graphic representation of data in Table 17.3

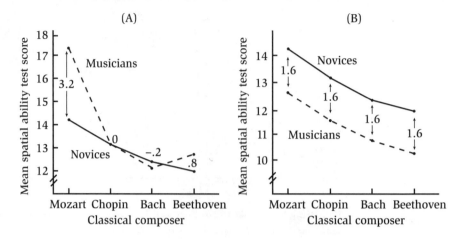

as the corresponding line for novices. That is, the two lines are parallel, which means that the distance between the two lines is the same at all points. When there is some amount of interaction (Figure 17.3A), musical background differences are different from one composer to another. From Table 17.3A, you can see that whereas musicians produced the higher means while listening to Mozart and Beethoven, novices had the higher mean during the Bach condition.

Different Types of Interactions

The (main) effects of the two factors in a two-way ANOVA are independent of each other. That is, either one could be significant while the other is not. Indeed, one factor could have a very large effect while the other has none at all. Or both effects, or neither effect, could be significant.

The size of the interaction in a two-way ANOVA is completely independent of the sizes of the main effects. Both main effects could be very large, while the amount of interaction is zero. Or there could be a large interaction with no main effects at all. Different relative amounts and directions of the two main effects can combine with different amounts of interaction to produce a variety of different patterns when the cell means are graphed. Two such patterns are shown in Figure 17.4.

In order to categorize two major types of cell-mean patterns, we will deal with an example of the simplest two-way ANOVA design: the 2 × 2 ANOVA. That is, each factor has only two levels. The first factor is sex, and the two levels are male and female. The second factor is drug type: The pill that is given at the beginning of the experiment contains caffeine for half of the males and half of the females, but only sugar (i.e., it is a placebo) for the other half of the

FIGURE 17.4

Two kinds of interaction patterns for caffeine and sex on test scores (2 × 2 factorial design)

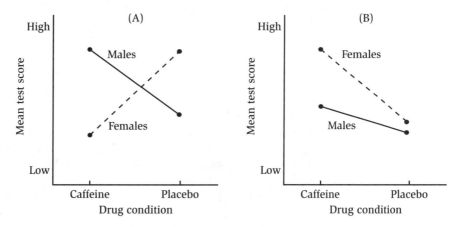

participants. The dependent variable is the score each participant obtains on a test of manual dexterity. For this experiment, two different kinds of interaction are shown in Figure 17.4.

In Figure 17.4A, women obtain higher average dexterity scores than men in the placebo condition. But when caffeine is administered, it is the men who achieve higher scores. This "reversal" effect leads to a large amount of interaction while virtually obliterating the main effects (e.g., when you average the men and women together for each drug condition, you get about the same mean for caffeine as you do for placebo). This pattern is often referred to as a *disordinal interaction*, because the effect of one factor changes its direction (order) depending on the levels of the other factor. For example, the gender difference changes its direction from the placebo to the caffeine condition.

There is a good deal of interaction in Figure 17.4B (the two lines are far from being parallel), but this time there is no reversal. Because the order of the effect for one factor does not change with different levels of the other factor (e.g., the gender difference favors females in both drug conditions), this pattern is called an *ordinal interaction*. With this pattern, it is not uncommon to find that both main effects are significant, as well as the interaction.

Notice that a large interaction can cause the main effects to be misleading. You could easily get a significant gender effect for the data depicted in Figure 17.4B, but it would be due almost entirely to the gender difference that is produced by the caffeine condition. Similarly, if you attained a significant drug effect for these data, it would be due mostly to the effect of caffeine on females, as there is not much of a caffeine/placebo difference for the males. The main effects are even more misleading in Figure 17.4A. Reporting that both main effects were small and not significant would seem to suggest that caffeine is no different from a placebo in its effect on manual dexterity and that there are no gender differences.

However, a quick look at Figure 17.4A shows that this is not the case. A large interaction, especially one that is statistically significant, is an indication that you should *not* focus your follow-up tests on the main effects (e.g., comparing pairs of row or column means), whether or not they are significant. Following up a significant interaction usually involves tests that are more specific; such comparison procedures will be described in the next section.

Following Up a Significant Interaction

A common approach to further specifying the source of a significant interaction is to test what are called *simple main effects*. A simple main effect is the effect of one factor at only one level of the other factor. This is easier to understand in terms of a graph of cell means. For example, in Figure 17.4A, each line is a simple main effect. The line that represents the men is the main effect of drug *only for the men;* hence it is a *simple* main effect. The same is true for the line representing the women. In addition, the cell means for the men and the women who were given caffeine represent the (simple) main effect of gender *only for the caffeine condition.* Similarly, there is a simple main effect for gender differences just for the placebo condition. You could highlight the simple main effects of gender by regraphing the cell means of Figure 17.4A so that the two genders would be specified along the horizontal axis. Then each line would represent the simple main effect of gender for one of the drug conditions.

Significant Interactions in a 2 × 2 ANOVA

In the 2 × 2 case, testing the simple main effects is just like testing cell-to-cell comparisons, and you can proceed by using Fisher's protected *t* test procedure. The cell-to-cell tests are protected if the *F* ratio for the interaction attains significance, as would be likely for the data shown in Figure 17.4A. However, not all of the possible cell-to-cell comparisons represent simple main effects. Of the six possible pairs of cells (i.e., $4 \cdot 3/2$), two pairs make little sense to test. If you were to compare men taking caffeine with women taking the placebo, or vice versa, and obtain a significant difference, you could not say which of the two factors (sex or drug versus placebo) is responsible, or whether both are. On the other hand, it would be meaningful to compare the two sexes separately for both the placebo and caffeine conditions, and the two drug conditions for each gender. Given a balanced two-way design, you could use the LSD formula to test these four differences of cell means:

$$\text{LSD} = t_{\text{crit}} \sqrt{\frac{2MS_{\text{W}}}{n}},$$

where n is the size of each cell.

In Figure 17.4A, it looks like all four of the simple main effects could easily be significant. However, the situation would likely be different for the pattern represented in Figure 17.4B. Again, the interaction could easily be significant. But whereas you could expect the simple main effect of drug condition to be significant for women, the relative flatness of the line representing men suggests that this simple main effect might fail to attain significance. Similarly, it looks like the simple main effect of sex could be significant for the placebo but not the caffeine condition.

The results you can obtain from testing simple main effects provide a more nuanced and specific story concerning the effects of your two factors, a story that can have practical implications. For example, if the simple effects of drug in Figure 17.4A were significant for both genders (albeit in different directions), the clear recommendation would be that a cup of coffee or two could improve performance for male workers but that females should avoid any source of caffeine before starting skilled manual work. On the other hand, the results in Figure 17.4B seem to suggest that females can benefit from caffeine, whereas the results for males are less clear. Moreover, this figure suggests a general female superiority in the skill being tested, which may only become noticeable, however, when both genders ingest caffeine before performing the task.

In general, the larger the interaction, the more the simple main effects differ from each other. A statistically significant interaction implies that the simple main effects differ from each other significantly. Specifying the source of a significant interaction becomes more complicated when one or both factors have more than two levels, because there are more options. The most common approach is to test simple main effects as an intermediate step before proceeding to cell-to-cell comparisons, as we will describe next.

Significant Interactions Involving Multilevel Factors

For an example involving a significant interaction with a factor that has more than two levels, we will return to the music experiment, with one modification. We subtracted 2 points from each of the five participants who lacked musical training and listened to Mozart. MS_W is unaffected, but the numerator MSs have changed, yielding the following F ratios for the data shown in Table 17.4: $F_{composer} (3, 32) = 2.84, p = .053; F_{background} (1, 32) = 4.47, p < .05; F_{interaction} (3, 32) = 3.42, p < .05$. Although the F ratio for composer is so close to being statistically significant that it would be tempting to apply pairwise comparisons to the composer (column) means, the significant two-way interaction suggests that tests of simple main effects may be more legitimate and informative. For example, to test the simple main effect of composer *just for the musicians,* you can perform a one-way ANOVA on the four cell means for the musicians, ignoring the cell means of the novices in finding MS_B and using MS_W from the original ("omnibus") two-way ANOVA. Given the equal cell sizes, we can use the following simplified formula from Chapter 15:

$$MS_B = ns_{\bar{X}}^2 = 5 \times \text{variance of } (17.4, 13.2, 12.2, 12.8) = 5(5.614) = 28.07$$

TABLE 17.4

Cell means for the music experiment, with one cell modified to produce a significant interaction

| Music background | Classical composer | | | | |
	Mozart	Chopin	Bach	Beethoven	Row mean
Novice	12.2	13.2	12.4	12.0	12.45
Musician	17.4	13.2	12.2	12.8	13.90
$\bar{X}_{musician} - \bar{X}_{novice}$	5.2	0.0	−.2	.8	1.45

Therefore, $F_{composer \, (for \, musicians)} = 28.07/4.7 = 5.97$, which substantially exceeds the critical value for $F_{.05}(3, 32) = 2.90$. (Note that our error df is df_w from the two-way ANOVA, because we are using MS_w from the two-way ANOVA.) Because we did not change any of the cell means for the musicians, this simple main effect would have been the same, and therefore statistically significant, for the data in Table 17.1. However, the interaction was not even close to significance before we changed one of the cell means for the novices, so we would not have been justified in testing simple main effects in the original data. Our follow-up tests would not have had the "protection" of having obtained a significant interaction.

Now that we know that the choice of musical composer affects the spatial ability (at least temporarily) of musicians, we still want to clarify this result further by conducting follow-up tests for each possible pair of composers. For this purpose, an appropriate multiple comparison procedure is Tukey's HSD test. In fact, we can use the same formula and the same values we used earlier to test pairs of column means, but with one important change:

$$\text{HSD} = q_{crit} \sqrt{\frac{MS_w}{n}} = 3.84 \sqrt{\frac{4.7}{5}} = 3.84(.97) = 3.72$$

Note that when we were comparing column means, we used rn (number of rows times size of each cell) as the number of subjects per group. In this latest test, we are comparing cell means, so it is appropriate to use just n as the number per group. The HSD is higher than it was for the column means (smaller groups can vary more easily by chance), but the Mozart condition is nonetheless significantly higher than the other three conditions, and none of the other composers differ significantly from each other. The test of the simple main effect of composer for novices is nowhere near statistical significance ($F < 1$), so no pairwise tests would be conducted among those cells.

Given the significant interaction in Table 17.4, there is another way that simple main effects could be tested. We would be justified in comparing the musicians to the novices for each composer. Because these simple main effects involve only two levels each, they are the same as cell-to-cell comparisons and would yield the same results whether conducted as one-way ANOVAs or t tests.

As the number of levels increases for each factor, so does the number of possible follow-up tests. When many comparisons are possible, it is likely that a researcher will plan to test just some of the comparisons, or use some multiple-comparison procedure that is better at controlling experimentwise alpha than Fisher's protected t tests.

Summary

In two-way ANOVA (or two-way *factorial design*), one of many complex forms of ANOVA, there are *two* independent variables. The statistical analysis makes possible a significance test (using the F ratio) of the effect of *each* independent variable, and of the effect of the *interaction* of the two variables—that is, the *joint* effect of the two variables over and above the separate effects of each one. Interaction is an important concept for behavioral science research.

1. Sums of Squares for a Balanced (i.e., Equal-n) Design

1. Total sum of squares (SS_T)

$$\text{Computing formula: } SS_T = \sum X^2 - N_T \overline{X}_G^2$$

where $\overline{X}_G$ is the grand mean

2. Between-groups sum of squares (SS_B)

$$\text{Computing formula: } SS_B = n \sum_{i=1}^{k} \overline{X}_i^2 - N_T \overline{X}_G^2,$$

where

k is the number of groups (i.e., cells), n is the number of scores in each cell, and $\overline{X}_i$ is any of the cell means

3. Within-groups sum of squares (SS_W)

$$\text{Computing formula: } SS_W = SS_T - SS_B$$

4. Sum of squares for factor 1, the "column" factor (SS_1):

$$\text{Computing formula: } SS_1 = rn \sum_{i=1}^{c} \overline{X}_i^2 - N_T \overline{X}_G^2,$$

where

r is the number of rows in the data table, c is the number of columns, and $\overline{X}_i$ can be any of the *column* means

5. Sum of squares for factor 2, the "row" factor (SS_2):

$$\text{Computing formula: } SS_2 = cn \sum_{i=1}^{r} \overline{X}_i^2 - N_T \overline{X}_G^2,$$

where

r, c, and n are defined as before, and $\overline{X}_i$ can be any of the *row* means

6. Sum of squares for interaction ($SS_{1\times2}$):

$$\text{Computing formula: } SS_{1\times2} = SS_B - SS_1 - SS_2$$

2. Degrees of Freedom

Total degrees of freedom:

$$df_T = N_T - 1,$$

where

$$N_T = \text{total number of observations}$$

Degrees of freedom within groups:

$$df_W = N_T - k,$$

where

$$k = \text{number of cells}$$

Degrees of freedom for the column factor (factor 1):

$$df_1 = c - 1,$$

where

$$c \text{ is the number of columns}$$

Degrees of freedom for the row factor (factor 2):

$$df_2 = r - 1$$

where

$$r \text{ is the number of rows}$$

Degrees of freedom for interaction:

$$df_{1 \times 2} = df_1 \times df_2 = (c - 1)(r - 1)$$

Also, note that $k = r \times c$, and $N_T = r \times c \times n$.

3. Mean Squares

Mean square within groups:

$$MS_W = \frac{SS_W}{df_W}$$

Mean square for factor 1:

$$MS_1 = \frac{SS_1}{df_1}$$

Mean square for factor 2:

$$MS_2 = \frac{SS_2}{df_2}$$

Mean square for interaction:

$$MS_{1 \times 2} = \frac{SS_{1 \times 2}}{df_{1 \times 2}}$$

4. *F* Ratios and Tests of Significance

Main effect of factor 1:

$$F = \frac{MS_1}{MS_W}$$

Main effect of factor 2:

$$F = \frac{MS_2}{MS_W}$$

Effect of interaction:

$$F = \frac{MS_{1 \times 2}}{MS_W}$$

Each computed F value is compared to the critical value from the F table for the degrees of freedom associated with the numerator and denominator *of that test.* If the computed F is less than the critical F, H_0 is retained; otherwise, H_0 is rejected in favor of H_1 (i.e., the effect is statistically significant).

5. Types of Interactions

A graph of the cell means for a two-way ANOVA allows you to see at a glance whether there is very little interaction (the lines on the graph are nearly parallel to each other), or a good deal of interaction. However, even an interaction that looks large (the lines sharply converge or diverge) could fail to attain statistical significance. If the *direction* of one factor's effect changes at different levels of the other factor, the interaction is said to be *disordinal.* If the lines converge or diverge while sloping in the same direction, the interaction is an *ordinal* one. A large interaction, especially a disordinal one, can lead to misleading main effects.

6. Follow-Up Tests (Multiple Comparisons) for a Two-Way ANOVA

1. If the interaction is *not* significant: In this case, the focus is on the main effects of each factor. If the F ratio for a factor is statistically significant, and that factor has more than two levels, pairwise comparisons among the column or row means may be conducted to ascertain which levels differ from which others. Fisher's protected t tests are acceptable when the factor has only three levels, whereas Tukey's test (or the modified LSD test) is recommended when there are four or more levels. Remember that when column or row means are being compared the value for n in the basic LSD or HSD formula should be the number of scores in each column (i.e., rn), or each row (i.e., cn), as appropriate.

2. If the interaction *is* significant: In this case, the focus usually turns to the *simple main effects*—that is, the effects of one factor at *each level* of the other factor. If the F ratio for a simple main effect is significant, and more than two levels are involved, cell-to-cell comparisons may be conducted to further specify the effect. LSD can be used when there are only three levels, and HSD for more than three levels, where n in these formulas is the size of each cell.

Exercises

1. The following table contains the statistics quiz scores for 18 students as a function of their phobia level and gender.

	Low phobia	Moderate phobia	High phobia
	5	8	5
Males	4	5	6
	4	7	9
	3	7	4
Females	4	5	9
	2	6	7

(a) Compute the two-way ANOVA for these data, and present your results in the form of an ANOVA summary table (see Table 17.2).

(b) Conduct the appropriate follow-up tests to determine which phobic levels differ significantly from which other levels. Are these follow-up tests justified by your results in part (a)? Explain.

2. An industrial psychologist wishes to determine the effects of satisfaction with pay and satisfaction with job security on overall job satisfaction. He obtains measures of each variable for a total group of 20 employees, and the results are shown in the following table. (Cell entries represent overall job satisfaction, where 7 = very satisfied and 1 = very dissatisfied.)

Satisfaction with job security	Satisfaction with pay	
	High	Low
	7	3
	7	1
High	6	2
	4	2
	6	2
	1	2
	2	1
Low	5	3
	2	1
	2	1

(a) Perform a two-way ANOVA on these data. Using an alpha of .05, what can the psychologist conclude?

(b) Graph the cell means for these data. What type of interaction do you see: ordinal or disordinal?

(c) Test all of the simple main effects. What specific conclusions can you draw from these tests?

3. Suppose that a 2 × 2 factorial design is conducted to determine the effects of caffeine and sex on scores on a 20-item English test. The cell means are given in the following table.

	Caffeine factor	
Sex	Caffeine	Placebo
Males	$\bar{X} = 17.3$	$\bar{X} = 12.0$
Females	$\bar{X} = 12.3$	$\bar{X} = 16.4$

(a) Given that $n = 7$ and $MS_w = 2.0$, compute the appropriate F ratios, and test each for significance at the .05 level.

(b) Graph the cell means for these data. What type of interaction do you see: ordinal or disordinal?

(c) Test all of the simple main effects. What specific conclusions can you draw from these tests?

4. For each of the following experiments, perform a two-way ANOVA and then the follow-up tests that are appropriate for your results. Use a graph of the cell means to explain the results you obtained.

(a) Experiment 1

	Factor 1		
Factor 2	1	2	3
1	8	14	1
	17	10	7
	2	3	15
2	18	6	3
	10	2	3
	19	2	7
3	5	16	4
	17	15	16
	6	9	1

(b) Experiment 2

	Factor 1		
Factor 2	1	2	3
1	2	17	8
	3	14	10
	1	15	7
2	4	18	6
	2	16	5
	3	17	9
3	3	19	10
	2	15	6
	1	16	7

(c) Experiment 3

	Factor 1		
Factor 2	1	2	3
	18	8	2
1	16	10	3
	17	7	1
	4	19	6
2	2	15	5
	3	16	9
	10	3	17
3	6	2	14
	7	1	15

Thought Questions

1. (a) What is a factorial design? (b) What is the difference in purpose between a two-way ANOVA and a one-way ANOVA? (c) What do we mean when we say that one factor in a two-way ANOVA has four levels and the second factor has two levels?

2. Complete the following table by stating what sums of squares, mean squares, and F tests are computed in *both* one-way ANOVA and two-way ANOVA, and what sums of squares, mean squares, and F tests are computed in a two-way ANOVA but *not* in a one-way ANOVA.

	Computed in *both* one-way and two-way ANOVA	Computed in two-way ANOVA but *not* in one-way ANOVA
Sums of squares		
Mean squares		
F tests		

3. A researcher conducts a two-way ANOVA. One factor is sex: male or female. The other factor is drug level: whether participants receive a pill designed to treat Obsessive-Compulsive Disorder or a placebo that looks and tastes the same but contains no medicine. Describe some of the interactions that might occur in this experiment.

4. What is the difference between a disordinal interaction and an ordinal interaction?

5. Give an example of how a large interaction in a two-way ANOVA could cause the main effects to be misleading.

6. (a) What is a simple main effect? (b) When should a researcher test simple main effects, and what procedure should the researcher use?

Computer Exercises

1. Using college major and sex as your independent variables, perform a two-way ANOVA on the math background quiz. Request descriptive statistics. Use the cell means to explain your results. (Advanced exercise: Redo the two-way ANOVA without the psychology majors.)

2. Redo exercise 1, replacing the college-major factor with the grouping variable you created (in Chapter 15) from the number of math courses taken.

3. Create a grouping variable based on a "median split" of the phobia scores, so that one group contains the students with the 50 lowest phobia scores, and the other has the 50 highest phobia scores. Then perform a two-way ANOVA on postquiz heart rate, using the new phobia grouping variable and the quiz conditions (last question easy, moderate, difficult, or impossible) as your two factors.

   (a) Request a graph of the cell means and refer to the graph to explain the results of the two-way ANOVA.

   (b) Test all of the possible pairs of levels for the quiz-condition factor.

4. Redo the two-way ANOVA in exercise 3 using postquiz anxiety as your dependent variable.

   (a) Request a graph of the cell means and refer to the graph to explain the results of the two-way ANOVA.

   (b) Regardless of your ANOVA results, test the simple main effect of quiz condition for each phobic group, and test all of the possible pairwise (cell-to-cell) comparisons for each of those simple main effects.

Bridge to SPSS

To perform a two-way ANOVA in SPSS, select "Univariate" from the Analyze/General Linear Model menu. Then, move your two independent variables into the Fixed Factor(s) space (we will not be discussing Random Factors in this text, but they are rarely used), and your dependent variable to its appropriately labeled space. If you want to create a plot of the cell means (and you probably will), click on the **Plots** button. If one factor has more levels than the other, the graph will look neater if you move that factor to the Horizontal Axis space and the other factor to Separate Lines. Don't forget to click the **Add** button before you click on **Continue.**

If you have a factor with more than two levels, and you know you will want to see pairwise comparisons among its levels (e.g., you expect the main effect of that factor to be significant), click on **Post Hoc** and, after moving over the factor(s) of interest, check the appropriate post hoc test (e.g., LSD for a three-level factor; Tukey for more than three levels). Under Options, you will likely want to check Descriptive statistics, in order to get the mean, SD, and n for each cell. However, for a balanced design, there is little reason to request Homogeneity tests, because it is routine to ignore all but the most extreme differences in cell variances if all the n's are the same. The other options are quite advanced, but we will describe one more of them briefly at the end of this section.

The easiest way to compute simple main effects in SPSS is to use Split File on one of the factors and perform a one-way ANOVA with the other factor. The only problem with this approach is that each one-way ANOVA will use its own error term rather than the within-cell error term from the original two-way ANOVA. To correct this you would have to calculate your own F ratios by dividing the numerator MSs from the one-way ANOVAs by MS_W from the two-way ANOVA (and then looking up critical values in Table F to make a decision about each null hypothesis). There is a way to get SPSS to print out these F ratios automatically, but it requires modifying a command in a Syntax Window, so it is not necessarily an easier procedure.

Like Compare Means/One-Way ANOVA, GLM/Univariate produces an ANOVA summary table as its main output. However, the summary table created by the latter procedure contains several extra rows, which are labeled in a way that can easily be confusing. So we will describe the output for a two-way ANOVA row by row. The first row is labeled "Corrected Model." The SS in this row corresponds to what we have been calling SS_B—the between-group SS that you get when you treat all the cells of the two-way design as the groups of a one-way ANOVA. The SS in the row labeled "Intercept" is equal to $N_T \times \overline{X}_G^2$; this quantity is sometimes called the "correction factor" (CF) in computational ANOVA formulas, because it is the quantity that gets subtracted in the formulas for SS_B and SS_T.

The next three rows represent the main effects of your two factors and their interaction, and are clearly labeled in terms of the variable names you assigned to your factors (the sum of the SS's in these three rows equals the SS for the "Corrected Model"). The following row, labeled "Error," contains what we have been referring to as SS_W, df_W, and MS_W. The row labeled "Total" is the sum of the Corrected Model, Intercept, and Error, and will generally be of no interest to you, but the last row, "Corrected Total," contains the sum of the SSs for the Corrected Model (i.e., SS_B) and for Error (i.e., SS_W), and is therefore equal to what we have been calling SS_T. The F ratio for the Corrected Model tests the differences among your cell means as a one-way ANOVA, and the F ratio for Intercept tests the grand mean of all your scores against a null hypothesis of zero. Unless you have some negative as well as positive scores in your data, this F ratio will generally be very large and totally uninteresting.

Finally, we mention one more statistic available from Options. First, note that under the two-way ANOVA summary table you will see a value for R Squared. This is the same as the statistic more commonly referred to as eta squared (η^2) in the context of ANOVA. It is equal to the SS for the Corrected Model divided by the SS for the Corrected Total—in other words, it is SS_B/SS_T.

(The Adjusted R Squared is the unbiased estimate of omega squared, as described in Chapter 15.) This tells you the proportion of variance accounted for by the cell means, but for a two-way ANOVA you are more likely to be interested in the variance proportions for each factor separately, as well as for the interaction. These "partial" eta squared values can be obtained by selecting "Estimates of effect size" under Options. (Whether partial eta squared gives a useful description of your data in a two-way ANOVA depends on the nature of the two factors; see Cohen, 2000, for a discussion of this issue.)

PREVIEW

Introduction

How can the advantage of the matched-pairs t test be extended to more than two conditions?

Calculating the One-Way RM ANOVA

How can the formulas for a two-way ANOVA be used to compute a one-way RM ANOVA?

How does the critical value for a one-way RM ANOVA compare to the critical value for the corresponding independent-samples ANOVA?

Rationale for the RM ANOVA Error Term

Why does it make sense to use the subject by treatment interaction as the error term for the RM ANOVA? How does this interaction compare to the variance of the difference scores when the RM ANOVA has only two levels?

Assumptions of the RM ANOVA

How are the usual ANOVA assumptions modified in the case of RM ANOVA? What is the sphericity assumption, and why is it important?

What precautions are recommended when conducting pairwise comparisons following a significant RM ANOVA?

The RM versus RB Design: An Introduction to Issues of Experimental Design

Under what conditions is the RM design highly recommended, and when is it problematic?

When is it advantageous to add an individual-difference factor to an ordinary one-way ANOVA?

What are the advantages and disadvantages of the treatment-by-block and the randomized-blocks (RB) design?

The Two-Way Mixed Design

What steps must be added to the two-way ANOVA procedure to obtain the two different error terms needed to compute a two-way mixed-design ANOVA?

What additional assumption is needed for the two-way mixed ANOVA as compared to the one-way RM ANOVA?

(continued next page)

Introduction

In Chapter 11 we demonstrated the advantage of matching subjects into pairs or measuring the same subject twice, as compared to giving two different treatments (or conditions) to two independent samples. Our goal in this chapter will be to show how ANOVA can be used to extend the same advantage to a situation in which the independent variable has three or more levels. The procedure we will describe in this chapter is commonly called the *repeated-measures (RM) ANOVA*, but it can be applied equally well to an experimental design in which subjects are matched across several conditions. The latter design is referred to as a *randomized-blocks (RB) design;* when there are only two conditions, it is identical to the matched-pairs design discussed in Chapter 11.

The trick that made it easy to compute a matched-pairs *t* test was to first calculate a difference score for each pair and then compute a one-sample *t* test to compare these difference scores to the mean for the null hypothesis (namely, zero). There is also a simple trick to calculating an RM ANOVA; it makes use of the two-way ANOVA formulas presented in the previous chapter. We will discuss the calculation procedure first and then explain why it makes sense that the RM ANOVA is computed this way.

Calculating the One-Way RM ANOVA

To demonstrate the power of the RM ANOVA, we will take a set of data for which we have already computed an independent-samples ANOVA and show how much larger the *F* ratio would be if the same data were analyzed accord-

| TABLE 18.1 |

Music experiment data from Table 15.1A presented as repeated measures

Subject number	Mozart	Chopin	Bach	Schubert	Beethoven	Subject $\bar{X}$
1	16	16	16	16	14	15.6
2	16	14	14	14	13	14.2
3	14	13	12	12	13	12.8
4	13	13	10	12	10	11.6
5	12	10	10	12	10	10.8
Column $\bar{X}$	14.2	13.2	12.4	13.2	12.0	13.0

ing to a repeated-measures design. For our example, we will use the data from Table 15.1A, for which the F ratio was quite small ($F = 3.60/4.28 = .84$). These data are reprinted in Table 18.1.

Note that if each row of data contains five scores *from the same person* (each obtained while he or she listened to a different one of the five classical composers included in this experiment), it is meaningful to calculate the means for the rows, as well as the columns, in the data set. The row means are therefore subject means. To view the data in Table 18.1 as coming from a two-way factorial design, you have to view the *second* factor (composer is the first factor) as the "subject" factor. Each particular subject is automatically at a different level of the subject factor by virtue of being a different person. Let us now apply the procedure of the previous chapter to begin the computation of a two-way ANOVA for the data in Table 18.1.

The first step, as in any ANOVA in which you have all of the raw data, is to calculate the total sum of squares. The same formula is used in both the one- and two-way ANOVAs, and in fact, SS_T was already calculated for these data in Chapter 15:

$$SS_T = \sum X^2 - N_T \bar{X}_G^2 = 4{,}325 - 25(13.0)^2 = 4{,}325 - 4{,}225 = 100$$

In an ordinary two-way ANOVA, the next step would be to calculate $SS_{between-cells}$. However, when dealing with a one-way RM ANOVA design, there is only one score per cell (i.e., $n = 1$), so $SS_{between-cells}$ is the same as SS_T (i.e., there is no SS_W component). As it turns out, this is not a problem; it simply saves us a step. Therefore, we can proceed to calculate SS_1 and SS_2 for the main effects of the two-way ANOVA. However, we can relabel these components as $SS_{treatment}$ (or SS_{treat}, for short) and $SS_{subject}$ (or SS_{sub}, for short), respectively, keeping in mind that the usual way to view the data from an RM ANOVA is with the subjects in the different rows, and the treatments in the different columns. Using the formulas from the previous chapter (keeping in mind that in this application $n = 1$), and relabeling appropriately, we obtain

$$SS_{treat} = r \sum \bar{X}_i^2 - N_T \bar{X}_G^2$$

$$= 5(14.2^2 + 13.2^2 + 12.4^2 + 13.2^2 + 12.0^2) - 4{,}225$$

$$= 5(201.64 + 174.24 + 153.76 + 174.24 + 144) - 4{,}225$$

$$= 5(847.88) - 4{,}225 = 4239.4 - 4{,}225 = 14.4$$

$$SS_{sub} = c \sum \bar{X}_j^2 - N_T \bar{X}_G^2$$

$$= 5(15.6^2 + 14.2^2 + 12.8^2 + 11.6^2 + 10.8^2) - 4{,}225$$

$$= 5(860.04) - 4{,}225 = 4300.2 - 4{,}225 = 75.2.$$

(The index j is used to represent the means for the latter summation, as a reminder that these means are different from the ones in the previous summation. The j means are found across rows or subjects, rather than columns or treatments.)

When applied to the one-way RM ANOVA, r (the number of rows) always equals the number of different subjects (or blocks), and c (the number of columns) always equals the number of levels of the IV. Also note that SS_{treat} agrees with the value that was calculated in Chapter 15 (albeit by a more tedious version of the same formula), when it was called just SS_B. The SS for the interaction term is found by subtraction, as usual:

$$SS_{inter} = SS_T - SS_{treat} - SS_{sub} = 100 - 14.4 - 75.2 = 10.4$$

The total df $(rc - 1)$ break down into three components in this design:

$$df_{treat} = c - 1; \; df_{sub} = r - 1; \; \text{and} \; df_{inter} = (c - 1)(r - 1)$$

Thus,

$$MS_{treat} = \frac{SS_{treat}}{df_{treat}} = \frac{14.4}{4} = 3.6 \text{ (compare to } MS_B \text{ in Chapter 15)}$$

$$\text{and } MS_{inter} = \frac{SS_{inter}}{df_{inter}} = \frac{10.4}{16} = .65$$

We will not bother to calculate MS_{sub} because it is not used in this design, for reasons that will be described shortly. Instead, it is MS_{inter} that is used as the denominator (i.e., error term) of the F ratio. Therefore,

$$F_{treat} = \frac{MS_{treat}}{MS_{inter}} = \frac{3.6}{.65} = 5.54$$

The Critical F for the RM ANOVA

The appropriate critical F at the .05 level is $F_{.05}(df_{treat}, df_{inter}) = F_{.05}(4, 16) = 3.01$. In fact, our calculated F is significant even at the .01 level, because $F_{treat} = 5.54 > F_{.01}(4, 16) = 4.77$. Notice how much larger the F for the RM ANOVA is (5.54) compared to the F for the independent-samples ANOVA calculated on the same data (.84). This difference is not due to the numerators of the two F ratios, which are the same (MS_{treat} and MS_B are based on the same column means). It is due to the difference in the denominators. Recall that the error term in the Chapter 15 ANOVA was based on SS_W, which was equal to 85.6. It is not a coincidence that the sum of SS_{inter} and SS_{sub} in the RM ANOVA (i.e., 10.4 + 75.2) also equals 85.6. In fact, put another way, it will always be true that $SS_{inter} = SS_W - SS_{sub}$.

SS_{inter} is almost always smaller than SS_W (it can never be larger), which works to the advantage of the RM ANOVA. It is also true that df_{inter} will *always* be smaller than df_W (16 versus 20, for this example), which means that the critical value for the RM ANOVA will always be *larger* than the critical value for the corresponding independent-samples ANOVA. This will make it more difficult to reject H_0, so the loss in degrees of freedom and corresponding increase in the critical value is clearly a disadvantage of the RM ANOVA. In practice, however, it is usually more than compensated for by the increase in the calculated F ratio. You may recall an analogous situation involving the matched-pairs t test. The connections between the RM ANOVA and the matched-pairs t test will become more obvious when we apply both statistical procedures to the same data set that has only two treatment levels.

Rationale for the RM ANOVA Error Term

Why does it make sense to use MS_{inter} as the error term for the RM ANOVA instead of MS_W, or even MS_{sub}? First, note that MS_{inter} refers to the interaction of the individual subjects with the treatment levels. Thus, it is a measure of how closely subjects follow the same pattern over the different levels of the treatment. Therefore, MS_{inter} can be thought of as a measure of the reliability of the various treatment effects. This concept can be visualized by graphing the data from an RM ANOVA as you would for the cell means of a two-way ANOVA, except in this case the cell means are really the individual scores. This graph is shown in Figure 18.1.

If all of the subjects in Figure 18.1 were to exhibit almost exactly the same profile over the treatment levels, the lines would be nearly parallel, and the amount of subject by treatment interaction would be quite small. As MS_{inter} decreases, the F ratio for the RM ANOVA increases, reflecting the increasing reliability of the treatment effects across the different subjects.

FIGURE 18.1

Graph of data in Table 18.1

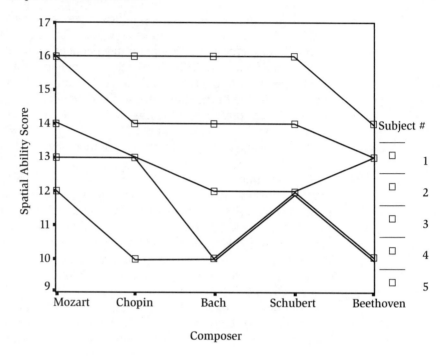

Comparing the Matched-Pairs *t* Test with the One-Way RM ANOVA for Two Conditions

To make the comparison with the matched-pairs *t* test, let us look at only the last two composers (i.e., 4 and 5) in Figure 18.1. The difference scores for the five subjects are 2, 1, –1, 2, and 2. The amount of subject by treatment interaction for the last two composers is directly related to the variability of these difference scores. If all the difference scores were the same, the variability of the difference scores would be zero, and so would MS_{inter}, because the lines on the graph would all be parallel to each other. The mean for the differences for the last two composers is $\Sigma D/N = 6/5 = 1.2$, and the (unbiased) standard deviation is 1.304. The matched *t* value for these two composers is therefore $1.2/(1.304/\sqrt{5}) = 1.2/.583 = 2.06$, which is not significant with only 4 degrees of freedom. It can be instructive to compare this result to the RM ANOVA for just the last two composers.

As an exercise, the reader should verify that

$$SS_T = 30.4; \; SS_{sub} = 23.4; \; SS_{treat} = 3.6; \text{ and } SS_{inter} = 3.4$$

$$MS_{treat} = \frac{3.6}{1} = 3.6; \; MS_{inter} = \frac{3.4}{4} = .85; \; F_{RM} = \frac{3.6}{.85} = 4.235$$

TABLE 18.2
Data from Table 18.1 for Schubert and Beethoven only

Subject number	Schubert	Beethoven	Subject $\overline{X}$
1	16	14	15.0
2	14	13	13.5
3	12	13	12.5
4	12	10	11.0
5	12	10	11.0
Column $\overline{X}$	13.2	12.0	12.6

As in the case of independent samples, squaring the matched t value yields the same value (within rounding error) as calculating the RM ANOVA on the same data: matched $t^2 = 2.06^2 = 4.24 = F_{RM}$. There is a simple relationship between the variance of the difference scores for two matched sets of scores (for the data in Table 18.2, s_D^2 is $1.304^2 = 1.7$) and MS_{inter} for the same data. The latter value is .85, which is exactly half of s_D^2, as will always be the case.

Assumptions of the RM ANOVA

The RM ANOVA makes the usual assumptions demanded by inferential parametric statistics:

1. The dependent variable has been measured on an interval or ratio scale.
2. The dependent variable follows a normal distribution in each population.
3. The observations are all mutually independent *within each sample.*

This last assumption has had to be modified, because the key element of an RM ANOVA is that the scores are *not* independent *across* samples. In fact, you are hoping that there is a fairly high positive correlation between the scores for every pair of samples.

Moreover, several statistical procedures, such as the pooled-variance t test and the ordinary independent-samples ANOVA (as presented in Chapter 15), require the assumption of homogeneity of variance. The one-way RM ANOVA described in this chapter also requires an appropriate homogeneity assumption, as described next.

The Sphericity Assumption

In the one-way independent-samples ANOVA, MS_W is found by averaging all of the sample variances. (A weighted average is used if the samples differ in size.) Averaging all of the sample variances to create a single error term leads to a straightforward statistical test only if you can assume that the variances of the populations represented by those samples are all the same. This homogeneity of variance (HOV) assumption can be tested for a one-way ANOVA. If the HOV test is significant (indicating *hetero*geneity of variance) and the samples differ considerably in size, statisticians recommend that the data be mathematically transformed to meet the assumptions, or an appropriately modified ANOVA procedure be used, or a nonparametric test (see Chapter 21) be substituted.

The error term in the RM ANOVA is also based on an average of the variances of the difference scores for every different pair of levels of the RM factor. (In the case of five composers, there are ten different pairs for which the variance of the difference scores can be calculated: 1 versus 2, 1 versus 3, 1 versus 4, 1 versus 5, 2 versus 3, and so forth.) The assumption that these variances of difference scores are all equal in the population is commonly referred to as the *sphericity assumption*. We have been referring to the error term of the RM ANOVA as MS_{inter}, based on the analogy with the two-way ANOVA, but it is more often referred to as the $MS_{residual}$ (for reasons we will not discuss here) or, most simply, as the MS_{error}. We will use the latter term to avoid confusion when we discuss the two-way mixed-design ANOVA, in which there is an interaction of the two independent variables.

Although a test of the sphericity assumption has been devised by Mauchly (1940), it is rarely used to make decisions about RM ANOVAs. However, because a lack of population sphericity generally leads to a higher Type I error rate than the alpha used to look up the critical value, it is becoming increasingly common to adjust the degrees of freedom downward in order to increase the critical value and make the test more conservative. The most popular *df* adjustment is the one devised by Greenhouse and Geisser (1959), but it is best left to statistical software that will also give you the corresponding adjusted *p* value.

Without statistical software, you can easily test your RM ANOVA by assuming the worst-case scenario (i.e., maximum violation of sphericity). Just use degrees of freedom of 1 for the numerator and $r - 1$ for the denominator to find the worst-case critical value. If your calculated *F* exceeds this very conservative criterion, you can declare your results statistically significant without worrying that your Type I error rate might be higher than you think it is. On the other hand, if your RM ANOVA is not significant using the usual (unadjusted) critical *F*, you cannot be making a Type I error at all, because you cannot reject the null hypothesis. (There is no adjustment that lowers your critical value to give you more power.) If your calculated *F* falls between the unadjusted and the worst-case critical *F* values, we advise the use of statistical software.

Returning to our example, in which the calculated *F* (5.54) was greater than the ordinary critical *F* (3.01), the worst-case critical *F* would be $F_{.05}$ (1, 4) = 7.71. Because the calculated *F* does not exceed the maximally adjusted critical *F*, you would need to obtain a more exact adjustment of your critical *F* from statistical software before you could confidently reject the null hypothesis.

Follow-Up Tests

Due to concerns about sphericity, some statisticians favor abandoning the RM ANOVA entirely in favor of a multivariate approach, but that topic is well beyond the scope of an introductory text. However, even those who want to retain the RM ANOVA approach in general may be concerned about the effects of a lack of sphericity on the multiple comparisons that follow a significant ANOVA to locate the significant results more specifically.

In our example involving the music of five different composers, the overall RM ANOVA was statistically significant. To determine which pairs of composers differ significantly, we could compute Tukey's HSD, substituting MS_{error} for MS_W in the formula given in Chapter 16. However, suppose that the interaction involving just Mozart and Chopin is considerably larger than it is for any other pair of composers. Using Tukey's HSD essentially compares those two composers with an error term that has been reduced by averaging in the much smaller interactions involving other pairs of composers.

Unless it is clear that the variability of the difference scores is quite similar for every pair of conditions in your RM ANOVA, the recommended (cautious) approach to follow-up tests is to use an error term based only on the conditions being compared. When conducting pairwise comparisons, this amounts to performing separate matched-pairs t tests for each pair of levels of your RM factor. When dealing with five RM levels, as in our music example, there are a total of ten matched t tests to conduct. Because of the danger of an increased experimentwise alpha when conducting so many individual follow-up tests, it is often recommended that the researcher use a Bonferroni adjustment to determine the alpha for each comparison (see page 325). In the music example, this would mean testing each pair of composers at the .005 level (i.e., .05/10).

The RM versus RB Design: An Introduction to Issues of Experimental Design

You may recall from Chapter 11 that the same matched-pairs t test formula is used whether the two measurements come from the same person, or two participants who were matched together. The matched version of the RM design is referred to as the *RB* design, for reasons we will soon make clear.

Problems with the RM Design

In Chapter 14 we showed how the power of a matched-pairs t test increases as the correlation between the two sets of scores increases. Similarly, the RM ANOVA gains power as the correlation between each pair of conditions increases. (If the correlations are not similar from one pair of factor levels to another, this is an indication that the RM ANOVA may not be appropriate for that data set.) Generally, the highest correlations (i.e., the best matching) are obtained when measuring the same subject under all of the conditions. Although a repeated-measures design works well when the different conditions can be randomly mixed together (e.g., when five different types of words are mixed together in one long list to be memorized), this design can be problematic when the conditions must be presented successively.

For example, the only reasonable way to conduct the music experiment in terms of repeated measures would be to test a particular subject's spatial ability only once for each composer. However, if the same order of composers were used for each subject, you would not be able to separate practice and/or fatigue effects (i.e., simple order effects) from the specific effects of each composer's music (e.g., think about the difference in spatial ability measured for the composer who is always presented first, as compared to the one who is always presented last). A possible solution is counterbalancing, as described near the end of Chapter 11. But the problems inherent in this approach increase rapidly with the number of conditions.

In the case of five conditions, *complete counterbalancing* is not feasible. It would require 120 subjects ($5 \times 4 \times 3 \times 2 \times 1 = 120$) just to have one subject assigned to each possible order. A form of counterbalancing can be achieved using the same number of orders as there are conditions, according to a design called the *Latin square.* However, any form of counterbalancing leaves your experimental design susceptible to complex carryover effects—that is, the effect of a particular composer could depend on which composer had been presented just before. Carryover effects can sometimes be avoided simply by allowing enough time or by inserting a distracting task between each pair of conditions. When serious carryover effects cannot be avoided (as described in Chapter 11), a design that involves the matching of participants on some relevant variable should be considered, as described in the next section.

Advantages and Disadvantages of the RB Design

When appropriate, the repeated-measures design is the most economical way to increase the power of an ANOVA test. It increases power by essentially increasing the effect size you are dealing with, which avoids the expense of increasing the size of the samples. Theoretically, the effect size of an ANOVA could be increased by producing greater differences among the factor levels (as by increasing the strength of your experimental manipulations). However, this approach is often not feasible or desirable (or even ethical, if a very strong manipulation could become dangerous). The alternative is to increase power by reducing variability (i.e., the denominator of any standardized measure of effect size), and the RM ANOVA does this by focusing on the *consistency* of subjects' responses (as represented by SS_{error}), while ignoring the subjects' overall differences on the dependent variable (as represented by SS_{sub}).

There are simpler (albeit less effective) ways to reduce the error term of an ANOVA (and therefore increase power). We will discuss three of these designs in this section.

Adding a Grouping Factor to a One-Way Independent-Samples ANOVA

Suppose that you are studying three methods for increasing vocabulary size in children by assigning a different method to each of three separate groups. After 6 months of applying these methods to your samples, your results could come out as depicted in Figure 18.2A. Notice that the subject-to-subject variability is large compared to any average differences among the groups. You then realize that your groups are mixed with respect to gender, and that vocabulary size may differ by gender, especially for the age group you are studying. By adding gender as a second between-groups factor, thus creating a two-way ANOVA, it is proper to calculate MS_W separately for each *cell* of the two-way design.

Looking at Figure 18.2B, you can see that the average of the six within-*cell* MS_w's is much smaller than the average of the three within-*group* MS_W's. This greatly reduces the denominator of the F ratio you will use to test the effect of the different methods. (The numerator of that F ratio would *not* change, because the means of the three methods would remain the same.) Adding a grouping factor based on preexisting individual differences (i.e., gender) allows you to convert *within-group* variability to *between-cell* variability.

Of course, we created an unusually dramatic example to illustrate this point. Adding a grouping factor to your ANOVA is not likely to have such a large effect. But as long as you can identify a preexisting individual-difference factor that is relevant to your dependent variable, it can be worth adding it to your ANOVA design. Moreover, you gain the opportunity to test whether the grouping variable interacts with your treatment factor (e.g., are the differences among the methods the same for both genders?).

The Treatment-by-Block Design

In the preceding example, the added factor (i.e., gender) was a categorical one. However, it is also quite possible to find an individual-difference factor that is related to your dependent variable and is at least crudely quantitative. In the case of children at a particular school, it should not be difficult to use existing information to classify the students into several levels of scholastic ability that can be expected to translate, on average, into differences in vocabulary size.

For convenience, you will want to make sure that the number of students included in each scholastic group (called a *block* in this context) is some multiple of the number of levels of your treatment factor. For example, if you are comparing three methods of instruction, you will want the number of children in each scholastic block to be some multiple of 3. Then, separately for each block, you would be able to assign, at random, exactly one third of the students to each of the three methods.

The data can be collected and then analyzed as they would be for any two-way ANOVA. Of course, the main effect of the blocking factor will not yield any new information, because you chose that factor for its obvious relationship to your dependent variable. However, the test of the main effect of the method

FIGURE 18.2

Reduction in error variance as a result of adding a relevant grouping factor to an ANOVA

A. Large within-group variability due partly to gender differences in each method group

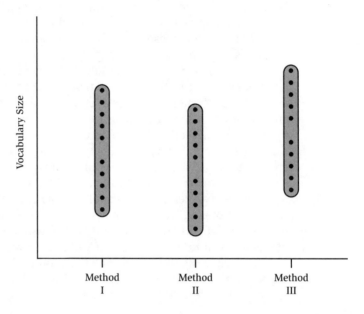

B. Reduced within-group variability as a result of adding gender as a second factor

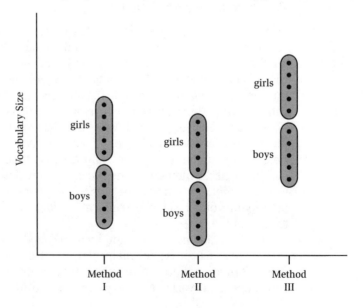

factor should become more accurate due to the reduction in the error term, and the interaction could show whether the relative superiority of one or another method depends on the initial level of the student.

The Randomized-Blocks (RB) Design

The most precise, and potentially the most powerful, form of the treatment by block design is the one in which the size of the block is equal to the number of different treatment conditions. If testing three vocabulary-enhancing methods, students would be matched into groups of three so that, within each block, the three students would be as similar as possible on whichever relevant criteria were available. The term *randomized-blocks design* usually refers to this special case of the treatment by block design, in which there is only one subject in each block/treatment combination (i.e., cell) and therefore no way to calculate MS_w. The data are analyzed as though the different subjects in a particular block were really different measurements of the same subject. The data can be arranged as in Table 18.1 (with block number replacing subject number), and then analyzed using the RM ANOVA procedure described earlier in this chapter. When the treatment factor has only two levels, the RB design becomes the matched-pairs design discussed in Chapter 11.

The responses of the subjects in the same block are generally not as similar as would be the responses of the same subject, and the RB design lacks the economy of measuring the same subject multiple times. But the RB design has the desirable feature of completely eliminating the possibility of carryover effects, as well as the need for counterbalancing. Unfortunately, the RB design is difficult to arrange if your subjects are not all known at the beginning of the study. For instance, if patients are being randomly assigned to one of three treatment methods as they arrive at a clinic seeking help (and meet the screening criteria of the study), they can be classified as belonging to one of several crudely defined blocks (in terms of gender, age, duration and intensity of symptoms, etc.), but they cannot be matched closely to patients who have not yet sought help at that clinic. When precise matching over your entire subject pool is not possible, it may still be helpful to create blocks along the way, in preparation for a treatment-by-block ANOVA.

The Two-Way Mixed Design

Now that you have learned how to conduct a one-way RM ANOVA as well as a two-way ANOVA, you have the tools you will need to analyze one of the most useful experimental designs in behavioral research: the two-way mixed design. There are a number of common situations that lead to this design. For example, subjects are assigned to one of two therapy conditions or to a control group, and they are then measured at the beginning of the experiment, at the midpoint, and again at the end. Or subjects are selected for being either high or low in visual imagery ability, and each is asked to memorize several lists of words that differ in how concrete the words are. Or subjects must read and respond to some opinions that they are told have been written by students, and others that ostensibly come from professors. For half of these subjects, the person conducting their experimental session is obviously a student, whereas for the other half, the experimenter is clearly a professor. Each of the three two-way factorial designs just described can be analyzed as a mixed-design ANOVA, in which one IV is a between-groups factor and the other is a *within-subjects* (i.e., RM) factor.

Calculating the Mixed-Design ANOVA

Just as we illustrated the calculation of the one-way RM ANOVA by taking a previous example of a one-way ANOVA and recasting it in terms of repeated measures, we will create a mixed design by taking the two-way ANOVA example from the previous chapter and imagining that the participants were matched across the four musical composers. (The analysis is the same whether the participants had been matched in blocks of four and then randomly assigned to the different composers, or each participant was measured four times, once for each composer.) The matching makes it meaningful to add subject means to Table 17.1, as shown in Table 18.3. Recall that the first five subjects have no musical training, whereas the second five are professional musicians.

When computing a two-way mixed ANOVA by hand, there are several reasonable ways to proceed. One instructive approach is to first calculate the numerators of the three F ratios, which we already did in the previous chapter. (Matching does not affect any of the numerators.) As a reminder, we will display a table of the cell means for this example (see Table 18.4), and briefly review the calculations of the numerator MSs.

TABLE 18.3

Music experiment data from Table 17.1 presented as repeated measures

Subject number	Mozart	Chopin	Bach	Beethoven	Subject $\overline{X}$
1	16	16	16	14	15.5
2	16	14	14	13	14.25
3	14	13	12	13	13.0
4	13	13	10	10	11.5
5	12	10	10	10	10.5
6	16	17	14	16	15.75
7	18	10	14	10	13.0
8	20	13	11	13	14.25
9	15	12	10	14	12.75
10	18	14	12	11	13.75

TABLE 18.4

Cell means by composer and subject group for the data in Table 18.3

Music training	Mozart	Chopin	Bach	Beethoven	Row mean
No training	14.2	13.2	12.4	12.0	12.95
Professional	17.4	13.2	12.2	12.8	13.90
Column means	15.8	13.2	12.3	12.4	13.425

$$SS_{\text{between-cell}} = SS_B = 107.4; \quad SS_{\text{composer}} = 80.1; \quad SS_{\text{training}} = 9.0;$$

$$SS_{\text{inter}} = 107.4 - 80.1 - 9.0 = 18.3;$$

$$MS_{\text{composer}} = \frac{80.1}{3} = 26.7; \quad MS_{\text{training}} = \frac{9.0}{1} = 9.0; \quad MS_{\text{inter}} = \frac{18.3}{3} = 6.1.$$

It is when we calculate the denominators of our F ratios that we must account for the fact that the participants are now matched across composers.

In the mixed-design ANOVA, the F ratio for the main effect of the between-groups factor can be calculated separately from the rest of the design. You can simply perform an ordinary one-way ANOVA on the subject means in Table 18.3, completely ignoring the particular scores on which these means are based, except that you should multiply your SS components by the number of scores that contribute to each subject mean (in this example, 4):

$$SS_T = \sum X^2 - N_T \overline{X}_G^2$$
$$= (15.5^2 + 14.25^2 + \ldots + 12.75^2 + 13.75^2) - 10\,(13.425)^2$$
$$= 1{,}826.56 - 1{,}802.31 = 24.25.$$

After multiplying by 4,

$$SS_T = 4 \times 24.25 = 97.$$

SS_B is based on the means of the two groups of subjects (the row means in Table 18.4). It was already calculated as SS_{training}, which is equal to 9.0 (because, to save effort, we are taking SS_{training} from the original two-way ANOVA, it should *not* be multiplied by 4).

Then

$$SS_W = SS_T - SS_B = 97 - 9 = 88,$$

$$MS_W = \frac{SS_W}{df_W} = \frac{88}{(10-2)} = \frac{88}{8} = 11.0,$$

and

$$MS_{\text{training}} = \frac{SS_{\text{training}}}{1} = \frac{9}{1} = 9.0.$$

Therefore,

$$F_{\text{training}} = \frac{9.0}{11.0} = .82.$$

Given that F for the between-groups factor is less than 1, it cannot be statistically significant.

All that remains is to calculate the error term for the within-subjects part of the ANOVA. Both the main effect of the RM factor and the interaction of the two factors use the same error term, which is based on the amount of subject by (RM) treatment interaction in each group. One straightforward way to obtain this error term is to subtract the SS_W just calculated for the between-groups factor from the $SS_{\text{within-cell}}$ from the original (i.e., unmatched) two-way ANOVA. $SS_{\text{within-cell}}$, which was just labeled SS_W in the previous chapter (when there was only one error term to talk about), was found to be 150.4. As in the one-way RM ANOVA, we will label the SS for the within-subject error term simply as SS_{error}. So $SS_{\text{error}} = SS_{\text{within-cell}} - SS_W = 150.4 - 88 = 62.4$. The degrees of freedom can be subtracted in the same way: $df_{\text{error}} = df_{\text{within-cell}} - df_W = 32 - 8 = 24$ ($df_{\text{within-cell}}$ is the same as df_W in the previous chapter). Therefore, $MS_{\text{error}} = 62.4/24 = 2.6$.

Finally, we can find the F ratios for the RM factor (composer), and the interaction of the two factors, from the previously computed numerator MSs and the just-calculated error term:

$$F_{\text{composer}} = \frac{MS_{\text{composer}}}{MS_{\text{error}}} = \frac{26.7}{2.6} = 10.3;$$

$$F_{\text{inter}} = \frac{MS_{\text{inter}}}{MS_{\text{error}}} = \frac{6.1}{2.6} = 2.35.$$

The critical value for both of these F ratios is $F_{.05}$ (3, 24) = 3.01. Therefore, the statistical conclusions from Chapter 17 have not changed: the main effect of composer is significant at the .05 level, and the interaction effect is not. However, it is important to note that the Fs for these two effects have nearly doubled, because the error term based on the matching of subjects (MS_{error}) is only a bit more than half as large as the original two-way ANOVA error term (2.6 versus 4.7). This will often be the case when subjects are matched or repeatedly measured.

Assumptions

In addition to all of the assumptions of the RM ANOVA, including sphericity, the mixed-design ANOVA also requires you to assume that the amount of interaction (in the population) between any two treatment levels is the same for each subgroup (i.e., level of the between-groups factor) in the design. For example, when there are only two repeated measurements (e.g., before and after some intervention) and two different groups (e.g., drug and placebo), the sphericity assumption does not apply (there is only one pair of treatment levels), but the 2×2 mixed-design ANOVA assumes that the amount of before-after interaction is the same for the placebo subjects as it is for those given the real drug.

Follow-Up Tests

If the interaction in a mixed design fails to approach significance, you can turn your attention to the main effects. Post hoc comparisons for a significant between-groups factor can use the MS_W error term from the original mixed-design ANOVA, unless there is a strong reason to be concerned about homogeneity of variance among the different groups (this is one reason it is a good idea to have the same number of participants or blocks at each level of the between-group factor). Following up a significant RM main effect evokes the same concern as expressed previously for the one-way design. Unless you can be quite confident in assuming sphericity in the population, it is recommended that each pair of levels of the RM factor be compared with an error term based on only those two levels.

   If the interaction in a mixed design *is* significant, the follow-up procedures are the same as for an independent-samples two-way ANOVA with a significant interaction (as described in the previous chapter), except for the error terms. The simplest and most conservative approach is not to use either error term from the original mixed-design ANOVA, but rather to base the error terms for your follow-up tests on only the data involved in those tests. For example, if, based on a significant interaction, you were to test the simple main effect of composer just for the group with no musical training, the recommendation is to use for your error term the subject by treatment interaction for only the untrained participants, rather than MS_{error} from the mixed-design ANOVA. Similarly, if comparing musicians to untrained participants only for the Mozart condition, base MS_W on the Mozart data only, instead of using MS_W from the original design.

The Before-After Case

A very common form of mixed-design ANOVA is one in which the RM factor is time, and it has only two levels (e.g., the dependent variable is measured at the beginning and end of some experimental treatment). Perhaps half the participants receive some new form of therapy, while the other half of them receive sham therapy. In such a case, there would be little interest in the *main* effect of time, because this effect would involve averaging the real with the sham therapy participants. Similarly, the main effect of group would not be of interest, because it would involve an average of the before scores (when no group difference is expected) with the after scores. The chief interest in this design is the group by time interaction. It is likely that you would want the before-after difference to be much larger in magnitude for the real, as compared to the sham, therapy recipients.

You do not need to conduct a mixed-design ANOVA to assess the amount of interaction in the design just described. If you calculate the before-after difference for each participant, and then compute the ordinary (independent-samples) one-way ANOVA on these difference scores, the *F* ratio you obtain will be exactly the same as the *F* ratio for the interaction effect of the mixed-design ANOVA. When there are only two groups in the study, you also have the option of conducting an independent-samples *t* test on the difference scores. Of course, the *p* value for the *t* test will be the same as for the *F* ratio from the corresponding ANOVA. If there are more than two levels of the between-groups factor, you can still compute a one-way ANOVA on the difference scores, and this *F* ratio will be the same as the *F* ratio for the interaction in the corresponding mixed-design ANOVA.

The One-Way RM ANOVA with Counterbalancing

By now it should be clear that if you are going to present the same participants with two or more conditions, one after another, you should not present these different conditions in the same order to all participants. What is less obvious is that even though simple order (e.g., practice) effects will be eliminated from the numerator of your *F* ratio by counterbalancing, order effects will increase the size of your denominator (i.e., error term) unless you add order as a between-groups factor to your analysis. Consider the simplest case: participants perform the same task under two different distraction conditions. If the performance of most participants is enhanced a bit by practice on whichever condition they receive second, this will cause participants receiving one order of the conditions to differ somewhat in the relative effects of the two conditions from participants receiving the conditions in the reverse order.

For instance, if the individual participants are graphed as in Figure 18.1, the lines representing participants receiving one of the orders will tend to slant a bit differently between the two conditions when compared to the lines of participants receiving the other order. Thus a simple order effect would cause the lines to be less parallel. This translates to a larger amount of subject by condition interaction, which forms the basis of the error term in an RM ANOVA. The solution to this problem involves creating a mixed design in which participants receiving different orders of the conditions are considered to be in different groups—that is, they are at different levels of a between-groups factor that we will refer to as *order*. If a mixed-design ANOVA is then computed, the subject by treatment interaction will be measured separately for each order group and then averaged. Participants from different levels of the order factor are separated in the analysis and therefore cannot interact with each other.

The amount of interaction caused by the simple order effects appears in the SS for the interaction of the two factors (order and the RM factor), rather than in the subject by treatment interaction. This reduces the error term when testing the main effect of the RM factor. A significant interaction between order and treatment just affirms that you have sizable order effects. A main effect of order, however, is worrisome, because there is no good reason for subjects from one order group to be performing better *overall* than the participants in another order group. This result suggests that you may have asymmetric carryover effects, and need to look more closely at your data. As discussed earlier, a randomized-blocks design would eliminate the possibility of such carryover effects, while providing much of the increased power associated with the RM design.

Summary

The repeated-measures (RM) ANOVA extends the advantages of the matched-pairs *t* test to studies in which more than two treatments or conditions are being compared. The significance test for the RM ANOVA uses the interaction of subjects with treatments as its error term and is therefore able to ignore overall subject-to-subject differences on the dependent variable. When the RM ANOVA is not feasible (e.g., comparing three methods for teaching young children to read), much of the power of the RM ANOVA can be gained by matching subjects into blocks, and then randomly assigning the members of the blocks to the different levels of the independent variable. This is called the randomized-blocks (RB) design. When each block contains the same number of subjects as there are different conditions, the data are analyzed in the same way as the RM ANOVA.

In the two-way mixed-design ANOVA, there is matching or repeated measures for one of the factors, but not the other. This necessitates the calculation of two separate error terms. One of these, MS_W, is based on the subject means within each group, and is used as the denominator for testing the main effect of the between-groups factor. The other, MS_{error}, is based on the subject by treatment interaction within each group, and is used as the denominator for testing the main effect of the RM factor, as well as its interaction with the between-groups factor. One important application of the mixed-design ANOVA involves the one-way RM design with counterbalancing. Adding order as a between-groups factor takes variability away from the error term of an RM ANOVA and puts it in the numerator of a new F ratio, which tests the interaction of the order by treatment effect.

I. One-Way RM ANOVA

The computational procedure outlined next can be applied in exactly the same way to data from either an RM or an RB design.

1. Sums of Squares

1. Total sum of squares (SS_T)

$$\text{Computing formula: } SS_T = \sum X^2 - N_T \, \overline{X}_G^2,$$

where $\overline{X}_G$ is the (grand) mean of all of the scores
2. Between-treatments sum of squares (SS_{treat})

$$\text{Computing formula: } SS_{treat} = r \sum \overline{X}_i^2 - N_T \, \overline{X}_G^2,$$

where r is the number of different subjects or blocks, and the $\overline{X}_i$'s are the means of the different treatments
3. Between-subjects sum of squares (SS_{sub})

$$\text{Computing formula: } SS_{sub} = c \sum \overline{X}_j^2 - N_T \, \overline{X}_G^2,$$

where c is the number of different treatments or conditions, and the $\overline{X}_j$'s are the means of the different subjects or blocks
4. Interaction (i.e., error) sum of squares (SS_{error})

$$\text{Computing formula: } SS_{error} = SS_T - SS_{treat} - SS_{sub}$$

2. Degrees of Freedom

Total degrees of freedom:

$$df_T = N_T - 1 = rc - 1$$

Degrees of freedom between treatments:

$$df_{treat} = c - 1$$

Degrees of freedom between subjects:

$$df_{sub} = r - 1$$

Degrees of freedom for interaction:

$$df_{error} = (c - 1)(r - 1)$$

3. Mean Squares

Mean square between treatments:

$$MS_{treat} = \frac{SS_{treat}}{df_{treat}}$$

Mean square for interaction:

$$MS_{error} = \frac{SS_{error}}{df_{error}}$$

4. F Ratio

$$F_{RM} \ (i.e., F_{treat}) = \frac{MS_{treat}}{MS_{error}}$$

$$df = (c-1), (c-1)(r-1)$$

5. The Sphericity Assumption

An important assumption that applies when an RM ANOVA has more than two levels is that the variability of the difference scores for any pair of conditions is the same as it is for any other pair of conditions in the population. A significant F ratio can be retested without assuming *sphericity* in the population by comparing it to a worst-case critical F based on 1 and $r-1$ degrees of freedom. Because a lack of population sphericity tends only to increase the F ratio when the null hypothesis is true, there is no need to retest an RM ANOVA that does not attain significance. However, if the F from an RM ANOVA is significant with the usual critical F, but not with the conservatively adjusted (worst-case F_{crit}), it is recommended that statistical software be used to adjust the critical F more precisely.

6. Alternative Experimental Designs

Carry-over effects can invalidate the results from an RM ANOVA conducted on an RM design. In such cases, the RB design may be preferable. Consult Table 18.5 for several error-reducing alternatives to the RM design.

II. Two-Way Mixed-Design ANOVA

There are several ways to begin the partitioning of the SS total from a mixed design, but all result in the same final SS components. Probably the easiest way to begin the analysis is by following the procedure for an ordinary two-way ANOVA, as shown next.

TABLE 18.5

Recommended experimental design that reduce the error term of a one-way ANOVA in various experimental situations

Experimental situation	Recommended experimental design
1. You have several different conditions, but trials of each can be mixed together randomly.	Repeated-measures ANOVA (each participant experiences all of the conditions).
2. You have several conditions that must be presented in order, but the effects of one condition are *not* likely to carry over into the next one.	Repeated-measures ANOVA with counterbalancing (equal number of participants receive the conditions in different orders).
3. You have several conditions that must be presented in order, but the effects of one condition *are* likely to carry over into the next, and you have a basis for matching participants into blocks.	Randomized-blocks ANOVA (match k participants in each block, where k is the number of different conditions, and then assign the members of each block randomly to the different conditions).
4. You have several conditions that must be presented in order, and the effects of one condition are likely to carry over into the next. You have a basis for matching participants but do not have all of your participants at the outset of the experiment.	Treatment-by-blocks (two-way) ANOVA (categorize participants as belonging to one or another level of some relevant blocking factor, and make sure that the same number of participants from each block is assigned to each condition).
5. You have several conditions that must be presented in order, and the effects of one condition are likely to carry over into the next. It is *not* feasible to match your participants, but you can categorize your participants into groups that differ on your dependent variable.	Two-way ANOVA with grouping factor (start with a one-way independent-samples ANOVA and then add the grouping factor to create a two-way ANOVA, thereby reducing the error term for your factor of interest).

1. Sums of Squares

1. Create a table of the cell means, and find the row and column means. Then calculate the SS for each of the two factors and their interaction as described in Chapter 17. We will label the SS for the between-groups factor as SS_{groups} and the SS for the repeated-measures factor as SS_{RM}; their interaction will be labeled SS_{inter}. Also, as in Chapter 17, calculate SS_T, and subtract SS_B to get SS_W, which we will call $SS_{within-cell}$ in the two-way mixed design.

2. Calculate the between-subjects sum of squares (SS_{sub}) as shown for the one-way RM ANOVA (ignore the fact that subjects belong to one group or another). Subtract SS_{group} from SS_{sub} to get SS_W for the mixed design.

3. Subtract SS_W from $SS_{within-cell}$ to obtain SS_{error}.

2. Degrees of Freedom

Total degrees of freedom:

$$df_T = N_T - 1 = nkc - 1$$

where k is the number of groups (i.e., levels of the between-groups factor), n is the number of subjects in each of the groups (we are considering only balanced designs), and c is the number of levels of the RM factor.

Numerator degrees of freedom:

$$df_{RM} = c - 1; \qquad df_{group} = k - 1; \qquad df_{inter} = (c - 1)(k - 1)$$

Denominator degrees of freedom:

$$df_{W} = k(n - 1); \qquad df_{error} = k(n - 1)(c - 1)$$

3. Mean Squares

Numerator mean squares:

$$MS_{groups} = \frac{SS_{groups}}{df_{groups}}; \qquad MS_{RM} = \frac{SS_{RM}}{df_{RM}}; \qquad MS_{inter} = \frac{SS_{inter}}{df_{inter}}$$

Denominator mean squares:

$$MS_{W} = \frac{SS_{W}}{df_{W}}; \qquad MS_{error} = \frac{SS_{error}}{df_{error}}$$

4. F Ratios

$$F_{groups} = \frac{MS_{groups}}{MS_{W}}; \qquad F_{RM} = \frac{MS_{RM}}{MS_{error}}; \qquad F_{inter} = \frac{MS_{inter}}{MS_{error}}$$

5. Additional Assumption

The mixed-design ANOVA requires all of the assumptions of the RM ANOVA, including sphericity, but in addition, it must be assumed that the variability of the difference scores for any pair of conditions is the same in each population that is represented by a different level of the between-groups factor.

Common Situations for Which the Two-Way Mixed Design Is Useful

1. *Measuring two or more independent groups over several points in time.* The simplest version of this situation, the before-after design, usually requires only a one-way ANOVA on the difference scores to yield all the information of interest. However, when more than 2 points in time are involved, a mixed-design ANOVA is called for.

2. *A one-way repeated-measures ANOVA with counterbalancing.* A mixed-design ANOVA is created by adding order (of treatments) as a between-groups factor to reduce the error term.

3. *Adding a grouping factor to a one-way repeated-measures or randomized-blocks ANOVA.* Each participant serves in several conditions, or participants are matched in blocks, but each participant is also categorized as belonging to one level or another of a preexisting individual-differences factor (e.g., psychiatric diagnosis).

4. *One experimental factor has levels that are easily repeated, but the other does not.* For example, the RM factor might involve several versions of the same task, while the levels of the between-groups factor consist of different general mind-sets for approaching the tasks (e.g., your performance on each of these tasks reflects your overall level of intelligence versus some individuals perform better on some versions of the task according to their individual skills and aptitudes).

Exercises

1. Redo exercise 5 from Chapter 11 as a one-way RM ANOVA. What is the relationship between the F ratio you calculated for this exercise and the t value you calculated for that exercise?

2. The following group means come from exercise 4 in Chapter 15. Compute the one-way RM ANOVA for these data, assuming that there are a total of 15 blocks of (matched) participants, and that $SS_{error} = 5,040$. Is the F ratio significant at the .05 level, based on the unadjusted df (i.e., assuming sphericity)? Would this F ratio be significant at the .05 level, given the worst-case adjustment of the df (i.e., assuming a maximum violation of sphericity)?

	Group				
	1	2	3	4	5
$\overline{X}$	23	30	34	29	26

3. The following data come from an experiment in which each participant has been measured under three different levels of distraction (the DV is the number of errors committed on a clerical task during a 5-minute period). Compute the one-way RM ANOVA for these data. Is the F ratio significant at the .01 level, assuming sphericity? Would this F ratio be significant at the .05 level, assuming a total lack of sphericity?

Sub. No.	Mild	Moderate	Strong
1	1	3	3
2	0	0	1
3	3	2	4
4	0	2	2
5	2	3	2
6	1	1	0
7	1	1	3
8	2	4	5
9	1	2	4
10	0	3	6
11	4	4	5
12	2	1	6

4. Suppose that, prior to performing the clerical tasks in the experiment of exercise 3, the first six participants took pills they thought to be caffeine but that were actually placebos; the remaining six participants ingested real caffeine pills.

   (a) Reanalyze the data in exercise 3 as a mixed-design ANOVA, adding drug condition (placebo versus caffeine) as the between-groups variable. Test each F ratio for significance at the .05 level.

   (b) Compare the SS components you found as part of your analysis in part (a) to the SS components you found in exercise 3. Which SS components are the same, and which combinations of SSs in part (a) add up to one of the SS components in exercise 3?

   (c) Compute separate one-way RM ANOVAs for the placebo and the caffeine participants, and test these simple main effects for significance at the .05 level. How do these tests relate to your analysis in part (a)?

   (d) If this design were completely counterbalanced for each of the two drug groups, how many participants would have been assigned to each possible treatment order within each group?

5. Suppose that participants are asked to memorize a list of words that range from very abstract to very concrete. The number of words recalled of each type for each participant are shown in the following table.

Participant number	Very abstract	Mildly abstract	Mildly concrete	Very concrete
1	2	5	11	14
2	0	8	4	11
3	7	9	13	20
4	3	12	10	15
5	3	7	8	6
6	2	6	6	9
7	5	8	7	7
8	4	9	5	8

   (a) Compute the one-way RM ANOVA for these data. Test the F ratio for significance at the .05 level. How many pairwise comparisons could be tested if your ANOVA were significant? What alpha would you use to test each of these comparisons, if you used a Bonferroni adjustment to keep the experimentwise alpha at .05?

   (b) Reanalyze the data as a mixed-design ANOVA, assuming that the first four participants were selected for their high scores on a spatial ability test, whereas the second group of four participants were chosen for their poor performance in spatial ability. Test each F ratio for significance at the .05 level.

   (c) Graph the cell means of the two-way mixed-design ANOVA, as described in part (b). Explain how the pattern of the cell means is consistent with the results you obtained in part (b).

Thought Questions

1. (a) What advantage does repeated-measures ANOVA have over ANOVA without repeated measures (where every score is derived from a different participant)? (b) Why might a researcher decide *not* to use repeated-measures ANOVA in spite of this advantage, and what alternatives would be considered?

2. What is the sphericity assumption in behavioral science research? Give an example of when it might be violated.

3. Give an example for which each of the following is appropriate: (a) Repeated-measures ANOVA. (b) The randomized blocks design. (c) The two-way mixed design. (d) The before-and-after form of the two-way mixed design. (e) One-way repeated-measures design with counterbalancing.

Computer Exercises

1. Perform an RM ANOVA to test for a significant change in anxiety level in all subjects over time (baseline, prequiz, and postquiz). Whether or not the ANOVA is significant, follow it with matched *t* tests (or two-level RM ANOVAs) for each pair of levels of the time factor.

2. Redo exercise 1 for heart rate.

3. Add gender to the analysis in exercise 1, and compute the mixed-design ANOVA. Request a plot of the cell means, and explain your ANOVA results in terms of the pattern in your graph. Follow the mixed-design ANOVA with separate one-way RM ANOVAs (i.e., simple main effects) for each gender.

4. Add the experimental factor (i.e., difficulty of the 11th quiz question) to the analysis in exercise 1, and compute the mixed-design ANOVA. Request a plot of the cell means, and explain your ANOVA results in terms of the pattern in your graph. Follow the mixed-design ANOVA with separate one-way ANOVAs for each measurement period (i.e., baseline, prequiz, and postquiz).

5. Redo exercise 4 using heart rate as the dependent variable instead of anxiety.

Bridge to SPSS

There is a fundamental difference between the ways in which data are entered for a repeated-measures design and for an independent-groups design. When the same subjects are measured at all the levels of your IV, there is no *one* column in your spreadsheet that contains your DV. Each level of your factor is represented by another column (i.e., variable) in your spreadsheet. You will have to tell SPSS which columns in your spreadsheet are the levels of your RM factor. If you are using an RB design, a single row does not literally represent one subject, but it does represent one *block,* which is treated as though it contained repeated measures of the same subject.

To perform an RM ANOVA in SPSS, select **Repeated Measures** from the **Analyze/General Linear Model** menu. The dialog box that opens will ask you to create a name for your RM factor. For example, if your matched blocks of subjects were randomly assigned across three methods for teaching reading, your three columns of final reading scores might be labeled: phonics, holistic, and traditional. In that case, it would be appropriate to type **method** in the space for Within-Subject Factor Name, or **methtype** (you are limited to eight characters), and then type **3** for Number of Levels and click **Add,** followed by **Define.** This action opens the main dialog box for Repeated Measures, where you are required to move three names (in this example) from the usual list of variables on the left to slots for the three levels of your RM factor on the right in a space labeled Within-Subjects Variables. You have the usual **Options, Plots,** and **Contrasts** available, but **Post Hoc** is only for any Between-Subjects Factors you specify. I will discuss that possibility when I get to the Mixed-Design ANOVA.

One-Way RM ANOVA Output

Much of the work required to interpret the default SPSS output for RM ANOVA consists of knowing which information you can safely ignore. After a box that just lists the variables that serve as the levels of your RM factor, you will see a box of data labeled **Multivariate Tests.** This box offers an alternative statistical solution to the RM ANOVA, which makes no assumptions concerning sphericity; ignore it if you have decided to perform an RM ANOVA (or learn more about the multivariate approach to RM data in a more advanced statistics text). The next box contains Mauchly's Test of Sphericity; if the **Sig.** for this test is less than .05, take note. This knowledge could affect your interpretation of the following box: Tests of Within-Subjects Effects. SPSS always presents four variations of the RM ANOVA in this box, whether you want to see them or not. The first variation, labeled **Sphericity Assumed,** is the ordinary RM ANOVA result, as described in this chapter. The next two rows of this box contain the results of two different formulas for reducing both the numerator and denominator *df* to accommodate possible violations of the sphericity assumption. The first of these, known as the Greenhouse-Geisser (G-G) correction, is by far the more conservative and more popular of the two; the Huynh-Feldt (H-F) correction is rarely used.

The fourth variation uses what we referred to as the worst-case *df* adjustment earlier in this chapter. There is no need to use this overly conservative adjustment, if the G-G solution is available. If your data seem very consistent with the sphericity assumption, it is reasonable to report the *p* value from the row labeled **Sphericity Assumed** (the *p* values change from row to row, but the calculated *F* values do not). However, if Mauchly's W test is significant (i.e., Sig. < .05), it is recommended that you report the *p* value according to the G-G correction, along with its (usually fractional) adjusted *df*.

The next output, Tests of Within-Subjects Contrasts, makes sense only if the levels of your RM factor are quantitative rather than qualitative. For example, you are measuring the time it takes your participants to solve anagrams (the letters of common words have been rearranged) of different lengths; anagrams containing five, six, seven, or eight letters each are presented in a random order. In this case, it may well be of interest to test the linear trend in your data: To what extent does the average time to solve an anagram increase as a linear function of the number of letters, and is this trend statistically significant. All of the possible higher-order trends (e.g., quadratic: To what extent do the means tend to increase at first, and then decrease at the highest levels of the factor, or vice versa?) are tested as well, and this output box is presented even if your RM factor has qualitative levels (e.g., participants perform a task while listening to four different types of music), in which case the results in this box are meaningless, as they are based on the arbitrary order in which you list the different types of music in the RM ANOVA dialog box.

The final box is generally ignored if you are conducting a one-way RM ANOVA, rather than a mixed-design ANOVA. If there are only RM factors, this box, Tests of Between-Subjects Effects, contains only a test of the intercept for your data. This is just a one-sample test to determine whether the grand mean of all your data is significantly greater than zero. If negative numbers are not possible in your data, the F ratio in this box will be surprisingly large, but of no practical interest.

Mixed-Design ANOVA

Requesting an analysis of a mixed-design ANOVA in SPSS begins the same way as for the one-way RM ANOVA. However, after you have defined the levels of your RM factor in the Repeated Measures dialog box, you can move one or more between-group factors (e.g., gender, order) into the space labeled **Between-Subjects Factors.** If you then click the **Post Hoc** button, you will see a list of those between-group variables under the heading **Factor(s).** Moving one or more of those factors to the right will make available all of the choices for post hoc tests. Unfortunately, pairwise comparisons for your RM levels cannot be requested from this box. In fact, the procedure for requesting post hoc tests for an RM factor is too complex to be described in this text (see the Cohen statistics web page, http://www.psych.nyu.edu/cohen/statstext.html, for advanced SPSS procedures).

The output box that was the most relevant to us for the RM design contains an additional analysis for the mixed design. In the Tests of Within-Subjects Effects box, the analysis for the interaction of the two factors is inserted between the RM factor and the error term; the latter is used as the denominator for both the RM main effect and the interaction. The Tests of Between-Subjects Effects box, which contains only a seldom-needed test of the intercept for a purely RM ANOVA, includes a test of the main effect of the between-groups factor in a two-way mixed design.

Part IV
Nonparametric Statistics

Chapter 19
Introduction to Probability and Nonparametric Methods

PREVIEW

Introduction

How do nonparametric and distribution-free statistical tests differ from parametric statistical tests?

Probability

How do we define the probability of a given event?

What is meant by the odds against a given event?

How do we compute the probability that *either* of two events will occur?

How do we compute the probability that one event *and then* another event will occur?

The Binomial Distribution

How can we use the laws of probability to construct a binomial distribution?

How can we use the binomial distribution to test a null hypothesis involving events with two possible outcomes?

How can we use the normal distribution as an approximation to the binomial distribution?

The Sign Test for Matched Samples

How can we use the binomial distribution as an alternative to the matched-pairs *t* test?

Under what conditions might you prefer the sign test to the matched-pairs *t* test?

Summary

Exercises

Thought Questions

Computer Exercises

Bridge to SPSS

Introduction

In the analysis of variance, as well as in the *t* test, the dependent variable is measured on a precise, quantitative (i.e., interval or ratio) scale. For example, the number of problems solved correctly on a task may be 6, 8, or 14. However, there are many possible dependent variables in behavioral research that cannot be measured precisely (at least at the present time). If we want to test some new form of imagery exercise that is designed to increase creativity, we may be able to assemble a panel of judges that can reliably determine whether one work of art or writing is more creative than another, or even rank several of these works in order. However, accurately quantifying the *amount* of creativity may not be feasible.

Alternatively, a behavioral outcome may have only two possible levels. For example, an (unknowing) participant may either return the wallet he or she found on the street (where the experimenter left it) or not. The independent variable in this study might also consist of just a few categories, such as the approximate economic level (wealthy, middle-class, or disadvantaged) of the neighborhood that corresponds to the wallet owner's address.

When both the independent and dependent variables in a study can only be categorized, or at best rank ordered, the parametric statistical methods discussed in previous chapters are not appropriate. Alternative methods will be described in this chapter and the two that follow.

Parametric versus Nonparametric Tests

A *parametric* statistical test is so labeled because it involves the estimation of the value of at least one population parameter. For example, the within-group sample variance calculated in the *t* and *F* tests is an estimate of the corresponding within-population variance. A *nonparametric* test, on the other hand, does not require such estimation. Also, the mathematical derivations of the *t* and *F* tests assume that each population being randomly sampled has a *normal* distribution. A *distribution-free* statistical test, by contrast, requires no assumption about the shape of the distribution in the population. While the terms *nonparametric* and *distribution-free* have different meanings, most statistical tests that meet one of these conditions also satisfy the other, so the terms tend to be used interchangeably in practice.

For convenience, we will use the term *nonparametric* to refer to any statistical test in which none of the variables has been measured quantitatively. Sometimes a nonparametric test is used when one or more variables was *originally* measured precisely, but those measurements have been transformed to a less precise ranking or categorical scale. (Reasons for this will be discussed later in this chapter.) For now, we will begin by considering the simplest possible situation in which you would use a nonparametric test: you are observing an outcome that is dichotomous—it can fall into only one of two possible categories.

If you want to make a statistical decision based on how many outcomes fall into one category or another, you need an appropriate null hypothesis distribution (NHD), just as you did for the t test or ANOVA. However, when the outcome is dichotomous, your NHD will not be a smooth mathematical curve like the t or F distributions. It will tend to have a rather boxy shape, which is known as the *binomial* distribution. For a small number of outcomes, it is not difficult to determine the entire binomial distribution exactly. To understand how this is done, you need to learn basic rules of probability as they apply to discrete events (as opposed to precise measurements).

Flipping a coin, which can land only as heads or tails, is the example that we will use to introduce the laws of probability. An *unbiased* coin is one that is just as likely to land heads as it is to land tails.

Probability

In Chapter 9 we discussed probability in terms of the area under a smooth distribution. However, when dealing with discrete events, probability can be defined more simply in terms of counting events, as you will see next.

Rules of Probability

After defining probability and odds, we will cover rules of probability.

Definition of Probability

The *probability* (P) of a given event is defined by the following fraction:

$$P(\text{event}) = \frac{\text{number of ways the specified event can occur}}{\text{total number of possible events}}$$

For example, if an unbiased coin is flipped and you wish to determine the probability that heads will come up, the solution is

$$P(\text{H}) = \frac{1}{2} = \frac{1 \text{ head}}{2 \text{ possible events: head or tail}}$$

Similarly, the probability of tails coming up is also 1/2. Decimals are often used to express probabilities, so we can also write $P(\text{H})$ (that is, the probability of obtaining a head on one toss of the coin), or $P(\text{T})$, as .50. These numbers express the fact that if the coin is fair, in the long run heads will occur half the time and tails will occur half the time.

To provide some further illustrations, let us assume that you have a standard 52-card deck of playing cards. The deck contains 52 cards divided into four suits (spades, hearts, diamonds, and clubs), each of which contains 13 cards (2 through 10, jack, queen, king, and ace). The deck is thoroughly shuffled, and one card is drawn. The probability that it is the king of diamonds is 1/52 (or .019); there is only one way for that event to occur (only one king of diamonds) and 52 possible equally likely events (cards that could be drawn). In fact, the probability of drawing any one specific card from the deck is 1/52. The probability of drawing a 9 is 4/52 or 1/13 (or .077), since there are four ways for this event to occur (9 of spades, 9 of hearts, 9 of diamonds, and 9 of clubs) out of the total possible 52 events. If we define a *spot card* as anything below a 10, the probability of drawing a spot card in clubs is 8/52, or 2/13 (or .15), for there are eight specific equally likely events (the 2, 3, 4, 5, 6, 7, 8, and 9 of clubs) in the 52-card deck.

Probability cannot be less than 0 or greater than 1. If an event has a probability of 1, that means that it must happen. The probability of drawing either a red or a black card from a standard deck is 1.00, since all of the cards in the deck are either red or black (that is, $P = 52/52 = 1.00$). The probability of drawing a purple card with yellow polka dots is zero ($P = 0/52 = 0$).

Odds

The odds against an event are defined as the ratio of the number of unfavorable outcomes to the number of favorable outcomes, all outcomes being equally likely. See, for example, the following table.

Outcome	Total events (T)	Number of ways of obtaining the event (W)	Number of ways of not obtaining the event (T – W)	Probability of event (W/T)	Odds against event (T – W to W)
King of diamonds	52	1	51	1/52	51 to 1
A nine	52	4	48	4/52 or 1/13	48 to 4 or 12 to 1
Spot card in clubs	52	8	44	8/52 or 2/13	44 to 8 or 11 to 2 ($5^{1}/_{2}$ to 1)

If the odds against your winning a game are (say) 12 to 1, you need to collect 12 times your wager when you win for the game to be fair. If you stand to win more than 12 times your bet, it is to your advantage to play the game. If you collect less than 12 times your bet when you win, you should refuse to play because you figure to lose in the long run.

The Probability of A or B

The probability of *either of two events* taking place is computed by using the following formula:

$$P(A \text{ or } B) = P(A) + P(B) - P(A \text{ and } B)$$

Example: Suppose that you will win a prize if you draw *either* a king *or* a club from a standard 52-card deck in a single try. The probability of winning is equal to

$$P(\text{king}) + P(\text{club}) - P(\text{king and club})$$

$$= 4/52 + 13/52 - 1/52$$

$$= 16/52 \text{ (or .31)}$$

To verify these calculations, let us tackle the problem the long way. There are the usual 52 total possible events, and the number of favorable events may be counted as follows:

King (4 favorable events)	Club (13 favorable events)
king of spades	ace of clubs
king of hearts	*king of clubs*
king of diamonds	queen of clubs
king of clubs	jack of clubs
	ten of clubs
	nine of clubs
	eight of clubs
	seven of clubs
	six of clubs
	five of clubs
	four of clubs
	three of clubs
	two of clubs

There appear to be 17 favorable events: 13 clubs and 4 kings. But the king of clubs has been counted twice, and there is only one king of clubs in the deck. Therefore, the probability of king *and* club (1/52) must be subtracted, and the resulting probability (16/52) shows that there are 16 separate and distinct favorable events (cards) out of the total of 52 in the deck.

If events A and B cannot happen simultaneously (in mathematical terminology, *are mutually exclusive*), then $P(A \text{ and } B) = 0$. For example, the probability of drawing a king or a queen from the deck is equal to $4/52 + 4/52 - 0/52 = 8/52$. The events are mutually exclusive because no card in the deck is *both* a king and a queen.

The Probability of A and Then B

Suppose that a card is drawn from a standard deck, looked at, and replaced in the deck. The deck is shuffled thoroughly, and a second card is drawn. We wish to know the probability of obtaining a king on the first draw *and then* the ace of spades on the second draw. We assume that the two draws are *independent*—

that is, what happens on the first draw does not affect the probabilities on the second draw (because of the shuffling). The solution is given by the formula

$$P(A \text{ and then } B) = P(A) \times P(B)$$

In the present example, the answer is

$$P(\text{king and then ace of spades}) = P(\text{king}) \times P(\text{ace of spades})$$
$$= 4/52 \times 1/52$$
$$= 4/2704 \text{ (or } .0015)$$

Conditional Probability

If the card drawn on the first try is *not* returned to the deck, the probability becomes $4/52 \times 1/51$ (or $4/2652$). Under this procedure, only 51 cards remain in the deck after the first draw, and the probability of success on the second draw is therefore $1/51$.

Drawing two cards from a deck *without* replacement results in two events that are *not* independent. That is, the probability of the second card drawn is changed by the first draw. In statistical language, the probability of the second event is *conditional* on the outcome of the first event. For example, the probability of the second card being a club is certainly less if the first card drawn happens to also be a club.

Alpha is another example of a *conditional probability.* Alpha is the probability of rejecting the null hypothesis *under the condition* that the null hypothesis is true. With alpha fixed at .05, we know that 5% of all experiments *for which the null hypothesis is actually true* will be statistically significant and therefore Type I errors, but we do *not* know what percentage of *all* experiments will be statistically significant at the .05 level.

To create a binomial distribution, as we are about to do, all of the events involved must be independent of all of the others. Therefore, we will not deal further with conditional probabilities in this chapter.

The Binomial Distribution

Using only the simple rules of probability we have just described, we can now explain how the binomial distribution arises and how it can be used.

Constructing the Binomial Distribution for $N = 2$

To return to the coin-tossing example, the probability of obtaining a head on each of two consecutive flips of a coin is $P(H) \times P(H)$, which is equal to $1/2 \times 1/2$ or $1/4$. This can be verified by listing all possible outcomes of two flips of the coin:

First flip	Second flip	Overall result	Probability
H	H	2 heads	1/4 (or .25)
H	T	1 head, 1 tail	1/4
T	H	1 head, 1 tail	1/4
T	T	2 tails	1/4

Of the four possible outcomes (all of equal probability), only one yields two heads, so this probability is 1/4. Similarly, the probability of two tails is 1/4, and the probability of obtaining one head and one tail irrespective of order is 2/4 or 1/2. Since the events are independent (that is, the results of the first flip do not affect the probabilities on the second flip), the probabilities are exactly the same if we flip two coins once. Notice also that the sum of the probabilities of the four possible outcomes is equal to 1.0.

The shape of a binomial distribution depends on two values: N, the number of events; and P, the probability of one of the two categories for each event. For coin tossing, the two categories are heads (H) and tails (T), and P is the probability of one of these. For a fair coin, P equals .5 for both heads and tails. This will *not* be the case for a biased coin, which will be more likely to fall heads up or tails up. In the general case, we choose one category to focus on and refer to it as X. Then we say that P is the probability of the X category occurring on any one event. (For flips of a coin, it is customary to choose heads as the X category). The probability of the other category (in this case, tails) is sometimes labeled Q. But when there are only two categories, it is simpler to refer to the probability of the other category as $1 - P$, because P plus Q (the sums of the probabilities of the two possible outcomes) must equal 1.

To construct a graph of a binomial distribution, place all of the possible values for X along the horizontal axis. The height of the bar for each value of X depends on the relative frequency of that value occurring. For $N = 2$, there are three possible values for X: 0 (no heads), 1 head, and 2 heads. From the preceding table and discussion, it should be easy to imagine the binomial distribution for $N = 2$ and $P = .5$. It would consist of three bars: the bars over 0 and 2 would reach a height of .25, while the bar in the middle ($X = 1$) would reach .5.

It is particularly easy to construct a binomial distribution when P (and therefore Q) equals .5. In that case, all of the possible sequences of the two categories have the same probability (e.g., HTTT is no more or less likely than THTH), and the task becomes one of counting how many sequences contain a particular number of Xs (e.g., heads). If instead X represents drawing a club from a standard deck of cards (with replacement), P equals .25. If we use Y to represent a card that is not a club ($Q = .75$), then a sequence like $XYYY$ is *more* likely than a sequence like $YXYX$, not because of the order but because one has more Ys (which are 3 times more likely) than the other. When $P = Q = .5$, the binomial distribution is conveniently symmetric, as you will see in the next section. Fortunately, $P = .5$ is often a reasonable value for the null hypothesis when dealing with dichotomous events, so the kind of binomial distribution that we will construct next has many uses.

Constructing the Binomial Distribution for $N = 6$ ($P = .5$)

If you toss a coin six times, the number of possible different sequences is $2 \times 2 \times 2 \times 2 \times 2 \times 2$ (or 2^6), which equals 64. When $P = .5$, the probability is the same for all 64 sequences, so $p = 1/64$ for each sequence. However, the probability for a particular value of X (e.g., 5) depends on how many of the 64 sequences have that value for X (e.g., how many sequences contain exactly five heads). So how many sequences have exactly five heads? Let us count the ways, which are labeled A through F in the following table:

	Possible outcomes					
	Flip 1	Flip 2	Flip 3	Flip 4	Flip 5	Flip 6
A	H	H	H	H	H	T
B	H	H	H	H	T	H
C	H	H	H	T	H	H
D	H	H	T	H	H	H
E	H	T	H	H	H	H
F	T	H	H	H	H	H

As you can see, there are six different sequences that contain exactly five heads. Using the "or" rule of probability, the probability that you will get five heads from a fair coin that is flipped six times is equal to

$$P(A \text{ or } B \text{ or } C \text{ or } D \text{ or } E \text{ or } F)$$

Since these events are mutually exclusive, this equals $1/64 + 1/64 + 1/64 + 1/64 + 1/64 + 1/64 = 6/64$ or .094.

Using the same procedures, we can compute the probability of any number of heads if a coin is flipped six times. However, writing out all of the possible sequences can be quite tedious,[1] so we will just present the end product in the following table:

Number of heads	Probability
0	$1/64 = .016$
1	$6/64 = .094$
2	$15/64 = .234$
3	$20/64 = .312$
4	$15/64 = .234$
5	$6/64 = .094$
6	$1/64 = .016$
	$64/64 = 1.000$

---

1. Mathematics makes use of special techniques, called *permutations* and *combinations,* to speed the calculation of the number of sequences for each X. Since an advanced knowledge of mathematics is not necessary for comprehension of the material in this book, it will be omitted.

Testing Null Hypotheses with the Binomial Distribution

The binomial distribution shown can be used to test some simple null hypotheses. Suppose a friend claims that he can taste the difference between two popular brands of root beer, and you decide to test his claim. You present the two brands of root beer in identical cups, and he has to tell you which cup contains which brand. Suppose your friend answers correctly six times in a row. What should you decide?

The appropriate null hypothesis is that your friend was just guessing, in which case P equals .5 for each test. Because being correct six times out of six tests is represented by only one sequence out of 64, the p value is .016. If you want to be conservative and perform a two-tailed test (your friend being *wrong* six times in a row would also suggest that he does detect some difference), the p value would be .032. In either case, using the .05 decision rule, you would reject the null hypothesis and conclude that your friend has a chance of being correct on each trial that is greater than .5.

If your friend were correct on only five of the six trials, the one-tailed p value would be .11. This is not significant at the .05 level, even for a one-tailed test. Notice that to get the p value in this case, you must add the probabilities of both one wrong, or .094, and zero wrong, or .016. Because zero wrong is further out in the tail of the binomial distribution, it contributes to the possibility of committing a Type I error.

If your friend is correct on 10 out of 12 repetitions of the taste test, you need the binomial distribution with $N = 12$, $P = .5$, to find his p value. This distribution is shown in Figure 19.1. (You can't read this accurately from the graph, but for $X = 10$, the one-tailed $p = .0161 + .0029 + .0002 = .0192$. So H_0 is rejected at the .05 level with either a one- or a two-tailed test.) We show the distribution for $N = 12$ so you can see its resemblance to the normal distribu-

FIGURE 19.1
Binomial distribution for $N = 12$, $P = .5$

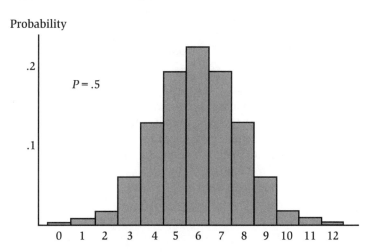

tion. As N increases, the binomial distribution becomes smoother and re- sembles the normal distribution more closely. (Theoretically, the two distribu- tions become identical when N is infinitely large.) When P is higher or lower than .5, the binomial distribution is skewed. The further P is from .5, the larger N needs to be before the binomial begins to resemble the normal distribution.

Using the Normal Distribution as an Approximation

It is not common to find tables of the binomial distribution for N greater than 20. Fortunately, if P is .5 (or even just close to .5) the resemblance to the nor- mal distribution becomes so close that a z score can be calculated and referred to a table of the standard normal distribution (like Table A in the Appendix).

It should be evident that the mean of a binomial distribution is NP (e.g., for $N = 12$ and $P = .5$, the mean is 6). It is not as obvious, but the standard devi- ation for a binomial distribution is $\sqrt{NPQ}$. This leads to the following z score formula that can be applied to the binomial distribution:

$$z = \frac{X - NP}{\sqrt{NPQ}}$$

For the example in which your friend identified the root beer brands cor- rectly 10 out of 12 times, the z score would be

$$z = \frac{10 - 6}{\sqrt{12(.5)(.5)}} = \frac{4}{\sqrt{3}} = 2.31$$

We can see from Table A that the p value corresponding to a z score of 2.31 is .0104. Although this p value leads to the same conclusion with respect to H_0 that we reached by calculating p exactly for the binomial distribution (.0192), it is noticeably different. With $P = .5$, N needs to be at least about 20 before the normal approximation to the binomial distribution becomes sufficiently accu- rate to use in null hypothesis testing.

The Formula for Proportions

Rather than dealing with the actual number of trials on which your friend was correct (i.e., X), or the number correct expected by chance (NP), it may be more convenient to deal with the *proportion* of trials on which your friend was correct (i.e., X/N), and the proportion expected by chance (i.e., $NP/N = P$). Be- cause we obtained the proportions by dividing by N, we also have to divide the standard deviation of the binomial distribution by N to get the standard devia- tion of the proportions:

$$\frac{\sqrt{NPQ}}{N} = \frac{\sqrt{NPQ}}{\sqrt{N^2}} = \sqrt{\frac{NPQ}{N^2}} = \sqrt{\frac{PQ}{N}}$$

Therefore, the z score for proportions is given by the following formula:

$$z = \frac{\frac{X}{N} - P}{\sqrt{\frac{PQ}{N}}}$$

This formula should seem familiar. To see why, let us change the notation. We will use a lowercase p to represent X/N, the proportion you observed in your sample. (For the example of 10 correct trials out of 12, $p = 10/12 = .833$.) Instead of using an uppercase P to represent the proportion under the null hypothesis, we will use the (lowercase) Greek letter pi, because this is the proportion of X in the entire population. Finally, because Q equals $1 - P$, it can now be written as $1 - \pi$. Using the modified notation, the previous formula can be written as

$$z = \frac{p - \pi}{\sqrt{\frac{\pi(1 - \pi)}{N}}}$$

This is the same formula as the z score for proportions in Chapter 10. If we apply this version of the formula to the root beer taste test example, it yields the same z score:

$$z = \frac{.833 - .5}{\sqrt{\frac{.5(1 - .5)}{12}}} = \frac{.333}{\sqrt{.02083}} = \frac{.333}{.1443} = 2.31$$

Applications of the Binomial Test

The use of z scores in conjunction with the normal distribution yields only an approximation to the exact p value you would get from the binomial distribution. As we mentioned in Chapter 10, this approximation is not sufficiently accurate for null hypothesis testing when *either $N\pi$ or $N(1 - \pi)$* is less than 5.

In Chapter 10, we applied the z-score proportion formula to the results of an election poll. This test can also be applied to experimental situations more central to behavioral research. For example, a developmental researcher may want to test whether 10-month-old infants spend more time looking at photographs of adult faces rated as attractive by other adults than faces rated as relatively unattractive. By exposing the infants to equal numbers of attractive and unattractive faces and measuring their gaze time for each type of face, each infant can be categorized as preferring attractive faces or preferring unattractive faces. (It is not likely that an infant will spend *exactly* the same amount of time looking at both types of faces, but it would be reasonable to delete from the data set any infant who exhibited very little preference.) The proportion of infants out of, say, 20 or more that prefers attractive faces can be tested against the null hypothesis of $\pi = .5$ using the preceding formula. (You can demonstrate for yourself that 15 out of 20 infants preferring attractive faces would allow rejection of H_0 at the .05 level with a two-tailed test.)

You can also test null hypotheses for which π is not .5. Imagine an observational study in which you find that out of 50 leading architects, 12 are left-handed. (There is some evidence that left-handers on the average have greater spatial ability than right-handers, because of the way the left and right sides of their brains are organized.) In this case, π is not .5. It is the actual proportion of left-handers in the population, which is closer to .15. The observed proportion is $p = 12/50 = .24$, and z is therefore as follows:

$$z = \frac{.24 - .15}{\sqrt{\dfrac{.15(.85)}{50}}} = \frac{.09}{.0505} = 1.78$$

This result would be significant at the .05 level only if a one-tailed test could be justified (which is not likely). Note that because $N\pi = 50 \times .15 = 7.5$, which is greater than 5, and $N(1 - \pi)$ is also greater than 5, the use of the normal approximation would be considered reasonably accurate in this case.

Simplified Formula for $P = .5$

In many common experimental situations, the null hypothesis will involve equal probabilities for the two alternatives. For this null hypothesis ($P = Q = .5$), the z–score formula that we started out with, $z = (X - NP)/\sqrt{NPQ}$, can be simplified to $z = (2X - N)/\sqrt{N}$, where X is the number of events that fall in (either) one of the two categories. We will have the opportunity to use this specialized version of the z score formula in the next section.

The Sign Test for Matched Samples

A particularly useful application of the binomial distribution is to serve as the null hypothesis distribution for a nonparametric alternative to the matched t test. At the beginning of this chapter, we mentioned the example of testing a new form of imagery exercise that is designed to increase creativity. Suppose that we match young art students into pairs based primarily on the creativity they have already shown in their paintings. (The matching won't be precise, of course, but even an approximate matching can be quite helpful.) The members of each pair are assigned randomly to either the imagery training condition, or to a control condition that provides some plausible but ineffective version of the training. At the end of the training period, each art student produces a painting. A panel of art instructors is asked to determine, for each pair of participants, whose painting exhibited the greater amount of creativity. Let us further suppose that, of the 30 pairs of participants in the study, the experimental participant is judged to be more creative in 18 cases, the control participant is found to be more creative in 10 cases, and no determination is made in 2 cases (each of these two comparisons is judged a tie). The conservative approach is to delete the two ties from the analysis and use 28 as N in the z score for proportions.

Because we don't have actual measurements of creativity, we cannot calculate difference scores and compute a matched-pairs t test. However, we can count how many of the creativity differences are positive and how many are negative. (We will define a difference as positive when the experimental participant is judged as more creative than his or her pair in the control condition.) The appropriate null hypothesis in such situations is that there will be equal numbers of positive and negative differences in the population (i.e., P, or π, = .5). We can use the binomial distribution to decide whether it is reasonable to reject the hypothesis that the signs of the difference scores in the population are just as likely to be positive as negative, and this is called *the sign test for matched samples*. Given that H_0 for the sign test is always that $P = .5$, as long as N is at least about 15 or 20, we can use the simplified version of the z-score formula shown and look up our p value in Table A in the Appendix. For this example, X is 18, so

$$z = \frac{2X - N}{\sqrt{N}} = \frac{36 - 28}{\sqrt{28}} = \frac{8}{5.29} = 1.51$$

From Table A, the one-tailed p value corresponding to this z score is .0655. Even with a one-tailed test, this z score would not allow rejection of the null hypothesis at the .05 level: There is not sufficient reason to believe that the imagery exercise increases creativity.

The sign test is particularly appropriate when you cannot make quantitative measurements, but you can determine the direction in which a variable changes (e.g., mental health has improved, stayed the same, or worsened). However, the sign test is sometimes used even when the dependent variable has been measured precisely and a matched t test can be computed. The matched t test is quite robust with respect to its assumption concerning normal distributions. Nevertheless, when you are dealing with fairly small samples and the distribution of the difference scores bears little resemblance to a bell-shaped curve (e.g., a few of the differences are very far from the others, or the difference scores form two distinct clumps), the sign test represents a useful alternative that is distribution-free. If nearly all the differences are in the same direction, you may obtain statistical significance with the sign test, even if the amounts of the difference scores are distributed in a strange way.

When applied to quantitative data, the sign test makes no use of the amounts of the differences. Therefore, it usually has considerably less power to detect a true population effect than a matched t test applied to the same data.

If you have precise measurements but are reluctant to perform a matched t test because of a combination of a fairly small sample size and an unusual distribution of difference scores, the *Wilcoxon* test is likely to give you more power than the sign test without requiring you to make questionable assumptions. The Wilcoxon test is based on rank ordering your difference scores and analyzing the ranks rather than the actual amounts. This test will be explained in detail in the last chapter, in which we describe statistical tests designed for ordinal data.

Summary

The rules of probability for discrete events can be described in terms of counting the number of events that fall into one category or another. When a fixed number of dichotomous events are counted in terms of how many events fell into either one of the two possible categories, it is easy to construct a binomial distribution, which can then be used to draw statistical inferences.

1. Probability

Definition:

$$P = \frac{\text{number of ways the specified event can occur}}{\text{total number of possible events}}$$

Odds against an event = number of unfavorable events to number of favorable events

Additive law:

$$P\ (A \text{ or } B) = P(A) + P(B) - P(A \text{ and } B)$$

Multiplicative law:

If A and B are independent events, $P(A \text{ and then } B) = P(A) \times P(B)$

2. Using the Normal Distribution as an Approximation to the Binomial Distribution

First, calculate

$$z = \frac{X - NP}{\sqrt{NPQ}},$$

where N is the total number of events, X is the number of events that fall into the category whose probability is P, and $Q = 1 - P$. Then look up the p value in Table A. (Double this value for a two-tailed test.)

If $P = Q = .5$, the formula can be simplified to

$$z = \frac{2X - N}{\sqrt{N}}$$

If we divide all of the terms of the first equation by N, we obtain the same z-score formula for proportions that we used in Chapter 10:

$$z = \frac{p - \pi}{\sqrt{\dfrac{\pi(1 - \pi)}{N}}}$$

3. The Sign Test for Matched Samples

For each matched pair of participants, determine the *sign* of the difference between them, using some arbitrary but consistent rule (e.g., if the participant in the experimental condition performs better than the paired participant in the control group, the difference is positive). If your DV has been measured precisely, you can calculate the difference as you would for a matched-pairs t test, but for this test you would note only the sign (positive or negative) of the difference score. Then apply one of the preceding formulas, wherein N is the number of pairs. Generally, the null hypothesis will be such that $P = Q = .5$.

Exercises

1. In the following problems, cards are drawn from a standard 52-card deck. Before a second draw, the first card drawn is replaced and the deck is thoroughly shuffled. Compute each of the following probabilities.

   (a) The probability of drawing a 10 on the first draw.

   (b) The probability of drawing either a deuce, a 3, a 4, a 5, a heart, or a diamond on the first draw.

   (c) The probability of drawing the ace of spades twice in a row.

   (d) The probability of drawing either a jack, a 10, a 7 of clubs, or a spade on the first draw *and then* drawing either the ace of diamonds or 9 of hearts on the second draw.

   (e) Recompute the probabilities asked for in parts (c) and (d) assuming that the first card drawn is *not* replaced.

2. The following questions refer to the throw of one fair, six-sided die.

   (a) What is the probability of obtaining an odd number on one throw?

   (b) What is the probability of obtaining seven odd numbers in seven throws?

3. One hundred slips of paper bearing the numbers from 1 to 100, inclusive, are placed in a large hat and thoroughly mixed. What is the probability of drawing

   (a) the number 17?

   (b) the number 92?

   (c) either a 2 or a 4?

   (d) a number from 7 to 11, inclusive?

   (e) a number in the 20s?

   (f) an even number?

   (g) an even number, and then a number from 3 to 19, inclusive? (The number drawn first is replaced prior to the second draw.)

   (h) a number from 96 to 100, inclusive, or a number from 70 to 97, inclusive?

4. Slips of paper are placed in a large hat and thoroughly mixed. Ten slips bear the number 1, 20 slips bear the number 2, 30 slips bear the number 3, and 5 slips bear the number 4. What is the probability of drawing

   (a) a 1?

   (b) a 2?

   (c) a 3?

   (d) a 4?

   (e) a 1 or a 4?

   (f) a 1 or a 2 or a 3 or a 4?

   (g) a 5?

   (h) a 2 and then a 3? (The number drawn first is not replaced prior to the second draw.)

5. Imagine that you want to test whether a particular coin is biased or fair by flipping the coin four times and counting the number of times it comes up heads.

   (a) How many different sequences can be produced by flipping the coin four times? How many different values can X (the number of heads) take on?

   (b) Graph the binomial distribution for $N = 4$ and $P = .5$ so that the height of each bar represents the probability that corresponds to each value of X.

   (c) If the coin were to land on tails four times in a row, could you reject the null hypothesis that the coin is fair? Explain.

6. Apply the sign test to the data from exercise 6 in Chapter 11, using one of the normal approximation formulas. Explain the difference in results between this exercise and the one in Chapter 11.

7. Suppose that after 6 months of a new form of treatment for chronic schizophrenia, 18 patients exhibited some improvement, 4 did not change, and 6 patients actually got worse.

   (a) Using the sign test, can you reject the null hypothesis (that the new treatment has no effect) at the .05 level? (Show the z score and p value that you used to answer this question.)

   (b) A more conservative way to conduct the binomial test is to assign half of the tied cases arbitrarily to each category (one pair is discarded if there is an odd number of ties). Redo part (a) after applying this approach to tied cases.

8. At a small rural college, incoming students are arranged into 320 *pairs* by the administration based on their high school credentials (the students do not know this). One member of each pair is chosen randomly to participate in an enriched orientation program. At the end of the first semester, it is found that 55% of enriched-program students are getting higher grades than the (control) students they have been matched with. Can you reject the null hypothesis at the .05 level with a two-tailed test? With a one-tailed test? Explain the basis for your statistical decisions.

Thought Questions

1. (a) Give an example of a psychological research study where the variables can be expressed as categories or as ranks, but not as a quantitative (i.e., interval/ratio) scale. (b) What kind of statistical analysis should be used for the data in such a study, parametric or nonparametric? Why?

2. You want to determine if a coin is biased in favor of falling heads up or tails up. (a) You flip the coin three times and obtain three heads. What should you decide? (b) Why is the informal experiment in part (a) badly designed? (c) What error in behavioral science research is similar to the one in part (a)? (d) Which error is more likely to result from the experiment in part (a), Type I or Type II? (e) Suppose you flip the coin six times and obtain six heads. What should you decide? (f) What distribution is used to reach a decision in part (a) and part (e)?

3. When should the normal distribution be used as an approximation to the binomial distribution?

4. A researcher wishes to determine if a particular form of psychotherapy will improve the mental health of patients who suffer from depression. If the researcher cannot obtain a quantitative measure of mental health but can con-

clude whether it has improved, stayed the same, or become worse for each patient, what application of the binomial distribution should the researcher use?

Computer Exercises

1. Perform a binomial test on the gender variable, with $P = .5$. Can you reject the null hypothesis that Sara's statistics class is a random sample from a population in which both genders are equally represented? Use the binomial test to compare the proportion of women in the class against the null hypothesis of $P = .55$. Can you reject the null hypothesis in this case?

2. Redo the binomial test on gender (with $P = .5$, only) separately for each college major.

3. In this exercise you will be testing the (two-valued) grouping variable you created from a median split of the phobia scores for the computer exercises in Chapter 17. Perform a binomial test for $P = .5$, separately for each gender. Explain the relationship between the tests of the two genders.

4. If you have not already done this for a previous exercise, create a variable that is the difference between baseline and prequiz heart rate. Then, recode this new variable so that negative difference scores are assigned a numeric score of 1, positive difference scores are assigned a score of 2, and zero differences are assigned as missing. Perform a binomial test on this new variable with $P = .5$. Compare the p value from this test with the p value you obtained for the matched-pairs t test on the same two variables in Chapter 11. Explain the relationship between these two alternative tests of the same difference scores.

5. If your software has the capability, request a sign test of the baseline versus the prequiz heart rates, and compare the results to those from the binomial test in the previous exercise.

6. Repeat exercise 5 for the baseline and prequiz anxiety scores (if your software does not have the sign test, repeat exercise 4 for the anxiety variable).

Bridge to SPSS

SPSS has a number of options for creating and deriving probabilities from a binomial distribution, and it makes some arbitrary choices without informing you. So you will need to read this section carefully.

The Binomial Test

If one of your variables has only two different numerical values, you can perform a binomial test on that variable by selecting **Binomial** from the Analyze/

Nonparametric Tests menu. Only numeric variables will appear in the list on the left side of the dialog box, from which they can be moved to the Test Variable List. The default value for the Test Proportion is .5, but it can be changed to any value between .001 and .999. For instance, suppose you have a variable called "prefhand" with string values of "right," "left," and "ambi." If you want to test whether you have a significantly greater proportion of left-handed people in your study than in the larger population, you can type your best estimate of the relevant population proportion in the Test Proportion box. However, before you can run the binomial test, you will first have to recode the words *right* and *left* into two different numbers, and replace the *ambi*'s with missing values. Under the list of variables, there is a Define Dichotomy choice, and if you use the default setting, **Get from data,** SPSS will *not* run the binomial test on any variable in the test list for which it reads three or more different values. However, there is another way to run the binomial test. If your test variable is numeric and multivalued, you can select **Cut point** to define your dichotomy, and then type in a value. SPSS will base the binomial test on the number of cases that fall below versus above the cut point on your test variable.

Assuming that the Test Proportion is left unchanged at the default value of .5, the basic output box for the binomial test gives you the N and the proportion for each of the two categories, and a *two-tailed p* value. If your total N is 25 or less, the p value you will get is labeled **Exact Sig. (2-tailed),** and it is based on adding the exact binomial probabilities for your value of X (the number out of N that fall in the first of your two groups) and all possible values for X that are more extreme than yours, in either tail. If your N is greater than 25, the p value you will get is labeled **Asymp. Sig. (2-tailed),** and it is based on calculating a z score corresponding to your value for X, and doubling the area beyond that z score. (Asymp. is short for *asymptotic*—a term that is meant to remind you that the normal approximation to the binomial distribution becomes perfect as N reaches infinity.) To improve the approximation when N is considerably less than infinite, SPSS uses a correction for continuity in its calculation of the z score for a binomial distribution; the magnitude of the numerator of the z score is reduced by .5 before it is divided by the denominator.) If you want a one-tailed p value, you will simply have to divide the two-tailed value that SPSS gives you in half.

If you change the Test Proportion to a value other than .5, you will be dealing with a binomial distribution that is not symmetrical, and you will no longer get two-tailed p values for your binomial test. In such cases, SPSS will give you a one-tailed p value and label it as such. Note that when P is not set to .5, it matters that SPSS automatically compares the proportion in the first group (defined as the group associated with the *lower* numerical value) to your test proportion. For example, if lefties are coded with a *higher* value than righties, your test proportion should be based on the population proportion of right-handed people in the population (e.g., .8). Otherwise, SPSS will compare the proportion of righties in your data (say, .7) with the population proportion of lefties that you typed in (e.g., .2), and will not give you the p value that you want.

Also note that SPSS always gives you the p value for the *tail* of the binomial distribution—that is, the portion of the binomial distribution that begins at your actual proportion and heads away from the test proportion. SPSS assumes that you would not want to know the p value if you picked the wrong tail. Of course, you can always subtract the one-tailed Sig. value that SPSS gives you from 1.0 to get the other portion of the binomial distribution.

The Sign Test

You could perform a sign test that compares two variables measured on the same cases (e.g., a "before" and an "after" variable) by computing a new variable that is the difference of the first two and then performing a binomial test on the difference scores using zero as the cut point. Fortunately, SPSS makes this procedure even easier by including the sign test as one of the choices in the dialog box that opens when you select **2 Related Samples** from the Analyze/Nonparametric Tests menu. Just select *two* variables from the list at the left of the dialog box, as you would for a matched-pairs t test, and move the *pair* over to the Test Pair(s) List. Then, under Test Type, click on the check box for **Sign.** When you click **OK,** SPSS will perform a binomial test by comparing the proportion of positive (or negative—the results are the same) difference scores (zero differences are excluded) to a test proportion (i.e., null hypothesis) of .5. The other two test choices are the Wilcoxon and McNemar tests. We will discuss the more popular of these, the Wilcoxon test, in the last chapter of this text.

Chapter 20
Chi Square Tests

PREVIEW

Chi Square and Goodness of Fit: One-Variable Problems

What are the procedures for testing the hypothesis that more than two population frequencies are distributed in a specified way?

What is the observed frequency? The expected frequency? The chi square ratio?

What is the correct statistical model to use in this situation?

How do we test chi square for statistical significance?

How does the chi-square test compare to the binomial test in the two-category case?

When should chi square *not* be used?

Chi Square as a Test of Independence: Two-Variable Problems

What are the procedures for testing the significance of the relationship between *two* variables when data are expressed in terms of frequencies?

How do we compute chi square from a 2×2 table?

Measures of Strength of Association in Two-Variable Tables

Why is it desirable to convert a statistically significant value of chi square into a measure that shows the strength of the relationship between the two variables?

What are three measures of strength of relationship? When should each of these measures be used?

Summary

Exercises

Thought Questions

Computer Exercises

Bridge to SPSS

Chi Square and Goodness of Fit: One-Variable Problems

Consider the following problem:

A publisher introduces three titles for a new literary magazine for women—*Today, Choice,* and *New Alternatives.* She wonders whether these titles will be equally popular among female consumers. To test the hypothesis of equal preference, she obtains a random sample of 177 women and asks them which *one* of the three titles they like best. She finds that 65 women prefer *Today,* 60 prefer *Choice,* and 52 prefer *New Alternatives.* Are these results sufficient reason to reject the null hypothesis that equal numbers of women *in the population* prefer each of the three titles? Or are these results likely to occur as a result of sampling error if the preferences in the population are in fact equal, in which case the null hypothesis of equality in the population should be retained?

In the previous chapter, you saw how to test null hypotheses when events are constrained to only two possible categories. In this chapter, you will learn how to deal with data that consist of the number of objects (usually persons) falling in any one of a number of categories. That is, the data are in terms of empirically observed *frequencies* for *more than two* categories that can then be compared to frequencies expected on the basis of some hypothesis.

The data for the problem given at the beginning of this chapter consist of frequencies or head counts—that is, *how many* prefer a particular alternative—and the objective is to decide whether or not it is reasonable to conclude that the several population frequencies are distributed in a specified way. Thus, in the example, the publisher knows how many women in the sample prefer one title to the other two. She would like to know if it is reasonable to conclude that the population from which her sample was randomly drawn is equally divided with regard to preference for the three titles.

Testing hypotheses about frequency data that fall in more than two category-sets is similar in strategy to the tests we performed on dichotomous data in the previous chapter. However, to find probabilities associated with sequences involving three or more outcomes for each event, we cannot use the binomial distribution. With three categories, we would need a trinomial distribution. In the general case of any number of possible categories, the appropriate statistical model would be the *multinomial distribution.*

Just as the normal distribution can be used to approximate the more exact results from the binomial distribution, a convenient statistic can be calculated from multicategory frequency data. The distribution of this statistic can be reasonably approximated by what is known as the *chi-square distribution.* (An exception does occur if you are dealing with very small frequencies, a problem we will discuss later in this chapter.) This statistic is named after the distribution it tends to follow, so it is called the *chi-square statistic* and is symbolized by the lowercase Greek letter chi (pronounced *kie* to rhyme with *pie*) squared: χ^2.

Because we may be dealing with any number of categories, we can no longer use X to represent the frequency of one category and $N - X$ as the number in the other category. Instead, we will need to keep track of the observed frequency (f_o) in each category. Similarly, rather than dealing with a single value that is expected for X according to the null hypothesis (i.e., NP), each category will have its own expected frequency (f_e). The chi-square statistic is based on the discrepancy between the observed and expected frequency for each category, as expressed in the following formula:

$$\chi^2 = \sum \frac{(f_o - f_e)^2}{f_e},$$

where

f_o = observed frequency

f_e = expected (null-hypothetical) frequency

$\sum$ is taken over all the categories

If the differences between the observed frequencies and the expected frequencies are small, χ^2 will be small. The greater the difference between the observed frequencies and those expected under the null hypothesis, the larger χ^2 will be. If the differences between the observed and expected values are so large collectively as to occur by chance only .05 or less of the time when the null hypothesis is true, the null hypothesis is rejected.

The problem given at the beginning of this chapter is concerned with differences in choice among different categories (or levels) of a *single* variable. In that example, the variable is magazine title preference, and each respondent selects one of three possible choices.

To analyze such a problem, the first step is to set up a table with the three alternatives and tabulate the observed frequencies. (See Table 20.1.) Next, the expected frequencies must be stated before χ^2 can be determined. The null hypothesis states that the three titles are equally preferred, so *if* it is true, you would expect the sample of 177 women to be equally divided among the three categories. Thus, the expected frequencies under the null hypothesis are 177/3, or 59, 59, and 59. (Note that the sum of the expected frequencies must be equal to the sum of the observed frequencies.) Is it likely or unlikely that observed frequencies of 65, 60, and 52 would occur if the population frequen-

TABLE 20.1

Chi-square test for literary title choices

Title	Observed frequency (f_o)	Expected frequency (f_e)	$f_o - f_e$	$(f_o - f_e)^2$	$\frac{(f_o - f_e)^2}{f_e}$
Today	65	59	6	36	.610
Choice	60	59	1	1	.017
New Alternatives	52	59	−7	49	.831

$$\chi^2 = \sum \frac{(f_o - f_e)^2}{f_e} = 1.458$$

FIGURE 20.1

Chi-square distribution for $df = 1$ and $df = 6$

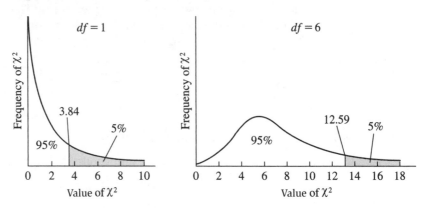

cies are exactly equal? In other words, are the observed frequencies of 65, 60, and 52 significantly different from the expected frequencies of 59, 59, and 59? To answer this question, χ^2 has been computed in Table 20.1. Note that *each* value of $(f_o - f_e)^2$ is divided by its own expected frequency. (All the expected frequencies happen to be equal in this particular problem, but this will not always be true since it depends on the particular null hypothesis.) The resulting three values are then summed to obtain χ^2, which is equal to 1.46.

In order to test the significance of χ^2 using a specified criterion of significance, the obtained value is referred to Table H in the Appendix with the appropriate degrees of freedom. Note that in this table, there is a different value of χ^2 for every df. Chi square, like t, yields a family of curves, with the shape of a particular curve depending on the df. (See Figure 20.1.) For the χ^2 distributions, however, the df is based on the number of *categories*, rather than on the sample size as in the case of the t distributions. In the one-variable case, the df are equal to $k - 1$, where k is equal to the number of categories of the variable. Thus, in the present problem, $df = 3 - 1 = 2$. For χ^2 to be significant at the .05 level, therefore, the obtained value must be equal to or greater than 5.99. Since the obtained value is only 1.46, the null hypothesis is retained; there is not sufficient reason to reject the null hypothesis that the frequencies in the population are equal. Therefore, we have an insufficient basis for concluding that any particular title or titles is (are) preferred.

The Relationship between the Binomial Test and the Chi-Square Test with Two Categories

Based on comments that some of her students have made, Sara believes that statistics students in general do not want their final examinations to be cumulative (i.e., encompassing all of the material from the beginning to the end of the course). Rather, the students seem to want the final exam to cover only the

TABLE 20.2

Chi-square test for attitude toward cumulative final examinations

Attitude	f_o	f_e	$f_o - f_e$	$(f_o - f_e)^2$	$\dfrac{(f_o - f_e)^2}{f_e}$
For	15	37.5	−22.5	506.25	13.5
Against	60	37.5	22.5	506.25	13.5
	75	75.0			

$$\chi^2 = \Sigma \frac{(f_o - f_e)^2}{f_e} = 27$$

second half of the course. She decides to use her own class as though it were a random sample of all statistics students, and she asks her students to turn in anonymous notes stating whether they want the final exam to be cumulative or not. Of the 75 students who hand in notes, Sara finds that 15 students are in favor of cumulative final exams and 60 students are against them. If the null hypothesis is that the population of statistics students is equally divided on this issue, the expected frequencies are 75/2 = 37.5 for each category. (f_e's frequently come out to fractional values, even though it is not possible for half a student to vote one way or the other.) The computation of the chi-square statistic for this problem is shown in Table 20.2.

Because the calculated chi-square statistic, 27, is larger than the critical value of 3.84 from Table H for 2 − 1 = 1 *df* using the .05 criterion of significance, the null hypothesis is rejected; it is *not* reasonable to assume that the student population is evenly divided on this issue. By inspecting the f_o, it may be concluded that a majority is opposed to final examinations that are cumulative. The χ^2 value of 27 would have been significant even if we used an alpha of .001 (e.g., we are performing 50 such tests and use the Bonferroni correction to adjust the alpha for each test), because 27 exceeds $\chi^2_{.001}(1) = 10.83$.

Because the situation just described involves only two categories (for and against), the null hypothesis can also be tested by using the binomial distribution. Given that $P = .5$ and N is rather large, we can use the shortcut formula from the previous chapter to create a z score:

$$z = \frac{2X - N}{\sqrt{N}} = \frac{2(60) - 75}{\sqrt{75}} = \frac{45}{8.66} = 5.196$$

If you square this z score, you will get 27, which is the value we calculated for chi square. (If in this formula you used 15, the number of students who voted "for," instead of 60, the z score would have the same magnitude but the opposite sign, which would make no difference at all after squaring.) Squaring the normal distribution yields a chi-square distribution with one degree of freedom. For example, the .05 critical value for χ^2 is 3.84, which equals 1.96 squared.

Some Precautions Involving the Use of χ^2

The χ^2 tests just described can only be validly performed when the observations are *independent*. That is, no response should be related to or dependent upon any other response. For example, it would be incorrect to apply χ^2 with $N = 100$ to the true-false responses of five schizophrenic patients to 20 questionnaire items. The 100 responses are not independent of each other, since the 20 responses given by each patient must be assumed to be mutually related. This assumption of independence is also critical to the validity of the binomial test.

Second, any subject must fall in *one and only one* category. Thus, in the problem involving the preference for literary titles, each subject was asked to choose the one title she most preferred.

Third, the computations must be based on all the subjects in the sample. In the previous example, a category of "for" as well as "against" had to be included so that χ^2 would be based on the total frequency of 75, the total size of the sample. As a check, the sum of the observed frequencies *must* be equal to the sum of the expected frequencies.

One final precaution is concerned with the size of the expected frequencies. Like the z score formula for the binomial test, chi square is actually an approximate test for obtaining the probability values for the observed frequencies (that is, the probability of getting the observed frequencies if the null hypothesis is true). This test is based on the expectation that within *any category*, sample frequencies are normally distributed about the population or expected value. Since frequencies cannot be negative, the distribution cannot be normal when the *expected* population values are *close to zero*. The sample frequencies cannot be much below the expected frequency, while they can be much above it—an asymmetric distribution.

Under certain conditions, therefore, you should *not* compute χ^2. For 1 *df*, *expected* frequencies should all be at least 5; this is consistent with the rule for the binomial test—that both NP and $N(1 - P)$ must be at least 5. For 2 *df*, expected frequencies should all exceed 2. With 3 or more *df*, if all expected frequencies but one are greater than or equal to 5 and if the one that is not is at least equal to 1, χ^2 is still a good approximation. In other words, the greater the *df*, the more lenient the requirement for minimum expected frequencies.

Chi Square as a Test of Independence: Two-Variable Problems

In the preceding section, χ^2 was used to test some a priori hypothesis about expected frequencies—that is, a hypothesis about f_e values formulated prior to the experiment—which involved frequency data concerning a single variable. Chi square can also be used, however, *to test the significance of the relationship between two variables when data are expressed in terms of frequencies of joint occurrence.*

TABLE 20.3

Hypothetical illustration of perfectly independent relationship between major and career preference, using frequency data

		Undergraduate Major		
		Economics	Psychology	Total Students
Career preference	Applied	40	60	100
	Academic	32	48	80
	Total	72 +	108 =	180

55.56% of the econ majors (40/72) prefer applied careers; 44.44% (32/72) prefer academia

55.56% of the psych majors (60/108) prefer applied careers; 44.44% (48/108) prefer academia

40.00% of the students who prefer applied careers are econ majors (40/100); 60.00% (60/100) are psych majors

40.00% of the students who prefer academia are econ majors (32/80); 60.00% (48/80) are psych majors

Thus, there is no relationship between major and career preference.

Suppose you want to find out if students majoring in psychology differ in their career preferences from students majoring in economics. If the two variables of major and career choice are *not* related (are *independent*), you would expect the proportion of psychology majors who prefer say, an academic to an applied career to be the same as the proportion of economics majors who prefer academia. (See Table 20.3.) Here, in contrast to one-variable problems, no a priori expected frequencies are involved. You are dealing with the relationship between two variables, each of which may have any number of categories or levels. (In this example, each variable has two levels.) The null hypothesis is that the two variables are independent, which (as you will see) implies a set of expected frequencies.

As an illustration, suppose you have a random sample of 108 psychology majors and a random sample of 72 economics majors. You ask each individual to state which of the two types of careers he or she prefers. With two categories of career type and two undergraduate majors, there are four possible combined categories or *cells:* econ-applied; econ-academic; psych-applied; psych-academic. The results are shown in Table 20.4.

Thus, 45 econ majors preferred applied careers, 55 psych majors preferred applied careers, 27 econ majors preferred academia, and 53 psych majors preferred academia. The total for the first column (called the *marginal frequency* for that column) indicates that the sample contains 72 (that is, 45 + 27) economics majors. The marginal frequency for the second column shows that the sample contains 108 psychology majors. Similarly, the row marginal frequencies indicate that 100 students of both majors preferred an applied career while 80 preferred academia. The total sample size, N, is equal to 180.

The null hypothesis is stated in terms of the independence of the two variables, undergraduate major and career preference.

TABLE 20.4

Table of frequencies relating undergraduate major to career preference (hypothetical data)*

| | | Undergraduate Major | | |
		Economics	Psychology	Total students
	Applied	45	55	100
		(40)	(60)	
Career Preference	Academic	27	53	80
		(32)	(48)	
	Total	72 +	108 =	180

			Calculations	
f_o	f_e	$f_o - f_e$	$(f_o - f_e)^2$	$\dfrac{(f_o - f_e)^2}{f_e}$
45	40	5	25	.625
55	60	−5	25	.417
27	32	−5	25	.781
53	48	5	25	.521
				$\chi^2 = 2.344$

*Within each cell, f_o is in the upper-left-hand corner and f_e is in parentheses.

H_0: major and career preference are independent (*not* related)

H_1: major and career preference *are* related

The expected frequencies are those of Table 20.3—the frequencies predicated on the independence of the two variables. The procedure for computing the expected frequencies can be summarized as follows: for any cell, the expected value is equal to the product of the two marginal frequencies common to the cell (the row total times the column total) divided by the total N. That is,

$$f_e = \frac{(\text{row total})(\text{column total})}{N}$$

For example, in Table 20.4, the expected frequency for the econ-applied cell is equal to

$$\frac{(100)(72)}{180} = 40$$

Precisely 72/180 or 40.00% of the sample are economics majors, and 100/180 or 55.56% of the sample prefer applied careers. So 40.00% of 55.56% or 22.22% of the 180 cases, or $(72/180)(100/180)(180) = 40$ of them, would be expected to be economics majors preferring applied careers if there were no relationship between major and career preference in the sample. The other f_e values may be found by the same rationale.

The computation of χ^2 is shown in Table 20.4. The resulting value of 2.34 is tested for statistical significance by referring to Table H in the Appendix with the proper df. For a two-variable problem, the df are equal to

$$df = (r - 1)(c - 1),$$

where

$$r = \text{number of rows}$$

$$c = \text{number of columns}$$

For the 2×2 table, the df are equal to $(2 - 1)(2 - 1) = 1$. The reason why there is one degree of freedom in a 2×2 table is as follows: Consider the expected frequency of 40 for the econ-applied cell. Having computed this value, the expected frequency for the psych-applied cell is fixed (not free to vary). This is because the total of the expected frequencies in the first row of the table, like the total of the observed frequencies, must add up to 100—the marginal frequency for that row. Thus, the expected frequency for the psych-applied cell is equal to

$$100 - 40 = 60$$

Similarly, the expected values in the first column must add up to the marginal frequency of 72. Having computed the expected value of 40 for the econ-applied cell, the expected frequency for the econ-academic cell is fixed; it must be

$$72 - 40 = 32$$

Finally, the expected frequency for the psych-academic cell is equal to

$$108 - 60 = 48$$

Thus, once any one f_e is known, all the others are automatically determined. In other words, only one f_e is free to vary; the values of the others depend upon its value. Therefore, the 2×2 table has one degree of freedom.

In a larger table, all but one of the values f_e in a given row or column are free to vary. Once they are specified, the last one is fixed by virtue of the fact that the expected frequencies must add up to the marginal frequency. An illustration of the degrees of freedom for a 4×3 table is shown in Figure 20.2.

Returning to the problem in Table 20.4, the minimum value of χ^2 required to reject H_0 for $df = 1$ and $\alpha = .05$ is 3.84. Since the obtained value of 2.34 is less than the tabled value, you retain the null hypothesis and conclude that

FIGURE 20.2

Illustration of degrees of freedom for a 4 × 3 table

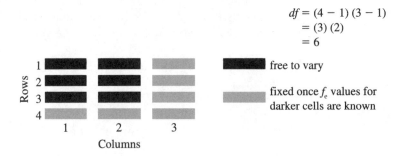

$$df = (4 - 1)(3 - 1)$$
$$= (3)(2)$$
$$= 6$$

■■■■ free to vary

▬▬▬▬ fixed once f_e values for darker cells are known

there is not sufficient reason to believe that the variables of undergraduate major and career preference are related.

Computing Formula for 2 × 2 Tables

For a 2 × 2 table, the following formula for χ^2 is equivalent to the one given previously and requires somewhat less work computationally:

Observed frequencies:

A	B
C	D

$$\chi^2 = \frac{N(AD - BC)^2}{(A + B)(C + D)(A + C)(B + D)}$$

As an illustration, consider the following 2 × 2 table:

50	70	120
19	41	60

69   111   180 = N

$$\chi^2 = \frac{180(50 \times 41 - 70 \times 19)^2}{(120)(60)(69)(111)}$$

$$= \frac{(180)(720)^2}{(120)(60)(69)(111)}$$

$$= 1.692$$

We leave it as an exercise for the reader to apply the 2 × 2 shortcut formula to the data in Table 20.4, and verify that it yields the same chi-square value as the longer method shown in that table.

Two-Way Chi-Square Example with Multiple Levels for Both Variables

The chi-square statistical procedure discussed in this section can be used for two-variable problems with any number of levels for each variable. To illustrate, consider a new environmental treatment that is designed to improve the general mental health of all inpatient psychiatric patients and facilitate the effectiveness of whatever other treatments they are receiving. (The environmental treatment could involve redecorating the ward in cheerful colors, playing soothing music, or even releasing pleasant aromas.) Suppose that this environmental manipulation is implemented in a large psychiatric facility in which 300 patients reside: 138 have been diagnosed with schizophrenia, 88 with bipolar disorder, 42 with major depressive disorder, and 32 with borderline personality disorder. After three months of living in the new environment, each patient is assessed by the hospital staff as having either improved, remained the same, or worsened with respect to his or her state of mental health. The (hypothetical) data for this experiment, along with the calculations needed to obtain the chi-square statistic, are displayed in Table 20.5.

As in the 2×2 chi-square design, the expected frequency for a given cell is obtained by multiplying the row total for the cell by the column total, and dividing by the total N. For example, f_e for the first (i.e., upper-left) cell is

TABLE 20.5
Table of frequencies relating treatment response to psychiatric diagnosis

Response	Psychiatric diagnosis				Row total
	Schizophrenic	Bipolar	Depressed	Borderline	
Improved	36	8	14	2	60
No change	84	72	18	26	200
Worse	18	8	10	4	40
Column Total	138	88	42	32	300

Calculations				
f_o	f_e	$f_o - f_e$	$(f_o - f_e)^2$	$\dfrac{(f_o - f_e)^2}{f_e}$
36	27.60	8.40	70.56	2.56
8	17.60	−9.60	92.16	5.24
14	8.40	5.60	31.36	3.73
2	6.40	−4.40	19.36	3.02
84	92.00	−8.00	64.00	.70
72	58.67	13.33	177.69	3.03
18	28.00	−10.00	100.00	3.57
26	21.33	4.67	21.81	1.02
18	18.40	−0.40	.16	0.01
8	11.73	−3.73	13.91	1.19
10	5.60	4.40	19.36	3.46
4	4.27	−0.27	.07	.02
				$\chi^2 = 27.55$

$$\frac{(60)(138)}{300} = 27.60.$$

The computed value of χ^2 of 27.55 (see bottom of Table 20.5) exceeds the tabled value for $(r-1)(c-1) = (3-1)(4-1)$ or 6 df of 12.59 at the .05 level of significance. So you can reject H_0, and conclude that psychiatric diagnosis and response to the new environment *are* related.

Note that if you ignore the middle row of the data ("No change") you could perform a sign test on the row totals to determine whether, across all diagnoses, patients were more likely to improve than to worsen. You could also perform sign tests for each diagnosis separately, but if you perform a two-way (4×2) chi-square test (without the middle row), you accomplish something that the sign test cannot do. You are testing the differences in the proportions of improvement among the four diagnoses against the null hypothesis that all four proportions are equal to each other (not that they are equal to .5). Adding the middle category of "No change" complicates the interpretation of the results, but it also gives you greater power to detect differences among the diagnostic groups.

If you perform smaller chi-square tests for follow-up purposes, you should use the Bonferroni correction. That is, the alpha you use for each of these tests should be .05 divided by the number of follow-up tests you plan to conduct.

One important application of the chi-square test is as an alternative to a parametric test when quantitative data has a very unusual distribution. (For example, it has multiple modes, or extreme outliers on one or both ends of the distribution.) For the environmental experiment just described, the researcher may have collected clinical ratings for each patient at the beginning and end of the 3-month period, with plans to perform a one-way ANOVA to compare the patient groups on the difference scores. However, the difference scores may be distributed so strangely that the researcher feels more comfortable simply categorizing those differences as exhibiting some improvement, some decline, or virtually no change at all. Considerable statistical power can be lost when converting precise measurements to just a few categories, but this conversion is justified (and even encouraged) if your data seriously violate the assumptions that underlie the planned parametric test. By just ignoring such violations you would be likely to commit a higher rate of Type I errors than the alpha you are using would indicate.

Measures of Strength of Association in Two-Variable Tables

The χ^2 test of independence allows you to make decisions about *whether* there is a relationship between two variables, using frequency data. Thus, if H_0 is rejected, you conclude that there *is* a statistically significant relationship between the two variables. As we pointed out in Chapter 14, however, statistical significance does not indicate the *strength* of the relationship; a significant result suggests only that the relationship in the population is unlikely to be zero. Here again, it is very desirable to have a measure of the strength of the relationship—that is, an index of the degree of correlation. We will discuss such a measure next.

The Phi Coefficient (ϕ) for 2 × 2 Tables

Recall that the chi-square statistic was not statistically significant for the relationship between undergraduate major and type of career preference. Suppose, however, that the researcher, undeterred, collects data for twice as many students, and the results come out proportionally the same as they did in Table 20.4. That is, the frequency in every individual cell is doubled as well. The data for these 360 students are shown in Table 20.6.

Using the convenient shortcut formula for 2 × 2 tables, we find that not only have N and all of the observed frequencies doubled, but the value for χ^2 is also exactly twice as large as it was in Table 20.4. This new value for χ^2 is now statistically significant: $4.688 > 3.84$. Does it seem reasonable that increasing N, without changing the proportions, should turn a nonsignificant result into one that *is* significant?

Just like t or F, χ^2 depends on sample size; it tells you about statistical significance, but says nothing about the size of the effect. To resolve this difficulty, you need a measure of the strength of the relationship between two dichotomous variables that depends only on the proportions, and does not change just because every frequency is, for instance, doubled. Such a measure does exist, and it is easy to calculate. For a 2 × 2 table, χ^2 can be converted to a correlation coefficient called the *phi coefficient* (symbolized by ϕ), where

$$\phi = \sqrt{\frac{\chi^2}{N}}.$$

TABLE 20.6

Table of frequencies relating undergrad major to career preference

		Undergraduate major		
		Economics	Psychology	Total students
Career preference	Applied	90	110	200
	Academic	54	106	160
	Total	144	216	360 = N

$$\chi^2 = \frac{360[(90 \times 106) - (110 \times 54)]^2}{200 \times 160 \times 144 \times 216} = \frac{4,665,600,000}{995,328,000}$$

$$= 4.688$$

Thus, for the data in Table 20.6,

$$\phi = \sqrt{\frac{4.688}{360}}$$

$$= \sqrt{.013}$$

$$= .114$$

If you compare Table 20.4 to Table 20.6, you will see that N gets doubled (from 180 to 360), but so does χ^2 (from 2.344 to 4.688). Because 4.688/360 equals 2.344/180, the ratio under the square root sign in the formula for ϕ does not change (it remains .013), and therefore ϕ is also .114 for the original data in Table 20.4.

The phi coefficient is interpreted as a Pearson r. In fact, it *is* a Pearson r; you would get the same answer of .114 if you assigned scores of 0 and 1 to major (for example, 0 = economics, 1 = psychology) and to career preference (0 = prefers academia, 1 = prefers an applied career), and then computed the correlation between the two variables using the usual formula for the Pearson r given in Chapter 12. Thus the absolute value of ϕ varies between 0 and 1. The larger the value of ϕ, the stronger is the relationship between the two variables. When the assignment of score values is arbitrary (as it is in the present case; it would be just as acceptable to score 1 for economics majors and 0 for psychology majors), the sign of ϕ is irrelevant, and ϕ is therefore reported without sign. Just as with the point-biserial r, you must look at the data to determine the direction of the findings (in our example, that the proportion of economics majors who prefer applied to academic careers is greater than that proportion for psychology majors).

In the present example, you would conclude from the value of ϕ that the relationship between major and career preference in the population, while likely to be greater than zero, is also likely to be fairly weak. In other words, there are likely to be numerous exceptions to the conclusion. This is evidenced, for instance, by the 54 out of 144 economics majors who expressed a preference for an academic career (see Table 20.6). Phi sums up this information conveniently in a readily interpretable correlation.

Note that there is no need to carry out a special significance test for ϕ. It has already been done with χ^2. In fact, the χ^2 test on a 2 × 2 table can just as well be viewed as testing the null hypothesis that the population ϕ value equals zero. When χ^2 is sufficiently large, this hypothesis is rejected, which obviously suggests that there is some degree of relationship other than zero.

Cramér's Phi Coefficient (ϕ_c)

When one (or both) of the two categorical variables whose relationship you are exploring has more than two levels, you cannot simply assign arbitrary numbers to their levels and calculate a Pearson r. The magnitude of the r will depend on how you assign the arbitrary numbers to the levels of any variable with more than two categories, so it will be uninterpretable. However, there is a strength-of-relationship index that is very similar to the phi coefficient and can be used with tables larger than 2×2. It is known as Cramér's ϕ, sometimes symbolized as ϕ_C. It is applicable to any $r \times c$ contingency table, and always varies between 0 and 1 regardless of the size of the table. It is simply

$$\text{Cramér's } \phi = \sqrt{\frac{\chi^2}{N(k-1)}},$$

where

$$k = \text{smaller of } r \text{ or } c \text{ (or, when } r = c, k = r = c)$$

For the example in Table 20.5, which is a 3×4 table,

$$\phi_C = \sqrt{\frac{27.55}{300(3-1)}}$$
$$= \sqrt{.0459}$$
$$= .21$$

This degree of relationship is somewhere between small and moderate in size.

Summary

Chi square is used with *frequency* data.

$$\chi^2 = \sum \frac{(f_o - f_e)^2}{f_e},$$

where

$$f_o = \text{observed frequency}$$
$$f_e = \text{expected frequency}$$

1. One-variable Problems

$$df = k - 1,$$

where

$$k = \text{number of categories of the variable}$$

Expected frequencies are readily determined from the null hypothesis. For example, if H_0 specifies that subjects in the population are equally divided among the k categories, f_e for each category is equal to N/k (where N = number of subjects in the sample).

2. Two-variable Problems: Test of Association

$$df = (r - 1)(c - 1),$$

where

$$r = \text{number of rows}$$

$$c = \text{number of columns}$$

For a cell in a given row and column, the expected frequency is equal to

$$f_e = \frac{(\text{row total})(\text{column total})}{N}$$

For a 2×2 table, the following formula for χ^2 is equivalent to determining expected frequencies and using the usual formula, and requires somewhat less work computationally:

$$\begin{array}{|c|c|} \hline A & B \\ \hline C & D \\ \hline \end{array} \quad \chi^2 = \frac{N(AD - BC)^2}{(A + B)(C + D)(A + C)(B + D)}$$

3. Measures of Strength of Association in Two-variable Tables

For 2×2 *tables*, compute the phi coefficient:

$$\phi = \sqrt{\frac{\chi^2}{N}}$$

ϕ is interpreted as a Pearson r.
For *larger tables*, compute Cramér's ϕ:

$$\text{Cramér's } \phi = \sqrt{\frac{\chi^2}{N(k - 1)}},$$

where

k = the *smaller* of r (number of rows) or c (number of columns);

k = either one if $r = c$

These two measures are statistically significant if χ^2 is statistically significant.

4. Some Precautions on the Use of χ^2

χ^2 should be used only when the observations are independent—that is, when no observation is related to or dependent upon any other observation. The significance test of χ^2 is not sufficiently accurate when either of the following conditions applies:

(a) $df = 1$, and any *expected* frequency is less than 5.

(b) $df = 2$, and any *expected* frequency is less than 3.

Exercises

1. Out of 100 psychiatric patients given a new form of treatment, 60 improved, while 40 got worse.

   (a) Use a chi-square test to decide whether you can reject the null hypothesis that the treatment is totally ineffective (i.e., that patients are equally likely to improve or get worse).

   (b) Redo the significance test in part (a) using the z score formula (i.e., normal approximation) for the binomial test. Explain the relationship between the z score you calculated in this part and the χ^2 value you calculated in part (a).

2. A developmental researcher has observed that in a random sample of 60 toddlers, 27 preferred blue toys, 19 preferred red toys, and 14 preferred green toys. Perform a chi-square test of the null hypothesis that, in the entire population of toddlers, the preference for these three colors is equally divided.

3. Repeat the previous exercise, except that this time there are 79 toddlers choosing among toys that come in a total of four different colors. The number of toddlers preferring each color is as follows:

   (a) 21 chose red, 14 chose blue, 26 chose yellow, 18 chose green.

   (b) The same toddlers were tested a year later with the following results: 28 chose red, 20 chose blue, 9 chose yellow, 22 chose green.

4. At University A, the typical grade distribution is A, 15%; B, 25%; C, 45%; D, 10%; F, 5%. The grades given by two professors are shown here. For each one (separately), test the null hypothesis that the professor is a typical grader, using a one-variable chi-square analysis.

	(a) Professor 1						(b) Professor 2				
	A	B	C	D	F		A	B	C	D	F
f_o	7	13	22	4	6		13	12	8	3	3

5. A psychologist wants to test the hypothesis that college women will do better on a particular type of problem-solving task than will college men. He obtains the following results:

	Result on problem-solving task	
Sex	Succeed	Fail
Male	12	18
Female	10	10

(a) Test the null hypothesis that sex and success on the problem-solving task are independent. Does this mean the same as a statement about whether or not the percent success differs between males and females?

(b) Calculate the phi coefficient for these data. Does it look like the psychologist is dealing with a small, medium, or large effect?

6. A bond issue is to be put before the voters in a forthcoming election. An opinion poll company obtains a random sample of 200 registered voters and asks them what party they belong to and how they intend to vote on the bond issue. The results are as follows:

	Prospective vote on bond issue		
Political party	Yes	No	Undecided
Democratic	20	30	10
Republican	30	30	20
Independent	10	40	10

(a) Test the null hypothesis that political party and prospective vote on the bond issue are independent. What is your conclusion?

(b) Calculate Cramér's ϕ for these data. Does it look like there's a strong association between party affiliation and attitude toward this particular bond issue?

7. Suppose that students majoring in the natural sciences, social sciences, and humanities were asked whether they were in favor of having greater student participation in academic decisions at their college. The data from the survey appear in the following table.

	Natural sciences	Social sciences	Humanities
In favor	20	18	16
Neutral	8	8	30
Against	6	19	18

(a) Compute the two-way chi-square test for these data. Can you reject the null hypothesis that students' attitudes on this question are not at all related to their academic areas? What critical value did you use to make your decision?

(b) Calculate the appropriate measure for the strength of relationship between the two variables, regardless of your decision in part (a). How strong does the relationship appear to be?

8. Repeat the previous exercise with the data in the following table. Note that the marginal frequencies have not changed, so you do not have to recompute the expected frequencies.

	Natural sciences	Social sciences	Humanities
In favor	11	17	26
Neutral	10	15	21
Against	13	13	17

(a) Now can you reject the null hypothesis that students' attitudes on this question are not at all related to their academic areas?

(b) Calculate the appropriate measure for the strength of relationship between the two variables, regardless of your decision in part (a). How strong does the relationship appear to be?

Thought Questions

1. A researcher wants to test the null hypothesis that three popular television shows are preferred equally by college students. She obtains a sample of 139 college students and finds that 57 prefer *Lost*, 44 prefer *Monday Night Football*, and 38 prefer *Desperate Housewives*. What statistical procedure should be used to test this null hypothesis? Why?

2. The same researcher wants to test the relationship between gender differences and preference for the three television shows. For the data in question 1, she finds the following: Of the 57 students who prefer *Lost*, 29 are female and 28 are male. Of the 44 who prefer *Monday Night Football*, 9 are female and 35 are male. Of the 38 who prefer *Desperate Housewives*, 30 are female and 8 are male. What statistical procedure should be used to test this null hypothesis? Why?

3. Suppose that the same researcher asks the 139 students to vote yes or no as to whether they like each of the three television shows and obtains the following results: For *Lost*, 92 yes and 47 no, for *Monday Night Football*, 61 yes and 78 no, for *Desperate Housewives*, 74 yes and 65 no. What type of chi-

square analysis should be used to analyze these data, if any? What assumption of chi-square tests is being violated in this example? Explain.

4. To use chi square for a one-variable problem, what is the minimum value that the expected frequencies must equal for: (a) 1 df? (b) 2 df? (c) 3 or more df?

5. (a) When using chi square for a two-variable problem, why is it desirable to compute either the phi coefficient or Cramér's phi coefficient when statistically significant results are obtained? (b) When should each of the coefficients in part (a) be used?

Computer Exercises

1. (a) Perform a one-way chi-square test to determine whether you can reject the null hypothesis that, at Sara's university, there are the same number of students majoring in each of the five areas represented in Sara's class, if you assume that Sara's students represent a random sample with respect to major area.

   (b) Perform the test in part (a) separately for both the males and the females in Sara's class.

2. Suppose that Sara obtains registration information from her university, and finds that the numbers of undergraduates who have declared each of the five majors are as follows: psychology, 400; pre-med, 310; biology, 270; sociology, 140; economics, 240. Can you reject the null hypothesis that Sara's statistics class is a random sample from the undergraduate population of her university?

3. Conduct a two-way chi-square analysis of Sara's data to test the null hypothesis that the proportion of females is the same for each of the five represented majors in the entire university population. Request a statistic to describe the strength of the relationship between gender and major.

4. Conduct a two-way chi-square analysis of Sara's data to test the null hypothesis that the (two-valued) grouping variable you created from a median split of the phobia scores is independent of gender. Request the phi coefficient for this relationship. Use your software to compute the correlation directly between the high/low phobia variable and gender, and compare this value to the phi coefficient.

5. Create a grouping variable that equals 1 if a student has taken no more than one college math course prior to registering for statistics and 2 if the student has taken two or more math courses. Test whether taking more than one prior math course is independent of a student's major. Request a statistic to describe the strength of the relationship between these two variables.

Bridge to SPSS

The Analyze menu selection that SPSS uses to access one-way chi-square tests bears no resemblance to the menu selection that leads to a two-way chi-square test. It is not obvious why this is so, but both types of the test are easily obtained, as described next.

One-Way Chi-Square Tests

If one of your variables has been coded with at least two different numerical values, you can perform a one-way chi-square test on that variable by selecting **Chi-Square** from the Analyze/Nonparametric Tests menu. The chi-square test dialog box is very similar to the one for the binomial test, but by necessity there are two major differences. First, replacing the Define Dichotomy choice is the selection of the Expected Range. As in the Define Dichotomy choice, the default setting is **Get from data.** In the chi-square test, this setting means that the number of categories for your one-way chi-square test (i.e., k) will be determined by the number of different values that SPSS reads for a variable that you selected (i.e., moved to the Test Variable list). The values of your test variable can be numeric codes that have been arbitrarily assigned to your categories (e.g., 1 = African American; 2 = European American; 3 = Asian American; etc.). However, the values can be real integer quantities, such as the number of children in a family. If there are quite a few possible values and you want to set some limits to avoid extreme values that occur quite infrequently, you can accomplish that by selecting **Use specified range** instead of **Get from data** and entering both upper and lower limits.

The second major difference from the binomial test is that Test Proportion is replaced by Expected Values. The default choice is **All categories equal,** and in the two-category case, this is equivalent to the binomial test's default Test Proportion of .5. This choice is often appropriate for experimental null hypotheses in which you want to see if some categorical distinction makes a difference to, or is even noticed by, your participants—for example, are people who find a wallet on the street (placed by a hidden experimental observer) more likely to return the wallet if it appears that the owner is poor, middle-class, or wealthy? The other choice for Expected Values is to actually type in your expected frequencies for all of the possible values of your test variable. You must add your f_e's to the Values box starting with the category with the lowest numerical value, and working your way up to the highest. For example, if you have coded right-handers as 1, left-handers as 2, and truly ambidextrous persons as 3, and the corresponding population proportions are 80%, 15%, and 5%, and your total N is 60, you would enter the following expected values in this order: 48, 9, and 3 (i.e., $.8 \times 60$, $.15 \times 60$, and $.05 \times 60$).

The basic output from the chi-square test consists of two boxes: one containing the observed and expected frequencies for each category (plus the residual, which is just $f_o - f_e$), and one containing the chi-square statistic. In addition to printing the value for χ^2 and its degrees of freedom $(k - 1)$, the latter box contains the p value for your test. This p value is labeled as **Asymp. Sig.** (asymptotic significance) to remind you that this is the area in the tail of the chi-square distribution that is beyond your computed χ^2 value. **Asymp. Sig.** is not an exact value from the appropriate multinomial distribution, but an approximation analogous to the normal approximation to the binomial distribution. That is why SPSS tells you, under this box, how many cells have f_e's less than 5. The chi-square approximation is not very accurate when several cells have f_e's less than 5 (or any cells have f_e's less than 1 or 2).

Two-Way Chi-Square Tests

Surprisingly, the Chi-Square Test dialog box from the Analyze/Nonparametric Tests menu does not accommodate the two-way chi-square test. Even more surprising, perhaps, is that the two-way test is accessed from the Analyze/Descriptive Statistics menu; choose **Crosstabs** (short for *cross-tabulations*) from that list. The descriptive function of **Crosstabs** is that it produces a matrix of rows and columns that makes it easy to see the joint frequencies of two categorical variables—that is, how frequently each possible combination of levels of the two variables is represented in the data set. For example, if you were to move *gender* to the Row space and *major* to the Column space, and then click **OK,** you would get a matrix with two rows (one for each gender) and five columns (one for each of the five majors represented in Sara's class). In each of the 10 cells of the matrix would be the number of students who fell into the two particular categories represented by that cell (e.g., female psychology majors). To test the null hypothesis that the two variables are independent of each other (i.e., not associated at all), click on the **Statistics** button.

The first choice (upper-left corner) in the Crosstabs: Statistics dialog box is **Chi-square.** This selection will give you the two-way chi-square statistic discussed in this chapter (it is called *Pearson chi-square,* after its originator, Karl Pearson), and its p value, which is labeled **Asymp. Sig.** for reasons we have already explained in the context of the one-way chi-square test (we cannot explain why it is also labeled as 2-sided, as this does not make sense in this context and therefore appears to be a labeling error on the part of SPSS). Two alternative statistics are included in the output box, but they are not needed for the simple cases we have been describing in this chapter, and will not be explained here. When both of your variables are dichotomous, two other statistics are added to the output box. The one labeled **Continuity Correction** is the same as the chi-square statistic, but made somewhat smaller by an adjustment analogous to the one described for SPSS's binomial test, when N is greater than 25. The other, **Fisher's Exact Test,** is based on the multinomial distribution rather than a chi-square approximation (it is analogous to SPSS's binomial test when N is 25 or less).

To obtain a measure of effect size from the Crosstabs: Statistics dialog box, you will want to check the second choice under **Nominal,** which is labeled **Phi**

and Cramér's V. Phi is the phi coefficient as described in this chapter, and Cramér's V is what we have been calling Cramér's ϕ. SPSS does not allow you to request only one of these statistics; you must request both or neither, even though they will yield identical results, unless *both* of your variables have more than two categories. In the latter case (i.e., when the two measures diverge), you should use Cramér's V, rather than phi, as your measure of effect size.

Chapter 21
Tests for Ordinal Data

PREVIEW

Introduction

What are the advantages and disadvantages of using ordinal tests?

What are some important considerations about significance tests based on ranks?

The Difference between the Locations of Two Independent Samples: The Rank-Sum Test

What are the procedures for testing the hypothesis that two independent samples of ranked data come from populations with equal locations?

What is the power efficiency of the rank-sum test?

When should the rank-sum test be used in place of the t test for two independent sample means?

How do we convert a significant result to a measure of strength of relationship?

Differences among the Locations of Two or More Independent Samples: The Kruskal-Wallis H Test

What are the procedures for testing the hypothesis that three or more independent samples of ranked data come from populations with equal locations?

What is the power efficiency of the Kruskal-Wallis H test?

When should the Kruskal-Wallis H test be used in place of the one-way analysis of variance?

What is the protected rank-sum test?

How do we convert a significant result to a measure of strength of relationship?

The Difference between the Locations of Two Matched Samples: The Wilcoxon Test

What are the procedures for testing the hypothesis that two matched samples of ranked data come from populations with equal values for location?

What is the power efficiency of the Wilcoxon test?

When should the Wilcoxon test be used in place of the matched t test?

How do we convert a significant result to a measure of strength of relationship?

The Relationship between Two Ranked Variables: The Spearman Rank-Order Correlation Coefficient

What is the procedure for computing the correlation between two variables when both consist of ranked data? When would you want to compute the Spearman correlation instead of the ordinary Pearson r?

(continued next page)

Introduction

In this chapter, we will consider some tests that are parallel to the t and F tests, but are applied to ordinal data and are both nonparametric and distribution-free. There are two main types of situations that give rise to ordinal data, and that may therefore call for such tests.

Suppose we can determine if one object has a greater amount of a continuous variable than another object, but we cannot measure this variable with any precision. For example, it may be reasonable to conclude that some junior executives at a given company have strong, moderate, or weak leadership qualities, without being able to quantify leadership much more precisely. To use the ordinal statistical procedures discussed in this chapter, we must at least be able to place all of the junior executives in order (i.e., to *rank* them) according to each one's amount of leadership ability. It is acceptable for some of the executives to be tied at the same rank, but a very high percentage of ties would make these procedures inappropriate.

Alternatively, the dependent variable may have already been measured on a precise, quantitative scale, but the distribution of the scores strongly violates the usual assumptions of parametric tests. The advantage of ordinal tests in these situations is that they do not require the population being sampled to be normally distributed. When we discussed the assumption of normality in connection with t and F tests, we stated that these tests were robust; moderate departures from normality of distributions did not seriously affect their validity. But it is not at all rare in the behavioral sciences to encounter data that are grossly nonnormally distributed. Consider, for example, a typical distribution of reaction times: the bulk of the reaction times will be fairly close to zero, a fair number will be relatively long, but none can be less than zero. Thus the distribution is quite asymmetrical, and therefore necessarily substantially *non*normal. So when we have reason to believe that some population distributions depart greatly from normality, ordinal methods (which require no assumption about population distribution shape) can be desirable. These methods do generally assume, however, that the population distributions being compared have the *same* shape and variability.

Of course, it is easy to rank order data that have already been measured precisely. However, whereas the original scores may be at varying distances from each other, their ranks are always one unit apart. Thus, measurement information is lost when scores are transformed to ranks. For example, suppose that the three lowest IQs of 72, 83, and 85 in a particular sample are converted into ranks of 1, 2, and 3. It is no longer possible to tell that the lowest IQ was well below the other two, or that the IQs ranked second and third were quite close in value. Thus, a considerable loss of the original interval information may occur. The ordinal tests discussed in this chapter compensate for this loss of information by being distribution-free, while suffering only a modest loss of power.

The Power Efficiency of Statistical Tests

It may have occurred to you to ask, "Why *ever* use parametric tests, which make normality assumptions about unobservable population distributions, when ordinal tests with nearly as much power are available? After all, one can never *know* that the shape of a population distribution is normal." The answer is that it can be quite costly to run subjects, and when populations are normally distributed, the sample size required by the parametric test (N_p) is smaller than that required by an alternative distribution-free test (N_d) in order to obtain the same amount of power. The ratio of these sample sizes expressed as a percent, or $(N_p/N_d) \times 100\%$, is called the *power efficiency* of the distribution-free test. Suppose that for a given difference between population means, a given significance criterion, α, and a specified power, a certain ordinal test requires a total sample of $N_d = 80$ cases. Its parametric alternative, however, requires only $N_p = 72$ cases. The power efficiency of the ordinal test would be $72/80 = 90\%$, so the parametric test requires only 90% as many cases to have the same probability of rejecting the null hypothesis.

When populations are normally distributed, the power efficiencies of ordinal tests are almost always less than 100%. This means that they require more cases in order to have the same power. Consequently, they have less power for the same number of cases. For this reason, you should *not* rush to use ordinal tests unless substantial nonnormality is believed to exist in the population. This is especially true when you are using two-tailed tests and when the sample sizes are *not* very small (say, 20 or more). But if you do have good reason to believe that a population distribution departs substantially from normality, or your data is already in the form of ranks or ordered categories (e.g., very small, small, moderate, etc.), an appropriate ordinal test should be chosen.

The Basics of Dealing with Data in the Form of Ranks

Among the most important and useful ordinal tests are those that deal with differences in *location* between populations, based on ranks. Recall from Chapter 4 that *location* is a general term describing where a distribution falls, often called its *central tendency*. In parametric statistics, the location of a population or sample is customarily indexed by its mean. When we conclude from a *t* test that scores in population 1 are larger than those in population 2, we mean literally that $\mu_1 > \mu_2$. But with ordinal tests, the same statement has a different meaning: if we draw at random a case from population 1 and another from population 2 and compare them, and do this repeatedly, more than half the time the case from population 1 will be larger than the case from population 2 (technically, population 1 is stochastically larger than population 2). This can be taken for all intents and purposes as an assertion that $\text{Mdn}_1 > \text{Mdn}_2$.

As previously mentioned, significance tests based on ranks are used when the original data come in the form of ranks (a relatively rare occurrence), or after a set of scores has been converted into ranks for the purpose of performing the test. In converting a set of *N* scores to ranks, it is customary to assign rank 1 to the smallest observation and rank *N* to the largest. If ties occur, the mean of the ranks in question is assigned to each of the tied scores.

What makes tests based on ranks work so simply is the fact that the data for any problems involving a total of *N* cases (where there are no ties) are the positive integers $1, 2, 3, \ldots, N$. Thus statistical functions of these data are simple functions of *N*. For example, it can easily be proved that the *sum* of the first *N* integers (ranks 1 to *N*) is as follows:

$$\sum R = 1 + 2 + 3 + \ldots + N$$
$$= \frac{N(N + 1)}{2}$$

Suppose that there are a total of 22 cases. Whatever their original raw scores may be, the sum of their *ranks* must be $(22)(23)/2 = 253$. And since the mean is equal to the sum divided by *N*, it therefore follows that the mean of a complete set of ranks (symbolized by $\bar{R}$) is equal to

$$\bar{R} = \frac{\sum R}{N}$$
$$= \frac{N(N + 1)}{2N}$$
$$= \frac{N + 1}{2}$$

Thus, the mean rank for 22 observations is simply $23/2 = 11.5$. The mean rank can be thought of as the expected rank of a case drawn at random from the *N* ranks, in the sense that the mean is the best guess as to the value of this case. Therefore, if we draw two cases at random when $N = 22$, the expected sum of the ranks (symbolized by T_E) is $2(11.5) = 23$. For three cases, it is $3(11.5)$ or 34.5. Generally, if we draw a subset of N_1 cases at random from the total N (N_T), their expected sum of ranks is N_1 times the mean rank:

$$T_E = N_1\bar{R}$$

$$= \frac{N_1(N_T + 1)}{2}$$

It can also be shown that if N_1 cases are randomly and repeatedly drawn from the complete set of N_T ranks, and the sum of the ranks (T) is obtained for each sample, the standard deviation of the resulting sampling distribution of T values (or the *standard error* of T) would be

$$\sigma_T = \frac{N_1 N_2 (N_T + 1)}{12},$$

where

$$\sigma_T = \text{standard error of } T$$

$$N_2 = N_T - N_1$$

The value of 12 in the denominator is a constant, and is not affected by any of the N_T values. Regardless of the shape of the population distribution of raw scores, this sampling distribution of a sum of a subset of ranks is approximately normal in form. This is *not* an assumption, but a provable mathematical property.

There now exist all the ingredients for a statistical test: a sample statistic (T) with a known (in this case, normal) sampling distribution, whose standard deviation is known (σ_T), and a null-hypothetical value (T_E). This leads us into the test of the difference in location between two independent samples. We will subsequently consider two other important applications of location tests based on ranks: a test of the differences in location among more than two independent samples, and a test of the difference in location between two matched (dependent) samples.

The Difference between the Locations of Two Independent Samples: The Rank-Sum Test

The first ordinal test that we will describe is the one that is sometimes used as a nonparametric alternative to the t test of two independent sample means. We begin with an example for which use of the ordinary t test would be questionable.

Rationale and Computational Procedures

Suppose that at the end of the semester Sara decides to use scores on the final exam to compare the performance of her most phobic students (those who rated their math phobia as 10) with that of her least phobic students (those who gave a rating of 0). The final exam scores for the ten least phobic and twelve most phobic students are shown in Table 21.1. As you can see, the normality assumption appears to be quite dubious. Since the samples are also small, a distribution-free test is appropriate.

The most powerful nonparametric test in this situation is known as the *rank-sum test* (sometimes referred to as the Mann-Whitney test). This ordinal statistical procedure is used to test the null hypothesis that two independent samples of ranked data come from populations with the *same* location (i.e., central tendency).

First, all 22 observations are subjected to a single ranking from the lowest ($X = 52$), which is assigned a rank of 1, to the highest ($X = 99$), which is assigned a rank of 22. The X scores are ignored from this point on, and the analysis proceeds solely with the ranks.

The question now is whether the ranks in Group 1 (or Group 2) are generally larger or smaller than one would expect by chance. The sum of the ten

TABLE 21.1
The rank-sum test for two independent samples

Least phobic (Group 1)		Most phobic (Group 2)	
X	R	X	R
55	3	52	1
62	7	53	2
69	11	56	4
78	15	58	5
79	16	60	6
84	18	63	8
92	19	64	9
96	20	65	10
98	21	71	12
99	22	74	13
		76	14
		81	17

$$T_1 = 152 \qquad T_2 = 101$$
$$N_1 = 10 \qquad N_2 = 12$$
$$\bar{R}_1 = \frac{152}{10} \qquad \bar{R}_2 = \frac{101}{12}$$
$$= 15.20 \qquad = 8.2$$

$$N_T = N_1 + N_2 = 22$$
$$\Sigma R = N(N + 1)/2 = (22)(23)/2 = 253$$
$$= T_1 + T_2 = 152 + 101 = 253$$

ranks in Group 1, symbolized by T_1, is 152. According to the null hypothesis, the expected sum of the ranks is

$$T_E = \frac{N_1(N_T + 1)}{2}$$

$$= \frac{(10)(23)}{2}$$

$$= 115$$

Is the observed T_1 of 152 a statistically significant departure from the null-hypothetical (expected) T_E value of 115? The analysis is quite similar to the normal curve procedures for tests about the mean of one population (see Chapter 9):

$$z = \frac{T_1 - T_E}{\sigma_T}$$

$$= \frac{T_1 - T_E}{\sqrt{\dfrac{N_1 N_2 (N_T + 1)}{12}}}$$

Instead of comparing a sample mean ($\overline{X}$) to a null-hypothesized population value (μ) and dividing by the standard error of the mean, as in Chapter 9, you compare the sample rank sum (T_1) to the null-hypothesized expected value (T_E) and divide by the standard error of T. (Remember that the value of 12 in the denominator is a constant, and has no relation to any of the N_T values.) And since the sampling distribution of T is approximately normal, you can determine whether the observed T_1 departs significantly from T_E by using the normal curve model and z.

For the data in Table 21.1, the results are

$$z = \frac{152 - 115}{\sqrt{\dfrac{(10)(12)(23)}{12}}}$$

$$= \frac{37}{15.17}$$

$$= 2.44$$

So the 37 rank-sum units by which Group 1 deviates from T_E place it 2.44 standard error units above the mean of a normal distribution of rank-sums. The computed z value of 2.44 exceeds the critical z value of ± 1.96 (for $\alpha = .05$, two-tailed). So you reject the null hypothesis, and conclude that the ranks in the least phobic group are significantly higher than chance expectation. This in turn implies that the ranks in the most phobic group are significantly lower than chance expectation, and therefore that the ranks for the least phobic students are generally higher than those for the most phobic. You can therefore conclude that the location of the two populations from which these samples were randomly drawn differs on X, with the first population being stochastically higher than the second. A more comprehensible way to say this is that the median of the first (least phobic) population is greater than the median of the second (most phobic) population (i.e., their final exam scores are higher).

It makes no difference which of the two sets of ranks you use to compute T and T_E. For Group 2, $T_2 = 101$, and T_E would now be equal to $(12)(23)/2$ or 138. The value of σ_T is unchanged, so z would equal $(101 - 138)/15.17$ or -2.44. And you would reach exactly the same conclusion, with the minus sign indicating that the group in question (Group 2) is the one with the lower location. Although you need compute only T_1 (or T_2) to carry out the statistical test, it is desirable to calculate both values (and verify that $T_1 + T_2 = N_T[N_T + 1]/2$) as a check against errors in ranking and/or calculating.

The rank-sum test for two samples depends on the fact that the sampling distribution of T is well approximated by the normal curve. This will be true provided that the samples are not too small, say at least 6 to 8 cases in each. With fewer than that, more accurate criterion values are needed, and tables of the small-sample exact distribution values of T (or of the closely related Mann-Whitney U statistic) are then required. This method is not included here because it is relatively rare that differences in location are large enough to be detectable with such small samples. Other statistical refinements, such as a correction for continuity that slightly reduces the absolute size of the numerator of the z formula and a procedure for reducing σ_T to take tied ranks into account, can be found in books devoted to nonparametric statistics, such as the one by Siegel and Castellan (1988).

The parametric analog of the rank-sum test is the t test for two independent sample means (Chapter 11). Relative to the t test, the rank-sum test has power efficiency ranging from 92% for small samples to 95% for large samples. Applying the pooled-variance formula to the final exam scores (X) in Table 21.1 yields a t value of 3.14, which, unlike the z for the corresponding rank-sum test, is significant at the .01 level.

For a given set of conditions, when populations are normally distributed, the same power is obtained using the t test with 92–95% of the sample size that would be required by the rank-sum test. Compared to other nonparametric tests, those based on ranks have fairly high power efficiencies, so they should be used when the normality assumption is in serious doubt. When this is not the case, the behavioral scientist usually cannot afford the luxury of what amounts to throwing away 5–8% of the cases.

Measure of Strength of Relationship: The Glass Rank Biserial Correlation

Throughout this book we have stressed the general insufficiency of merely computing a test of statistical significance, which indicates only whether or not there is some (nonzero) effect in the population, and the desirability of indexing the *strength* of an observed relationship. For example, in the case of the parametric t test for two independent sample means, the point biserial r served as such a measure (Chapter 13). The point biserial r is the product moment (Pearson) correlation between the dichotomous variable, membership in Group 1 or Group 2, and the continuous variable under study.

An analogous measure of the strength of the relationship between the group membership dichotomy and the *rank* values for two groups is provided by the Glass rank biserial correlation coefficient, symbolized by r_G. It is computed using the following formula:

$$r_G = \frac{2(\bar{R}_1 - \bar{R}_2)}{N_T},$$

where

$$\bar{R}_1 = \text{mean of ranks in Group 1}$$
$$\bar{R}_2 = \text{mean of ranks in Group 2}$$
$$N_T = \text{total number of observations}$$

The r_G coefficient is *not* a product moment (Pearson) r computed on the rank values. However, it has the same limits: it may take on values from -1 to $+1$, with its sign depending on which group is called Group 1, and the magnitude is interpreted much like that of any other correlation coefficient. The maximum value of $+1$ or -1 occurs when there is no overlap in ranks between the two groups, with one group containing all the highest ranks while the other group contains all the lowest ranks. (By contrast, r_{pb} equals $+1$ or -1 only when the values within each group are identical, that is, when the variance within each group is zero. This is clearly a higher standard than nonoverlap between groups.)

For the data in Table 21.1, $\bar{R}_1 = 15.20$ and $\bar{R}_2 = 8.42$, and $N_T = 22$. Thus,

$$r_G = \frac{2(15.20 - 8.42)}{22}$$

$$= .62$$

This indicates a fairly high degree of relationship between group membership and ranking on X.

Differences among the Locations of Two or More Independent Samples: The Kruskal-Wallis *H* Test

The next ordinal test we will describe is a fairly common nonparametric replacement for the one-way ANOVA you learned about in Chapter 15.

Rationale and Computational Procedures

When the locations of more than two independent samples are to be compared, a distribution-free test based on ranks is provided by the Kruskal-Wallis H test. This procedure is analogous to the parametric F test of one-way analysis of variance, and it uses the same logic. However, because statistics based on ranks are simple functions of N, the computation of H is much easier than is the computation of F. In fact, H is a simple function of just the sum of squares between groups (SS_B) exactly as defined in Chapter 15, except that SS_B is computed on the ranks instead of the scores. Also, just as the t test is a special case of one-way ANOVA where there are only two groups, the rank-sum test described previously is a special case of the Kruskal-Wallis H test where there are only two groups. That is, when k (the number of groups) is equal to 2, the rank-sum test and the Kruskal-Wallis H test yield the same p values.

By way of illustration, the data from Table 16.1 have been converted into ranks. (See Table 21.2.) The total of $N = 27$ observations have been ranked from the lowest (rank $= 1$) to the highest (rank $= 27$) and organized into $k = 3$ groups, in exactly the same order as they appeared in Table 16.1. Tied scores were assigned mean ranks in the usual manner. For example, there are two scores of 9 that should occupy ranks 5 and 6, and each has been assigned the rank of 5.5 (the mean of 5 and 6). The next highest score, 10 (which is not tied), receives a rank of 7.

The sum of the ranks for each of the k groups is now obtained; $T_1 = 113.5$, $T_2 = 189.5$, and $T_3 = 75$. (To guard against errors in ranking or summing, the

---

TABLE 21.2

The Kruskal-Wallis H test for $k = 3$ independent samples

Natural sciences (Group 1)		Social sciences (Group 2)		Humanities (Group 3)	
X	R	X	R	X	R
15	19	17	21	6	2
18	22	22	27	9	5.5
12	12	5	1	12	12
12	12	15	19	11	8.5
9	5.5	12	12	11	8.5
10	7	20	24	8	4
12	12	14	16.5	13	15
20	24	15	19	14	16.5
		20	24	7	3
		21	26		
$T_1 = 113.5$		$T_2 = 189.5$		$T_3 = 75$	
$N_1 = 8$		$N_2 = 10$		$N_3 = 9$	

$$N_T = N_1 + N_2 + N_3 = 27$$
$$\Sigma R = N_T(N_T + 1)/2 = (27)(28)/2 = 378$$
$$= T_1 + T_2 + T_3 = 113.5 + 189.5 + 75 = 378$$

sum of all T values should be verified as equal to ΣR or $N_T[N_T + 1]/2$, as shown at the bottom of the table.) The next step is to compute the sum of squares between groups, SS_B, for the ranks. Any appropriate ANOVA computing formula may be used, but the following one is particularly convenient in that it capitalizes on the fact that the data are in rank form:

$$SS_B = \frac{T_1^2}{N_1} + \frac{T_2^2}{N_2} + \ldots + \frac{T_k^2}{N_k} - \frac{N_T(N_T + 1)^2}{4}$$

Substituting the values from Table 21.2 gives

$$SS_B = \frac{(113.5)^2}{8} + \frac{(189.5)^2}{10} + \frac{(75)^2}{9} - \frac{27(28)^2}{4}$$

$$= 5826.31 - 5292.00$$

$$= 534.31$$

The final step is to compute the Kruskal-Wallis H statistic:

$$H = \frac{12SS_B}{N_T(N_T + 1)}$$

The value of 12 in the numerator is a constant, and it arises from the fact that the variance of a full set of N untied ranks is equal to $(N + 1)^2/12$. In our example,

$$H = \frac{(12)(534.31)}{(27)(28)}$$

$$= 8.48$$

Under the null hypothesis that the locations of the k populations are identical, H is distributed approximately as χ^2 with $k - 1$ degrees of freedom. Thus the computed H value of 8.48 is referred to Table H of the Appendix, and it is found to be larger than the value of 5.99 that corresponds to the .05 criterion of significance for 2 df. You should therefore reject the null hypothesis that the three populations have equal locations.

The chi-square approximation used to test H for statistical significance is a good one unless the size of any group is very small. If there are no more than three groups, each group should have at least five cases in it; otherwise the Kruskal-Wallis H test should not be used. With more than three groups, as few as two cases in a group are sufficient. The existence of tied ranks tends to make the H test conservative (smaller and less likely to yield statistical significance), but this tendency is slight unless ties are very long and numerous. It is possible to correct for ties, and to perform this test for very small samples (see Siegel &

Castellan [1988]). Finally, as compared to the analogous parametric *F* test in a one-way ANOVA, the *H* test has power efficiency ranging from 90% for small samples to 95% for large samples. The same comments apply here as for the rank-sum test.

Multiple Comparisons: The Protected Rank-Sum Test

We have seen that when the overall *F* test in an analysis of variance is statistically significant, an additional procedure is necessary in order to determine which populations differ significantly. When there are only three groups, as in the preceding example, the protected *t* test (Fisher's LSD method) can be used to serve this purpose. Similarly, if and only if a Kruskal-Wallis *H* is statistically significant, a method called the *protected rank-sum test* may be used to determine which pairs of populations differ significantly in location. As with the protected *t* test, you may perform the pairwise rank-sum tests for three independent samples using an alpha of .05; the tests are protected against a larger experimentwise Type I error rate by the precondition that *H* be significant. (When $k > 3$, a Bonferroni adjustment of alpha is recommended.)

To illustrate, let us return once again to the data in Table 21.2. Since *H* was statistically significant, any or all of the three pairs of groups (1 versus 2, 1 versus 3, or 2 versus 3) may be compared by using the protected rank-sum test. In order to do so, however, *the scores must be reranked for each test.* For example, if Groups 1 and 2 are being compared, the third group is ignored. The third score in Group 2 is ranked 1 (the lowest score), the fifth score in Group 1 is now ranked 2, the score right below this one is now ranked 3, and so on until the highest score in these two groups (the second score in Group 2) receives a rank of 18. Thus $N_1 = 8$, $N_2 = 10$, and $N_T = 18$ for this comparison. Upon reranking it is found that $T_1 = 59.5$ (and $T_2 = 111.5$), $T_E = (8)(19)/2 = 76$, and $\sigma_T = \sqrt{(8)(10)(19)/12} = 11.25$. Therefore, using the formula for the rank-sum test given previously, we have

$$z = \frac{T_1 - T_E}{\sigma_T}$$

$$= \frac{59.5 - 76}{11.25}$$

$$= -1.47$$

This *z* value is not statistically significant. When Group 1 and Group 3 are compared, a nonsignificant *z* value of 1.73 is obtained. But when Group 2 and Group 3 are compared, a statistically significant *z* value of 2.69 results. Therefore the conclusion is that the locations of these three populations are not the same because the location (or median) of population 2 is greater than that of population 3. However, the data do not warrant concluding that the location of population 1 differs from either of the other two.

Measure of Strength of Relationship: η_R^2

A measure of the strength of the relationship between membership in one of the k groups and rank on the dependent variable may be obtained by computing a form of eta squared. This is the same index that was used in connection with one-way ANOVA, but applied to ranks rather than scores. Just as η^2 for scores was a function of F and dfs, so η_R^2 may be found from H, k, and N_T:

$$\eta_R^2 = \frac{H - k + 1}{N_T - k},$$

where

$$k = \text{number of groups}$$

$$N_T = \text{total number of observations}$$

For example, the ranked attitude scores in Table 21.2 yielded an H of 8.48. Therefore, for these data,

$$\eta_R^2 = \frac{(8.48 - 3) + 1}{27 - 3}$$

$$= \frac{6.48}{24}$$

$$= .27$$

For the continuous score data in Table 16.1, η^2 was equal to .298 ($SS_B/SS_T = 170.21/572$)—a quite similar value. This similarity will usually be the case. Thus, by either route we find that the observed relationship in the sample is fairly strong.

Just as the statistical significance of η^2 is automatically given by F, so the significance of η_R^2 is given automatically by H. So as with the other measures of strength of relationship that we have discussed, there is no need to conduct an additional significance test for η_R^2.

The Difference between the Locations of Two Matched Samples: The Wilcoxon Test

The final ordinal test of location we will describe is the nonparametric alternative to the matched-pairs t test. Like the latter test, this ordinal test can be used whether the pairs of scores come from matched participants or the same participant measured twice.

Rationale and Computational Procedures

We saw in Chapter 11 that when a comparison is to be made between the means of two matched or dependent samples, a different procedure is used than when the samples are independent. For each of the N matched pairs, the difference (D) between the X_1 and X_2 values is found, and the null hypothesis tested is that the population mean of the D values is zero. Rejection of this null hypothesis necessarily implies that μ_1 and μ_2 are not equal.

The same distinction applies for the appropriate rank-based test of the difference in location between two samples. The rank-sum test discussed earlier is used with independent samples, while a different technique (called the *Wilcoxon matched-pairs signed ranks test*) is used with dependent samples. The Wilcoxon test also uses $D = X_1 - X_2$ values, but considers only the ranks of the absolute values of these difference scores.

As an example, let us consider an investigation into the question of whether sensitivity training improves extrasensory perception (ESP) scores. A sample of 12 subjects is tested for ESP before (X_2) and again after (X_1) a series of 10 training sessions, and the results are shown in Table 21.3. In this experiment, therefore, the samples are dependent because the two observations in each pair come from the same subject. (It should be noted, however, that this matched design is obtained whenever there is some connection between the observations making up a pair. More exactly, it holds whenever there is a non-zero population correlation between the paired observations.)

The first two columns in Table 21.3 give the posttraining (X_1) and pretraining (X_2) ESP scores for the 12 subjects. The third column shows each subject's

TABLE 21.3

The Wilcoxon test for two matched samples

Subject	X_1	X_2	D $(= X_1 - X_2)$	$R_{|D|}$	$R(+)$	$R(-)$
1	33	38	−5	7		7
2	45	43	+2	2	2	
3	50	42	+8	10	10	
4	45	44	+1	1	1	
5	46	49	−3	3.5		3.5
6	45	41	+4	5.5	5.5	
7	28	22	+6	8	8	
8	43	46	−3	3.5		3.5
9	32	32	0			
10	40	31	+9	11	11	
11	34	27	+7	9	9	
12	40	44	−4	5.5		5.5

$$\Sigma R = 66 \qquad T_1 = 46.5 \qquad T_2 = 19.5$$
$$(= T_1 + T_2)$$

$N = 11$ (deleting subject 9 for whom $D = 0$)

$\Sigma R = N(N + 1)/2 = (11)(12)/2 = 66$

change or difference score, where $D = X_1 - X_2$. The D values are positive when the ESP score has increased following sensitivity training, and negative when it has decreased. As was the case in the parametric matched t test, all further analyses focus on these D scores.

First, all cases where $D = 0$ are dropped. Case 9 in the table is therefore deleted, and the analysis proceeds on the basis of $N = 11$. (For this test, we will let N stand for the number of *pairs*, and not use the symbol N_T.) Then, *ignoring the signs* of the D values, they are rank ordered from the smallest (rank $= 1$) to the largest (rank $= N$), with ties being resolved in the usual way. This has been done in the column for $R_{|D|}$. This results in the familiar set of ranks from 1 to N whose statistical properties are known; for example, their sum must equal $N(N + 1)/2$, which for $N = 11$ is equal to $(11)(12)/2$ or 66.

If the population locations of X_1 and X_2 are the same, then (ignoring pairs where $D = 0$) the sum of the ranks of the absolute D values should be approximately equally divided between those that are positive $(R+)$ and those that are negative $(R-)$. That is, there should be an equal number of cases where $X_1 > X_2$ and where $X_1 < X_2$. Since the sum of *all* the ranks equals $N(N + 1)/2$, the expectation under the null hypothesis is that the sum of the ranks for the positive Ds and the sum of the ranks for the negative Ds will *each* equal half the sum. That is, the expected result under the null hypothesis is

$$T_E = \frac{1}{2} \frac{N(N + 1)}{2}$$

$$= \frac{N(N + 1)}{4}$$

For the data in Table 21.3,

$$T_E = \frac{(11)(12)}{4}$$

$$= 33,$$

which is half of 66, the sum of all the ranks.

In the columns headed $R(+)$ and $R(-)$ in Table 21.3, the $R_{|D|}$ values for positive and negative Ds have been segregated. The sum of the ranks of the positive D values, T_1, is equal to 46.5. The sum of the ranks of the negative D values, T_2, is equal to 19.5. Except as a check, only one of these values is needed, so let us choose $T_1 = 46.5$. This value departs 13.5 rank-sum units from the value expected under the null hypothesis, $T_E = 33$. You are then left with the question of whether or not this departure is sufficiently unlikely to reject the null hypothesis, using (say) the $\alpha = .05$ decision rule.

A method for answering this question can be easily derived. In repeated random sampling, T_1 (and also T_2) is approximately normally distributed when the null hypothesis is true. The standard deviation of the sampling distribution of this matched-pairs signed ranks T (the standard error), symbolized by σ_{T_M}, is

$$\sigma_{T_M} = \sqrt{\frac{(2N + 1)T_E}{6}}$$

Thus we have a sampling distribution that is approximately normal, whose mean is T_E and whose standard deviation is σ_{T_M}, and the null hypothesis of equal positive and negative rank sums. This gives us all the ingredients for a significance test using the normal curve model:

$$z = \frac{T_1 - T_E}{\sigma_{T_M}},$$

$$= \frac{T_1 - T_E}{\sqrt{\dfrac{(2N + 1)T_E}{6}}}$$

For data in Table 21.3, we found that the null hypothesis leads to an expected value of T_1 (and T_2) of $T_E = 33$. The observed $T_1 = 46.5$. Therefore,

$$z = \frac{46.5 - 33}{\sqrt{\dfrac{[(2)(11) + 1](33)}{6}}}$$

$$= \frac{13.5}{\sqrt{\dfrac{(23)(33)}{6}}}$$

$$= 1.20$$

Thus the observed departure of 13.5 rank-sum units from the null-hypothetical expected value of 33 is only a little more than one standard error, and far less than the value of 1.96 needed to reject H_0, using the two-tailed .05 criterion of significance. Therefore, the data do *not* justify the conclusion that 10 sessions of sensitivity training will improve ESP scores in the population from which this sample was randomly drawn. The results do not permit the conclusion that no effect exists, of course, since the probability of a Type II error has not been determined. Only if the population effect were very large would there be a reasonably good chance of rejecting the null hypothesis with such a small sample.

Here again, it does not matter whether T_1 or T_2 is used in the statistical test, since both are necessarily at equal distances from T_E. The only effect of replacing T_1 with T_2 is to change the sign of z.

Relative to the matched t test, the Wilcoxon test has power efficiency ranging from 92% for small samples to 95% for large samples. This means that if the parametric assumptions of the t test for matched samples were valid, our choice of the Wilcoxon test would result in somewhat lower power than the t test would have; our $N = 11$ for the Wilcoxon test is about as powerful as a t test using $N = (.92)(11) = 10$ pairs. (A t test applied to the 12 D values is also not significant; it equals 1.28, very close to the z of 1.20.) Note, however, that the Wilcoxon test should not be used if the sample size is smaller than about 8, since the approximation to normality will then not be sufficiently accurate.

A considerably cruder alternative to both the Wilcoxon and matched-pairs t test is the *sign* test, described in Chapter 19. Applied to the data in Table 21.3, the X value of the sign test is either 4 (the number of negative signs) or 7 (the number of positive signs), N is 11, and P (the null hypothesis) is .5. Because N is too small for the normal approximation to be accurate, the probabilities of the binomial distribution should be added for the X values of 7, 8, 9, 10, 11, and 4, 3, 2, 1 (for a two-tailed test). In this case, it is easier to subtract the probabilities for $X = 5$ and $X = 6$ from 1.0. The exact binomial p value for these data is .549. Note that the two-tailed p value associated with $z = 1.20$ is .230, so it appears that the sign test has much less power than the Wilcoxon test. This is true in general. The sign test ignores virtually all of the quantitative information in the data. Because of this, it has a power efficiency that is usually below 70% with respect to the matched-pairs t test. The sign test should only be used when the difference of each pair cannot be quantified precisely enough for the differences to be ranked but the directions for most of the differences can be determined.

Measure of Strength of Relationship: The Matched-Pairs Rank Biserial Correlation

The matched-pairs rank biserial correlation, symbolized by r_C, expresses the strength of the relationship between condition (such as posttest versus pretest) and the dependent variable. Another way to describe r_C is that it indexes the degree of relationship between the sign of D and its rank. It is computed as follows:

$$r_C = \frac{4(T_1 - T_E)}{N(N + 1)}$$

The r_C index can take on values from -1 to $+1$. It is equal to zero when T_1 does not differ from the null hypothetical value T_E, and it equals ± 1 when all D values have the same sign. It is not a product-moment correlation coefficient, however, but is part of the same system as r_G. The sign of r_C indicates whether the positive or negative sums of ranks is larger.

In Table 18.3, the Wilcoxon test was not statistically significant. Therefore, there is little reason to compute r_C for these data. As a guideline that you may use when you do have statistically significant results that you wish to convert to r_c, however, we will illustrate the calculation of r_c for these data:

$$r_c = \frac{4(46.5 - 33)}{(11)(12)}$$

$$= .41$$

This value cannot be statistically significant, since the Wilcoxon test for the same data did not yield significance. It may be used to describe the relationship within this particular sample, but there is insufficient reason to conclude that the corresponding population correlation is different from zero.

The Relationship between Two Ranked Variables: The Spearman Rank-Order Correlation Coefficient

Thus far, we have looked at ordinal alternatives to the independent-samples t test, one-way ANOVA, and the matched-pairs t test. We now turn our attention to the ordinal alternative to the Pearson r, which is called the *Spearman rank-order correlation coefficient,* symbolized as r_s.[1] As in the case of the ordinal tests previously discussed, r_s is commonly used when a dependent variable has been measured precisely, but its distribution makes the use of parametric tests questionable, and the sample size is not large. Even if only one of the two variables that you are correlating (e.g., IQ and annual income) seems to violate the distributional assumptions of parametric tests, both variables must be converted to ranks in order to calculate r_s. You *cannot* replace one variable with ranks and correlate it with the raw scores of the other variable.

Rationale and Computational Procedures

Suppose you wish to determine the relationship between the IQ scores and incomes of 10 entrepreneurs (as in Table 21.4). The income values are extremely skewed, while the IQ scores appear to have a normal distribution. To compute r_s, you must rank order *both* income *and* IQ. The entrepreneur with the lowest IQ gets a rank of 1 for IQ, the next to lowest is assigned the rank of 2, and so on. These ranks then replace the original IQ scores, which are no longer used. The same procedure is used to determine rank order by income. Finally, r_s is calculated by applying any formula for the Pearson r to the *ranks* rather than to the original scores.

---

1. The Greek letter rho, ρ, is also commonly used to designate the rank-order correlation coefficient. In order to avoid confusion between this statistic and the population parameter for the Pearson correlation coefficient, which is also symbolized by rho, we will use r_s for the Spearman coefficient.

TABLE 21.4

Ten entrepreneurs both measured and ranked for IQ and for annual income (1 = least, 10 = most)

Entrepreneur's first name	IQ score	Ranks for IQ	Annual income (in thousands of dollars)	Ranks for income	D (X – Y)	D² (X – Y)²
John	108	3	97	4	–1	1
Joseph	107	2	72	1	1	1
Martha	114	5	223	6	–1	1
William	124	9	255	7	2	4
Robert	98	1	88	3	–2	4
Sophia	132	10	974	10	0	0
Donald	120	8	650	9	–1	1
Manuel	113	4	85	2	2	4
Richard	117	7	148	5	2	4
Nancy	115	6	403	8	–2	4
						$\Sigma D^2 = 24$

To make sure that your ranks are properly paired, you can start by listing your participants (in any order), along with their scores on both variables. Then list the participants in IQ order in a separate place, and assign ranks. Next to each IQ score in the original table, write the appropriate rank. Again in a separate place, list the participants in order by income and assign ranks, and then write each participant's income rank next to his or her income in the original table (see Table 21.4). You can then apply a Pearson r formula to the two sets of ranks, or use a shortcut formula for r_s after calculating the difference for each pair of ranks and then summing the squared differences, as shown in Table 21.4.

The shortcut formula for the Spearman correlation coefficient is

$$r_s = 1 - \frac{6 \sum D^2}{N(N^2 - 1)},$$

where

$$D = \text{difference between a pair of ranks}$$

$$N = \text{number of pairs}$$

If you applied one of the formulas for the Pearson product moment correlation coefficient (Chapter 12) to rank-order data by treating the ranks as scores, and if there were no tied ranks, you would get exactly the same value for r_s. The shortcut formula for r_s takes advantage of certain relationships that hold when the N scores are the integers from 1 to N.

Like r, then, r_s varies between –1.0 and +1.0. A high positive value of r_s indicates a strong tendency for the paired ranks to be equal. Conversely, a high negative value of r_s indicates a strong tendency for the paired ranks to be opposite, as would occur if entrepreneurs with the higher ranks for IQ were to have the lower ranks for income. A zero value would indicate no relationship between the two sets of ranks.

In our example, the calculation of ΣD^2 is shown in Table 21.4; r_s is equal to

$$r_s = 1 - \frac{6(24)}{10(10^2 - 1)}$$

$$= 1 - \frac{144}{990}$$

$$= 1 - .15$$

$$= .85$$

Dealing with Tied Ranks

In the preceding example, if Joseph and John were equal in IQ both would share second place. This would be expressed numerically by *averaging* the two ranks in question, and assigning this average as the rank of each person. The ranks in question are 2 and 3, so the average of these ranks, or 2.5, is the rank that would be given to both John and Joseph. The next entrepreneur would receive a rank of 4. What if three entrepreneurs were tied for the 4th rank? In this case, ranks 4, 5, and 6 would be averaged, and each of these three participants would receive a rank of 5. The next participant would be ranked 7th.

When there are tied ranks, the above formula will overestimate the absolute value of r_s. But unless there are many ties, and particularly long ties (that is, three- or more-way ties), this overestimate is likely to be trivial (less than .01 or .02).

Testing the Significance of the Rank-Order Correlation Coefficient

Although the formula for r_s and the formula for the Pearson r yield the same numerical result in the absence of tied ranks, the significance of the two coefficients *cannot* be tested in the same manner when N is very small (especially when it is less than 10). To test the null hypothesis that the ranks are independent in the population from which the sample was drawn, you can use Table I in the Appendix. The minimum values of r_s needed for statistical significance are shown in the table for values of N from 5 to 30. (Note that when using this table, you need only refer to N—the number of pairs of ranks—rather than degrees of freedom.)

To use Table I for the problem involving the data in Table 21.4, you would look up the minimum value necessary for r_s to be statistically significant when $N = 10$. Using the two-tailed .05 criterion, this value is .648. Since the absolute value of the obtained r_s (.85) is greater than the tabled value, you reject H_0 and conclude that there is a nonzero relationship between the two sets of ranks in the population.

When N is greater than 30, the critical values for testing a Pearson r for statistical significance will give a very good approximation. That is, you can refer the computed Spearman correlation coefficient to Table C in the Appendix with $N - 2$ degrees of freedom.

This test of significance is not, in general, as *powerful* as the test for the Pearson r. That is, it is *not* as likely to detect nonzero relationships. On the other hand, when one of a pair of variables is substantially skewed, transformation into ranks followed by the computation of r_s may well provide a better measure of their correlation than the Pearson r computed on the original data. This is the case for the data in Table 21.4. If you calculate the Pearson r for the raw IQ and income scores, you will see that it equals .78, which is less than r_s (.85).

When to Use the Spearman Correlation Coefficient

In some instances the data for both of your variables may be in the form of ranks. Suppose that you wish to determine whether the creativity of abstract paintings can be judged in a reliable way. You ask two art instructors to independently rank the same 10 paintings in order of the creativity they express. The Pearson r for these two sets of ranks *is* a Spearman correlation coefficient (by definition), and therefore its critical value may be found in Table I (unless the number of rank-ordered paintings grows larger than 30). Even if only one of the two variables has been measured ordinally (e.g., you are correlating the creativity ranks from the first art instructor with the price being asked for each painting), it is necessary to compute r_s, so you will have to convert the measurements on the second variable to ranks before computing the correlation.

If both variables have been measured on interval/ratio scales and you are worried about the distribution of both variables in the population—or even just one of them, as in the IQ/income example—both sets of measurements should be converted to ranks and r_s should be computed. Even if each variable follows an approximately normal distribution, if the relationship between them follows a monotonic curve (e.g., the curve begins steeply and then levels off but never reverses its direction) rather than a straight line, the Pearson r of the ranks (i.e., r_s) will be larger than the Pearson r of the raw scores. This is true because r_s measures the degree to which the relationship of two variables is monotonic, whereas the Pearson r applied to the raw scores measures the degree to which the relationship conforms to a single, straight line.

Summary

When there is reason to believe that the shape of a population distribution is substantially nonnormal, and the samples are not very large, nonparametric statistical tests, such as the ordinal tests described in this chapter, may be desirable.

1. Basic Considerations

The main advantage of nonparametric and distribution-free statistical tests is that they do *not* require the population(s) being sampled to be normally distributed, so they are applicable when gross nonnormality is suspected. The primary disadvantage of these methods is that when normality does exist, they are less powerful than the corresponding parametric tests (more likely to lead to a Type II error). A numerical measure of the *power efficiency* of a nonparametric test is

$$\frac{N_p}{N_d} \times 100\%,$$

where

N_p = sample size required by a parametric test to obtain a specified level of power for a specified criterion of significance and a specified difference between population means

N_d = sample size required by the corresponding nonparametric test to obtain the same power under the same conditions

The power efficiency of a nonparametric test is almost always less than 100%, but the power of the ordinal tests described in this chapter is quite good. Nonetheless, it is wasteful to use these methods when parametric tests are applicable.

2. The Difference between the Locations of Two Independent Samples: The Rank-Sum Test

1. Parametric analog: t test for the difference between two independent means (Chapter 11).
   Power efficiency: Approximately 92–95%

2. Computational procedures: Rank *all* scores from 1 (smallest) to N (largest), regardless of which group they are in. In case of ties, follow the usual procedure of assigning the mean of the ranks in question to each of the tied scores. Then compute

$$z = \frac{T_1 - T_E}{\sqrt{\dfrac{N_1 N_2 (N_T + 1)}{12}}},$$

where

$$T_1 = \text{sum of ranks in group 1}$$

$$T_E = N_1(N + 1)/2$$

$$N_1 = \text{number of observations in group 1}$$

$$N_2 = \text{number of observations in group 2}$$

$$N_T = \text{total number of observations}$$

Do *not* use the preceding formula if there are fewer than six cases in any group. Use an exact table of critical values, such as Table A.15 in Cohen (2000).

3. Measure of strength of relationship: If the value of z computed in the rank-sum test is statistically significant, a measure of the strength of the relationship between group membership and the rank values may be found by computing the *Glass rank biserial correlation* (r_G):

$$r_G = \frac{2(\bar{R}_1 - \bar{R}_2)}{N_T},$$

where

$\bar{R}_1 = \text{mean of ranks in group 1}$

$\bar{R}_2 = \text{mean of ranks in group 2}$

$N_T = \text{total number of observations}$

The r_G coefficient is *not* a Pearson r, but it does fall between the limits of -1 and $+1$.

3. Differences among the Locations of Two or More Independent Samples: The Kruskal-Wallis *H* Test

1. Parametric analog: F test of one-way ANOVA (Chapter 15)

Power efficiency: Approximately 90–95%

2. Computational procedures: Rank *all* scores from 1 (smallest) to N (largest), regardless of which group they are in. In case of ties, follow the usual procedure of assigning the mean of the ranks in question to each of the tied scores. Then compute the sum of squares between groups (SS_B) for the ranks, using either an appropriate formula from Chapter 15 or the following somewhat simpler one, which is especially designed for ranked data:

$$SS_B = \frac{T_1^2}{N_1} + \frac{T_2^2}{N_2} + \ldots + \frac{T_k^2}{N_k} - \frac{N_T(N_T + 1)^2}{4},$$

where

$$T_1 = \text{sum of ranks in group 1}$$

$$T_2 = \text{sum of ranks in group 2}$$

$$T_k = \text{sum of ranks in group } k$$

$$N_1 = \text{number of observations in group 1}$$

$$N_2 = \text{number of observations in group 2}$$

$$N_k = \text{number of observations in group } k$$

$$k = \text{number of groups}$$

$$N_T = \text{total number of observations}$$

Once SS_B has been obtained, compute

$$H = \frac{12 SS_B}{N_T(N_T + 1)}$$

The value of H is then referred to the χ^2 table with $k - 1$ degrees of freedom. If H equals or exceeds the tabled value, reject the null hypothesis that all populations have equal locations. Otherwise retain H_0. Do *not* use this procedure if there are only two or three groups *and* any group has fewer than five cases.

3. Multiple comparisons: If (and only if) H is statistically significant, the *protected rank-sum test* may be used to determine which pairs of populations differ significantly in location. First the two groups being compared must be *reranked,* with all other groups being ignored for purposes of this comparison. Then, the rank-sum test described previously is computed (with N equal to the number of observations *in these two groups*). This test may be performed when there are more than three groups involved, but in that case, the alpha used for each comparison should be reduced with a Bonferroni correction or other experimentwise alpha adjustment.

4. Measure of strength of relationship: If H is statistically significant, a measure of the strength of relationship between group membership and rank on the dependent variable may be obtained by computing eta squared applied to ranks (η_R^2):

$$\eta_R^2 = \frac{H - k + 1}{N_T - k},$$

where

$$k = \text{number of groups}$$

$$N_T = \text{total number of observations}$$

4. The Difference between the Locations of Two Matched Samples: The Wilcoxon Test

1. Parametric analog: matched t test (Chapter 11)

   Power efficiency: Approximately 92–95%

2. Computational procedures: First obtain the D score for each subject by subtracting X_2 from X_1. Next, discard any case where $D = 0$ (and reduce N accordingly). Then, *ignoring the sign* of the Ds, rank them from the smallest (rank = 1) to the largest (rank = N). Finally, compute

$$z = \frac{T_1 - T_E}{\sqrt{\dfrac{(2N + 1)T_E}{6}}},$$

where

T_1 = sum of ranks for those D values that are positive (the sum of the ranks for those D values that are negative may instead be used)

$T_E = N(N + 1)/4$

N = number of pairs (excluding cases where $D = 0$)

Do *not* use this procedure if N is less than about 8.

3. Measure of strength of relationship: If the value of z computed in the Wilcoxon test is statistically significant, a measure of the strength of the relationship between the condition (X_1 versus X_2) and the dependent variable may be found by computing the *matched-pairs rank biserial correlation* (r_C):

$$r_C = \frac{4(T_1 - T_E)}{N(N + 1)},$$

where T_1, T_E, and N have the same meaning as in the Wilcoxon test. The r_C coefficient is *not* a Pearson r, but it does fall between the limits of -1 and $+1$.

5. The Spearman Rank-Order Correlation Coefficient

With ranked data, you can compute the Pearson r for the two sets of ranks, or you can use the shortcut formula for the Spearman rank-order correlation coefficient:

$$r_S = 1 - \frac{6 \sum D^2}{N(N^2 - 1)},$$

where

$$D = \text{difference between a pair of ranks}$$

$$N = \text{number of pairs}$$

When $N < 31$, r_s should be compared to a critical value from Table I in order to determine statistical significance. However, for $N > 30$, the critical values for Pearson r in Table C provide a good approximation.

Exercises

1. An operator of a certain machine must turn it off quickly if a danger signal occurs. To test the relative effectiveness of two types of signals, a small group of operators is randomly divided into two groups. Those in group 1 operate machines with a newly designed signal, while those in group 2 use machines with the standard signal. The signal is flashed unexpectedly, and the reaction time of each operator (time taken to turn off the machine after the signal occurs) is measured in seconds. The actual results (not ranks) are shown below. (a) Use the rank-sum test to determine whether there is a significant difference between the two groups. (b) Compute the appropriate measure of strength of relationship.

Group 1	Group 2
5	3
3	17
4	13
10	2
1	8
3	16
5	6
2	9
7	11
	8

2. Redo exercise 3 from Chapter 11 using the rank-sum test instead of a t test. Does your statistical conclusion differ from the one you made in the Chapter 11 exercise? Why would the rank-sum test not be very accurate for the data in this exercise?

3. In Experiment 1, Sara is comparing scores on a practice final exam between the students who performed most poorly on the midterm (group 1), and those who got the highest midterm scores (group 2). Experiment 2 also

compares scores on the practice final, but in this case, group 1 consists of the students who received the highest scores on the first quiz, and group 2 contains the students who received the lowest scores.

(a) Perform the rank-sum test for each experiment. Can you reject the null hypothesis in each case?

(b) Calculate the appropriate measure for the strength of relationship between the two variables, for each experiment. How strong does the relationship appear to be in each case?

Experiment 1		Experiment 2	
Group 1	Group 2	Group 1	Group 2
43	80	96	43
53	45	78	54
57	62	41	59
41	83	60	70
62	46	53	45
54	87	54	83
63	56	63	57
46	70	46	80
59	75	80	50
50	78	56	87
54	89	75	57
57	96	46	62
57		57	
80		62	
60		89	

4. A psychology professor uses three different methods of instruction in three small classes, with the assignment of students to classes being random, and gives each class the same final examination. Following are the results. (a) Test the null hypothesis that method of instruction has no effect on examination scores, using the Kruskal-Wallis H test.

Group 1	Group 2	Group 3
94	60	86
97	97	42
100	96	61
72	57	73
99	93	40
96	90	63
98	92	87
97		65
		67

(b) Calculate the appropriate measure of the strength of relationship between method of instruction and examination scores, and comment briefly on the apparent size of the effect.

(c) Perform the appropriate multiple comparison test on each possible pair of groups, and comment briefly on the results.

5. For each of the two (separate) experiments that follow, perform the Kruskal-Wallis H test. If an experiment yields statistically significant results, compute eta squared and also perform all possible multiple comparisons, indicating which pairs of groups differ significantly.

(a) Experiment 3				(b) Experiment 4		
Group 1	Group 2	Group 3		Group 1	Group 2	Group 3
36	43	26		36	33	43
8	33	28		33	6	36
33	6	19		22	26	28
14	11	36		14	19	38
26	22	46		28	28	43
43	24	9		11	8	46
28	28	31		26	30	42
35	36	38		31	9	48
42	40			35	24	
30				36		
48				40		

6. A psychology instructor develops a training method that is designed to improve the examination scores of poor students. The performance of a sample of 12 such students on the posttest (X_1) following training, and the pretest (X_2) prior to training, is shown. (a) Test the null hypothesis that the training method has no effect, using the Wilcoxon test. (b) Compute the appropriate measure of strength of relationship.

S	X_1	X_2
1	77	68
2	64	64
3	56	52
4	56	57
5	71	69
6	54	58
7	76	70
8	57	60
9	63	61
10	68	61
11	71	73
12	66	66

7. For each of the two (separate) experiments that follow, perform the Wilcoxon test. If an experiment yields statistically significant results, also compute r_c.

(a) Experiment 5			(b) Experiment 6		
S	X_1	X_2	S	X_1	X_2
1	12	9	1	15	15
2	13	8	2	25	8
3	23	16	3	9	16
4	17	21	4	13	9
5	19	14	5	11	23
6	20	9	6	19	14
7	15	17	7	10	21
8	14	9	8	12	18
9	22	14	9	15	17
10	18	13	10	14	17
11	25	10	11	9	14
12	11	10	12	11	15
13	20	15	13	20	13
14	15	15	14	10	10
15	10	11	15	20	22

8. Ten subjects participate in a problem-solving experiment. Two judges are asked to rank order the solutions with regard to their creativity (1 = most creative, 10 = least creative). The experimenter wishes to know if the judges are in substantial agreement. Following are the rankings; what should the experimenter decide?

Subject	Judge 1	Judge 2
1	5	4
2	7	9
3	2	2
4	9	8
5	1	3
6	4	1
7	10	10
8	3	7
9	6	5
10	8	6

9. (a) Convert the data in part (a) of exercise 3 in Chapter 12 to ranks, separately for each variable, in order to compute the Spearman rank-order correlation coefficient. Test r_s for statistical significance by using Table I. Compare r_s to the Pearson r that you calculated for the Chapter 12 exercise.

(b) Redo part (a) for the data in part (b) of exercise 3 in Chapter 12.

Thought Questions

1. Parametric statistical tests are based on certain assumptions about unobservable population distributions. If these assumptions are incorrect, the parametric tests are likely to yield misleading results (and should therefore not be used). Yet we never know for certain what the population distributions are, so we cannot know for certain if these assumptions are justified. Nonparametric tests do *not* require such assumptions. Why, then, do psychological researchers often use parametric tests?

2. Give an example of when each of the procedures discussed in this chapter should be used: (a) Rank-sum test. (b) Glass rank biserial correlation. (c) Kruskal-Wallis *H* test. (d) Protected rank-sum test. (e) Eta squared. (f) Wilcoxon test. (g) Matched-pairs rank biserial correlation. (h) Spearman rank-order correlation coefficient.

Computer Exercises

1. Separately for each of the five majors, use the rank-sum test to determine whether male students differ significantly from female students with respect to (a) statistics quiz scores. (b) prequiz anxiety scores. (c) math phobia ratings.

2. Using college major as the grouping variable, perform the Kruskal-Wallis test to determine whether there are significant differences for the following DVs (compare your results with the corresponding ANOVA results you obtained for computer exercise 2 in Chapter 15): (a) the math background quiz. (b) the statistics quiz.

3. (a) Use the Kruskal-Wallis procedure to test whether the different quiz conditions (last question easy, moderate, difficult, or impossible) had a significant effect on postquiz anxiety scores. Regardless of the significance of your test, perform all of the possible pairwise comparisons as ordinal tests. Which of these pairwise tests would be significant after a Bonferroni adjustment of your alpha for each comparison?

   (b) Repeat part (a) for the postquiz heart rates.

4. (a) Separately for male and female students, perform the Wilcoxon test to determine whether there is a significant increase in heart rate from baseline to the prequiz measurement. Compare your results to those you obtained in computer exercise 6 in Chapter 11.

   (b) Repeat part (a) for the anxiety scores.

5. Separately for male and female students, compute the Spearman correlation coefficient between the baseline and the prequiz heart rates. How do these results relate to those you obtained in part (a) of the previous exercise?

Compute the corresponding Spearman correlations for the anxiety scores, as well.

Bridge to SPSS

The rightmost column in Variable View, labeled **Measure,** allows you to define each of your variables as either Scale (i.e., interval or ratio), Ordinal, or Nominal. Although this designation can affect the way SPSS displays your output, surprisingly, it has no effect on the statistical analyses SPSS performs. As long as you keep Type set to its default value of Numeric, SPSS will treat your data as interval/ratio when you request a parametric test, and will rank your data when you request an ordinal test.

The Rank-Sum Test

You can perform the rank-sum test in SPSS by selecting **2 Independent Samples** from the Analyze/Nonparametric Tests menu. The first (and default) choice in the dialog box under Test Type is the one that produces the rank-sum test, and it is labeled **Mann-Whitney U.** Just as in the Independent-Samples *t* test dialog box, you must specify the two levels of the Grouping Variable that you wish to compare (even if there *are* only two levels), as well as the list of Test Variables (DVs) on which you would like the two groups to be compared.

This test produces two boxes of output. The first is descriptive and contains the *N*s, sums, and means of the ranks for each group. The second box contains three Test Statistics: the Mann-Whitney U (mentioned in this chapter), the Wilcoxon W (the lower of the two sums of ranks), and *Z*, which is the *z* score we showed you how to calculate for this test. The *p* value associated with *Z* (SPSS uses an uppercase *Z*, to represent the same statistic for which we have been using the lowercase *z*) comes from the normal distribution and is labeled **Asymp. Sig (2-tailed).** The U and W statistics are provided so that you can look up their critical values from an appropriate statistical table, but that step is not necessary, because the **Exact Sig.** is also provided. Moreover, the Exact Sig will differ very little from the Asymptotic Sig, unless the samples are quite small.

The Kruskal-Wallis *H* Test

To compute the Kruskal-Wallis *H* test, select **K Independent Samples** from the Analyze/Nonparametric Tests menu. Again, it is the first (and default) choice in the dialog box under Test Type that you will want to use, and it is appropriately labeled **Kruskal-Wallis H.** The main difference between this dialog box (titled **Tests for Several Independent Samples**) and the one for two independent samples is that you are asked to Define Range instead of Define Groups. You must enter integers to define the minimum and maximum values of interest for your Grouping Variable. Those integers entered, and all integer values between them, will each define a different group in the analysis. If your grouping variable contains the integers from 1 to 5, and you want to perform the Kruskal-Wallis test only on groups 2, 3, and 5, you can enter **2** as the minimum of the range and **5** as the maximum, but you will then have to use Select Cases to exclude cases that have a value of 4 on the grouping variable. For example, click the **If** button in the Select Cases box, and then type in **group** $\sim$ **= 4,** where "$\sim$ =" means "not equal."

Like the Mann-Whitney rank-sum test, the Kruskal-Wallis procedure creates two boxes of output, the first of which contains the size and mean rank for each group. The second box contains only the H statistic, the formula for which was given earlier in this chapter, along with its df (one less than the number of groups being compared), and its approximate p value, labeled **Asymp. Sig.** The H statistic is actually labeled **Chi-Square** in the output box, because that is the distribution from which the (asymptotic) p value is obtained. (Note that for a small N it may be desirable to find the exact p value for H, but for larger N the chi-square distribution with $df = k - 1$ serves as a good approximation).

The relation between the Kruskal-Wallis and the rank-sum tests is perfectly analogous to the relation between the one-way ANOVA and the independent-samples t test. If you run the Kruskal-Wallis test on just two groups, the chi-square value you will obtain is just the square of the z score produced by the rank-sum test for the same two groups. And, of course, the p value will be the same for both tests.

The Wilcoxon Test

Any time that your data have been entered in such a way that a paired-samples t test can be run, you can perform the Wilcoxon Signed Ranks test (as SPSS refers to it) instead. Just select **2 Related Samples** from the Analyze/Nonparametric Tests menu, and make sure that the first choice under Test Type (Wilcoxon) has been checked. Choose *two* variables from the list on the left, and move the pair to the Test Pair(s) List, as you would for a paired-samples t test. Repeat this process for each pair of variables that you would like to test.

The Wilcoxon test creates difference scores for each pair of variables to be tested and then ranks these differences by magnitude, temporarily ignoring the signs. SPSS does not show you these difference scores, or their actual ranks, but the first output box for the Wilcoxon procedure gives the N, sum, and mean rank separately for the positive and negative differences. The number of ties (i.e., differences that are equal to zero—not identical difference scores) is also noted. The second output box contains only the z score (labeled **Z**) obtained from the Wilcoxon approximation formula we included earlier in this chapter, along with its two-tailed p value.

The Spearman Rank-Order Correlation Coefficient

The Spearman correlation cannot be obtained from the Analyze/Nonparametric Tests menu, although it could have easily been included in the procedure for two related samples. Instead, as you may recall, **Spearman** is one of the choices (the default is **Pearson**) when you open the dialog box for Bivariate Correlations (select **Bivariate** from the Analyze/Correlate menu). Unless the data for the two variables to be correlated have already been entered in terms of ranks, the Spearman correlation coefficient (labeled **Spearman's rho** by SPSS) will differ from the Pearson r, as will its Sig. value. However, either correlation coefficient can be the larger, depending on how the data are distributed for each variable and how the data are distributed bivariately.

Appendix

Statistical Tables

TABLE A
Percent area under the normal curve between the mean and z

z	.00	.01	.02	.03	.04	.05	.06	.07	.08	.09
0.0	00.00	00.40	00.80	01.20	01.60	01.99	02.39	02.79	03.19	03.59
0.1	03.98	04.38	04.78	05.17	05.57	05.96	06.36	06.75	07.14	07.53
0.2	07.93	08.32	08.71	09.10	09.48	09.87	10.26	10.64	11.03	11.41
0.3	11.79	12.17	12.55	12.93	13.31	13.68	14.06	14.43	14.80	15.17
0.4	15.54	15.91	16.28	16.64	17.00	17.36	17.72	18.08	18.44	18.79
0.5	19.15	19.50	19.85	20.19	20.54	20.88	21.23	21.57	21.90	22.24
0.6	22.57	22.91	23.24	23.57	23.89	24.22	24.54	24.86	25.17	25.49
0.7	25.80	26.11	26.42	26.73	27.04	27.34	27.64	27.94	28.23	28.52
0.8	28.81	29.10	29.39	29.67	29.95	30.23	30.51	30.78	31.06	31.33
0.9	31.59	31.86	32.12	32.38	32.64	32.89	33.15	33.40	33.65	33.89
1.0	34.13	34.38	34.61	34.85	35.08	35.31	35.54	35.77	35.99	36.21
1.1	36.43	36.65	36.86	37.08	37.29	37.49	37.70	37.90	38.10	38.30
1.2	38.49	38.69	38.88	39.07	39.25	39.44	39.62	39.80	39.97	40.15
1.3	40.32	40.49	40.66	40.82	40.99	41.15	41.31	41.47	41.62	41.77
1.4	41.92	42.07	42.22	42.36	42.51	42.65	42.79	42.92	43.06	43.19
1.5	43.32	43.45	43.57	43.70	43.82	43.94	44.06	44.18	44.29	44.41
1.6	44.52	44.63	44.74	44.84	44.95	45.05	45.15	45.25	45.35	45.45
1.7	45.54	45.64	45.73	45.82	45.91	45.99	46.08	46.16	46.25	46.33
1.8	46.41	46.49	46.56	46.64	46.71	46.78	46.86	46.93	46.99	47.06
1.9	47.13	47.19	47.26	47.32	47.38	47.44	47.50	47.56	47.61	47.67
2.0	47.72	47.78	47.83	47.88	47.93	47.98	48.03	48.08	48.12	48.17
2.1	48.21	48.26	48.30	48.34	48.38	48.42	48.46	48.50	48.54	48.57
2.2	48.61	48.64	48.68	48.71	48.75	48.78	48.81	48.84	48.87	48.90
2.3	48.93	48.96	48.98	49.01	49.04	49.06	49.09	49.11	49.13	49.16
2.4	49.18	49.20	49.22	49.25	49.27	49.29	49.31	49.32	49.34	49.36
2.5	49.38	49.40	49.41	49.43	49.45	49.46	49.48	49.49	49.51	49.52
2.6	49.53	49.55	49.56	49.57	49.59	49.60	49.61	49.62	49.63	49.64
2.7	49.65	49.66	49.67	49.68	49.69	49.70	49.71	49.72	49.73	49.74
2.8	49.74	49.75	49.76	49.77	49.77	49.78	49.79	49.79	49.80	49.81
2.9	49.81	49.82	49.82	49.83	49.84	49.84	49.85	49.85	49.86	49.86
3.0	49.87									
3.5	49.98									
4.0	49.997									
5.0	49.99997									

TABLE B
Critical values of t

	Level of significance for one-tailed test					
	.10	.05	.025	.01	.005	.0005
	Level of significance for two-tailed test					
df	.20	.10	.05	.02	.01	.001
1	3.078	6.314	12.706	31.821	63.657	636.619
2	1.886	2.920	4.303	6.965	9.925	31.598
3	1.638	2.343	3.182	4.541	5.841	12.941
4	1.533	2.132	2.776	3.747	4.604	8.610
5	1.476	2.015	2.571	3.365	4.032	6.859
6	1.440	1.943	2.447	3.143	3.707	5.959
7	1.415	1.895	2.365	2.998	3.449	5.405
8	1.397	1.860	2.306	2.896	3.355	5.041
9	1.383	1.833	2.262	2.821	3.250	4.781
10	1.372	1.812	2.228	2.764	3.169	4.587
11	1.363	1.796	2.201	2.718	3.106	4.437
12	1.356	1.782	2.179	2.681	3.055	4.318
13	1.350	1.771	2.160	2.650	3.012	4.221
14	1.345	1.761	2.145	2.624	2.977	4.140
15	1.341	1.753	2.131	2.602	2.947	4.073
16	1.337	1.746	2.120	2.583	2.921	4.015
17	1.333	1.740	2.110	2.567	2.898	3.965
18	1.330	1.734	2.101	2.552	2.878	3.922
19	1.328	1.729	2.093	2.539	2.861	3.883
20	1.325	1.725	2.086	2.528	2.845	3.850
21	1.323	1.721	2.080	2.518	2.831	3.819
22	1.321	1.717	2.074	2.508	2.819	3.792
23	1.319	1.714	2.069	2.500	2.807	3.767
24	1.318	1.711	2.064	2.492	2.797	3.745
25	1.316	1.708	2.060	2.485	2.787	3.725
26	1.315	1.706	2.056	2.479	2.779	3.707
27	1.314	1.703	2.052	2.473	2.771	3.690
28	1.313	1.701	2.048	2.467	2.763	3.674
29	1.311	1.699	2.045	2.462	2.756	3.659
30	1.310	1.697	2.042	2.457	2.750	3.646
40	1.303	1.684	2.021	2.423	2.704	3.551
60	1.296	1.671	2.000	2.390	2.660	3.460
120	1.289	1.658	1.980	2.358	2.617	3.373
∞	1.282	1.645	1.960	2.326	2.576	3.291

TABLE C
Critical values of the Pearson r

df ($= N - 2$; N = number of pairs)	Level of significance for one-tailed test			
	.05	.025	.01	.005
	Level of significance for two-tailed test			
	.10	.05	.02	.01
1	.988	.997	.9995	.9999
2	.900	.950	.980	.990
3	.805	.878	.934	.959
4	.729	.811	.882	.917
5	.669	.754	.833	.874
6	.622	.707	.789	.834
7	.582	.666	.750	.798
8	.549	.632	.716	.765
9	.521	.602	.685	.735
10	.497	.576	.658	.708
11	.476	.553	.634	.684
12	.458	.532	.612	.661
13	.441	.514	.592	.641
14	.426	.497	.574	.623
15	.412	.482	.558	.606
16	.400	.468	.542	.590
17	.389	.456	.528	.575
18	.378	.444	.516	.561
19	.369	.433	.503	.549
20	.360	.423	.492	.537
21	.352	.413	.482	.526
22	.344	.404	.472	.515
23	.337	.396	.462	.505
24	.330	.388	.453	.496
25	.323	.381	.445	.487
26	.317	.374	.437	.479
27	.311	.367	.430	.471
28	.306	.361	.423	.463
29	.301	.355	.416	.456
30	.296	.349	.409	.449
35	.275	.325	.381	.418
40	.257	.304	.358	.393
45	.243	.288	.338	.372
50	.231	.273	.322	.354
60	.211	.250	.295	.325
70	.195	.232	.274	.302
80	.183	.217	.256	.283
90	.173	.205	.242	.267
100	.164	.195	.230	.254

TABLE D

Power as a function of δ and significance criterion (α)

	One-tailed test (α)					One-tailed test (α)			
	.05	.025	.01	.005		.05	.025	.01	.005
	Two-tailed test (α)					Two-tailed test (α)			
δ	.10	.05	.02	.01	δ	.10	.05	.02	.01
0.0	.10[a]	.05[a]	.02	.01	2.5	.80	.71	.57	.47
0.1	.10[a]	.05[a]	.02	.01	2.6	.83	.74	.61	.51
0.2	.11[a]	.05	.02	.01	2.7	.85	.77	.65	.55
0.3	.12[a]	.06	.03	.01	2.8	.88	.80	.68	.59
0.4	.13[a]	.07	.03	.01	2.9	.90	.83	.72	.63
0.5	.14	.08	.03	.02	3.0	.91	.85	.75	.66
0.6	.16	.09	.04	.02	3.1	.93	.87	.78	.70
0.7	.18	.11	.05	.03	3.2	.94	.89	.81	.73
0.8	.21	.13	.06	.04	3.3	.96	.91	.83	.77
0.9	.23	.15	.08	.05	3.4	.96	.93	.86	.80
1.0	.26	.17	.09	.06	3.5	.97	.94	.88	.82
1.1	.30	.20	.11	.07	3.6	.97	.95	.90	.85
1.2	.33	.22	.13	.08	3.7	.98	.96	.92	.87
1.3	.37	.26	.15	.10	3.8	.98	.97	.93	.89
1.4	.40	.29	.18	.12	3.9	.99	.97	.94	.91
1.5	.44	.32	.20	.14	4.0	.99	.98	.95	.92
1.6	.48	.36	.23	.16	4.1	.99	.98	.96	.94
1.7	.52	.40	.27	.19	4.2	.99	.99	.97	.95
1.8	.56	.44	.30	.22	4.3	[b]	.99	.98	.96
1.9	.60	.48	.33	.25	4.4		.99	.98	.97
2.0	.64	.52	.37	.28	4.5		.99	.99	.97
2.1	.68	.56	.41	.32	4.6		[b]	.99	.98
2.2	.71	.59	.45	.35	4.7			.99	.98
2.3	.74	.63	.49	.39	4.8			.99	.99
2.4	.77	.67	.53	.43	4.9			.99	.99
					5.0			[b]	.99
					5.1				.99
					5.2				[b]

[a]Values inaccurate for *one-tailed* test by more than .01.

[b]The power at and below this point is greater than .995.

TABLE E

δ as a function of significance criterion (α) and power

	One-tailed test (α)			
	.05	.025	.01	.005
	Two-tailed test (α)			
δ	.10	.05	.02	.01
.25	0.97	1.29	1.65	1.90
.50	1.64	1.96	2.33	2.58
.60	1.90	2.21	2.58	2.83
.67	2.08	2.39	2.76	3.01
.70	2.17	2.48	2.85	3.10
.75	2.32	2.63	3.00	3.25
.80	2.49	2.80	3.17	3.42
.85	2.68	3.00	3.36	3.61
.90	2.93	3.24	3.61	3.86
.95	3.29	3.60	3.97	4.22
.99	3.97	4.29	4.65	4.90
.999	4.37	5.05	5.42	5.67

TABLE F
Critical values of F (α = .05 in standard type, α = .01 in boldface)

n_2	n_1 degrees of freedom (for numerator mean square)											
	1	2	3	4	5	6	7	8	9	10	11	12
1	161	200	216	225	230	234	237	239	241	242	243	244
	4,052	**4,999**	**5,403**	**5,625**	**5,764**	**5,859**	**5,928**	**5,981**	**6,022**	**6,056**	**6,082**	**6,106**
2	18.51	19.00	19.16	19.25	19.30	19.33	19.36	19.37	19.38	19.39	19.40	19.41
	98.49	**99.00**	**99.17**	**99.25**	**99.30**	**99.33**	**99.34**	**99.36**	**99.38**	**99.40**	**99.41**	**99.42**
3	10.13	9.55	9.28	9.12	9.01	8.94	8.88	8.84	8.81	8.78	8.76	8.74
	34.12	**30.82**	**29.46**	**28.71**	**28.24**	**27.91**	**27.67**	**27.49**	**27.34**	**27.23**	**27.13**	**27.05**
4	7.71	6.94	6.59	6.39	6.26	6.16	6.09	6.04	6.00	5.96	5.93	5.91
	21.20	**18.00**	**16.69**	**15.98**	**15.52**	**15.21**	**14.98**	**14.80**	**14.66**	**14.54**	**14.45**	**14.37**
5	6.61	5.79	5.41	5.19	5.05	4.95	4.88	4.82	4.78	4.74	4.70	4.68
	16.26	**13.27**	**12.06**	**11.39**	**10.97**	**10.67**	**10.45**	**10.27**	**10.15**	**10.05**	**9.96**	**9.89**
6	5.99	5.14	4.76	4.53	4.39	4.28	4.21	4.15	4.10	4.06	4.03	4.00
	13.74	**10.92**	**9.78**	**9.15**	**8.75**	**8.47**	**8.26**	**8.10**	**7.98**	**7.87**	**7.79**	**7.72**
7	5.59	4.74	4.35	4.12	3.97	3.87	3.79	3.73	3.68	3.63	3.60	3.57
	12.25	**9.55**	**8.45**	**7.85**	**7.46**	**7.19**	**7.00**	**6.84**	**6.71**	**6.62**	**6.54**	**6.47**
8	5.32	4.46	4.07	3.84	3.69	3.58	3.50	3.44	3.39	3.34	3.31	3.28
	11.26	**8.65**	**7.59**	**7.01**	**6.63**	**6.37**	**6.19**	**6.03**	**5.91**	**5.82**	**5.74**	**5.67**
9	5.12	4.26	3.86	3.63	3.48	3.37	3.29	3.23	3.18	3.13	3.10	3.07
	10.56	**8.02**	**6.99**	**6.42**	**6.06**	**5.80**	**5.62**	**5.47**	**5.35**	**5.26**	**5.18**	**5.11**
10	4.96	4.10	3.71	3.48	3.33	3.22	3.14	3.07	3.02	2.97	2.94	2.91
	10.04	**7.56**	**6.55**	**5.99**	**5.64**	**5.39**	**5.21**	**5.06**	**4.95**	**4.85**	**4.78**	**4.71**
11	4.84	3.98	3.59	3.36	3.20	3.09	3.01	2.95	2.90	2.86	2.82	2.79
	9.65	**7.20**	**6.22**	**5.67**	**5.32**	**5.07**	**4.88**	**4.74**	**4.63**	**4.54**	**4.46**	**4.40**
12	4.75	3.88	3.49	3.26	3.11	3.00	2.92	2.85	2.80	2.76	2.72	2.69
	9.33	**6.93**	**5.95**	**5.41**	**5.06**	**4.82**	**4.65**	**4.50**	**4.39**	**4.30**	**4.22**	**4.16**
13	4.67	3.80	3.41	3.18	3.02	2.92	2.84	2.77	2.72	2.67	2.63	2.60
	9.07	**6.70**	**5.74**	**5.20**	**4.86**	**4.62**	**4.44**	**4.30**	**4.19**	**4.10**	**4.02**	**3.96**

TABLE F

			n_1 degrees of freedom (for numerator mean square)								
14	16	20	24	30	40	50	75	100	200	500	∞
245	246	247	248	259	251	252	253	253	254	254	254
6,142	**6,169**	**6,208**	**6,234**	**6,258**	**6,286**	**6,302**	**6,323**	**6,334**	**6,352**	**6,361**	**6,366**
19.42	19.43	19.44	19.45	19.46	19.47	19.47	19.48	19.49	19.49	19.50	19.50
99.43	**99.44**	**99.45**	**99.46**	**99.47**	**99.48**	**99.48**	**99.49**	**99.49**	**99.49**	**99.50**	**99.50**
8.71	8.69	8.66	8.64	8.62	8.60	8.58	8.57	8.56	8.54	8.54	8.53
26.92	**26.83**	**26.69**	**26.60**	**26.50**	**26.41**	**26.35**	**26.27**	**26.23**	**26.18**	**26.14**	**26.12**
5.87	5.84	5.80	5.77	5.74	5.71	5.70	5.68	5.66	5.65	5.64	5.63
14.24	**14.15**	**14.02**	**13.93**	**13.83**	**13.74**	**13.69**	**13.61**	**13.57**	**13.52**	**13.48**	**13.46**
4.64	4.60	4.56	4.53	4.50	4.46	4.44	4.42	4.40	4.38	4.37	4.36
9.77	**9.68**	**9.55**	**9.47**	**9.38**	**9.29**	**9.24**	**9.17**	**9.13**	**9.07**	**9.04**	**9.02**
3.96	3.92	3.87	3.84	3.81	3.77	3.75	3.72	3.71	3.69	3.68	3.67
7.60	**7.52**	**7.39**	**7.31**	**7.23**	**7.14**	**7.09**	**7.02**	**6.99**	**6.94**	**6.90**	**6.88**
3.52	3.49	3.44	3.41	3.38	3.34	3.32	3.29	3.28	3.25	3.24	3.23
6.35	**6.27**	**6.15**	**6.07**	**5.98**	**5.90**	**5.85**	**5.78**	**5.75**	**5.70**	**5.67**	**5.65**
3.23	3.20	3.15	3.12	3.08	3.05	3.03	3.00	2.98	2.96	2.94	2.93
5.56	**5.48**	**5.36**	**5.28**	**5.20**	**5.11**	**5.06**	**5.00**	**4.96**	**4.91**	**4.88**	**4.86**
3.02	2.98	2.93	2.90	2.86	2.82	2.80	2.77	2.76	2.73	2.72	2.71
5.00	**4.92**	**4.80**	**4.73**	**4.64**	**4.56**	**4.51**	**4.45**	**4.41**	**4.36**	**4.33**	**4.31**
2.86	2.82	2.77	2.74	2.70	2.67	2.64	2.61	2.59	2.56	2.55	2.54
4.60	**4.52**	**4.41**	**4.33**	**4.25**	**4.17**	**4.12**	**4.05**	**4.01**	**3.96**	**3.93**	**3.91**
2.74	2.70	2.65	2.61	2.57	2.53	2.50	2.47	2.45	2.42	2.41	2.40
4.29	**4.21**	**4.10**	**4.02**	**3.94**	**3.86**	**3.80**	**3.74**	**3.70**	**3.66**	**3.62**	**3.60**
2.64	2.60	2.54	2.50	2.46	2.42	2.40	2.36	2.35	2.32	2.31	2.30
4.05	**3.98**	**3.86**	**3.78**	**3.70**	**3.61**	**3.56**	**3.49**	**3.46**	**3.41**	**3.38**	**3.36**
2.55	2.51	2.46	2.42	2.38	2.34	2.32	2.28	2.26	2.24	2.22	2.21
3.85	**3.78**	**3.67**	**3.59**	**3.51**	**3.42**	**3.37**	**3.30**	**3.27**	**3.21**	**3.18**	**3.16**

(continued)

TABLE F

n_2	1	2	3	4	5	6	7	8	9	10	11	12
	n_1 degrees of freedom (for numerator mean square)											
14	4.60	3.74	3.34	3.11	2.96	2.85	2.77	2.70	2.65	2.60	2.56	2.53
	8.86	**6.51**	**5.56**	**5.03**	**4.69**	**4.46**	**4.28**	**4.14**	**4.03**	**3.94**	**3.86**	**3.80**
15	4.54	3.68	3.29	3.06	2.90	2.79	2.70	2.64	2.59	2.55	2.51	2.48
	8.68	**6.36**	**5.42**	**4.89**	**4.56**	**4.32**	**4.14**	**4.00**	**3.89**	**3.80**	**3.73**	**3.67**
16	4.49	3.63	3.24	3.01	2.85	2.74	2.66	2.59	2.54	2.49	2.45	2.42
	8.53	**6.23**	**5.29**	**4.77**	**4.44**	**4.20**	**4.03**	**3.89**	**3.78**	**3.69**	**3.61**	**3.55**
17	4.45	3.59	3.20	2.96	2.81	2.70	2.62	2.55	2.50	2.45	2.41	2.38
	8.40	**6.11**	**5.18**	**4.67**	**4.34**	**4.10**	**3.93**	**3.79**	**3.68**	**3.59**	**3.52**	**3.45**
18	4.41	3.55	3.16	2.93	2.77	2.66	2.58	2.51	2.46	2.41	2.37	2.34
	8.28	**6.01**	**5.09**	**4.58**	**4.25**	**4.01**	**3.85**	**3.71**	**3.60**	**3.51**	**3.44**	**3.37**
19	4.38	3.52	3.13	2.90	2.74	2.63	2.55	2.48	2.43	2.38	2.34	2.31
	8.18	**5.93**	**5.01**	**4.50**	**4.17**	**3.94**	**3.77**	**3.63**	**3.52**	**3.43**	**3.36**	**3.30**
20	4.35	3.49	3.10	2.87	2.71	2.60	2.52	2.45	2.40	2.35	2.31	2.28
	8.10	**5.85**	**4.94**	**4.43**	**4.10**	**3.87**	**3.71**	**3.56**	**3.45**	**3.37**	**3.30**	**3.23**
21	4.32	3.47	3.07	2.84	2.68	2.57	2.49	2.42	2.37	2.32	2.28	2.25
	8.02	**5.78**	**4.87**	**4.37**	**4.04**	**3.81**	**3.65**	**3.51**	**3.40**	**3.31**	**3.24**	**3.17**
22	4.30	3.44	3.05	2.82	2.66	2.55	2.47	2.40	2.35	2.30	2.26	2.23
	7.9	**5.72**	**4.82**	**4.31**	**3.99**	**3.76**	**3.59**	**3.45**	**3.35**	**3.26**	**3.18**	**3.12**
23	4.28	3.42	3.03	2.80	2.64	2.53	2.45	2.38	2.32	2.28	2.24	2.20
	7.88	**5.66**	**4.76**	**4.26**	**3.94**	**3.71**	**3.54**	**3.41**	**3.30**	**3.21**	**3.14**	**3.07**
24	4.26	3.40	3.01	2.78	2.62	2.51	2.43	2.36	2.30	2.26	2.22	2.18
	7.82	**5.61**	**4.72**	**4.22**	**3.90**	**3.67**	**3.50**	**3.36**	**3.25**	**3.17**	**3.09**	**3.03**
25	4.24	3.38	2.99	2.76	2.60	2.49	2.41	2.34	2.28	2.24	2.20	2.16
	7.77	**5.57**	**4.68**	**4.18**	**3.86**	**3.63**	**3.46**	**3.32**	**3.21**	**3.13**	**3.05**	**2.99**
26	4.22	3.37	2.98	2.74	2.59	2.47	2.39	2.32	2.27	2.22	2.18	2.15
	7.72	**5.53**	**4.64**	**4.14**	**3.82**	**3.59**	**3.42**	**3.29**	**3.17**	**3.09**	**3.02**	**2.96**

TABLE F

				n_1 degrees of freedom (for numerator mean square)							
14	16	20	24	30	40	50	75	100	200	500	∞
2.48	2.44	2.39	2.35	2.31	2.27	2.24	2.21	2.19	2.16	2.14	2.13
3.70	**3.62**	**3.51**	**3.43**	**3.34**	**3.26**	**3.21**	**3.14**	**3.11**	**3.06**	**3.02**	**3.00**
2.43	2.39	2.33	2.29	2.25	2.21	2.18	2.15	2.12	2.10	2.08	2.07
3.56	**3.48**	**3.36**	**3.29**	**3.20**	**3.12**	**3.07**	**3.00**	**2.97**	**2.92**	**2.89**	**2.87**
2.37	2.33	2.28	2.24	2.20	2.16	2.13	2.09	2.07	2.04	2.02	2.01
3.45	**3.37**	**3.25**	**3.18**	**3.10**	**3.01**	**2.96**	**2.89**	**2.86**	**2.80**	**2.77**	**2.75**
2.33	2.29	2.23	2.19	2.15	2.11	2.08	2.04	2.02	1.99	1.97	1.96
3.35	**3.27**	**3.16**	**3.08**	**3.00**	**2.92**	**2.86**	**2.79**	**2.76**	**2.70**	**2.67**	**2.65**
2.29	2.25	2.19	2.15	2.11	2.07	2.04	2.00	1.98	1.95	1.93	1.92
3.27	**3.19**	**3.07**	**3.00**	**2.91**	**2.83**	**2.78**	**2.71**	**2.68**	**2.62**	**2.59**	**2.57**
2.26	2.21	2.15	2.11	2.07	2.02	2.00	1.96	1.94	1.91	1.90	1.88
3.19	**3.12**	**3.00**	**2.92**	**2.84**	**2.76**	**2.70**	**2.63**	**2.60**	**2.54**	**2.51**	**2.49**
2.23	2.18	2.12	2.08	2.04	1.99	1.96	1.92	1.90	1.87	1.85	1.84
3.13	**3.05**	**2.94**	**2.86**	**2.77**	**2.69**	**2.63**	**2.56**	**2.53**	**2.47**	**2.44**	**2.42**
2.20	2.15	2.09	2.05	2.00	1.96	1.93	1.89	1.87	1.84	1.82	1.81
3.07	**2.99**	**2.88**	**2.80**	**2.72**	**2.63**	**2.58**	**2.51**	**2.47**	**2.42**	**2.38**	**2.36**
2.18	2.13	2.07	2.03	1.98	1.93	1.91	1.87	1.84	1.81	1.80	1.78
3.02	**2.94**	**2.83**	**2.75**	**2.67**	**2.58**	**2.53**	**2.46**	**2.42**	**2.37**	**2.33**	**2.31**
2.14	2.10	2.04	2.00	1.96	1.91	1.88	1.84	1.82	1.79	1.77	1.76
2.97	**2.89**	**2.78**	**2.70**	**2.62**	**2.53**	**2.48**	**2.41**	**2.37**	**2.32**	**2.28**	**2.26**
2.13	2.09	2.02	1.98	1.94	1.89	1.86	1.82	1.80	1.76	1.74	1.73
2.93	**2.85**	**2.74**	**2.66**	**2.58**	**2.49**	**2.44**	**2.36**	**2.33**	**2.27**	**2.23**	**2.21**
2.11	2.06	2.00	1.96	1.92	1.87	1.84	1.80	1.77	1.74	1.72	1.71
2.89	**2.81**	**2.70**	**2.62**	**2.54**	**2.45**	**2.40**	**2.32**	**2.29**	**2.23**	**2.19**	**2.17**
2.10	2.05	1.99	1.95	1.90	1.85	1.82	1.78	1.76	1.72	1.70	1.69
2.86	**2.77**	**2.66**	**2.58**	**2.50**	**2.41**	**2.36**	**2.28**	**2.25**	**2.19**	**2.15**	**2.13**

(continued)

TABLE F

n_2	n_1 degrees of freedom (for numerator mean square)											
	1	2	3	4	5	6	7	8	9	10	11	12
27	4.21	3.35	2.96	2.73	2.57	2.46	2.37	2.30	2.25	2.20	2.16	2.13
	7.68	5.49	4.60	4.11	3.79	3.56	3.39	3.26	3.14	3.06	2.98	2.93
28	4.20	3.34	2.95	2.71	2.56	2.44	2.36	2.29	2.24	2.19	2.15	2.12
	7.64	5.45	4.57	4.07	3.76	3.53	3.36	3.23	3.11	3.03	2.95	2.90
29	4.18	3.33	2.93	2.70	2.54	2.43	2.35	2.28	2.22	2.18	2.14	2.10
	7.60	5.42	4.54	4.04	3.73	3.50	3.33	3.20	3.08	3.00	2.92	2.87
30	4.17	3.32	2.92	2.69	2.53	2.42	2.34	2.27	2.21	2.16	2.12	2.09
	7.56	5.39	4.51	4.02	3.70	3.47	3.30	3.17	3.06	2.98	2.90	2.84
32	4.15	3.30	2.90	2.67	2.51	2.40	2.32	2.25	2.19	2.14	2.10	2.07
	7.50	5.34	4.46	3.97	3.66	3.42	3.25	3.12	3.01	2.94	2.86	2.80
34	4.13	3.28	2.88	2.65	2.49	2.38	2.30	2.23	2.17	2.12	2.08	2.05
	7.44	5.29	4.42	3.93	3.61	3.38	3.21	3.08	2.97	2.89	2.82	2.76
36	4.11	3.26	2.86	2.63	2.48	2.36	2.28	2.21	2.15	2.10	2.06	2.03
	7.39	5.25	4.38	3.89	3.58	3.35	3.18	3.04	3.04	2.86	2.78	2.72
38	4.10	3.25	2.85	2.62	2.46	2.35	2.26	2.19	2.14	2.09	2.05	2.02
	7.35	5.21	4.34	3.86	3.54	3.32	3.15	3.02	2.91	2.82	2.75	2.69
40	4.08	3.23	2.84	2.61	2.45	2.34	2.25	2.18	2.12	2.07	2.04	2.00
	7.31	5.18	4.31	3.83	3.51	3.29	3.12	2.99	2.88	2.80	2.73	2.66
42	4.07	3.22	2.83	2.59	2.44	2.32	2.24	2.17	2.11	2.06	2.02	1.99
	7.27	5.15	4.29	3.80	3.49	3.26	3.10	2.96	2.86	2.77	2.70	2.64
44	4.06	3.21	2.82	2.58	2.43	2.31	2.23	2.16	2.10	2.05	2.01	1.98
	7.24	5.12	4.26	3.78	3.46	3.24	3.07	2.94	2.84	2.75	2.68	2.62
46	4.05	3.20	2.81	2.57	2.42	2.30	2.22	2.14	2.09	2.04	2.00	1.97
	7.21	5.10	4.24	3.76	3.44	3.22	3.05	2.92	2.82	2.73	2.66	2.60
48	4.04	3.19	2.80	2.56	2.41	2.30	2.21	2.14	2.08	2.03	1.99	1.96
	7.19	5.08	4.22	3.74	3.42	3.20	3.04	2.90	2.80	2.71	2.64	2.58

TABLE F

				n_1 degrees of freedom (for numerator mean square)							
14	16	20	24	30	40	50	75	100	200	500	∞
2.08	2.03	1.97	1.93	1.88	1.84	1.80	1.76	1.74	1.71	1.68	1.67
2.83	**2.74**	**2.63**	**2.55**	**2.47**	**2.38**	**2.33**	**2.25**	**2.21**	**2.16**	**2.12**	**2.10**
2.06	2.02	1.96	1.91	1.87	1.81	1.78	1.75	1.72	1.69	1.67	1.65
2.80	**2.71**	**2.60**	**2.52**	**2.44**	**2.35**	**2.30**	**2.22**	**2.18**	**2.13**	**2.09**	**2.06**
2.05	2.00	1.94	1.90	1.85	1.80	1.77	1.73	1.71	1.68	1.65	1.64
2.77	**2.68**	**2.57**	**2.49**	**2.41**	**2.32**	**2.27**	**2.19**	**2.15**	**2.10**	**2.06**	**2.03**
2.04	1.99	1.93	1.89	1.84	1.79	1.76	1.72	1.69	1.66	1.64	1.62
2.74	**2.66**	**2.55**	**2.47**	**2.38**	**2.29**	**2.24**	**2.16**	**2.13**	**2.07**	**2.03**	**2.01**
2.02	1.97	1.91	1.86	1.82	1.76	1.74	1.69	1.67	1.64	1.61	1.59
2.70	**2.62**	**2.51**	**2.42**	**2.34**	**2.25**	**2.20**	**2.12**	**2.08**	**2.02**	**1.98**	**1.96**
2.00	1.95	1.89	1.84	1.80	1.74	1.71	1.67	1.64	1.61	1.59	1.57
2.66	**2.58**	**2.47**	**2.38**	**2.30**	**2.21**	**2.15**	**2.08**	**2.04**	**1.98**	**1.94**	**1.91**
1.98	1.93	1.87	1.82	1.78	1.72	1.69	1.65	1.62	1.59	1.56	1.55
2.62	**2.54**	**2.43**	**2.35**	**2.26**	**2.17**	**2.12**	**2.04**	**2.00**	**1.94**	**1.90**	**1.87**
1.96	1.92	1.85	1.80	1.76	1.71	1.67	1.63	1.60	1.57	1.54	1.53
2.59	**2.51**	**2.40**	**2.32**	**2.22**	**2.14**	**2.08**	**2.00**	**1.97**	**1.90**	**1.86**	**1.84**
1.95	1.90	1.84	1.79	1.74	1.69	1.66	1.61	1.59	1.55	1.53	1.51
2.56	**2.49**	**2.37**	**2.29**	**2.20**	**2.11**	**2.05**	**1.97**	**1.94**	**1.88**	**1.84**	**1.81**
1.91	1.89	1.82	1.78	1.73	1.68	1.64	1.60	1.57	1.54	1.51	1.49
2.54	**2.46**	**2.35**	**2.26**	**2.17**	**2.08**	**2.02**	**1.94**	**1.91**	**1.85**	**1.80**	**1.78**
1.92	1.88	1.81	1.76	1.72	1.66	1.63	1.58	1.56	1.52	1.50	1.48
2.52	**2.44**	**2.32**	**2.24**	**2.15**	**2.06**	**2.00**	**1.92**	**1.88**	**1.82**	**1.78**	**1.75**
1.91	1.87	1.80	1.75	1.71	1.65	1.62	1.57	1.54	1.51	1.48	1.46
2.50	**2.42**	**2.30**	**2.22**	**2.13**	**2.04**	**1.98**	**1.90**	**1.86**	**1.80**	**1.76**	**1.72**
1.90	1.86	1.79	1.74	1.70	1.64	1.61	1.56	1.53	1.50	1.47	1.45
2.48	**2.40**	**2.28**	**2.20**	**2.11**	**2.02**	**1.96**	**1.88**	**1.84**	**1.78**	**1.73**	**1.70**

(continued)

TABLE F

n_2	n_1 degrees of freedom (for numerator mean square)											
	1	2	3	4	5	6	7	8	9	10	11	12
50	4.03	3.18	2.79	2.56	2.40	2.29	2.20	2.13	2.07	2.02	1.98	1.95
	7.17	**5.06**	**4.20**	**3.72**	**3.41**	**3.18**	**3.02**	**2.88**	**2.78**	**2.70**	**2.62**	**2.56**
55	4.02	3.17	2.78	2.54	2.38	2.27	2.18	2.11	2.05	2.00	1.97	1.93
	7.12	**5.01**	**4.16**	**3.68**	**3.37**	**3.15**	**2.98**	**2.85**	**2.75**	**2.66**	**2.59**	**2.53**
60	4.00	3.15	2.76	2.52	2.37	2.25	2.17	2.10	2.04	1.99	1.95	1.92
	7.08	**4.98**	**4.13**	**3.65**	**3.34**	**3.12**	**2.95**	**2.82**	**2.72**	**2.63**	**2.56**	**2.50**
65	3.99	3.14	2.75	2.51	2.36	2.24	2.15	2.08	2.02	1.98	1.94	1.90
	7.04	**4.95**	**4.10**	**3.62**	**3.31**	**3.09**	**2.93**	**2.79**	**2.70**	**2.61**	**2.54**	**2.47**
70	3.98	3.13	2.74	2.50	2.35	2.23	2.14	2.07	2.01	1.97	1.93	1.89
	7.01	**4.92**	**4.08**	**3.60**	**3.29**	**3.07**	**2.91**	**2.77**	**2.67**	**2.59**	**2.51**	**2.45**
80	3.96	3.11	2.72	2.48	2.33	2.21	2.12	2.05	1.99	1.95	1.91	1.88
	6.96	**4.88**	**4.04**	**3.56**	**3.25**	**3.04**	**2.87**	**2.74**	**2.64**	**2.55**	**2.48**	**2.41**
100	3.94	3.09	2.70	2.46	2.30	2.19	2.10	2.03	1.97	1.92	1.88	1.85
	6.90	**4.82**	**3.98**	**3.51**	**3.20**	**2.99**	**2.82**	**2.69**	**2.59**	**2.51**	**2.43**	**2.36**
125	3.92	3.07	2.68	2.44	2.29	2.17	2.08	2.01	1.95	1.90	1.86	1.83
	6.84	**4.78**	**3.94**	**3.47**	**3.17**	**2.95**	**2.79**	**2.65**	**2.56**	**2.47**	**2.40**	**2.33**
150	3.91	3.06	2.57	2.43	2.27	2.16	2.07	2.00	1.94	1.89	1.85	1.82
	6.81	**4.75**	**3.91**	**3.44**	**3.14**	**2.92**	**2.76**	**2.62**	**2.53**	**2.44**	**2.37**	**2.30**
200	3.89	3.04	2.65	2.41	2.26	2.14	2.05	1.98	1.92	1.87	1.83	1.80
	6.76	**4.71**	**3.88**	**3.41**	**3.11**	**2.90**	**2.73**	**2.60**	**2.50**	**2.41**	**2.34**	**2.28**
400	3.86	3.02	2.62	2.39	2.23	2.12	2.03	1.96	1.90	1.85	1.81	1.78
	6.70	**4.66**	**3.83**	**3.36**	**3.06**	**2.85**	**2.69**	**2.55**	**2.46**	**2.37**	**2.29**	**2.23**
1000	3.85	3.00	2.61	2.38	2.22	2.10	2.02	1.95	1.89	1.84	1.80	1.76
	6.66	**4.62**	**3.80**	**3.34**	**3.04**	**2.82**	**2.66**	**2.53**	**2.43**	**2.34**	**2.26**	**2.20**
∞	3.84	2.99	2.60	2.37	2.21	2.09	2.01	1.94	1.88	1.83	1.79	1.75
	6.64	**4.60**	**3.78**	**3.32**	**3.02**	**2.80**	**2.64**	**2.51**	**2.41**	**2.32**	**2.24**	**2.18**

TABLE F

			n_1 degrees of freedom (for numerator mean square)								
14	16	20	24	30	40	50	75	100	200	500	∞
1.90	1.85	1.78	1.74	1.69	1.63	1.60	1.55	1.52	1.48	1.46	1.44
2.46	**2.39**	**2.26**	**2.18**	**2.10**	**2.00**	**1.94**	**1.86**	**1.82**	**1.76**	**1.71**	**1.68**
1.88	1.83	1.76	1.72	1.67	1.61	1.58	1.52	1.50	1.46	1.43	1.41
2.43	**2.35**	**2.23**	**2.15**	**2.06**	**1.96**	**1.90**	**1.82**	**1.78**	**1.71**	**1.66**	**1.64**
1.86	1.81	1.75	1.70	1.65	1.59	1.56	1.50	1.48	1.44	1.41	1.39
2.40	**2.32**	**2.20**	**2.12**	**2.03**	**1.93**	**1.87**	**1.79**	**1.74**	**1.68**	**1.63**	**1.60**
1.84	1.80	1.73	1.68	1.63	1.57	1.54	1.49	1.46	1.42	1.39	1.37
2.37	**2.30**	**2.18**	**2.09**	**2.00**	**1.90**	**1.84**	**1.76**	**1.71**	**1.64**	**1.60**	**1.56**
1.84	1.79	1.72	1.67	1.62	1.56	1.53	1.47	1.45	1.40	1.37	1.35
2.35	**2.28**	**2.15**	**2.07**	**1.98**	**1.88**	**1.82**	**1.74**	**1.69**	**1.62**	**1.56**	**1.53**
1.82	1.77	1.70	1.65	1.60	1.54	1.51	1.45	1.42	1.38	1.35	1.32
2.32	**2.24**	**2.11**	**2.03**	**1.94**	**1.84**	**1.78**	**1.70**	**1.65**	**1.57**	**1.52**	**1.49**
1.79	1.75	1.68	1.63	1.57	1.51	1.48	1.42	1.39	1.34	1.30	1.28
2.26	**2.19**	**2.06**	**1.98**	**1.89**	**1.79**	**1.73**	**1.64**	**1.59**	**1.51**	**1.46**	**1.43**
1.77	1.72	1.65	1.60	1.55	1.49	1.45	1.39	1.36	1.31	1.27	1.25
2.23	**2.15**	**2.03**	**1.94**	**1.85**	**1.75**	**1.68**	**1.59**	**1.54**	**1.46**	**1.40**	**1.37**
1.76	1.71	1.64	1.59	1.54	1.47	1.44	1.37	1.34	1.29	1.25	1.22
2.20	**2.12**	**2.00**	**1.91**	**1.83**	**1.72**	**1.66**	**1.56**	**1.51**	**1.43**	**1.37**	**1.33**
1.74	1.69	1.62	1.57	1.52	1.45	1.42	1.35	1.32	1.26	1.22	1.19
2.17	**2.09**	**1.97**	**1.88**	**1.79**	**1.69**	**1.62**	**1.53**	**1.48**	**1.39**	**1.33**	**1.28**
1.72	1.67	1.60	1.54	1.49	1.42	1.38	1.32	1.28	1.22	1.16	1.13
2.12	**2.04**	**1.92**	**1.84**	**1.74**	**1.65**	**1.57**	**1.47**	**1.42**	**1.32**	**1.24**	**1.19**
1.70	1.65	1.58	1.53	1.47	1.41	1.36	1.30	1.26	1.19	1.13	1.08
2.09	**2.01**	**1.89**	**1.81**	**1.71**	**1.61**	**1.54**	**1.44**	**1.38**	**1.28**	**1.19**	**1.11**
1.69	1.64	1.57	1.52	1.46	1.40	1.35	1.28	1.24	1.17	1.11	1.00
2.07	**1.99**	**1.87**	**1.79**	**1.69**	**1.59**	**1.52**	**1.41**	**1.36**	**1.25**	**1.15**	**1.00**

TABLE G

Critical values of the studentized range statistic (q) for $\alpha = .05$

df for error term	Number of groups																		
	2	3	4	5	6	7	8	9	10	11	12	13	14	15	16	17	18	19	20
1	17.97	26.98	32.82	37.08	40.41	43.12	45.40	47.36	49.07	50.59	51.96	53.20	54.33	55.36	56.32	57.22	58.04	58.83	59.56
2	6.08	8.33	9.80	10.88	11.74	12.44	13.03	13.54	13.99	14.39	14.75	15.08	15.38	15.65	15.91	16.14	16.37	16.57	16.77
3	4.50	5.91	6.82	7.50	8.04	8.48	8.85	9.18	9.46	9.72	9.95	10.15	10.35	10.52	10.69	10.84	10.98	11.11	11.24
4	3.93	5.04	5.76	6.29	6.71	7.05	7.35	7.60	7.83	8.03	8.21	8.37	8.52	8.66	8.79	8.91	9.03	9.13	9.23
5	3.64	4.60	5.22	5.67	6.03	6.33	6.58	6.80	6.99	7.17	7.32	7.47	7.60	7.72	7.83	7.93	8.03	8.12	8.21
6	3.46	4.34	4.90	5.30	5.63	5.90	6.12	6.32	6.49	6.65	6.79	6.92	7.03	7.14	7.24	7.34	7.43	7.51	7.59
7	3.34	4.16	4.68	5.06	5.36	5.61	5.82	6.00	6.16	6.30	6.43	6.55	6.66	6.76	6.85	6.94	7.02	7.10	7.17
8	3.26	4.04	4.53	4.89	5.17	5.40	5.60	5.77	5.92	6.05	6.18	6.29	6.39	6.48	6.57	6.65	6.73	6.80	6.87
9	3.20	3.95	4.41	4.76	5.02	5.24	5.43	5.59	5.74	5.87	5.98	6.09	6.19	6.28	6.36	6.44	6.51	6.58	6.64
10	3.15	3.88	4.33	4.65	4.91	5.12	5.30	5.46	5.60	5.72	5.83	5.93	6.03	6.11	6.19	6.27	6.34	6.40	6.47
11	3.11	3.82	4.26	4.57	4.82	5.03	5.20	5.35	5.49	5.61	5.71	5.81	5.90	5.98	6.06	6.13	6.20	6.27	6.33
12	3.08	3.77	4.20	4.51	4.75	4.95	5.12	5.27	5.39	5.51	5.61	5.71	5.80	5.88	5.95	6.02	6.09	6.15	6.21
13	3.06	3.73	4.15	4.45	4.69	4.88	5.05	5.19	5.32	5.43	5.53	5.63	5.71	5.79	5.86	5.93	5.99	6.05	6.11
14	3.03	3.70	4.11	4.41	4.64	4.83	4.99	5.13	5.25	5.36	5.46	5.55	5.64	5.71	5.79	5.85	5.91	5.97	6.03
15	3.01	3.67	4.08	4.37	4.59	4.78	4.94	5.08	5.20	5.31	5.40	5.49	5.57	5.65	5.72	5.78	5.85	5.90	5.96
16	3.00	3.65	4.05	4.33	4.56	4.74	4.90	5.03	5.15	5.26	5.35	5.44	5.52	5.59	5.66	5.73	5.79	5.84	5.90
17	2.98	3.63	4.02	4.30	4.52	4.70	4.86	4.99	5.11	5.21	5.31	5.39	5.47	5.54	5.61	5.67	5.73	5.79	5.84
18	2.97	3.61	4.00	4.28	4.49	4.67	4.82	4.96	5.07	5.17	5.27	5.35	5.43	5.50	5.57	5.63	5.69	5.74	5.79
19	2.96	3.59	3.98	4.25	4.47	4.65	4.79	4.92	5.04	5.14	5.23	5.31	5.39	5.46	5.53	5.59	5.65	5.70	5.75
20	2.95	3.58	3.96	4.23	4.45	4.62	4.77	4.90	5.01	5.11	5.20	5.28	5.36	5.43	5.49	5.55	5.61	5.66	5.71
24	2.92	3.53	3.90	4.17	4.37	4.54	4.68	4.81	4.92	5.01	5.10	5.18	5.25	5.32	5.38	5.44	5.49	5.55	5.59
30	2.89	3.49	3.85	4.10	4.30	4.46	4.60	4.72	4.82	4.92	5.00	5.08	5.15	5.21	5.27	5.33	5.38	5.43	5.47
40	2.86	3.44	3.79	4.04	4.23	4.39	4.52	4.63	4.73	4.82	4.90	4.98	5.04	5.11	5.16	5.22	5.27	5.31	5.36
60	2.83	3.40	3.74	3.98	4.16	4.31	4.44	4.55	4.65	4.73	4.81	4.88	4.94	5.00	5.06	5.11	5.15	5.20	5.24
120	2.80	3.36	3.68	3.92	4.10	4.24	4.36	4.47	4.56	4.64	4.71	4.78	4.84	4.90	4.95	5.00	5.04	5.09	5.13
∞	2.77	3.31	3.63	3.86	4.03	4.17	4.29	4.39	4.47	4.55	4.62	4.68	4.74	4.80	4.85	4.89	4.93	4.97	5.01

Source: Adapted from Biometrika Tables for Statisticians, Vol. 1, 3rd ed., by E. Pearson & H. Hartley, Table 29. Copyright © 1966 University Press. Used with the permission of the Biometrika Trustees.

TABLE H
Critical values of chi square

df	Level of significance					
	.20	.10	.05	.02	.01	.001
1	1.64	2.71	3.84	5.41	6.63	10.83
2	3.22	4.61	5.99	7.82	9.21	13.82
3	4.64	6.25	7.82	9.84	11.34	16.27
4	5.99	7.78	9.49	11.67	13.28	18.46
5	7.29	9.24	11.07	13.39	15.09	20.52
6	8.56	10.64	12.59	15.03	16.81	22.46
7	9.80	12.02	14.07	16.62	18.48	24.32
8	11.03	13.36	15.51	18.17	20.09	26.12
9	12.24	14.68	16.92	19.68	21.67	27.88
10	13.44	15.99	18.31	21.16	23.21	29.59
11	14.63	17.28	19.68	22.62	24.72	31.26
12	15.81	18.55	21.03	24.05	26.22	32.91
13	16.98	19.81	22.36	25.47	27.69	34.53
14	18.15	21.06	23.68	26.87	29.14	36.12
15	19.31	22.31	25.00	28.26	30.58	37.70
16	20.46	23.54	26.30	29.63	32.00	39.25
17	21.62	24.77	27.59	31.00	33.41	40.79
18	22.76	25.99	28.87	32.35	34.81	42.31
19	23.90	27.20	30.14	33.69	36.19	43.82
20	25.04	28.41	31.41	35.02	37.57	45.32
21	26.17	29.62	32.67	36.34	38.93	46.80
22	27.30	30.81	33.92	37.66	40.29	48.27
23	28.43	32.01	35.17	38.97	41.64	49.73
24	29.55	33.20	36.42	40.27	42.98	51.18
25	30.68	34.38	37.65	41.57	44.31	52.62
26	31.80	35.56	38.89	42.86	45.64	54.05
27	32.91	36.74	40.11	44.14	46.96	55.48
28	34.03	37.92	41.34	45.42	48.28	56.89
29	35.14	39.09	42.56	46.69	49.59	58.30
30	36.25	40.26	43.77	47.96	50.89	59.70

Note. For *df* greater than 30, the value obtained from the expression $\sqrt{2\chi^2} - \sqrt{2df - 1}$ may be used as a *t* ratio.

Critical values of r_s (Spearman rank-order correlation coefficient

No. of pairs (N)	Level of significance for one-tailed test			
	.05	.025	.01	.005
	Level of significance for two-tailed test			
	.10	.05	.02	.01
5	.900	1.000	1.000	—
6	.829	.886	.943	1.000
7	.714	.786	.893	.929
8	.643	.738	.833	.881
9	.600	.683	.783	.833
10	.564	.648	.746	.794
12	.506	.591	.712	.777
14	.456	.544	.645	.715
16	.425	.506	.601	.665
18	.399	.475	.564	.625
20	.377	.450	.534	.591
22	.359	.428	.508	.562
24	.343	.409	.485	.537
26	.329	.392	.465	.515
28	.317	.377	.448	.496
30	.306	.364	.432	.478

Source. G. E. Olds, *Ann. Math. Statistics* 9 (1938); 20 (1949). Reproduced by permission of the publisher.

Answer Key

Chapter 1

1. (a) $\sum X + \sum Y$

   (b) $\sum G + \sum P^2$

   (c) $\sum X^2 - 6 \sum XY + 4(\sum X)^2 + 2 \sum Y^2$

3. (a) $\sum X = 60$; $\sum X^2 = 450$; $(\sum X)^2 = 3{,}600$

   (b) $\sum X = 55$; $\sum X^2 = 685$; $(\sum X)^2 = 3{,}025$

5. Data set 3:

   $N = 14$

   $\sum X = 1176$; $\sum X^2 = 100{,}288$; $(\sum X)^2 = 1{,}382{,}976$; $\sum XY = 96{,}426$;
   $\sum(X + Y) = 2{,}305$
   $\sum Y = 1129$; $\sum Y^2 = 93{,}343$; $(\sum Y)^2 = 1{,}274{,}641$; $\sum X \sum Y = 1{,}327{,}704$;
   $\sum(X - Y) = 47$

Chapter 2

1.

Score	Univ. A		Univ. B		Univ. C	
	f	cf	f	cf	f	cf
20	1	50	0	50		
19	0	49	1	50		
18	2	49	0	49		
17	4	47	3	49		
16	4	43	2	46		
15	5	39	0	44		
14	2	34	4	44		
13	7	32	4	40		
12	7	25	8	36		
11	5	18	5	28	1	10
10	4	13	6	23	0	9
9	4	9	4	17	2	9
8	1	5	3	13	0	7
7	0	4	2	10	1	7

(continues)

Score	Univ. A		Univ. B		Univ. C	
	f	cf	f	cf	f	cf
6	1	4	2	8	1	6
5	0	3	2	6	2	5
4	1	3	0	4	2	3
3	0	2	2	4	0	1
2	1	2	1	2	0	1
1	0	1	1	1	0	1
0	1	1	0	0	1	1

3.

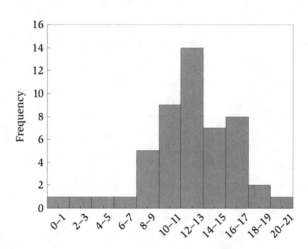

5.

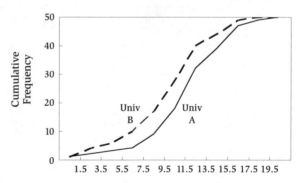

7. (1) h or b;   (2) b;   (3) c;   (4) a;   (5) d;   (6) g

Chapter 3

1.		L%	LRL	h	I%	PR
	(a)	8%	4.5	1	4%	10%
	(b)	34%	9.5	1	12%	40%

3.

		LRL	SFB	f	h	Score
	(a)	7.5	10	3	1	8.3
	(b)	12.5	36	4	1	12.9

Chapter 4

1. University A: $\overline{X}$ = 12.34; University B: $\overline{X}$ = 10.52; University C: $\overline{X}$ = 6.00; University D: $\overline{X}$ = 11.00

3. LRL = 11.5, SFB = 18, f = 7, h = 1, Mdn = 12.5

5. Mode = 12

Chapter 5

1. University A: σ^2 = 15.42, σ = 3.93, s^2 = 15.74, s = 3.97
   University B: σ^2 = 15.65, σ = 3.96, s^2 = 15.97, s = 4.00
   University C: σ^2 = 9.00, σ = 3.00, s^2 = 10.00, s = 3.16
   University D: σ^2 = 16.00, σ = 4.00, s^2 = 20.00, s = 4.47

3. Range = 20, 18, 11, 11

5. 21.25. This variance is larger than the ordinary variance of 20.00; the variance from the mean will be less than the variance from any other point in the distribution.

Chapter 6

1. University A:

	12.5	
10.4		15.2
0		20

University B:

	10.9	
8.3		12.9
1		19

3.

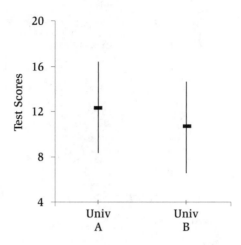

Chapter 7

1.

	$\overline{X}$	σ	σ^2
(a)	14.8	4	16
(b)	4	4	16
(c)	25.6	12.8	163.84
(d)	2	1	1
(e)	7	2	4

3. Psychology z score $= -1.60$; English z score $= -1.00$. This student performed relatively better on the English test.

5.

S	z_x	z_y
1	+1.25	+0.65
2	−1.54	−1.85
3	+0.10	+0.50
4	−0.97	−0.36
5	+0.77	+1.28
6	+0.77	−0.13
7	+1.54	+0.81
8	−2.03	−2.39
9	+0.10	+0.34
10	+0.29	+0.26
11	−0.29	+0.81
12	+0.87	+0.81
13	−0.68	−0.44
14	−0.19	−0.28

Chapter 8

1. $z = -0.90$, area between mean and $z = 31.59\%$; Answer $= 18.41\%$

3. $z = -2.25$ (area $= 48.78\%$); $z = -1.25$ (area $= 39.44\%$); Answer $= 9.34\%$

5. $z = +1.65$; Answer $= 665$

7. (a) $p = .184$;   (b) $p = .376$;   (c) $p = .093$;   (d) $p = .050$

Chapter 9

1. (a) $\sigma_{\bar{X}} = 0.5$

   (b) $z = -1.60$, one-tailed $p = .0548$, two-tailed $p = .1096$

   (c) $p > .05$ for both one- and two-tailed tests, so retain H_0 in both cases

   (d) $z = +4.80$, reject H_0 at .05 and .01

3. (a) $z = +1.50 < +1.96$ (two-tailed z_{crit}), retain H_0;
   $z = +1.50 < +1.65$ (one-tailed z_{crit}), not significant for a one-tailed test, either.

   (b) $z = +2.40 > +1.96$; reject H_0 for both the one- and two-tailed tests.

Chapter 10

1. (a) $s_{\bar{X}} = .56$; $t = 2.96$. Reject H_0

   (b) $s_{\bar{X}} = .57$; $t = -0.92$. Retain H_0

3. (a) $s_{\bar{X}} = .63$; $t = -0.62$; $df = 8$. Retain H_0

   (b) $s_{\bar{X}} = .63$; $t = -6.17$; $df = 8$. Reject H_0

   (c) $t s_{\bar{X}} = 1.45$; CI $= 0.66 - 3.56$. When the CI includes the null hypothesis mean, retain the null; when the null hypothesis mean falls outside of the CI, reject the null.

5. $z = (.6 - .5)/\sqrt{(.5)(.5)/100} = 2.0$; $p < .05$. Reject H_0; conclude that the electorate will support the new constitution.

Chapter 11

1. $s^2_{pooled} = 15.86$; $df = 98$; $t = 1.82/.80 = 2.28$; reject H_0. This is a possible Type I error. On average, the scores for University A were higher (M $= 12.34$) than the scores for University B (M $= 10.52$); this difference was found to be statistically significant, t (98) $= 2.28$, $p < .05$.

3. $s_1^2 = 9.49$; $s_2^2 = 10.00$; $s_{pooled}^2 = 9.75$; $df = 8$;
$t = 7/1.97 = 3.55$; $p < .05$. Reject H_0; ethnic groups differ in performance.

5. $\Sigma D = 10$; $\overline{D} = 1$; $s_D^2 = 4.67$; $df = 9$; $t = 1.46$; $p > .05$. Retain H_0; there is not sufficient reason to conclude that the two techniques differ.

7. $\Sigma D = 47$; $\overline{D} = 3.36$; $s_D = 18.54$; $df = 13$; $t = 0.68$; $p > .05$. Retain H_0.

Chapter 12

1. (a) $\mu_x = 80$; $\sigma_x = 8.02$; $\mu_y = 3$; $\sigma_y = .60$; $r_{xy} = +.67$

(b) $\Sigma z_x z_y = 4.70$; $r_{xy} = +.67$. This is a highly positive correlation, which tells us that there is a strong tendency for students who do well in the first semester to also do well in their sophomore year, and that those who do poorly in the first semester tend to do poorly in their sophomore year.

(c) $\Sigma CY = 61$; $\mu_c = 3$; $\sigma_c = 1.41$; $\mu_y = 3$; $\sigma_y = .60$; $r_{cy} = -.34$, $df = 5$, $p > .05$. Retain H_0; there is not sufficient reason to believe that the correlation is different from zero.

(d) $\Sigma CX = 1695$; $\mu_c = 3$; $\sigma_c = 1.41$; $\mu_x = 80$; $\sigma_x = 8.02$; $r_{cx} = .19$, $df = 5$, $p > .05$.
Retain H_0; there is not sufficient reason to believe that the correlation is different from zero.

3. (a) $\Sigma XY = 96,426$; $\overline{X} = 84$; $s_x = 10.76$; $\overline{Y} = 80.64$; $s_y = 13.29$; $r_{xy} = .855$, $df = 12$, $p < .05$. Retain H_0.

(b) $\Sigma z_x z_y = 11.98$; $r_{xy} = .855$.

(c) $\Sigma XY = 94,502$; $\overline{X} = 84$; $s_x = 10.76$; $\overline{Y} = 80.64$; $s_y = 13.29$; $r_{xy} = -.18$, $df = 12$, $p < .05$. Retain H_0.

5. $b_{yc} = -.14$; $a_{yc} = 3.42$; $Y' = -.14C + 3.42$; $Y' = 2.3$

Chapter 13

1. $t = 2.28$; $df = 98$; $r_{pb}^2 = t^2/(t^2 + df) = .05$; $r_{pb} = .224$.

$$t = \frac{.224\sqrt{98}}{\sqrt{1 - .224^2}} = \frac{2.2175}{\sqrt{.95}} = 2.28;$$ the two t values are equal.

3. $\sigma_Y = 4.72$; $\sqrt{pq} = .5$; $r_{pb} = -.74$; 55% of the variance accounted for by group membership.

5.

t	N_1	N_2	r_{pb}
2.11	12	8	.445
2.75	12	8	.544
6.00	12	8	.816
2.11	19	23	.316
2.75	19	23	.399
6.00	19	23	.688
2.11	51	51	.206
2.75	51	51	.265
6.00	51	51	.514

Chapter 14

1. (a) $d = 20/100 = .20$; $\delta = .20\sqrt{25} = 1.0$; for a two-tailed test, power $= .17$; for a one-tailed test, power $= .26$. Power is higher for the one-tailed test, because you are putting all of your alpha in just one tail, leading to a smaller critical value to beat.

   (b) $d = 50/100 = .50$; $\delta = .50\sqrt{25} = 2.5$; power $= .71$ (two-tailed), or power $= .80$ (one-tailed). These power values are higher because the effect size increased from .20 to .50. As d increases, power increases.

   (c) $\delta = .20\sqrt{100} = 2.0$; power $= .52$ (two-tailed), or power $= .64$ (one-tailed). Larger samples yield higher values for delta (all else equal), and thus increase the likelihood of correctly rejecting H_0. So, power increases as N increases.

   (d) For .05, two-tailed: $N = (2.80/.20)^2 = 196$; for .01, two-tailed: $N = (3.40/.20)^2 = 289$.

   (e) For .05, two-tailed: $N = (2.80/50)^2 = 31$; for .01, two-tailed: $N = (3.40/.50)^2 = 46$

3. (a) $d = .10/\sqrt{(.5)(.5)} = .10/.50 = .20$; $\delta = .20\sqrt{81} = 1.8$; Power $= .22$. He is very unlikely to reject H_0 even when specified H_1 is true, so the experimental plan is not good.

   (b) Power improves to .44, but he still has better than half a chance of failing to reject H_0 when the specified H_1 is true.

   (c) $N = (2.63/.20)^2 = 173$

5. $\rho = .52$; $N = (2.47/.52)^2 + 1 = 24$

7. (a) $n = 2(41)(31)/(41 + 31) = 35.31$; $g = \sqrt{2/35.31}\,(1.19) = .283$; $n = 2(2.47/.283)^2 = 152$.

   (b) $d = \sqrt{2/35.31}\,(2.8) = .67$

9. $\delta = \sqrt{1/.6}\,\sqrt{50/2}\,(.72) = 4.65$; power $= .99$

11. (a) $g = \sqrt{2/10}$ (1.45) $= .65$; $\delta = \sqrt{10/2}$ (.65) $= .29$; power $= .06$

   (b) $\delta = \sqrt{1/.5}\ \sqrt{2/10}$ (.65) $= 2.01$; power $= .52$

Chapter 15

1. (a) There appears to be less within-group variability in Experiment 1 and the between-group variability is equal, so the results of Experiment 1 are more likely to be statistically significant.

   (b) $\sum X^2 = 302$; $\bar{X}_G = 4$; $SS_T = 62$; $SS_B = 40$; $SS_W = 22$; $MS_B = 20$; $MS_W = 1.83$; $F(2,12) = 10.93$, $p < .05$. Reject H_0; conclude that reward type affects performance. $\eta^2 = 40/62 = .65$.

   (c) $\sum X^2 = 490$; $\bar{X}_G = 4$; $SS_T = 250$; $SS_B = 40$; $SS_W = 210$; $MS_B = 20$; $MS_W = 17.5$; $F(2,12) = 1.14$, $p > .05$. Retain H_0: there is not sufficient reason to conclude that reward type affects performance. $\eta^2 = 40/250 = .16$.

   (d) There is much more within-group (error) variation in Experiment 2, thus group differences comprise a smaller part of the total variance. In Experiment 1, most of the total variation is due to between-groups differences.

   (e) Est. $\omega^2 = 36.34/63.83 = .57$

3. (a) Experiment 1:

Source	SS	df	MS	F	p
Between-groups	173.36	2	86.68	1.63	> .05
Within-groups	797.70	15	53.18		
Total	971.06	17			

There is not sufficient evidence to reject the null hypothesis that the means of the three populations are equal, $F(2,15) = 1.63$, $p > .05$, $\eta^2 = .217$.

   (b) Experiment 2:

Source	SS	df	MS	F	p
Between-groups	527.98	2	263.99	8.77	< .01
Within-groups	451.64	15	30.11		
Total	979.62	17			

The three population means are not all equal, $F(2,15) = 8.77$, $p < .01$, est. $\omega^2 = .46$.

Chapter 16

1. Exp. 1: LSD = $2.179\sqrt{3.66/5}$ = 1.82; Exp. 2: LSD = $2.179\sqrt{35/5}$ = 5.64. LSD is justified only for Experiment 1 because H_0 is rejected in that case. All pairs of means differ significantly for Experiment 1.

3. Exp. 1: LSD = $2.131\sqrt{106.36/6}$ = 8.97; no pairs of means differ.
   HSD = $3.67\sqrt{53.18/6}$ = 10.93; no pairs of means differ.

   Exp. 2: LSD = $2.131\sqrt{60.22/6}$ = 6.75; Group 1 differs from Groups 2 and 3.
   HSD = $3.67\sqrt{30.11/6}$ = 8.22; Group 1 differs from Groups 2 and 3.

   LSD values are smaller than HSD, which increases the chance of finding a significant difference between pairs of means. LSD is generally more powerful than HSD.

Chapter 17

1. (a)

Source	SS	df	MS	F	p
Phobia	32.44	2	16.22	6.34	< .05
Gender	2.00	1	2.00	.78	> .05
Phobia × Gender	1.33	2	.67	.26	> .05
Error	30.67	12	2.56		
Total	66.44	17			

   (b) LSD = $2.179\sqrt{5.12/6}$ = 2.01. Therefore, the low phobia group differs from the moderate and high phobia groups. The F value for phobia is statistically significant, so these follow-up tests comparing the marginal means of the phobia groups are justified.

3. (a) $MS_{caffeine}$ = 2.52; MS_W = 2.0; $F_{caffeine}(1,24)$ = 1.26, $p > .05$
   MS_{sex} = .63; MS_W = 2.0; $F_{sex}(1,24)$ = .32, $p > .05$
   MS_{inter} = 154.63; MS_W = 2.0; $F_{inter}(1,24)$ = 77.32, $p < .01$

   (b) Graph shows a disordinal interaction

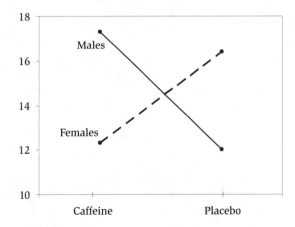

(c) The significant interaction justifies the testing of the four simple main effects. Thus, men given caffeine scored significantly higher than men given placebos, $t(24) = 7.01$, $p < .01$, whereas, women with caffeine had lower scores than women given placebos, $t(24) = -5.42$, $p < .01$. Men with caffeine had higher scores than women with caffeine, $t(24) = 6.61$, $p < .01$, but men given placebos had lower scores than women given placebos, $t(24) = -5.82$, $p < .01$. In general, these results show that caffeine increases performance for men, but decreases performance for women.

Chapter 18

1. $SS_{total} = 91.0$; $SS_{RM} = 5.0$; $SS_{sub} = .65$; $SS_{inter} = 21.0$; $MS_{RM} = 5.0$; $MS_{inter} = 2.33$; $F(1,9) = 2.14$, $p > .05$. Relationship is that $F = t^2$.

3. $SS_{total} = 100.0$; $SS_{RM} = 24.5$; $SS_{sub} = 46.1$; $SS_{inter} = 29.4$; $MS_{RM} = 12.25$; $MS_{inter} = 1.336$; $F(2,22) = 9.17$, $p < .01$, sphericity assumed. Adjusted $F_{.05}(1,11) = 4.84$; therefore, F is significant at the .05 level without assuming sphericity.

5. (a) $SS_{total} = 551.5$; $SS_{RM} = 260.5$; $SS_{sub} = 155.5$; $SS_{inter} = 135.5$; $MS_{RM} = 86.83$; $MS_{inter} = 6.45$; $F(3,21) = 13.46$, $p < .01$; $4(4-1)/2 = 6$ pairwise comparisons; $\alpha_{pc} = .05/6 = .00833$

   (b) $SS_{groups} = 33.89$; $SS_{W} = 121.61$; $SS_{RM} = 260.5$; $SS_{G\times RM} = 99.11$; $SS_{S\times RM} = 36.39$; $F_{ability} = 33.89/20.27 = 1.67$, $p > .05$; $F_{word} = 86.83/2.02 = 42.99$, $p < .01$; $F_{inter} = 33.04/2.02 = 16.36$, $p < .01$.

   (c) Graph of cell means

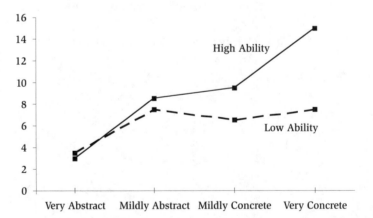

You can see from the graph that there is some interaction, as the lines increasingly diverge with greater concreteness. There is also a visible main effect for word concreteness, due chiefly to the high ability participants. Also, the high ability participants are somewhat higher than low ability participants across word conditions, but the (usually) larger error term for the between-group test prevented this result from attaining significance.

Chapter 19

1. (a) $p = 4/52 = 1/13 = .077$
   (b) $p = 42/52 - 8/52 = 34/52 = .654$
   (c) $p(A \text{ and } B) = 1/52 \cdot 1/52 = .00037$
   (d) $p(A \text{ and } B) = 20/52 \cdot 2/52 = .0148$
   (e) $p(A \text{ and } B) = 1/52 \cdot 0 = 0; p(A \text{ and } B) = 20/52 \cdot 2/51 = .0151$

3. (a) $1/100 = .01$
   (b) $1/100 = .01$
   (c) $.01 + .01 = .02$
   (d) $5/100 = .05$
   (e) $10/100 = .10$
   (f) $50/100 = .50$
   (g) $.50 \cdot .17 = .085$
   (h) $.05 + .28 - .02 = .31$

5. (a) $2^4 = 16; 4!/2! = 24/2 = 12$
   (b) Binomial distribution for N = 4 and P = .5

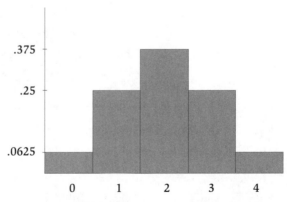

   (c) $z = (.0625 - .5)/\sqrt{(.5)(.5)/4} = -1.75, p < .05$. Reject the null hypothesis, conclude that the coin is weighted more heavily to land "tails."

7. (a) $z = [18 - 28(.5)]/\sqrt{28(.5)(.5)} = 1.51, p = .0655$; retain H_0.
   (b) $z = [20 - 28(.5)]/\sqrt{28(.5)(.5)} = 2.27, p = .0116$; reject H_0.

Chapter 20

1. (a) $\chi^2 = 4.0$; $df = 1$; $p < .05$. Reject H_0; conclude that patients are more likely to improve with new treatment

   (b) $z = [60 - 100(.5)]/\sqrt{100(.5)(.5)} = 2.0$; relationship is $z^2 = \chi^2$

3. (a) $\chi^2 = [(21 - 19.75)^2/19.75] + [(14 - 19.75)^2/19.75] + [(26 - 19.75)^2/19.75] + [(18 - 19.75)^2/19.75] = 3.89$. Retain H_0; $3.89 < \chi^2_{.05}(3) = 7.82$

   (b) $\chi^2 = 9.56$; $df = 3$; $p < .05$. Reject H_0; $9.56 > \chi^2_{.05}(3) = 7.82$

5. (a) $\chi^2 = [(12 - 13.2)^2/13.2] + [(10 - 8.8)^2/8.8] + [(18 - 16.8)^2/16.8] + [(10 - 11.2)^2/11.2] = .49$. Retain H_0; $.49 < \chi^2_{.05}(1) = 3.84$. This is equivalent to saying that the percent success is not significantly different between the sexes.

   (b) $\phi = \sqrt{.49/50} = .10$; small effect

7. (a) $\chi^2 = 18.84$; $df = 4$; $p < .01$. Reject H_0; $18.84 > \chi^2_{.01}(4) = 13.28$

   (b) $\phi_c = \sqrt{18.84/(143)(2)} = .26$; moderate relationship.

Chapter 21

1. (a) $\Sigma R = (19)(20)/2 = 190$; $T_1 = 63.5$; $T_2 = 126.5$. Based on group 1, $T_E = 90$ and $\sigma_T = 12.25$, so $z = -26.5/12.25 = -2.16$; $p < .05$. Conclude that the new signal (group 1) is superior.

   (b) $r_G = -.59$, indicating a strong relationship between group membership and reaction times, such that group 1 reacts more quickly.

3. (a) Exp. 1: $\Sigma R = 378$; $T_1 = 159.5$; $T_2 = 218.5$. Based on group 1, $T_E = 210$ and $\sigma_T = 20.49$, so $z = -50.5/20.49 = -2.46$; $p < .05$. Reject H_0.

   Exp. 2: $\Sigma R = 378$; $T_1 = 213.5$; $T_2 = 164.5$. Based on group 1, $T_E = 210$ and $\sigma_T = 20.49$, so $z = +3.5/20.49 = 0.17$; $p > .05$. Retain H_0.

   (b) Exp. 1: $r_G = -.56$. Exp. 2: no need to calculate r_G ($= .04$), because rank-sum test is not statistically significant.

5. (a) Exp. 3: $\Sigma R = 406$; $df = 2$; $H = 12(40.99)/812 = 0.61$, $p > .05$ (not significant).

   (b) Exp. 4: $H = 12(966.45)/812 = 14.28$, $p < .01$; reject H_0. $\eta^2 = 966.45/3745.25 = .258$. Group 1 vs. 2, $z = 25/13.16 = 1.90$, $p > .05$ (not significant, but close). Group 2 vs. 3, $z = 33.5/10.39 = 3.22$, $p < .01$. Group 1 vs. 3, $z = 34.5/12.11 = 2.85$, $p < .01$.

7. (a) Exp. 5: $N = 14$; $z = (95.5 - 52.5)/\sqrt{29(52.5)/6} = 2.70$, $p < .05$; reject H_0. $r_c = .82$.

   (b) Exp. 6: $N = 13$; $z = (33.5 - 45.5)/\sqrt{27(45.5)/6} = -0.84$, $p > .05$; retain H_0.

9. (a) $r_s = 1 - (6 \cdot 104)/2730 = .77 > .648$ (critical r_s for $N = 10$ for a .05, two-tailed test); reject H_0. $r_s = .77 < r_{xy} = .855$. The Spearman correlation throws away some of the quantitative information in the data, and is therefore often smaller (and therefore has less power) than the corresponding Pearson r calculated on the raw data. However, for some data patterns, r_s will be higher than r. Also, the critical value for r_s will be higher than the corresponding critical value for r, although the difference becomes negligible when N is large.

(b) $r_s = 1 - (6 \cdot 586)/2730 = -.28 > -.648$, so $p > .05$; retain H_0. This is a case in which r_s is actually larger in magnitude than the corresponding r_{xy}—that is, $|-.28| > |-.18|$.

Data from Sara's Experiment

gender	major	cond	phobia	math	bkgd	sqz	hr_b	hr_p	hr_a	anx_b	anx_p	anx_a
1	1	1	1	3	43	6	71.0	68.0	65.0	17.0	22.0	20.0
1	1	1	1	4	49	9	73.0	75.0	68.0	17.0	19.0	16.0
1	1	1	4	1	26	8	69.0	76.0	72.0	19.0	14.0	15.0
1	1	1	4	0	29	7	72.0	73.0	78.0	19.0	13.0	16.0
1	1	1	10	1	31	6	71.0	83.0	74.0	26.0	30.0	25.0
1	1	2	4	1	20	7	70.0	71.0	76.0	12.0	15.0	19.0
1	1	2	4	2	13	3	71.0	70.0	66.0	12.0	16.0	17.0
1	1	2	4	1	23	7	77.0	87.0	84.0	17.0	19.0	22.0
1	1	2	4	1	38	8	73.0	72.0	67.0	20.0	14.0	17.0
1	1	2	5	0		7	78.0	76.0	74.0	20.0	24.0	19.0
1	1	4	3	1	21	8	72.0	74.0	68.0	21.0	27.0	22.0
1	1	2	5	1	29	8	74.0	72.0	73.0	21.0	25.0	22.0
1	1	2	4	0	32	8	73.0	74.0	74.0	32.0	35.0	33.0
1	1	3	4	1		5	72.0	83.0	77.0	18.0	27.0	28.0
1	1	4	8	0		3	76.0	76.0	79.0	14.0	18.0	21.0
1	1	4	4	1	37	8	68.0	67.0	74.0	15.0	19.0	18.0
1	1	2	7	0	18	1	73.0	76.0	78.0	19.0	23.0	20.0
1	1	4	0	3	32	10	74.0	74.0	75.0	20.0	12.0	18.0
1	1	4	5	1	37	7	77.0	78.0	73.0	39.0	39.0	40.0
1	2	1	4	2	21	7	78.0	79.0	73.0	18.0	13.0	16.0
1	2	1	3	2		7	70.0	63.0	66.0	18.0	12.0	14.0
1	2	2	4	1		7	74.0	75.0	73.0	15.0	11.0	20.0
1	2	2	4	0	25	7	74.0	84.0	77.0	19.0	27.0	23.0
1	2	2	0	3	47	8	75.0	75.0	71.0	23.0	28.0	24.0
1	2	3	1	3	41	6	76.0	73.0	72.0	18.0	24.0	26.0
1	2	3	3	1	22	4	73.0	71.0	79.0	18.0	13.0	19.0
1	2	3	4	1	35	8	71.0	74.0	76.0	18.0	22.0	25.0
1	2	4	1	4	26	7	71.0	76.0	75.0	14.0	10.0	18.0
1	2	4	0	6	39	8	74.0	79.0	79.0	17.0	12.0	16.0
1	2	1	5	1	22	4	73.0	78.0	69.0	21.0	14.0	17.0
1	3	1	2	0	10	7	74.0	72.0	72.0	15.0	21.0	16.0
1	3	1	1	1	20	8	76.0	69.0	71.0	17.0	25.0	19.0
1	3	4	4	1	26	8	76.0	74.0	81.0	17.0	26.0	15.0
1	3	1	9	1	21	8	75.0	83.0	73.0	18.0	21.0	23.0
1	3	1	2	1	30	6	69.0	69.0	64.0	22.0	16.0	18.0
1	3	2	8	1	35	6	71.0	70.0	75.0	20.0	27.0	22.0
1	3	2	0	0	40	8	77.0	79.0	74.0	21.0	14.0	19.0
1	3	3	3	0		7	78.0	76.0	84.0	24.0	27.0	25.0
1	3	4	4	1	44	6	67.0	67.0	73.0	12.0	19.0	17.0
1	3	4	3	1	35	8	78.0	73.0	78.0	19.0	12.0	17.0
1	3	4	4	1	26	7	77.0	78.0	78.0	21.0	15.0	15.0
1	4	4	2	1	42	7	69.0	70.0	64.0	13.0	24.0	22.0
1	4	1	1	1	39	7	71.0	63.0	66.0	15.0	21.0	13.0
1	4	1	0	1		9	71.0	72.0	67.0	20.0	23.0	21.0
1	4	2	5	1		5	75.0	76.0	70.0	16.0	18.0	23.0

gender	major	cond	phobia	math	bkgd	sqz	hr_b	hr_p	hr_a	anx_b	anx_p	anx_a
1	4	2	3	1	15	3	76.0	79.0	71.0	19.0	21.0	17.0
1	4	3	4	1	24	7	74.0	76.0	75.0	22.0	27.0	23.0
1	4	3	4	1		7	74.0	74.0	69.0	30.0	36.0	32.0
1	4	4	10	0	26	5	78.0	80.0	80.0	19.0	24.0	24.0
1	4	4	2	1	33	8	72.0	64.0	68.0	20.0	14.0	22.0
1	4	1	5	0	38	8	71.0	82.0	79.0	20.0	26.0	26.0
1	4	4	7	1	14	5	68.0	78.0	73.0	20.0	29.0	30.0
1	4	4	1	0	29	6	72.0	79.0	76.0	22.0	27.0	24.0
1	5	1	2	0		8	72.0	67.0	67.0	16.0	20.0	22.0
1	5	3	3	5	45	9	76.0	79.0	75.0	15.0	8.0	17.0
1	5	3	4	1	28	8	73.0	78.0	77.0	19.0	13.0	18.0
1	5	4	2	2	31	8	74.0	78.0	82.0	27.0	21.0	24.0
2	1	1	0	3	33	10	72.0	67.0	68.0	16.0	25.0	15.0
2	1	1	1	1	32	8	74.0	84.0	76.0	17.0	19.0	14.0
2	1	1	7	0	15	3	73.0	73.0	71.0	19.0	16.0	16.0
2	1	2	1	4	34	9	70.0	73.0	65.0	11.0	19.0	9.0
2	1	2	5	0	26	8	73.0	74.0	76.0	16.0	20.0	17.0
2	1	3	5	1	26	8	80.0	82.0	86.0	18.0	27.0	20.0
2	1	3	1	2	32	5	67.0	68.0	73.0	20.0	25.0	24.0
2	1	3	3	0	21	8	65.0	75.0	69.0	26.0	29.0	23.0
2	1	4	3	1	43	8	71.0	72.0	76.0	18.0	13.0	16.0
2	1	4	5	1		8	72.0	75.0	68.0	21.0	26.0	27.0
2	2	1	3	1	37	6	70.0	73.0	77.0	15.0	23.0	14.0
2	2	2	1	2		8	69.0	67.0	64.0	14.0	17.0	15.0
2	2	2	5	0	30	7	69.0	70.0	74.0	18.0	15.0	15.0
2	2	3	0	2	30	8	68.0	72.0	71.0	10.0	13.0	15.0
2	2	3	0	4	30	9	69.0	70.0	74.0	15.0	21.0	17.0
2	2	3	2	2	28	5	71.0	74.0	67.0	15.0	17.0	17.0
2	2	3	6	2	46	8	68.0	74.0	71.0	16.0	10.0	17.0
2	2	3	2	4	34	8	68.0	70.0	69.0	18.0	21.0	19.0
2	2	3	3	2		7	76.0	79.0	71.0	19.0	13.0	15.0
2	2	4	2	3	32	9	70.0	62.0	71.0	17.0	23.0	19.0
2	2	4	5	0	33	7	68.0	71.0	77.0	18.0	21.0	19.0
2	2	4	10	0	14	6	69.0	78.0	76.0	20.0	25.0	23.0
2	2	4	4	2	29	7	76.0	79.0	71.0	22.0	15.0	20.0
2	3	1	3	1	9	7	71.0	69.0	76.0	13.0	10.0	13.0
2	3	1	3	1	11	4	72.0	83.0	73.0	14.0	16.0	15.0
2	3	1	8	1	30	6	76.0	78.0	71.0	15.0	18.0	17.0
2	3	1	3	1	15	5	76.0	67.0	71.0	18.0	12.0	17.0
2	3	2	3	1	32	3	72.0	70.0	67.0	15.0	9.0	13.0
2	3	2	2	0	25	6	68.0	70.0	73.0	16.0	20.0	19.0
2	3	2	1	0	22	5	74.0	78.0	72.0	20.0	27.0	18.0
2	3	2	1	3	31	7	64.0	74.0	70.0	22.0	25.0	19.0
2	3	3	1	4		8	70.0	71.0	69.0	10.0	16.0	14.0
2	3	3	8	1	18	4	71.0	73.0	77.0	15.0	19.0	21.0
2	3	3	3	1	11	4	72.0	75.0	76.0	24.0	17.0	21.0
2	4	1	0	1	11	6	71.0	78.0	72.0	16.0	21.0	15.0
2	4	3	4	0	28	7	73.0	77.0	79.0	24.0	18.0	20.0
2	4	4	0	2	37	9	72.0	71.0	73.0	17.0	11.0	17.0
2	5	2	2	2	39	7	70.0	70.0	64.0	17.0	11.0	14.0
2	5	2	0	1	33	7	74.0	73.0	71.0	17.0	18.0	17.0

gender	major	cond	phobia	math	bkgd	sqz	hr_b	hr_p	hr_a	anx_b	anx_p	anx_a
2	5	3	0	2	28	8	70.0	66.0	65.0	17.0	12.0	13.0
2	5	3	2	2	38	9	65.0	65.0	69.0	18.0	14.0	19.0
2	5	3	7	2		8	69.0	70.0	71.0	23.0	28.0	24.0
2	5	4	1	4	41	8	72.0	68.0	73.0	17.0	11.0	18.0

Key

Gender: 1 = Female; 2 = Male.

Major: 1 = Psychology; 2 = Pre-Med; 3 = Biology; 4 = Sociology; 5 = Economics.

Condition: 1 = Easy; 2 = Moderate; 3 = Difficult; 4 = Impossible.

Phobia: 0 = No phobia to 10 = Extreme phobia.

Math = Number of math courses taken prior to statistics course.

Bkgd = Score on Math Background Quiz (a blank for this value indicates that a student did not take the quiz).

Sqz = Score on stats quiz (number correct, ignoring the eleventh question).

HR_b = Baseline heart rate (in beats per minute).

HR_p = Pre-quiz heart rate.

HR_a = Post-quiz heart rate (measured After quiz).

Anx_b = Baseline anxiety score (before quiz announcement).

Anx_p = Pre-quiz anxiety score.

Anx_a = Post-quiz anxiety score (measured After quiz).

Glossary of Terms

A priori **(planned) comparison**   In analysis of variance, a significance test between two or more group means that was planned before the results were in.

Absolute values   Numerical values with the signs ignored; thus all absolute values are treated as positive.

Alpha   The probability of committing a Type I error (i.e., rejecting the null hypothesis when the null hypothesis is true).

Alternative hypothesis   The hypothesis which states that the null hypothesis is *not true* and specifies some other value or set of values for the population parameter(s) in question.

Analysis of variance   Procedures for testing hypotheses about the equality of population means.

Area of rejection   All numerical results of a statistical test that will cause the null hypothesis to be rejected.

Bar chart   A graph in which the heights of the bars show how often each measure or range of measures was obtained. Spaces between adjacent bars are used to indicate that the data come from a discrete variable.

Beta   The probability of committing a Type II error (i.e., failing to reject the null hypothesis when the null hypothesis is *not* true).

Between-group variance   In analysis of variance, variability based on differences among the means of the various groups.

Bimodal distribution   A distribution that has two pronounced peaks when graphed as a frequency polygon.

Bivariate normal distribution   A joint distribution of two variables, wherein scores on one variable are normally distributed for each score value of the other.

Bonferroni correction (or adjustment)   A reduction in the alpha used for each of several planned comparisons based on dividing the desired experiment-wise alpha by the number of tests planned.

Box-and-whisker plot   A pictorial description of the median, first and third quartiles, and lowest and highest scores of one or more groups (it helps in the identification of outliers).

Carry-over effects   In a repeated-measures design, it is the persistence of the effect of one condition that affects a participant's response to subsequent conditions; they can produce misleading results.

Central tendency   The general location of a set of scores.

Chi square   The statistical model used to test hypotheses when data are in the form of frequencies.

Class interval   One set of score values in a grouped frequency distribution.

Complex comparison (or contrast)   In analysis of variance, a significance test involving a weighted combination of three or more group means.

Confidence interval   A range of values within which a specified population parameter has a given probability of falling.

Confidence limits   The upper and lower end points of a confidence interval.

Constant   A numerical value that is exactly the same for all cases or subjects; the converse of *variable*.

Continuous variable   A variable for which it is theoretically possible for any value to occur between any specified pair of score values.

Control group   A group that does *not* receive the treatment whose effects are being investigated by the researcher. Used as a baseline against which to evaluate the performance of the experimental group.

Correlation coefficient   A measure of the extent to which scores on one variable are related to scores on a second variable.

Counterbalancing   In a repeated-measures design, it is a system of assigning different orders of the RM conditions to different participants, so that no one condition will benefit from order effects more than any other condition.

Cramér's phi   A measure of the strength of the relationship between two variables, both of which are categorical and have more than two levels.

Criterion   The variable being predicted in a linear regression analysis; a dependent variable.

Criterion of significance   A numerical value or decision rule that specifies when the null hypothesis is to be rejected.

Critical interval   When computing percentiles, the class interval in which the specified raw score or critical case number falls.

Cumulative frequency distribution   A listing that shows how many times a given score or less was obtained.

d   The standardized difference between two population means (a measure of effect size).

Decile   A transformed score that divides the number of cases into ten equal parts.

Degrees of freedom   The number of quantities that are free to vary when we estimate the value of a parameter from a statistic.

Delta   In power analysis, an index that combines the population effect size and the sample size.

Dependent variable   A variable that changes with changes in one or more independent variables.

Descriptive statistics   Mathematical procedures for summarizing and describing the characteristics of a set of data.

Deviation score   The difference between a score and the mean of the set of scores of which it is a member.

Dichotomous variable   A variable with only two categories.

Discrete variable   A variable for which it is *not* theoretically possible for any value to occur between any specified pair of score values.

Distribution-free statistical test   A statistical test that does *not* require any assumptions about the shape of the distribution in the population.

Effect size   How large the phenomenon we wish to investigate is in the population; the extent to which the null hypothesis is false.

Error variance   In analysis of variance, differences among scores or group means that *cannot* be explained by the experimental treatment(s).

Eta squared   The proportion of variance accounted for in ANOVA.

Experimental group   A group that receives the treatment whose effects are being investigated by the researcher.

Experimental (or empirical) sampling distribution   A distribution whose elements are statistics (for example, sample means) obtained by drawing repeated samples from the population and computing that statistic for each sample.

Experimentwise error rate   The rate of occurrence of *any* (one or more) Type I errors when a *series* of individual statistical tests is conducted within the same study.

_F_ distributions   The statistical model used to test hypotheses when the analysis involves the comparison of variance estimates.

Factorial design   A procedure used to study the relationship of two or more independent variables (factors) to a dependent variable.

Five-number summary   A procedure for summarizing important numerical characteristics of a set of data: the median, first and third quartiles, and lowest and highest scores.

Frequency   The number of times a specified score or range of scores was obtained.

Frequency polygon   A graph showing how often each score or range of scores was obtained.

Generalize   Apply results obtained from a sample to a specific population.

Glass rank biserial correlation   A measure of the strength of the relationship between membership in one of two independent samples and a set of ranked data.

Grouped frequency distribution   A listing of sets of two or more score values (class intervals) together with the number of times that scores in each class interval were obtained.

Histogram   A bar graph in which there is no space between adjacent bars (for use with continuous data).

Homogeneity of variance   In a *t* test or analysis of variance, equality of the variances for all treatment populations.

Hypothesis testing   Procedures for deciding whether to retain or reject the null hypothesis about one or more population parameters.

Independent events   Events whose occurrence or nonoccurrence is unrelated to the occurrence (or probability of occurrence) of specified other events.

Independent samples   Samples such that any element in one sample has no connection of any kind with any element in another sample.

Independent variable   A variable whose variation is studied with regard to its effect on another (dependent) variable(s).

Inferential statistics   Mathematical procedures for drawing inferences about characteristics of a population, based on what is observed in samples from that population.

Interaction   The joint effect of two or more independent variables on a dependent variable, over and above their separate (main) effects.

Interval estimate   A synonym for confidence interval.

Interval size   The number of scores in each class interval in a grouped frequency distribution.

J-curve   A distribution that looks like the letter J or its mirror image when graphed as a frequency polygon.

Kruskal-Wallis _H_ test   A nonparametric procedure for testing hypotheses about differences among the locations of two or more independent populations, used when data are in the form of ranks.

Least squares regression line   The regression line that minimizes the sum of squared errors in prediction (the sum of squared deviations between the predicted scores and actual scores).

Linear regression Procedures for determining the straight line that will enable us to predict scores on one variable (the criterion) from scores on another variable (the predictor), while minimizing the amount of (squared) error.

Lower real limit The lower end point of a class interval in a grouped frequency distribution.

Marginal frequency A column or row total in a two-way table of joint frequencies.

Matched-pairs rank biserial correlation A measure of the strength of the relationship between membership in one of two matched samples and a set of ranked data.

Matched samples Samples such that each element in one sample is paired with one element in the other sample.

Matched _t_ test Procedure for testing a hypothesis about the difference between two population means, using matched samples, or two measurements on each participant.

Mean A measure of the central tendency of a set of scores, obtained by summing all scores and dividing by the number of scores.

Mean-on-spoke representation A graphic method that depicts the mean and standard deviation of one or more groups.

Mean square In analysis of variance, an estimate of the population variance that is obtained by dividing a sum of squares by its associated degrees of freedom.

Median The score such that exactly half the scores in the group are higher and exactly half the scores are equal or lower; the score corresponding to the 50th percentile.

Midpoint The value halfway between the lower real limit and the upper real limit of a class interval.

Mode The score that occurs most often in a frequency distribution.

Multiple comparisons In analysis of variance, procedures for testing hypotheses about differences between specified pairs of means.

Mutually exclusive events Events that cannot happen simultaneously.

Negatively skewed distribution A distribution with some extremely low scores, resulting in a frequency polygon with a pronounced tail at the left.

Nonparametric statistical test A statistical test that does not involve the estimation of any population parameters.

Normal distribution A particular bell-shaped, symmetric, and unimodal distribution defined by a specific mathematical equation.

Null hypothesis The hypothesis that specifies the value of a population parameter or a difference between two or more population parameters (usually zero), and that is assumed to be true at the outset of the statistical analysis.

Odds against an event The ratio of the number of unfavorable outcomes to the number of favorable outcomes.

One-tailed test of significance A statistical test wherein the null hypothesis can only be rejected if results are in the direction predicted by the experimenter.

Order effects In a repeated-measures design, simple order effects can be produced on later conditions from the practice or fatigue of having been involved in previous conditions. Simple order effects can be neutralized by counterbalancing, but carryover effects may not; see also carry-over effects.

Parameter A numerical quantity that summarizes some characteristic of a population.

Pearson _r_ A measure of the strength of the linear relationship between two variables, both of which are continuous.

Percentile A score at or below which a given percent of the cases fall.

Percentile rank   The percent of cases in a specific reference group that fall at or below a given score.

Phi coefficient   A measure of the strength of the relationship between two variables, both of which are dichotomous (that is, they have only two categories).

Point-biserial correlation coefficient   A measure of the strength of the relationship between one dichotomous and one continuous variable.

Point estimate   A single statistic used to estimate the value of the corresponding parameter.

Pooled variance   In the significance test of the difference between two means, an estimate of the population variance (assumed to be the same for both populations) obtained from a weighted average of the sample variances.

Population   *All* of the cases in which a researcher is interested; a (usually very large) group of people, animals, objects, or responses that are alike in at least one respect.

Population variance estimate   An estimate of the variability in a population, obtained by dividing the sum of squared deviations from the sample mean by $N - 1$.

Positively skewed distribution   A distribution with some extremely high scores, resulting in a frequency polygon with a pronounced tail at the right.

Post hoc comparison   In analysis of variance, a significance test between two group means that was not planned prior to obtaining the results.

Power efficiency of a nonparametric test   How many fewer cases, expressed as a percent, that are required by a parametric test to have the same power as the nonparametric test when the assumptions of the parametric test are met.

Power of a statistical test   The probability of obtaining a statistically significant result if the null hypothesis is actually false; the probability of rejecting a false null hypothesis.

Predicted score   In linear regression, the score on the criterion that is estimated for subjects with a specified score on the predictor.

Predictor   In linear regression, the variable from which criterion scores are estimated; an independent variable.

Probability of an event   The number of ways the specified event can occur, divided by the total number of possible events.

Protected *t* test   In analysis of variance, a procedure for conducting multiple comparisons between pairs of group means that requires the ANOVA to be statistically significant before proceeding.

Quartile   A transformed score that divides the number of cases into four equal parts.

Random sample   A sample drawn in such a way that each element in the population has an equal chance of being included in the sample.

Randomized-blocks design   This is an extension of the matched-samples design to more than two conditions. Participants are matched in blocks according to the number of different levels of the factor, and then one member of each block is randomly assigned to each condition.

Range   The largest score minus the smallest score.

Rank   A measure that shows where a given case falls with respect to others in the group, but gives no indication of the distance between the cases. Thus, ranks provide less information than do scores.

Rank-sum test   A nonparametric procedure for testing hypotheses about the difference in location between two populations; used when data are in the form of ranks.

Raw score   A score not subjected to any statistical transformations, such as the number correct on a test.

Rectangular distribution   A distribution wherein each score occurs with the same frequency.

Regular frequency distribution   A listing of every score value, from the lowest to the highest, together with the number of times that each score was obtained (its frequency).

Repeated-measures ANOVA   Procedure for testing differences between two or more population means by measuring each participant under all of the conditions (i.e., levels) of the independent variable; it is an extension of the matched t test that can also be applied to any number of matched samples.

Restriction of range   Low variability, caused by the way in which the samples were defined, that will usually underestimate the correlation between that variable and other variables.

Robust statistical test   A statistical test that gives fairly accurate results even if the underlying assumptions are not met.

Sample   Any subgroup of cases drawn from a clearly specified population.

Sample size   The number of cases in a sample.

Sampling error   Differences between the value of a statistic observed in a sample and the corresponding population parameter (thus, error), caused by the accident of which cases happened to be included in the sample.

Scatter plot   A graph showing the relationship between two variables, where each score is expressed as a point.

Sign test   A nonparametric method for testing hypotheses about differences in location between two matched populations; an alternative to the matched-pairs t test.

Significance test   A procedure for deciding whether to retain or reject a null hypothesis.

Simple main effect   In a two-way ANOVA, it is the effect of one factor at only one level of the other factor.

Skewed distribution   A distribution with some extremely low scores (negatively skewed, skewed to the left) or some extremely high scores (positively skewed, skewed to the right), resulting in a frequency polygon with a pronounced tail in one direction.

Slope   In linear regression, the average rate of change in the criterion per unit increase in the predictor.

Spearman (rank-order) correlation coefficient   A measure of the strength of the relationship between two variables, both of which are in the form of ranks.

Sphericity   In an RM ANOVA, the assumption that the variance of the difference scores is the same, in the population, for every pair of levels of the RM factor.

Standard deviation   A measure of the variability of the scores in a specified group, or how much the scores differ from one another; the positive square root of the variance.

Standard error   The standard deviation of some statistic in a sampling distribution (rather than scores), which tells us how trustworthy the single statistic we have on hand is an estimate of the corresponding parameter. Examples of parameters that are estimated include a population mean (*standard error of the mean*), a population proportion (*standard error of a proportion*), and the difference between two population means (*standard error of the difference*).

Standard error of estimate   In linear regression, a measure of the variability (average error) in prediction.

Standard scores   A synonym for z scores.

Statistic   A numerical quantity that summarizes some characteristic of a sample.

Statistical model   A summary of the probability of all possible events of a specified type (for example, each possible value of a sample mean drawn at random from one population) under specified conditions (for example, that the null hypothesis is true). Examples include the normal distribution, the t, the F, and the chi square distributions.

Statistical significance   Occurs when the results of a statistical analysis indicate that the null hypothesis can be rejected.

Stem-and-leaf display   A pictorial description of a set of data that combines features of the frequency distribution and the histogram.

Sum of squares   The sum of the squared deviations of observations from their mean.

Summation sign   A mathematical symbol that represents the sum of a set of numbers.

Symmetric distribution   A distribution wherein one half is the mirror image of the other half.

t distributions   The statistical model used to test hypotheses about the mean of one population when the population standard deviation is *not* known, the differences between the means of two populations (independent or matched samples), the significance of certain correlation coefficients, and certain multiple comparison procedures in the analysis of variance.

T scores   Transformed scores that have a mean of 50 and standard deviation of 10.

Theoretical sampling distribution   An estimate of an experimental sampling distribution that is determined mathematically (rather than by drawing repeated samples).

Theta   In power analysis, an alternative hypothesis for the difference between two means that is *not* equal to zero and is expressed in raw units.

Transformed score   A score that has been altered mathematically to show its standing relative to a specified group.

Two-tailed test of significance   A statistical test of two population means wherein the null hypothesis may be rejected regardless of the direction of the results.

Type I error   Rejecting a null hypothesis that is actually true.

Type II error   Retaining a null hypothesis that is actually false.

Unimodal distribution   A distribution that has one pronounced peak when graphed as a frequency polygon.

Upper real limit   The upper end point of a class interval in a grouped frequency distribution.

Variability   The extent to which the scores in a specified group differ from one another, or how spread out or scattered the scores are.

Variable   Any characteristic that can take on different values.

Variance   A measure of the variability of the scores in a specified group, or how much the scores differ from one another; the square of the standard deviation.

Wilcoxon test   A nonparametric procedure for testing hypotheses about the difference between the locations of two matched populations, used when data are in the form of ranks.

Within-group variance   In analysis of variance, differences among the scores within the groups. Reflects variation that cannot be explained by the experimental treatment(s) (error variance).

Y-intercept   The point at which the regression line crosses the Y-axis.

z scores   Transformed scores that have a mean of 0 and standard deviation of 1.

References

American Psychological Association. (2001). *Publication manual of the American Psychological Association* (5th ed.). Washington, DC: Author.

Cohen, B. H. (2000). *Explaining psychological statistics* (2nd ed.). New York: Wiley.

Cohen, J. (1988). *Statistical power analysis for the behavioral sciences* (2nd ed.). Hillsdale, NJ: Erlbaum.

Ewen, R. B. (2000). *Study guide to accompany introductory statistics for the behavioral sciences* (5th ed.). New York: Wiley.

Greenhouse, S. W., & Geisser, S. (1959). On methods in the analysis of profile data. *Psychometrika, 24,* 95–112.

Hayter, A. J. (1986). The maximum familywise error rate of Fisher's least significant difference test. *Journal of the American Statistical Association, 81,* 1000–1004.

Kline, R. B. (2004). *Beyond significance testing: Reforming data analysis methods in behavioral research.* Washington, DC: American Psychological Association.

Mauchly, J. W. (1940). Significance test for sphericity of a normal n-variate distribution. *Annals of Mathematical Statistics, 11,* 204–209.

Rauscher, F. H., Shaw, G. L., & Ky, K. N. (1993). Music and spatial task performance. *Nature, 365,* 611.

Siegel, S., & Castellan, N. J., Jr. (1988). *Nonparametric statistics for the behavioral sciences* (2nd ed.). New York: McGraw-Hill.

Tukey, J. W. (1977). *Exploratory data analysis.* Reading, MA: Addison-Wesley.

Index